The Irwin Guide
to Using
The Wall Street Journal

About the author...

MICHAEL B. LEHMANN is a Professor of Economics at the University of San Francisco. He is a graduate of Grinnell College and received his Ph.D. from Cornell University.

Professor Lehmann lectures extensively on business and investment conditions and has developed a popular seminar based on this book, which he offers to investors, the business community, and corporations as an in-house training program.

The Irwin Guide
to Using
The Wall Street Journal

Fifth Edition

Michael B. Lehmann

IRWIN
Professional Publishing®
Chicago • London • Singapore

Times Mirror
Higher Education Group

Library of Congress Cataloging-in-Publication Data

Lehmann, Michael B.
  The Irwin guide to using the Wall Street journal / Michael B.
Lehmann. — 5th ed.
        p. cm.
  Rev. ed. of: The Business One Irwin guide to using the Wall Street
journal. 4th ed. 1993.
  Includes index.
  ISBN 0-7863-0483-9
  1. Business cycles—United States. 2. Economic indicators—United
States. 3. Investments—United States. 4. Wall Street journal.
I. Lehmann, Michael B. Business One Irwin guide to using the Wall
Street journal. II. Irwin Professional Publishing. III. Wall
Street journal. IV. Title.
HB3743.L44   1996
332.6—dc20   95–45386

Printed in the United States of America
1 2 3 4 5 6 7 8 9 0 Q 2 1 0 9 8 7 6 5

PREFACE

When I first proposed this book to Irwin, they asked me if its purpose was to show the reader "how to be your own economist." Not exactly, I said. The objective was to show the reader "how to use *The Wall Street Journal* to be your own economist."

After all, the *Journal* is the authoritative source for business news in America; it is published coast to coast; and it has the largest daily circulation of any newspaper in the country. By focusing on a handful of key statistical reports in the *Journal*, you can acquire a surprisingly quick and firm comprehension of the ups and downs of the American business economy. This book will facilitate that comprehension, clearly and accurately—but, I hope, in a pleasing and nontechnical manner.

The *Irwin Guide to Using The Wall Street Journal* is designed to help you develop a sound overview of our economy, thus making your grasp of economic events as well as your business and investment decisions more informed and more confident. But it is not a get-rich-quick manual. You should always seek competent professional counsel before placing business or personal capital at risk.

Michael B. Lehmann

ACKNOWLEDGMENTS

Jane O'Neil did most of the work. She collected *The Wall Street Journal* articles, executed the primary revision of the text, and organized the text editing. Her efforts were invaluable to me.

Lee Bihlmayer and her crew at Desktypography in San Francisco did the graphics, layout, production management, and typesetting. If you need the job done right, call Lee.

Bob Meier of DeKalb, Illinois, revised the list of suggested further reading in Appendix E, which he had kindly contributed to the fourth edition.

My thanks also to Stanley Nel, Dean of the University of San Francisco's College of Arts & Sciences, and Jack Clark, the university's Vice President for Academic Affairs, for their past and continuing support of my writing and research efforts.

Finally, my thanks to Amy Ost, my editor at Irwin, who is a pleasure to work with and for.

M.B.L.

CONTENTS

PART III
FINE TUNING: REFINING YOUR SENSE
OF THE ECONOMY AND THE RIGHT
INVESTMENT DECISIONS

PART I

THE BIG PICTURE: THE ECONOMIC CLIMATE AND THE INVESTMENT OUTLOOK

CHAPTER 1

INTRODUCTION

GOLD VERSUS STOCKS

Some say that we learn best by doing...that we should plunge right in.

Give it a try. Examine Chart 1–1 on page 3 with an investor's eye. The vertical axis provides values for the Dow Jones Industrial Average and the price of gold. Years are on the horizontal axis. Where would you have placed your assets—into gold or stocks—at two critical junctures or turning points: 1970 and 1980? And where will you keep them for the remainder of the 1990s?

Before you answer, you should be aware that the U.S. Treasury had set the price of gold at $35 an ounce from 1934 to 1971. Since the Treasury stood ready to buy or sell gold at $35 an ounce, and since the United States had most of the world's gold, there was no reason for any seller of gold to take one penny less than $35 or any buyer to pay one penny more than $35. So the price just sat at $35, year after year.

Just in case the stagnant price was not disincentive enough, Americans were prohibited by law from owning gold as an investment. Gold was to be used exclusively by the Treasury to settle international accounts. All that changed dramatically in the early 1970s, when the United States stopped selling gold for international settlement purposes and Americans were granted permission to own gold as an investment.

Although Americans were not permitted to own gold until December 31, 1974, place yourself in the hypothetical position of an investor who could have chosen between gold and stocks in 1970. With the wisdom of hindsight, can there be any doubt about your choice?

Look at Chart 1–1 again. You already know that gold was $35 in 1970. The Dow Jones Industrial Average, which most people view as a proxy for the stock market, began and ended the 1970s at about 800. It fluctuated in a limited range for these 10 years, going nowhere. Had you bought stock

CHART 1–1
**Gold vs. Stocks: Gold-Engelhard High Price through 1987, Average
Thereafter; Dow Jones Industrial Average**

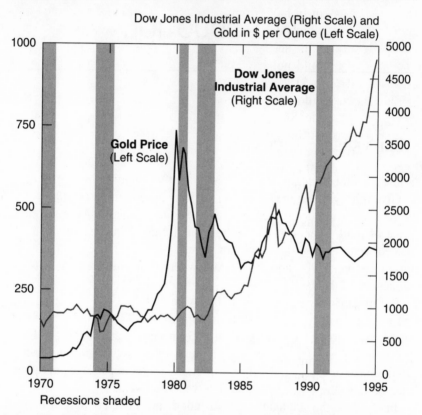

Source: U.S. Bureau of Mines, *Minerals Yearbook*; Standard & Poor's *Statistical Service*; Phyllis S.
Pierce, ed., *The Dow Jones Investor's Handbook* (Homewood, IL: Dow Jones-Irwin, 1995); *Barron's*.

in 1970, you would have enjoyed no investment appreciation. Gold, on the
other hand, exploded in value, climbing to over $800 by early 1980. The
smart money was in gold, not stocks.

Your choice was equally clear in 1980. Gold stood at over $800 an
ounce; the Dow was under 1000. Then gold began to plunge. By mid-
decade it had fallen to around $300. The price rose briefly to $500 in late
1987 but by the end of the decade was down around the $400 mark. Stock
prices, on the other hand, broke free in 1982, climbing intermittently until,
in a burst of activity, the Dow topped 2700 in August of 1987. Then came
the crash and the recovery that followed, so that the Dow had made up its
loss and reached 3000 by the end of the decade.

Looking back over the 1980s, there's no doubt that you should have taken all your money out of gold and put it all in stocks at the beginning of the decade. Stocks more than tripled (from under 1000 to over 3000), while gold was cut in half (from over $800 to under $400). You would have done very well in stocks, *despite the crash*. And even though the gain was not as great as the spectacular appreciation of gold during the 1970s, remember, you could not have bought gold until December 31, 1974, when the price was $186.

But what do you do now? The Dow broke 3000 in 1990 and approached 5000 by mid-decade. Should you stay with stocks?

Your response at this point might well be, "Now wait a minute, there are other investment avenues. I don't have to restrict my choice to gold or stocks. Besides, gold's performance has been so poor for so long, why consider it?" True, not every investment need be in the stock market or in gold, but most investments will be either "goldlike" or "stocklike" in their behavior. Conditions favorable to the stock market will also favor other paper investments such as bonds, while tangible investments such as commodities, collectibles (art, stamps), and real estate, will move with gold. So, to simplify the discussion at this point, continue as if stocks and gold were the only investment opportunities. (Short-term money market investments will also be discussed later.) The principles illustrated will be easy to apply later to the full spectrum of investment possibilities.

In the meantime, diversification is one time-honored method for protecting investment income from the vagaries of the economic climate. Yet, putting half your money in stocks and half in gold in 1970 would have gained you much less over these decades. Diversification by itself is not an optimal strategy. Your store of investments must be minded. Investments must be shifted from gold (i.e., tangibles) to stocks (i.e., paper investments) and back again as conditions change. Investment timing is the key.

In order to call these moves, you will have to know why gold and stocks behaved as they did. What force propelled gold upward in the 1970s and held stocks back? And was it the same force or a different one that boosted stocks and depressed gold in the 1980s? Could the same force have generated such remarkably different turns of events?

Yes. Could and did. In a word, *inflation* was responsible for both sets of events. But you need to modify that word in order to describe the 70s and 80s accurately. *High* inflation drove gold upward and held stocks down in the 70s, and *low* inflation had the opposite effect in the 1980s—raising stocks and depressing gold.

That means you will need to forecast the investment climate fot the remainder of the 1990s from the perspective of inflation. In order to do that, you will not only have to make an educated guess with respect to inflation, you will also need to know how to forecast inflation based on the readily available economic data. And that forecast must be completed reasonably far in advance, so that your actions can anticipate investment trends (long-run movements in gold and stocks) before they occur. You don't want to react to events after the profitable opportunities have passed. You want to beat the market to the punch...and that's not easy.

Investor's Tip

- Diversification by itself is not an optimal strategy.
- Timing is the key
- Buy gold, commodities, and other tangibles when high (more than 8 percent) inflation threatens; sell if you expect low (less than 7 percent) inflation.
- Buy stocks, bonds, and other paper investments if you anticipate low inflation; get out when high inflation looms.

ON YOUR OWN

This means you will have to use the investment data on your own, without an interpreter. You will have to decipher the Dow Jones Industrial Average, GDP, capacity utilization, price/earnings ratio, housing starts, advance/decline line, auto sales, and other statistical series and reports. You must use them to gain an understanding of developing business and investment trends so that your judgments and opinions are not merely based on (and therefore biased by) popular analyses and secondary sources.

It's worth some time and effort to learn how to deal with the data on your own, because until you come to grips with the data you can't honestly say that you have formed your own opinion about current economic and business events, let alone about what the future holds. The news media now serve as intermediaries between you and the data. Furthermore, no matter how many experts are quoted, you still aren't dealing with the facts, only with someone else's interpretation of them.

And these interpretations are often contradictory—and therefore confusing. At some point you have to wonder: Do the "experts" know what they're talking about? And while you are waiting for them to sort things out, your investment opportunities may have passed.

On the other hand, your desire to master the data may also stem from your own business needs. Will demand for your product be weak or strong two quarters from now or two years from now? Is this the time to lay in additional inventory, hire key personnel, and build more plant? Or, despite the current level of orders, would it be more prudent to cancel those plans? Can you beat the competition to the punch, one way or another? Are interest rates likely to rise or to fall? Is disinflation (as deflation is sometimes called) merely a buzzword, or has inflation really been licked? That's just a hint of the issues you can begin to analyze on your own; all it takes is learning to come to grips with a small number of regularly released statistical reports.

You may also wish to conduct your own analysis of current economic events because they form the foundation for so many other social and political developments. Were President Reagan's tax cut and supply-side economics responsible for the early 1980s decline in inflation, or should the Federal Reserve System take the credit? And how serious are the problems of the federal government's budget deficit and the balance-of-trade deficit? Do your answers to these questions reflect your analysis of the data, your political point of view, or the opinions of your favorite commentator? Maybe they should reflect all three, but they can reflect only the last two until you learn to deal with the numbers on your own. Once you do that, your own judgment will be of greater importance to you and others.

Don't misunderstand: Dispensing with expert advice is not the objective. Even the world's leading authority on a subject must consult other experts as a continual check on his or her understanding. This challenges the authority and helps prevent sloppy thinking. The point is: If you become the expert by handling the data on your own, you will know whether or not the other experts make sense. Otherwise, you'll never be certain whether you're receiving sound or flimsy advice.

If you want to be your own economist and investment advisor, if you wish to master the daily data, you need two things: (1) a readily available, reliable, and comprehensive statistical source and (2) a guide to organizing and interpreting the information you receive.

As to the first requirement, *The Wall Street Journal* is your best source of investment, business, and economic information; you really don't need

anything else. It contains all the reports necessary to conduct your own analysis.

With respect to the second requirement, this book can be your guide. In it, the nature of the statistics will be explained so that what they measure and how they are computed will be clear. GDP, capacity utilization, the price/earnings ratio, and the Dow Jones Industrial Average cannot remain vague and indefinite terms if you are going to be in control of the information.

For example, if the *Journal* reports that the money supply has increased, it is important to know that this fact has virtually nothing to do with the availability of currency. The money supply is composed largely of checking accounts; currency is the petty cash of the economy.

Understanding the nature of the various statistical series is, of course, not enough. You must be able to place them in both historical and contemporary context. For instance, the price/earnings (P/E) ratio for the Dow stocks hit a high of 22 in August 1987, just as the Dow peaked immediately prior to the October crash. A year later the P/E ratio was only 12, and the outlook for stocks was bright. The savvy investor understood these developments and was prepared to act on them.

These essential skills will develop and gain strength with each chapter. Your historical perspective will deepen, providing the background or benchmark for evaluating contemporary events. When a *Journal* article states that the trade deficit is the largest ever, or that the Dow Jones Industrial Average has hit a new high, the comparison can provide perspective only if you grasp the frame of reference: Knowledge of the past aids evaluation of the present by providing a standard against which recent developments are measured. For instance, auto sales and housing starts may be slightly higher or lower than they were a year ago, but if you know that current levels of activity are substantially higher than those of the early 90s, those recession years are behind us.

As you read on, you will become aware that none of the statistical reports stands alone. Understanding the relationships among them provides insight into the economy's operation and the investment scene; each is a piece of the puzzle, and together they compose the picture. For instance, mortgage interest rates and home construction have been featured in the *Journal* lately, and there is a simple, vital link between them: As mortgage interest rates fall, home construction increases.

Consider another example. In 1985 we asked our major trading partners to intervene in the foreign exchange markets in order to depress the value

of the dollar. The hope was that cheaper dollars—and hence cheaper prices for American goods in world markets—would boost our exports and reduce our balance-of-trade deficit. Thus, the statistical reports on the value of the dollar and on our ability to export are inextricably linked, as you will see in more detail in Chapter 16.

All of the statistics analyzed in this book can be interrelated in this fashion, so they need not be a series of isolated events, released piecemeal on a day-to-day basis. Instead, they will form an unfolding pattern that clearly reveals the direction of economic and business activity.

Finally, you need a framework, a device to give a coherent shape to these historical insights and contemporary interrelationships. The business cycle, the wavelike rise and fall of economic activity, provides that necessary framework. You are already familiar with the cycle in your own investing, business, or personal situation, and the news media have provided increased coverage of the ups and downs of the economy in recent years. Economic expansion and contraction, easy or tight credit conditions, inflation, and unemployment are recurring facts of life. Who escapes them?

The business cycle is the best vehicle for illuminating the *Journal*'s regularly appearing statistical series. Its phases bring life and meaning to the statistical reports and establish the perspective through which the illustrations and examples in the book are interwoven into a unified exposition.

Each chapter will introduce one or more statistical series, and each will be devoted to a theme (such as the money and credit markets) that is used to describe and explain the statistical series introduced in the chapter, beginning with the simplest and most basic elements of the business cycle and proceeding to additional topics that will complete your understanding. This step-by-step progression of topics will not, however, prevent you from breaking into any chapter, out of order, if you wish to examine a particular statistical series or group of series. Indeed, you may already have a firm grasp of some of these topics and need only to fill in the missing elements to round out your comprehension of the essential workings of American business. A complete listing of all the statistical series discussed in this guide can be found in the appendices following Chapter 17.

Each chapter will describe its statistical series in the context of the business cycle and explain the relationship of the new series to the overall picture. Analysis will be based on charts drawn from official publications so that you can visualize the data and put the current information in perspective. Recent articles in *The Wall Street Journal* containing the statis-

tical series will be reproduced and discussed so that you can interpret the data in light of the visual presentation made by the charts. Finally, you will be alerted to what future developments can be expected.

You will enjoy putting the puzzle together yourself. Anyone can do it, with a little help. The ebb and flow of the business cycle will channel the stream of data that now floods you in seemingly random fashion, and you will experience a genuine sense of accomplishment in creating order out of something that may previously have appeared chaotic.

A word of caution before you begin. This will not be an economics or business cycle course or text, nor will it be a precise forecasting device. There will be no formula or model. The business cycle is used strictly as a vehicle to make the statistical information usable in as easy a manner as possible. The objective is not to make a professional economist out of you, but to enable you to conduct your own analysis of the data just as soon as you are able. You will dive into the data and "get your hands dirty" by taking apart the cycle, analyzing it, and reassembling it. When you have finished this book, you will feel confident that you can deal with the data on your own.

Returning to Chart 1–1 and the example at the beginning of this chapter, you will be able to forecast the outlook for inflation and decide whether stocks (paper investments) or gold (tangible investments) are best for you. But a full discussion of that choice must wait until Chapter 8.

Now, before exploring the business cycle in detail, take time for a leisurely overview.

CHAPTER 2

THE BUSINESS CYCLE

A BIT OF HISTORY

The business cycle is nothing new. It's been a characteristic of every capitalist economy in the modern era. Nations have endured boom followed by bust, prosperity and then depression—periods of growth and confidence trailing off into a decade of despair.

It is all so familiar to us that images of its human effects are scattered among our popular stereotypes. Men in top hats peer at ticker tape emerging from a little glass dome. They wheel and deal, corner wheat markets, play with railroads, and organize steel companies. Fortunes are quickly won and just as quickly lost. Former tycoons are seen selling apples on street corners. Factory gates shut and signs go up saying, "No help wanted." Soup kitchens appear, and desperate families flee the dust bowl in Model A pickup trucks.

These caricatures—based on real history, actual power, blows of ill fortune, human suffering—persist in our collective consciousness, permanently etched by the Great Depression. Although the stock market collapse of 1929 is the most notorious such event in our history, it is by no means unique. Cycles in the American economy can be traced and analyzed going back to the beginning of the 19th century.

The settlement of the West is an example. The frontier assumes such importance in our history and folklore that we tend to think of the westward migration as a smooth, if hazardous, inevitable flow, driven by the doctrine of Manifest Destiny. It didn't happen that way. The settlement of the West proceeded in a cyclical pattern.

Farmers and ranchers were (and are) business people. The sod house and subsistence farming of the 1800s were temporary inconveniences, converted as quickly as possible to growing cash crops and raising livestock for the market. The settlers wanted to know the bottom line, the dif-

ference between revenue and expense. They wanted the best price for their cotton, corn, cattle, wheat, and hogs. They wanted to maximize production and minimize cost by using modern cultivation techniques and the latest equipment. Railroads and banks concerned them, because transportation and interest rates affected the cost of doing business and thus their profit margin. Finally, and most important, farmers wanted their capital to grow. They expected their net worth to increase as their farms appreciated in value and their mortgages were paid.

This experience was not confined to the United States; European settlers in Canada, Australia, and Argentina produced the same commodities under similar conditions. All were part of the growing world economy. Every farmer and rancher counted on industrialization and urbanization at home and in Europe to build demand for his or her commodities.

And worldwide demand for food and fiber did increase rapidly. Farmers responded by boosting production as best they could on existing holdings. Eventually, however, their output reached its limit, even though demand continued to grow. As a result, prices began to creep, and then race, upward. The venturesome dreamed of moving west and doubling or tripling their acreage. Record crop and livestock prices made the costs of moving and financing a new spread seem manageable, and existing farms could always be sold to the less intrepid. Thousands upon thousands of families streamed across the frontier, claiming millions of acres offered by generous government policies or buying from speculators who held raw land.

Nobody planned the westward migration; nobody coordinated it; nobody governed it. Each individual made his or her own calculation of the market. Farmers borrowed in order to purchase land and building materials and to buy livestock, seed, and equipment. Newly opened banks faced an insatiable demand for credit. Towns sprang up at railroad sidings where grain elevators and livestock yards were constructed. Merchants and Main Street followed. High prices brought a land boom, and the land boom brought settlement and opened the West.

It took a while for the newly converted prairie to produce a cash crop. But when it did, thousands of new farms began dumping their output on the market. The supply of agricultural commodities increased dramatically. Shortage changed to surplus, and prices dropped. Time after time during the 19th century, commodity prices fell to record lows after a period of inflation and the subsequent land rush.

Many farmers were wiped out. They could not pay their debts while commodity prices scraped bottom, and banks foreclosed on farm property.

If a bank made too many loans that went bad, then it was dragged down too. Merchants saw their customers disappear and had to close up shop. Settlers abandoned their land, and boomtowns became ghost towns.

Prices inevitably remained low for years, and most farmers, living on returns far below expectations, barely made it. In every instance, it took a while before the steady growth in world demand absorbed the excess agricultural commodities.

But as time passed, the cycle would repeat itself. After the inflation that accompanied the Civil War, western settlement continued to occur in waves until the end of the century, despite 30 years of deflation. The process happened at least half a dozen times until the frontier closed in the last years of the 19th century.

By the turn of this century, progress had been spectacular. Many thousands of acres of prairie had been transformed into productive field and pasture. Commodities worth billions of dollars were produced annually for the domestic and world markets. Billions of dollars of wealth had been created in the form of improved farmland. But the discipline of the business cycle governed the advance. For every two steps forward, there had been one step backward, as those who borrowed or lent the least wisely, settled the poorest land, or had the worst luck went broke.

Things haven't changed. Agriculture's fortunes are still guided by the cycle. Remember the boom of the early 70s? Consumption of beef was up; President Nixon negotiated the wheat deal with Russia; the Peruvian anchovy harvest had failed, and soy beans were used to fill the gap (as a protein extender). Agricultural commodity prices doubled, even tripled, causing farm income to shoot up. As a result, farmers spent the rest of the decade investing heavily in land and equipment. Ultimately, supply outstripped demand, and farm prices deteriorated throughout the early 80s.

We've seen the result. It's nothing that hasn't happened before: foreclosures, bankruptcies, falling land values, broken families, and ruined lives. Eventually, of course, prices stabilized—until the next cycle comes along to start the process all over again.

Oil presents a similar picture. Billions were spent on exploration, recovery, and production projects in Texas, Louisiana, Oklahoma, Wyoming, Colorado, and Alaska when prices were high. Houston, Dallas, Denver, and Anchorage were boomtowns in the early 1980s. Then, when prices fell (and they always do), the money dried up. Soon you could get a condominium in Anchorage or Denver for $15,000 because whole city blocks of new housing developments were abandoned—left by their owners for bank foreclosure.

What was true for farming and oil was equally true for the nation's railroads: They developed in the same cyclical pattern. On the eve of World War I, America's railway system was complete, representing a total capital investment second only to that of agriculture. It was a remarkable feat of creative engineering and equally creative financing.

We marvel at the colorful exploits of the Goulds, Fisks, Drews, Vanderbilts, Stanfords, Hills, and others. History refers to some of them as "robber barons"; they seemed to skim off one dollar for every two invested, and it's a wonder that the railway system was ever completed or operated safely. Yet there it was, the largest in the world, a quarter of a million miles of track moving the nation's freight and passenger traffic with unparalleled efficiency.

Promoters speculatively pushed the railroads westward in anticipation of the freight and passenger traffic that settlement would bring. Federal, state, and local governments, vying for the routes that would generate progress and development, gave the railroad companies 10 percent of the nation's land. Improving rights-of-way; laying track; building trestles, stations, and marshaling yards; and purchasing locomotives and rolling stock required the railway company to raise more capital than had ever been mobilized for any other single business venture. The companies floated billions of dollars in stocks and bonds, and investors eagerly ventured their capital to take advantage of prospective success. Flush with funds, the railroads raced toward the Pacific Coast, hoping that revenue would grow quickly enough to justify their huge investment. Periodically, however, the generous rate of expansion exceeded the growth in traffic. Prospects for profits, which had seemed so bright, grew dim. Investors stopped providing funds, and railroad track construction came to a halt. Since operating revenues could not recover costs, many railroads were forced into receivership and were reorganized. Stock and bond prices plunged, wiping out investors long after the promoters had made off with their killings.

Eventually, traffic grew sufficiently to justify existing lines and raise hopes that construction could profitably resume. Investors were once again lured into advancing their funds, and a new cycle of railway expansion began. It, too, was followed by a bust, and then by another wave of construction, until the nation's railway system was complete.

The tracks spanned a continent, from New York, Philadelphia, and Baltimore to Chicago, and from there to New Orleans, Los Angeles, San Francisco, Portland, and Seattle. Profit had motivated the enterprise, and enormous tangible wealth had been created. Losses had periodically

and temporarily halted the undertaking and impoverished those who had speculated unwisely or who had been duped. Construction had proceeded in waves. It was an unplanned and often disorganized adventure, but, given the institutions of the time, no other method could have built the system as rapidly.

In this century, we have seen the business cycle not only in the heroic proportions of the Roaring Twenties and the Great Depression, but also during every succeeding business expansion or recession. We're in the cycle now, and we will be tomorrow and next year.

Business activity always expands and then contracts. There are periods when production, employment, and profits surge ahead, each followed by a period when profits and output fall and unemployment increases. Then the entire cycle repeats itself once again. During the expansion, demand, production, income, and wealth grow. Homes and factories are constructed, and machinery and equipment are put in place. The value of these assets also grows as home prices and common stock prices increase. But then comes the inevitable contraction, and all the forces that mark the expansion shift into reverse. Demand, production, and income fall. The level of construction and the production of machinery and equipment are drastically curtailed. Assets lose their value as home prices and common stock prices fall.

No doubt you already realize that business cycles occur and repeat themselves in this way. But why? No completely satisfactory theory has yet been created. No one can accurately predict the length and course of each cycle. Economics, unlike physics, cannot be reduced to experiments and repeated over and over again under ideal conditions. There is no economic equivalent to Galileo on the Tower of Pisa, proving that objects of unequal weight fall with equal speed, because the economic "tower" is never quite the same height; the "objects" keep changing in number, size, and even nature; and the "laws of gravity" apply unequally to each object.

Yet one thing is certain: The business cycle is generated by forces within the economic system, not by outside forces. These internal forces create the alternating periods of economic expansion and contraction. And you should recognize that certain crucial features of the cycle endure.

A THUMBNAIL SKETCH

First, the forces of supply and demand condition every cycle. Our ability to enjoy increasing income depends on our ability to supply or create

increased production or output; we must produce more to earn more. But the level of demand, and the expenditures made in purchasing this output, must justify the level of production. That is, we must sell what we produce in order to earn. With sufficient demand, the level of production will be sustained and will grow, and income will increase; if demand is insufficient, the reverse will occur. During the expansionary phase of the cycle, demand and supply forces are in a relationship that permits the growth of production and income; during the contractionary phase, their relationship compels a decrease in production and income.

Second, neither consumers nor businesses are constrained to rely solely on the income they have generated in the process of production. They have recourse to the credit market; they can borrow money and spend more than they earn. Spending borrowed funds permits demand to take on a life of its own and bid up a constantly and rapidly growing level of production. This gives rise to the expansionary phase of the cycle. Eventually, the growth in production becomes dependent on the continued availability of credit, which sustains the growth in demand. But once buyers can no longer rely on borrowed funds (because of market saturation, the exhaustion of profitable investment opportunities, or tight credit), demand falls and, with it, the bloated level of production and income. The contractionary phase has begun.

Third, every expansion carries with it the inevitability of "overexpansion" and the subsequent contraction. Overexpansion may be impelled by businesses that invest too heavily in new plant and equipment in order to take advantage of a seemingly profitable opportunity, or by consumers who borrow too heavily in order to buy homes, autos, or other goods. But when businesses realize that the expected level of sales will not support additional plant and equipment, and when consumers realize that they will have difficulty paying for that new home or car, then businesses and consumers will curtail their borrowing and expenditure. Since production and income have spurted ahead to meet the growth in demand, they fall when the inevitable contraction in demand takes place.

Fourth, during contractions, production and income recede to a sustainable level; that is, they fall to a level not reliant on a continuous growth in credit. The contraction returns the economy to a more efficient level of operation.

Fifth, every contraction sows the seeds of the subsequent recovery.
Income earned in the productive process, rather than bloated levels of borrowing, maintains the level of demand. Consumers and businesses repay their debts. Eventually, lower debt burdens and interest rates encourage consumer and business borrowing and demand. The economy begins expanding once more.

And there is progress over the course of the cycle. Overall growth takes place because some, or even most, of the increase in output remains intact. Nor is all the created wealth subsequently destroyed. The abandoned steel mills of the "rust belt" will be scrapped, but the plant and equipment used to make personal computers will remain on-stream. Residential construction completed in 1986 turned a profit for its developers, while homes completed in 1990, at the peak of the cycle, were liquidated at a loss after standing empty for a year. And so on. The tree grows, but the rings in its trunk mark the cycles of seasons that were often lush but on occasion were beset by drought.

Yet the American economy grew steadily throughout the 1980s after the recession of 1981–82. Had the business cycle been repealed? Some seemed to think so, just as others had thought so before them, only to be disappointed by the next recession.

Why did the economy just keep growing in the 1980s? Why didn't it stop? Did President Reagan and his supply-side policies deserve the credit? Was the Federal Reserve responsible?

Why did the economy lurch into recession in 1990? The chapters that follow will not only discuss the cycle's dynamic, they will also describe the forces that "stretched out" the cycle in the 1980s and postponed recession's expected return. And they will also discuss the cycle's dynamic in the 1990s: what we can reasonably expect for the remainder of the decade and what its impact on investors will be.

But as you may already suspect, the business cycle does not operate in a vacuum. It is conditioned, shortened and stretched, and initiated and forestalled by the institutions of our economy. So, before embarking on an investigation of the cycle, take a quick look at Chapter 3, which discusses the attempts to influence the economy since World War II.

CHAPTER 3

THE TRANSFORMATION
OF THE POSTWAR ECONOMY

To this point, we have discussed the business cycle as if it were independent and autonomous. In fact, in modern history, the American business
cycle has been influenced by a variety of attempts to guide and direct it.
The economic events of the 15 years from 1965 to 1980 provide a vivid
example of well-intentioned economic meddling gone awry.

During these years, the federal government and the Federal Reserve
System attempted to stimulate demand for goods and services with liberal
spending, tax, and credit policies. Their objective was to boost the economy higher and faster, thereby generating increased employment opportunities. They thought that as supply rose to meet demand, increased
production would accomplish their objectives. Unfortunately, as demand
grew more rapidly than supply, prices spiraled upward. As inflation
became more severe, the only solution appeared to be a periodic reversal
of those policies of liberal spending, tax, and credit—which invariably
helped plunge the economy into recession. These policy reversals exacerbated the cycle so that inflation *escalated* during boom and unemployment
rose during bust.

The actions of the Federal Reserve and federal government had their
origin in the 1930s, when economists were attempting to cope with the
ravages of the Great Depression. At that time, it was obvious that
the economy was stagnating due to insufficient demand for the goods and
services business could produce. The factories were there; the machines
were there; the labor was there; only the customers were missing. The
great question of the day was, "How can we generate effective demand for
goods and services?"

Traditional economists had no solution to the problem. They viewed the
Depression as a trough in a particularly severe cycle that would correct

itself with time. Therefore, they prescribed laissez-faire (leave it alone) as the best possible course of action. Why not? It had always worked in the past.

A new generation of economists surveyed the scene and came up with a different diagnosis. They saw the Great Depression as inaugurating an era in which demand was (and might remain) chronically depressed. To deal with the problem, they recommended a two-pronged solution.

First, stimulate demand directly. Clearly, consumers were not going to spend more, for many were unemployed, and those who were working were afraid to spend, because they might lose their jobs. Business was not going to buy new factories and machinery, since existing facilities were underutilized. Only the government was in a position to spend more. Such government spending would involve deficit financing as the level of expenditures exceeded tax revenues, but the New Dealers were prepared to run the risk. If the government had to borrow now, it could pay back later. In this way, the government would be the employer of last resort, hiring people to build dams, bridges, roads, and parks.

Second, the Federal Reserve System (the nation's central bank, known as the Fed) could push interest rates down and thereby depress the cost of borrowing money. This would motivate businesses (to the extent that they could be motivated) to borrow funds in order to buy equipment and machinery and to build additional factories and other establishments. Making credit easy was a way of stimulating economic activity.

These policies, applied in the late 30s, were interrupted by World War II, which generated boom conditions. But when the war came to an end, it was feared that the economy would again slip back into a chronic state of depression. That anxiety was unfounded, but it was so strongly felt that the ideological revolution of the 1930s survived. The new school of economists believed it was the government's duty to stimulate demand until the economy reached its maximum potential of full employment. This attitude meshed with other liberal and progressive views regarding government's responsibility for the social welfare of all.

Conservatives, on the other hand, continued to believe that laissez-faire was the best policy. Thus, throughout the Eisenhower years, the conservative administration drew fire from progressive economists for not implementing the lessons that had been learned in the 30s. They wanted additional federal spending and easy money in order to spur the economy.

When John F. Kennedy ran for office in 1960, he charged that the Eisenhower administration's conservative policies had reduced the rate of economic growth, and he promised to get the economy moving again.

After he took office in 1961, he made good on that pledge by inviting the new school of economists into his administration, urging them to apply the progressive policies that had been developed under Roosevelt.

They did prescribe those policies, but with a new wrinkle. Rather than stimulate demand directly with increased government spending, they proposed putting more purchasing power in the pockets of consumers by cutting taxes. The government would still have to borrow to meet the deficit, but this time it would do so to pay for a shortfall of revenue rather than a growth in expenditure. One way or the other, demand would grow.

Increased consumer spending was just as good as government spending—and, as a rule, politically more advantageous. The extra spending would stimulate economic growth and create jobs as production expanded to meet the surge in consumer demand. At the same time, President Kennedy's economists urged the Federal Reserve to maintain an easy policy so that liberal credit would be available at low rates of interest for consumer and business needs.

These views remained in fashion for two decades. A generation of students was trained to believe that an inadequate level of demand was the paramount problem facing the economy and that they should study economics in order to determine how the federal government and the Federal Reserve could best stimulate the level of economic activity to provide full employment. They all recognized that excessive stimulation of demand could lead to inflation, but they felt that inflation would not be a severe problem until the economy attained full employment.

In each recession the Federal Reserve depressed interest rates, and the government stimulated spending directly with tax cuts for consumers and business. Demand roared ahead in short order, and, when it exceeded supply at current prices, prices surged upward. At this point the federal government and the Federal Reserve reversed course and employed policies designed to dampen inflation. They slammed on the brakes, raising taxes and interest rates, depressing demand temporarily, and causing recession. But as soon as the inflation rate dropped, they reversed course and helped bring on the next round of expanding demand and inflation.

No one—not the economists, not the government, not the Federal Reserve—realized that World War II had profoundly changed the underlying circumstances and that policies appropriate for the 30s were not suited for the 60s and 70s. The Great Depression, which preceded the war, was a time of inadequate demand. But government borrowing from banks during the war, and the expenditures of those funds, had placed a wealth of liquid assets at the consumer's disposal. When the war ended, con-

sumers were prepared to spend those funds, and they were also increasingly prepared to borrow in order to supplement their expenditures. In the postwar world, demand, buttressed by borrowing, would chronically exceed supply, thus bidding prices upward. Excessive demand, not inadequate demand, would be the problem.

Thus began the first American peacetime period with significant and continuing inflation. In all other eras, inflation had been the product of wartime government spending financed by borrowing, while peacetime had been a period of stable prices or even deflation. Consequently, government spending financed by borrowing, whether in time of war or peace, was viewed by almost everyone as the single source of inflation, and this mindset spilled over into the postwar world. No one comprehended that a new economic dynamic was at work in which inflation would be generated by private (consumer and business) borrowing and spending. Ever greater waves of borrowing by the private sector (not government) would drive the inflationary cycle.

The new generation of economists and their students, whose intellectual mold had been cast during the New Deal, were like generals who conduct a war by fighting the previous campaign. But the real issue facing the postwar world was how to keep demand under control, how to restrain it and prevent it from generating inflation. The Eisenhower years, when demand did seem to stall, confused economists, making them believe that the chronically depressed conditions of the 1930s were a real possibility in the postwar world.

This was a major miscalculation. In fact, the escalating inflation of the 70s showed us that the potential runaway horse of the economy was champing at the bit—and all the while economists and policy makers were wondering how to apply the spurs more vigorously.

By 1980, after two decades of inappropriate policies, the Federal Reserve was determined to come to grips with the problem. New Deal economics had to be discarded. The spurs had to be removed, the reins taken in hand, and the runaway horse restrained. So the Fed tightened up; interest rates reached the stratosphere, borrowing and spending dried up, and the economy came closer to collapsing in 1981–82 than at any time since the war. After the recession of 1981–82 contained demand and eliminated inflation, the Fed slowly began to ease up. But the Fed was determined not to return to the errors of the past; it would not let credit become easy, or demand grow too rapidly, or inflation get out of control again.

Thus, the Fed acted single-handedly to stretch out the business cycle and forestall recession. By squashing the cycle flat in the early 1980s, and

then restraining inflation in the mid and late 80s, the Fed interrupted the cycle's regular and periodic oscillations. This created a period of steady expansion during which the economy did not overheat. Inflation had been brought under control, giving the edge to stocks and other paper assets over gold and similar tangible investments.

But the recession of 1990–91 brought an end to the Fed's run of good luck. Why? What had gone wrong? Was the Federal Reserve or the federal government to blame once again?

The Fed responded to the recession by letting interest rates fall sharply and holding them there until recovery was well under way. Then, mindful of its overriding long-run concern with inflation, the Fed sent interest rates upward when the economy expanded rapidly in 1994 and 1995. The Fed hoped its preemptive strike would cool the economy before it overheated, instigate a "soft landing," and prevent a repeat of the cyclical excess of the 1970s.

So before you consider *The Wall Street Journal*'s reports on business cycle developments, read Chapters 4 and 5 to review the role of the Federal Reserve System and the federal government in today's business and investment scene.

CHAPTER 4

THE FEDERAL RESERVE SYSTEM: MONETARY POLICY AND INTEREST RATES

THE FED AND INFLATION

Chart 1–1 on page 4 provides graphic evidence that inflation and the business cycle had the greatest imaginable impact on economic conditions and investment values from 1970 to 1990. Because the Federal Reserve System (the Fed) is the only modern American institution that has been able to constructively control and shape these forces, you should begin by learning how to use *The Wall Street Journal* to decipher the Fed's operations.

The Fed is your first order of business because the power of the Fed squashed the business cycle flat in the early 1980s, bringing an end to excessive inflation for the foreseeable future. Before that, during the high-inflation 70s, business cycle fluctuations had grown more severe and inflation's pace had accelerated. *Thus, the Fed's stand against inflation in 1981–82 was the most important turning point in our post World War II economic history.* And, as you already know, the Fed's anti-inflation policies of the late 80s were crucial in postponing recession and stretching out the cycle.

The business cycle and inflation had spun out of control in the late 1960s and 70s because consumers and businesses had borrowed ever more heavily to finance ever larger expenditures on homes, cars, and other durable goods, as well as plant, equipment, and inventory. As oceans of borrowing supported tidal waves of spending (i.e., demand for goods and services), supply could not keep pace, and prices rose.

To understand this phenomenon, consider a hypothetical example in which people had just as much to spend at the end of a given year as at the

beginning, but had increased their output of goods and services by 5 percent during that year. Prices would have to fall by 5 percent before the same amount of spending (demand) could absorb an additional 5 percent of goods and services (supply). And if folks continued each year to produce 5 percent more while their spending did not grow, then prices would fall by 5 percent year after year. We would have chronic deflation.

Similarly, if people's ability to spend (demand) grew by 20 percent while output (supply) grew by 5 percent, you can imagine prices being bid up by 15 percent in that year. And if their spending continued to grow by 20 percent a year while their output grew by only 5 percent, you can imagine chronic inflation of 15 percent. Now you understand how changing supply and demand generate deflation and inflation.

You may ask, "How is it possible for spending (demand) to grow more rapidly than the output (supply) of society? You can spend only what you have, after all." No, not if people have access to credit provided by banks. For instance, suppose you earn $50,000 a year and your income is a measure of the value of the goods and services that you produce or supply for the market. Also, suppose that your spending (demand) is limited by your income. Demand and supply ($50,000) are equal, so prices don't change. Now suppose that you have access to bank credit, so that you can borrow $200,000 to have a house built. Your demand (spending) rises to $200,000, even though your income (supply) remains at $50,000. Demand exceeds supply in this case, and if your situation is repeated often enough in others, prices rise. Whenever demand exceeds supply at current prices, a situation made possible by borrowing (credit), inflation (rising prices) occurs.

The $200,000 provided by the banks was *not* produced and saved by someone else, thereby equating earlier supply with new demand. It was created out of thin air by the banking system, and that is why your bank-financed spending is inflationary. It also serves to illustrate the point that you have to understand the banking and credit system to comprehend the reasons for the ever-escalating business cycle and inflation of 1965–80.

And finally, you should also be aware that the decline in borrowing in the early 1990s signaled the drop in demand that led to both the recession of 1990–91 and the reduced inflation that accompanied it.

Private borrowing by consumers and businesses has always been a feature of our economy, but it did not begin to reach heroic proportions and grow at an explosive pace until the late 1960s. From that point on, credit doubled every five years. There was no way production could keep pace with these surges in demand, so rising inflation filled the gap.

But borrowing and spending did not grow smoothly. They surged forward periodically, generating the wavelike action of the business cycle. The rise of borrowing and spending carried inflation with it; interest rates rose too, as spiraling borrowing drove up the cost of credit. Steep increases in prices and interest rates eventually choked off the boom, discouraging consumers and businesses from continued borrowing and spending. The wave crashed and the cycle completed itself as the economy contracted into recession.

The Fed exacerbated the worst aspects of the cycle in the late 60s and throughout the 70s by attempting to alleviate them. Reining in credit expansion at the peak of the cycle in order to curb inflation merely contributed to the severity of the inevitable downturn and made recession worse. Easing up during recession, in order to encourage borrowing and spending and thus pull the economy out of a slump, contributed to the excesses of the next boom. And with each wave of the cycle, inflation and interest rates ratcheted higher and higher.

The Fed reversed course in 1981–82 and brought an end to 15 years of escalating inflation and cyclical instability by applying a chokehold of high interest rates. The economy was brought to the brink of collapse. But when the Fed relaxed its grip and interest rates declined from exorbitant to merely high, the manic rounds of boom and bust had ceased. The economy set out on a healthy expansion without inflation that lasted through the late 80s until Iraq's invasion of Kuwait eroded consumer sentiment, casting a pall over borrowing and spending that led to the 1990–91 recession.

That recession prompted the Fed to let interest rates fall to their lowest level in years, as the economy languished in the doldrums of an anemic recovery. But by late 1994, the Fed had ratcheted rates up again in order to rein in a rapidly expanding economy. At mid-decade, the Fed had not abandoned its 15-year struggle against inflation.

Borrowing and Inflation

- Bank lending finances spending; spending generates inflation.
- The Fed controls bank lending and can thereby control inflation.
- But a drop in borrowing and spending will reduce inflation and, if sufficiently sharp, will lead to recession.

But what is the Fed? How does it work? What, exactly, did it (and does it) do? Start your investigation with a bit of background.

THE FED'S HISTORY

The United States was the last major industrial nation to establish a central bank. The modern German state commissioned a central bank in 1875; the Bank of France was founded in 1800; and the Bank of England had entered its third century of operation when the Federal Reserve System was created in 1913.

America's tardiness was due to our traditional suspicion of centralized financial power and authority. Historically, we have felt more comfortable with small banks serving a single community. In fact, some states limited branch banking until recently. For instance, the First National Bank of Chicago became one of the nation's biggest, even though Illinois law severely constrained its branch facilities in downstate Illinois. Similarly, the big New York City banks (until after World War II) were hampered by legislation that confined them to the city and its suburbs and kept their branches out of upstate New York. On the other hand, California's liberal branch banking laws once helped Bank of America build its position as the nation's largest bank. To this day, a rational, nationwide scheme for organizing our banking institutions does not exist.

Recall how many banks failed in the 1980s and the disaster that struck the savings and loan industry. There were many causes, but surely the small size and limited resources of many of our banks and S&Ls were contributing factors. Japan and Germany have a fraction of the number of banks that we have. Massive financial institution failure is unthinkable in those countries.

Alexander Hamilton proposed a central bank shortly after the country's founding. The two early attempts to create one failed when confronted with the nation's suspicion of the Eastern financial community. Consequently, our economy grew until the eve of World War I without benefit of coordination or control of its banking activity. Banking, like the sale of alcohol following the repeal of Prohibition, was largely subject to local option.

Under these circumstances, the banks had to fend for themselves, and the business cycle created perils for them as well as opportunities for profit. During recessions, when business income was down (usually

following periods of speculative excess), banks found it difficult to collect on loans.

At the same time, nervous business persons and investors made large withdrawals, sometimes demanding payment in gold or silver specie. These precious metal coins composed the ultimate reserve for deposits; however, no bank possessed enough of them to secure every depositor, and the banking system functioned on the assumption that only a minority of depositors would demand their funds on any one day. When panic set in and a queue formed out the door and around the block, a bank could be wiped out in a matter of hours. As rumor spread, one bank after another failed, until only the most substantial institutions, with the greatest specie reserve, were left standing. The chain reaction damaged many people, not the least of whom were innocent depositors who could not reach their funds in time.

Congress took up the issue after the panic of 1907. In that crisis—as the story goes—J.P. Morgan kept New York's most important bankers locked up in his home overnight until they agreed to contribute a pool of specie to be lent to the weakest banks until the run subsided. It worked—but the near-disaster had made it clear that the time had come to establish an American central bank that could lend to all banks in time of panic; the nation's financial system could no longer rely on the private arrangements of J.P. Morgan. Thus, Congress established the Federal Reserve System in 1913. All member banks were required to make deposits to the system, creating a pool of reserves from which financially strapped banks could borrow during a crisis.

The system was originally conceived as a lender of last resort. In times of severe economic stress, it would use the pooled reserves of the banking system to make loans to banks under stress. When conditions improved, the loans were to be repaid. As time went by, however, the Fed discovered two things: first, that the reserve requirement could be used to control banking activity; and second, that control over the banking system provided a means of influencing the business cycle.

The reasoning was straightforward. Bank lending is a key ingredient in the business cycle, driving the cyclic expansion of demand. It cannot, however, grow beyond the limits set by bank reserves; so, when the Fed wants to give the economy a boost by encouraging banks to lend more, it increases reserves. On the other hand, by decreasing reserves and thereby shrinking available credit, the Fed exerts a restraining effect on the economy.

OPEN-MARKET OPERATIONS

The mechanism used by the Fed to manipulate the banking system's reserves is astonishingly simple: It buys or sells securities on the open market. Briefly put, when the Fed buys securities, the sellers deposit the proceeds of the sale in their banks, and the banking system's reserves grow. On the other hand, when the Fed sells securities, buyers withdraw funds from their banks in order to make the purchases, and bank reserves fall.

This illustration may help you understand the process. Imagine that the Fed, a government-securities dealer, and all banks (not an individual bank) are the only players in this example. Keep in mind that there are trillions of dollars of U.S. Treasury securities outstanding and that anyone (domestic and foreign corporations, individuals, state, local, and foreign governments, private banks, and central banks) can buy them. Billions of dollars of securities are traded each day in New York City.

The Fed increases and reduces bank reserves by its actions in this market. It trades in U.S. Treasury securities rather than some other instrument because the government securities market is so broad and Federal Reserve activities have a relatively small impact on that market.

When the Fed purchases a security from one of the dealers, it pays the dealer by instructing the dealer's bank to credit the checking account of the dealer by the amount of the transaction. At the same time, the Fed pays the bank by crediting the bank's reserve account at the Fed.

Returning to the example, Treasury bills are denominated in amounts of $10,000. Thus, when the Fed buys a Treasury bill from a securities dealer, it instructs the dealer's bank to credit the dealer's account by $10,000 to pay for the Treasury bill. At the same time, the Fed credits the dealer's bank's reserve account by $10,000. As a result of the transaction, the dealer has exchanged one asset (Treasury bills ↓ $10,000) for another (checking account ↑ $10,000), the bank's assets (reserves at the Fed ↑ $10,000) and liabilities (dealer's checking account ↑ $10,000) have both increased, and the Fed's assets (Treasury bills ↑ $10,000) and liabilities (bank reserves ↑ $10,000) have both increased.

You may ask, "What gives the Fed the authority to execute these transactions: to pay for a Treasury bill by instructing the dealer's bank to credit the dealer's checking account and then to compensate the bank by crediting its reserve account at the Fed? It's as if the Fed has the right to fund the purchase of an asset by creating its own liability." That's how it works.

The Fed has the right under the authority vested in it by the Federal Reserve Act of 1913.

In other words, the Fed can increase the nation's bank reserves by purchasing U.S. Treasury securities from securities dealers, and all it need do to pay for those securities is inform the banks that it has provided them with more reserves. And that's not all; be aware that, unless the Fed continues to buy those securities and pay for them by crediting the banks' reserve accounts, bank reserves won't grow. The Fed can halt the economy's expansion by no longer purchasing Treasury bills. Once the Fed stops buying, bank reserves stop growing, and so must bank lending. If the Fed wishes to keep a growing economy supplied with bank reserves, it must increase its holdings of Treasury securities over the long haul.

But suppose the Fed wishes to slow the economy's growth temporarily by curtailing banks' ability to lend. Easy—it just stops *buying* securities and starts *selling* them. The securities dealer pays for the Treasury bill it acquires (dealer's assets ↑) when the Fed instructs the dealer's bank to debit the dealer's bank account (dealer's assets ↓). The Fed collects from the dealer's bank by debiting the bank's reserve account at the Fed (bank's assets ↓), and the bank is compensated when it debits the dealer's checking account (bank's liabilities ↓). Consequently, bank lending must cease because the banks are deprived of reserves. Meanwhile, the Fed has merely reduced its assets (Treasury securities ↓) as well as its liabilities (bank reserves ↓).

Consider a few additional points. Don't worry whether or not the securities dealer is willing to buy or sell Treasury securities. There are dozens of dealers competing for the Fed's (and everyone else's) business. There's as much likelihood of the Fed not being able to find a buyer or seller for its Treasury securities as there is of someone not being able to buy or sell a share of stock at the market price. If one stockbroker won't do it, another will.

Also, don't be confused because these open-market operations involve the buying and selling of Treasury securities. Remember, the Fed is not an agency of the U.S. government. The Fed could just as easily deal in common stock or automobiles, but it wouldn't do that because it does not want its actions to upset the stock market or the car market. Nonetheless, keep in mind that the Fed could pay for shares of stock or autos by instructing banks to credit stockbrokers' or auto dealers' accounts (and then credit those banks' reserve accounts) in the same fashion that it instructs banks to credit U.S. Treasury securities dealers' accounts. Then, the Fed would

credit the reserve accounts of the banks that held the stockbrokers' and car dealers' accounts. If the Fed sold common stock or used cars, it would drain away bank reserves just as surely as when it sold Treasury bills in the open market.

Finally, keep in mind that the discussion refers to all banks collectively, not to individual banks. This distinction is important. Banks can competitively drain one another of reserves to augment their ability to lend, but this activity does not increase the entire system's reserves, though it does explain the fierce rivalry among banks for deposits. When deposits are moved from one bank to another, the reserves of the first bank fall and those of the second bank increase. The first bank must restrain its lending, while the second bank can lend more. This competitive reshuffling of reserves, however, has not altered the overall level of reserves, and so the lending ability of the banking system remains the same.

To resume the historical account, the Fed has exercised increasing power over the economy since 1913. Periodically, this has led to conflict with the president and Congress. On occasion, politicians took the Fed to task for being too restrictive, for not permitting the economy to grow rapidly enough. At other times, the Fed was criticized for being too lenient and permitting demand to grow so rapidly that inflation threatened.

Why the conflict? Shouldn't the Fed's policy reflect the wishes of Congress and the president? Maybe, but it need not, for—as many do not realize—the Fed is not an agency of the U.S. government, but a corporation owned by banks that have purchased shares of stock. Federally chartered banks are required to purchase this stock and be members of the Federal Reserve System; state-chartered banks may be members if they wish. All banks, however, are subject to the Fed's control.

True, the Fed does have a quasi-public character, because its affairs are managed by a Board of Governors appointed by the president of the United States with the approval of Congress. Nonetheless, once appointed, the Board of Governors is independent of the federal government and is free to pursue policies of its own choosing. New laws could, of course, change its status. That's why the chairman of the board is so frequently called upon to defend the policies of the Fed before Congress, and why Congress often reminds the Fed that it is a creature of Congress, which can enact legislation to reduce, alter, or eliminate the Fed's powers. Indeed, legislators and others do suggest from time to time that the Fed be made an agency of the U.S. government in order to remove its autonomy. So far, however, Congress has kept it independent, and it is

likely to remain so, exercising its best judgment in guiding the nation's banking activity.

In some ways, the Fed's control over the banking system's reserves is the most important relationship between any two institutions in the American economy. The Fed can increase or reduce bank reserves at will, making it easier or more difficult for the banks to lend, thus stimulating or restricting business and economic activity.

THE FED AND THE MONEY SUPPLY

But how is it that bank lending increases the supply of money? Where does the money come from? There is an astonishingly simple answer to these questions: The banks create it by crediting the checking account deposits of their borrowers. Thus, bank lending creates money (deposits).

And the only limits to the money supply are:

1. The Fed's willingness to provide the banks with reserves, so that they can lend.
2. The banks' ability to find borrowers.

It may sound strange that banks create money, but, nonetheless, it's true.

The reason so much controversy surrounds the money supply is that many people misunderstand its nature. Checking accounts (or demand deposits, as they are formally called) constitute three-quarters of the money supply, and currency and coins in circulation together make up the remaining quarter. The one-quarter of the money supply that exists as cash comes from a two-tiered source: The U.S. Treasury mints coins and prints paper money for the Fed, and the Fed distributes them.

These arrangements have an interesting and important history. Before the Civil War, with the exception of the two short-lived attempts at a central bank that were mentioned earlier, all paper money was issued by private banks and was called bank notes. These bank notes resembled modern paper currency and entered circulation when banks lent them to customers.

The banks' incentive to issue bank notes to borrowers, instead of gold and silver coins, came from the limited supply of gold and silver coins (specie). If banks wished to lend more than the specie on hand, they would have to issue bank notes. Each bank kept a specie reserve that was no

more than a fraction of its outstanding bank notes. This reserve was used to satisfy those who demanded that a bank redeem its notes with specie; as long as the bank could do so, its notes were accepted at face value and were "good as gold." Bank notes and minted coins circulated together.

After the Civil War, checking accounts replaced bank notes. They were safer and more convenient, because the customer (borrower) had to sign them and could write in their exact amount. In modern times, all customers, whether depositors or borrowers, began to make use of checking accounts. The private bank note passed into history.

The U.S. Treasury first issued paper money during the Civil War, and it continued to do so until some time after World War II. During the 20th century, however, most of our paper money has been issued by the Federal Reserve System, and today the Fed has that exclusive responsibility; if you examine a piece of currency, you will see that it is a "Federal Reserve Note." Thus, ironically, bank notes constitute all of our currency today, just as they did before the Civil War, but the notes are issued by the central bank rather than by a host of private banks.

Since the Treasury prints currency at the Fed's request to meet the public's needs, the common notion that the federal government cranks out more paper money to finance its deficits has no factual basis. The amount of paper money in circulation has nothing to do with the deficits of the federal government. When the federal government runs a deficit (expenditures exceed revenue), the Treasury borrows by issuing bonds that are bought by investors; the government gets the money, and the investors get the bonds. If a bond is sold to a bank (and banks are major purchasers of U.S. Treasury securities), the bank pays for it by crediting the checking account of the U.S. Treasury, thus increasing the total volume of all checking accounts. This is called *monetizing the debt*; it enlarges the money supply but does not affect currency in circulation. (If the bond is purchased by the Fed, the transaction is also characterized as monetizing the debt, and the effect is similar to an expansionary monetary policy in which the Fed buys U.S. Treasury securities through open-market operations.)

By contrast, the Fed issues paper money in response not to the budget deficits of the *federal government*, but to the *public's* requirements for cash. It supplies banks with currency, and the banks pay for it with a check written on their reserve account. Checks written to "cash" by bank customers then determine the amount of currency circulating outside banks. This demand for currency has no impact on the money supply because checking accounts decrease by the amount currency increases when the check is "cashed."

How then does the money supply grow? It increases in the same fashion that outstanding bank notes grew in the 19th century. When banks lend, they create demand deposits (checking accounts) or credit an existing demand deposit. The more that banks lend, the more that the money supply (which is mostly demand deposits) increases. Today, as 100 years ago, bank reserves set the only limit on bank lending and, therefore, on the money supply. The difference is that, instead of keeping specie as reserves, the banks must maintain reserves with the Fed.

Remember: Bank loans create deposits (checking accounts), not the other way around. As long as the banking system has sufficient reserves, it can make loans in the form of demand deposits (money). You must abandon the notion that depositors' funds provide the wherewithal for bank lending. That may be true for the traditional mortgage-lending activity of a savings and loan association, but it is not true for commercial banks. After all, where would depositors get the funds if not by withdrawing them from another checking account? But this actually does not increase deposits for the entire system; it only reshuffles deposits among banks. The total is unchanged.

Thus, demand deposits (checking accounts), and with them the money supply, grow when banks lend, and it makes no difference who the borrower is. When a business borrows from its bank in order to stock goods for the Christmas season, the bank creates a deposit (money) on which the business writes checks to pay for merchandise. If you borrow from your bank to buy a car, the loan creates a demand deposit that increases the money supply. Therefore, as you can see, it is not just the federal government that "monetizes debt" when it borrows from the banking system; businesses and consumers "monetize" their debt too.

One last point must be made about the nature of bank reserves. A hundred years ago, these reserves consisted of gold and silver specie; today, they are deposits that banks maintain with the Federal Reserve System. Of what do these reserves consist, if not specie? They are merely checking accounts that the banks have on deposit with the Fed, very much like the checking account you have at your own bank.

Recall that the banks' checking accounts (reserves) increase when the Fed buys securities from a government securities dealer. In other words, banks' reserves are nothing more than accounts the banks maintain at the Fed, accounts that grow at the Fed's discretion whenever it buys securities in the open market.

If it sounds like a house of cards, or like bookkeeping entries in a computer's memory, that's because it is. Nothing "backs up" the money sup-

ply except our faith in it, expressed every time we accept or write a check. Those checking accounts, and hence the money supply, built on borrowing, *must keep growing* if the economy is to grow over the business cycle. The forward surge of the cycle, when demand grows rapidly and pulls the economy's output with it, is founded on spenders' ability and willingness to borrow and to go into debt.

This, then, is the critical significance of the money supply: It measures the increase in demand made possible by bank lending. With that in mind, it is now time to discuss the price borrowers are willing to pay for those funds.

THE FED AND INTEREST RATES

Every commodity has a price; the *interest rate* is the price of money. As with any commodity, that price fluctuates according to the laws of supply and demand.

The demand for money increases and interest rates rise during economic expansion as consumers and businesses finance increased spending. They do so by drawing on three sources of funds: current savings, liquidation of financial assets, and borrowing from banks and other financial intermediaries. It's easy to see that an increase in the demand for funds will drive up interest rates.

During recessions, however, as the economy moves from trough to recovery, cash becomes plentiful again. Savings grow, financial assets accumulate, and debt is repaid. Interest rates fall as the supply of funds exceeds the demand for funds at current rates.

The cyclical rise and fall of interest rates would occur with or without the Federal Reserve System. Yet the Fed's influence on interest rates is so pervasive that it is now time to study the Fed's actions in detail.

Begin with a summary statement of the Fed's objectives and actions that refers to neither the money supply nor interest rates, which will be developed later:

- *Expansionary policy*: If the Fed buys securities, thus increasing member bank reserves, the banks will be able to lend more, stimulating demand. Such an expansionary policy has traditionally been pursued during a period of recession, when the economy is at the bottom of the business cycle.

- *Contractionary policy*: If the Fed sells securities, and bank reserves are reduced, the banks will not be able to lend as much, which will curtail the share of demand that depends on borrowing and, hence, will reduce the total level of demand. This policy has been followed at the peak of the cycle to restrain the growth of demand and inflationary increases in prices.

These relationships can be easily summarized in the following manner: (Read ↑ as "up," ↓ as "down," and → as "leads to.")

Expansionary policy: Fed buys securities → Bank reserves ↑ →
Bank lending ↑ → Demand ↑
Contractionary policy: Fed sells securities → Bank reserves ↓ →
Bank lending ↓ → Demand ↓

Now include money in the analysis.

The Fed was traditionally activist, alternately pursuing easy (supplying banks with reserves) or tight (depriving banks of reserves) money policies, depending on the state of the business cycle. During periods of recession and through the recovery stage and the early period of expansion, the Fed's easy money policy contributed to rapid growth in the money supply (demand deposits or checking accounts), as banks lent money (demand deposits or checking accounts) freely in response to plentiful reserves. As the expansionary phase of the cycle reached its peak, the Fed switched to a tight money policy, restricting the growth of bank reserves and, hence, the money supply.

The Fed's actions with respect to the money supply may be added to the earlier set of directed arrows and summarized as shown:

Expansionary policy: Fed buys securities → Bank reserves ↑→
Bank lending ↑→ Money supply ↑→ Demand ↑
Contractionary policy: Fed sells securities → Bank reserves ↓→
Bank lending ↓→ Money supply ↓→ Demand ↓

As you can imagine, the Fed's actions also have an impact on interest rates. The Fed traditionally pursued an "easy money" policy to hold interest rates down and promote relaxed credit conditions in order to boost demand during the recovery phase of the cycle. Eventually, when the expansion was fully under way, the peak of the cycle was not far off, and

credit availability was constricting on its own, the Fed switched to a "tight money" policy, which reduced the supply of credit even further and drove up interest rates.

The Fed's actions with respect to *interest rates* may be included with the directed arrows and summarized as follows:

Easy money policy: Fed buys securities → Bank reserves ↑→ Interest Rates ↓→ Bank lending ↑→ Money supply ↑→ Demand ↑.

Tight money policy: Fed sells securities → Bank reserves ↓→ Interest Rates ↑→ Bank lending ↓→ Money supply ↓→ Demand ↓.

FEDERAL RESERVE POLICY AND THE POSTWAR BUSINESS CYCLE

With these principles in mind, you can examine the Fed's record of expansionary (low interest rates) and contractionary (high interest rates) monetary policies since World War II (see Charts 4–1 and 4–2 on pages 39 and 40). Remember that the Fed's objective had always been to counteract the natural swing of the cycle, stimulating demand at the trough with low interest rates, making it easy for the banks to lend, and curbing inflation at the peak with high interest, making it difficult for the banks to lend. The peaks and valleys of the cycle are reflected in these oscillations. Recessions are shaded in gray.

The economic events that began in the early 70s clearly illustrate these ideas. Do you recall the feverish inflationary boom of 1973, when demand for autos and housing was so insistent that the United Auto Workers Union was complaining of compulsory overtime and there were shortages of lumber? The demand for borrowed funds was very strong, and bank lending grew apace. Accordingly, the Fed instituted a tight money policy (see Charts 4–1 and 4–2 for years 1973 and 1974), forcing interest rates upward.

CHART 4–1
Short-Term Interest Rates: The Prime Rate, the Federal Funds Rate, and the Treasury Bill Rate

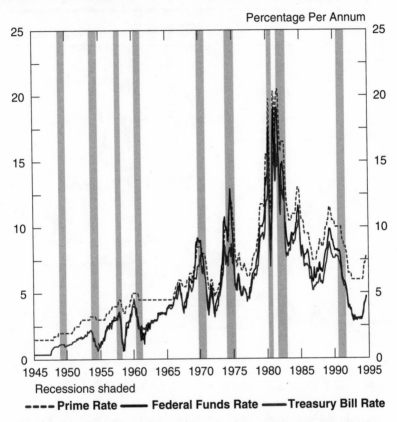

Percentage Per Annum

Recessions shaded

- - - - Prime Rate ——— Federal Funds Rate ———Treasury Bill Rate

Source: U.S. Department of Commerce, *Business Cycle Indicators*, Series 109, 114, and 119.

As the Fed applied the brakes and raised interest rates, the boom came to a halt. More than 2 million people were thrown out of work when the full force of recession hit in late 1974 and early 1975. So, the Fed switched to an easy money policy to stimulate the economy from 1975 through 1977, and interest rates fell. By 1977 the economy was expanding once more, and the Fed reversed itself again, adopting a tight money policy. It was 1974 all over again, except that inflation was even more severe. While the Fed pursued its traditional tight money policy, President Carter instituted voluntary wage and price controls.

CHART 4–2
Long-Term Interest Rates: Secondary Market Yields on FHA Mortgages, Yield on New Issues of High-Grade Corporate Bonds, and Yield on Long-Term Treasury Bonds

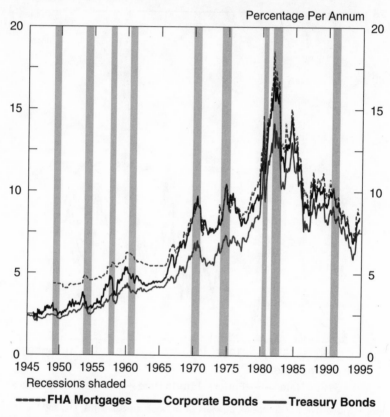

Recessions shaded

------ FHA Mortgages ——— Corporate Bonds ——— Treasury Bonds

Source: U.S. Department of Commerce, *Business Cycle Indicators*, Series 115, 116, and 118.

President Carter reshuffled his cabinet in 1979, appointing Fed Chairman G. William Miller to the position of Secretary of the Treasury, and asking Paul Volcker, President of the Federal Reserve Bank of New York, to replace Mr. Miller. Paul Volcker accepted the appointment and immediately rallied the members of the Board to maintain the fight against inflation, obtaining a commitment from them to pursue the struggle beyond the cycle's present phase. Interest rates were at a postwar high, the cyclical peak had arrived, and a downturn was inevitable.

The 1980 downturn was so sharp that the Board of Governors set aside its inflation-fighting stance temporarily, providing banks with sufficient

reserves and lowering interest rates to prevent undue hardship. Paul Volcker's battle plan, which will be described more fully in a moment, had been postponed by the exigencies of the moment.

In summary, then, the overall aim of the Fed since World War II had been to curb and, ultimately, reverse the extremes of the cycle: to dampen inflation and to stimulate a depressed economy.

THE MONETARIST CRITIQUE

However, another look at interest rates on pages 39 and 40 reveals that the Fed's policies contributed to the cycle's severity. Like an inexperienced driver with one foot on the gas and the other on the brake, attempting to achieve a steady speed but only able to surge forward after screeching to a halt, the Fed alternately stimulated and restrained the economy. Record interest rates at the cyclical peaks of the late 60s and the middle and late 70s provide evidence of the Fed's desperate attempts to bring inflationary expansion under control. Yet these sudden stops were partly the result of previous attempts, such as those made in 1972 and 1976, to stimulate rapid expansion by providing borrowers with low interest rates. As the economy accelerated and inflation began to go out of control, the Fed hit the brakes.

Meanwhile, the business cycle of the 1970s rose higher and higher, with inflation becoming more severe with each boom and unemployment becoming more severe with each bust. The Fed's policies had failed.

In the 70s, a growing group of economists began to criticize the Fed's policy, accusing the Fed of contributing to the severity of the business cycle instead of reducing cyclical fluctuations. In their view, the Fed's contractionary policy, applied at the peak of the cycle, only added to the severity of the impending recession, while its expansionary policy, during the early stages of recovery, only set the stage for the subsequent inflations.

These economists, known as the *monetarist* school, believe that the rate of increase in the money supply is the single most important determinant of business cycle conditions. If the money supply grows rapidly, the economy expands; if the money supply does not grow rapidly, or even contracts, economic activity also contracts. The monetarists also believe that because other forces intrinsic to the economy will lead to normal cyclical activity and fluctuation in the rate of growth in the money supply, the Fed's best course of action is to attempt to keep the money supply's

growth on an even keel, preferably at a low rate, reflecting the economy's long-range ability to increase output. According to the monetarists' view, anything beyond that rate will lead to inflation, and attempts to reduce the swings of the cycle will instead only exacerbate them.

It's as if the monetarists were saying, "If you want a comfortable temperature, set the thermostat and leave it. Don't fiddle with it by alternately raising and lowering it every time you feel a little chilly or a bit too warm, because this will just cause wide swings in temperature, which only heighten discomfort rather than reduce it."

The Road to Hell Is Paved with Good Intentions

- The effect of the Fed's policies in the 70s was the opposite of its intentions.
- The Fed's policies increased the amplitude of the cycle's swings.
- The rate of inflation rose over the course of the cycle.

DEBT AND THE CYCLE

Now, although the Fed was unable to control the cycle or inflation in the 70s, it was not solely responsible for the course of events. You can see tidal waves of consumer and business borrowing (referred to earlier) in Chart 4–3, doubling every five years: $100 billion in 1969, $200 billion in 1974, and $400 billion in 1979. This borrowing drove demand forward during the expansionary phase of the cycle, creating the inflationary conditions that provoked the Fed's tight money policy and the subsequent crash into recession. The downturn would have occurred in the Fed's absence; the Fed's policies just made it more severe. Unfortunately, after recession took hold, the quick shift to an easy money policy fostered the next giant wave of borrowing, spending, and inflation, and this inevitably produced (once the wave's internal energy was spent and the Fed tightened up) a major collapse.

CHART 4–3
Total Private Borrowing

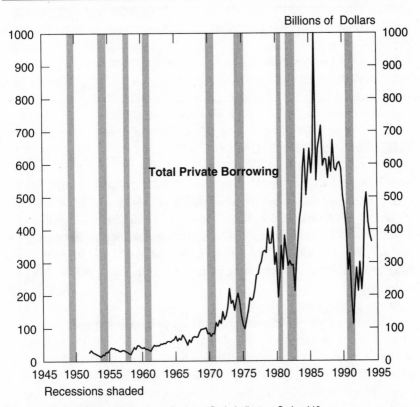

Billions of Dollars

Total Private Borrowing

1945 1950 1955 1960 1965 1970 1975 1980 1985 1990 1995
Recessions shaded

Source: U.S. Department of Commerce, *Business Cycle Indicators*, Series 110.

Be sure to notice as well that interest rates rose over time due to the ever-escalating demand for funds. You saw this in Charts 4–1 and 4–2 on pages 39 and 40, when consumer and business borrowing doubled every five years in the 1970s. Since the demand for funds continuously exceeded the supply of funds at current prices, interest rates (the price of borrowed money) climbed in the long run.

You can see that by the mid-80s interest rates had fallen from their record peak,s although private borrowing reached an all-time high. More about this later.

Inflation's Engine: The 1970s

- Explosive borrowing → explosive spending → explosive inflation.

THE FED'S REVOLUTION

Although the Fed may not have been entirely responsible for the debacle of the late 70s, the monetarists' criticism of its "stop-go" policies had hit home. In October 1979, shortly after Paul Volcker began his term of office, the Fed announced an accommodation with the monetarist position. Henceforth, Mr. Volcker said, the Fed would set targets for monetary growth that it believed were consistent with an acceptable (low) rate of inflation.

In the summer of 1980, Mr. Volcker persuaded the Fed that it would have to renew immediately its commitment to halting inflation, a commitment that it had suspended briefly during the recession of the previous spring. After earlier recessions, the Fed had always reverted to an expansionary policy of a year or two's duration (see Charts 4–1 and 4–2 on pages 39 and 40). Following the 1980 slump, however, the Fed decided to prevent rapid recovery and expansion by maintaining a very tight money policy during the early phases of recovery. Mr. Volcker persuaded the Board of Governors that inflation had become so severe that the economy could not tolerate the usual easy-money-aided recovery. The rate of inflation had risen over each successive cycle and had barely declined during the 1980 recession. Rapid stimulation and recovery of demand would quickly bid prices up once again. This time, tight money was the only appropriate remedy, even if it stunted the recovery.

In consequence, the Fed's 1980, 1981, and 1982 tight money policies drove the prime rate to 21.5 percent and first mortgage rates to 18 percent, unleashing the worst recession since World War II. For the first time, the Fed had stopped a recovery in its tracks and watched the economy slide off into back-to-back recessions. The Fed had made up its mind that restraining demand in order to control inflation was worth the price of economic contraction.

But the Fed relaxed its grip in the summer of 1982, first, because inflation had been wrung out of the economy and unemployment had reached

an intolerable level; and second, because there were strong signs that Congress was losing patience with the Fed's restrictive policies. The Fed had accomplished its objective, so there was no need to further antagonize those who had the power to terminate the Fed's independent status. Yet, despite the eventual relaxation, you should realize that the Fed's 1981 policies marked a major shift in strategy that had significant and far-reaching consequences for our economy. *If severe inflation has been eliminated for the foreseeable future, it is no exaggeration to say that the Fed beat it back single-handedly.*

The Fed Beats Back Inflation: Early 80s

- Restrictive policy → Bank reserves ↓→ Interest rates ↑→

Events in the 1980s nonetheless required the Fed's constant vigilance. When the Fed permitted easier conditions in late 1982, the economy roared ahead, as you can see from Chart 4–3 on page 43. Business and consumer borrowing grew rapidly in 1983, reaching $500 billion (a record high at the time) by early 1984. Was this to be a repeat of earlier inflationary cycles, where demand, financed by easy credit, would be permitted to leap upward, bidding the rate of inflation to a new record? Would the bitter and wrenching experience of 1981–82, which had brought inflation under control, have been suffered in vain?

Fortunately, because there was so much slack in the economy due to the recession's severity, inflation did not immediately reappear. But, immediate action was required to avoid just such a painful reoccurrence. So the Fed fine-tuned a mini-slowdown, restricting bank reserves and forcing up interest rates (Charts 4–1 and 4–2 on pages 39 and 40). That solved the problem; the growth in demand was stymied, and the economy cooled off.

The Fed's policies in the early 80s were a radical departure from those of the 60s and 70s. The 1981–82 recession and the mini slowdown of 1984 signaled a new era, a major turning point in postwar economic history. The Fed had abandoned its old game plan: spurring the economy onward during slack conditions only to apply a chokehold when boom and inflation got out of hand, and then dealing with a repeat performance in the next cycle but on a new, higher plateau. General restraint over the course of the cycle was the new master strategy.

Paul Volcker knew that easy conditions and a pro-growth attitude had contributed to the disaster of the 70s. He also knew that he was on a tightrope, and that the cautious attitude described above could not lapse into complacency. But by the mid-80s, new appointees to the Board of Governors who favored an easy-money policy had begun to undermine Mr. Volcker's go-slow approach. You will notice on pages 39 and 40 that interest rates fell, signaling dramatically easier conditions.

Why did these new appointees to the Board of Governors pursue a policy which appeared to be such a reckless reversal of the Fed's success-ful approach? And why were they appointed? Because President Reagan and his advisers, who called themselves "supply-side" economists, wanted supply-siders on the Board. Supply-siders favor easy credit and low interest rates. By 1987, at the end of Paul Volcker's second four-year term as the Board's chair, he was the only veteran of the tight money cam-paigns of the early 80s. As the supply-siders pushed easier and easier conditions, Mr. Volcker informed President Reagan that he did not wish to be appointed to another term as chair—a term in which the Board's policy of restraint could be undone by a new majority that favored easy money and in which easy money could once again unleash the forces of inflation upon the economy.

President Reagan appointed Alan Greenspan to succeed Paul Volcker. Many observers were pessimistic and did not believe that Mr. Greenspan would be any more successful in controlling the supply-siders. But these fears were unfounded, because, under Mr. Greenspan, the Board con-tinued to be responsible, refusing to permit a rekindling of the inflation of the 1970s.

You can see in Chart 4–3 on page 43 that private borrowing did not increase in the late 1980s, fluctuating around $600 billion annually. Thus, the Board maintained sufficient restraint to prevent the headlong expan-sion of private borrowing and, with it, the explosion in demand that precedes a new round of inflation.

(The big jump in borrowing in the last quarter of 1985 was due to state and local government borrowing in anticipation of tax law changes that never came about. State and local borrowing is included with these private borrowing figures, but it is usually quite small.)

The Fed Controls Inflation: Late 80s

- Moderate restraint → Moderately high interest rates →
  Moderate borrowing → Moderate spending → Moderate
  inflation.

Instead, Mr. Greenspan's board had to confront a new problem at the turn of the 90s. Recession forced them to temporarily suspend the struggle against inflation. As private borrowing plunged to levels not seen since the 1970s (see Chart 4–3 on page 43), the Fed eased and short-term interest rates fell to 17-year lows, although long-term rates held steady (see Charts 4–1 and 4–2 on pages 39 and 40).

FINE-TUNING AND DEREGULATION

All of this raises the issue of economic "fine-tuning." How did the Fed manage to bring about an effective mini slowdown in 1984, when it seemed incapable of such sensitive fine-tuning in the 70s? And why should we be optimistic that the Fed can fine-tune in the future? The answer is partly that the Fed had a relatively small and easy task before it in 1984. But that's not all. In the 70s and earlier, interest rate regulations restricted the Fed to operating a switch that was either "off" or "on." But deregulation in the late 70s and early 80s permitted a metamorphosis; the switch became a valve, allowing the flow of credit to be more finely calibrated.

The history of this transition deserves some explanation. Until the end of the 70s, banks and savings and loan companies were not permitted to pay more than a statutory maximum of slightly over 5 percent on consumer savings accounts. During the rapid expansions of 1968–69 and 1973–74, Treasury bill interest rates climbed to well above 5 percent, providing an incentive for large depositors to withdraw their funds from these financial intermediaries and invest them in Treasury bills in order to earn the higher market return.

This process was called *disintermediation* (a coinage only an economist could love), because savers bypassed the financial intermediaries to invest their funds directly in Treasury bills; S&Ls suffered severely due to their dependence on consumer savings accounts.

The upshot was that, as soon as boom conditions developed and the Fed began exercising a tight money policy, driving interest rates up, an ocean of deposits drained out of the banks and especially out of the S&Ls. The savings and loans literally ran out of money. They couldn't make mortgage loans, even if borrowers were willing to pay exorbitant rates of interest.

You can understand, then, why the Fed's tight money policies during these earlier periods did not cause credit to constrict gradually as interest rates climbed; instead, the availability of credit suddenly dried up for certain key areas of the economy (e.g., residential construction almost shut down).

Then, when the boom peaked and the economy slipped off into recession, the Fed switched to an easy money policy. As soon as Treasury bill interest rates fell below the statutory maximum that banks and S&Ls were able to pay, depositors sold their Treasury bills and redeposited the funds, propelling a tidal wave of deposits back into the financial intermediaries. As a result, S&Ls practically gave money away to finance home building.

These fund flows out of and then back into the banks and S&Ls exacerbated the business cycle. In 1969 and 1974, analysts didn't talk about tight conditions; they talked about the "credit crunch" and how it had stopped the economy in its tracks. Then, as deposits came flooding back into the system in 1970–72 and 1975–77, demand, fueled by cheap credit, took off like a rocket.

By 1980, deregulation had begun to remove interest rate ceilings from consumer savings accounts. The new, flexible-rate accounts were even called "T-bill accounts" for a while, because they were pegged to the Treasury bill rate and were designed to prevent savers from defecting to the savings account's chief competitor, the Treasury bill, as interest rates rose.

When the Fed made its desperate stand against inflation in 1981–82, deregulation had been partially accomplished: The T-bill accounts prevented a run on the savings and loan companies' deposits. These accounts required a minimum deposit of $10,000, however, so many savers were attracted by recently created money market mutual funds that had much smaller minimum deposit requirements. The money market funds invested in commercial paper and other short-term instruments, thus providing yields slightly higher than those of Treasury bills. Consequently, banks and S&Ls still faced a partial drain on their deposits.

But deregulation had begun to work. The S&Ls did not run out of money in 1981–82, although they were obliged to raise mortgage rates to prohibitive levels as T-bill account interest rates went up with the yield on Treasury bills. Residential construction was, at last, constrained by the price borrowers had to pay for funds rather than by the availability of those funds.

After the Fed eased up in mid-1982, and as the economy rebounded strongly in 1983, banks and S&Ls received permission to offer "money market accounts," which competed directly with the money market funds. Although deregulation was not 100 percent complete, depositors now had little reason to keep their funds elsewhere, and so a large volume of funds returned to the banks and S&Ls from the money market mutual funds.

Now that the Fed had a finely honed scalpel, it could maintain interest rates at sufficiently low levels to encourage demand, but it could easily nudge them upward whenever inflationary conditions threatened. And it would not have to fear disintermediation, the destructive flows of funds out of banks and S&Ls.

Early 1984 provided the first test; to confirm the results, review the interest rate record in Charts 4–1 and 4–2 on pages 39 and 40 once again. Interest rates collapsed in late 1982, but the Fed didn't wait long before it began to tighten up again. Demand had roared ahead throughout 1983; and, by the end of the year, there were many alarming signs that inflation was about to be rekindled. Although the Fed had allowed interest rates to drift upward throughout 1983, more decisive, positive action was required by early 1984.

Recall from Charts 4–1 and 4–2 that the Fed's tight money policy in the spring of 1984 had forced interest rates quickly upward, inducing the mini-slowdown of 1984. There was talk of recession, but the Fed had carefully tuned the slowdown and did not let it develop into recession. Once the danger was past, the Fed permitted interest rates to drop sharply, and demand began to grow once again.

Although deregulation became suspect in the late 80s because of the excesses and consequent failures associated with unregulated lending practices by the savings and loan industry, the deregulation of interest rates helped the Fed alter the course of America's economic history.

By the early 1990s, of course, the Fed faced a different problem. Private borrowing tumbled so steeply during the 1990–91 recession (see page 43) that the Fed redirected its efforts to stimulating demand with low interest

rates. But a glance at page 40 reveals that long-term rates remained high enough to restrain houshold mortgage borrowing and corporate borrowing. Chart 4–3 on page 43 shows that private borrowing peaked in the mid-90s at levels below that of the mid-80s. The Fed's restraint had worked.

THE NEW CREDIT RATIONING

Recall once again the credit craziness of the late 70s, when rampant recourse to borrowed funds pumped up the inflationary balloon. Many observers suggested credit rationing as a solution. That was the only way, they argued, to provide funds for productive business investment in new technology and capital goods, while curtailing unproductive consumer expenditures financed by installment plans, credit cards, and so forth. Otherwise, industry had to compete with consumers in the capital markets for scarce funds. Consumers, the argument continued, were notoriously insensitive to interest rates; all they cared about was the size of the monthly payment, and this could be held down by stretching out the length of payment.

Consequently, as consumers borrowed more and more for second homes, boats, the latest electronic gadget, or whatever, business was forced to pay ever higher interest rates as it competed for scarce funds. This not only limited industry's ability to modernize and improve our nation's capital stock, it also added *business* debt-financed demand on top of *consumer* debt-financed demand (see Chart 4–3 on page 43). Too many dollars chased too few goods (i.e., supply could not keep pace with demand at current prices), and, therefore, prices inevitably rose too quickly. So, the advocates of credit rationing recommended their solution.

They suggested that legal minimums be set for auto and home loan down payments and that legal maximums be established for the term of the loan: for instance, 50 percent minimum down payments, with a 10-year maximum loan term for housing and 2 years for autos. Yet, there was no way Congress would enact, or the President sign, such legislation. The auto and construction industries would not permit it.

Then, beginning in the early 80s, the Fed stepped in and throttled inflation with its tight money policy. Inflation collapsed; the Fed was the victor and remained vigilant ever-after.

The Fed has a unique opportunity in the 1990s to keep interest rates at just the right level to maintain an adequate, but not too rapid, growth in demand without inflation. But that means that interest rates in the 1990s (especially long-term rates) cannot return to the low levels of yesteryear, especially when compared to the rate of inflation. The Fed will keep interest rates well above the rate of inflation, except for an occasional counter-cycle dip to temporarily deal with recession. *High interest rates (which is not to say chronically rising rates) are the new credit rationing, and they will be with us for many years.*

Investors should keep that in mind. And they should be aware that the Fed's anti-inflation posture will bode ill for gold and other tangibles but well for stocks and other paper investments. Chapter 8 will discuss all of this in greater detail.

SUMMARY

To summarize this experience, think of the economy as a frisky horse where the rider (the Fed) must continually pull back on the reins (tight money) in order to prevent a runaway, breakneck gallop (inflation). The rider has learned a lesson the hard way, by periodically letting the reins go slack and permitting the horse to break into a gallop, only to be thrown from the horse as it reared when the rider desperately yanked on the reins (pre-1981–82 stop-go policy).

The stop-go policy is over; the Fed has a firm grip on the reins. Its present governors know it must restrain borrowing with high interest rates into the foreseeable future in order to dampen both the business cycle and inflation.

CHAPTER 5

FEDERAL FISCAL POLICY

THE CONVENTIONAL WISDOM

The federal deficit needs no introduction. It's been an issue for debate in every presidential election campaign since 1980. The federal government borrowed $200 billion in some years of that decade and over a trillion dollars throughout the decade. By the early 1990s, the annual deficit had risen to around $300 billion, and the outstanding debt has increased to more than $3 trillion. This chapter will deal principally with one aspect of that issue: the deficit's impact on the rate of inflation.

Chapter 4 asserted that the Fed had "single-handedly" overcome inflation in the 1980s by the exercise of monetary policy. This runs contrary to the conventional wisdom that it is federal deficits that generate inflation. How do we reconcile the conventional wisdom that deficits generate inflation with the earlier analysis of the Fed's role? Let's look at the evidence.

The facts portrayed in Chart 5–1 on page 54 show that the deficit grew dramatically in 1975 and 1981–82 and shrank to an insignificant number in 1979. If the conventional wisdom made sense, inflation should have jumped in 1975 and 1981–82 with the increase in the federal deficit and subsided in 1979 when the budget balanced.

But that didn't happen. As a matter of fact, the opposite occurred. Inflation narrowed in 1975 and 1981–82 and peaked in 1979. In other words, not only do the facts not support the conventional wisdom, they seem to indicate the opposite. Inflation fell with the increases in the federal deficit (1975 and 1981–82) and rose when the deficit declined (1979). Does this mean that balanced budgets *generate* inflation, while deficits *reduce* inflation? Now that *would* be a scoop.

CHART 5–1
Federal Government Expenditures, Receipts, and Deficit

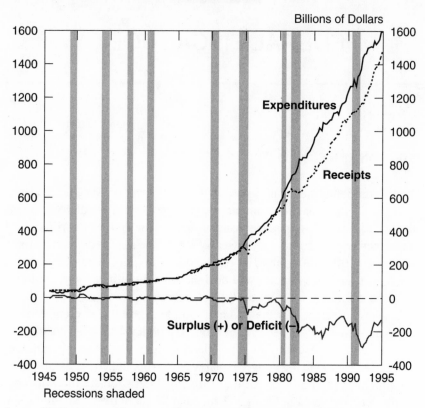

Source: U.S. Department of Commerce, *Business Cycle Indicators*, Series 500, 501, and 502.

To resolve the problem, you must put the federal deficit in perspective. Chart 4–3 on page 43, reproduced as Chart 5–2 on page 55, depicts private borrowing. Compare it with the federal deficit in Chart 5–1. Recall that private borrowing includes mortgage borrowing to support residential construction, installment credit to finance the purchase of autos and other consumer durables, and business indebtedness to pay for expenditures on plant, equipment, and inventory. But it also includes (unfortunately, because it is confusing) borrowing by state and local governments, for reasons that need not be developed here.

Keep in mind that both charts portray annual borrowing, not outstanding debt. By the early 1990s, outstanding federal debt was over $4 trillion and outstanding private debt was around $15 trillion. Each

year's borrowing adds to the outstanding figure, so that an annual federal deficit of $100 billion would boost the outstanding federal figure from $4 trillion to $4.1 trillion, and annual private borrowing of $200 billion might lift the private total to $15.2 trillion. (Don't confuse either of these with the balance of trade deficit, to be examined in Chapter 16.)

Now compare private borrowing with the federal deficit in 1975, and note that both were approximately $100 billion. Then, they move in opposite directions: The federal deficit shrinks to nothing in 1979, and private borrowing balloons to $400 billion. Total borrowing grew from $200 billion in 1975 ($100 billion of private plus $100 billion of federal) to $400 billion in 1979 (all private).

CHART 5–2
Total Private Borrowing

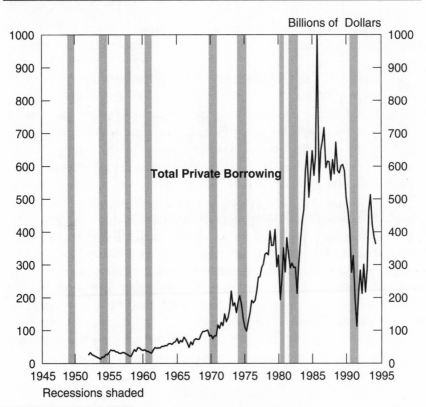

Source: U.S. Department of Commerce, *Business Cycle Indicators*, Series 110.

This explains the burst of inflation in the late 70s. Total borrowing doubled, financing the huge increase in demand (greater than the economy's increase in production at current prices) that drove up inflation. Thus, the growth in private borrowing in the late 70s overwhelmed the decline in federal borrowing, generating rapid price increases.

On the other hand, if you continue to look at the record in Charts 5–1 and 5–2, you'll notice that private borrowing slumped in 1981 and 1982, dropping to almost $200 billion annually from its $400 billion peak in 1979. The federal deficit, however, popped back up from next to nothing in 1979 to about $200 billion in 1982. Once again, when you add private and federal borrowing, you see an offset: the total is $400 billion in both years ($400 billion private in 1979 with no federal deficit and $200 billion for each in 1982). When total borrowing stopped growing from 1979 through 1982, the rate of inflation subsided as demand came into line with supply.

This illustrates the fallacy in the conventional wisdom and explains why inflation seemed to behave so perversely when compared to the federal deficit. You can't ignore private borrowing when analyzing inflation. As a matter of fact, the explosion of private borrowing from 1970 to 1973 ($100 billion to $200 billion) and from 1975 to 1979 ($100 billion to $400 billion) explains that decade's two great rounds of inflation. Inflation did not grow in the 1980s, because private borrowing fluctuated in a narrow range (except for 1985) and demonstrated no upward trend after 1984. By the end of the decade, private borrowing was still fluctuating around $600 billion annually, the level it had reached more than five years earlier. When it plunged to $200 billion in the early 90s, inflation withered. Federal borrowing's growth to $400 billion was not large enough to offset private borrowing's decline. Another development also requires clarification: the burst of private borrowing in late 1985. This burst was due to state and local governments' trying to beat an anticipated change in tax laws that never came to pass. Some Congressmen had suggested that interest paid on state and local bonds no longer be tax-exempt. Enactment of this legislation would have increased state and local interest payments, because their bonds had paid below-market rates for years due to the tax-exempt benefit to investors (i.e., bond holders were willing to receive below market yields, provided they were tax-exempt). State and local governments moved up their borrowing in anticipation of the 1986 change that never came to pass.

But the main point to bear in mind is that the large federal deficits of the 1980s and early 90s have not generated inflation, despite the

attention paid them. The recessionary drop in private borrowing overshadowed them.

For instance, the drop in private borrowing (see page 55) during the 1990–1991 recession was far larger than the surge in federal borrowing, keeping total borrowing—and hence, inflation—below 1980's levels. By the mid 90s the two remained below 1980's highs.

Investor's Tip

- Forget about the federal deficit; it won't influence our rate of inflation for the foreseeable future, and, therefore, it won't influence the value of your investments.

ALONG CAME KEYNES

Nonetheless, you ought to consider the federal government's deficits in some detail for no other reason than that they have drawn so much attention. In order to sort out the continuing debate surrounding the federal government's taxing and spending programs and their impact on the economy, you must go back to the 19th and early 20th centuries. Economics then was governed by an axiom known as *Say's Law*: "Supply creates its own demand." This meant that economic recession and depression and their accompanying unemployment were temporary and self-correcting phenomena. After all, capitalists produce goods for market, and workers offer their labor for hire *so that they, in turn, can demand goods in the marketplace*. If the goods cannot be sold or the labor is not hired, then a lower price or wage will be asked, until price and wage cutting permit all of the goods or labor to be sold. No goods will remain chronically unsold and no labor will remain chronically unemployed as long as prices and wages remain flexible.

Using this line of reasoning, 19th-century economists argued that recession and its concomitant unemployment were transitory phenomena and should generate neither a great deal of concern nor any corrective policy prescription by the government. Society and government ought to let well enough alone (i.e., follow the policy of laissez-faire) and let market forces prevail. The operation of the market would eventually restore full employment.

With Say's Law as their guide, no wonder economists could not understand the Great Depression, which began in 1929 and hit bottom in 1933. Nor could they understand why the economy's performance remained anemic for so long after 1933. After all, they reasoned, the economy should naturally return to conditions of full production and full employment as business cut prices in order to sell products and workers took wage cuts in order to find employment. If the economy continued in a slump, that was the fault not of the economists and their theories, but of employers and employees who refused to cut prices and wages.

The economists' logic did not help the businesses that were failing or the workers who were out of jobs. Prices and wages had fallen, yet conditions remained dismal; something was dreadfully wrong, and somebody had to do something about it.

In America, President Roosevelt was elected. He responded with massive public-works programs, which, by the way, were funded by federal deficits. The economics community was horrified, and they insisted that the federal government's efforts would merely deny resources to the private sector, and thus provide no net benefit. F.D.R. ignored economic theory. He was a practical man with a practical solution: if people were out of work, then the government would be the employer of last resort and put them to work building roads, parks, bridges, dams, and other public projects.

In 1936, an Englishman named John Maynard Keynes (rhymes with *brains*) gave intellectual credentials to F.D.R.'s practical policies by proposing that the problem was the economists' theories, not the economy. Keynes tackled Say's Law (and the economics establishment) at the knees by declaring that demand *could* be chronically insufficient and the economy *could* be chronically plagued with substantial excess capacity and unemployment. Keynes scolded his fellow economists for arguing that their theories were right and that the problem lay with the practical world of business and work that was not living up to theoretical expectations. Science—even "the dismal science" of economics—dictates that a theory that does not conform to the facts must be discarded.

Keynes declared that it was ridiculous to expect price and wage cuts to solve the economy's problem. A totally new approach had to be devised. He believed the only answer was to boost demand by the use of some exogenous (outside) force. Workers could not be expected to buy more under conditions of actual and threatened unemployment, nor business to spend more on plant and equipment when excess capacity and weak

profits were the rule. But if consumers and business would not spend, how could the economy pull out of its slump? Through government spending, Keynes argued, even if the government had to borrow funds. Once government began to spend on public works, the people who were employed on these projects would spend their earnings on privately produced goods and services. In a multiplier effect, the total level of demand would be lifted and full employment restored. When the pump-priming operation was over and the private economy was back on its feet, the government could gradually withdraw from the economic scene. Pump-priming by government intervention became known as *Keynesian* economics.

Keynesian (rhymes with "brainsian") theory came to dominate economics, rendering Say's Law archaic. The next generation of economists pushed Keynesian theory a bit further, reasoning that a tax cut could be as effective in priming the pump as an increase in government expenditures. Reducing taxes would increase consumers' disposable income and their consumption expenditures. The new generation believed this would be as effective as an increase in government expenditures for restoring demand to a level sufficient to ensure full employment.

Economists now argued that it didn't matter how the pump was primed, whether through expenditure increases or tax cuts. Putting more into the expenditure stream than was removed from the income stream (in the form of taxes) would always create a net boost in total demand. If government expenditures increased while tax revenues remained the same, the increase in public expenditures would boost demand. If government expenditures remained the same while taxes were cut, the increase in private consumption expenditures would boost demand. In either case, or in both together, the increased government deficit and the borrowing needed to fund that deficit made possible a net addition to total demand.

The increase in the deficit measures the increase in demand, and the government finances that deficit by borrowing from the public through the sale of U.S. Treasury securities. Now, it might seem that borrowing from the public would have the same effect as taxing the public, since it removes funds from the private sector, and would thus neutralize the spending increase. After all, if the public refrains from spending to buy government bonds, isn't the public's expenditure reduced? The answer is yes, if the bonds are purchased by private citizens; however, this is generally not the case. The largest share of bonds is sold to the banking system, which purchases them by creating a demand deposit (checking account) for the government. This is known as "monetizing"

the debt, as described in Chapter 4. The fact that the government borrows from the banks permits an increase in government spending without a decrease in private spending.

The federal government's attempts to influence economic activity through its power to tax and spend is known as *fiscal policy*. Although this chapter discusses fiscal policy in the context of the need to stimulate demand in order to deal with recession, it should be clear that fiscal policy could also be employed to deal with inflation. For example, increasing taxes or reducing government expenditures, which would create a surplus, drains spending from the economy, reducing total demand and, consequently, cooling inflation.

As the discussion of fiscal policy continues, remember that it is not the same thing as *monetary policy*, which was discussed in Chapter 4.

Monetary policy refers to the actions of the Federal Reserve System; *fiscal policy* refers to the actions of the federal government. Monetary policy works through its influence on the banking system, the money supply, bank lending, and interest rates, whereas fiscal policy works through its direct impact on aggregate demand.

Also keep in mind that fiscal policy is the province solely of the federal government, not of state or local government. Only the federal government has the flexibility to run the necessary budget deficits or surpluses large enough to influence total demand. Most state and local governments are limited, either de facto or de jure, to operating with a balanced budget.

THE KENNEDY TAX CUT

Keynesian economics, with its emphasis on fiscal policy, had won the hearts and minds of academic economists by the early 1960s. Not everyone, however, was convinced. When President Kennedy assumed office in 1961 and proposed a tax cut to stimulate the level of economic activity, Republicans and conservative Democrats in Congress attacked it as fiscally irresponsible. They demanded a balanced budget and argued that tax cuts would generate unacceptable deficits. President Kennedy's Keynesian reply was that the deficits would disappear as soon as the tax cut stimulated the level of demand, output, and income, providing even greater tax revenues, despite the decline in the tax rate. These arguments did not immediately persuade Congress, and the tax cut did not pass until the spring of 1964, following President Kennedy's assassination.

The nation enjoyed full employment and a balanced budget in 1965,

and Keynesian fiscal policy became an accepted method of "fine-tuning" the economy. Indeed, this technique became so legitimate that it was employed by the next two Republican presidents. President Nixon cut taxes to deal with the 1970 recession, and President Ford cut taxes to deal with the 1974–75 recession. In each case, the Federal Reserve also pursued an easy money policy in order to stimulate demand. Conservatives joined liberals and Republicans agreed with Democrats that tax cuts were necessary to get the economy moving.

By the late 1970s, however, severe inflation prompted a new and growing group of economists to conclude that attempts to stimulate demand with easy money and easy fiscal policies had gone awry. Escalating inflation, which reduced real income, had drawn more and more people into the labor force. The new entrants to the labor force, usually the secondary or tertiary wage earners in the family, had fewer skills and thus were more difficult to employ. Unemployment grew as inflation escalated. The economy had the worst of both worlds. Thus, this new group of economists and politicians argued that what was known as "full-employment policy," actually the Keynesian prescription of stimulating demand through easy monetary and fiscal policies, had been a failure.

Moreover, they continued, increased inflation had discouraged savings and investment. Rising prices penalized savers for their thrift, because the value of real savings fell. This encouraged personal indebtedness rather than saving, and inasmuch as saving is the ultimate source of all funds for investment, the level of investment was bound to shrink over time. These critics charged that the lack of savings and the resulting lack of investment were reflected by the low levels of business investment in new machinery and technology and by the resulting decline in productivity.

Finally, they attacked the progressive income tax, which propelled people into higher tax brackets despite a drop in real income. Higher marginal tax rates, they said, removed the incentive to work more and to work harder. Why should businesses invest in new ideas, new products, and more efficient ways of doing things if higher taxes confiscated the profits? Why should workers put in more hours on the job if higher taxes reduced the additional pay to a meaningless figure?

SUPPLY-SIDE ECONOMICS

The views of these economists and politicians came to be called *supply-side* economics, which they developed in contrast to *demand-side*, or

Keynesian, economics. The supply-siders argued that it was more important to support policies that bolstered the economy's ability to supply or
produce more goods than to enhance demand. Therefore, the supply-side
economists advocated drastic federal income tax reductions over a three-
year period, with deficits to be avoided by a parallel reduction in federal
spending. Federal expenditure programs, in their view, tended to over-
regulate private activity and to waste tax dollars in a variety of boon-
doggles and unnecessary transfer payments.

Supply-side theory claimed that a massive, across-the-board tax cut
would accomplish two major objectives. First, it would provide incentives
for increased work, thus boosting output. A greater supply, or output, of
goods and services would dampen inflation. Second, increased disposable
income would lead to increased savings, providing a pool of funds to
finance investment. Once again, the supply of goods and services would
be stimulated, and increased output would reduce inflation.

Supply-side economics was a total contradiction of Keynesian fiscal
policy, which had prevailed for almost half a century. It was widely and
correctly viewed as a device to restrict and contract the federal government, and so it was admired and promoted by conservatives and viewed
with suspicion by liberals. The supply-siders began to make their voices
heard during President Carter's administration, placing him in a potential
quandary. He had pledged to balance the federal budget by the end of his
first term in office. Rapid economic expansion and inflation had pushed
revenues upward more rapidly than expenditures; consequently, his goal
was in sight by late 1979. The tax cut proposed by the supply-siders would
have postponed that goal, unless, of course, it was accompanied by large
reductions in federal expenditures, which, as a Democrat, President Carter
could not endorse.

The 1980 recession created an even sharper dilemma for him. He might
have advocated a tax cut (the traditional Keynesian prescription for recession), but this would have played into the hands of the supply-siders, who
would have demanded compensating spending cuts. By now the supply-
siders had a presidential candidate, Ronald Reagan, as their principal
spokesman. The situation was further complicated for President Carter by
the fact that the supply-side tax cut favored upper-income groups, rather
than the lower-income groups traditionally targeted for tax cuts by the
Democrats. Thus, political circumstances precluded President Carter from
trying to deal with the 1980 recession by means of tax reductions.

After his inauguration in 1981, as the economy slid into the 1981–82
recession, President Reagan pushed for and obtained the supply-side tax

cuts. What a strange historical reversal: 20 years after President Kennedy battled Republicans and conservatives for his tax cut, President Reagan now had to battle Democrats and liberals for his. Whereas Democrats had once advocated tax cuts to stimulate the economy and the Republicans had opposed those cuts, it was now the Republicans who were advocating tax cuts over the opposition of the Democrats. The parties had done a complete about-face.

The shift of the mantle of fiscal conservatism from Republicans to Democrats is one of the most important political changes since World War II. President Reagan's supply-side tax cut of 1981–83 accompanied the recession of 1981–82. It generated a chaotic reduction in federal revenue, because a smaller proportion of a declining level of income was collected in taxes. Meanwhile, total expenditures continued to grow, despite reductions in the budget left by President Carter. Democrats criticized the resulting deficit and demanded that the tax cuts be rescinded. Republicans insisted that there be no tax increase, despite the deficits.

The debate occurred in the midst of recession and recovery. The Republicans contended that any tax increase would jeopardize the supply-side expansion. The Democrats countered that continued deficits and the accompanying government borrowing drove up interest rates and jeopardized the expansion. Beneath the economic details of the debate, both sides had ideological positions to defend. The Democrats realized that continued deficits put relentless pressures on domestic expenditures. Only a tax increase could generate the revenue that made these expenditure programs affordable. The Republicans were also aware that the only way to deliver a knockout punch to the domestic programs, while increasing military expenditures, was to hold taxes down and let the clamor to end the deficits force legislators to curtail domestic spending. So, the real battle was over domestic programs, not taxes, the deficit, or even supply-side economics. Indeed, there are some political analysts who believe that the whole supply-side argument was only a cynical "Trojan Horse," the sole purpose of which was to decimate federal assistance programs and repeal the New Deal.

In the end, no compromise of these issues was attained. The Democrats held on to the social programs, the Republicans held on to the military programs, and President Reagan made it clear that he would veto any tax increase. The deficit remained. Finally, in a desperate attempt to at least seem to be doing something about the problem, Congress passed the Gramm-Rudman Balanced Budget Act in late 1985, mandating gradual elimination of deficits over a five-year period. The political fight was

pushed into the future. The Democrats hoped that military expenditures would be cut and taxes raised, the Republicans and the president hoped that domestic expenditures would be cut, and they all hoped that this procrustean bed would dismember someone else.

In any event, the Gramm-Rudman Act failed in its objective, because Congress and the President ignored it. By the early 90s, it was a dead letter.

CROWDING OUT

Meanwhile, the argument over supply-side economics (never the real issue) was lost in the shuffle, as the political wrangling over the impact of the deficit continued. The Democrats insisted that the increased federal borrowing due to the tax cut would crowd-out private borrowing (and hence capital expenditures). Ironically, Republicans had criticized President Carter's (shrinking) deficits in the late 1970s on precisely the same grounds. Yet, you have seen that private borrowing exploded in those years. The inconsistencies in the political debate provide further evidence that the real issues were not (and are not) economic.

Indeed, any fear about "crowding out" was misplaced, for it was the actions of the Federal Reserve that largely determined whether private borrowing at reasonable rates was possible. Whenever the Fed pursues a tight money policy, private borrowers must compete with the government for funds; whenever the Fed pursues a sufficiently easy policy, there is room for both private and public borrowing. The point is that difficulty or ease of credit conditions is determined largely by the Fed and not by any crowding-out dynamic.

Keep in mind that the Fed's objective throughout the 80s was to restrain the expansion rather than stimulate it, so perhaps a little crowding out, if it helped prevent credit conditions from becoming too easy, was not so unhealthy. Tight money restricted consumer borrowing more than business borrowing, allocating funds (and resources) away from consumption expenditures and toward investment expenditures in new plant and equipment. And as the economy and tax revenues grew in the late 80s, private borrowing held its own, while federal borrowing shrank (see Chart 5–1 on page 54 and Chart 5–2 on page 55). Then, the recession of 1990–91 and the full impact of the S&L crisis hit, multiplying the deficit, but without crowding-out private borrowing.

Forget about Crowding Out

• The Fed's influence on interest rates is far more important than the federal government's borrowing.

In order to relate this discussion of fiscal policy to the business cycle, you need to know how *not* to relate it. Please realize that the huge federal deficits were responsible for neither the 1981–82 recession nor the subsequent recovery and expansion. The Federal Reserve's tight money policy generated the recession; the recession choked off inflation; and the stifling of inflation, along with the release of the Fed's grip, is what produced recovery and expansion in the mid and late 80s.

Thus, President Reagan's administration should be neither blamed for the recession nor lauded for the recovery and expansion or inflation's demise. Those phenomena were created by monetary policy, not fiscal policy.

BALANCING THE BUDGET

You can see from Chart 5–1 on page 54 that the federal deficit has grown enormously with each recession—for two chief reasons. First, recession reduced receipts because of lower personal income tax revenues, unemployment (the unemployed paid no income tax), and lower profits-tax revenues. Second, tax cuts accompanied the recessions of 1970, 1974–75, and 1981–82. In addition, note that federal expenditures continued to grow during each recession despite revenue's setback, generating the budget gap. Since the deficit grew with each successive recession, closing this deficit gap became more difficult and took longer every time.

In order to close the continuing deficit gap, receipts must grow more rapidly than expenditures. How long will it take? That's hard to say. The gap began to shrink in the late 80s until the S&L crisis and the 1990–91 recession hit, and it shrank once again as a growing economy generated additional tax revenues in 1993 and 1994 and President Clinton's tax increases took hold. Another recession, however, will bring about renewed deficits by reducing tax revenues. If future deficits are to be avoided, a substantial budgetary surplus must be built to provide a cushion for the inevitable decline in revenue that accompanies recession.

With or without a balanced-budget amendment to the U.S. Constitution, continually balanced budgets require surpluses in most years to cushion against the inevitable revenue shortfalls of recession. Tax-cuts, of course, also complicate the goal. It remains to be seen whether or not the nation can generate fiscal responsibility by the new millennium.

CHAPTER 6

THE POSTWAR BUSINESS CYCLE: THE ROLE OF CONSUMER DEMAND

CONSUMER DEMAND AND INFLATION

Chapter 4 developed three concepts:

1. The Fed's policies aided and abetted inflation through the end of the 1970s and exacerbated the business cycle.
2. The Fed's 1981–82 tight money policy was the major turning point in our post-World War II economic history, ending inflation's upward spiral.
3. Fighting inflation continues to be the Fed's primary concern, and, therefore, interest rates will remain relatively high (when compared with the rate of inflation) despite weak economic conditions.

This chapter will build on these concepts by analyzing the role of the consumer in the post-World War II business cycle, showing how consumer demand led the business cycle by generating ever higher waves of inflation, until that inflation broke on the rocks of the Fed's 1981–82 tight money policy. It will also illustrate how the Fed's fine-tuning smoothed out consumer demand after the 1981–82 crackdown, thereby limiting inflation and postponing recession until the start of the Persian Gulf War.

To begin the analysis of inflation, start with a definition and consider that definition in its historical context. *Inflation* is an increase in prices due to excessive spending financed by borrowing from banks. "Too many dollars chasing too few goods" is a standard way of putting it. Economists are

more formal: "Inflation occurs when demand exceeds supply at current prices and prices are bid up."

Both explanations conjure up the image of a gigantic auction at which customers bid for both goods and services. The more money the customers have to spend, the higher prices go. Where do they get the money? From banks that create it.

Now look at inflation's record in Chart 6–1. Although we wait and hope for it to subside, we tend to assume that inflation, like death and taxes, is inevitable. In fact, however, chronic inflation is a recent problem. Before the late 1940s, severe inflation was a temporary phenomenon, usually associated with war. When the federal government's wartime expenditures overshot tax revenues and the government covered the difference by selling bonds to the banking system or by printing paper money (which

CHART 6–1
Wholesale Prices

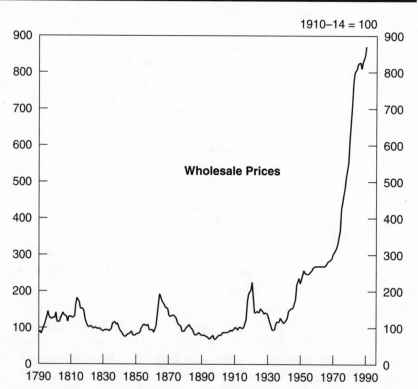

1910–14 = 100

Source: U.S. Bureau of the Census, *Historical Statistics of the U.S.* (Washington, D.C., 1975), Series E52 and 23; U.S. Department of Commerce, *Business Cycle Indicators*, Series 334.

the federal government has not done recently), prices increased swiftly. That's how the conventional wisdom arose that government deficits cause inflation.

From 1789 until after World War II, except for war-related inflations, prices in America fell more often than they rose. As a matter of fact, prices were actually lower in 1914, on the eve of World War I, than they were in 1815, at the end of the Napoleonic Wars and the War of 1812!

Prices dropped during the 19th century because supply grew more rapidly than demand. Railroads and steamships opened new continents and made their agricultural products available throughout the world. Business mobilized the technological advances of the Industrial Revolution to produce standard items of consumption in large quantities at considerably lower cost. Occasionally, prices rose during the upswing of the business cycle, because investment expenditures were financed by bank borrowing or because there were temporary shortages of agricultural commodities. But these increases were more than offset in recession years, when prices tumbled as huge additions to supply were brought to market.

The institutions that, in our day, enabled and encouraged headlong private borrowing and spending had not yet evolved. A hundred years ago it wasn't easy to obtain a home mortgage. Typically, the purchase of a new home required a 50-percent down payment with interest-only mortgage payments on a seven-year loan, followed by a balloon payment of the entire principal. If you go back far enough, most of the major consumer durables that we now buy on credit were available exclusively to a small portion of the population on a cash-only basis, if they existed at all.

It was not until after World War II that vast amounts of consumer borrowing came into common use, financing residential construction, autos, and other goods. At the same time, new institutions evolved to facilitate business borrowing.

Only the Civil War and World Wars I and II had provided great inflationary experiences; even the period between World War I and World War II was a time of deflation (falling prices). War brought inflation, and peace brought deflation, because government borrowed and spent more massively in wartime than business borrowed and spent in peacetime. The difference was more a matter of degree than a matter of kind; peacetime investment expenditures and borrowing by farmers, railroads, and manufacturers, though substantial, were usually not large enough to boost the growth in demand beyond the increase in supply. Thus, prices fell in most years, because supply exceeded demand at current prices.

To summarize, prices fell unless there was a rapid increase in demand (spending) financed by bank borrowing or the printing press (greenbacks during the Civil War). Only when outside financing provided a boost did demand take on a life of its own and grow more rapidly than supply. It made little difference whether it was government spending for war or business spending for investment, as long as banks printed bank notes or created demand deposits or the government printed paper money. Once demand grew more rapidly than supply, and too many dollars chased too few goods, prices rose.

History does not note or dwell upon the pre-World War II examples of private borrowing and spending that generated inflation, because there were so few of them; they were insignificant when compared to wartime episodes.

But what was responsible for the post-World War II inflationary experience? Why did prices rise so steadily? The answer lies in consumer spending. This period marked the first time that consumers borrowed continually and prodigiously to finance purchases of luxury goods. The level of activity grew decade after decade, and with each cycle, so that in the 1970s tidal waves of credit roared through the system, rapidly swelling demand to record levels.

It started in the 1920s, a kind of brief test run for the full-scale activity that followed World War II. Credit-backed demand included kitchen and laundry appliances; furniture and furnishings; electronic equipment such as television sets, VCRs, stereos, and personal computers; residential construction; and automobiles. All were financed by credit, and the terms became more liberal over time, even as interest rates rose. The American consumer was encouraged—indeed, came to feel obligated—to mortgage the future so that present expenditures could exceed present income, with borrowing covering the difference.

The economy's health thus developed a dependence on the chronic fix of greater consumer expenditures, financed by borrowing. These circumstances were entirely different from the circumstances of the 19th century; during that era, consumers were largely confined to standard items of consumption purchased with current income (not debt), and economic growth was propelled by increased supply, which pushed prices downward. Now the situation became quite different. Full production and employment became the hostages of ever larger waves of consumer expenditure on discretionary purchases financed by borrowing.

CONSUMER DEMAND AND THE BUSINESS CYCLE

Unfortunately, these surges in consumer demand always led to their own demise, because expansion brought inflation, which depleted real incomes and generated the downturn of the cycle. Only then did inflation abate, real income recover, and expansion begin anew. Thus, every boom inevitably went bust, and each recession was also self-correcting and carried with it the seeds of economic recovery.

But why did the business cycle always rebound from recession, never falling into permanent depression, and why wasn't expansion continuous?

Well, to begin with, every expansion ended inevitably in recession, because every expansion was fueled by credit. Consumers and businesses borrowed to buy new homes, cars, factories, and machinery. The more they borrowed and spent, the faster demand grew, pushing production into high gear in order to keep pace with demand. But, sooner or later, the upward spiral of borrowing and spending came to an end. The strain on productive facilities forced costs higher, pushing prices up, too. Inflation depressed consumer sentiment, and consumers responded by curtailing their expenditures. Consumers also found that their incomes could not support the burden of additional debt repayment. Businesses, having accomplished their targeted growth in plant and equipment, cut back or ceased their expenditures in this area. Once business and consumer borrowing and spending started to decline, the slump began, and production and income fell. Inflation subsided with the drop in demand.

The recessions hit bottom just before consumers recovered their confidence, due to inflation's decline, and began spending again. Components of demand that were financed by credit stopped shrinking. Remember that these components were a limited, though highly volatile, share of total demand. (The demand for many items that were not financed by credit, such as food and medical care, hardly declined at all during recession.) As consumers and businesses ceased borrowing and turned their attention to liquidating their expansion-generated debts, the price of credit, namely interest rates, fell until, finally, the debt burden and interest rates were low enough that consumers and businesses could borrow and spend again. At this juncture, auto production, home construction, and business investment in new plant and equipment stopped falling, the slide ended, and economic recovery was in sight.

Generally speaking, expansion ceased when consumers were no longer willing to borrow and spend; contraction ended when their confidence returned. In the 1970s, these cyclical changes in consumer

confidence were closely tied to the rate of inflation. Rapid economic expansion brought swiftly rising prices with an attendant and sobering drop in real income and consumer confidence. Recession cooled the pace of inflation, encouraging a resurgence of confidence.

In the 1980s, the Fed interrupted the normal course of the cycle by implementing its tight money policy of 1981–82, and then strongly influenced the cycle through its new posture toward inflation. The Fed squashed the cycle flat and squeezed high inflation out of the system, permitting the economy to expand gradually and steadily in the mid and late 80s.

Yet the Fed could not repeal the business cycle. When Iraq invaded Kuwait, and it appeared that we would be drawn into the conflict, consumer sentiment plunged and dragged the economy down with it. Consumer demand led the economy out of recession, too, as surging demand for homes and cars brought robust production and employment by the mid 1990s. By then, the Fed had signaled its concern over inflation, raising interest rates frequently in 1994.

Chapter 4, which examined the Federal Reserve System and the money and credit markets, described the 70s cycle and the new climate of the 80s and 90s in financial terms. Look at the cycle now from a different perspective, weaving in the elements of production, income, and consumer demand.

Consumers borrowed heavily in 1972 and 1973 to make record purchases of new homes and automobiles. Business responded by adding plant and equipment to meet the demand and by stockpiling inventory to satisfy customer orders. The sharp growth in consumer and business demand boosted prices rapidly, and the rate of inflation increased from 4 percent in 1972 to 12 percent in 1974. Interest rates moved in parallel fashion. Soon consumers became discouraged, because their incomes failed to keep pace, so their expenditures on homes, autos, and other goods plunged.

This led to a general decline in production, and, by early 1975, unemployment was at a postwar record high. The cycle was complete. The drop in demand reduced both inflation and interest rates, thereby restoring consumer confidence and spending. Recovery and expansion brought boom conditions. Rising inflation and interest rates returned in 1978, eroding consumer confidence once again. Consumer demand fell, and the 1980 recession began; another cycle had come full circle.

Recovery from the 1980 recession had barely begun when the Fed strangled the credit markets in 1981–82. The ensuing recession, designed

to curb inflation, had the typical impact on consumer confidence (dramatic improvement due to reduced inflation), and as soon as the Fed relaxed its grip, consumer expenditures surged forward in 1983.

But why didn't the 80s repeat the experience of the 70s? Why didn't burgeoning consumer demand, backed by exploding credit, drive inflation upward once again? Because the Fed fine-tuned demand by maintaining interest rates at relatively high levels. Even though Saddam Hussein had to spoil it all by invading Kuwait and plunging us into recession, the Fed continued to maintain its vigilant stance against inflation, despite the temporary interest rate dip of the early 1990s. As soon as the economy perked up, the Fed drove rates north once more. Thus, you should now learn which signposts to observe in order to follow the dynamic of inflation and consumer demand.

So far, the business cycle has been painted with fairly broad strokes. The time has come to take up a finer brush, so that essential details and connections can be clearly drawn. This chapter shows you how to use *The Wall Street Journal* to understand each step in the growth of consumer demand.

The first statistical series to be examined in this chapter is the *consumer price index* (CPI), whose fluctuations chart the course of inflation. Lower inflation leads to improved consumer sentiment and demand, which drives economic expansion forward. You can gauge the latter through data on auto sales, consumer credit, and housing starts, which will serve as the leading indicators of consumer demand.

CONSUMER PRICE INDEX (CPI)

The Bureau of Labor Statistics' CPI release usually appears mid-month in *The Wall Street Journal*. In the Wednesday, September 14, 1994 article on pages 74–76, the sixth paragraph informs you of the CPI's 0.3 percent increase in August. Although multiplying the monthly data by 12 will provide a rough approximation of inflation's annual rate for that month, you can see from the same paragraph that the CPI had increased 2.9 percent in the year ending August 1994. (See pages 78 and 79.)

The CPI compares relative price changes over time. An index must be constructed because consumers purchase such a wide variety of goods and services that no single item could accurately reflect the situation. (See Chart 6–2 on page 77.)

Mostly Sunny

Despite Some Threats, U.S. Inflation Outlook Seems Rather Bright

---

Labor Costs, a Crucial Factor, Are Rising Only Slowly; People Don't Act Worried

---

Bargain-Hunting Is in Vogue

By DAVID WESSEL
Staff Reporter of THE WALL STREET JOURNAL

Stanley Boyd, vice president for sales at San Francisco's Fairmont Hotels, would love to raise prices, but can't get away with it. "There's an overabundance of luxury hotel rooms nationwide," he complains. "And consumers going out today are spending the same amount for dinner for two at first-class hotels as they did seven years ago."

John Dermody, a restaurant worker shopping in downtown Washington, D.C., observes, correctly, that some clothing prices are actually falling. "I think it is because of more competition," he says, and industry executives concur. "There is a Banana Republic here that can sell stuff cheaper than the department store across the street."

Last spring, Long Island Rail Road workers agreed to a new three-year contract. The union called it "a big win." The Metropolitan Transit Authority, which runs the railroad, called it "ransom" to end a strike.

The price tag: an average annual wage increase of just 2.9%.

On Wall Street, inflation alarms are ringing. "Higher inflation is on the way," warns Erich Heinneman, chief economist for Ladenburg, Thalmann & Co., who sees an inflation rate of 5% by this time next year. Judging from market action in recent days, many bond traders seem to agree.

CPI ⎯ But elsewhere in America, the inflation dog isn't barking. Despite a recent surge in prices for certain commodities, there is little reason to believe the longer-term inflation outlook has deteriorated. Except for momentary spikes, inflation appears securely rooted in a 3% to 4% range. After accounting for yesterday's report of a 0.3%

increase in consumer prices in August, consumer prices are up just 2.9% over the past year. The consensus of private forecasters sees a rise to just 3.3% next year, according to the latest surveys.

Two Crucial Factors

Why? For a significant acceleration of inflation, two things must occur: The pace of wage increases must pick up substantially, and inflationary psychology must infect the economy. So far, neither seems to be happening. Nor is the economy currently experiencing Fed policies that have lifted inflation in the past: a surging money supply or interest rates so low that they overstimulate the economy.

"Wages are, across the economy, roughly 70% of business costs. If the 70% stay in check, there's a severe limit on how much more costs can accelerate," says Federal Reserve Vice Chairman Alan Blinder. "In a competitive economy, prices are based on costs. I think low rates of wage inflation act as a safeguard against sustained outbursts of inflation."

Yet financial markets, conditioned by history, are uneasy — and unwilling to bet on the optimistic inflation scenario. Wage increases, after all, usually come after the inflationary virus has begun to spread.

A Few Clouds

And some of the conditions that have preceded past bouts of inflation are becoming evident. Commodity prices are on the rise. Gold prices are up. Manufacturers, though still finding it tough to raise prices, say they are forced to pay more for materials; two-thirds of those surveyed by the Atlanta Federal Reserve Bank expect material prices to keep climbing, the bank said yesterday. Factories find it takes a bit longer to get deliveries. Reports of shortages of construction workers, truck drivers and skilled machinists are popping up.

Michael Niemera of Mitsubishi Bank's New York office, who tends a computer model that attempts to predict inflation nine months ahead, anticipates that the inflation rate will hit a peak of 5.5% next spring and then recede. "The model is suggesting it's a bubble," he says. He doesn't consider that "far-fetched."

Perhaps. But the preponderance of evidence, most forecasters agree, is for a much milder increase in inflation, largely because no substantial surge in wages is in sight.

Despite all the well-publicized cautions about inflation, the most recent union contracts and surveys asking employers about plans for next year give little hint that an inflationary mentality is taking

hold where it makes the most difference — in wages. "Are wages a problem now? No — except in baseball," says Fed Governor Lawrence Lindsey.

Contracts signed in the second quarter called for average annual wage increases of only 2.4%, the Labor Department says. Just last month, Westinghouse Electric Corp. agreed to a four-year contract with 5,000 workers that calls for raises of 2.5% in 1995, 2.5% in 1996 and 3.0% in 1997. Fewer than one-fourth of union workers are covered by cost-of-living adjustment clauses, down from about 40% five years ago.

Moreover, a survey of 1,850 big companies released yesterday by Towers Perrin found that "larger organizations are holding the line on salary increases," says Susan Rowland, a principal in the employee-benefits consulting firm. "They're basically the same as last year," she adds. Employers are planning 1995 increases of 3.8% for hourly, nonunion employees, for instance, the same as this year. And she cautions that employers usually end up paying raises slightly less than planned. Similar surveys by other consulting firms show similar results.

Of course, the wage outlook could shift in the coming months and pressures for increases could build, especially if unemployment falls further or if more and more employers find it hard to hire workers. But minus that, wage pressures seem likely to remain tame. "The wage-setting mechanism is different than it was 20 years ago," says Larry Michel, an economist at the Economic Policy Institute in Washington. "Unions don't have the power to push up wages, and I don't think there are many people walking into their bosses to say, 'I want a 5% raise or else I'm going to leave for a better job.' Today, the fear is that if you leave, you'll get a worse job."

Despite the fears haunting the bond markets, there are few signs that consumers and workers expect a new round of serious inflation. "Inflation expectations . . . are a bit higher than at the start of the year, but they are still at relatively low levels," says Richard Curtin, who oversees the University of Michigan consumer surveys. Consumers see inflation running about 3.1% in the year ahead and about 3.5% over the next five years — a more optimistic outlook than they have held at any time since the 1960s.

"It does have an effect on their behavior," Mr. Curtin says. In the 1970s, consumers tried to beat price increases by buying sooner, contributing to the inflation problem. "Right now, consumers are more on the other side: They have tended to act to resist price increases," he says.

Indeed, Marlene Budram, interviewed at City Place in Silver Spring, Md., times her shopping to coincide with sales. She says she usually buys a lot in September and then waits "until November or December because sales are the best then." And she indicates she certainly intends to follow that strategy this year.

"People are comparison-shopping more and more," says Carol Johnson, a Banana Republic saleswoman browsing with her husband in a Washington shopping mall earlier this week. "They're not going to buy something at full price if they can go somewhere else and get a good deal."

It pays off. The consumer-price figures released yesterday show that higher prices for coffee, gasoline and new cars, among other things, pushed up the August inflation index. But apparel prices fell 1.0%, the second monthly decline, reflecting end-of-

Consumer Prices

Year-to-year percent change

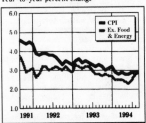

season sales of summer clothes and smaller-than-usual increases for fall and winter wear, the Labor Department said. Prices for men's suits, for instance, are off 0.9% over the past year. Women's coats and jackets are down 2.3%.

"In order to keep the consumer interested in coming into the stores for men's and women's apparel, the issue has been not fashion for the past few years, but how cheap is cheap," says Alan Millstein of Fashion Network Report, an industry newsletter based in New York.

And it isn't just the price of clothing that is holding down the inflation rate. Restaurant prices are up only 1.6% over the past year, the Labor Department says.

"Our costs are rising, but our prices are not because of competition," says George Protonentis, who manages the Campus Sugar Bowl in the Brooklyn borough of New York. Not that he doesn't feel some pressure to increase prices. "We had someone try to raise prices on us today," he said yesterday. "French fries: $15.75 to

(continued)

$17.65 for 25 cases of fries." But with a McDonald's nearby, menu prices at the Campus Sugar Bowl aren't going up.

The same forces are restraining prices for beer, wine and liquor. Wine prices are down 0.7% over the past year, and beer and liquor prices are up less than three-quarters of a percentage point, the government says. "There isn't a big growth in the business," says Jim Surdyk, who runs Surdyk's Liquor in Minneapolis. "There has been an antidrinking movement," and the producers "have to steal customers away from competitors."

At the same time, the pace of price increases in the service industries—which account for nearly 60% of the consumer price index — appears to be moderating. Overall, service prices have risen just 3.3% over the past year, a gain close to a 10-year low. Health-care price increases, restrained in part by fear of health-care reform and by aggressive efforts by big employers, have slowed. (Some analysts worry that this positive development may reverse itself now that the Clinton health-care overhaul has been derailed.)

In this relatively calm sea, however, there are a few waves. Auto makers are clearly taking advantage of strong demand and the strong yen, which forces up Japanese import prices. So far this year, new-car prices have risen at a 4.6% pace, the Labor Department says. Oil prices were up this summer, contributing to a 1.4% increase in energy prices in August and a 1.8% increase in July; but oil prices have since softened somewhat.

Import prices for goods other than oil are on the rise as well, the result of the decline in the dollar's value over the past several months. "Obviously, that ultimately means you've generated some inflation," says Donald Ratajczak of Georgia State University. "If we thought the dollar was going to continue to plummet, we'd have to raise our inflation estimate."

As it is, he forecasts a 3.8% inflation rate next year, slightly higher than the consensus, and he doubts that the inflation rate will fall until the next recession hits.

Nevertheless, inflation is − and seems likely to remain−at levels that, less than a decade ago, would have been unimaginable. At the end of the 1980s, the inflation rate kicked up from about 4% to a little over 5%. In response, the Federal Reserve helped provoke a recession that brought the inflation rate below 3%. Now, the economy has been growing for three years and is fully recovered from the recession. The Fed has tried to hold onto the gains it made against inflation. It will be a year or more before the Fed, the markets and the country at large know whether it has succeeded.

—Chris Georges and Josh Chetwynd contributed to this article

CONSUMER PRICES

Here are the price indexes (1982-1984 = 100) and percentage change for the components of the Labor Department's consumer price index for all urban consumers for August. The percentage changes from the previous month are seasonally adjusted.

| | | % chg. from | |
| | | July | August |
	Index	1994	1993
All items	134.6	+0.3	+2.9
Minus food & energy	155.0	+0.3	+2.9
Food and beverage	145.6	+0.3	+2.7
Housing	145.2	+0.3	+2.5
Apparel	133.1	−1.0	−0.6
Transportation	136.2	+1.0	+4.4
Medical care	212.4	+0.4	+4.6
Entertainment	150.3	+0.0	+3.0
Other	200.6	+0.2	+3.1

August consumer price indexes (1982-1984 equals 100), unadjusted for seasonal variation, together with the percentage increases from August 1993 were:

All urban consumers	149.0	+2.9
Urban wage earners & clerical	146.5	+2.9
Chicago	149.8	+2.5
Detroit	145.3	+3.9
Los Angeles	152.0	+1.4
New York	159.1	+2.4
Philadelphia	155.7	+3.4
San Francisco	149.4	+2.2
Dallas	142.2	+3.0
Houston	139.2	+4.7
Pittsburgh	145.7	+3.8

After a base period (1982–84) is selected and assigned an index number of 100.0, prices for other periods are then reported as percentage changes from this base. For instance, if prices rose 5 percent, the index would be 105.0. If prices fell by 10 percent, the index would be 90.0.

CHART 6–2
Consumer Price Index (CPI) (1982–84 = 100); Change in Index at
Annual Rates (smoothed)

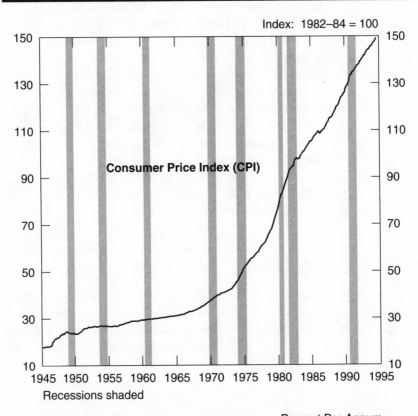

Index: 1982–84 = 100

Consumer Price Index (CPI)

Recessions shaded

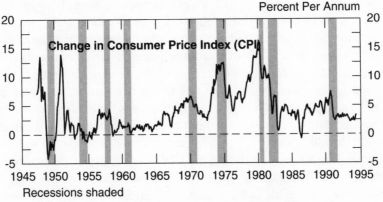

Percent Per Annum

Change in Consumer Price Index (CPI)

Recessions shaded

Source: U.S. Department of Commerce, *Business Cycle Indicators*, Series 320 and 320c.

CPI–Sixth Paragraph

But elsewhere in America, the inflation
dog isn't barking. Despite a recent surge in
prices for certain commodities, there is
little reason to believe the longer-term
inflation outlook has deteriorated. Except
for momentary spikes, inflation appears
securely rooted in a 3% to 4% range. After
accounting for yesterday's report of a 0.3%
increase in consumer prices in August,
consumer prices are up just 2.9% over the
past year. The consensus of private forecasters sees a rise to just 3.3% next year,
according to the latest surveys.

The Bureau of Labor Statistics (BLS) calculates the CPI by compiling
a list of the goods and services purchased by the typical consumer, including such items as food, clothing, shelter, public utilities, and medical care.
These make up the "market basket." The base-period price of each item is
recorded and assigned a weight according to its relative importance in the
basket. Changes in the price of each item are noted, and the percentage
change in the total price is reflected in the change of the index number.

The ways consumers spend are continuously shifting, because tastes
change, as do incomes and the relative prices of goods. New goods and
services are frequently introduced. It would be impossible, however, to
generate a consistent index of consumer prices if the components of the
market basket were constantly changed; a balance must be struck between
the need for consistency and the need for an accurate reflection of consumer buying patterns. Therefore, the BLS revises the contents of the market basket only occasionally, after conducting a survey of consumer
expenditure patterns.

Contrary to the popular image, the CPI is not really a "cost-of-living"
index. The BLS's market basket is fixed; the individual consumer's is not.
Substitutions are made with changes in prices and with changes in
income. Your cost of living can vary (or can be made to vary) indepen-
dently of any change in the CPI.

CPI–Chart

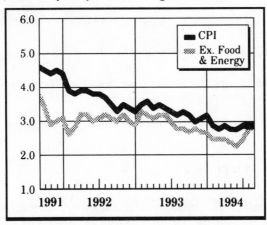

Consumer Prices

Year–to–year percent change

Source: *The Wall Street Journal*, September 14, 1994. Reprinted by permission of *The Wall Street Journal*, ©1994 Dow Jones & Company, Inc. All rights reserved worldwide.

A final point should be made. In the early 80s, the BLS replaced the cost of home ownership with an imputation (or estimate) of the rental value of owner-occupied homes. The cost of home ownership, which includes mortgage interest rates and home purchase prices, had swiftly escalated in the late 1970s, so that this component of the CPI pulled the entire index upward. Many found this an unjustified upward bias. Accordingly, the BLS adjusted the shelter component to estimate the increase in rental value of an owner-occupied home, which more closely approximates its usage value than does actual appreciation in price. Ironically, interest rates and home prices fell soon afterward, so that the old index, had it remained in use, would have displayed a downward bias and risen less rapidly than the new index.

Make a mental note that the *Journal*'s September 14, 1994 report updates Chart 6–2 on page 77 and confirms inflation's continued abatement since the late 70s peak; the CPI increased by about 5 percent annually in the mid and late 80s and then fell to half that level with the 1990–91 recession. As always, weak demand had done the trick.

Despite the surge in demand at mid decade, the CPI remained in the 3% range. It will take a sustained boom to jolt inflation upward again, and the Fed appears intent upon avoiding that.

Investor's Tip

- If the CPI increases by 8 percent or more (at an annual rate) for three months running, watch out!
- If that performance is repeated over the next three months, the Fed has failed.
- Bail out of paper investments like stocks and bonds; get into gold and other tangible assets.

CONSUMER SENTIMENT

Let's now consider the impact of inflation on economic recovery in general and on the consumer's leading role in particular.

The Survey Research Center at the University of Michigan compiles the *Index of Consumer Expectations*. Consumers are asked a variety of questions regarding their personal financial circumstances and their outlook for the future. Responses are tabulated according to whether conditions are perceived as better or worse than a year earlier, and an index is constructed comparing the outcome to that for a base year (1966). *The Wall Street Journal* occasionally reports this index, but more often publishes the Conference Board's index of consumer confidence. (See the Wednesday, September 28, 1994 article on page 81.) A glance at Chart 6–3 on page 82 shows you that the Michigan and Conference Board indexes have similar records, although the Conference Board index is more volatile.

Compare the CPI with the Michigan index (see Chart 6–4 on page 83), and you will find that inflation and consumer sentiment moved in opposite directions during the 1970s, as consumers responded to the rate of inflation.

U.S. Consumer Confidence Fell In September

By Lucinda Harper
Staff Reporter of The Wall Street Journal

Consumer Confidence

Index (1985=100)

WASHINGTON—Americans seem to be slipping into a bit of a funk: Their confidence drooped for the third straight month in September, a widely followed index suggests.

Consumer Confidence —
The Conference Board said its consumer confidence measure fell two points to 88.4 in September. Since June, the index has fallen roughly four points.

Fabian Linden, executive director of the board's Consumer Research Center, said most of September's decline resulted from lower expectations for the immediate months ahead among the 5,000 U.S. households surveyed. Although optimists continue to outnumber pessimists, the number of Americans fearing the economy will worsen in the coming months was up significantly, the survey found.

Overall, buying plans for cars and homes were down from August. Attitudes about job prospects, current economic conditions and plans to buy household appliances were little changed.

The recent drops in consumer confidence don't necessarily mean the economy is headed for bad times. Mr. Linden said that, historically, the current level of the board's index is associated with a "reasonably lively economy." And despite September's decline, most areas of the country had improved spirits during the month. The West North Central and East South Central regions of the country, in particular, reported big jumps in confidence.

Separately, the Commerce Department boosted its estimate of the increase in building permits issued in August to 1.3% from 1%. Building permits are often a precursor of future construction activity.

All figures have been adjusted for normal seasonal variations.

Consumer Confidence–Second Paragraph

The Conference Board said its consumer confidence measure fell two points to 88.4 in September. Since June, the index has fallen roughly four points.

CHART 6–3
Consumer Sentiment: Michigan and Conference Board Surveys

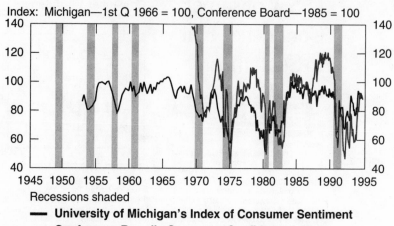

Index: Michigan—1st Q 1966 = 100, Conference Board—1985 = 100

Recessions shaded
— **University of Michigan's Index of Consumer Sentiment**
— **Conference Board's Consumer Confidence Index**

Source: U.S. Department of Commerce, *Business Cycle Indicators*, Series 58 and 122.

Begin by comparing the 1955–65 period with 1965–80. The principal difference between these periods is the moderate rate of inflation in the first decade and the cyclical increase of inflation after that. With each boom (1969, 1974, 1979), the rate of inflation hit a new high and consumer sentiment reached a new low. Although the mid-70s recession was worse than the 1970 recession, the rate of inflation did not drop to as low a number. No wonder consumer sentiment deteriorated for 15 years: Inflation and the attendant swings of the business cycle were becoming more severe. Once inflation's grip was broken in the early 80s, however, consumers began feeling positively upbeat again for the first time in 20 years. The key had been the interruption of the inflationary boom/bust cycle.

Note the dramatic improvement in consumer sentiment after 1980, as inflation slackened due to the recession forced on the economy by the Fed's 1981–82 tight money policy. Then, when the Fed relaxed its grip and the economy began to recover, consumer sentiment exploded in the most dramatic gain since the construction of the index. Consumer sentiment remained robust for the rest of the 1980s, a dramatic testimony to consumers' relief that ever-increasing inflation was behind them.

CHART 6–4
Index of Consumer Sentiment and Change in CPI at Annual Rate

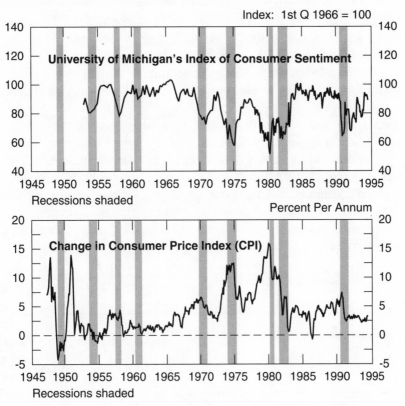

Index: 1st Q 1966 = 100

University of Michigan's Index of Consumer Sentiment

Recessions shaded

Percent Per Annum

Change in Consumer Price Index (CPI)

Recessions shaded

Source: U.S. Department of Commerce, *Business Cycle Indicators*, Series 83 and 320c.

But consumers are influenced by more than inflation. Employment opportunities, interest rates, and current events (like the Persian Gulf war) all play a role. Consumer psychology is complicated. Yet you can see the singular impact of inflation before the Fed came to grips with it in the early 1980s; inflation and consumer sentiment demonstrated a clear and predictable inverse relationship.

Iraq's invasion of Kuwait on August 2, 1990 broke that relationship and depressed consumer sentiment for two reasons. First, consumers expected that gasoline prices would rise quickly. Second, and even more important, no one knew whether we would be drawn into the conflict and what the consequences would be. How many lives would be lost? How long would the fighting last? As a result, consumer sentiment plunged dramatically and drastically without a severe and protracted surge of inflation.

Consumer sentiment remained in the doldrums until the fighting stopped, and then snapped back, only to fade as the recession lingered. For the first time in two decades, consumer sentiment seemed to follow the cycle rather than lead it. But by late 1994, consumer confidence had climbed out of the doldrums and was back in its 1980s range. What would restrain it now that the Fed successfully held inflation in check?

By the mid-1990s, both consumer sentiment and consumer demand were robust once more. Would the Fed's continued anti-inflation vigilance keep them strong?

Here's the nub of this discussion: *Consumer sentiment drives consumer borrowing and spending.* Strong consumer sentiment propels consumer demand forward, while low consumer sentiment depresses consumer demand. That's why inflation traditionally brought on recession (it depressed consumer sentiment) and why low inflation generated recovery and expansion (it boosted consumer sentiment). Low inflation in the 1980s maintained consumer sentiment and postponed the cycle's peak and the next recession. Credit the Fed's fine-tuning for that. Events in the Persian Gulf depressed consumer sentiment and led to the 1990–91 recession. Credit Saddam Hussein for that.

Feelings Are Facts

- When consumer sentiment falters, watch out for recession.

CONSUMER DEMAND

The Wall Street Journal regularly publishes articles on three indicators of consumer demand that merit your close attention: new-vehicle sales, consumer credit, and housing starts. Let's examine each in turn.

New-Vehicle Sales

Around the 5th, 15th, and 25th of the month, *The Journal* reports new-vehicle sales data compiled by the manufacturers. Look at the Wednesday, September 7, 1994 report on pages 85 and 86.

Vehicle Sales In August Rose 10.1% in U.S.

Boom at GM Led Rebound From the Year Before; Economy's Help Cited

By DOUGLAS LAVIN
Staff Reporter of THE WALL STREET JOURNAL

DETROIT — Led by a boom at **General Motors** Corp., U.S. sales of cars and light trucks in August rose 10.1% from a year earlier and rebounded substantially from July's relatively weak sales rate.

The strong August vehicle sales underscore that the economic expansion continues at a moderate pace. "It is steady as she goes," said Lincoln Merrihew, an economist at DRI/McGraw-Hill.

In August, purchases totaled 1,298,453 domestically built and imported cars and light trucks, compared with 1,136,010

New-Vehicle Sales

U.S. car and truck sales; in millions at seasonally adjusted annual rate

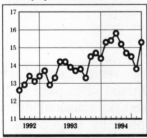

in the year-earlier month. GM said the latest report means the industry is on track to meet sales projections of 15.3 million vehicles this year.

Indeed, August vehicle sales were equivalent to an annual sales pace of 15.3 million units, based on seasonal adjustment factors supplied by the Commerce Department. In July, vehicle sales were running at a revised rate of 13.8 million units a year, the factors indicated.

Mr. Merrihew of DRI/McGraw-Hill cautioned that the sales growth from August 1993 was somewhat exaggerated by an unusually poor year-earlier period at GM. GM's August sales posted a 16.9% gain from a year earlier. "It's a nice, healthy sales year, but the growth isn't exploding as it was in the beginning of the year," Mr. Merrihew said. In February and March, auto sales were up 20% from the previous year.

The percentage change in sales is calculated on a daily basis and adjusted for months in which there were fewer business days open for selling. There were 27 selling days this year and only 26 last year.

Robust August sales at GM pushed up figures for the entire industry. GM sold 412,783 vehicles in August, up 16.8% from the 340,422 it sold last year. It was GM's best August since 1990, with strong gains across the product lineup.

"It feels better than last year," said a jovial William E. Hoglund, a GM executive vice president. "The new products are looking strong." GM's car sales have been hurt in recent months by lengthy plant closings for conversion to new models, but now the plants are operating again and shipping the new compact Chevrolet Lumina and subcompact Chevrolet Cavalier to dealers.

GM showed strong sales growth even in some divisions which had been lagging. Sales were up a stunning 91.9% at Saturn, in part because the division continues to add new dealerships; up 39.3% at Oldsmobile; and up 29.9% at Cadillac.

The favorable comparisons partly reflect lackluster August 1993 sales, which were hurt because of tight supplies caused by the company's annual two-week vacation shutdown in late July. This year, the shutdown came in early July, which had the effect of hurting July sales and pushing some deliveries into August.

GM increased its market share to 31.8% from about 30% a year ago. **Toyota Motor** Corp. was another big gainer. Its share increased to 9.8% from 8.7% a year ago. **Ford Motor** Co. and **Chrysler** Corp lost market share even though their sales rose. At Ford, market share dropped to 24% from 26.3%. Chrysler's share dropped to 12.6% from 13.3% a year ago.

Dealers reported strong demand for new cars and said sales were hampered by short supplies of some models. Greg Sutliff, who owns several Chevrolet and Saturn dealerships in central Pennsylvania, said he had a record month but only because he was able to purchase additional vehicles from an out-of-state dealership that was changing hands. Other dealers

(continued)

said higher interest rates are holding down sales.

"It's inventory and interest rates," said Mark Lawrence, who owns a Chrysler-Plymouth dealership in Richmond, Va. Sales there were off slightly from August 1993, Mr. Lawrence said, although he believes he will finish 1994 ahead of 1993.

Truck sales continued to lead sales growth in the industry, with both Chevrolet and Chrysler posting truck-sale records. But car sales grew more slowly, and at Ford they declined 9.4%.

Much of Ford's car-sales decline came from a drop in sales of the Ford Tempo and Mercury Topaz, which are being phased out and will be replaced at the end of this month by the Ford Contour and Mercury Mystique. Ford truck sales made up for the drop in car sales. Altogether Ford sold 311,237 light vehicles, up 0.5% from 298,240 a year ago.

Chrysler sold 163,858 vehicles last month, up 5% from the year earlier. The relatively modest increase comes as the manufacturer continues to decrease sales of imported cars, which were down 65% from last year, and gears up to build more cars domestically. Later this year dealers will be receiving their first shipments of the Chrysler Cirrus, production of which was formally kicked off last week.

Toyota reported its best August, with sales up 23.4%, thanks largely to special leasing promotions and financing subsidies on the Camry. Strong sales growth came despite a decline in sales at Toyota's Lexus division, off 13.1% for the month.

The headline and first paragraph refer to a 10.1 percent increase in car and light truck (pickups and vans) sales. But you need the *seasonally adjusted annual rate* to make a comparison with the data included in the chart accompanying the article. The fourth paragraph and the accompanying chart report the August new-vehicle sales at a *seasonally adjusted annual rate* of 15.3 million units. (See Chart 6–5 on page 87 for a historical comparison.)

New-Vehicle Sales–Fourth Paragraph

Indeed, August vehicle sales were equivalent to an annual sales pace of 15.3 million units, based on seasonal adjustment factors supplied by the Commerce Department. In July, vehicle sales were running at a revised rate of 13.8 million units a year, the factors indicated.

CHART 6–5
New-Vehicle Sales

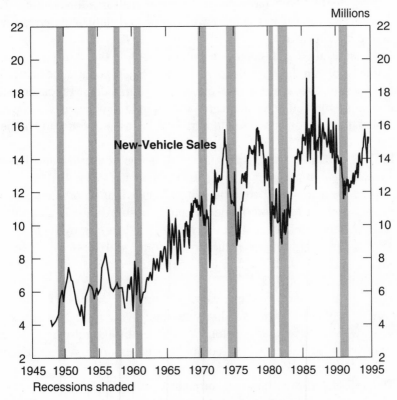

Recessions shaded

Source: U.S. Department of Commerce, *Economics and Statistics Administration.*

The well-equipped auto has symbolized the American consumer economy since the 1920s. The automobile industry pioneered such now familiar techniques as planned obsolescence, mass production, and mass marketing and advertising campaigns in the 1920s and 30s. Henry Ford's Model T was the first mass-produced automobile. His assembly line production methods were state-of-the-art; his marketing concept, however, was vintage 19th century. He emphasized the cheapest possible serviceable car at the lowest price. Henry Ford reduced the price of a Model T to $300 in the early 1920s and provided customers with any color they wanted, as long as it was black. Ford dominated the market until the late 1920s, when General Motors saw the profit potential in continually inflating the product by offering colors, options, and model changes and

increased size, weight, and speed. This strategy enabled GM to take the sales lead from Ford; from then on, competition in autos meant more (and different) car for more money, not the same car for a lower price. The option of less car for less money was eliminated until the German and Japanese imports arrived.

Ford had grafted 20th-century technology onto 19th-century marketing techniques, driven the price down as far as it could go, and seen sales go flat in the mid-1920s, as the market became saturated. GM pioneered the 20th-century marketing technique of product inflation on a mass scale and gambled that the consumer would borrow ever more in order to buy next year's model.

Product inflation boosts sales by cajoling the consumer into buying something new at a higher price. The customer isn't swindled, just convinced by marketing and advertising techniques that he or she needs an improved product for more money. Planned obsolescence is a corollary, because style and model changes, as well as product improvement, aid in persuading the consumer that the present (and still serviceable) model should be replaced with a better, more expensive model, not a lower cost repeat of the old model.

That set the pattern for American marketing of consumer goods. You can see it in your kitchen, laundry room, and living room, not just your driveway. TV replaced radio, color TV replaced black-and-white TV, and VCRs are now perceived as near-compulsory accessories. With each innovation, the price goes up and so does debt.

The 1970s and 80s, however, brought a rude shock to the domestic automobile manufacturers. The American public was no longer willing to buy whatever the manufacturers wished to sell. Consumers balked at continued product inflation, especially if it meant buying features, such as increased size and weight, that were no longer attractive. In addition, consumers were willing to accept less car for less money, especially if it meant a better made and more fuel efficient vehicle. As a result, the domestic manufacturers lost market share to the imports, and they have only recently stemmed the tide.

Yet auto sales remained a leading indicator of economic activity. You can see that sales turned down as soon as escalating inflation eroded consumer sentiment (see Charts 6–4 and 6–5 on pages 83 and 87) and recovered quickly when inflation subsided and consumer sentiment improved. Auto sales have led the cycle into both expansion and contraction.

This will help you understand auto sales' role in the economy and why you should regularly track them. It's not just that the auto industry, along

with the cluster of industries that depends upon it (e.g., rubber tire, steel, glass, upholstery, fuzzy dice), represents a significant share of total economic activity. It's also that the fortunes of the auto industry lead the cycle, foretelling recession and prosperity. What's good for GM may not necessarily be good for America, but GM's sales are a reliable leading indicator of overall economic activity.

Investor's Tip

- New-vehicle sales above 15 million threaten inflation; 20 million assure inflation.

Consumer Credit

The Wall Street Journal publishes the Commerce Department's release on consumer installment debt in the second week of the month. Changes in consumer credit have been an important barometer of consumer activity, because consumers have borrowed heavily to finance purchases of autos and other expensive and postponable items. The Tuesday, November 8, 1994, article reproduced on page 90 informs you that consumers borrowed $10.57 billion at a seasonally adjusted monthly rate in September, for an approximate increase of $125 billion (times 12) at an annual rate.

Chart 6–6 on page 91 illustrates consumer credit's gradual and cyclical rise until the 1970s. Then, it exploded. You can see the cyclical maximum of $10 billion in the late 60s, $20 billion in the early 70s, $50 billion in the late 70s, and $80 billion by the mid 1980s. No wonder the Fed maintained its guard throughout the 80s; indeed, it's amazing that inflation was not more severe in the face of this stimulus to demand.

Investor's Tip

- Consumer credit growth of $100 billion threatens inflation; sustained growth of $125 billion assures inflation.
- There's no threat of inflation when consumer credit fails to grow.

Credit Usage For September Increased 14.6%

Data Post 22nd Rise in Row; Car Loans Made Up Bulk Of Consumer Debt Rise

By LUCINDA HARPER

Staff Reporter of THE WALL STREET JOURNAL

WASHINGTON—Americans increased their use of credit at a 14.6% annual rate in September—less than August's huge 21.3% but still the 22nd rise in a row, the Federal Reserve said.

Consumer Credit

Car loans made up the biggest part of September's $10.57 billion rise in consumer installment debt, jumping at a 21.7% annual rate after climbing at a 17.8% rate the month before. Revolving credit, which includes bank and department-store cards, rose at a 8.6% rate after increasing at a 29.7% pace in August. A catch-all category that includes loans for boats, school tuition and taxes rose at a 13.5% rate; in August the rate was 14.5%.

Analysts are uncertain just how much this recent borrowing binge reflects pent-up demand and how much reflects marketing on the part of credit-card companies.

"There is something of a credit-card interest-rate war going on now in a battle to get new customers and induce them to spend," said David Orr, chief economist of First Union Corp., Charlotte, N.C. Some airlines offer free mileage when a particular credit card is used, and many people find it more convenient to use a credit card for items, such as groceries, for which they used to pay cash. Mr. Orr said small businesses have also begun making purchases on credit cards instead of using invoices. In January, the Fed will release a report estimating how much of installment-debt balances are related to convenience usage.

But no matter how much of the increase is based on technical factors, it is obvious that consumer spending has picked up for durable goods. Stephen Roach, senior economist for Morgan Stanley & Co., says a key question for the economic outlook is whether consumers can afford to service the recent surge of new debt. Mr. Roach says the evidence suggests they can because debt as a percentage of disposable income is still about a percentage point lower than its cyclical peak in 1990.

All figures have been adjusted for normal seasonal variations.

Here are the seasonally adjusted totals of consumer installment credit for September, in billions, and percentage changes from August at an annual rate:

Total	$880.20	14.6%
Automobile	315.31	21.7
Revolving	323.66	8.6
Other	241.22	13.5

Consumer Credit–Second Paragraph

Car loans made up the biggest part of September's $10.57 billion rise in consumer installment debt, jumping at a 21.7% annual rate after climbing at a 17.8% rate the month before. Revolving credit, which includes bank and department-store cards, rose at a 8.6% rate after increasing at a 29.7% pace in August. A catch-all category that includes loans for boats, school tuition and taxes rose at a 13.5% rate; in August the rate was 14.5%.

CHART 6–6
Change in Consumer Installment Credit

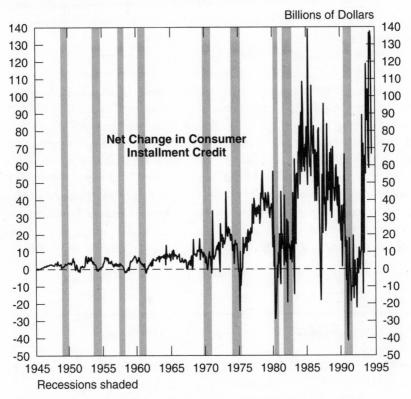

Billions of Dollars

Net Change in Consumer Installment Credit

Recessions shaded

Source: U.S. Department of Commerce, *Business Cycle Indicators*, Series 113.

Both consumer sentiment and consumer credit fell steeply in the 1990–91 recession, and you can see their historical relationship when you compare Chart 6–6 with Chart 6–4 on page83. In 1991, consumers actually reduced their installment debt for the first time since World War II. By mid-decade, however, consumer sentiment had recovered, and consumers were once again borrowing at record levels. No wonder the Fed had signaled concern over rising inflation.

Housing Starts

The Commerce Department's monthly release on *housing starts* is usually published in *The Wall Street Journal* between the 17th and the 20th of the

month. Always direct your attention to the seasonally adjusted monthly figure, presented at an annual rate. The first paragraph and the chart accompanying the Thursday, September 22, 1994 story on page 93 tell you that there were 1.44 million home and apartment unit construction starts in August of 1994.

The cyclical sensitivity of housing starts to consumer sentiment and the availability of mortgage credit is striking. (See Chart 6–7 on page 94.) Housing starts turned down well before the onset of recession, as soon as rising inflation reduced consumer confidence and the Fed slammed on the brakes, drying up mortgage credit. But you can see that they turned back up even before the recession ended, as consumer confidence returned with the decline of inflation and the Fed's switch to an easy money policy.

You have already reviewed the dramatic impact of the Fed's 1981–82 tight money policy on residential construction. The Fed's policy put a new home beyond the reach of most consumers, and mortgage borrowing and housing starts plunged. Although housing starts and mortgage borrowing recovered in the mid-1980s, housing starts did not surpass the record levels of the early 70s (2.5 million at an annual rate in 1972). That fit well with the Fed's plan of restraint.

Investor's Tip

- As housing starts approach 2 million, inflation looms.
- It will be a long time before housing starts recover their past glory and threaten inflation.

Residential construction withered during the 1990–91 recession, but had made a modest recovery by mid decade. Unfortunately for many households, home prices have risen more rapidly than incomes in many areas of the country, putting a brake on housing demand.

What was said earlier about industries related to auto sales can be repeated for residential construction. Lumber, cement, glass, roofing materials, heating, plumbing and electrical supplies, kitchen and laundry appliances, and furniture and furnishings are all part of the cluster of industries that fluctuate with housing starts. The Fed's policy of restraint holds all of these activities in check, thereby maintaining moderate levels of inflation in those industries as well.

Housing Starts Edged Up 2.1% During August

But Economists Say Drop In Single-Family Homes Could Hinder Economy

By Josh Chetwynd
Staff Reporter of The Wall Street Journal

Housing
Starts

WASHINGTON — Housing starts grew moderately in August, rising 2.1% to an annual rate of 1,442,000 units, the Commerce Department reported.

But economists said that the overall increase isn't a good indicator of the home-building sector's health. A drop in single-family home construction last month means that housing starts could soon become a drag on the economy.

Single-family starts, which represent the largest portion of new-home construction, fell 2.7% to an annual rate of 1,167,000 after rising 3.1% in July to a 1,199,000 pace.

Economists attributed this drop to higher interest rates and poor job and income expectations. Many analysts believe that the decrease will continue at a steady pace into next year.

"Single-family starts are slowing at a fairly moderate pace, but it will take a skyrocketing of mortgage rates or something close to a recession for it to fall off the cliff," said David Berson, chief economist of the Federal National Mortgage Association.

Adjustable-Rate Effect

The decline has been limited because of a greater use of adjustable-rate mortgages, according to David Seiders, chief economist of National Association of Home Builders.

"More buyers, who might have postponed buying, are shifting to adjustable-rate mortgages because interest rates are lower in the early years and [the borrowers] are enticed by lenders who are aggressively marketing" the loans, Mr. Seiders said. "It is helping to soothe the effect of higher interest rates on the sector."

In contrast, multifamily homes starts continued to increase in August. Construction starts on homes with two-to-four units rose 3.1% to an annual rate of 33,000 after increasing 68.4% in July to a rate of 32,000. Starts on homes with five or more units were up 33% last month to an annual rate of 242,000 after rising 4% in July to a rate of 182,000.

Apartment Builders

The growth in multifamily starts has been stimulated by apartment builders taking advantage of a low-income tax credit for new or rehabilitated homes. Congress reinstated this credit last fall. Nevertheless, expansion in this area provides only a small indication of future growth because multifamily starts aren't tied closely to future interest rates.

Regionally, housing starts rose 15.2% in the Northeast and 14% in the South, while starts declined 14% in the West and 6.8% in the Midwest. The variation represents areas with the greatest increase in multifamily starts and isn't a good sign of regional growth, according to Merrill Lynch economist Bruce Steinberg.

Total building permits for new houses, often an indicator of future growth, rose a modest 1% in August to an annual rate of 1,350,000. Permits for single-family units increased 1% in August to a yearly rate of 1,047,000, while multifamily permits were unchanged at a rate of 303,000.

All figures have been adjusted for normal seasonal variation.

Housing Starts

Annual rate, in millions of dwelling units.

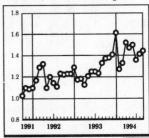

HOUSING STARTS in August rose to a seasonally adjusted rate of 1,442,000 units from a revised 1,413,000 units in July, the Commerce Department reports.

Housing Starts–First Paragraph

WASHINGTON – Housing starts grew moderately in August, rising 2.1% to an annual rate of 1,442,000 units, the Commerce Department reported.

CHART 6–7
Housing Starts

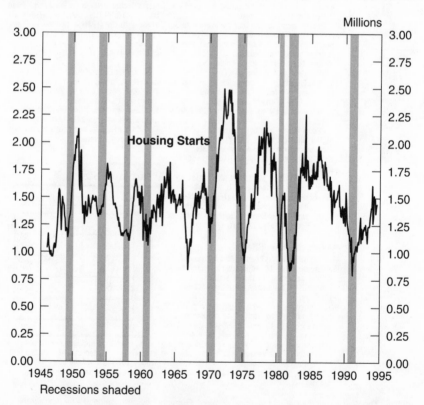

Source: U.S. Department of Commerce, *Business Cycle Indicators*, Series 28.

SUMMING UP: THE CYCLE AND ITS CONSEQUENCES

Now you can see how much the modern American economy has come to depend on product inflation and ever larger volumes of debt. These sustain the growth in demand required to maintain production and income at adequate levels. Moreover, consumer debt and consumer demand have been the leading edge of the post-World War II business cycle. Paradoxically, their strong growth led to cyclical problems with inflation, which periodically tended to choke off credit, demand, and economic expansion, generating recession.

In summary, as the cycle moved from *peak* to *contraction*, rapidly rising inflation depressed consumer real income and consumer sentiment, bringing on a collapse in consumer demand and inevitable recession.

CPI ↑→ Consumer sentiment ↓→ Consumer demand ↓
(Auto sales ↓ + Consumer credit ↓ + Housing starts ↓)

Recession let the steam out of the economy, cooling inflation. The temporary reduction in the rate of inflation permitted the business cycle to resume its course after each recession. Reduced inflation encouraged consumers to indulge in a new wave of borrowing and spending, moving the cycle from *recovery* to *expansion* and launching another round of inflation.

CPI ↓→ Consumer sentiment ↑→ Consumer demand ↑
(Auto sales ↑ + Consumer credit ↑ + Housing starts ↑)

There was no human villain in this drama. Blame the inanimate forces of credit and inflation, which periodically swept over the economy to leave recession's wreckage behind. The Fed finally came to grips with the problem in 1981 when, in its attempt to bring inflation under control, it tightened credit sufficiently to turn recovery into recession.

There are no villains, but there are victims. There is no doubt who bore the burden of recession: the unemployed. Their loss of income is not shared by the rest of us as the economy contracts. Moreover, unemployment hits hardest those industries that depend heavily on big-ticket consumer expenditures financed by borrowing. It is worst in construction, autos, and other durable goods industries, and in the steel and nonferrous metal industries. Workers in communications, services, finance, and government are largely spared.

Through no fault of their own, therefore, workers (and their families) in a narrow band of industries must bear most of the cycle's burden. They are not responsible for the economy's fluctuations, but they are the chief victims in every downturn. Someone must build the homes and cars and mill the lumber and steel. Yet, as if caught in a perverse game of musical chairs, those who do are always left without a seat when the music stops.

WHAT NEXT?

Is the next recession inevitable? Yes, because all economic expansions end in recession. The 1990–91 recession departed from the cyclical pattern described above when the Persian Gulf crisis depressed consumer sentiment even though there was no surge of inflation. That recession created so much slack that it did not appear that the old cyclical pattern of inflation and recession would reappear. Severe inflation was no longer a concern.

But what have we learned from the past? A strong and rapid expansion, driven by large increases in consumer and business borrowing and ending in virulent inflation, will produce a sharp and severe recession. A mild and gradual expansion, lacking excessive borrowing and ending with only slight inflation, will produce a mild recession.

Data on auto sales, consumer credit, and housing starts in the late 80s provided evidence that the excesses of the 70s can be avoided if the Fed has the resolve to keep interest rates at restrictive levels. It is better to avoid the rapid growth of demand and the resurrection of inflation, the lethal twins that have killed all previous booms. If demand grows slowly because credit is restrained, expansion will last longer and will not be set back so severely by the next recession.

That explains the Fed's preemptive strike against inflation in the mid 90s, as it forced interest rates upward to cool the interest-sensitive borrowing that finances consumer purchases of new vehicles and new homes.

Investor's Tip

- If housing starts exceed 1.8 million, consumer credit $125 billion, and new-vehicle sales 15 million for more than a quarter year, inflation is around the corner.

CHAPTER 7

THE POSTWAR BUSINESS CYCLE: THE ROLE OF COSTS AND INFLATION

INTRODUCTION

This chapter will develop the relationship between production, costs, and prices, so that you will be able to understand the dynamic whereby rapid growth is transformed into severe inflation. By fathoming this dynamic, you will see why there is little likelihood of inflation's resurgence in the 1990s.

You can find inflation's bellwether in the statistical series that chart output and efficiency. Gross national product, industrial production, and capacity utilization measure the economy's output; productivity measures its efficiency. As output increases, efficiency decreases, and inflation (as reported by the producer price index) inevitably becomes a problem.

At the peak of the cycle, when output is at its maximum, production facilities are strained to the point where production costs rise sharply. Overburdened equipment fails, accelerating the expense of maintenance and repair. The quantities of labor added to the production process are relatively greater than the increase in output. Inevitable inefficiencies force up costs and, consequently, prices, even though the product itself has not changed. As the obvious result, inflation increases rapidly.

With the recession's drop in production, the strain on facilities and labor eases. Costs fall, inflation declines, and the stage is set for a new round of expansion and growth.

The connections between output, efficiency, and inflation form this chapter's central theme. Turn now to an examination of the statistical releases that will be of particular importance in charting the course of pro-

duction and the interaction of efficiency and inflation as the economy moves from trough to recovery.

GROSS DOMESTIC PRODUCT (GDP)

GDP is a good place to start. As the broadest available measure of economic activity, it provides the official scale with which fluctuations in the economy are measured.

The Wall Street Journal publishes data from the U.S. Department of Commerce's quarterly release on the GDP about 25 days after the close of each quarter. Then, around the 25th of the two subsequent months, it reports revisions of the data. The fourth quarter of 1994 figures appeared in the Monday, January 30, 1995 *Journal* on pages 99 and 100.

Look for the following features: *constant-dollar (real) GDP*, *current dollar (nominal) GDP*, the *rate of inflation*, and the *statistical summary*.

Constant-Dollar (Real) GDP

The headline, accompanying chart, and third paragraph tell you the economy grew at a 4.5 percent annual rate in the fourth quarter of 1994. What does this mean?

Constant-dollar (real) GDP measures the final output of goods and services produced in the U.S. in one year, without including the impact of changed prices on the value of those goods. Thus, this year's output (as well as last year's output, next year's, or any year we wish to measure) is calculated in the prices of the base year (1987).

This kind of aggregate measure was once referred to as the Gross National Product (GNP), and there is a slight difference between the two. Put simply, GNP measures the output and earnings of Americans, no matter where they live and work, whereas GDP measures output and earnings in the U.S. regardless of the earner's nationality. For instance, GNP includes the profits of American corporations overseas and excludes the profits of foreign corporations in America, while GDP excludes the former and includes the latter.

Economy Grew At 4.5% Rate In 4th Quarter

Full-Year 4% Pace Was Best Since 1984; Two Gauges Of Inflation Were Low

By LUCINDA HARPER
Staff Reporter of THE WALL STREET JOURNAL

WASHINGTON – The economy ended 1994 with its strongest growth in a decade and, at least by one measure, its lowest inflation rate in 30 years.

But the combination is a rare one, not likely to be repeated soon. "It's hard to get any better than this," said James Smith, professor of finance at the University of North Carolina's business school.

The Commerce Department said gross domestic product, the value of goods and services produced in the U.S., surged at an annual rate of 4.5% in the fourth quarter, compared with a 4% rate in the third quarter. The strong performance helped push growth for the year to 4%, the best showing since a 6.2% rate in 1984.

At the same time, the government's fixed-weighted price index, which meas-

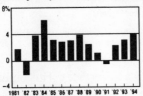

Robust Growth
Percentage change in GDP, adjusted for inflation

Source: Commerce Department, Bureau of Economic Analysis

ures prices paid by U.S. residents for a specific list of goods, rose at a 2.5% rate in the fourth quarter and 2.6% for the year, the smallest since the government started reporting the figure in 1983. The rise in the implicit price deflator – a measure that varies with purchasing patterns – was only 2.1% for the year, the smallest since a 1.8% rise in 1964.

Commerce Chief's View

The figures were of great satisfaction to the Clinton administration, which the Republicans rebuked for raising taxes almost two years ago, saying the move would choke off the economic recovery. "His detractors at the time told us that the president's proposals would be a recipe for disaster," Commerce Secretary Ron Brown said. "Now we know they were wrong."

The strength in economic growth during the final phase of the year was broad-based. Investment outside the residential sector jumped at a 17.6% annual rate, following a third-quarter increase at a 14.1% rate. Investment in durable equipment rose the most, but there was a big rise in structures as well. The economy was also helped by strong consumer spending, a reflection of more jobs and growing consumer confidence. Spending rose at a 4.6% annual rate, helped by an increase in durable goods, such as autos and light trucks, at an 18.4% rate.

The unquestionable strength in these sectors is another harbinger of an expected interest-rate boost when the Federal Reserve meets to set its rate policy tomorrow and Wednesday. Many analysts expect the Fed to raise rates by half a percentage point.

Greenspan Defends Moves

The Fed has been criticized for raising interest rates before seeing any evidence of worsening inflation, but Fed Chairman Alan Greenspan replied in remarks prepared for delivery over the weekend: "If we had waited until inflation had become evident, it would have been too late.

"To successfully navigate a bend in the river, the barge must begin the turn well before the bend is reached," Mr. Greenspan said, offering a new monetary-policy metaphor. "Even so, currents are always changing and even an experienced crew cannot foresee all the events that might occur as the river is being navigated. A year ago, the Fed began its turn, and we do not yet know if it has been successful."

There were some indications that the higher interest rates have begun to cut down on growth in some areas. Residential investment, the sector most sensitive to changes in rates, fell at a 2.6% rate in the fourth quarter. That was the second quarterly decline in a row.

But many analysts expect more widespread slowing in the coming months as the Fed's interest-rate boosts to date begin filtering down the pipeline. "The economic

GDP

Inflation

(continued)

theme for 1995 will be a soft landing," said John Mueller, chief economist for Lehrman Bell Mueller Cannon Inc., economic consulting firm in Arlington, Va.

Economists expect consumers to shift their focus away from expensive durable goods to nondurable goods such as clothes and cosmetics. Business investment is expected to taper off from its extraordinarily high levels. The Blue Chip Economic Indicators newsletter, a survey of the nation's top economists, finds they expect 1995 economic growth to slow to 3.1%.

Productivity gains are expected to narrow, leading many analysts to anticipate larger price increases this year than last despite a slowdown in growth. The Blue Chip economists see an inflation rate of 3.3%.

The extent to which the economy slows depends, in part, on inventories. Businesses added $10.9 billion to their stockpiles in the fourth quarter. It's unclear whether that buildup was voluntary, because of an expected increase in demand, or involuntary, meaning those goods could get stuck on the shelf if demand falls off too much. If the latter occurs, factories could sharply curb production and possibly lay off workers.

Laura Tyson, chairwoman of the Council of Economic Advisers, said it is difficult to tell why inventories increased so much in the fourth quarter and suggested the numbers could be revised to show a smaller buildup. "Everyone knows they are based on very partial information and subject to big revisions," Ms. Tyson said. The Commerce Department's figures will be revised twice in the coming months.

Friday's report also showed a huge drop in federal government spending, re-

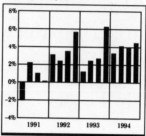

Real GDP

Percentage change at annual rate.

REAL GROSS DOMESTIC PRODUCT increased at a 4.5% annual rate in the fourth quarter, the Commerce Department reports.

suming a trend of leaner government. Federal purchases dropped at a 15.6% annual rate, mainly because of defense cuts, reversing an unusual third-quarter increase at a 10.9% rate.

All figures have been adjusted for normal seasonal variations.

GROSS DOMESTIC PRODUCT

Here are some of the major components of the gross domestic product expressed in seasonally adjusted annual rates in billions of constant (1987) dollars:

	4th Qtr. 1994	3rd Qtr. 1994	
GDP	5,426.8	5,367.0	Statistical
less: Inventory chng	68.0	57.1	Summary
equals: final sales	5,358.8	5,310.0	
Components of Final Sales			
Personal Consumption	3,625.1	3,584.7	
Nonresidential Invest.	708.2	680.0	
Residential Invest.	228.7	230.2	
Net Exports	−124.1	−117.0	
Gov't Purchases	920.9	932.0	

GDP includes only final goods and services. This eliminates measuring the same thing more than once at various stages of its production. For instance, bread purchased by the consumer appears in GDP, but both the flour from which the bread is baked and the wheat from which the flour is milled are omitted, because the value of the bread comprises the value of all its ingredients. Thus, the economy's output of *all* goods and services is far greater than its output of *final* (GDP) goods and services. We use very little steel, chemicals, or advertising agency services directly. Their value is subsumed in our purchases of well-promoted Chevrolets and Saran Wrap.

The third paragraph refers to a 4.5 percent increase in final output in the fourth quarter of 1994. This measurement was made at a *seasonally adjusted annual rate*. Adjusting for seasonal factors merely means correcting the distortion in the data arising from the measurement being taken during this rather than any other quarter. Obviously, no seasonal adjustment is required when a whole year's data is measured, but when the year is divided up and data extracted for a run of months, the risk of distortion attributable to the season is great. For instance, retail trade is particularly heavy around Christmas and particularly light immediately after the first of the year; you could not make a useful comparison of the first quarter's retail sales with the last quarter's without first making a seasonal adjustment.

GDP–Third Paragraph

The Commerce Department said gross domestic product, the value of goods and services produced in the U.S., surged at an annual rate of 4.5% in the fourth quarter, compared with a 4% rate in the third quarter. The strong performance helped push growth for the year to 4%, the best showing since a 6.2% rate in 1984.

The reference to "annual rate" shows that the data for the fourth quarter, which of course covers only three months' activity, has been multiplied by four to increase it to a level comparable to annual data.

The constant-dollar or real GDP calculation is made in order to compare the level of output in one time period with that in another without inflation's distorting impact. If the inflation factor were not removed, you would not know whether differences in dollar value were due to output changes or price changes. Real GDP gives you a dollar value that measures output changes only.

One last point should be made before moving on. The first paragraph said that 1994 ended "with its strongest growth in a decade." A glance at the accompanying chart shows a steady and robust rise in GDP, indicating

economic recovery and expansion from the slump of 1990–91. At a yearly rate of four percent, the economy is growing at a good pace. It is well above the rate of population growth, providing a substantial per capita gain, without getting to an unsustainable rate of more than five percent, which, for any length of time, strains our productive capacity.

Current-Dollar (Nominal) GDP

Nominal (current-dollar) GDP includes inflation and is therefore higher than real (constant-dollar) GDP, which does not. Before adjustment for inflation (i.e., including current, inflated prices), GDP was slightly more than the real figure (at 1987 prices) of $5.427 trillion reported in the statistical summary at the end of the article.

Rate of Inflation

The fourth paragraph of the article reports that the *fixed-weighted price index* "…rose at a 2.5 percent annual rate in the fourth quarter…" This index yields the broadest measure of inflation, since GDP is the most broadly based yardstick of economic activity. The more familiar consumer price index includes consumption expenditures only, while this index includes production for business and government use as well. The producer price index, which is explained later in this chapter, covers wholesale prices of goods, but not services.

Inflation–Fourth Paragraph

At the same time, the government's fixed-weighted price index, which measures prices paid by U.S. residents for a specific list of goods, rose at a 2.5% rate in the fourth quarter and 2.6% for the year, the smallest since the government started reporting the figure in 1983. The rise in the implicit price deflator – a measure that varies with purchasing patterns–was only 2.1% for the year, the smallest since a 1.8% rise in 1964.

Statistical Summary

The statistical summary at the end of the article provides a convenient breakdown of the major GDP components.

Statistical Summary—End of Article

GROSS DOMESTIC PRODUCT

Here are some of the major components of the gross domestic product expressed in seasonally adjusted annual rates in billions of constant (1987) dollars:

	4th Qtr. 1994	3rd Qtr. 1994
GDP	5,426.8	5,367.0
less: inventory chng	68.0	57.1
equals: final sales	5,358.8	5,310.0
Components of Final Sales		
Personal Consumption	3,625.1	3,584.7
Nonresidential Invest.	708.2	680.0
Residential Invest.	228.7	230.2
Net Exports	−124.1	−117.0
Gov't Purchases	920.9	932.0

Source: *The Wall Street Journal*, January 30, 1995. Reprinted by permission of *The Wall Street Journal*, ©1995 Dow Jones & Company, Inc. All rights reserved worldwide.

Now you are ready to put GDP's current performance in historical perspective. Compare it with Chart 7–1 on page 104.

The top graph portrays the actual level of GDP, while the bottom graph depicts quarterly percentage changes at annual rates. When the bottom series is above the zero line, GDP has increased; a drop in GDP is indicated by points below the zero line.

As you look at these graphs, pay special attention to the setback to GDP growth during the recession of 1990–91. "Two consecutive quarters of declining GDP" is the traditional definition of recession.

Industrial production and capacity utilization will mirror GDP's performance and also provide important additional detail, so you should now become acquainted with these series.

CHART 7–1
Gross Domestic Product (GDP) in Constant (1987) Dollars;
Quarterly Change in GDP at Annual Rates

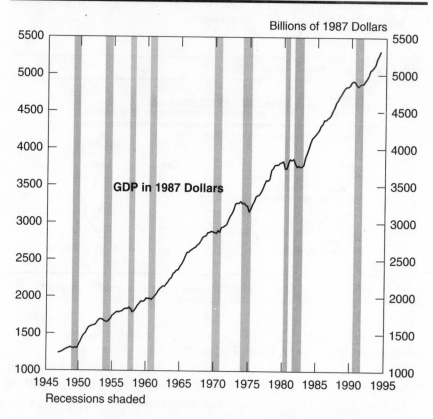

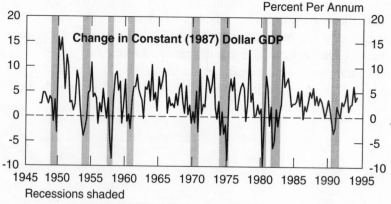

Source: U.S. Department of Commerce, *Business Cycle Indicators*, Series 50 and 50c.

INDUSTRIAL PRODUCTION

The Wall Street Journal reports data from the Federal Reserve's report on *industrial production* in an article that usually appears mid-month. A typical report was published on Wednesday, January 18, 1995 (see pages 106–108). The headline, accompanying chart, second paragraph, and statistical table at the end of the story summarize matters, while the article provides detail and commentary.

The index of industrial production measures changes in the output of the mining, manufacturing, and gas and electric utilities sectors of our economy. Industrial production is a narrower concept than GDP, because it omits agriculture, construction, wholesale and retail trade, transportation, communications, services, finance, and government. Industrial production is also more volatile than GDP, because GDP, unlike industrial production, includes activities that are largely spared cyclical fluctuation, such as services, finance, and government. The brunt of cyclical fluctuations falls on the mining, manufacturing, and public utilities sectors. Nonetheless, GDP and industrial production move in parallel fashion.

Industrial production is measured by an *index*, a technique that focuses on the relative size and fluctuation of physical output without concern for its dollar value. To construct the index, a base year (1987) was selected to serve as a benchmark and assigned a value of 100.0. (Think of it as 100 percent.) Data for all other months and years is then expressed in relative proportion (numerical ratio) to the data for the base year. For example, according to the statistical summary at the end of the article, industrial production had an index value of 121.4 in December of 1994. This means that industrial production was 21.4 percent higher than the average rate of production in 1987.

These developments are reflected in the rate of capacity utilization and in the efficiency with which the economy operates.

Industrial Production Surged 1%, Biggest Monthly Jump Since 1992

Strong Showing Contradicts Other Reports Signaling Slowdown in Economy

ECONOMY

By LUCINDA HARPER

Staff Reporter of THE WALL STREET JOURNAL

WASHINGTON—Industrial production across the country surged last month, raising doubts about earlier signs of a slowing economy.

The Federal Reserve said output at the nation's factories, mines and utilities jumped 1.0% in December, the largest monthly gain since November 1992. When compared with the same month a year ago, factory output was up 5.8%.

The jump in industrial production, the Fed report said, means U.S. factories were operating at 85.4% of capacity in December. That was up from 84.7% in November and was the highest level of capacity since October 1979.

The strong industrial production report seemed to contradict last week's government report on retail sales, which showed that sales declined 0.1% in December and suggested that consumer spending — and thus the economy—may be slowing down.

Schedules Set in Advance

Analysts point out, however, that production schedules for December were planned several months in advance and were likely set before consumer spending began to show signs of weakness. "The strong production last month was more a reflection of what was going on well before," when consumer spending was very strong, said Stuart Hoffman, chief economist for PNC Bank Corp. in Pittsburgh.

Although in any given month a big rise in production coupled with weak consumer spending isn't a problem, if it happens repeatedly the economy could be in for trouble. That's because inventories will build up, and factories will cut production and possibly lay off workers.

But so far, such a major slowdown doesn't seem to be at hand. While consumer spending and housing sales have tapered in recent months, the economy still has a lot of momentum. "The signs we are slowing down are very weak and very

(Labels at left:)

Industrial Production

Capacity Utilization

Industrial Production

Index, 1987=100, seasonally adjusted.

THE INDUSTRIAL PRODUCTION index rose in December to 121.4 after seasonal adjustments from a revised 120.3 in November, the Federal Reserve reports.

modest," said Mark Zandi, chief economist for Regional Financial Associates in West Chester, Pa.

Jobs increased at a healthy pace last month, the unemployment rate fell and the manufacturing sector stayed strong. As a result, most analysts think that when the Fed meets later this month it will again raise short-term interest rates in an effort to slow economic growth and put off inflation.

"Clearly, the manufacturing sector is operating all-out," said Mr. Zandi. "There is no doubt we will begin to see inflation in this sector."

The increase in industrial production during December was broad-based. Production of business equipment jumped 1.1%, after a 0.4% rise the month before. Materials production rose 1.3%, following a 0.8% rise. Mining production, which has faltered virtually all year, was up 1.2%. The only major industry group to fall during the month was utility production, which analysts blamed on unseasonably warm weather.

Analysts noted a pickup in production of nondurable goods, which rose at a healthy pace for the second straight month. As interest rates rise, consumers

traditionally turn their attention away from durable goods and focus on items with a shorter lifespan, such as clothes and cosmetics. In December, production of chemicals, textile-mill products and food all had significant increases.

Stock prices largely shrugged off the reports, ending mixed in heavy trading. Every major index except the Dow Jones Industrial Average showed moderate gains.

Making More

Change in production of selected goods, December 1994 vs. December 1993

	% CHANGE
Consumer goods	+ 3.4%
Furniture, carpeting	+ 5.5
Autos and trucks	+ 4.4
Appliances, TVs, air conditioners	+ 4.2
Clothing	+ 0.7
Business equipment	+ 9.8
Info. processing	+14.0
Industrial	+ 8.9
Defense and space equip.	− 8.0
Oil- and gas-well drilling	− 2.4
TOTAL	+ 5.8%

Source: Federal Reserve Board

Statistical Summary

Here is a summary of the Federal Reserve Board's report on industrial production in December. The figures are seasonally adjusted.

	% change from	
	Nov. 1994	Dec. 1993
Total	1.0	5.8
Consumer goods	0.9	3.4
Business equipment	1.1	9.8
Defense and space	0.4	−8.0
Manufacturing only	1.0	6.7
Durable goods	1.3	8.2
Nondurable goods	0.7	4.9
Mining	1.2	1.5
Utilities	−0.8	−0.6

The industrial production index for December stood at 121.4% of the 1987 average.

Source: *The Wall Street Journal*, January 18, 1995. Reprinted by permission of *The Wall Street Journal*, ©1995 Dow Jones & Company, Inc. All rights reserved worldwide.

Statistical Summary–End of Article

Here is a summary of the Federal Reserve Board's report on industrial production in December. The figures are seasonally adjusted.

	% change from	
	Nov. 1994	Dec. 1993
Total	1.0	5.8
Consumer goods	0.9	3.4
Business equipment	1.1	9.8
Defense and space	0.4	−8.0
Manufacturing only	1.0	6.7
Durable goods	1.3	8.2
Nondurable goods	0.7	4.9
Mining	1.2	1.5
Utilities	−0.8	−0.6

The industrial production index for December stood at 121.4% of the 1987 average.

Source: *The Wall Street Journal*, January 18, 1995. Reprinted by permission of *The Wall Street Journal*, ©1995 Dow Jones & Company, Inc. All rights reserved worldwide.

Industrial Production–Second Paragraph

The Federal Reserve said output at the nation's factories, mines and utilities jumped 1.0% in December, the largest monthly gain since November 1992. When compared with the same month a year ago, factory output was up 5.8%.

CHART 7–2
Industrial Production Index (1987 = 100)

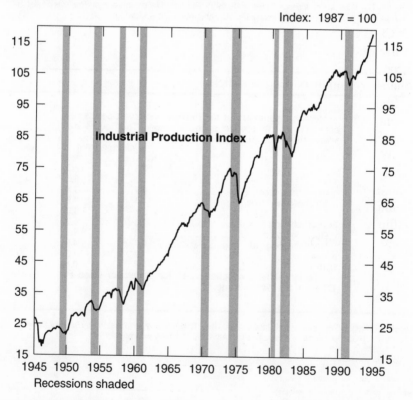

Index: 1987 = 100

Industrial Production Index

Recessions shaded

Source: U.S. Department of Commerce, *Business Cycle Indicators*, Series 47.

CAPACITY UTILIZATION

The Wall Street Journal publishes information from the Federal Reserve's monthly statistical release on *capacity utilization,* or, as it is often called, *the factory operating rate,* along with the industrial production figures. The third paragraph of the January 18, 1995 article on pages 106 and 107 informs you of December's 85.4 percent rate.

Capacity utilization is the rate at which mining, manufacturing, and public utilities industries operate, expressed as a percentage of the maximum rate at which they could operate under existing conditions. Putting the matter differently, think of capacity utilization as measuring what these industries are currently producing compared (in percentage terms) to the most they could produce using all of their present resources. Thus, if an industry produces 80 tons of product in a year, while having plant and equipment at its disposal capable of producing 100 tons a year, that industry is operating at 80 percent of capacity; its capacity utilization is 80 percent.

Capacity utilization is a short-run concept determined by a company's current physical limits; at any moment in which capacity utilization is reported, it is assumed that the company's plant and equipment cannot be increased, although labor and other inputs can. This defines the short run. Although manufacturing industry continually adds new plant and equipment, it is useful to snap a photograph at a particular moment to enable measurement and comparison.

What bearing does capacity utilization have on the efficiency or productivity of industry? Consider a hypothetical analogy. Your car operates more efficiently at 50 miles per hour than at 70 miles per hour if its maximum speed is 80, for you will obtain better gas mileage at the lower speed. Efficiency is expressed as a relationship between inputs (gas gallons) and outputs (miles driven). Your car's engine operates more efficiently at lower speeds, or at lower levels of capacity utilization.

You are therefore confronted with the problem of diminishing returns: As your speed increases, you obtain fewer miles for each additional gallon of gas. At 50 miles per hour, you can go 30 miles on an additional gallon of gas; at 52 miles per hour, 29 miles on an additional gallon; at 54 miles per hour, 28 miles; and so on. Your output (miles) per unit of input (gallon) falls as you push toward full capacity utilization (maximum speed).

Likewise, as capacity utilization increases, an industry also passes the point of diminishing returns. This may be at 70 percent, 80 percent, or

90 percent of capacity utilization, depending on the industry, but the point will ultimately be reached where the percentage increases in output will become smaller than the percentage increases in input. For instance, a 15 percent increase in labor input, once we have passed the point of diminishing returns, may provide only a 10 percent increase in output. This phenomenon does not occur because of some mystical mathematical relationship, nor because people are just like automobile engines. There are common-sense reasons for it, and you probably know many of them already.

First, at low levels of capacity utilization, there is ample time to inspect, maintain, and repair equipment; accidental damage can be held to a minimum; and production increases can be achieved easily in a smoothly efficient plant. Above a certain level of capacity utilization, however, management finds it more difficult to inspect, maintain, and repair equipment because of the plant's heavier operating schedule. Perhaps a second shift of workers has been added or additional overtime scheduled. There is less time for equipment maintenance, and accidental damage becomes inevitable. The labor force is in place and on the payroll, and production does increase, but not as rapidly as does labor input, because equipment frequently breaks down.

Second, as production increases and more labor is hired, the last people hired are less experienced and usually less efficient than the older workers; furthermore, crowding and fatigue can become a problem if more overtime is scheduled. Poor work quality and accidental damage result. All of this ensures that output will not increase as rapidly as labor input.

Third, low levels of capacity utilization occur at the trough of a recession. Business firms typically suffer a sharp drop in profit, if not actual losses, and, under these circumstances, the employer reduces the work force as much as possible. In fact, he or she usually reduces it more than the drop in output, once the decision to cut back has been made. Why more than the drop in output? Because by the trough of recession, the seriousness of the situation is recognized, and industry has embarked on a thorough restructuring. The alarm has sounded and costs (work force) are slashed. That's why recession often generates the sharpest increases in efficiency.

Even after output has begun to recover, an extended period of labor reduction may continue as part of a general cost-cutting program. As recovery boosts capacity utilization, however, hiring additional workers becomes inevitable. When a factory reaches full capacity utilization near the peak of a boom, the cost-cutting program will be long forgotten as

management scrambles for additional labor in order to meet the barrage of orders. At this point, additions to labor are greater than increments in output, even though (to repeat) output will be rising somewhat.

You can summarize business's decisions regarding labor as follows. During rapid expansion and into economic boom, when orders are heavy and capacity utilization is strained, business will sacrifice efficiency and short-run profits to maintain customer loyalty. Management adds labor more rapidly than output increases in order to get the job done. But, when the recession hits in earnest, and it becomes apparent that orders will not recover for some time, management cuts labor costs to the bone with layoffs and a freeze on hiring. This is especially true during a prolonged recession, such as that of 1981–82, which followed on the heels of an earlier recession (in 1980) and an incomplete recovery. Even after recovery and expansion begin, however, business will still attempt to operate with a reduced labor force in order to reap the benefits of cost cutting in the form of higher profits. Operating efficiency (productivity) improves rapidly, and it will not be threatened until the expansion heats up and boom conditions develop.

Remember the motor in your car? Efficiency is expressed as the relationship between inputs (fuel) and outputs (distance traveled). It is useful to think of the economy as if it were a machine, like the engine. Since your engine is fixed in size (at any moment in time), you can only push a finite amount of fuel through it. Depressing the accelerator rapidly increases your speed and the distance traveled, but the increment in fuel used is greater than the increment in speed and distance. Hence, the efficiency of your engine falls, despite your greater speed and distance. You are getting fewer miles per gallon, and it's taking more fuel to go a mile, because you are driving faster.

Just as a bigger engine would help you accelerate more quickly, more industrial capacity would permit the economy to operate more efficiently. But, for the moment, the economy is limited to the amount of capacity at hand, making it useful to speak about the rate of capacity utilization now. And it is important to realize that, like your car engine, the economy becomes less efficient if it is pushed too hard.

Now compare capacity utilization's historical record with that of GDP, noting once again the figure reported in the January 18, 1995 *Journal* article (see Chart 7–3 on page 112). Each of the series examined thus far (GDP, industrial production, capacity utilization) tells the same story. The economy has moved well past the trough of the cycle in 1990–91, and was expanding rapidly by mid decade.

CHART 7–3
GDP and Capacity Utilization

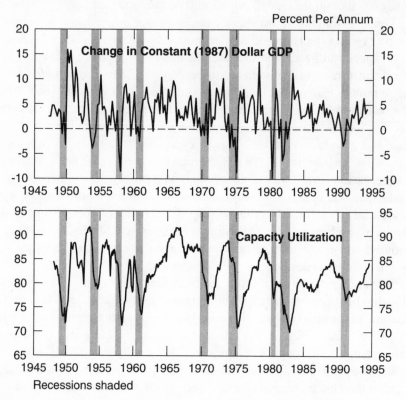

Source: U.S. Department of Commerce, *Business Cycle Indicators*, Series 50c and 82.

The mid-80s capacity utilization plateau (hovering around 80 percent for almost five years) and the 1990–91 recession explain the low inflation rates we have had since 1982. The economy had not been pushed to a sufficiently high level of capacity utilization to produce the inefficiencies that generate rapidly rising costs and prices.

But you can see from the third paragraph of the January 18, 1995 *Journal* that capacity utilization was at its highest level since 1979 (85.4 percent) in December of 1994. Some economists believe high capacity utilization no longer signals inflation because of the increased availability of imports. But the most prudent reaction is to raise the inflation alarm when it moves beyond 85 percent.

Capacity Utilization–Third Paragraph

The jump in industrial production, the Fed report said, means U.S. factories were operating at 85.4% of capacity in December. That was up from 84.7% in November and was the highest level of capacity since October 1979.

Source: *The Wall Street Journal*, January 18, 1995. Reprinted by permission of *The Wall Street Journal*, ©1995 Dow Jones & Company, Inc. All rights reserved worldwide.

When you examine the 1970s, on the other hand, you can see that the rate of capacity utilization periodically rose to the 90 percent level, generating the inefficiency that brings on inflation. That's why the severe cyclical fluctuations of the 70s were bad for the economy and the slow, steady growth of the 80s was good.

Capacity Utilization and Inflation

- Robust consumer demand for housing, autos, and other durables leads to surging capacity utilization and inflation.
- Capacity utilization over 85% generates inflation.

The next series in this chapter, labor productivity and unit labor costs, will provide the statistical measurements needed to calibrate these fluctuations in efficiency.

LABOR PRODUCTIVITY AND UNIT LABOR COSTS

The Wall Street Journal reports figures from the U.S. Department of Labor's preliminary release on *labor productivity* about a month after the end of the quarter and publishes a revision about a month later. The Thursday, November 10, 1994 article presents third quarter 1994 data. (See page 114.)

Productivity Increased 2.7% In 3rd Quarter

Labor Costs Barely Budged, A Sign That Inflationary Pressures Were Muted

---

By CHRISTOPHER GEORGES
Staff Reporter of THE WALL STREET JOURNAL

WASHINGTON — Productivity rose in the third quarter, while inflationary pressures remained mild.

Labor Productivity

The Labor Department reported that productivity of non-farm businesses, or output per hour of work, rose at a 2.7% annual rate from July through September. The increase marks a turnaround from the second quarter, when productivity dropped at a 2.1% rate.

But the third-quarter improvement included a barely perceptible 0.1% annual rate of increase in unit labor costs. Because labor represents about two-thirds of the cost of a product, the report suggested inflationary pressures remained muted last summer.

"It's a very positive development as far as inflation is concerned," said Marilyn Schaja, an economist at Donaldson, Lufkin & Jenrette. "It's not the whole picture, but an encouraging sign."

One contrary signal that wage-based inflation may have picked up came in last week's October employment report, which showed a 0.7% increase in hourly earnings from September, the largest gain in nearly five years.

Analysts agreed that yesterday's productivity report would have little impact on the Federal Reserve Board's thinking on raising interest rates. Most economists expect the central bank to raise short-term rates next week for the sixth time this year.

The productivity advance, analysts said, was largely a result of businesses working their employees harder and longer rather than adding to payrolls. Analysts had said that the second-quarter drop in productivity, which often moves erratically from quarter to quarter, largely reflected declines in the service sector.

Output and Hours

Third-quarter output rose 3.9% at an annual rate, while the number of hours worked increased at a 1.2% rate. Manufacturing productivity, which was up 5.3%, outpaced the overall improvement. Manufacturing showed a 7.1% surge in output and a 1.7% gain in the number of hours worked.

Unit labor costs in manufacturing fell at a 2.1% annual rate, slower than the 6.8% decline three months earlier.

Total business productivity, including farming, rose 3.1%, compared with a 2% drop in the second quarter.

The second paragraph and the third paragraph from the end of the article inform you that third-quarter output rose at an annual rate of 3.9 percent, while labor input increased by only 1.2 percent, boosting productivity (output per worker) by 2.7 percent. The calculation is simple: 3.9 minus 1.2 equals 2.7.

Chart 7–4 on page 116 presents the record for all business (including farms). The series are similar.

Labor productivity measures output or production per unit of labor input (e.g., output per hour) and is *the most important gauge* of our nation's efficiency. Its significance cannot be overemphasized, for *per capita real income cannot improve*—and thus the country's standard of living cannot rise—*without an increase in per capita production.*

Labor Productivity–Second Paragraph

> The Labor Department reported that productivity of non-farm businesses, or output per hour of work, rose at a 2.7% annual rate from July through September. The increase marks a turnaround from the second quarter, when productivity dropped at a 2.1% rate.

Output and Hours–Third Paragraph from End of Article

> Third-quarter output rose 3.9% at an annual rate, while the number of hours worked increased at a 1.2% rate. Manufacturing productivity, which was up 5.3%, outpaced the overall improvement. Manufacturing showed a 7.1% surge in output and a 1.7% gain in the number of hours worked.

Unit labor cost measures the cost of labor per unit of output. Thus, unit labor cost is the *inverse* of labor productivity, since unit labor costs fall as labor productivity rises, and vice versa. Unit labor cost tells you how much added labor is required to produce an additional unit of output. Because labor is hired for a wage, requiring more labor time to produce each unit of output will raise labor costs per unit of output, and vice versa.

Consider, for instance, a factory that assembles hand-held calculators. If the production of a calculator has required an hour of labor and a technological innovation permits the production of two calculators per hour, labor productivity has doubled from one to two calculators per hour. The output per hour of work is twice what it was.

CHART 7–4
Productivity: Output per Hour, All Persons, Private Business Sector
(1982 = 100); Change in Output per Hour (smoothed)

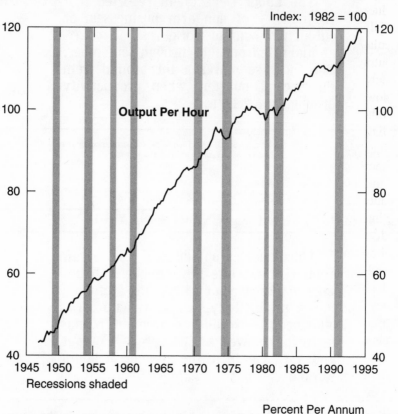

Recessions shaded

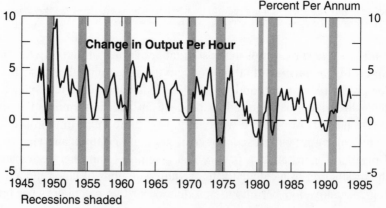

Recessions shaded

Source: U.S. Department of Commerce, *Business Cycle Indicators*, Series 370 and 370c.

If the wage rate is $10 per hour, and before the innovation an hour of work was required to produce a calculator, the labor cost per unit of output was then $10. After the innovation, however, two calculators can be produced in an hour, or one calculator in half an hour, so unit labor cost has fallen to $5. Note that as labor productivity doubled, from one to two calculators per hour, unit labor costs were halved, from $10 to $5 per unit of output. The gain in labor productivity drove down unit labor costs without any change in the wage rate.

Now compare the record of labor productivity and unit labor costs with the other indicators examined so far (see Chart 7–5 on page 118).

GDP, industrial production, and capacity utilization together define the business cycle in the 1970s. Since 1970, their fluctuations have indicated prosperity and recession. You can also see that labor productivity plunged and unit labor costs soared with the peak of each cycle in the 1970s. Labor productivity improved and unit labor costs declined with each recession and into the next recovery. But as soon as expansion got under way, labor productivity's growth began to weaken and unit labor costs began to rise, until productivity slumped and costs peaked at the end of the boom.

And this brings you full circle to the discussion of efficiency included in the earlier investigation of capacity utilization: The economy's efficiency deteriorated in the 70s with each boom and improved in each recession and into recovery. All that this section has done is to provide the labels and devices (labor productivity and unit labor costs) necessary to measure that efficiency. During boom conditions, efficiency (labor productivity) declines and expenses (unit labor costs) mount. During recession the opposite is true.

At first you might ask yourself, "Why would management ever place itself in the position of risking a drop in the efficiency of its operations in order to push output and capacity utilization too far? Why not limit production to an efficient level of operations, at, say, 80 percent capacity utilization, rather than risk declining productivity at 90 percent of capacity utilization?"

The answer is easy, if you put yourself in management's shoes. Suppose you're the boss at Bethlehem Steel, and Ford Motor Co. is your best customer. Suppose also that you're running two production shifts at your mill, sixteen hours a day, and a small maintenance crew is employed during the remaining eight-hour shift. The maintenance crew inspects, maintains, and repairs the equipment so that everything is up and running during the daily sixteen hours of production.

CHART 7–5
GDP, Capacity Utilization, Labor Productivity, and Unit Labor Cost

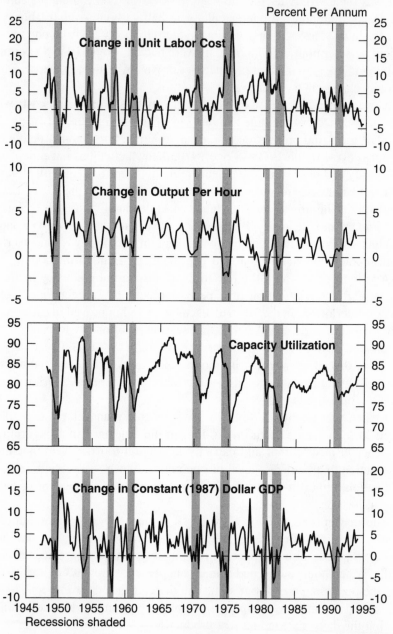

Recessions shaded

Source: U.S. Department of Commerce, *Business Cycle Indicators*, Series 50c, 62, 82 and 370c.

Now Ford calls and says their Taurus model has been a big success and they need more steel in a hurry. Do you tell Ford that you're sorry, that you're running flat out, that you have no idle capacity, and that they should come back during the next recession when you have plenty of idle capacity and would be happy to take their order? Only if you want to lose your best customer. No, you tell them you will move heaven and earth to fill their order, and you cancel the maintenance shift and put on another production shift.

Putting on another shift of workers increases the size of your production crew (and labor costs) by 50 percent (from sixteen to twenty-four hours a day), yet your output increases by only 30 percent because of periodic breakdowns in equipment that cannot be properly maintained. But if you only require a 30 percent increase in output in order to fill the order, you may very well be willing to put up with a 50 percent increase in labor hours and costs. Sure, output per worker (productivity) falls on this order, and maybe you won't turn a profit either. That's okay as long as you keep your best customer. You're interested in maximizing your profit in the long run, not the short run.

As a result, you've met your deadline by pushing your mill's output to the maximum. Productivity has declined and costs have increased. But that's acceptable, especially if you can pass those higher costs on in the form of higher prices (the subject of the next section of this chapter).

The charts inform you that productivity growth was moderate during the 80s, as output grew more rapidly than labor input. The economy was far better off than in the 70s, when periodic declines in productivity were associated with excessive rates of capacity utilization.

Notice as well that productivity improved nicely coming out of the 1990–91 recession. That illustrates, once again, that efficiency rebounds in the trough of the cycle and during recovery.

Productivity and the Cycle

- The economy is like your car's engine—far more efficient at a steady, moderate pace than in stop-and-go traffic.
- If you push the accelerator to the floor and rev the engine (high capacity utilization), efficiency (productivity) drops.

Perhaps by now you are wondering about the long-run influences on productivity. Our economy's efficiency depends on more than cyclical developments. What about industry's efforts to improve efficiency? Where do these fit in?

An economy's productivity improves when enterprise mobilizes improved technology and additional capital goods to raise output per worker and an increasing share of the economy's work shifts to those enterprises that have upgraded their technology and capital goods. These changes occur year-in and year-out, regardless of short-run developments and the cycle's phase. But pushing production to the limit can set these efforts back in the short run.

Turn now to the object of all the effort to contain costs: producer prices.

PRODUCER PRICES

The *producer price index*, until recently referred to as the wholesale price index, is compiled by the U.S. Department of Labor and shows the changes in prices charged by producers of finished goods—changes that are, of course, reflected in the prices consumers must pay. Data from the Labor Department's news release on producer prices is usually published by *The Wall Street Journal* in mid-month.

The Monday, September 12, 1994 article on page 121 is an example, and the headline, accompanying chart, and first paragraph tell you that the producer price index rose 0.6 percent in August of 1994.

Chart 7–6 (see page 123) confirms that in the early 90s, inflation, as measured by the producer price index, was still well below the double-digit levels of the 1970s. The drop since the 1979–80 peak has been dramatic.

You can also see from Chart 7–7 on page 124 that in the 70s the cyclical trends in producer prices mirrored those of unit labor costs. With each boom in output and capacity utilization, productivity dropped and unit labor costs rose, driving producer prices up. Then, when recession hit and output and capacity utilization fell, improved labor productivity and lower unit labor costs were reflected in reduced inflation. The 1981–82 recession illustrates the principle: Inflation's trend followed unit labor costs downward. As the economy's efficiency improved, stable prices followed on the heels of stable costs. Inflation remained low throughout the 1980s and early 90s because unit labor costs increased at a moderate pace.

Economists Say Jump in Prices Is Overstated

Wholesale Level Rise of 0.6% In August Roils Markets As Stocks, Bonds Fall

By PAULETTE THOMAS
Staff Reporter of THE WALL STREET JOURNAL

Producer
Prices

WASHINGTON — The unanticipated 0.6% jump in wholesale prices in August rekindled financial-market fears that inflation is accelerating, and added to pressure on the Federal Reserve to raise interest rates further.

But several economists said the report wasn't as bad as it looked.

"It's a little troublesome, but I'm not convinced that this is the beginning of an upturn in inflation," said Edward Yardeni of C.J. Lawrence, a New York brokerage house. "Inflation is on the rise, but not as much as the markets think," said Donald Ratajczak of Georgia State University. Marilyn Schaja of Donaldson, Lufkin & Jenrette called the report "disappointing, but not devastating."

Although some economists boosted their inflation forecasts a bit based on the report, most still expect tomorrow's consumer price report, a much broader inflation gauge, to be less alarming, rising perhaps 0.4%. Over the past year, they note, the producer price index has risen just 1.9%, and that is magnified because it reflects, in part, recovery of tobacco prices from a 26% plunge in August 1993.

Commodities, including coffee, tobacco and energy, were the chief culprits in the Labor Department's producer price index. Excluding food and energy prices, which tend to be volatile from month to month, producer prices rose 0.4% in August.

Biggest Rise in Four Years

Still, the surge in producer prices, the largest single-month increase since October 1990, followed a sizable 0.5% increase in July and was stronger than the 0.2%-to-0.4% increase expected by most economists. Financial markets, braced for any

trace of inflation, hit the panic button. Yields on 30-year bonds rose to 7.70%, a peak for this business cycle. The Dow Jones Industrial Average fell 33.65 points to 3874.81 (see articles on page C1).

"It was capitulation on the part of the benign-inflation camp," said Gene Sherman, economist with M.A. Schapiro & Co.

The report also undermined the Federal Reserve's argument that it raised interest rates early enough in this business cycle to avoid an increase in the inflation rate. Reflecting this view, Robert Parry, president of the San Francisco Federal Reserve Bank, said in a speech in Portland, Ore., Friday: "It is dangerous to wait until the problems show up in the inflation data. . . . Our actions this year were warranted to guard against an increase in future inflation. . . ."

Fed policy makers have increased short-term interest rates by 1¾ percentage points since February. The last increase was a one-half percentage point hike on Aug. 16. Friday's report added to widespread expectations that the Fed will keep increasing rates, if not at the Sept. 27 meeting of policy makers, then at the Nov. 15 meeting.

PRODUCER PRICES
Here are the Labor Department's producer price indexes (1982 = 100) for August, before seasonal adjustment, and the percentage changes from August 1993.

Finished goods	126.6	1.9%
Minus food & energy	137.2	1.9%
Intermediate goods	119.4	2.4%
Crude goods	101.4	0.8%

Producer Prices

Percentage change from previous month, seasonally adjusted

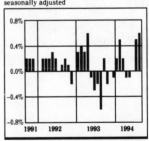

PRODUCER PRICES of finished goods rose a seasonally adjusted 0.6% in August, the Labor Department reports.

Producer Prices—First Paragraph

WASHINGTON – The unanticipated 0.6% jump in wholesale prices in August rekindled financial-market fears that inflation is accelerating, and added to pressure on the Federal Reserve to raise interest rates further.

Source: *The Wall Street Journal*, September 12, 1994. Reprinted by permission of *The Wall Street Journal*,

"But isn't it true," you may ask "that moderate wage increases have restrained unit labor costs recently? Perhaps the emphasis on productivity is misplaced and we should instead focus attention on wages as the driving force propelling prices upward."

True, wage increases subsided in the low-inflation 80s and have remained low ever since, contributing to the meager growth in unit labor costs. But generally speaking, *wage rates follow the cycle, they do not lead it.* Wages lagged behind prices during inflation's surge in the late 70s and fell less rapidly than prices in the early 80s. If boom conditions return, and sharp cost increases due to declining productivity are the result, expect wage increases to lag behind inflation once again.

Even the full employment of the late 80s didn't generate "wage inflation," because employers remained loath to grant wage increases in excess of inflation. Competition for workers in some markets did boost wages rapidly in some occupations in some locales, but this was not a nationwide phenomenon.

CHART 7–6
Producer Price Index (1982 = 100);
Quarterly Change in Index at Annual Rates (Smoothed)

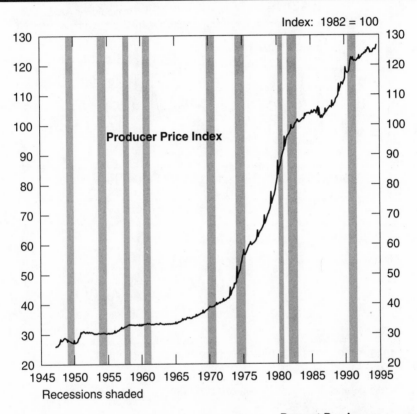

Index: 1982 = 100

Recessions shaded

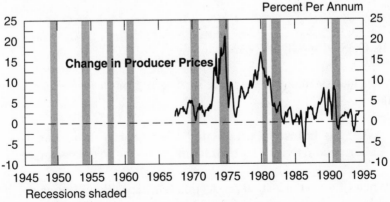

Percent Per Annum

Recessions shaded

Source: U.S. Department of Commerce, *Business Cycle Indicators*, Series 334 and 334c.

CHART 7–7
Changes in Unit Labor Cost and Producer Prices

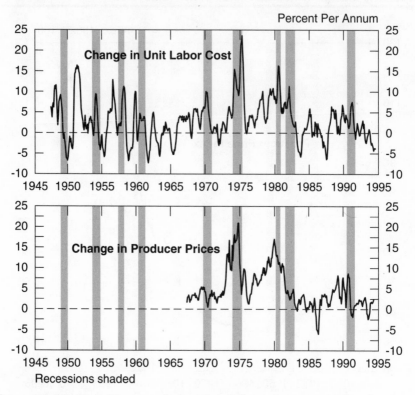

Source: U.S. Department of Commerce, *Business Cycle Indicators*, Series 62 and 334c.

THE COST/PRICE DYNAMIC

To conclude, summarize the cycle's progress from *trough* to *recovery* as follows:

> **GDP ↓→ Industrial production ↓→ Capacity utilization ↓→**
> **Labor productivity ↑→ Unit labor costs ↓→ Producer prices ↓**

When GDP and industrial production fall, capacity utilization declines. This leads to an increase in labor productivity and a drop in unit labor costs, driving down the rate of inflation as measured by producer prices.

Like the reveler's hangover, recession grips the economy following the bender of boom and inflation. Rest is the only cure, and recovery is marked not by a renewed round of expansion and growth, but by a slack period in which steadiness is restored.

But it would surely be naive to assume that low inflation will be forever with us. What forces can propel it upward once again? Why may we have a renewed round of price increases?

If you ask a business person why prices rise, he or she will answer, "Rising costs," probably referring to personal experience. When you ask an economist the same question, the response will be, "Demand exceeds supply at current prices, and therefore prices rise," probably referring to the textbook case. These points of view seem to have nothing in common, yet an analysis of economic expansion shows that they meld into a single explanation. Consider an idealized (and hypothetical) situation.

Suppose all the indicators of economic expansion (demand)—auto sales, consumer credit, housing starts—are strong. This will initiate broad-based growth as incomes increase in the construction, auto, and other durable goods industries, spilling over and boosting demand for other consumer goods. Boom conditions will intensify as business invests in additional factories and machinery to meet the rush in orders.

As the expansion unfolds, capacity utilization increases with the growth in demand and production. Soon factories move from, say, 70 percent to 90 percent of their rated maximum. Productive facilities strain to meet the demands and retain the loyalty of customers.

Next, high levels of capacity utilization drive labor productivity down and unit labor costs up; efficiency is sacrificed for increased output. Machinery that is always in use cannot be adequately maintained, and so it breaks down. Inexperienced workers often do not make the same contribution as old hands. The amount of labor employed increases more rapidly than output, and, as output per worker falls, the labor cost per unit of output rises. This generates a surge in production costs.

Finally, rapidly increasing costs are translated into rapidly increasing prices, and a renewed round of inflation begins.

All the forces that led to a reduction in the rate of inflation are now reversed as the cycle moves from *expansion* to *peak*.

$$\text{GDP } \uparrow \rightarrow \text{ Industrial production } \uparrow \text{ Capacity utilization } \uparrow \rightarrow$$
$$\text{Labor productivity } \downarrow \rightarrow \text{ Unit labor costs } \uparrow \rightarrow \text{ Producer prices } \uparrow$$

So the practical (business person's) and the theoretical (economist's) explanations of inflation are not at odds. During expansion, demand bids production to a level that is inefficient and costly. The business person experiences the increased cost and attributes inflation directly to that experience. The economist sees increased demand as the ultimate cause of the production gain that drives costs up. Each explanation covers different aspects of the single phenomenon, economic expansion.

THE 1970s AS AN ILLUSTRATION

The late 1970s illuminate the process graphically. You will need the same statistical series employed earlier to illustrate expansion's impact on inflation: *GDP, industrial production, capacity utilization, labor productivity* and *unit labor costs*, and the *producer price index*. Each of these statistical series has already been introduced, so excerpts from *The Wall Street Journal* will not be presented again.

Although subsequently eclipsed by the 1981–82 recession, the 1974 recession established a postwar record at the time. GNP declined for four quarters, and industrial production tumbled 15 percent. By the spring of 1975, the unemployment rate was over 9 percent.

Like all recessions, however, this one prepared the way for the subsequent recovery. Capacity utilization fell to a postwar low, and labor productivity began to rise immediately. The resulting decline in unit labor costs cut the rate of inflation.

At the same time, the Federal Reserve System switched from a tight to an easy money policy, reducing interest rates and providing ample credit. A sharp recovery and strong expansion began as the decline in the rate of inflation dramatically improved consumer real income and boosted consumer sentiment. At long last, consumers were pulling ahead of inflation; their pleasure was reflected in demand's rapid increase.

By 1977–78, new housing starts were 2 million annually and domestic automobile sales peaked at approximately 10 million, while consumer installment borrowing hit annual rates of $50 billion.

The evidence of a robust economic expansion was all around as GNP and industrial production surged ahead. Rapid growth in demand, produc-

tion, and capacity utilization had its inevitable result: The nation's factories and other productive facilities were strained, and increases in the labor force no longer made a proportional contribution to output (see Chart 7–5 on page 118).

In 1979, labor productivity stopped improving and began to fall. As a result, unit labor costs increased steadily, and by early 1980 the rate of inflation, as measured by the producer price index, had reached 15 percent (see Chart 7–7 on page 124).

Declining labor productivity is the focal point of this analysis. Once output is pushed past the point of diminishing returns, unit labor costs become an inevitable problem. Most people believe that rising wages are chiefly responsible for this condition; wages do play a minor role, naturally, but unit labor costs will increase swiftly even if wage gains run well below the rate of inflation (i.e., even if real wages are falling).

Falling real wages, coupled with the forward surge in labor costs, creates one of the cruelest features of inflation. Because labor productivity has declined, there is less per capita output and, therefore, less real income per person. Declining real income pits one segment of American society against another, fighting over a shrinking pie. Labor management relations become especially bitter in these periods of boom without prosperity. Employers blame workers' wages for rising labor costs and shrinking profits, while workers blame employers' profits for shrinking real wages; in reality, neither one is responsible for the other's misfortune.

In such times, the public's support for wage and price controls becomes insistent (although, of course, management has a greater interest in controlling wages and labor has a greater interest in controlling prices). Yet you can see from this chapter's analysis that rising costs due to reduced efficiency (falling labor productivity) are responsible for the increase in prices that captures everyone's attention. No one's greed is to blame. Therefore, controls designed to limit greed are bound to be ineffective.

There have been two recent attempts at wage and price controls: the first under President Nixon in 1971–72 and the second under President Carter in 1979–80. President Nixon's controls were certain to "succeed," because they were implemented during the transition from recovery to expansion, while capacity utilization was low and labor productivity was high. As a result, the rate of inflation was still falling from its 1970 cyclical peak. It would have continued to decline in any event and remain low until the expansion gained strength. The controls did slightly dampen inflation, but their impact was marginal.

President Carter's controls were destined to "fail," just as President Nixon's were destined to succeed, because President Carter's were implemented during the virulent expansion of 1977–79. As labor productivity fell and unit costs climbed, business merely passed its increased costs on to the consumer. Rising prices reflected rising costs, not greed, and business did not earn excessive profits.

Keep in mind also that more stringent wage controls could not have restrained business costs. Some of the increase in unit labor costs was due to the increase in wage rates, but most of it was due to declining productivity caused by high capacity utilization. Workers were no more culpable than their employers.

This is an important point. We really can't blame the declines in labor productivity in the 1970s on the American worker, as some are prone to do. Productivity lapses in that decade occurred cyclically, when the economy overheated, and thus they really reflected the limitations of plant and equipment under extreme conditions rather than failures of diligence in the labor force.

Harking back to World War II for an example of successful wage and price controls is not the answer, either. Wage and price (and profit) controls worked then because the economy was on a war footing. About half of the economy's output was devoted to the war effort, much of it under a system of planning and direct resource allocation that operated outside ordinary market relationships. You couldn't bid up the price of a car (none were produced because the auto plants were converted to war production) or buy all the gasoline and steak you wanted (these were rationed). And despite the patriotism aroused by the war effort, black markets arose to subvert the controls. Therefore, it's doubtful whether such a system could work to contain peacetime inflation, for which, unlike war-induced inflation, there is no end in sight.

Imposing wage and price controls during the expansionary phase of the business cycle (as was attempted in the late 70s) is a little like trying to stop the rattle of a boiling kettle by taping down the lid. Demand heats the expansion, and inflation is the natural result. Turning down the heat is the only practical solution.

Investor's Tip

- Moderate levels of consumer demand (auto, housing, consumer credit) → Moderate capacity utilization → Moderate inflation.
- Booming new-vehicle sales (15 million +) + Housing starts (1.8 million +) + Consumer credit ($125 billion +) → High capacity utilization (85+ percent) → rapid (8 + percent) producer price inflation.
- A booming economy is your first hint that you should anticipate inflation by disposing of paper investments and buying tangible investments.

Finally, there's the question of "supply-side shocks." These are sudden increases in the price of important commodities (imposed by the sellers) or reductions in supply due to forces beyond our control. Some believe that the late 70s' inflation was due to these sorts of shocks, but this argument should be taken with a grain of salt. First, any explanation that places the blame on others should be suspect; if you wish to find fault, it is always best to look in the mirror. Second, neither OPEC, nor the Russian wheat deal, nor the failure of the Peruvian anchovy harvest can explain the price explosions of the 70s. They may have contributed to the inflation, but they did not cause it. If demand had been weak, prices would have remained stable. After all, prices stopped climbing as soon as recession hit in 1981–82, well before the oil price collapse of early 1986.

And whether you are dealing with free-market farm prices or OPEC, repealing the laws of supply and demand is not easy. Farm prices eased down in the commodity deflation of the 80s, while oil prices collapsed in a matter of months in early 1986. In both cases, high prices and profits in the 70s had attracted investment in new productive facilities and therefore created excess capacity (supply). Once supply exceeded demand at current prices, the price collapse was inevitable.

CONCLUSION

The expansion of the late 80s did not generate inflation as virulent as that of 1977–79 because the Fed restrained the growth in demand by restraining the growth in credit. The 1980s confirm the Fed's resolve to keep demand under control by restraining credit and keeping interest rates high.

The Fed's posture had not changed by the mid 90s. It raised interest rates at the first sign of robust expansion, holding demand, output, costs, and prices in check.

CHAPTER 8

―――

STOCKS VERSUS GOLD

――――――――――――――――――――――――――――――――

If you return to the comparison of stocks' and gold's performance (see Chart 8–1 on page 132) first mentioned in Chapter 1, you will note, to repeat, that stocks did poorly in the high-inflation 70s and well in the low-inflation 80s and early 90s, and that gold performed in the opposite fashion. Recall the promise in Chapter 1 that you would be able to forecast stocks' and gold's future performance once you had mastered (1) an understanding of the forces that shaped inflation and (2) an ability to use *The Wall Street Journal* to analyze those forces. Now is the time to put your knowledge to work.

GOLD

Compare gold's performance to an index of a dozen commodity prices (including gold) presented in Chart 8–2 on page 133, and recall the suggestion in Chapter 1 that you view gold as a proxy for all tangible investments. When you mention commodities as an investment, most people think of gold.

The similarity in movement between gold prices and the commodity index is easily explained. All commodity prices (and gold is a commodity) measure inflation, which is, after all, nothing more than rising prices. Copper, cattle, hogs, lumber, wheat, and gold will move along the same path in the long run, because the price of each is subject to the same supply and demand forces. When demand exceeds supply at current prices because spenders have access to credit, all prices rise. Sure, there are occasions when a commodity will defy the price trend for a while because of circumstances peculiar to its production and market. But these are exceptional cases.

CHART 8–1
Gold versus Stocks: Gold–Engelhard High Price through 1987,
Average Thereafter; Dow Jones Industrial Average

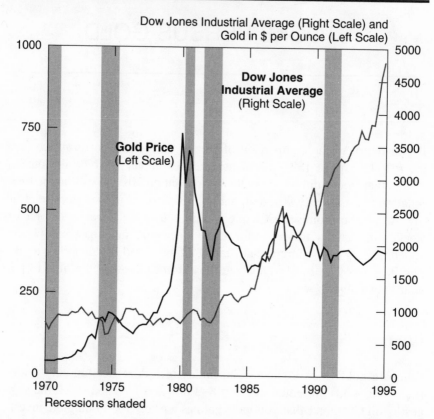

Source: U.S. Bureau of Mines, *Minerals Yearbook*; Standard & Poor's *Statistical Service*; Phyllis S.
Pierce, ed., *The Dow Jones Investor's Handbook* (Homewood, IL: Dow Jones-Irwin, 1995); *Barron's*.

Gold is a good investment (as are most tangibles) in times of high and
rising inflation, because its price climbs more rapidly than standard measures of inflation such as the CPI. In times of low inflation, gold prices
will be weak or actually fall. Why does gold beat the averages during a
period of severe inflation and then fall when inflation subsides (although
prices generally are still rising)?

CHART 8–2
Gold and Dow Jones Commodity Futures Index

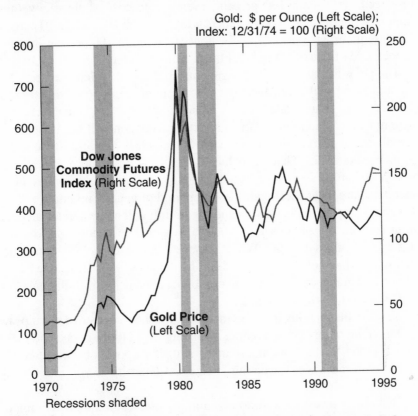

Gold: $ per Ounce (Left Scale);
Index: 12/31/74 = 100 (Right Scale)

Dow Jones
Commodity Futures
Index (Right Scale)

Gold Price
(Left Scale)

Recessions shaded

Source: U.S. Bureau of Mines, *Minerals Yearbook*; Standard & Poor's Statistical Service; Phyllis S.
Pierce, ed., *The Dow Jones Investor's Handbook* (Homewood, IL: Dow Jones-Irwin, 1995); *Barron's*

What is true for gold is true for commodities in general. All occupy a
position early in the production chain, before a great deal of value has
been added in the productive process. Value added, which is the labor and
technology applied to raw materials that turn them into useful products,
acts as a cushion between the prices we pay for the finished product and
the volatile prices paid for the commodities from which the product
was fashioned.

Consider an example. If air travel increases, airlines order more planes
from the aircraft manufacturers. Aircraft prices may rise 10 percent with
the costs of designing, developing, manufacturing, and assembling. Most
of these costs are payments to people. Yet the price of aluminum, the air-

craft's principal ingredient, may rise 50 percent in the face of rapidly growing demand. And bauxite, the raw material from which aluminum is produced, may jump 100 percent, even as the cost of electricity (aluminum's other principal ingredient) hardly grows at all. Thus, a 10 percent increase in airplane prices may be consistent with a 100 percent increase in the price of bauxite, a mineral taken from the ground.

The point is that prices of the raw material out of which the aircraft is manufactured will surge far more rapidly than the price of the aircraft, because the value added costs (design, engineering, manufacturing, assembly, etc.) required for the aircraft's production will not increase as rapidly as the costs of the raw materials (which had very little value added in their production). That's why bauxite prices will rise more than aircraft prices, tomato prices more than ketchup prices, and cattle prices more than hamburgers at McDonald's—in a period of general inflation.

Conversely, a drop in the demand for aircraft will not generate a decline in aircraft prices, as labor and other value added costs continue to grow. Yet bauxite prices may fall. Wheat was six dollars a bushel in the summer of 1973 but had not regained that level by the mid-1990s. Thus, the prices of finished goods will continue to climb in a climate of low inflation, even as raw material prices slump.

It's as if fluctuations in the demand for finished goods had a whipsaw effect on the price of commodities, with slight variations at one end magnified in the fluctuations at the other end. It's a kind of reverse ripple effect, with the waves escalating in size and intensity as you move away from the splash.

That's why investors want to position themselves in the raw commodity and not in finished goods during high inflation. And gold is the raw commodity investment vehicle—par excellence. This explains why gold surges whenever there's a whiff of inflation. But look out when deflation hits. Gold will fade along with all other commodities.

Chart 8–3 on page 135 provides an illustration by presenting a number of price indexes, from raw commodity prices to semifinished goods to the CPI.

The sharp break presented by the early 1980s is never lost, but is clearly muted as you go up the productive process from raw to finished goods. Commodity prices rise most steeply among all the indexes and actually fall in the 80s. The CPI rises least rapidly of all the indexes in the 1970s, yet continues to rise most rapidly in the 1980s, a period in which many commodity prices fell.

CHART 8–3
Price Index Comparisons: Dow Jones Commodity Futures Index, Raw Industrial Materials (spot), Producer Price Index, Consumer Price Index

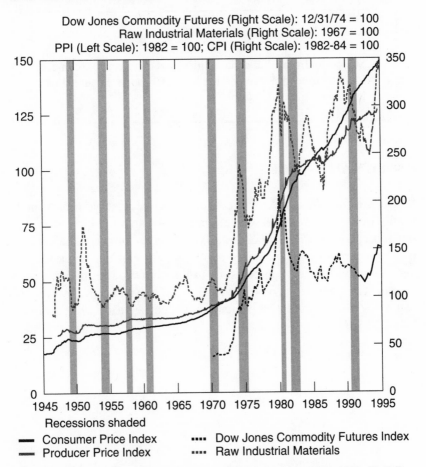

Dow Jones Commodity Futures (Right Scale): 12/31/74 = 100
Raw Industrial Materials (Right Scale): 1967 = 100
PPI (Left Scale): 1982 = 100; CPI (Right Scale): 1982-84 = 100

Recessions shaded

— Consumer Price Index   ▪▪▪▪ Dow Jones Commodity Futures Index
— Producer Price Index   ▪▪▪▪ Raw Industrial Materials

Source: U.S. Department of Commerce, *Business Cycle Indicators*, Series 320 and 320c. Phyllis S. Pierce, ed., *The Dow Jones Investor's Handbook* (Homewood, IL: Dow Jones-Irwin, 1995); Knight-Ridder, Commodity Research Bureau.

As a general rule, commodity prices rise more rapidly than consumer prices in high inflation, but rise less rapidly than consumer prices when inflation is low (and can actually fall).

Once again, the farther back you go in the chain of production, the more volatile the price index. Gold is no exception to this rule. Glance back to Chart 8–2 on page 133 and you can see gold's explosion in the 70s and its weak performance in the 80s and early 90s. It will stay weak in the 90s if

inflation remains in check. It will climb to its 1980 high of about $900 an ounce only if inflation is rekindled.

Investor's Tip

- Stay away from gold, commodities, and other tangibles unless inflation exceeds 8 percent at a seasonally adjusted annual rate for at least a quarter year.

PROFITS AND STOCKS

Stocks are more complex than commodities, because you must analyze profits first. You can't measure a company's value until you know how much it can earn. *The Wall Street Journal* survey of corporate profits for over 500 corporations, including industry-wide statistics on earnings and net income (see below), appears about two months after the close of the quarter. The fourth paragraph of the Monday, November 7, 1994 report on pages 137–141 reports a 34 percent gain over the year-earlier quarter.

Companies' Profits Rose 39%, Exceeding Expectations

By FRED R. BLEAKLEY
Staff Reporter of THE WALL STREET JOURNAL.

CORPORATE PROFITS continued to surge during the third quarter, surprising many analysts who thought the earnings party that began in early 1992 would be winding down.

Corporate America attributed the strong profit performance to a healthy U.S. economy, which lifted the fortunes of companies in virtually every industry, and to manufacturing price gains and improved overseas sales. There were record third-quarter profits at Ford Motor, record sales at Apple Computer and robust earnings among most banks, pharmaceutical companies, airlines and heavy-equipment makers, among others.

According to a Wall Street Journal survey, 679 major companies reported net income rose a cumulative 39% from the 1993 period. That's a strong pickup from the 26% gain in the second quarter.

After-tax profit from continuing operations increased 34% from a year earlier. That's nearly as high as the 39% growth for second-quarter operating profit and well ahead of the 11% first-quarter growth rate for the group.

Earnings have been so strong for so long that some analysts think the current trend of double-digit growth rates is unsustainable. Although economic indicators show that the fourth quarter opened on very strong footing, analysts say it will be hard enough to match the lofty operating-profit levels of last year's fourth quarter, let alone show as strong a growth rate as that period's 38% pace.

"People should not be deluded into thinking we are in a very easy profit environment," says Gail Fosler of the Conference Board. She expects about half the rate of growth next year as this year, at first, followed by a leveling off of the economy in the second half.

However, many economists expect the economy to slow, making it tougher to grind out earnings growth in 1995. "The year-over-year momentum is now at its peak," says Donald Straszheim, chief economist of Merrill Lynch & Co. "It will be hard to find large companies in 1995 whose earnings growth is as fast or faster than it was this year." He expects to see continued benefits from the dramatic cost cutting and restructuring of recent years, but he says earnings still will decelerate due to a "materially slower economy."

Other economists also expect higher interest rates and a drop-off in consumer spending to begin slowing the economy next year. For the third quarter, gross domestic product grew 3.4%, faster than most economists had expected.

More analysts than usual were surprised by the strength of earnings in the third quarter. Typically fewer than half the consensus estimates come in under the mark, according to Zacks Investment Research, which tracks Wall Street forecasts. This time, 54% of posted results for companies in the Dow Jones industry groups outper-

Corporate Profits

Year-to-year percentage change in net income for companies in the Dow Jones Equity Market Index

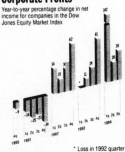

* Loss in 1992 quarter

formed analysts' estimates, the second highest percentage in 10 years of counting, says Ben Zacks of the Chicago firm.

Earnings jumped, says Nancy Lazar, an economist with ISI Group, because costs are unusually low for the current stage of economic growth. She attributes this to efficient inventory control and the wave of corporate layoffs and equipment investment that lifted productivity, or goods produced per hour of labor.

Steel, chemical and paper companies got a big boost from higher product prices, as did other raw-material producers and parts makers. Caterpillar and Deere were among heavy-equipment companies that were able to pass along higher costs to business customers. But generally, price increases have yet to trickle down to the end consumer.

The extra boost from exports and sales by foreign affiliates stemmed from better-than-expected growth in European economies, said Joseph Carson, chief economist for Dean Witter Reynolds. He expects "multinational companies will get an extra lift from overseas earnings for another six to nine months."

The stronger economy in the U.S. prompted stronger loan demand and helped bank profitabil-

ity. But new bond financing remained at low levels, held down by the rise in long-term interest rates this year. Higher rates also damped Wall Street's profits by curbing stock-market volume.

Among industry groups, the Big Three auto makers earned a record $2.32 billion for the quarter, three times the $773 million they earned a year earlier. But while Ford and Chrysler had excellent quarters, General Motors' performance was a disappointment. Although GM was profitable overseas and in its nonautomotive operations, it shocked Wall Street with a $328 million loss in its core North American operations despite the strong U.S. vehicle market. Two labor strikes and slow launches of several key vehicles hurt GM's performance, although demand for its trucks and sport-utility vehicles is high.

Auto makers are benefiting from the rising value of the yen against the dollar, which has given their vehicles a $2,000 to $3,000 price advantage over Japanese vehicles. It has allowed the U.S. companies to raise prices and trim incentives.

The third quarter is normally the auto industry's weakest, because of production shutdowns for model changeovers and vacations. But the fourth quarter is a different story. David Healy of S.G. Warburg is forecasting that the industry will earn $3.7 billion this quarter, compared with $2.68 billion a year earlier.

Computer makers' returns exceeded expectations, thanks to continued strength in computer sales. The biggest surprise came from Apple, which benefited from strong shipments of its new Power Mac computers and higher gross margins from cost cutting. Compaq's profit surged 88%, as lower prices helped it increase computer shipments.

PC shipments in the U.S. had been expected to slow to 10% year-over-year growth in the quarter from 20% in the second. But the unusually strong period a year earlier, but in fact grew 13% as computer makers continued to catch up with backlogged orders, according to International Data, a market research firm in Framingham, Mass.

Makers of large hardware showed mixed results. IBM said its mainframe revenue grew for the first time in two years. That and an increase in sales of midrange computers helped Big Blue beat analysts' expectations. Unisys, on the other hand, suffered from a decline in its mainframe sales.

Sales of workstations surged, resulting in huge profit gains for both Sun Microsystems and Silicon Graphics. Digital Equipment said sales of its Alpha workstation jumped 138% in the quarter, resulting in a narrowed loss on a 3.6% gain in revenue.

The pharmaceutical industry's sales and earnings perked up after a year and a half of slowing growth. Companies such as Johnson & Johnson, Schering-Plough and Pfizer reported double-digit growth in domestic drug sales. Analysts were hard-pressed to explain the pharmaceutical industry's revival, except to note that the sales rise coincided with the death of health-care reform.

(continued)

Many retailers expect to report disappointing earnings for their fiscal quarter ended Oct. 30, mainly because unusually warm weather made it difficult to inspire consumers to buy heavy clothing.

Retailers that stand to buck the trend are those that sell office supplies, electronics and the like. Consumers are spending more leisure and work time at home, stirring up demand for these products. The retail operations of Sears Roebuck, the only big retailer to report earnings so far, logged a healthy gain due to strong sales of home-related items. The drop in Sears's net income reflects a one-time gain a year earlier; operating profit rose 24%.

The weak quarter raises red flags for the critical Christmas season. But analysts see strong fourth-quarter gains, partly because consumer-confidence levels are up from a year earlier. They also cite pent-up demand for apparel.

BASIC MATERIALS

Steelmakers enjoyed further robust demand, with most steel mills operating at or near capacity.

Steel producers also were aided by higher prices. In July, major steelmakers pushed through a 2% spot-market price increase for their biggest product, flat-rolled sheet steel. On top of that, some began selling steel to Chrysler during the quarter under new supply contracts, with price increases of as much as 10%.

Analysts expect steelmakers to post strong earnings again in the fourth quarter as surging demand persists. And major steelmakers plan a 5% to 6% price increase effective with Jan. 1 shipments.

Aluminum producers' earnings were bolstered by soaring demand. Prices also climbed for aluminum ingot as demand picked up world-wide, which in turn drew down hefty inventories and pushed up prices on the London Metal Exchange. And aluminum makers began increasing prices on fabricated products. Analysts expect aluminum makers to post strong profits for the current quarter as strong demand continues.

Forest-products concerns turned in strong profits, propelled by a boom in new housing starts this fall and a continuing rebound in the pulp and paper sector. On the timber side, some analysts were skeptical that the strong housing market would continue.

Paper earnings continued to rebound from the industry's long-running slump. Earnings for some categories lagged slightly behind some analysts' estimates because end-product pricing hasn't caught up with price increases of raw materials. Profits by big paper makers such as Weyerhaeuser, International Paper and Louisiana-Pacific were boosted by substantial price increases in major paper grades. Analysts expect pulp and paper profits to continue to climb if the economy doesn't slump.

Chemical makers' earnings rose dramatically on strong demand from a booming U.S. economy, coupled with a substantially improved European market. The industry marked the third full quarter of its cyclical upturn.

Pricing, which previously hadn't played much of a role, became much more prominent. For companies that manufacture "building-block" chemicals, including ethylene and methanol, surging prices made the quarter a barn-burner.

The benefits weren't spread evenly, however. A number of chemical companies that purchase such commodity chemicals to produce value-added products found profits under temporary pressure, because they were unable to immediately pass along the higher prices.

DuPont's year-earlier net reflects a $1.3 billion restructuring charge, only partially offset by a $265 million tax credit; operating profit rose 85%. W.R. Grace's year-earlier figure was lowered by a $300 million provision related to asbestos issues.

ENERGY

Oil-company profits generally rose because of a resurgence in the petrochemical business. Increased sales and—more importantly—sharply higher profit margins boosted earnings at chemical subsidiaries twofold and more at many companies. Slightly higher oil prices also aided industry profits, but that was almost offset by a sharp decline in domestic natural-gas prices. Most companies' operating profits rose, although one-time items caused net income to fall at some. Exxon's net slid but operating profit rose 9.6%; the company had

a $306 million gain in the 1993 period. Excluding one-time items, operating profit at Amoco also rose. Atlantic Richfield's latest period included gains totaling $200 million.

Despite weak natural-gas prices, many pipeline companies turned in strong earnings. Continued cost cutting helped bolster interstate pipeline activity, which increased volume only moderately. Companies continued to profit from their less-regulated operations, such as natural-gas marketing activities.

INDUSTRIAL

Major railroads boosted earnings, aided by the strong economy, gains in rail traffic and recovery from last year's Midwest flooding. Coal traffic rebounded. Intermodal shipments of highway trailers and containers on rail flatcars soared, as truckers put more of their long-haul freight on the rails. Excluding a $425 million charge to write down disposal of a unit in the latest quarter, Union Pacific said profit from continuing operations rose 24%. Conrail's earnings grew 28%, excluding nonrecurring items in the 1993 quarter.

Among trucking companies, less-than-truckload carriers are benefiting from the strong economy, increased freight rates and continuing recovery from a Teamsters strike earlier this year. Excluding a special item in the latest period, Yellow's earnings rose 26%. Yellow and other truck companies said the new Teamster contract permits them to transport more freight by rail, lowering their costs, and analysts expect fourth-quarter earnings increases. Roadway said its earnings would have risen but for an operating loss at its new air-freight unit, a write-off of intrastate operating rights and a special performance-recovery plan at a unit in the latest quarter.

Air-freight couriers faced increasing profit pressures as growth slowed in the U.S. overnight-delivery market. While total volume grew in the double digits, a market shift from high-priced overnight services to cheaper next-afternoon and two-day deliveries continued to drive down prices and force further cost cutting. Analysts say the trend is likely to continue in the fourth quarter, forcing the carriers to rely more heavily on overseas markets. For the latest quarter, Federal Express's domestic profit fell 10%, but strong performance overseas and tax benefits aided the company's earnings. Airborne Freight's slower U.S. growth and higher aircraft-repair bills resulted in an unexpected profit decline.

Strong production out of U.S. factories continued to be good news for makers of heavy trucks, engines and rail cars. The strength is expected to continue in the fourth quarter. Cummins Engine and Eaton, two big suppliers, said production of heavy trucks is running at record levels. In the 1993 quarter, Navistar International had a pretax charge of $513 million to restructure health and life-insurance benefits for its retirees.

Makers of heavy equipment continued to post robust profits, boosted by the growing U.S. economy. Caterpillar's strong operating performance came in spite of a strike by the United Auto Workers union through the quarter; Cat had a gain of $336 million from a tax settlement and tax credit a year earlier.

Industry Profits: The Turnarounds

		1994 QUARTER	1993 QUARTER
PROFIT vs. LOSS	Telephone	$1,625,495	−$356,082
	Chemicals, Commodity	1,352,427	− 341,658
	Transportation Equipment	241,300	− 173,000
	Pollution/Waste Management	314,100	− 58,834
	Steel	290,764	− 70,677
	Recreation-Other	262,400	− 75,800
	Paper Products	239,208	− 170
	Aluminum	127,300	− 51,700
NARROWER LOSS	Recreation-Entertainment	−$32,000	− 133,000
LOSS vs. PROFIT	Oil/Drillers	−$17,359	12,274
	Oil/Secondary Firms	−118,487	180,952

CONSUMER CYCLICAL

With fixed mortgage rates shooting past 9%, the housing market appears to be past its peak, and most publicly held builders are seeing their stock prices sag. Still, demand and earnings remain at healthy levels for most. Dwindling refinancings hurt the mortgage-banking business of Centex, the nation's biggest builder, even though home-building revenue jumped 22%. Pulte's net income fell on margin pressures, but home-building revenue rose 15%; likewise for Kaufman & Broad. Ryland's year-earlier loss stemmed from a restructuring charge.

Home builders' profits are likely to tail off next year. Mark Zandi, chief economist with Regional Financial Associates, estimates that housing starts will fall to 1.3 million from a strong 1.43 million this year.

Hotel and casino companies reported mixed results based on strengthening in the hotel business and competition in traditional gambling markets. Casino operators such as Mirage Resorts posted strong gains as their new projects attracted visitors to Las Vegas, but others felt the pinch of competition from the newcomers.

Toy results were tempered by economic sluggishness abroad, along with a growing preference by children for Japan's Mighty Morphin Power Rangers over other toys. A soft market in Europe had its greatest impact on the industry's biggest players.

Analysts predict improved fourth-quarter results over a year ago, thanks largely to a growing trend among retailers to spread out Christmas orders more evenly between the third and fourth quarters, unlike the previous custom of placing the bulk of orders by October.

Broadcasting companies continued to record strong gains due to strong advertising demand, a trend that is expected to continue well into the next quarter. Although CBS had gains at its local television stations due to advertising demand, the company reported sharply lower net income, which it attributed to higher taxes and a one-time gain in the 1993 quarter. The CBS network also recorded lower sales, due to the loss of professional football and baseball programming, although that contributed to higher operating profit because of the absence of rights fees for the sports.

Newspaper publishers had one of their strongest quarters in several years due to continued improvement in advertising linage at several major metropolitan newspapers, such as those owned by Gannett and Knight-Ridder. Analysts expect the positive advertising trend, especially for classified ads, to continue along with the generally strong economic conditions in most regions.

Publishers with broadcast operations also were largely helped by strong ad revenue gains. But the Major League Baseball strike pinched some companies. Tribune has TV stations in several major league cities and owns the Chicago Cubs; reduced revenue from the baseball broadcasts was offset by improved performance from the company's publishing group. Times Mirror's continuing operations rose; the year-earlier results reflect a gain from an asset sale.

Strong demand for air travel boosted profits for the nation's airlines in what is expected to be the first profitable year for the industry since 1989. The Air Transport Association is predicting 1994 industry profits of $1.1 billion.

Industry-by-Industry Quarterly Earnings

The table shows earnings reported for the third quarter of 1994 and those for the like quarter of 1993, with percentage changes. Where individual company reports cover three-month periods other than calendar quarters, the nearest comparable periods have been used. For all dollar figures, 000s have been omitted. The table reflects the fact that many companies have closed down facilities, sold off assets or otherwise restructured operations. The "net income" columns include both income from operations and the gains or losses associated with such moves. The "net on continuing operations" columns, insofar as possible, exclude such gains and losses. In cases in which the after-tax gains or losses haven't been reported, they are retained in "net on continuing operations."

	NET ON CONTINUING OPERATIONS			NET INCOME		
BASIC MATERIALS	3rd QTR 1994	3rd QTR 1993	% CHG	3rd QTR 1994	3rd QTR 1993	% CHG
8 Steel	$290,764	–$35,677	—	$290,764	–$70,677	—
4 Aluminum	127,300	–45,200	—	127,300	–51,700	—
4 Other nonferrous metals	102,853	47,121	+ 118	102,853	47,121	+ 118
3 Mining, diversified	27,843	40,797	– 32	27,843	40,797	– 32
4 Precious metals	25,100	42,835	– 41	25,100	42,835	– 41
6 Forest products	391,367	106,744	+ 267	391,367	98,744	+ 296
10 Paper	227,608	–11,070	—	239,208	–170	—
9 Chemicals/commodity	1,342,427	–343,356	—	1,352,427	–341,658	—
4 Chemicals/specialty	625,272	66,131	+ 846	625,272	66,131	+ 846
Total (62 cos.)	$3,160,534	–$131,677	—	$3,182,134	–$168,577	—

ENERGY

10 Integrated oils	$3,573,000	$3,600,000	– 1	$3,573,000	$3,431,000	+ 4
15 Secondary oils	–106,487	22,331	—	–118,487	180,952	—
5 Drillers	–17,359	12,653	—	–17,359	12,274	—
7 Oilfield equip/svcs	256,213	85,286	+ 200	255,013	80,886	+ 215
8 Pipelines	246,863	9,829	+2412	270,662	57,352	+ 372
4 Coal	52,540	66,122	– 21	52,540	66,122	– 21
Total (49 cos.)	$4,004,770	$3,802,221	+ 5	$4,015,369	$3,828,586	+ 5

INDUSTRIAL

7 Railroads	$860,300	$224,100	+ 284	$437,300	$231,600	+ 89
5 Trucking	58,404	63,785	– 8	48,824	63,785	– 23
6 Air-freight couriers	109,397	73,383	+ 49	109,397	73,383	+ 49
3 Marine transport	35,814	31,465	+ 14	35,814	31,465	+ 14
3 Transportation equip.	241,300	–170,900	—	241,300	–173,000	—
3 Factory equipment	30,347	32,625	– 7	30,347	32,625	– 7
7 Heavy machinery	461,873	491,489	– 6	461,972	499,567	– 8
8 Electrical components	559,277	497,005	+ 13	559,277	497,005	+ 13
5 Building materials	67,671	66,442	+ 2	67,661	66,442	+ 2
7 Building materials	330,608	263,169	+ 26	296,101	264,060	+ 12
6 Containers/pkging	146,101	147,279	– 1	146,101	146,279	0
15 Indust/comm serv	553,392	395,274	+ 40	553,392	399,569	+ 38
4 Pollution management	314,100	–58,834	—	314,100	–58,834	—
16 Diversified indust	748,113	570,662	+ 31	426,362	586,462	– 27
Total (97 cos.)	$4,516,897	$2,627,144	+ 72	$3,727,948	$2,660,408	+ 40

CONSUMER, CYCLICAL

3 Auto manufacturers	$2,327,000	$773,100	+ 201	$2,327,000	$773,100	+201
10 Auto parts	480,377	379,697	+ 27	506,177	381,317	+ 33
7 Home builders	84,141	50,704	+ 66	82,593	58,479	+ 41
6 Furnishings/appliances	261,092	154,436	+ 69	261,092	154,436	+ 69
9 Apparel retailers	245,476	223,061	+ 10	289,140	236,464	+ 22
8 Broadline retailers	1,325,070	1,357,015	– 2	1,325,070	1,268,515	+ 4
5 Drug-based retailers	141,341	127,653	+ 11	149,741	136,861	+ 9
10 Specialty retailers	532,909	431,493	+ 24	299,896	443,832	– 32
2 Lodging	41,011	30,511	+ 34	41,011	30,211	+ 36
5 Restaurants	473,732	414,930	+ 14	472,694	414,930	+ 14
5 Casinos	144,708	122,728	+ 18	141,935	111,691	+ 27
1 Entertainment	–32,000	–111,000	—	–32,000	–133,000	—
4 Other recreational pdts	262,400	–77,200	—	262,400	–75,800	—
5 Toys	219,736	204,559	+ 7	219,736	204,559	+ 7
3 Broadcasting	222,544	226,712	– 2	222,544	226,712	– 2
13 Publishing	583,853	192,243	+ 204	596,358	254,701	+ 134
2 Advertising	35,554	27,176	+ 31	35,554	27,176	+ 31
5 Airlines	441,882	391,862	+ 13	555,882	384,862	+ 44
5 Footwear	213,115	210,107	+ 1	213,115	209,192	+ 2
5 Clothing/fabrics	217,784	179,726	+ 21	217,784	171,126	+ 27
Total (113 cos.)	$8,221,725	$5,309,513	+ 55	$8,187,722	$5,279,364	+ 55

(continued)

	NET ON CONTINUING OPERATIONS			NET INCOME		
	3rd QTR 1994	3rd QTR 1993	% CHG	3rd QTR 1994	3rd QTR 1993	% CHG
CONSUMER, NONCYCLICAL						
20 Food	$1,415,504	$1,382,374	+2	$1,352,704	$1,328,753	+2
11 Food retailers	422,698	348,707	+21	404,823	336,585	+20
8 Beverages	1,684,165	1,027,758	+64	1,684,165	991,016	+70
7 Health-care providers	435,119	227,012	+92	412,119	49,504	+732
6 Medical supplies	587,631	566,670	+4	586,631	153,470	+282
9 Pharmaceuticals	3,526,552	2,569,834	+37	3,526,552	2,570,106	+37
3 Cosmetics/personal care	248,524	216,424	+15	248,524	222,824	+12
3 Durable household pdts	165,659	140,981	+18	165,659	140,981	+18
7 Non-dur household pdts	1,243,910	1,033,283	+20	1,243,910	1,065,793	+17
4 Consumer services	40,286	25,319	+59	40,286	28,121	+43
5 Tobacco	1,704,098	1,233,162	+38	1,704,098	1,205,756	+41
Total (83 cos.)	$11,474,146	$8,771,524	+31	$11,369,671	$8,093,509	+40
TECHNOLOGY						
12 Computers/information	$1,482,230	$310,749	+377	$1,546,733	$259,773	+496
4 Office equipment	274,877	240,141	+14	285,583	227,422	+26
5 Semiconductors	882,501	737,873	+20	882,501	742,773	+19
14 Software/processing	630,770	268,084	+135	630,770	263,284	+140
9 Communications	1,720,308	1,459,948	+18	1,720,308	1,449,848	+19
14 Aerospace/defense	798,159	824,745	-3	768,786	783,635	-2
11 Diversified tech	1,237,478	1,007,577	+23	1,246,174	1,000,024	+25
5 Industrial tech	75,700	57,239	+32	80,700	56,050	+44
4 Advanced medical devices	139,657	124,199	+12	139,657	124,199	+12
6 Biotechnology	96,143	81,463	+18	96,143	81,463	+18
Total (86 cos.)	$7,337,823	$5,112,018	+44	$7,397,305	$4,988,421	+48
FINANCIAL SERVICES						
8 Money-center banks	$2,926,217	$2,922,705	0	$2,926,217	$2,922,705	0
15 Central-states banks	1,688,854	1,478,752	+14	1,688,854	1,478,752	+14
15 Eastern banks	1,379,825	1,193,564	+16	1,379,825	1,193,564	+16
9 Southern banks	1,201,705	1,052,467	+14	1,201,705	1,052,467	+14
8 Western banks	542,985	499,967	+9	542,985	499,967	+9
7 Insurance/full line	566,600	433,500	+31	569,800	712,500	-20
6 Insurance/life	334,381	8,157	+9999	334,381	8,157	+9999
7 Property/casualty	1,355,682	1,230,359	+10	1,396,082	1,226,859	+14
6 Savings & loans	252,379	203,472	+24	252,379	203,472	+24
5 Real estate invest	51,805	28,175	+84	51,805	28,175	+84
7 Div financial serv	1,274,884	1,076,895	+18	1,274,884	1,181,595	+8
10 Securities	544,975	1,004,148	-46	544,975	997,448	-45
Total (110 cos.)	$12,120,292	$11,132,161	+9	$12,163,892	$11,505,661	+6
UTILITIES						
17 Telephone	$3,775,495	$2,936,818	+29	$1,625,495	$-356,082	—
45 Electric	5,462,342	4,865,001	+12	5,462,342	4,917,401	+11
8 Gas	-4,607	9,485	—	33,519		
5 Water	54,477	53,463	+2	54,477	49,046	+11
Total (75 cos.)	$9,287,707	$7,864,767	+18	$7,175,833	$4,618,684	+55
CONGLOMERATES						
4 Conglomerates	$1,709,300	$1,507,200	+13	$1,755,300	$1,573,200	+12
TOTAL (679 cos.)	$61,833,194	$45,994,871	+34	$58,975,174	$42,379,256	+39

But increased competition from low-cost rivals continued to sting major U.S. carriers. With fares down about 4% this year, airlines carried more passengers this summer but earned less for each ticket sold. UAL's results reflect a $96 million charge related to its employee buyout in the quarter.

Analysts expect discount carriers to garner even more market share through the rest of the year, suggesting that revenue pressures are far from over.

CONSUMER NONCYCLICAL

Several packaged-foods concerns reported record results for the quarter, helped by lower commodity costs and strong sales gains. Archer-Daniels-Midland benefited from a rebound from last year's costly Midwest floods. A number of diverse factors pulled down other companies' results, from a pesticide problem that hurt General Mills' cereal volume to higher marketing expenses and a slump in European pet-food sales for Quaker Oats.

Profits at the major beverage companies exceeded expectations, as soft-drink sales volume soared over the summer. Coca-Cola and PepsiCo each posted a 6% gain in domestic sales volume, buoyed by strong sales of new packages such as Coke's 20-ounce contour bottle and Pepsi's one-liter Big Slam. Despite heavy supermarket discounting, Coke Enterprises, the big Coke bottler, benefited from growing sales in single-serve channels, such as convenience stores. Overseas, Coke and Pepsi posted better-than-expected volume gains.

Health-maintenance companies posted another quarter of strong earnings gains, aided by increased membership and favorable trends in medical costs. HMO membership is climbing 10% a year, with some of the biggest increases coming at large, publicly traded companies. Medical costs declined slightly as a percentage of total revenue at both U.S. Healthcare and Humana. Analysts predicted the upward earnings trend would continue this quarter, due to the big HMOs' success in reducing patient stays in hospitals and in negotiating discounts from medical providers. Some HMOs also contend that their low-cost health plans will gain appeal as employers no longer expect the U.S. health-care system to be overhauled by Congress anytime soon.

Earnings at the nation's tobacco companies rebounded from last year's costly cigarette price war. Philip Morris and RJR Nabisco Holdings reported strong cigarette profits in the U.S. and abroad. RJR benefited from aggressive cost cutting in its tobacco business. The profit recovery is expected to continue in the fourth quarter.

TECHNOLOGY

Makers of microchips continued to post earnings gains, driven by the personal-computer boom.

Intel, the king of PC microprocessor chips, managed a 28% sales jump. But profits grew less than half as fast, as falling prices on its 486 chips reduced Intel's gross profit margin by nearly three percentage points. Archrival Advanced Micro Devices, not a factor in the 486 market a year ago, rose above the pricing pressure by boosting its unit sales sharply. But AMD cautioned that pricing and spending on new factories will cause fourth-quarter profits to fall below third-quarter levels. National Semiconductor's earnings came in below analysts' projections, but most of them expect a slight recovery in its current period.

Bolstering chip makers' fourth-quarter outlook is the traditionally strong selling season for PCs and new software that demands faster machines that can store more data. Next year, however, the industry's growth rate is expected to fall to about half the 29% growth rate predicted for 1994.

The software industry prospered overall during the seasonally slow third quarter, in part on the strength of U.S. PC demand.

PC sales are especially robust in the consumer market, where buyers are enticed by low prices and new multimedia features such as sound and video. Microsoft, as usual, dominated the industry's profits in the quarter, boosted not only by its fast-growing line of consumer programs but also by its market-share gains in areas like word processing and spreadsheets.

Microsoft's ever-rising fortunes came at the expense of competitors like Lotus Development and Borland International. But Borland's operating loss shrank substantially from the prior quarter because of new-product revenue. Another big Microsoft competitor, Novell, struggled to digest its recent $1 billion acquisitions of WordPerfect and Borland's Quattro Pro spreadsheet business. Oracle, on the other hand, benefited from brisk sales of its database software and its fast-growing service business.

Defense companies pulled out another quarter of strong profits, despite shrinking revenues from many of the planes, weapons and systems they make. Boeing's profit slipped from the weakness lingering in commercial-airplane markets. Profits from continuing operations rose at General Dynamics and Litton Industries, which took an $86 million charge to settle a lawsuit.

While most companies met analysts' estimates, McDonnell Douglas's results were slightly better than expectations. Martin Marietta, which is awaiting antitrust clearances for its proposed merger with Lockheed, showed a similar increase. . Lockheed's operating profit rose despite a 9% decline in sales and a drop in net.

FINANCIAL

While the generally positive trend among banks continues several good quarters for the industry, the differences between the individual banks are becoming more pronounced.

Big banks that focus on securities underwriting and trading, including J.P. Morgan and Bankers Trust New York, suffered sharp setbacks because of rising interest rates. But other institutions, particularly those that stress consumer businesses, reported strong gains. Citicorp, the nation's largest bank, reported a strong increase, mostly thanks to its retail operations.

Throughout the nation, most banks were helped by increased lending. Bank analysts think loan growth will continue for the rest of the year, helping the industry to continue its overall earnings gains. Many banks also will continue to benefit from continued tight expense control and moderate credit costs.

Property and casualty insurers turned in mixed results as the industry continued to experience weak prices. Continued strict underwriting discipline and dominance in high-margin specialty businesses boosted American International Group's net. But for many, improved operating performance was overwhelmed by additions to reserves or pollution claims and still-further upward revisions in damage estimates for January's California earthquake. Year-to-year comparisons of net income also were unfavorable for many because of bountiful capital gains from a rallying bond market a year earlier. Many companies reported realized capital losses in the latest quarter as the bond market continued to be bearish.

The bearish bond market generally also hurt year-to-year comparisons for life insurers. However, after a sluggish first half, life-insurance sales rebounded strongly for many. Combined with favorable mortality experience, many saw operating earnings' growth. Annuity sales also continued robustly. Many managed to widen their spreads—the difference between what insurers earn on their investments and what they credit to policyholders.

Thrifts' earnings continued to be pushed down by rising interest rates reflected in higher deposit costs. Despite that and an industrywide slump in mortgage volume, some of the nation's best-run savings and loans, such as Golden West Financial and Washington Federal Savings, still have relatively high levels of profitability. Washington Federal's return on assets, for example, is a lofty 2.38%, while 1% is considered respectable.

However, industry giants H.F. Ahmanson and Great Western Financial continue to post mediocre returns, at slightly more than half the 1% level. Great Western's year-earlier results included a big nonrecurring charge for problem assets. Some analysts say profit comparisons will continue to suffer until loan volumes pick up, a difficult feat in the aftermath of an almost unprecedented boom in refinancing that ended last year.

Securities-industry profits slumped as higher interest rates continued to depress the stock and bond markets. Revenue fell in virtually every business segment, including investment banking, proprietary trading and commission fees. But asset-management revenue climbed, helping cushion some firms, such as Merrill Lynch and Dean Witter Discover from the severity of the downturn. Even with its strong asset-management franchise, Merrill's profit was off considerably.

Securities-industry analysts say that as long as interest rates continue to rise, stock and bond markets will be skittish, squashing profitability for securities firms. In such a climate, analysts say, diversified firms like Merrill will outperform trading giants like Salomon.

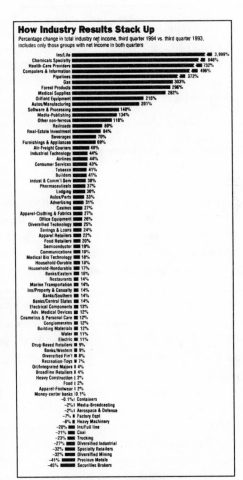

How Industry Results Stack Up

Percentage change in total industry net income, third quarter 1994 vs. third quarter 1993, includes only those groups with net income in both quarters

Industry	% Change
Ins/Life	3,999%
Chemicals Specialty	846%
Health-Care Providers	732%
Computers & Information	496%
Pipelines	372%
Gas	303%
Forest Products	296%
Medical Supplies	282%
Oilfield Equipment	215%
Autos/Manufacturing	201%
Software & Processing	140%
Media-Publishing	134%
Other non-ferrous	118%
Railroads	89%
Real-Estate Investment	84%
Beverages	70%
Furnishings & Appliances	69%
Air-Freight Couriers	49%
Industrial Technology	44%
Airlines	44%
Consumer Services	43%
Tobacco	41%
Builders	41%
Indust & Comm'l Serv	38%
Pharmaceuticals	37%
Lodging	36%
Autos/Parts	33%
Advertising	31%
Casinos	27%
Apparel-Clothing & Fabrics	27%
Office Equipment	26%
Diversified Technology	25%
Savings & Loans	24%
Apparel Retailers	22%
Food Retailers	20%
Semiconductor	19%
Communications	19%
Medical Bio Technology	18%
Household-Durable	18%
Household-Nondurable	17%
Banks/Eastern	16%
Restaurants	14%
Marine Transportation	14%
Ins/Property & Casualty	14%
Banks/Southern	14%
Banks/Central States	14%
Electrical Components	13%
Adv. Medical Devices	12%
Cosmetics & Personal Care	12%
Conglomerates	12%
Building Materials	12%
Water	11%
Electric	11%
Drug-Based Retailers	9%
Banks/Western	9%
Diversified Fin'l	8%
Recreation-Toys	7%
Oil/Integrated Majors	4%
Broadline Retailers	4%
Heavy Construction	2%
Food	2%
Apparel-Footwear	2%
Money-center banks	0.1%
Containers	-0.1%
Media-Broadcasting	-2%
Aerospace & Defense	-2%
Factory Eqpt	-7%
Heavy Machinery	-8%
Ins/Full line	-20%
Coal	-21%
Trucking	-23%
Diversified Industrial	-27%
Specialty Retailers	-32%
Diversified Mining	-32%
Precious Metals	-41%
Securities Brokers	-45%

UTILITIES

The regional Bells turned in a solid performance during the quarter, driven by strong growth in cellular services and a recovering U.S. economy. Other local and long-distance players likewise benefited from the improving economy. Ameritech, Bell Atlantic and Nynex, as expected, took one-time charges related to work-force reductions and changes in accounting that negatively affected earnings.

In the fourth quarter, the Bells are expected to continue to show solid gains, buoyed by explosive increases in cellular subscriptions. ✦

CORPORATE PROFITS-Fourth Paragraph

> After-tax profit from continuing operations in-
> creased 34% from a year earlier. That's nearly as
> high as the 39% growth for second-quarter operat-
> ing profit and well ahead of the 11% first-quarter
> growth rate for the group.

Profits measure efficiency by comparing revenues to costs. Recall that the economy's efficiency improves during the early phases of the cycle and deteriorates during the latter phases. Thus, profits grow during recovery and expansion and deteriorate during peak and contraction.

A bit of logic reveals the relationship between general changes in economic efficiency over the cycle and the specific measurement of profit. Efficiency rises early in the cycle, because factories operate with excess capacity and produce less than maximum output. The general reduction in costs due to enhanced productivity increases the spread between prices and costs, known as the profit rate or profit per unit of output. As sales increase, total profit grows because of both higher output and higher profits per unit of output.

Efficiency deteriorates late in the cycle as factories strain to produce maximum output. Costs rise as productivity falls, and industry is forced into a "profit squeeze," meaning that costs push up against prices. Total profits fall as sales volume stops growing, or actually contracts with the onset of recession, and profit per unit of output (the profit rate) falls.

It may help to think of it in these terms: Costs rise as output increases and industry reaches full capacity utilization. As costs come up from below, they bump prices upward. But competition prevents management from raising prices as rapidly as it would like. If costs rise more rapidly than prices, the margin between price and cost is squeezed. Profit margins decline.

On the other hand, management has the opportunity to rebuild its profit margins in the slack period following recession. Costs are no longer rising as rapidly, because capacity utilization is low. This provides management with the opportunity to recover profit margins by raising prices more rapidly than costs.

Thus, paradoxically, profit margins shrink when prices rise most rapidly, typically before the peak of the cycle, and grow when inflation abates in the slack period immediately after recession and when recovery begins.

That's why both productivity and profitability recovered nicely as the economy emerged from the 1990–91 recession. There's a strong correlation between productivity and profit margins. As the economy's efficiency improves, so does the spread between price and cost. Business earns more per unit of output. But in the superheated economy at the business cycle's peak, such as during the highly volatile 1970s, efficiency and profitability deteriorated. Profit margins shrank.

Chart 8–4 on page 144 depicts the ratio of price to unit labor cost (i.e., the relative strength of prices and unit labor cost) and is therefore a proxy for profit margins. This informs you of the extent of labor cost's encroachment on prices and of business's ability to hold down labor costs in relation to the prices received. Keep in mind that the ratio of price to unit labor cost is a fraction in which price is the numerator (top half) and cost the denominator (bottom half). In boom conditions, when costs are rising rapidly and pushing prices upward, profit margins are squeezed, because competition prevents management from raising prices as rapidly as costs increase. Thus, the value of the fraction (ratio of price to unit labor cost) falls as the denominator (cost) rises more rapidly than the numerator (price).

In recession and recovery from recession, management can rebuild profit margins, because costs are no longer rising rapidly. Management raises prices somewhat more quickly than costs increase, and profit margins are rebuilt. As a result, the ratio of price to unit labor cost rises as the numerator of the fraction now gains more rapidly than the denominator.

Each of the cycles in the 1970s demonstrates the same sequence of events. Start with a typical recovery and expansion, such as the recovery and expansion of 1971–72 or 1975–77. Unit labor cost was kept down by good gains in labor productivity due to modest levels of capacity utilization. As a result, the ratio of price to unit labor cost (our proxy for the term profit margins) improved and held up well. Since sales volume and output were growing, total real profits grew sharply.

Then, in 1973 and 1978–79, as production and capacity utilization peaked, labor productivity declined and unit labor cost increased. As a result, the ratio of price to unit labor cost fell, pinching profit margins. Since, at the peak of the cycle, sales and output had also stalled, real profits tumbled and continued to fall throughout the ensuing recessions of 1974–75 and 1980.

CHART 8–4
Ratio, Price to Unit Labor Cost, Nonfarm Business

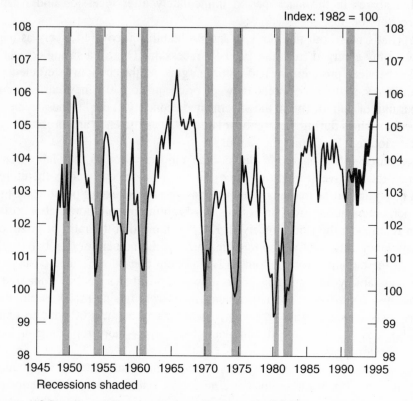

Index: 1982 = 100

Recessions shaded

Source: U.S. Department of Commerce, *Business Cycle Indicators*, Series 26.

Chapter 7 discussed wage and price controls, and Chart 8–4 (above) illustrates the foolishness of this adventure. The rate of inflation declined in 1971–72, during President Nixon's controls, despite rising profit margins (ratio of price to unit labor cost). Since profit margins rose, why didn't inflation climb with them? Because the rate of cost increase subsided due to improved productivity brought about by the recovery phase of the business cycle. In other words, the drop in costs exceeded any increase in margins.

The rate of inflation rose in 1979–80, during President Carter's controls, despite falling profit margins (ratio of price to unit labor cost). Since profit margins fell, why weren't controls effective in limiting inflation? Because the inflation was not due to excessive profit margins; it was due to the increasingly rapid rise in costs brought on by cyclical expansion's

negative impact on productivity. Controls could not stem the rising spiral of prices.

To summarize, profits, when calculated for the entire economy, measure efficiency, not greed. Prices simply can't be controlled by limiting profits.

You can see in Chart 8–4 on page 144 that profit margins recovered in the mid-80s, as low rates of capacity utilization boosted labor productivity and held down unit labor costs, providing an increased spread between prices and costs (improved profit margins).

Profit margins stumbled in the late 80s because the economy grew too languidly and slid even further with the start of the 1990–91 recession, an anomaly caused by the Persian Gulf war. Keep in mind, however, that margins did not fall as severely as they had in the 70s during the cyclical course of boom conditions.

The important point (see Chart 8–5 on page 147) is that inflation's cyclical squeeze on profit margins and real earnings in the 1970s regularly depressed the stock market so that it could not advance out of the trading range in which it was trapped. Inflation is murder on profit margins and, therefore, is the death of the stock market. On the other hand, once inflation subsided, continued strong margins provided a boost to the stock market in the 1980s that continued through the mid 1990s.

Investor's Tip

- Stay away from stocks if the annual inflation rate exceeds 8 percent for a quarter.

STOCKS AND THE PRICE/EARNINGS RATIO

Let's return to the Dow Jones Industrial Average. You know that the price of a share of stock reflects the ability of the corporation to earn profits. This relationship is expressed as the price/earnings (P/E, or price divided by per share earnings) ratio between the price of the stock and the profits per share of stock earned by the corporation (profits divided by number of shares outstanding). The price/earnings ratio answers this question: "What is the price an investor must pay to capture a dollar of earnings?" For

instance, a P/E ratio of 10 might mean that a company earned $10 per share per annum and that a share sold for $100, or it might mean that a company earned $7 per share per annum and that a share sold for $70, and so on.

The investor, of course, seeks the highest yield consistent with safety. The earnings yield is annual profit expressed as a percentage of market price. If you earn $100 a year on an investment of $1,000, the yield is 10 percent. A P/E ratio of 10 (10/1) represents a 10 percent yield, because earnings are ⅒ (10 percent) of the price per share. Similarly, a P/E ratio of 5 (5/1) is the equivalent of a 20 percent yield, because earnings per share are one fifth (20 percent) of invested capital. A P/E ratio of 20 (20/1) represents a 5 percent earnings yield. And so on.

Chart 8–5 on page 147 shows that the Dow's P/E ratio fell from the end of World War II until the beginning of the Korean War, because earnings grew while share prices languished. Following the uncertainties of the 1930s and World War II, investors were still tentative about the market.

Then the great bull market (stock prices fall in a bear market) of the 1950s began, and the P/E ratio rose as investors bid up share prices more rapidly than earnings increased. Investors were at last convinced of a "return to normalcy" and were willing to stake their future in shares of stock. The market was clearly "undervalued" (a P/E ratio of seven was roughly a 15 percent earnings yield), so it is not surprising that stock prices climbed rapidly. Stocks were a good buy, because their price was very low compared to their earnings per share and their potential for even higher earnings. As investors rushed into the market, stock prices soared. Enthusiasm was so great and share prices advanced so rapidly that the P/E ratio rose despite stronger earnings per share.

The P/E ratio had climbed to more than 20 (a 5 percent yield) by the early 60s, so the market was no longer undervalued. The ratio plateaued or fell slightly to the end of the 60s, because share prices were no longer increasing faster than corporate earnings. The great bull market had ended.

During the 70s, investors became frightened of the impact of inflation and severe cyclical fluctuation on profit margins, since margins fell sharply with each burst of inflation. At the first hint of declining margins, investors unloaded their shares and stock prices plunged. As a result, the Dow remained mired within a range for a decade, fluctuating between the high 500s and just over 1,000. Investors had been so badly burned by the market's decline in 1969 and 1974 that they refused to be swayed by the strong recovery of profits after each recession.

CHART 8–5
**Dow Jones Industrial Average (Price), Earnings per Share,
and Price/Earnings Ratio**

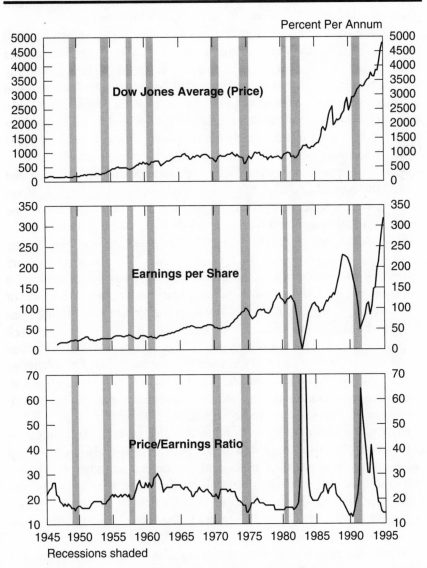

Recessions shaded

Source: Phyllis S. Pierce, ed., *The Dow Jones Investor's Handbook* (Homewood, IL: Dow Jones-Irwin, 1995); *Barron's*.

Yet nominal (not adjusted for inflation) profits rose over the decade, and thus the P/E ratio fell, so that by the early 1980s it was almost as low as it had been at the outset of the Korean War. The market had not kept pace with nominal earnings, and stocks were undervalued once again.

To some, this indicated that we were on the verge of another bull market. The situation seemed similar to that of the late 1940s, with investors hesitant after years of bad news, yet willing to take the plunge when it became clear that the fundamentals had changed. One indication of this sentiment was that stock prices fell little in the recessions of 1980 and 1981–82 when compared with those of 1970 and 1974. (Ignore the early 80s P/E surge. It was clearly the temporary consequence of the collapse in earnings associated with the 1981–82 recession.) It was as if investors were positioning themselves for the bull market that was just around the corner.

There were two very auspicious signs. First, the breaking of the boom-and-bust inflationary spiral with the back-to-back recessions of 1980 and 1981–82 was a key signal that henceforth corporations could enjoy high profit margins. Second, the low P/E ratio meant that stocks were undervalued. Growing earnings would generate rising share prices, and when sufficient numbers of investors realized that the earnings improvement was permanent, the P/E ratio would rise to higher levels as buying pressure drove stock prices up.

The bull market of the 80s began in the summer of 1982, when it became clear that the Fed had loosened its monetary vise. The decline in interest rates mattered to investors, because interest-earning assets are an alternative to stocks. As interest rates fell, investors moved out of interest-earning instruments and into stocks.

But Chart 8–5 on page 147 demonstrates that investors responded too enthusiastically to the improved profit potential. Speculation bid share prices up much faster than either real or nominal earnings. By August 1987 the Dow had doubled its 1985 level and stood at more than 2700, while earnings per share at $125 were not much greater than they had been four years earlier. The P/E ratio climbed to 22, higher than it had been since the early 60s.

Clearly the market was overvalued, ripe for a correction. It began to fold after its peak of 2722.42 on August 25, 1987, and declined 500 points by October 16. Then, on October 19, it crashed another 500 points.

Yet earnings per share continued to grow in a climate of low inflation. They exceeded $200 by early 1989, sending the P/E back down to 12. Now the Dow was undervalued once again, and investors began to

recover from their post crash jitters. By early 1990, investors had propelled the Dow passed its 1987 high; in the summer of 1990 it reached 3000.

What was the source of their bullish attitude? Strong margins, low inflation, and a low P/E. What did investors have to fear? Either inflation's return or speculation; the first because of its depressing impact on profit margins, the second because excessive stock market appreciation would create overvaluation (a high P/E) of the kind that existed before the 1987 crash.

Then Iraq invaded Kuwait. As consumer sentiment collapsed and recession unfolded, the Dow fell to 2400. But consumer sentiment rebounded with the success of Desert Storm, and the stock market anticipated economic recovery. The Dow quickly regained the 3000 range and remained there for some time.

Unfortunately, the economic recovery took longer than forecast, and earnings continued to decline. The 1990–91 recession repeated the experience of 1981–82 by sharply depressing earnings. Moreover, as you can see in Chart 8–5 on page 147, the drop in earnings drove the P/E ratio to absurdly high figures. Was that a sign of speculation and a signal for investors to sell?

Clearly not. Abysmal earnings for the Dow stocks, not speculation, had generated the extraordinary P/E ratios. Circumstances at the close of the 1990–91 recession were quite different from those before the crash of 1987. Depressed earnings, not speculation, were responsible for the extraordinarily high P/E ratio.

By the mid 1990s, the P/E had fallen back to 15 as earnings passed the $300 per share level. The Dow was poised for and achieved another ascent above the 4000 level.

Investor's Tip

- If the P/E exceeds 15, be cautious: stocks may be overvalued. If the P/E reaches 20, get out unless you have firm evidence that speculation is absent (such as the unusually depressed earnings of 1981–82 and 1990–91).

P/E RATIOS & YIELDS ON INDEXES				
	--P/E Ratios--		Dividend Yields	
	1/20/95	Yr. Ago	1/20/95	Yr. Ago
DJ Industrials	17.2	35.9	2.77%	2.59%
DJ Tranportations ..	40.5	....	1.43%	1.06%
DJ Utilities	16.3	13.6	6.89%	6.00%
S&P 500	17.01	23.26	2.87%	2.68%

Price earnings ratios for the Dow Jones Averages are based on per share earnings for the most recent four quarters of $224.37 for the 30 Industrials; $37.56 for the 20 transportation issues; $11.50 for the 15 utilities.

Source: *The Wall Street Journal*, January 23, 1995. Reprinted by permission of *The Wall Street Journal*, ©1995 Dow Jones & Company, Inc. All rights reserved worldwide.

Follow the earnings and P/E for the Dow stocks each Monday on the third page (C3) of the *Journal*'s third section, called Money and Investing. An example from the Monday, January 23, 1995 *Journal* appears above.

STOCKS VS. GOLD

Smart investors picked stocks and stayed away from gold in the 1980s and 1990s. The Fed had inflation under control, which was a good omen for stocks (and bonds and other paper investments) and a bad omen for gold (and commodities and other tangible investments).

As for the crash of 1987, that proved to be a correction for excessive speculation in stocks, for which a lofty P/E ratio was an omen. The smart money left the market when it became overvalued (P/E exceeded 20), and returned immediately after the crash.

WHAT ABOUT REAL ESTATE?

In general, invest in tangible assets when inflation is high and invest in paper assets when inflation is low.

Then what happened to real estate in the 1980s? Why did this tangible asset soar in many locales despite low rates of inflation?

Don't confuse the real estate markets of the 1970s and 80s. The rising tide of inflation lifted all the boats in the inflationary 70s. Whether you owned urban, suburban, or rural real estate, all values rose. Like Rip Van

Winkle, you could have gone to sleep in 1970 and awakened in 1980 to find an increase in the value of your assets, no matter where their location. But most real estate markets languished in the 1980s, because most of America is rural, and farmland values collapsed with agricultural commodity prices in the early 80s. There were important exceptions, such as California and the Northeast, whose values soared with local job conditions, but those situations were local, not general. The oil boomlets are another illustration of this phenomenon.

These special situations collapsed too, of course, so that the 1990s began with all real estate markets in slack condition. And since low inflation should continue from the 1980s right through the 90s, real estate should not be a good investment in the 90s. Sure, special situations and local booms will continue to occur, but that will be against a backdrop of generally weak conditions. Remember, too, that falling interest rates drove much of the mid-80s boom (where it did occur) and that interest rates are not likely to decline so dramatically in the 90s.

PART II

YOUR CHOICE OF
INVESTMENTS

CHAPTER 9

THE STOCK MARKET

A FIRST GLANCE: MARKETS DIARY

Chapter 8 compared the fortunes of stocks and gold in conditions of high and low inflation. Now it's time to study these competing investments in depth.

Start with stocks, not only because they are a more common investment, but also because you have seen that our economy's health and the stock market's health are inextricably intertwined.

You probably want to plunge right in and find out how you can make money in the market and use *The Wall Street Journal* to see how much you've made, but slow down a little instead and take the time for a step-by-step approach.

The stock market is a good barometer of economic activity, because it reflects the value of owning the businesses responsible for most of our economy's output. *The Dow Jones Industrial Average* is the most popular indicator of stock market performance, and that's why Chapters 1 and 8 employed it to portray the entire market.

The Dow represents share prices of 30 blue-chip industrial corporations, chosen because their operations cover the broad spectrum of industrial America, although you can see from the list presented below that not all of these firms are literally "industrials" (e.g., American Express, AT&T, McDonald's, and Woolworth are in financial services, communications, and retailing). (Dow Jones publishes separate indexes for public utilities and transportation companies.)

There are broader stock market barometers that include more corporations, but the Dow Industrials remains the most closely watched average because it was first and, more significant, because its handful of blue-chip companies do reflect stock market activity with surprising precision. Other measures of the stock market's performance will be mentioned shortly.

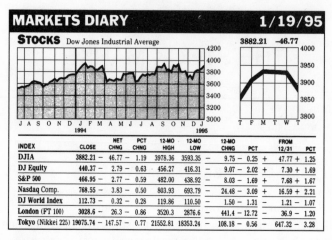

You probably already know a fair bit of the information in the next several pages, but it will provide a good basis for some more complex ideas presented later in this chapter.

Every day, on the first page (Cl) of the third section, *The Wall Street Journal* publishes a summary account of the activity of the stock market as measured by several major indexes. It is always the lead item under the heading **Markets Diary** (see the excerpt from the Friday, January 20, 1995 *Journal* above). The Dow Jones Industrial Average is featured in the two charts under the **Stocks** caption. The chart on the left pictures the fluctuations in the Dow over the past year-and-a-half, while the one on the right shows the Dow's weekly movement. The table just below the charts features four major domestic indexes, the DJ world index, and two international indexes to be discussed more fully below.

You should use this chart and table for your first quick assessment of the previous day's stock market activity. Notice that, while the majority of the indexes dropped slightly over the past twelve months (percentage change), the London market fell by a significantly larger margin.

But take a moment to consider the Dow Industrials in more detail.

CALCULATING THE DOW

Each day, on the third page (C3) of the last section, the *Journal* publishes in chart form a detailed summary of the **Dow Jones Averages** over the past six months (see pages 158 and 159). It records the progress of the 30 industrials, the 20 stocks in the transportation average, and the 15 stocks in the utility average, as well as trading volume.

After glancing at the top chart of the Dow Jones Averages, your first question—once you know what this index signifies—probably is, "How can an average of stock market prices be over $4,000? I don't know of *one* stock that trades that high, much less 30 of them."

The answer involves the manner in which the Dow deals with "stock splits." Companies split their stock (say, two for one) to prevent the stock from becoming too expensive. Shareholders receive two shares for each share they own, and the stock's price is halved; thus, the total value of the shares remains the same.

This usually occurs when the price of a "round-lot" transaction (100 shares) climbs too high. Round-lot transactions are popular with large investors because of the lower commission per share, and it's much easier to buy a round lot at $50 than $100 a share. Most companies would rather split their stock than see it become too expensive and discourage investors' purchases.

The 30 Stocks in the Dow Jones Industrial Average (April 12, 1995)

Alcoa	Goodyear
Allied-Signal	IBM
American Express	International Paper
AT&T	McDonald's
Bethlehem Steel	Merck
Boeing	Minnesota Mining & Manufacturing
Caterpillar	JP Morgan
Chevron	Phillip Morris
Coca-Cola	Procter & Gamble
Disney	Sears
DuPont	Texaco
Eastman Kodak	Union Carbide
Exxon	United Technologies
General Electric	Westinghouse
General Motors	Woolworth

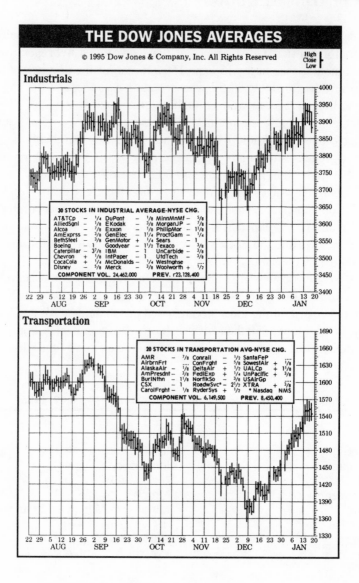

THE DOW JONES AVERAGES

High
Close
Low

Industrials

30 STOCKS IN INDUSTRIAL AVERAGE-NYSE CHG.

AT&TCp	−	1/4	DuPont	−	1/8	MinnMnMf	−	5/8
AlliedSgnl	−	1/8	EKodak	−	3/8	MorganJP	−	7/8
Alcoa	−	7/8	Exxon	−	1/8	PhilipMor	−	1 1/8
AmExprss	−	3/8	GenElec	−	1 1/4	ProctGam	−	1/4
BethSteel	−	3/8	GenMotor	+	1/4	Sears	−	1
Boeing	−	1	Goodyear	−	1 1/2	Texaco	−	3/8
Caterpillar	−	3 7/8	IBM	−	1	UnCarbide	−	3/8
Chevron	+	1/8	IntPaper	−	1	UtdTech	−	3/8
CocaCola	+	1/4	McDonalds	−	3/8	Westnghse	−	3/8
Disney	−	5/8	Merck	−	3/8	Woolworth	+	1/2

COMPONENT VOL. 24,462,000   PREV. r23,128,400

4000
3950
3900
3850
3800
3750
3700
3650
3600
3550
3500
3450
3400

22 29 5 12 19 26 2 9 16 23 30 7 14 21 28 4 11 18 25 2 9 16 23 30 6 13 20
AUG   SEP   OCT   NOV   DEC   JAN

Transportation

20 STOCKS IN TRANSPORTATION AVG-NYSE CHG.

AMR	−	7/8	Conrail	−	1/2	SantaFeP		....
AirbrnFrt		....	ConFrght	−	5/8	SowestAir	+	1/8
AlaskaAir	−	1/8	DeltaAir	+	1/2	UALCp	+	1 1/8
AmPresdnt	−	3/8	FedlExp	+	1/4	UnPacific	+	3/8
BurlNthn	−	1 1/8	NorflkSo	−	3/8	USAirGp		....
CSX	−	1	RoadwSvc*	−	2 1/2	XTRA	+	5/8
CarolFrght	−	1/8	RyderSys	+	1/2	* Nasdaq NMS

COMPONENT VOL. 6,149,500   PREV. 8,450,400

1690
1660
1630
1600
1570
1540
1510
1480
1450
1420
1390
1360
1330

22 29 5 12 19 26 2 9 16 23 30 7 14 21 28 4 11 18 25 2 9 16 23 30 6 13 20
AUG   SEP   OCT   NOV   DEC   JAN

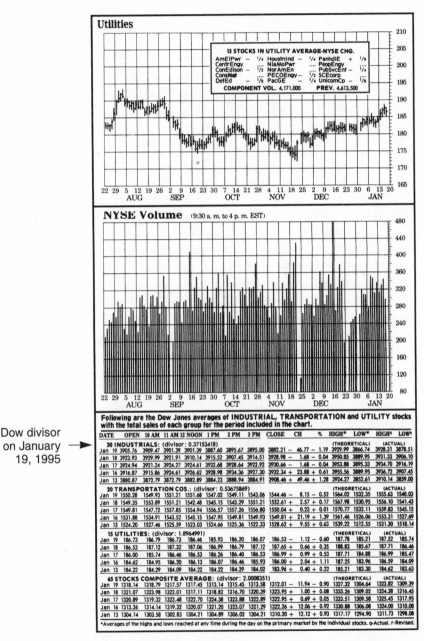

Utilities

15 STOCKS IN UTILITY AVERAGE-NYSE CHG.

AmElPwr	– 1/4	HousInInd	– 1/4	PanhdlE	+ 1/8
CentrEngy	....	NiaMoPwr	....	PeopEngy	....
ConEdison	– 1/2	NorAmEn	...	PubSvcEnt	– 1/4
ConsNat	....	PECOEngv	– 1/2	SCEcorp	...
DetEd	– 1/8	PacGE	– 1/4	UnicomCp	– 1/8

COMPONENT VOL. 4,171,000   PREV. 4,613,500

NYSE Volume (9:30 a. m. to 4 p. m. EST)

Dow divisor on January 19, 1995 →

Following are the Dow Jones averages of INDUSTRIAL, TRANSPORTATION and UTILITY stocks with the total sales of each group for the period included in the chart.

30 INDUSTRIALS: (divisor: 0.37153418)

DATE	OPEN	10 AM	11 AM	12 NOON	1 PM	2 PM	3 PM	CLOSE	CH	%	HIGH* (THEORETICAL)	LOW*	HIGH⁰ (ACTUAL)	LOW⁰
Jan 19	3905.76	3909.47	3901.39	3901.39	3887.60	3895.67	3895.00	3882.21	– 46.77	– 1.19	3929.99	3866.74	3928.31	3878.51
Jan 18	3923.93	3929.99	3921.91	3910.14	3915.52	3907.45	3914.51	3928.98	– 1.68	– 0.04	3950.85	3889.95	3931.33	3906.10
Jan 17	3924.94	3921.24	3924.27	3924.61	3932.68	3928.64	3922.92	3930.66	– 1.68	– 0.04	3953.88	3895.33	3934.70	3916.19
Jan 16	3916.87	3915.86	3924.61	3926.62	3928.98	3934.36	3927.30	3932.34	+ 23.88	+ 0.61	3955.56	3889.95	3936.72	3907.45
Jan 13	3880.87	3872.79	3872.79	3882.89	3884.23	3888.94	3884.91	3908.46	+ 49.46	+ 1.28	3924.27	3852.61	3910.14	3859.00

20 TRANSPORTATION COS.: (divisor: 0.53675869)

DATE	OPEN	10 AM	11 AM	12 NOON	1 PM	2 PM	3 PM	CLOSE	CH	%	HIGH* (THEORETICAL)	LOW*	HIGH⁰ (ACTUAL)	LOW⁰
Jan 19	1550.28	1549.93	1551.21	1551.68	1547.02	1549.11	1543.06	1544.46	– 8.15	– 0.52	1564.02	1532.35	1555.63	1540.03
Jan 18	1549.35	1553.89	1551.21	1542.48	1545.15	1543.29	1551.21	1552.61	+ 2.57	+ 0.17	1567.98	1530.95	1556.10	1541.43
Jan 17	1549.81	1547.72	1557.85	1554.94	1556.57	1557.26	1556.80	1550.04	+ 0.23	+ 0.01	1570.77	1532.11	1559.83	1545.15
Jan 16	1531.88	1534.91	1543.52	1545.15	1547.95	1549.81	1549.93	1549.81	+ 21.19	+ 1.39	1561.46	1526.06	1553.31	1527.69
Jan 13	1524.20	1527.46	1525.59	1523.03	1524.66	1525.36	1522.33	1528.62	+ 9.55	+ 0.63	1539.22	1512.55	1531.30	1518.14

15 UTILITIES: (divisor: 1.8964991)

DATE	OPEN	10 AM	11 AM	12 NOON	1 PM	2 PM	3 PM	CLOSE	CH	%	HIGH* (THEORETICAL)	LOW*	HIGH⁰ (ACTUAL)	LOW⁰
Jan 19	186.73	186.79	186.73	186.46	185.93	186.20	186.07	186.53	– 1.12	– 0.60	187.78	185.21	187.52	185.74
Jan 18	186.53	187.12	187.32	187.06	186.99	186.79	187.12	187.65	+ 0.66	+ 0.35	188.83	185.67	187.71	186.46
Jan 17	186.00	185.74	186.46	186.53	186.26	186.40	186.53	186.99	+ 0.99	+ 0.53	187.71	184.88	186.99	185.47
Jan 16	184.62	184.95	186.20	186.13	186.07	186.46	185.93	186.00	+ 2.04	+ 1.11	187.25	183.96	186.59	184.09
Jan 13	184.22	184.29	184.09	184.22	184.22	184.29	184.02	183.96	+ 0.40	+ 0.22	185.21	183.30	184.62	183.63

65 STOCKS COMPOSITE AVERAGE: (divisor: 2.0008351)

DATE	OPEN	10 AM	11 AM	12 NOON	1 PM	2 PM	3 PM	CLOSE	CH	%	HIGH* (THEORETICAL)	LOW*	HIGH⁰ (ACTUAL)	LOW⁰
Jan 19	1318.14	1318.79	1317.57	1317.45	1313.14	1315.45	1313.58	1312.01	– 11.94	– 0.90	1327.32	1304.64	1323.82	1309.39
Jan 18	1321.07	1323.98	1322.01	1317.11	1318.82	1316.70	1320.39	1323.95	+ 1.00	+ 0.08	1333.26	1309.02	1324.38	1316.45
Jan 17	1320.89	1319.32	1323.48	1322.70	1324.38	1323.88	1322.89	1322.95	+ 0.69	+ 0.05	1333.51	1309.58	1325.45	1317.95
Jan 16	1313.26	1314.14	1319.32	1320.07	1321.20	1323.07	1321.29	1322.26	+ 12.06	+ 0.92	1330.88	1306.08	1324.00	1310.08
Jan 13	1304.14	1303.58	1302.83	1304.21	1304.89	1306.02	1304.21	1310.20	+ 12.12	+ 0.93	1317.17	1294.90	1311.73	1298.08

*Averages of the highs and lows reached at any time during the day on the primary market by the individual stocks. q-Actual. r-Revised.

Source: *The Wall Street Journal*, January 20, 1995. Reprinted by permission of *The Wall Street Journal*, ©1995 Dow Jones & Company, Inc. All rights reserved worldwide.

Here's how this applies to the Dow Jones Industrial Average. Suppose you are calculating the average of a group of 30 stocks (such as the Dow) by adding the share prices of all of them and dividing by 30. If (to make the arithmetic simple and the point clear) each of the 30 were selling at $100, obviously the average would be $100 ($3,000 ÷ 30). However, if each of the 30 happened to split two for one, then each would be worth $50, per share; that is, the average price per share of these 30 stocks would suddenly be $50 not $100. Clearly, it makes no sense to reduce the average because of such splits, since someone who owns the stock has exactly as much equity (percentage ownership) value after a split as before it.

Reducing the divisor from 30 to 15 is one solution: 30 shares at $50 each ($1,500) divided by 15 (not 30) keeps the average at 100. Future stock splits can be handled in a similar fashion with an appropriate adjustment in the divisor.

Another, though less important, reason for changing the divisor is that occasionally Dow Jones replaces one of the 30 industrial stocks with another. Here, too, it wouldn't make sense to change the average; just because one stock is substituted for another doesn't mean the market, itself, has changed. Therefore, the divisor is adjusted at the same time, to keep the average constant.

Now consider a real-life example (see page 161) using the Dow on June 11, 1992 and on April 12, 1995. Add the share prices of all 30 companies in the Dow. The total for June 11, 1992 is $1,616.125, and, when you divide that by a divisor of 0.48220767, you get $3,351.51—the Dow average for June 11, 1992. Repeating the same calculation for April 12, 1995 provides the Dow average for the day—$4,197.81. Note that the 30 industrial stocks remained the same between June 1992 and March 1995, but the divisor dropped from 0.48220767 to 0.36143882 because some of the 30 industrials split over the last few years. For instance, Allied Signal, Alcoa, Chevron, General Electric, and 3M split two for one, so that their 1995 prices are sharply lower than their 1992 prices. Others, such as Woolworth and IBM, did not split, but simply dropped in value.

The point is: Since the sum of the Dow stocks fell (from 1,616.125 to 1,517.25) between June 11, 1992 and April 12, 1995, the divisor's decline from 0.48220767 to 0.36143882 (reflecting stock splits) drove all of the Dow's increase (from $3,351.51 to $4,197.81) between those dates.

Calculating the Dow

Company	NYSE Price	
	June 11, 1992	*April 12, 1995*
AT&T	43	51.375
Allied Signal	57.875	39.25
Alcoa	75.75	42.625
American Express	23.875	35
Bethlehem Steel	16.375	15.5
Boeing	44.25	55.875
Caterpillar	56.75	55.875
Chevron	73.375	45
Coca Cola	42.75	58.375
Disney	36.75	55
DuPont	52	61.875
Eastman Kodak	39.875	52.125
Exxon	63.25	66.875
General Electric	76.625	54.75
General Motors	43	44.25
Goodyear	66.375	38.625
IBM	92	87.125
International Paper	66.375	75.375
McDonald's	44.5	34.5
Merck	49.25	42.875
Minnesota Mining & Manufacturing	95.25	57.625
JP Morgan	55.25	60.625
Philip Morris	72.375	67.625
Procter & Gamble	99.375	67.875
Sears	41.375	52.75
Texaco	66	65
Union Carbide	27.5	30.75
United Technologies	50.625	68.875
Westinghouse	18.25	15.375
Woolworth	26.125	18.5
Total	1,616.125	1,517.25
Sum of Stock Prices	1,616.125	1,517.25
Divisor	0.48220767	0.36143882
= The DJIA	= 3,351.51*	= 4,197.81*

*The Dow average onJune 11, 1992 and April 12, 1995.

The figures used on page161 to compute the Dow are the closing prices for the New York Stock Exchange (NYSE). NYSE *Composite Transactions* prices (to be discussed below) vary slightly from the prices used here. Why the discrepancy? Because the composite includes the closing prices of NYSE stocks listed on other exchanges such as the Pacific Stock Exchange, which continues its operations for half an hour after the New York Exchange closes.

Compare the April 12, 1995 Dow Jones Industrials divisor of 0.36143882 shown below with the June 11, 1992 divisor of 0.48220767 used in the previous example. The divisor fell by 0.12076885 between June 1992 and April 1995 due to splits in several of the stocks in the Dow.

Dow → divisor on April 12, 1995

Following are the Dow Jones averages of INDUSTRIAL, TRANSPORTATION and UTILITY stocks with the total sales of each group for the period included in the chart.

DATE	OPEN	10 AM	11 AM	12 NOON	1 PM	2 PM	3 PM	CLOSE	CH	%	HIGH*	LOW*	HIGH⁹	LOW⁹
30 INDUSTRIALS: (divisor: 0.36143882)											(THEORETICAL)		(ACTUAL)	
Apr 12	4190.20	4184.66	4185.70	4187.78	4191.58	4192.27	4200.92	4197.81 + 10.73 + 0.26			4221.67	4163.57	4201.96	4182.24
Apr 11	4209.91	4208.18	4195.38	4187.08	4189.16	4194.35	4194.00	4187.08 − 11.07 − 0.26			4229.97	4168.06	4216.83	4182.93
Apr 10	4181.21	4185.70	4190.20	4195.73	4194.69	4196.42	4200.23	4198.15 + 5.53 + 0.13			4219.94	4163.91	4203.69	4180.86
Apr 7	4203.69	4189.85	4194.00	4175.33	4181.21	4169.45	4187.43	4192.62 − 12.79 − 0.30			4226.86	4154.23	4211.29	4169.45
Apr 6	4208.53	4218.21	4212.33	4204.03	4203.34	4207.49	4201.96	4205.41 + 4.84 + 0.12			4239.31	4179.13	4224.09	4197.96
20 TRANSPORTATION COS.: (divisor: 0.53675869)											(THEORETICAL)		(ACTUAL)	
Apr 12	1643.66	1639.24	1644.13	1649.95	1645.99	1648.79	1654.37	1654.61 + 10.95 + 0.67			1662.53	1633.42	1656.24	1638.89
Apr 11	1649.72	1649.72	1645.99	1644.83	1643.20	1643.66	1645.06	1643.66 − 2.33 − 0.14			1657.87	1636.44	1652.28	1642.26
Apr 10	1641.10	1642.03	1646.92	1646.69	1645.99	1645.76	1643.66	1645.99 + 1.75 + 0.11			1656.94	1633.18	1648.20	1639.70
Apr 7	1628.76	1629.46	1630.85	1631.09	1634.58	1645.53	1645.99	1644.24 + 6.63 + 0.40			1659.03	1617.11	1647.16	1627.13
Apr 6	1628.99	1632.95	1634.11	1630.62	1630.16	1629.92	1630.16	1637.61 + 8.62 + 0.53			1647.39	1620.84	1639.70	1627.59
15 UTILITIES: (divisor: 1.8964991)											(THEORETICAL)		(ACTUAL)	
Apr 12	191.67	191.27	191.60	191.93	191.87	192.13	192.06	191.87 − 0.19 − 0.10			192.72	190.55	192.20	191.08
Apr 11	193.65	193.38	192.53	192.26	192.59	192.66	192.39	192.06 − 1.32 − 0.68			194.11	191.14	193.71	191.93
Apr 10	193.25	193.05	193.05	193.12	193.18	193.12	193.18	193.38 − 0.66 − 0.34			194.17	192.06	194.04	192.59
Apr 7	193.32	193.18	193.32	192.99	193.18	192.79	193.25	194.04 + 0.92 + 0.48			194.44	192.06	194.04	192.66
Apr 6	193.58	193.65	193.25	193.45	193.12	193.45	193.12	193.12 − 0.59 − 0.30			194.63	192.26	193.71	192.79
65 STOCKS COMPOSITE AVERAGE: (divisor: 1.9709993)											(THEORETICAL)		(ACTUAL)	
Apr 12	1400.43	1397.96	1399.67	1401.95	1401.51	1402.65	1405.70	1405.00 + 4.76 + 0.34			1412.35	1391.68	1406.14	1397.36
Apr 11	1407.60	1407.03	1402.84	1400.75	1401.00	1402.14	1402.21	1400.24 − 3.93 − 0.28			1413.94	1393.90	1409.18	1399.42
Apr 10	1399.61	1400.50	1402.65	1403.67	1403.35	1403.54	1403.79	1404.17 + 0.85 + 0.06			1411.91	1393.14	1404.74	1399.35
Apr 7	1400.43	1397.96	1399.23	1395.55	1397.77	1398.21	1402.08	1403.32 + 0.35 + 0.02			1414.00	1386.99	1403.54	1394.53
Apr 6	1401.64	1404.55	1403.41	1401.13	1400.56	1401.57	1400.30	1402.97 + 2.67 + 0.19			1413.31	1392.76	1406.58	1399.61

Averages of the highs and lows reached at any time during the day on the primary market by the individual stocks. q-Actual. r-Revised.

Source: *The Wall Street Journal*, April 13, 1995. Reprinted by permission of *The Wall Street Journal*, ©1995 Dow Jones & Company, Inc. All rights reserved worldwide.

So much for the Dow; you are now ready to move on to a more detailed analysis of the other stock market indicators and stock market performance.

STOCK MARKET DATA BANK

The Stock Market Data Bank appears daily on the second page (C2) of the third section. See pages 164 and 165 for an example from the Friday, January 20, 1995 *Wall Street Journal*. It presents a comprehensive summary of stock market activity in seven sections: **Major Indexes, Most Active Issues, Diaries, Price Percentage Gainers and Losers, Volume Percentage Leaders**, and **Breakdown of Trading in NYSE Stocks**. Look at it after you have examined the **Markets Diary** in order to get a more detailed view of the previous day's trading activity.

Major Indexes on page 166 lists the Dow averages as well as a variety of other domestic indexes in greater detail than provided in the **Markets Diary** on the first page (Cl) of the third section. These statistics permit you to compare the performance of your own investments with the broadest gauges of stock market activity.

The Dow Jones Equity Market Index is a very broad-based index (June 30, 1982=100) of about 700 stocks (see page 166). A more detailed discussion appears on page 216.

The **New York Stock Exchange Composite** tracks the movements of all stocks listed on that exchange. Notice that this composite, like most others, is broken out into a number of components.

Since this index includes all stocks listed (about 3,000), rather than a sample like the Dow, you may wonder why it isn't preferred to the Dow. Because most investors aren't interested in all the stocks listed, just the most important ones. For that reason, the next measure of the market strikes a compromise.

The Standard and Poor's 500 includes some stocks not listed on the New York exchange, and it is a composite. Since it weights (measures the importance of) its constituent companies by their market value (share price multiplied by the number of share outstanding), unlike the Dow which weights by price alone, and since it includes far more companies then the Dow, most observers prefer this index to the Dow.

NASDAQ (National Association of Securities Dealers Automated Quotations) stocks are traded over-the-counter (electronically), not on an organized exchange, and usually represent ownership of smaller and less widely-held companies.

STOCK MARKET DATA BANK 1/19/95

MAJOR INDEXES

HIGH	LOW (†365 DAY)		CLOSE	NET CHG	% CHG	†365 DAY CHG	% CHG	FROM 12/31	% CHG
DOW JONES AVERAGES									
3978.36	3593.35	30 Industrials	3882.21	− 46.77	− 1.19	− 9.75	− 0.25	+ 47.77	+ 1.25
1862.29	1371.89	20 Transportation	1544.46	− 8.15	− 0.52	− 269.54	− 14.86	+ 89.43	+ 6.15
226.01	173.94	15 Utilities	186.53	− 1.12	− 0.60	− 33.88	− 15.37	+ 5.01	+ 2.76
1447.06	1224.18	65 Composite	1312.01	− 11.94	− 0.90	− 101.91	− 7.21	+ 37.60	+ 2.95
456.27	416.31	Equity Mkt. Index	440.37	− 2.79	− 0.63	− 9.07	− 2.02	+ 7.30	+ 1.69
NEW YORK STOCK EXCHANGE									
267.71	243.14	Composite	254.38	− 1.59	− 0.62	− 8.85	− 3.36	+ 3.44	+ 1.37
327.93	298.30	Industrials	321.51	− 1.85	− 0.57	− 1.23	− 0.38	+ 3.41	+ 1.07
230.70	197.30	Utilities	200.11	− 0.95	− 0.47	− 25.48	− 11.29	+ 1.70	+ 0.86
285.03	212.94	Transportation	233.72	− 0.68	− 0.29	− 45.77	− 16.38	+ 11.26	+ 5.06
224.90	190.17	Finance	201.11	− 2.06	− 1.01	− 17.63	− 8.06	+ 5.31	+ 2.71
STANDARD & POOR'S INDEXES									
482.00	438.92	500 Index	466.95	− 2.77	− 0.59	− 8.03	− 1.69	+ 7.68	+ 1.67
184.79	162.44	400 MidCap	172.74	− 0.79	− 0.46	− 7.37	− 4.09	+ 3.30	+ 1.95
104.45	88.14	600 SmallCap	94.31	− 0.67	− 0.71	− 6.86	− 6.78	+ 0.14	+ 0.15
NASDAQ									
803.93	693.79	Composite	768.55	− 3.83	− 0.50	− 24.48	− 3.09	+ 16.59	+ 2.21
851.80	703.27	Industrials	762.64	− 3.89	− 0.51	− 67.77	− 8.16	+ 8.83	+ 1.17
960.18	858.96	Insurance	953.22	− 6.92	− 0.72	+ 31.27	+ 3.39	+ 27.35	+ 2.95
787.92	662.57	Banks	726.16	− 3.52	− 0.48	+ 31.97	+ 4.61	+ 29.09	+ 4.17
356.61	307.55	Nat. Mkt. Comp.	342.79	− 1.74	− 0.51	− 8.32	− 2.37	+ 7.55	+ 2.25
342.72	282.87	Nat. Mkt. Indus.	309.69	− 1.55	− 0.50	− 23.36	− 7.01	+ 3.65	+ 1.19
OTHERS									
487.89	420.23	Amex	439.53	− 0.44	− 0.10	− 45.28	− 9.34	+ 5.86	+ 1.35
258.31	235.50	Russell 1000	248.87	− 1.64	− 0.65	− 5.38	− 2.12	+ 4.23	+ 1.73
271.08	235.16	Russell 2000	251.01	− 1.30	− 0.52	− 12.36	− 4.69	+ 0.65	+ 0.26
278.44	254.01	Russell 3000	267.69	− 1.63	− 0.61	− 6.38	− 2.33	+ 4.25	+ 1.61
305.87	266.56	Value-Line(geom.)	280.75	− 1.40	− 0.50	− 20.45	− 6.79	+ 3.23	+ 1.16
4804.31	4373.58	Wilshire 5000	4616.18	− 28.65	− 0.62	− 111.60	− 2.36	+ 75.56	+ 1.66

†-Based on comparable trading day in preceding year.

MOST ACTIVE ISSUES

NYSE	VOLUME	CLOSE	CHANGE
TelefMex	7,615,200	34 1/2	− 1 3/4
ChilgenerADR	5,100,300	x22 1/2	− 3/8
IntGameTech	4,259,500	13 1/4	+ 1/4
Citicorp	4,097,900	39 3/8	− 1 3/8
RJR Nabisco	3,698,700	5 5/8	......
Caterpillar	3,499,400	54 3/4	− 3 7/8
Chrysler	2,793,600	49 1/4	− 7/8
PlgrmPrm rt	2,742,400	5/64	......
FleetFnl	2,598,400	31	− 2 1/8
FordMotor	2,486,400	27 1/2	− 3/4
YPF ADR	2,462,100	20 5/8	− 1/2
GenElec	2,441,000	51	− 1 1/4
Westnghse	2,277,300	14 1/8	+ 1/8
GrpTelevADR	2,110,700	22 3/4	− 2 1/8
SantaFePac	2,076,600	18 1/4	......
NASDAQ			
Intel	9,187,000	70 11/16	+ 1 5/16
Microsoft	4,194,300	63 1/2	− 1 9/16
VLSI Tech	3,565,700	12 3/8	− 2
SunMicrsys	3,369,800	33 11/16	− 15/16
Novell	3,087,100	18	+ 1/8
MCI Comm	3,081,700	18 13/16	− 1/8
Pharmos	3,061,400	7/8	+ 5/32
LDDS Comm	2,950,200	22 1/4	− 1/8
AppleCptr	2,806,200	45 7/8	+ 1/4
Atmel	2,774,700	34 3/8	− 2 1/8
AlteraCp	2,768,200	47 1/4	+ 3 1/8
OracleCp	2,756,600	44 3/4	+ 1 1/2
BayNtwrk	2,593,400	31 7/8	+ 3/4
AMEX			
ViacomVar rt	5,712,000	3/4	+ 1/16
ViacomB	1,134,800	45	......
InterDigital	1,008,800	8	− 3/8
CheynSftwr	860,800	15 1/4	− 1/8
IvaxCp	642,000	21 3/8	+ 1/2

DIARIES

NYSE	THU	WED	WK AGO
Issues traded	2,958	2,957	2,944
Advances	748	1,061	1,128
Declines	1,423	1,171	1,057
Unchanged	787	725	759
New highs	38	54	27
New lows	38	26	61
zAdv vol (000)	78,684	133,491	145,241
zDecl vol (000)	175,916	169,187	119,366
zTotal vol (000)	297,757	344,568	312,508
Closing tick[1]	−139	+251	+354
Closing Arms[2] (trin)	1.18	1.15	.88
zBlock trades	6,820	7,289	7,307
NASDAQ			
Issues traded	5,114	5,115	5,112
Advances	1,413	1,560	1,705
Declines	1,791	1,693	1,554
Unchanged	1,910	1,862	1,853
New highs	76	113	73
New lows	78	60	57
Adv vol (000)	129,449	157,362	148,667
Decl vol (000)	157,768	148,397	116,117
Total vol (000)	331,863	348,333	302,235
Block trades	6,217	6,444	5,491
AMEX			
Issues traded	750	760	739
Advances	228	251	268
Declines	303	274	278
Unchanged	219	235	193
New highs	14	18	10
New lows	12	10	14
zAdv vol (000)	5,396	6,628	7,549
zDecl vol (000)	7,329	4,888	5,930
zTotal vol (000)	17,035	18,202	15,667
Comp vol (000)	17,820	21,256	19,425
zBlock trades	n.a.	273	296

PRICE PERCENTAGE GAINERS . . .

NYSE	VOL	CLOSE	CHANGE	% CHG
UDC Homes.pfA	2,500	5 7/8	+ 1	+ 20.5
SunEngy	49,200	4 1/2	+ 1/2	+ 12.5
UDCHomes.pfB	7,700	5 5/8	+ 5/8	+ 12.5
HuntgInt	68,600	3 5/8	+ 3/8	+ 11.5
EvergreenHlth	135,600	11 1/2	+ 1 1/8	+ 10.8
CoramHlthcr	965,000	19 3/4	+ 1 3/4	+ 9.7
BriggsStrat	234,000	34 7/8	+ 2 1/4	+ 6.9
UnoRestr	43,600	15 1/2	+ 1	+ 6.9
ChartInd	5,800	4 1/8	+ 1/4	+ 6.5
PittstonSvc	70,700	27 5/8	+ 1 5/8	+ 6.3
Genesco	56,900	2 1/8	+ 1/8	+ 6.3
WorldCp	341,700	9	+ 1/2	+ 5.9
CarlPlastc	40,300	4 1/2	+ 1/4	+ 5.9
WahlcoEnvSys	7,600	2 1/4	+ 1/8	+ 5.9
StdFedBk	623,300	25 1/2	+ 1 3/8	+ 5.7
CorrctnCpwt	2,700	11 7/8	+ 5/8	+ 5.6
RollinsEnvr	130,300	4 7/8	+ 1/4	+ 5.4
HancockFab	84,100	9 3/4	+ 1/2	+ 5.4
TexfiInd	5,800	2 1/2	+ 1/8	+ 5.3
TCC	2,100	2 1/2	+ 1/8	+ 5.3
NASDAQ NNM				
Cnfertech	2,570,800	7 5/8	+ 2 1/8	+ 38.6
BirdMedTech	60,100	4 1/2	+ 1	+ 28.6
Penederm	24,100	7	+ 1 3/8	+ 24.4
CPIAero	11,800	4	+ 3/4	+ 23.1
IGLabs	5,200	3 1/2	+ 5/8	+ 21.7
IntJensen	48,200	12	+ 2	+ 20.0
AmVngrd	33,200	9	+ 1 1/2	+ 20.0
Comshare	158,200	16 3/4	+ 2 3/4	+ 19.6
KTelInt	9,700	5 3/8	+ 7/8	+ 19.4
CableMaxx	51,900	6 1/4	+ 1	+ 19.0
MegatestCp	677,700	9 5/8	+ 1 1/2	+ 18.5
CambrdgeSound	115,600	4 1/8	+ 5/8	+ 17.9
Astronic	4,600	2 1/2	+ 3/8	+ 17.6
HerleyInd	245,400	3 13/16	+ 9/16	+ 17.3
AMEX				
PnWbrHKpwt95	146,800	4 13/16	+ 13/16	+ 20.3
LaserTch	61,700	4 7/16	+ 11/16	+ 18.3
Audiovox	154,000	8	+ 3/4	+ 10.3
BearStnHKpwt	18,500	6 1/8	+ 1/2	+ 8.9
PLMEq2	4,200	7 7/8	+ 5/8	+ 8.6

AND LOSERS

NYSE	VOL	CLOSE	CHANGE	% CHG
DescSAADR	55,600	11 3/8	− 2 5/8	− 18.8
AcmeElec	296,300	16 5/8	− 3 1/4	− 16.4
GenData	1,305,000	30	− 5 1/2	− 15.5
IntlCeram	95,700	16 1/8	− 2 7/8	− 15.1
BrdwyStore	86,500	5 1/2	− 7/8	− 13.7
TCWDWTermTr	295,500	7 1/8	− 1 1/8	− 13.6
CGDinaADRL	71,400	3 5/8	− 1/2	− 12.1
TCWDWTr2000	204,000	6 1/2	− 7/8	− 11.9
VitroSA	341,800	11 1/2	− 1 3/8	− 10.7
GrupoDesarADRB	128,900	4 1/4	− 1/2	− 10.5
CGDinaADR	423,900	5 3/8	− 5/8	− 10.4
EmpricaADR	1,415,000	9 1/8	− 1	− 9.9
GrpRadioADR	26,800	10 1/8	− 1	− 9.0
GrpTelevADR	2,110,700	22 3/4	− 2 1/8	− 8.5
GrupoSidekB	3,700	6 3/4	− 5/8	− 8.5
EmprModrnADR	280,900	14	− 1 1/4	− 8.2
GrpSidekADR	87,600	7 1/8	− 5/8	− 8.1
Aracruz	64,400	11 5/8	− 1	− 7.9
GrpDurangoADR	4,100	10 1/4	− 7/8	− 7.9
BufetIndADR	83,400	18 3/4	− 1 1/2	− 7.4
NASDAQ NNM				
Cyberonics	3,700	3 3/4	− 1 3/4	− 31.8
HerblfInt	2,416,000	12 5/8	− 5 1/8	− 28.9
CardioImag	821,600	7 1/4	− 2 3/8	− 24.7
MWave	53,900	11 3/4	− 3 3/4	− 24.2
AEREngyRes	57,100	4	− 1	− 20.0
WavePhore	102,700	6 3/4	− 1 1/8	− 14.3
PetFdWrhse	287,300	3 1/8	− 1/2	− 13.8
VLSITech	3,565,700	12 5/8	− 2	− 13.7
Infrasonc	31,000	3 1/4	− 1/2	− 13.3
DairyMrtB	2,200	3 11/16	− 9/16	− 13.2
AirMethod	73,600	1 3/4	− 1/4	− 12.5
Octagon	35,000	1 3/4	− 1/4	− 12.5
SearchCap	9,400	1 3/4	− 1/4	− 12.5
EmisphereTch	64,300	3 1/8	− 7/16	− 12.3
AMEX				
BethlehemCp	235,800	3 3/8	− 2	− 37.2
Polyphase	64,300	2 1/8	− 7/8	− 29.2
UtdGuardn	3,700	2 1/16	− 1/4	− 10.8
UtdFoodsA	10,700	2 3/8	− 1/4	− 9.5
SilvrdoFod	12,800	3 1/4	− 5/16	− 8.8

VOLUME PERCENTAGE LEADERS

NYSE	VOL	%DIF*	CLOSE	CHANGE
ChilgenerADR	5,100,300	10000.0	x22 1/2	− 3/8
StarterCp	1,315,900	1317.3	9 3/4	.....
IntstBaker	497,800	1260.2	14 7/8	.....
EdisonBros	784,700	1247.6	14 1/8	− 1/2
ThorInd	118,500	954.6	19 1/8	.....
AcmeElec	296,300	944.6	16 5/8	− 3 1/4
ReadersDigB	122,100	923.3	43 3/4	− 1/2
EvergreenHlth	135,600	728.9	11 1/2	+ 1 1/8
NewfieldExpl	113,900	688.1	18 7/8	− 1/8
ArcadnPtnr	184,000	655.8	23 7/8	− 1
StdFedBk	623,300	604.2	25 1/2	+ 1 3/8
AmericusInc	102,300	583.6	6 3/4	− 1/2
GenData	1,305,000	544.3	30	− 5 1/2
CalgnCarb	410,100	539.1	10 5/8	− 1/4
CoramHlthcr	965,000	521.4	19 3/4	+ 1 3/4
EastUtil	237,700	516.6	21 7/8	− 3/8
BallyEntmt	1,464,200	504.0	7 7/8	+ 3/8
CarltonXCAP	40,300	492.0	21 3/32	+ 3/32
Rhodes	205,600	484.7	12 3/4	+ 1/4
IBPInc	1,283,600	456.5	31 1/4	+ 1/4

NASDAQ NNM	VOL	%DIF*	CLOSE	CHANGE
Cnfertech	2,570,800	7352.2	7 5/8	+ 2 1/8
ResBcshMtg	805,200	6523.3	9	+ 1/8
PremierRdio	351,000	2830.4	9	......
AcmatA	302,500	2459.2	9 5/16	+ 1/16
Theraptcun	215,300	2140.8	5 3/8	......
LibertyBcp	185,000	2023.5	31 3/8	+ 5/16
II-VI	332,100	1675.9	9 3/4	+ 1
HerblfInt	2,416,000	1562.4	12 5/8	− 5 1/8
ZingTech	200,200	1510.7	6 1/16	− 5/8
CairnEngy	304,300	1146.5	7 13/16	+ 5/16
JeffriesGp	75,800	1123.8	29 5/8	− 3/4
LaddFurn	1,569,400	1104.6	5	......
CardioImag	821,600	1000.2	7 1/4	− 2 3/8
ElectroRtl	63,200	938.4	5 3/8	− 1/4
MariettaCp	199,000	889.5	10 3/4	− 1/4
SymixSys	69,200	874.0	8	+ 3/4
AMEX				
CenterptProp	575,900	6425.0	18 1/4	......
TejasPwr	139,500	1642.7	9 1/8	− 1/8
Audiovox	154,000	622.9	8	+ 3/4
Semtech	109,400	527.5	5 1/4	− 1/8
USFGPchld	52,200	453.1	17	− 3/8

*Common stocks of $5 a share or more with average volume over 65 trading days of at least 5,000 shares.
a – has traded fewer than 65 days on any exchange.

BREAKDOWN OF TRADING IN NYSE STOCKS (9:30 a.m. to 4 p.m. EST)

BY MARKET	Thur	Wed	WK AGO
New York	297,756,780	344,567,620	312,508,110
Chicago	13,339,500	15,287,100	13,616,400
Pacific	7,420,800	8,473,100	7,713,100
NASD	27,314,430	29,578,450	28,990,530
Phila	5,149,190	5,167,000	3,752,400
Boston	4,140,100	4,965,000	4,422,900
Cincinnati	6,127,100	6,459,600	5,862,400
Composite	361,247,900	414,497,870	376,865,840

NYSE first crossing 141,500 shares, value $978,375 (est.)
Second (basket) 16,159,228 shares, value $726,852,546
[1]The net difference of the number of stocks closing higher than their previous trade from those closing lower; NYSE trading only.
[2]A comparison of the number of advancing and declining issues with the volume of shares rising and falling. Generally, an Arms of less than 1.00 indicates buying demand; above 1.00 indicates selling pressure.
z-NYSE or Amex only.

½-HOURLY	Thur	Wed	WK AGO
9:30-10	38,540,000	40,420,000	38,780,000
10-10:30	28,330,000	33,910,000	29,810,000
10:30-11	23,450,000	29,420,000	25,830,000
11-11:30	22,110,000	29,100,000	25,030,000
11:30-12	21,230,000	26,830,000	20,050,000
12-12:30	18,420,000	22,140,000	19,990,000
12:30-1	17,130,000	14,270,000	16,560,000
1-1:30	17,010,000	17,080,000	16,250,000
1:30-2	16,220,000	27,420,000	21,620,000
2-2:30	15,170,000	18,210,000	20,410,000
2:30-3	18,710,000	23,080,000	21,250,000
3-3:30	25,530,000	24,390,000	22,750,000
3:30-4	35,906,780	38,297,620	34,178,110

Source: *The Wall Street Journal*, January 20, 1994. Reprinted by permission of *The Wall Street Journal*,

STOCK MARKET DATA BANK   1/19/95

MAJOR INDEXES

HIGH	LOW (†365 DAY)		CLOSE	NET CHG		% CHG	†365 DAY CHG		% CHG	FROM 12/31		% CHG
DOW JONES AVERAGES												
3978.36	3593.35	30 Industrials	3882.21	− 46.77	−	1.19	− 9.75	−	0.25	+ 47.77	+	1.25
1862.29	1371.89	20 Transportation	1544.46	− 8.15	−	0.52	− 269.54	−	14.86	+ 89.43	+	6.15
226.01	173.94	15 Utilities	186.53	− 1.12	−	0.60	− 33.88	−	15.37	+ 5.01	+	2.76
1447.06	1224.18	65 Composite	1312.01	− 11.94	−	0.90	− 101.91	−	7.21	+ 37.60	+	2.95
456.27	416.31	Equity Mkt. Index	440.37	− 2.79	−	0.63	− 9.07	−	2.02	+ 7.30	+	1.69
NEW YORK STOCK EXCHANGE												
267.71	243.14	Composite	254.38	− 1.59	−	0.62	− 8.85	−	3.36	+ 3.44	+	1.37
327.93	298.30	Industrials	321.51	− 1.85	−	0.57	− 1.23	−	0.38	+ 3.41	+	1.07
230.70	197.30	Utilities	200.11	− 0.95	−	0.47	− 25.48	−	11.29	+ 1.70	+	0.86
285.03	212.94	Transportation	233.72	− 0.68	−	0.29	− 45.77	−	16.38	+ 11.26	+	5.06
224.90	190.17	Finance	201.11	− 2.06	−	1.01	− 17.63	−	8.06	+ 5.31	+	2.71
STANDARD & POOR'S INDEXES												
482.00	438.92	500 Index	466.95	− 2.77	−	0.59	− 8.03	−	1.69	+ 7.68	+	1.67
184.79	162.44	400 MidCap	172.74	− 0.79	−	0.46	− 7.37	−	4.09	+ 3.30	+	1.95
104.45	88.14	600 SmallCap	94.31	− 0.67	−	0.71	− 6.86	−	6.78	+ 0.14	+	0.15
NASDAQ												
803.93	693.79	Composite	768.55	− 3.83	−	0.50	− 24.48	−	3.09	+ 16.59	+	2.21
851.80	703.27	Industrials	762.64	− 3.89	−	0.51	− 67.77	−	8.16	+ 8.83	+	1.17
960.18	858.96	Insurance	953.22	− 6.92	−	0.72	+ 31.27	+	3.39	+ 27.35	+	2.95
787.92	662.57	Banks	726.16	− 3.52	−	0.48	+ 31.97	+	4.61	+ 29.09	+	4.17
356.61	307.55	Nat. Mkt. Comp.	342.79	− 1.74	−	0.51	− 8.32	−	2.37	+ 7.55	+	2.25
342.72	282.87	Nat. Mkt. Indus.	309.69	− 1.55	−	0.50	− 23.36	−	7.01	+ 3.65	+	1.19
OTHERS												
487.89	420.23	Amex	439.53	− 0.44	−	0.10	− 45.28	−	9.34	+ 5.86	+	1.35
258.31	235.50	Russell 1000	248.87	− 1.64	−	0.65	− 5.38	−	2.12	+ 4.23	+	1.73
271.06	235.16	Russell 2000	251.01	− 1.30	−	0.52	− 12.36	−	4.69	+ 0.65	+	0.26
278.44	254.01	Russell 3000	267.69	− 1.63	−	0.61	− 6.38	−	2.33	+ 4.25	+	1.61
305.87	266.56	Value-Line(geom.)	280.75	− 1.40	−	0.50	− 20.45	−	6.79	+ 3.23	+	1.16
4804.31	4373.58	Wilshire 5000	4616.18	− 28.65	−	0.62	− 111.60	−	2.36	+ 75.56	+	1.66

†-Based on comparable trading day in preceding year.

Source: *The Wall Street Journal*, January 20, 1994. Reprinted by permission of *The Wall Street Journal*, ©1994 Dow Jones & Company, Inc. All rights reserved worldwide.

The **AMEX** index measures all the stocks (about 1,000) traded on the American Stock Exchange. Most of these companies were traditionally between the New York and over-the-counter companies in size, but this distinction has evaporated with the rapid growth of many of the over-the-counter companies. This exchange was once known as the Curb Exchange, because its business was conducted in the street and it had no premises.

The **Russell 1000**, **Russell 2000**, and **Russell 3000** track stocks issued by smaller companies.

The **Value-Line** composite is prepared by the investment service of the same name. It contains about 1,700 stocks traded on the two major exchanges as well as over-the-counter.

The **Wilshire 5000** measures all the 5,000 or so stocks that are actively traded on the two major exchanges as well as over-the-counter. This excludes several thousand stocks that are not actively traded.

Now, take a look at **Most Active Issues** (C2) below, which lists the day's most heavily traded stocks on the three major markets: New York Stock Exchange (NYSE), the National Association of Security Dealers Automated Quotation (NASDAQ) system in the over-the-counter (OTC) market, and the American Stock Exchange (AMEX). For instance, under NASDAQ you can see that over 9 million shares of Intel changed hands on Thursday, January 19, 1995.

MOST ACTIVE ISSUES

NASDAQ	VOLUME	CLOSE	CHANGE	
Intel	9,187,000	$70^{11}/_{16}$	$+$	$1^{5}/_{16}$
Microsoft	4,194,300	$63^{1}/_{2}$	$-$	$1^{9}/_{16}$
VLSI Tech	3,565,700	$12^{5}/_{8}$	$-$	2
SunMicrsys	3,369,800	$33^{11}/_{16}$	$-$	$^{15}/_{16}$
Novell	3,087,100	18	$+$	$^{1}/_{8}$
MCI Comm	3,081,700	$18^{13}/_{16}$	$-$	$^{1}/_{8}$
Pharmos	3,061,400	$^{7}/_{8}$	$+$	$^{5}/_{32}$
LDDS Comm	2,950,200	$22^{1}/_{4}$	$-$	$^{1}/_{8}$
AppleCptr	2,806,200	$45^{7}/_{8}$	$+$	$^{1}/_{4}$
Atmel	2,774,700	$34^{5}/_{8}$	$-$	$2^{1}/_{8}$
AlteraCp	2,768,200	$47^{1}/_{4}$	$+$	$3^{1}/_{8}$
OracleCp	2,756,600	$44^{3}/_{4}$	$+$	$1^{1}/_{2}$
BayNtwrk	2,593,400	$31^{7}/_{8}$	$+$	$^{3}/_{4}$

9.187 million shares of Intel changed hands due to heavy buying pressure

The Diaries provide another important measure of the day's trading activity: *advances versus declines, new highs versus new lows,* and the *volume of the stocks advancing and declining.* On Thursday, January 19, 1995, 748 issues advanced and 1,423 declined on the New York exchange. The decliners were far more actively traded: 175,916 to 78,684. These figures confirm the Dow's big drop that day (46.77 points).

Closing tick and *closing Arms (trin)* are even finer measures of stock market strength or weakness.

A *tick* is a measure of movement in closing stock prices; a positive (+) tick means prices were rising at the end of the day, and the negative (–) tick indicates falling prices. The closing tick nets all stocks whose last trade was higher than the previous trade (+) on the NYSE against

all stocks whose last trade was lower (–); a "+" closing tick means that more stocks were rising than falling, and a "–" closing tick means that more stocks were falling than rising. On January 19, 1995, 139 more stocks were falling than at their last trade, and so the closing tick for the day was –139.

The *Arms index (trin)*, named for Richard W. Arms, Jr., its creator, measures market strength. A trin less than one indicates money flowing into stocks (bullish sign), while a trin greater than one (1.18 on January 19, 1995) indicates money flowing out of stocks (bearish sign). The Arms index is computed by dividing two ratios:

$$\frac{\dfrac{\text{Advances}}{\text{Declines}}}{\dfrac{\text{Advance volume}}{\text{Decline volume}}} = \frac{\dfrac{748}{1{,}423}}{\dfrac{78{,}684}{175{,}916}} = \frac{0.52565}{0.442816} = 1.1752 = \text{Arms index}$$

DIARIES

NYSE	THU	WED	WK AGO	
Issues traded	2,958	2,957	2,944	
Advances	748	1,061	1,128	Declining issues nearly
Declines	1,423	1,171	1,057	◄— doubled advances
Unchanged	787	725	759	
New highs	38	54	27	
New lows	38	26	61	
zAdv vol (000)	78,684	133,491	145,241	
zDecl vol (000)	175,916	169,187	119,366	Negative (–) tick indicates more
zTotal vol (000)	297,757	344,568	312,508	stocks declined than advanced
Closing tick[1]	–139	+251	+354	◄— in last trade
Closing Arms[2] (trin)	1.18	1.15	.88	◄— Arms index of more than one
zBlock trades	6,820	7,289	7,307	indicates selling pressure

Source: *The Wall Street Journal*, January 20, 1995. Reprinted by permission of *The Wall Street Journal*, ©1995 Dow Jones & Company, Inc. All rights reserved worldwide.

In this example, a trin of more than one indicates that the (denominator) ratio of the volume of advancing stocks to declining stocks (78,684/175,916) was less than the (numerator) ratio of advancing stocks to declining stocks (748/1,423), *and, therefore, a disproportionate share of the trading volume was in declining stocks (a bearish sign).* A trin of less than one would indicate the opposite.

This example, drawn from the January 20, 1995 *Journal*, is complex because it employs actual trading data for January 19, 1995. Consider, instead, the simple hypothetical examples on the next page. The first illustrates a bull (rising) market, the second a bear (falling) market.

Use hypothetical numbers of your own to create additional examples. This will establish your understanding of the Arms index.

Bull Market

$$\frac{\dfrac{\text{Advances}}{\text{Declines}}}{\dfrac{\text{Advance volume}}{\text{Decline volume}}} = \frac{\dfrac{1}{1}}{\dfrac{2}{1}} = \frac{1}{2}$$

Although advances and declines were equal, advance volume was twice decline volume, and, therefore, a trin of $\frac{1}{2}$ is a bullish sign.

$$\frac{\dfrac{\text{Advances}}{\text{Declines}}}{\dfrac{\text{Advance volume}}{\text{Decline volume}}} = \frac{\dfrac{1}{2}}{\dfrac{1}{1}} = \frac{1}{2}$$

Although declines exceeded advances, advance volume equaled decline volume, and a trin of $\frac{1}{2}$ remained a bullish sign.

Bear Market

$$\frac{\dfrac{\text{Advances}}{\text{Declines}}}{\dfrac{\text{Advance volume}}{\text{Decline volume}}} = \frac{\dfrac{1}{1}}{\dfrac{1}{2}} = 2$$

Although advances and declines were equal, decline volume was twice advance volume, and, therefore, a trin of 2 is a bearish sign.

$$\frac{\dfrac{\text{Advances}}{\text{Declines}}}{\dfrac{\text{Advance volume}}{\text{Decline volume}}} = \frac{\dfrac{2}{1}}{\dfrac{1}{1}} = 2$$

Although advances exceeded declines, decline volume equaled advance volume, and a trin of 2 remained a bearish sign.

As an investor, you want to know the percentage performance of your stocks. A $1 rise in the price of a stock that you purchased at $100 a share is an event to note, but if you had paid $2 a share for the stock, the same $1 rise is a cause for celebration. In the first case, your investment increased by 1 percent, in the second, by 50 percent. In **Price Percentage Gainers and Losers** (page 170) you can track this daily. On January 19, 1995, DescSAADR lost 18.8% of its value. You may notice that it was a bad day for other ADRs, too. ADRs (American Depository Receipts) will be discussed later in the chapter.

AND LOSERS

NYSE	VOL	CLOSE	CHANGE	% CHG
DescSAADR	55,600	11⅜ −	2⅝ −	18.8
AcmeElec	296,300	16⅝ −	3¼ −	16.4
GenData	1,305,000	30 −	5½ −	15.5
IntlCeram	95,700	16⅛ −	2⅞ −	15.1
BrdwyStore	86,500	5½ −	⅞ −	13.7
TCWDWTermTr	295,500	7⅛ −	1⅛ −	13.6
CGDinaADRL	71,400	3⅝ −	½ −	12.1
TCWDWTr2000	204,000	6½ −	⅞ −	11.9
VitroSA	341,800	11½ −	1⅜ −	10.7
GrupoDesarADRB	128,900	4¼ −	½ −	10.5
CGDinaADR	423,900	5⅜ −	⅝ −	10.4
EmprIcaADR	1,415,000	9⅛ −	1 −	9.9
GrpRadioADR	26,800	10⅛ −	1 −	9.0
GrpTelevADR	2,110,700	22¾ −	2⅛ −	8.5
GrupoSidekB	3,700	6¾ −	⅝ −	8.5
EmprModrnADR	280,900	14 −	1¼ −	8.2
GrpSidekADR	87,600	7⅛ −	⅝ −	8.1
Aracruz	64,400	11⅝ −	1 −	7.9
GrpDurangoADR	4,100	10¼ −	⅞ −	7.9
BufetIndADR	83,400	18¾ −	1½ −	7.4

◄——— DescSAADR loses 18.8% of its value in one day

Volume Percentage Leaders represent the stocks that traded the largest volume of shares on January 19, 1995. The percentage difference refers to the increase in volume over the average for the previous 65 trading days.

The **Breakdown of Trading in NYSE Stocks** on page 171 provides trading volume on all stock exchanges of securities listed on the New York Stock Exchange, as well as trading volume by half-hours. As mentioned earlier in the discussion on how to compile the Dow, shares listed on the NYSE trade on a variety of exchanges as well as electronically, and, therefore, the composite of all trades will be greater than the New York volume. Trading of all NYSE stocks on all exchanges was a composite volume of 361,247,900 shares on January 19, 1995.

Finally, the **Diaries** component of the **Stock Market Data Bank** on page 168 listed the number of stocks that hit new highs and lows (i.e., the number that closed higher or lower than at any time in the past 52 weeks). You saw that on January 19, 1995, 38 reached new highs and 38 reached new lows. **NYSE Highs/Lows** (in the front-page indexes of the first and last sections) lists these stocks. Consider the example on page 171 from the Friday, January 20, 1995 *Journal*.

BREAKDOWN OF TRADING IN NYSE STOCKS (9:30 a.m. to 4 p.m. EST)

BY MARKET	Thur	Wed	WK AGO	½-HOURLY	Thur	Wed	WK AGO
New York	297,756,780	344,567,620	312,508,110	9:30-10	38,540,000	40,420,000	38,780,000
Chicago	13,339,500	15,287,100	13,616,400	10-10:30	28,330,000	33,910,000	29,810,000
Pacific	7,420,800	8,473,100	7,713,100	10:30-11	23,450,000	29,420,000	25,830,000
NASD	27,314,430	29,578,450	28,990,530	11-11:30	22,110,000	29,100,000	25,030,000
Phila	5,149,190	5,167,000	3,752,400	11:30-12	21,230,000	26,830,000	20,050,000
Boston	4,140,100	4,965,000	4,422,900	12-12:30	18,420,000	22,140,000	19,990,000
Cincinnati	6,127,100	6,459,600	5,862,400	12:30-1	17,130,000	14,270,000	16,560,000
Composite	361,247,900	414,497,870	376,865,840	1-1:30	17,010,000	17,080,000	16,250,000
				1:30-2	16,220,000	27,420,000	21,620,000
				2-2:30	15,170,000	18,210,000	20,410,000
				2:30-3	18,710,000	23,080,000	21,250,000
				3-3:30	25,530,000	24,390,000	22,750,000
				3:30-4	35,906,780	38,297,620	34,178,110

NYSE first crossing 141,500 shares, value $978,375 (est.)
Second (basket) 16,159,228 shares, value $726,852,546
‡The net difference of the number of stocks closing higher than their previous trade from those closing lower; NYSE trading only.
‡A comparison of the number of advancing and declining issues with the volume of shares rising and falling. Generally, an Arms of less than 1.00 indicates buying demand; above 1.00 indicates selling pressure.
z-NYSE or Amex only.

NYSE HIGHS/LOWS

Thursday, January 19, 1995

NEW HIGHS — 38

AlcoStd	CptrAssoc	Loctite	SPS Tech
AlexBrown	Continuum	LoneStar n	SiliconGrph
AlleghanyCp	CoramHlthcr n	MGIC Inv	SunHlthcr
AmHotel	CorrctnCp	McKesson n	TomHilfiger s
BectonDksn	CorrctnCp wt	MicronTech s	TrigenEngy n
Belo AH A	GA PwCp pfA n	NetwkEqpt	Unifi
Bowtr dp pfB n	HewlettPk	Olin pfA	UnoRestr
CMAC	IdexCp	ParkerHan	WyleLabs
Ceridian	ItelCp	Pfizer	Zeneca
Ceridian dep pf		SCI Fin n	

NEW LOWS — 38

AmericusInc n	EK ChorChina	GrpRadioADR	PubSvcEG pfJ
AustriaFd	EQK Rlty	Hibernia	Reedlnt n
BCE Inc	EdisonBros	IntegraFnl	SpartonCp
BankBost pfC	ElPasoGas	IntlCeram n	StrtGlob
BrdwyStore	Elcor	Kellwood s	StrideRite
BrdwyStore wt	FdltyAdvKor n	LAGear	TCW TmT
CabotO&G	Fleming	Minn P&L	TCW T2000
DescSA ADR n	GrrityOil dp pf n	NYSE&G pf	ToysRUs
CG DinaADR	GrpDrgADR n	Ogden pf	TurkishFd
CG DnADR L n		PatrickPete	

s-Split or stock dividend of 25 percent or more in the past 52 weeks. High-low range is adjusted from old stock. n-New issue in past 52 weeks and does not cover the entire 52 week period.

ODD-LOT TRADING

NEW YORK – The New York Stock Exchange specialists reported the following odd-lot transactions (in shares):

	Customer Purchases	Short Sales	Other Sales	Total Sales
January 18, 1995	963,715	83,931	1,421,870	1,505,801

Odd-lot sales exceeded odd-lot purchases

THE ODD-LOT TRADER

So far this discussion has proceeded without regard to the magnitude of individual investments, except for the observation that companies split their stock chiefly in order to keep its price within the small investor's reach. Remember that round lots are trades of 100 shares whose commission per share is lower than that on *odd-lot* (less than 100 shares) transactions. Yet many small investors still trade in odd lots because they cannot afford to deal in round lots. For instance, Alcoa closed at $88.38 on Wednesday, January 18, 1995, putting the cost of a round-lot purchase at $8,837.50 ($88.375 multiplied by 100) and out of the reach of many small investors. See page 173.

Many market analysts used to believe that odd-lot transactions were a contrary (negative) indicator, because they saw the small investor as a market follower who buys more as the market peaks and sells more as it bottoms out (the opposite of the savvy, big time trader who gets in at the bottom and out at the top). Therefore, according to this wisdom, a high ratio of odd-lot buying to selling is a sign of a market peak (time to sell), while the opposite indicates a market trough (time to buy). However, since a great many small investors in recent years have abandoned odd-lots in favor of mutual funds, this omen has become less significant to analysts.

The Journal provides a daily record of **Odd-Lot Trading** for the day preceding the previous trading day. You'll find it beneath NYSE Highs/Lows. See the example on page 171 from the Friday, January 20, 1995 issue that indicated sales of 1,505,801 and purchases of 963,715 on January 18, 1995. According to the contrarian wisdom outlined above, this was a *buy* signal for the savvy investor.

A more detailed report appears on Mondays (also beneath NYSE Highs/Lows). See for yourself when examining the **Odd-Lot Trading** report from the Monday, February 13, 1995 *Wall Street Journal* on page 173. Odd-lot sales (1,329,626 shares) exceeded odd-lot purchases (987,503) on Thursday, February 9, 1995 in NYSE trading by odd-lot specialists, and orders to sell plus short sales (6,466,122 + 301,332 = 6,767,454) exceeded orders to buy (4,826,456) by all NYSE member firms for the week ended Friday, January 27, 1995.

29½	22⅝ ♣ Allstate	ALL	.72	3.0	19	2012	24⅜	24	24⅜	...
31⅜	24	ALLTEL	AT	.96f	3.1	20	2280	30¾	30⅜	30½ – ⅛
7½	4⅝	Allwaste	ALW	...	15	1335	5⅝	5½	5⅝	...
35	21⅝	Alumax	AMX	...	dd	4421	29	28⅜	28½ – ⅜	
90¼	64¼ ♣ Alcoa	AA	1.60a	1.8	18	4054	88½	87	88⅜ +1¼	◄
28⅞	17	Alza	AZA	...	48	4827	21⅜	20¾	21¼ + ¼	
8¼	4¾	AmaxGold	AU	.06j	...	dd	3380	5½	5¼	5½ + ¼

Cost of a round-lot
purchase:
$8,837.50
($88.375 × 100)

ODD-LOT TRADING

NEW YORK – The New York Stock Exchange specialists reported the following odd-lot transactions (in shares):

	Customer Purchases	Short Sales	Other Sales	Total Sales
February 9, 1995	987,503	58,503	1,271,123	1,329,626

New York Stock Exchange odd-lot trading for all member firms dealing in odd-lots, for the week ended January 27, 1995:

	Shares	Values
Customers' Orders to Buy	4,826,456	$189,482,258
Customers' Orders to Sell	6,466,122	$232,339,748
Customers' Short Sales	301,332	$12,416,832

Round-Lot transactions (in shares) for the week ended January 27, 1995:

	Purchases	Sales (incl. Short Sales)	Short Sales
Total	1,621,857,570	1,621,857,570	113,452,180
For Member Accounts:			
As Specialists-a,b	128,857,620	129,503,180	40,204,700
As Floor Traders	1,370,800	1,579,900	464,200
Others-a	197,650,080	186,851,625	19,510,380

a-Including offsetting round-lot transactions arising from odd-lot dealer activity by specialists and other members.
b-Includes transactions effected by members acting as Registered Competitive Market Makers.

American Stock Exchange round-lot and odd-lot trading statistics for the week ended January 27, 1995:

	Purchases	Sales (incl. Short Sales)	Short Sales
Total	83,056,680	83,056,680	3,405,183
For Member Accounts:			
As Specialists	8,173,945	8,403,530	1,506,660
As Floor Traders	329,400	398,800	182,800
Others	3,714,176	3,797,519	261,300
Customer odd-lots	293,758	174,793	....

Odd-lot sales exceeded odd-lot purchases on February 9, 1995, and odd-lot orders to sell exceeded odd-lot orders to buy for the week ended January 27, 1995

FOLLOW YOUR STOCK

Suppose now that you have studied the various stock market indicators and indexes, decided that the time was right to get into the market, and did

so. You will want to follow the progress of your investment. Here's how you do it.

If you own shares of British Petroleum, you can follow their daily performance in *The Wall Street Journal* by turning to **New York Stock Exchange Composite Transactions**. Recall that this composite report includes a small amount of trading activity on regional exchanges. You'll find a reference to all exchanges in the index on the front pages of the first (A1) and third (C1) sections.

In the accompanying Thursday, January 19, 1995 excerpts (pages 175 and 176), the first and second columns tell you the highest and lowest value of one share of the stock in the past 52 weeks, expressed in dollars and fractions of a dollar. **British Petroleum** stock was as low as $58.375 (58⅜) and as high as $85.25 (85¼) in the year preceding January 18, 1995.

Footnotes and symbols, including arrows and underlining, are fully explained in the box on the lower left of the first page of the Composite listings.

The third and fourth columns give the company name and stock ticker symbol (**BP**).

The fifth column of data reports the latest annual cash dividend of $2.21 per share. The dividend is expressed as a percentage of the closing price in the next column ($2.21 ÷ $79.125 = 2.79 percent, rounded to 2.8 percent).

The seventh column shows the price-earnings (P/E) ratio, which is obtained by dividing the price of the stock by its earnings per share. (This important statistic is discussed in detail in Chapter 8.) On January 18, British Petroleum's stock was worth 22 times the profits per share of stock.

The eighth column informs you of the number of shares traded that day, expressed in hundreds of shares: 352,300 shares of British Petroleum traded on January 18, 1995. If a *z* appears before the number in this column, the figure represents the actual number (not hundreds) of shares traded.

The ninth, tenth, and eleventh columns reveal the stock's highest, lowest, and closing (last) price for the trading day. On Wednesday, January 18, 1995, British Petroleum stock traded as high as 79⅝ and as low as 79, before closing at 79⅛.

The last column provides the change in the closing price of the stock from the price at the close of the previous day. You can see that this stock closed at a price 62.5 cents (⅝ of a dollar) lower than the previous closing price.

NEW YORK STOCK EXCHANGE COMPOSITE TRANSACTIONS

Quotations as of 5 p.m. Eastern Time
Wednesday, January 18, 1995

	52 Weeks Hi	Lo	Stock	Sym	Div	Yld %	PE	Vol 100s	Hi	Lo	Close	Net Chg
	33⅝	23	♣Acordia	ACO	.60	1.8	17	21	32⅞	32½	32⅝	– ⅛
	13¾	5¾	ActavaGp	ACT	.09j	...	dd	463	9⅛	8¾	9⅛	+ ⅜
	18⅜	11¼	Acuson	ACN		...	26	1128	16	15⅝	15⅞	+ ¼
	18⅜	15⅜	AdamsExp	ADX	1.60e	10.0	...	220	16⅛	16	16	...
n	19¾	16⅞	PensnProvdSA ADR	PVD		...	...	100	18	17¾	17¾	– ¼
	32¼	18½	AdvMicro	AMD		...	11	23406	32¼	31½	32⅛	+ ⅝
	64½	48⅜	AdvMicro pf		3.00	4.7	...	279	64½	63	63¾	+ ¼
	6⅞	5	Advest	ADV		...	15	113	5⅜	5¼	5¼	– ⅛
	20	15	Advo	AD	.10	.6	17	105	18	17¾	17¾	...
n▲	13¾	8¼	Advocat	AVC		...	...	133	13⅞	13⅝	13⅞	+ ⅛
	66⅛	49⅜	AEGON NV	AEG	2.21e	3.4	11	7	65	65	65	– ⅛
	5	3⅜	♣Aeroflex	ARX		...	12	357	3 29/32	3¾	3 29/32	...
n	26⅜	25	AetnaMIPS pfA		.25e	1.0	...	532	26⅜	26	26¼	+ ⅛
	65¾	42¼	AetnaLife	AET	2.76	5.4	dd	1915	50⅞	50¼	50⅞	+ ⅜
	14¾	8¼	♣AgnicoEgl	AEM	.10	1.0	...	532	10¼	9⅞	9⅞	...
n	19⅝	14⅝	AgreeRlty	ADC	1.80	11.3	...	26	15⅞	15⅞	15⅞	...
	22¾	15¼	Ahmanson	AHM	.88	5.2	10	2282	17	16⅝	17	+ ⅛
	27¼	22⅛	Ahmanson pfC		2.10	8.6	...	189	24½	24⅛	24⅜	...
	52	39¾	Ahmanson pfD		3.00	7.2	...	22	41⅝	41½	41⅝	+ ⅛
	28¼	24½	Ahmanson pf		2.40	9.4	...	30	25¾	25½	25½	– ¼
	31	24	AholdADR	AHO	.61e	2.0	...	199	30⅞	30⅜	30⅜	– ⅜
	3⅝	13/16	vjAileen	AEE		...	...	245	⅞	13/16	⅞	+ 1/16
	50⅜	38¾	AirProduct	APD	.98	2.1	23	1570	46⅝	46¼	46⅜	– ¼
	39⅞	18	AirbornFrght	ABF	.30	1.3	11	990	22⅝	22⅛	22⅜	+ ½
	29⅞	19⅝	♣Airgas	ARG		...	31	899	25⅜	24½	25	+ ½
	17	10⅞	Airlease	FLY	1.88	13.0	11	30	14⅝	14½	14½	...
	30⅝	19⅞	AirTouch	ATI		...	...	13258	28¼	27¾	28¼	...
	26⅞	22	AlaPwr pfA		1.90	8.2	...	24	23¼	23⅛	23⅛	+ ¼
n	23½	18⅜	AlaPwr pfC		1.60	7.9	...	1	20¼	20¼	20¼	+ ¼
	26½	21⅞	AlaPwr pfH		1.90	8.2	...	22	23¼	23¼	23¼	...
	25	18	AlaPwr pfB		1.70	8.4	...	8	20¼	20⅛	20⅛	– ⅛
	18⅞	13⅛	AlaskaAir	ALK	.05j	...	28	1373	15⅛	14⅞	15⅛	...
	21¼	16⅛	♣AlbanyInt	AIN	.35	1.8	26	548	19⅝	19⅜	19½	+ ⅛
n	17⅝	12½	Albemarle	ALB	.20	1.4	...	485	14⅜	13½	13⅞	– ⅜
	27½	19⅜	♣AlbertoCl	ACV	.28	1.1	17	38	26½	26⅜	26⅜	– ⅛
	24⅞	17¾	♣AlbertoCl A	ACVA	.28	1.2	15	90	23⅝	23⅜	23½	...
	30⅞	25⅛	Albertsons	ABS	.44	1.5	19	2286	29⅞	29¼	29½	– ½
	28⅛	19¾	Alcan	AL	.30	1.1	79	4714	27⅛	26½	27	+ ⅜
	26⅝	15⅜	AlcatelAsthom	ALA	.53e	3.0	...	1022	18	17¾	17⅞	...
	67⅜	49½	AlcoStd	ASN	1.00	1.5	51	1163	67¼	66¼	66¼	–1⅛
▲	32⅜	23¼	♣AlexBrown	AB	.70	2.1	6	418	32⅞	32⅛	32¾	+ ⅝
	22¾	14	Alex&Alex	AAL	.10	.5	dd	510	20⅞	20⅛	20¾	+ ¼
	58¾	48⅞	Alexanders	ALX		...	9	14	50½	50¼	50¼	– ¼
	14⅝	11⅛	AllAmTerm	AAT	1.20a	10.0	...	142	12	11⅞	12	...
	152⅞	136¾	AlleghanyCp	.Y	t	...	10	46	152⅞	151½	152	– ½
	24⅝	17	AllegLud	ALS	.48	2.4	83	278	20¼	19⅞	20	– ⅜
	25¾	19¾	AllegPwr	AYP	1.64	7.3	12	540	22¾	22½	22½	– ⅛
	25⅝	13½	AllenGp	ALN	.20f	.8	22	1008	25⅛	24⅛	24⅞	– ⅜
	30⅞	20	Allergan	AGN	.44	1.6	17	1091	27⅞	27⅛	27⅞	+ ⅛
n	20	15½	AllncAll	AMO	.25p	...	...	92	17¼	17	17¼	+ ⅛
	26⅞	16½	AllncCapMgt	AC	1.64	8.8	11	211	18¾	18½	18⅝	...
	7¼	4⅜	AllncEntn	CDS		...	...	427	5⅝	5⅜	5½	...
	1¾	5/32	AllncEntn wtB			...	...	25	⅜	⅜	⅜	...
	10½	8⅝	AllncGlblEnv	AEF		...	...	64	9⅛	9	9	...
	16⅛	8⅞	AllianceWrld II	AWF	1.42a	12.9	...	1685	11	10¾	11	...
	19½	9⅞	AllianceWrld	AWG	1.68a	15.1	...	410	11¼	10¾	11⅛	+ ⅜
	40⅝	21¾	AlliantTech	ATK		...	47	262	38¼	37	37⅜	– ⅞
	27⅝	21½	AlldIrishBk	AIB	1.17e	4.7	...	7	24¾	24¾	24¾	...
	29¼	25½	AlldIrishBk pf		2.97	11.2	...	36	26½	26⅜	26½	...
	17⅜	12	AlliedPdts	ADP		...	10	462	15⅞	15¼	15⅝	– ¼
s	40⅝	30⅜	AlliedSgnl	ALD	.67	1.9	14	3917	36¼	35¾	36⅛	...
	20¾	14¼	♣AllmrPC	APY	.16	.9	11	293	18⅝	18½	18½	...
	11⅜	8¾	AllmrST	ALM	.84a	8.7	...	24	9¾	9⅝	9⅝	...
	10¼	8¼	AllmonTr	GSO	.57e	6.4	...	542	9	8⅞	8⅞	– ⅛
	29½	22⅝	♣Allstate	ALL	.72	3.0	19	2012	24⅜	24	24⅜	...
	31⅜	24	ALLTEL	AT	.96f	3.1	20	2280	30¾	30⅜	30½	– ⅛
	7½	4⅝	Allwaste	ALW		...	15	1335	5⅝	5½	5⅝	...
	35	21⅝	Alumax	AMX		...	dd	4421	29	28⅜	28½	– ⅜
	90¼	64¼	♣Alcoa	AA	1.60a	1.8	18	4054	88½	87	88⅜	+1¼
	28⅞	17	Alza	AZA		...	48	4827	21⅜	20¾	21¼	+ ¼
	8¼	4¾	AmaxGold	AU	.06j	...	dd	3380	5½	5¼	5½	+ ¼

	52 Weeks Hi	Lo	Stock	Sym	Div	Yld %	PE	Vol 100s	Hi	Lo	Close	Net Chg
	10¾	8⅛	BlkrkMuni	BMT	.62	6.8	...	209	9⅛	9	9⅛	+ ⅛
	15⅜	11¼	BlkrkMuni2008	BRM	.89	6.8	...	197	13⅛	13	13⅛	...
	14¼	9⅝	BlackrockInvQty	BKN	.90	8.0	...	782	11⅜	11⅛	11¼	+ ⅛
	9⅜	6⅝	BlackRockInv	BQT	.65	9.1	...	205	7¼	7⅛	7⅛	– ⅛
	10⅞	8¼	BlackRockMuni	BMN	.62	6.7	...	905	9¼	9⅛	9¼	+ ⅛
	15⅝	11⅝	BlkrkNY2008	BLN	.86	6.5	...	73	13¼	13⅛	13¼	...
	12⅜	8⅛	BlackRockNoAm	BNA	1.05	12.4	...	617	8⅝	8½	8½	...
	9¾	6⅝	BlackRockStrat	BGT	.62	8.6	...	477	7⅜	7⅛	7¼	...
	10	7⅞	BlackRockTgt	BTT	.65	7.9	...	969	8⅜	8¼	8¼	– ⅛
	10⅛	7⅞	BlackRock1998	BBT	.58	6.8	...	1012	8½	8⅜	8½	+ ⅛
	9⅞	7⅛	BlackRock1999	BNN	.58	7.5	...	525	7⅞	7¾	7¾	– ⅛
	9⅜	7	BlackRock2001	BLK	.58	7.9	...	1157	7½	7⅜	7⅜	– ⅛
	23	15¾	♣BlanchHldg	EWB	.32	1.5	18	9	21⅜	21⅜	21⅜	+ ⅛
	48¾	33	BlockHR	HRB	1.25	3.6	19	5510	35	34¾	35	...
	8⅜	6	BluChipValFd	BLU	.75e	11.8	...	130	6½	6⅜	6⅜	– ¼
n	29⅛	18¼	BlythInd	BTH		...	...	1	28⅛	28⅛	28⅛	– ¼
	50⅛	42⅛	Boeing	BA	1.00	2.0	17	8948	49¾	49⅛	49¼	– ⅜
▲	30⅝	19	BoiseCasc	BCC	.60	2.0	dd	8559	30¾	29½	30	+ ⅛
	27¾	23⅜	BoiseCasc depF		2.35	9.3	...	56	25½	25	25⅜	+ ¼
	26¾	19	BoiseCasc depG		1.58	6.0	...	234	26⅛	25¾	26⅛	+ ½
	21½	10	BoltBerNew	BBN		...	dd	2515	15⅞	15	15⅝	+ ⅝
	32¾	8⅝	Bombay	BBA		...	16	2120	9⅛	8⅞	8⅞	– ⅛
	26⅜	10	BordChm un	BCU	1.88e	7.6	12	2584	24¾	24	24¾	– ¼
	15¾	11	BordenInc	BN	.04m	.3	dd	3603	13⅜	13	13⅛	+ ⅛
	34	21⅝	BorgWarAuto	BWA	.60	2.4	10	73	25¾	24⅞	24⅞	– ⅞
	21⅞	8¼	BorgWarner	BOR		...	...	33	9⅞	9¾	9⅞	+ ⅛
	24⅛	18½	BostCelts	BOS	1.50e	7.0	9	14	21½	21⅛	21⅜	...
	29⅛	21½	BostEdsn	BSE	1.82f	7.5	10	267	24⅜	24¼	24¼	...
	26½	22	BostEdsn pfA		2.06	8.7	...	42	23¾	23¼	23¾	+ ⅜
	26	20½	BostEdsn pfB		1.94	8.3	...	17	23⅞	23½	23½	...
	19⅛	12	BostonSci	BSX		...	24	1979	18½	18¼	18⅜	...
▲	29⅝	20⅜	Bowater	BOW	.60	2.0	dd	4843	30	28¾	30	+1⅜
n	27¼	21	Bowater dep pfB		1.65	6.2	...	76	26¾	26⅝	26¾	+ ½
n	25⅜	20½	Bowater dep pfC		2.10	9.0	...	49	24½	23¼	23¼	+ ⅜
	19⅜	10½	BoydGaming	BYD		...	49	24	11⅜	11⅛	11⅜	...
	17¼	10½	Bradlees	BLE	.60	5.3	6	149	11⅜	11¼	11⅜	+ ⅛
s	19¼	13⅝	Bradley R E	BTR	1.32f	8.6	16	39	15½	15⅜	15⅜	– ⅛
	36⅞	18¾	BrazilFd	BZF	2.46e	8.4	...	597	30	29⅛	29⅛	– ¾
s	23½	12½	BrazEqtyFd	BZL	3.83e	19.1	...	303	20⅝	19⅞	20	– ½
	44	17⅛	♣BreedTech	BDT	.10e	.4	13	6186	26⅜	25	25⅜	– ½
s	45⅛	30½	BriggsStrat	BGG	1.00	3.1	9	745	33⅞	32½	32⅝	– ⅞
	17¼	7½	BrillAuto	CBA	.08	1.0	...	120	8¼	8⅛	8¼	...
s	33⅝	15	BrinkerInt	EAT		...	22	2675	20⅜	19⅝	20⅛	– ¼
	61	50	BrisMyrsSqb	BMY	2.96f	5.0	15	7834	59⅝	59	59⅜	+ ⅛
	74⅛	54⅞	BritAir	BAB	1.49e	2.5	...	271	60⅛	59¾	59¾	...
	54⅛	39	BritGas	BRG	2.80e	5.7	...	30	48¾	48¾	48¾	+ ½
	85¼	58⅜	BritPetrol	BP	2.21e	2.8	22	3523	79⅝	79	79⅛	– ⅝
n	25¼	22⅞	BritSkyBdcst	BSY		...	...	4652	24⅛	24	24⅛	+ ⅛
	27¼	18⅛	BritSteel	BST	.69e	2.8	...	2571	24⅝	24⅜	24⅝	+ ⅝
	71¾	53⅞	♣BritishTele	BTY	3.29e	5.2	...	1888	63⅜	62¾	63	+ ¾
▼	**13¼**	**6⅝**	**BrdwyStore**	**BWY**		**...**	**dd**	**2732**	**6⅝**	**6⅜**	**6⅜**	**– ⅜**
	4½	**1¾**	**BrdwyStore wt**			**...**	**...**	**110**	**1⅞**	**1¾**	**1⅞**	**– ⅛**
	62⅜	45	BrokenHill	BHP	1.34e	2.3	...	58	59½	59¼	59½	+ ¾
	5⅜	1¼	BrookeGp	BGL		...	1	133	3¾	3⅝	3⅝	...
	28¼	21½	♣BklynUnGas	BU	1.39f	6.1	12	301	22⅝	22½	22⅝	...
	8	5¼	BrownShrp	BNS		...	dd	14	6⅝	6½	6½	– ¼
	38⅞	29¾	BrownGp	BG	1.60	5.3	dd	253	30¼	30	30⅛	– ⅛
s	32¼	26¾	♣BrownFormn A	BFA	.99f	3.3	15	13	30⅜	30⅛	30¼	...
s	32½	26⅛	♣BrownFormn B	BFB	.99f	3.2	15	576	30⅞	30⅜	30¾	– ⅛
	32⅞	24¼	♣BrownFer	BFI	.68	2.3	20	3977	30⅛	29¾	29⅞	– ¼
	25⅜	17	♣Brunswick	BC	.44	2.2	18	4982	20½	20⅛	20⅜	+ ⅛
	18⅝	13½	BrushWell	BW	.32	2.1	14	197	15⅞	15½	15½	– ½
	41	30⅞	♣BuckeyePtr	BPL	2.80	7.9	9	37	35⅞	35¼	35¼	– ½
	49¼	26½	BuenosAirADR	BAE	.46e	1.4	...	245	34½	33½	33⅞	– ⅝
	54¾	18¼	BufetIndADR	GBI	.09p	...	...	214	20½	19¾	20¼	– ¼
	28⅜	9¾	BurlgtnCoat	BCF		...	10	1242	10¼	9⅞	9⅞	– ⅜
	17⅛	9¼	BurlgtnInd	BUR		...	10	1353	10½	10¼	10⅜	– ⅛
	66⅝	46½	BurlgtnNthn	BNI	1.20	2.3	13	8972	54⅛	52¾	52¾	+ ⅛
	75	52⅞	BurlgtnNthn pfA		3.13	5.3	...	609	59⅞	58¾	59¼	+1¼
	25	14⅛	BurlngtnRes	BRU	1.88e	11.0	...	231	17⅜	17	17⅛	– ⅛
	49⅝	33⅛	BurlgtnRes	BR	.55	1.6	29	4709	35⅛	34⅜	35	+ ⅞
	19⅛	12⅝	BurnhmPacif	BPP	1.44	11.2	14	1001	13¼	12⅞	12⅞	– ⅛
n	27	15¼	BushBoake	BOA		...	...	336	25⅛	24¾	25	+ ⅛
	33⅜	17	BushInd	BSH	.08	.4	13	184	20¼	20	20⅛	+ ⅛

← British Petroleum

Source: *The Wall Street Journal*, January 19, 1995. Reprinted by permission of *The Wall Street Journal*,

	61	50	BrisMyrsSqb	BMY	2.96f	5.0	15	7834	59⅝	59	59⅜	+	
	74⅛	54⅞	BritAir	BAB	1.49e	2.5	...	271	60⅛	59¾	59¾		
	54⅛	39	BritGas	BRG	2.80e	5.7	...	30	48¾	48¾	48¾	+	
	85¼	58⅜	BritPetrol	BP	2.21e	2.8	22	3523	79⅝	79	79⅛	–	◄— British Petroleum
n	25¼	22⅞	BritSkyBdcst	BSY		...	...	4652	24⅛	24	24⅛	+	
	27¼	18⅛	BritSteel	BST	.69e	2.8	...	2571	24⅝	24⅜	24⅝	+	
	71¾	53⅞ ♣	BritishTele	BTY	3.29e	5.2	...	1888	63⅜	62¾	63	+	
▼	**13¼**	**6⅝**	**BrdwyStore**	**BWY**		...	**dd**	**2732**	**6⅝**	**6⅜**	**6⅜**	–	

British Petroleum

Source: *The Wall Street Journal*, January 19, 1995. Reprinted by permission of *The Wall Street Journal*,

You may wonder why share prices are quoted with figures such as ⅛, which must be converted into fractions of a cent. Because trading is usually conducted in round lots of 100 shares, and payment for a round lot eliminates the problem. For instance, $79\frac{1}{8} \times 100 = \$7{,}912.50$.

Shares of other companies, usually smaller than those listed on the NYSE, trade on the American Stock Exchange (AMEX). *The Wall Street Journal*'s AMEX report, called **American Stock Exchange Composite Transactions**, is identical in form to **NYSE Composite Transactions**.

Over-the-counter (OTC) stocks are not traded on an exchange. Instead, dealers have established a market for them using a computer network referred to as NASDAQ (National Association of Securities Dealers Automated Quotations). You can follow this market in **NASDAQ National Market Issues**, which is similar to the New York and American Exchange listings. Take a look at the reprint from the Thursday, January 19, 1995 *Journal* (on pages 177 and 179), using **Apple Computer (AAPL)** as an example.

The first two columns give the high and low prices for the past year. The column after the price-earnings ratio lists sales in hundreds, informing you that 1,139,800 shares of Apple Computer traded on Wednesday, January 18, 1995.

The next three columns provide the high (45⅝), low (44¾), and closing (45⅝) prices of the day, and the final column tells you that Apple Computer's stock closed at a price \$0.63 higher than its price at the previous close.

Smaller companies with smaller capitalizations are listed as **NASDAQ Small-Cap Issues** and show trading volume, closing price, and price change only (see page 178).

With this information, you can track the performance of any share of stock traded on the New York or American exchanges or the OTC market.

NASDAQ NATIONAL MARKET ISSUES

Quotations as of 4 p.m. Eastern Time
Wednesday, January 18, 1995

	52 Weeks Hi	Lo	Stock	Sym	Div	Yld %	PE	Vol 100s	Hi	Lo	Close	Net Chg
	18 1/4	9	AAON Inc	AAON		...	18	139	14 1/4	13 3/4	13 3/4	...
n	14	12	ABC Bcp	ABCB	.29e	2.4	...	92	12 5/8	12	12	- 1/4
	23 1/4	15 3/4	ABC RailPdt	ABCR		...	20	15	21 3/4	21 1/2	21 1/2	...
n	20 1/4	10 1/4	ABR InfoSvc	ABRX		...	...	116	19	18 1/2	18 1/2	- 1/2
	16 3/4	11	ABS Ind	ABSI	.20	1.7	13	22	12	12	12	+ 1/4
	30	11 7/8	ABT BldgPdt	ABTC		...	8	58	14 1/2	13 3/4	13 3/4	- 1/4
	26 1/4	12 3/4	ACC	ACCC	.12	.8	dd	139	15 3/4	15	15 1/4	...
	22 1/2	**5 1/2**	**ACS Ent**	**ACSE**		...	**dd**	**1341**	**11 1/4**	**9 1/4**	**10**	+ 1/2
	40 3/4	31 1/4	ACX Tch	ACXT		...	30	284	40 1/4	39 1/2	39 3/4	+ 1/4
	50 3/4	31 3/4	ADC Tel	ADCT		...	34	1758	50	47 1/4	49 3/4	+2 1/8
	16 1/4	10 3/4	ADESA	SOLD		...	22	1000	15 3/4	15 1/4	15 1/2	+ 1/8
n	46 3/4	20 5/8	ADTRAN Inc	ADTN		...	...	721	44 1/2	43 1/2	44 1/4	+1 1/4
	10 1/4	7	AEL Ind A	AELNA		...	23	1	9 3/4	9 3/4	9 3/4	...
	21	12 1/4	AEP Ind	AEPI	.08	.4	12	9	18 1/4	17 1/2	18 1/4	+ 3/4
	10 1/2	3 5/8	AER EngyRes	AERN		...	...	237	5 3/8	4 5/8	5	- 1/4
n	17 1/4	8 7/8	AES China A	CHGNF		...	...	1258	9 1/2	9	9 3/8	- 1/8
s	24 1/2	15 3/4	♣AES Cp	AESC	.67b	3.7	17	1214	18 1/2	17 3/4	18	- 1/2
	17 3/4	10	AFC Cable	AFCX		...	...	168	13 1/4	12 1/2	12 1/2	...
	31 1/2	24 7/8	AMCOR Ltd	AMCRY	.99e	3.5	...	4	28	28	28	- 1/2
	31 1/4	17 3/4	APS Hldg	APSI		...	11	46	27	26 3/4	26 3/4	- 1/2
	9 3/4	1 3/4	A PealnPod	APOD		...	dd	271	2 3/4	2 1/2	2 5/8	- 1/8
	15 3/8	7 1/2	A+ Comm	ACOM		...	dd	176	13 1/4	12 3/4	13 1/4	...
	7 1/4	2 3/8	ARI Netwk	ARIS		...	dd	7	2 7/8	2 13/16	2 13/16	+ 1/16
	33	10 3/8	AST Rsrch	ASTA		...	cc	2787	15 1/2	15	15 3/16	- 3/16
	6	3 1/8	ATSMed	ATSI		...	cc	54	4 1/8	3 7/8	4 1/8	...
	3 3/8	13/16	AW Cptr A	AWCSA		...	dd	17	1 1/2	1 5/16	1 5/16	- 1/16
	10 3/4	7	AamesFnl	AAMS	.30	3.6	8	944	8 3/4	8 1/4	8 5/8	+ 1/8
	15 3/4	**11**	**AaronRents**	**ARONA**	**.04m**	**.3**	**11**	**6**	**12 1/4**	**12 1/4**	**12 1/4**	-1
n	8 7/8	7 1/4	AascheTransp	ASHE		...	...	191	8 1/2	8	8 1/2	+ 1/8
	11 1/2	**3**	**Abaxis**	**ABAX**		...	...	**260**	**3 5/8**	**3 3/8**	**3 7/16**	- 3/16
	29 1/2	14 1/2	AbbeyHlthcr	ABBY		...	38	1790	25 1/2	24 1/2	24 9/16	-1 1/16
	19 1/4	10 1/4	AbingtnSav	ABBK	.40	2.9	10	66	13 3/4	13 1/2	13 3/4	+ 1/4
	9	**4**	**Abiomed**	**ABMD**		...	**dd**	**19**	**5 1/4**	**5 1/4**	**5 1/4**	- 5/16
n	16 5/8	5 5/8	AbleTelecom	ABTE		...	...	1007	8	7 11/16	8	+ 1/4
	13 1/2	9	AbraxasPete	AXAS		...	dd	209	9 3/8	9 1/4	9 3/8	- 3/8
	22 3/8	7 1/2	AccessHlth	ACCS		...	dd	558	17 1/4	16 3/4	17 1/4	+ 1/4
	27 1/4	12 7/8	AcclmEntn	AKLM		...	13	8174	14 5/8	14	14 3/8	- 1/4
n	14 5/8	10 5/8	AccuStaff	ASTF		...	...	373	14 1/4	13 3/4	14 1/4	+ 3/8
	13	5 3/4	♣AceCashExp	AACE		...	16	5	8 3/4	8 3/4	8 3/4	...
	17 1/2	13 1/4	Aceto	ACET	.36f	2.6	10	12	14	13 3/4	14	- 1/2
	10	8 1/4	Acmat A	ACMTA		...	8	12	9 3/8	9 1/4	9 1/4	- 1/8
	27 1/4	15	AcmeMetals	ACME		...	7	229	19 1/4	18 3/4	19 1/4	+ 1/2
	14 1/2	7 1/4	Actel	ACTL		...	...	604	10	9 5/8	9 3/4	...
	6 1/8	3 7/16	ActionPerf	ACTN		...	...	1764	5 1/4	4 7/8	5 1/4	+ 1/8
	1 3/16	7/16	ActionPerf wt			...	...	67	7/8	55/64	7/8	+ 3/32
	24 3/4	15 7/8	ActiveVoice	ACVC		...	22	116	22 1/2	21 3/4	21 3/4	- 3/4
s▲	15 1/2	9 1/4	Acxiom	ACXM		...	24	1521	16	14 3/4	15 3/4	+ 1/2
	13 1/2	6 1/8	AdacLabs	ADAC	.48	5.7	8	547	8 1/2	7 3/4	8 3/8	+ 3/8
	7	4 1/4	Adage	ADGE		...	29	13	5	5	5	...
s▲	**25 1/8**	**14**	**Adaptec**	**ADPT**		...	**19**	**83636**	**30**	**27 7/8**	**29 5/8**	+5 1/8
	19 3/4	8	AddintnRes	ADDR		...	dd	63	11 1/2	11 1/8	11 1/2	+ 3/8
	23 1/4	8 1/4	AdelphiaComm	ADLAC		...	dd	134	10 1/8	9 3/4	10 1/8	+ 7/16
n	21 3/4	13 1/2	ADFlexSol	AFLX		...	...	254	19 1/2	18 3/4	19 1/2	...
n	20 3/4	19 3/8	Adia adr	ADIAY		...	...	47	20 1/4	19 7/8	19 7/8	- 1/8
	38 1/2	21 1/2	♣AdobeSys	ADBE	.20	.6	cc	12746	33 1/2	32 1/4	32 5/16	- 3/16
	17	9	AdvCircuit	ADVC		...	11	440	13 5/8	13 1/4	13 1/4	- 3/8
s	30 1/4	14 3/4	AdvRoss	AROS		...	12	252	20 3/64	19 1/8	20 3/64	+ 35/64
	7 1/2	3 1/2	AdvLogicRsrch	AALR		...	dd	40	5 1/8	4 7/8	4 7/8	...
	7	4	AdvMktg	ADMS		...	25	66	5 13/16	5 3/4	5 3/4	...
	6 5/16	2 1/8	AdvNMRSys	ANMR		...	...	680	3 5/8	3 1/2	3 1/2	- 1/32
	7 3/4	3 5/8	AdvPolymer	APOS		...	dd	160	4 7/8	4 5/8	4 11/16	...
	10 1/2	3 7/8	AdvPromoTch	APTV		...	...	1411	4 1/2	4 1/4	4 1/4	- 1/8
	5	1 5/8	AdvSemi	ASMIF		...	...	54	4 1/2	4 1/4	4 1/2	- 1/8
	19 1/2	12 1/2	AdvTchLab	ATLI		...	dd	36	17	16 1/2	16 1/2	- 1/8
	7 1/4	4 1/4	♣AdvTchMatrl	ATMI		...	21	332	6	5 3/4	6	+ 1/4
	9 1/2	**4 1/4**	**AdvTissue**	**ATIS**		...	...	**1202**	**8 7/8**	**8**	**8 1/4**	- 5/8
	41 3/4	24 1/4	Advanta A	ADVNA	.27f	.8	13	2117	32 1/2	30 1/2	32 1/2	+1 1/2
	37 1/2	23 1/4	Advanta B	ADVNB	.32f	1.1	12	1869	30	28 1/2	30	+1
	26 3/4	20	Am Life pf	ALHCP	2.16	10.5	...	25	20 5/8	20 1/8	20 5/8	...
s	19 7/8	12 1/16	AmMgtSys	AMSY		...	21	668	18 1/2	17 1/2	18 1/8	- 3/8
	17 1/2	**5**	**AmMedElec**	**AMEI**		...	**11**	**587**	**6 1/2**	**5 1/8**	**5 9/16**	- 13/16
	21	11 1/2	♣AmMobile	SKYC		...	...	22	14 3/4	14 3/4	14 3/4	...
	18 1/4	**2 7/8**	**AmMobSys**	**AMSE**		...	...	**27**	**3 3/4**	**3 1/2**	**3 1/2**	- 1/2
	54	44 1/4	AmNatlIns	ANAT	2.36f	4.9	7	101	48	46 3/4	48	+ 1/2
	10 1/4	5 3/8	AmOilField	DIVE		...	dd	1623	5 3/4	5 3/8	5 1/2	+ 1/8
	17	6 3/4	AmPacCorp	APFC		...	dd	254	7 3/4	7 1/2	7 1/2	...

	52 Weeks Hi	Lo	Stock	Sym	Div	Yld %	PE	Vol 100s	Hi	Lo	Close	Net Chg
	2 7/8	1 1/2	AmPhysnSvc	AMPH		...	11	124	2 5/8	2 3/8	2 3/8	...
	30 1/2	14 1/2	AmPwrConv	APCC		...	23	8548	17 1/4	16 3/8	16 1/2	- 5/8
n	15	10	AmPublish A	AMPC	.03	.2	...	2994	12 3/4	12	12 1/4	- 3/8
	7 1/2	4 1/2	AmRecCtrs	AMRC	.24	3.8	17	5	6 1/4	6 1/4	6 1/4	...
	15 1/4	6	AmRecHldg	AMRE		...	11	18	6 3/4	6 1/4	6 1/4	...
	14 1/2	**10**	**AmSaftyRazr**	**RAZR**		...	**16**	**330**	**13 1/4**	**12 13/16**	**13**	- 3/4
	23 3/8	15 1/8	AmSavFla	ASFL		...	9	181	19 13/16	19 3/4	19 3/4	...
sn	21	8	AmSensors	SNIFF		...	...	580	16 7/8	15 3/4	16 3/4	- 1/4
	6 3/8	2 1/2	AmSftwr A	AMSWA	.24j	...	dd	532	3 1/8	2 7/8	3	...
	5 1/4	2 3/4	AmStudios	AMST	.08	2.8	16	42	3 1/8	2 7/8	2 7/8	- 1/8
s	26 5/32	16 21/64	AmSuprcnd	AMSC		...	...	183	24 1/2	23 1/4	23 7/8	- 5/8
	27	**9 1/4**	**AmTelecastg**	**ATEL**		...	**dd**	**3370**	**11 5/8**	**11**	**11 5/8**	+ 3/4
	18	10 7/8	AmTrvlrs	ATVC		...	10	156	16 13/16	16 1/2	16 1/2	- 3/8
	6 13/16	**3 1/4**	**AmUtdGlbl**	**AUGI**		...	**11**	**351**	**4 1/8**	**3 13/16**	**3 7/8**	- 1/4
	2 1/8	7/8	AmUtdGlbl wt			...	...	40	15/16	15/16	15/16	+ 1/16
	16 1/2	5 3/4	AmVngrd	AMGD		...	6	29	7 1/2	7 1/2	7 1/2	-1 1/2
	9 1/2	2 1/2	AmWhiteCros	AWCI		...	dd	62	2 7/8	2 3/4	2 7/8	...
	7 1/2	3 7/8	AmWoodmk	AMWD	.39t	7.3	8	55	5 3/8	5	5 3/8	...
	6 5/8	3 1/2	AmhostProp	HOST		...	dd	432	4 1/4	4	4 3/16	+ 3/16
n	13 1/8	8	AmeriLink	ALNK		...	...	160	11 3/8	11	11	...
	16 3/4	4 1/2	AmerstarCno	ASCA		...	...	26	6 3/8	5 3/4	6 1/8	- 1/8
	19	7	Ameriwood	AWII		...	4	11	7	7	7	...
	26 1/4	19	AMFED Fnl	AMFF	.24	1.1	12	407	22 3/4	22	22 1/2	+ 1/2
	61 1/8	34 3/4	Amgen	AMGN		...	20	5763	59 1/4	58	58 1/2	- 1/4
	3 1/2	1 1/8	Amistar	AMTA		...	9	10	2 1/16	2 1/16	2 1/16	...
	9 1/4	5 1/2	AMRESCO	AMMB	.20	3.1	4	235	6 3/4	6 1/2	6 1/2	...
	15	5 1/2	Amrion	AMRI		...	17	224	7	6 5/8	7	...
	2 5/8	**11/16**	**AmserHlthcr**	**AMSR**		...	**dd**	**110**	**2 1/2**	**2 1/4**	**2 3/8**	- 1/8
	33 3/4	7 5/8	AmtechCp	AMTC	.08	.8	13	1360	10	9 5/8	9 3/4	- 1/4
	10 3/4	6	Amtran	AMTR		...	15	14	8 1/2	8 1/8	8 1/8	+ 3/8
	22 1/2	13 1/2	AMTROL	AMTL	.20	1.3	...	54	15 3/4	15	15	...
	15 1/4	4 3/4	AmylinPharm	AMLN		...	...	1702	5 3/4	5	5 1/2	...
	20	14 5/8	Analogic	ALOG		...	16	71	19	18 3/8	19	+ 1/4
	17	13 3/4	Anly&Tech	AATI	.24f	1.5	14	2	15 1/2	15 1/2	15 1/2	...
	21 3/4	14 1/2	AnlyInt	ANLY	.52	2.5	17	411	21 1/4	20 3/4	20 3/4	- 3/4
	3 5/8	**2**	**Anaren**	**ANEN**		...	**dd**	**26**	**2 7/8**	**2 3/4**	**2 7/8**	+ 3/8
▲	33 1/2	22	AnchrBcpWis	ABCW	.30	.9	11	597	34 1/4	32 3/4	34 1/4	+1 1/8
n	19 1/2	10 1/2	AnchorGaming	SLOT		...	15	236	17 1/8	16 1/2	16 13/16	- 5/16
	21 3/4	13 1/2	AndovrBcp	ANDB	.40	2.6	8	116	15 1/4	15	15 1/4	...
	3	1 1/4	AndovrTog	ATOG		...	dd	6	1 1/2	1 5/16	1 1/2	- 1/16
s	54 1/4	25	♣AndrewCp	ANDW		...	31	1635	54	52 1/2	53	- 7/8
	21 1/4	13 1/2	Andros	ANDY		...	12	91	16 3/4	16 1/4	16 3/4	+ 1/4
n	7 1/4	5 1/8	AndyneCptg	ADYNF		...	...	1	5 1/2	5 1/2	5 1/2	...
	6 1/2	1 3/4	Anergen	ANRG		...	...	60	2 1/4	2 1/4	2 1/4	+ 5/16
n	13 1/4	5 1/4	♣Anesta	NSTA		...	...	200	5 1/2	5 3/8	5 3/8	- 1/4
	38 1/2	15	ANTEC Cp	ANTC		...	...	190	19 3/4	19 1/4	19 5/8	...
	12 5/8	2 3/4	ApertusTech	APTS		...	dd	1913	10 7/8	10 1/4	10 7/16	- 3/16
	27 3/4	**6 7/8**	**Aphton**	**APHT**		...	...	**511**	**9 1/2**	**8 3/4**	**8 7/8**	- 5/8
	18 1/2	11 1/2	ApogeeEnt	APOG	.32f	2.0	29	45	16 1/4	15 3/4	16 1/4	...
n	19 3/4	12	Apogee	APGG		...	...	96	16 3/4	16 1/4	16 3/8	+ 1/8
n	19	11	♣ApolloGp A	APOL		...	...	392	19	18 1/8	18 5/8	- 3/8
	48 1/16	24 5/8	AppleCptr	AAPL	.48	1.1	18	11398	45 5/8	44 3/4	45 5/8	+ 5/8 ← Apple Computer
s	18 3/4	10 3/4	AppleSouth	APSO	.02	.1	30	2146	14 1/2	13 3/4	14	...
s	25 1/4	11	Applebee	APPB	.05e	.3	34	4678	19 1/4	18 1/4	19	+ 3/4
	14 3/4	**3 1/2**	**ApplncRecyc**	**ARCI**		...	**dd**	**109**	**3 3/4**	**3 1/2**	**3 1/2**	- 1/4
	7 3/8	4 5/8	ApldBiosci	APBI		...	dd	378	5 7/8	5 5/8	5 7/8	...
n	30 1/4	13 3/4	♣ApldDigital	ADAX		...	...	596	29 1/4	28	28 1/4	...
	12 3/8	3 7/8	ApldExtr	AETC		...	33	4513	12 1/8	11 5/8	11 13/16	- 11/32
	13	4 1/2	ApldImuSci	AISX		...	...	196	5 5/8	5 3/8	5 3/8	- 1/8
s	33	15	ApldInnovt	AINN		...	35	209	26 1/2	25 1/4	25 3/4	- 3/4
	54 1/2	36 1/4	♣ApldMatl	AMAT		...	18	15826	45	43 1/2	44	- 1/4
	6 1/2	2 5/8	ApldMicbio	AMBI		...	38	107	3 1/8	2 7/8	3	...
	9 3/4	**4 3/4**	**♣ApldSciTech**	**ASTX**		...	**42**	**20**	**6 1/4**	**6**	**6 1/4**	+ 3/8
	1 1/2	9/32	ApldSciTech wt			...	...	80	5/16	5/16	5/16	- 3/32
	7 3/4	**3 1/4**	**♣ApldSignal**	**APSG**		...	**15**	**369**	**6**	**4 3/4**	**6**	+1
n	52	31 1/4	BabySuperstr	BSST		...	...	79	51	50 1/4	50 1/4	- 1/16
▲	**4 3/16**	**1 3/4**	**BachmnInfo**	**BACH**		...	**dd**	**4750**	**4 5/8**	**3 3/4**	**4 3/8**	+ 1/2
	20 1/4	7	BackBay	PAPA		...	13	27	8 1/8	7 3/4	7 3/4	- 3/8
	16 1/2	5 1/8	Bailey	BAIB		...	9	572	8 7/8	8 9/16	8 5/8	+ 1/8
	22 3/8	13 5/8	BakrJInc	JBAK	.06	.4	8	334	15 1/8	14 1/2	14 1/2	- 5/8
s	7 3/4	3 9/16	Balchm	BLCC	.03e	.6	22	4	5 3/8	5 1/4	5 3/8	- 3/4
	18 1/2	10 1/4	BaldwPiano	BPAO		...	7	2gg				...
	17	6 1/2	BallyGaming	BGII		...	dd	3268	7 1/8	6 3/4	6 15/16	+ 1/16
n	13 1/4	10 1/2	BallyGrand	BGLV		...	...	10	11 3/8	11 3/8	11 3/8	+ 1/2
n	5	3 1/8	BallyGrand wt			...	...	107	3 3/4	3 1/2	3 1/2	- 1/16
	9 1/4	6 1/2	Baltek	BTEK	.08j	...	22	9	6 3/4	6 3/4	6 3/4	+ 1/4

Source: The Wall Street Journal, January 19, 1995. Reprinted by permission of *The Wall Street Journal*, ©1995 Dow Jones & Company, Inc. All rights reserved worldwide.

178 Chapter 9

NASDAQ SMALL-CAP ISSUES

Issue	Div	Vol 100s	Last	Chg
A&A Fd g		310	7/16	+1/32
ACR		365	1/2	−1/16
ACTV		803	3 7/8	+ 1/8
ADM Tr		40	9/32	...
AFP		12	13/16	+ 1/8
AGBag		372	1 1/2	...
AGP &Co		1996	3/4	−5/32
APA		17	3 1/4	...
ASV Inc		19	3	...
ATC Env		494	14 3/4	−7/16
ATC EnC		45	6 3/8	− 1/8
Abatix		140	2 1/8	−1/16
AberRs		209	5	−11/64
AcrnVn		588	7/8	−1/16
AcresGm		5	5 1/4	...
AcreG un		5	5 1/4	...
Acrody un		339	2 3/4	+1/16
Activisn		93	6 1/4	...
Actrade		20	1 13/16	...
Acuity		10	7 1/4	+ 1/2
AdapSol		789	5	...
AdapSl wt		11	1 1/8	− 1/8
Admar		194	1 1/32	...
AdvDep		30	2 7/8	...
AdvDp wt		25	5/16	...
AdvEnv		170	11/32	−1/32
AdvMam		232	12 3/8	...
AMam wt		40	9 1/8	...
AdvMat		620	3/8	− 1/4
AdvMedP		14	3/8	− 1/2
AdvSurg		205	1 7/16	−1/16
AdvLfe s		50	2 1/8	−1/16
AdvntTc		1035	5/32	...
AerSyE		175	49/64	−1/64
AffinTel		237	4 3/32	−3/32
AgesHlt		79	1 1/2	...
Air LA		34	1 13/16	+1/16
AirInt		512	1/16	...
AirInt pf		60	9/16	+1/16
Ajay		96	1/2	−1/32
Alamar		630	1 1/16	−1/16
Alamr wt		75	5/32	...
Alanco		6631	1 9/16	−1/16
Alden		1	2 1/4	...
♣AllACm		17	6 1/4	...
AllPrd un		833	9 5/8	...
AllQuote		23	1 3/8	+ 1/8
AllnImg		54	13/16	+1/16
AldCAdv		2	3 1/2	−1/16
AldDevic		330	5 3/8	− 5/8
AlphHsp		324	5 1/2	− 1/4
AlphH wt		10	3/4	...
AlphaSo		965	1/8	+1/32
Alpnet		25	5/16	...
AlterSal		12	9/32	−1/16
Ambanc	.84	8	32	...
AmBcpNV	2.10t	7	13 1/2	+ 1/2
ABingo		1871	6 9/16	...
ABingo wt		2404	2 13/16	−1/32
ABsCpt		1002	3 3/8	+ 1/8
AmCasn		200	11/16	+3/32
AmCine s		257	4 3/4	...
AmCin wt		118	3 1/8	− 3/8
AmDentl		31	5/8	+1/16
AGamEnt		11	13/16	+1/16
AMdAlt		245	2 5/8	+ 1/8
AmMdTc		95	27/32	+1/16
APacBk		1	15/32	+5/32
APacMin		100	5/8	+1/16
AmResCp		306	4 5/8	...
AmRes s		10	5 7/8	...
AmSfCls		174	1 7/16	...
AmToys		1232	11 1/4	...
AToys wt		954	6 5/8	+ 1/8
AToy nwt		616	6 3/4	+ 3/8
AmersGF		474	4 1/2	+ 1/2
Amerlgn		143	12 1/2	...
Ames wt		122	2	− 1/8
AmesDS		559	2 11/16	−1/16
Amnex		533	2 15/16	...
Ampal pf	.32	4	17 1/2	−1
Amtch wt		702	1 3/64	+3/64
Amtech		5	4 5/8	...
AnlySur		80	6 1/8	+ 1/4
AncorCm		519	5 1/4	− 3/8
Angeion		1203	3	− 1/8
AnikaRs		13	1 5/8	− 1/8
Appltre s		1505	1 1/8	−3/16
ApBiomet		377	3 7/8	− 3/4
ApldLsr		260	1 1/8	− 1/8
ApLsr wtA		280	11/32	+1/16
AquaCre		10	3 1/8	...
AquC wtA		341	1 1/4	...
AquC wtB		861	13/16	−3/32
AquaC un		129	5 1/16	− 1/8
Aquanat		6501	2	+ 1/8
ArizInst		203	1	...
Arman wt		100	3/16	...
Arman		343	1 1/8	−1/16
Artagp wt		1200	1 1/2	−1
Artgph pf	.60	78	1/2	...
Artagp un		4	7 1/2	...
AstroSc		953	2 9/16	+3/16

Issue	Div	Vol 100s	Last	Chg
CntMne		627	1 13/16	− 1/8
CentCas		45	1 3/4	+ 1/8
Cerprbe	.03e	2	5 1/4	+ 1/4
ChalInt		30	2 3/8	...
Chantal		1379	2 9/32	+1/16
Chapral		182	23/32	−1/16
ChtBnc	.24b	63	14	− 1/4
ChrtBk	.60b	4	15 1/4	...
ChefsInt		139	5/8	+1/16
Chemex		112	3/4	...
Cherke sh		24	2 1/2	+ 1/4
ChesterH		1730	1/4	−1/32
ChfCon		12	5 3/4	...
ChldBrd		69	4 1/16	−1/16
Childrbc		1094	1 15/16	...
Childr wt		1630	3/4	+1/16
ChinaIndl		359	2 11/16	−1/16
Chinl wtA		25	5/32	...
ChromCS		144	3 7/8	+ 1/8
ChmCS wt		178	1 7/16	...
ChrchllD	.50e	33	45	+2 1/2
ChchTch		1419	27/32	−3/32
Clattis		5	3 1/2	− 1/4
CineRide		831	6 3/4	+ 1/8
CinRd wt		96	1 7/16	−3/16
CircRsh		5	1 5/8	+ 1/8
CtzFBk pf	2.19	10	22 5/8	...
Classics		110	2 1/2	+1/16
CluckWd		10	5 7/8	...
CstFncl s	.45e	1	19	− 5/8
Cohesant		338	5 1/2	+ 1/2
Cohes wt		278	1 1/4	− 1/2
ComCnt s		210	13/32	− 1/8
CmndCr		1074	1/4	+1/16
CmceG		40	3 1/2	− 1/4
ComWld		52	5	− 1/4
CmtyFin	.51t	50	9 3/4	+ 3/4
CmtyMdT		452	4 5/8	...
CtyMT wt		137	15/16	−3/16
Compartr		3689	1/16	...
Complnk		206	3 7/8	− 1/8
CmpMd s		510	1 3/8	+ 1/8
CptConc		3495	1	+1/32
CptMkt s		136	1 1/32	−1/16
CptM wtA		345	3/8	−1/32
CptMk wtB		2185	13/32	+ 1/8
CmpTel		243	13 5/8	+ 1/8
Computne		520	3 3/4	− 1/4
Comtrx		3	1	...
ConcptT		25	3 3/4	+ 3/8
Concept		26	1 5/8	+ 3/8
Congind s		21	1 9/32	−3/32
ConsSv pf	1.52	6	27 3/4	− 1/4
ConHCre		260	15/16	− 1/8
ConsNev		10	15/16	+ 1/8
ConRam		405	4	...
ConTech		272	7/8	−1/32
CtlCC un		369	7 1/4	...
Continum		101	1	+1/16
Cornucp		131	1 1/8	−1/32
CorpRen		158	9 3/4	...
Cortx wt		500	1/32	...
Cortex s		52	2 5/8	+ 1/8
Corvita		1	4 1/8	+ 1/8
Cosmetic		45	2	− 5/8
Cosmtc un		64	4 5/8	− 7/8
Cosmo hs		45	1 3/8	− 1/8
CtryStr		274	6	...
CtrySt wt		175	1 7/8	...
CtryWTr		264	4 1/8	− 3/8
CrLr wt		10	1/16	− 1/8
CreatL s		1897	2 3/8	− 3/8
CreatMd		5	2 11/16	...
CreaM wt		727	1 1/4	+ 1/4
CrePrg		16	2 1/8	−1/16
CreTch		672	4 1/2	+3/16
CreatCa		122	5 3/8	+ 1/8
CrdDept		17	5 1/4	...
CrockrRl		1	8 1/4	+ 5/8
Crockr wt		40	1	+ 1/8
CwnCas		5870	3	−1 1/4
Crystal		57	3 1/2	...
Crystal un		120	3/4	− 1/8
CurrTec h		154	3/8	−1/32
CMathes		110	1 7/16	...
Cusac g		492	21/32	+1/32
Cusac wt		437	7/32	+1/32
Cusac pf		31	9	+ 1/4
♣Cyanotc		47	15/16	−1/16
Cybrnet		477	1 1/8	...
Cybr wtB		355	5/32	...
Cybr wtA		694	5/16	...
Cybrnet pf	.19e	286	1 7/8	...
CyclMed		19	4 7/8	+ 1/8
Cypros		988	14 1/2	+ 3/8
Cypr wtA		10	9 1/4	...
Cypr wtB		379	5 1/2	+ 1/8
Cytoprb s		1	7/8	− 1/8
D&K Whl		46	7	− 3/8
DMI Frn		31	1 7/8	+13/64
DMI Inc		155	9/16	−3/32
DSI Ind		210	1/16	...
Danngr		6	4 1/4	− 1/8

Issue	Div	Vol 100s	Last	Chg
FFSSiou	.72a	3	23	...
FtFnPlk s	.30	10	10	+ 3/4
FtIndp	.20	41	14 1/2	− 1/4
FstKent	.15e	10	16 3/4	− 1/4
FtLesprt	.44	1	16 1/2	−1 1/2
FtLbty pf	1.94	9	28 1/2	− 1/4
FtNatEnt		36	3/8	...
FUtdSv	.24e	1	27	...
Fstmark		23	4 3/4	...
FlaGam		148	2 1/2	...
vjFlaWt h		170		...
FluroS un		63	10 3/4	+ 3/8
FocusEn		99	2 1/4	+ 1/4
Focus wt		277	7/16	−3/16
Fonar		1469	1 11/16	−3/32
FoodIntg		20	1 1/4	...
FoodTch		1	4 3/8	+ 1/8
ForeInd		284	1 13/16	...
Forum		162	9 1/8	+ 1/8
Foxmor		36	2 1/4	+ 1/4
FrkBncp		10	4 3/8	− 1/4
FrankOp		1679	1 3/16	−1/16
FrnkOp wt		1739	1/4	...
FrJuice		2	1 13/16	−3/16
FrontrAir		84	3	− 1/4
FrontA wt		103	7/16	−5/32
FrntNat		10	3 3/8	...
FrtNt wt		10	7/8	...
FullHse		423	5 3/4	− 1/4
FullHs wt		20	3 3/8	...
FutMed		277	7/16	...
Futurebio		617	3	...
Futrbi wt		285	1 1/16	...
Futrbi un		73	7 1/2	+ 3/8
GB Fds		198	6	− 3/8
GFS Bcp		1	14 1/2	− 1/2
GTEC 56pf	.90	1	10 3/4	...
GTEC 5pf	1.00	7	12	...
GlxyFd		36	1 3/4	...
GameFn		10	4 1/2	...
GamngCp		723	1 7/16	+3/16
Gamng wt		55	3/8	+1/16
Gamng un		23	1 29/64	−7/64
GarmGph		32	2	+1/32
GtwyKY n		1048	11 1/4	...
Gentnr		286	27/32	+1/32
Gentnr wt		115	3/16	+1/32
GeoWste		61	7/16	−1/16
Geores		31	1 1/16	...
GllmnClo		12	3 9/16	−3/16
GlenF wt		170	2 5/8	− 1/8
Glenway	.68	5	17 1/2	−2
GlbCasn		119	1 1/16	+1/32
GlbRsc s		2	4 1/4	+ 1/4
GlbSpill		1073	1 3/8	+1/16
GlobTele		313	5 1/8	+ 1/8
GlbTel wt		854	2 3/16	+1/16
GoldRs		26	6 35/64	−29/64
GldStd		916	3 7/8	−1/16
GldEg wt		50	3/4	+ 1/4
GldQual		835	7/16	+1/32
♣GoldTri		200	1	+1/32
GoodT wtB		50	9/32	...
GoodTm		30	1 1/4	...
GrandG		87	1 1/32	+1/32
Grand wt		350	1/8	+1/32
Grand un		545	1 3/16	+5/32
GrndToy		212	1 5/8	− 1/2
GrToy wt		220	9/32	−3/32
GrntSt	.60c	1	5/32	...
GraphixZ		28	3 7/8	...
GrMonk		147	2 1/2	+ 3/8
GtARc pf		2	13/16	...
GrtPines		8	3	...
GtTrain n		297	6 1/4	...
GtTrn wt		364	1 1/8	− 5/8
GrnMtn		13	8 7/8	− 1/2
GrnstRs		70	1 1/8	+ 1/8
GrnstR		172	7/16	−1/16
GrntrSf s		20	2 7/32	−1/32
GrnwPh		356	7/32	−1/16
GManning		210	2 3/8	+ 1/4
GMann wt		38	15/32	+3/32
GthEnvr		20	4 1/2	+ 1/4
GthFn	.38t	3	11 1/4	+ 1/2
Gulfwest		71	2 3/4	...
HERC		10	3	...
HainFood		258	4 11/16	− 1/8
HamPlsR		113	2	...
HamP wtA		2	3/4	...
HamP wtB		4	1/2	...
HanovGld		65	1 1/2	+ 1/8
Hansen		6	1 11/16	−3/16
Haristn		187	4 1/16	−3/16
HarmBrk		100	1 15/16	−1/16
HrmHld		752	3 3/4	...
HarveyU		169	4 3/4	− 1/8
HaupD un		3237	3 3/4	+ 1/8
HwkEn		75	1/2	+1/16
HltcrTc		20	1 19/32	+1/32
Hlthwtch		24	15/16	...
HlthPln		475	8 1/8	...
♣HemaC		2331	2 1/8	− 7/8
Hemagn		17	2	...

Issue	Div	Vol 100s	Last	Chg
Jordan		481	7/8	+1/16
Judicate		110	2 3/4	...
JuniprF		175	1/4	...
KnCtyL	1.44	53	45 1/8	−1 3/8
KellyRus		15	2 3/8	...
KendSqr		335	1/16	...
KiddePr	.17	2	23 1/2	+2
KngsRd		4	3/8	− 1/8
KooKR		2966	6 1/8	+ 1/4
Krantor		220	2 7/16	+3/16
Krantr un		705	2 1/2	+1/16
KrauseF		120	2 1/8	− 1/8
LF Bcp	.60e	2	30 1/2	−2
LaTeko		816	2 5/8	− 1/8
LaMan		36	7/16	+1/16
LabSpec		159	3 1/2	+ 1/4
LabSpc wt		91	1 1/4	...
Lafay un		12	9 3/4	...
LakeAriel	.52a	23	16 1/4	−1
vjLamont		90	9/16	...
Langer		10	7/8	−7/64
LarDav		444	2 1/8	...
LasVDsc		20	1 5/8	...
LasVEnt		2339	1 1/32	+1/32
LasVE wtA		8	7/16	− 1/8
LaserFr		193	3 5/8	+ 1/8
LsrSght		1180	12 13/16	−3/16
Lasrtch		902	1 7/32	+1/32
LsrVide		2205	4 1/2	+ 1/2
LsrV wtA		13	1 13/16	...
LsrV wtB		6466	15/16	+7/16
LsrVis		195	7 11/16	−3/16
LsrVs wt		80	1 15/16	−1/64
Lasrgt wt		1664	8 1/4	+ 1/4
Lasergte		103	13 1/2	− 1/8
LatexRs		1164	31/32	+1/32
Latex wt		1	3/16	−1/32
LauriCa s	.32	7	17	...
Leadvle		5	5/8	+1/16
LeakX		63	1 3/4	− 1/2
Leak X wt		10		...
Leggons		10	13/16	+1/16
LeisMkt		432	1 3/4	−1/16
LetchInd	.40a	2	20 5/8	+ 5/8
Licon s		10	11/32	...
♣LfeMed		1310	3 1/8	+ 1/4
LfMd wtA		446	9/16	+1/16
LfeMd un		24	4 1/4	+2
Lifecell		3	3	+ 1/4
Lifeway		7	1 3/16	...
LincSnk		32	1 7/8	− 1/4
Linda un		119	5 3/4	...
LiveEnt n		14	3 5/8	...
LneStar		786	1/2	...
LouG pf	1.86	1058	22 3/4	+ 1/4
LucileFr		148	3 5/8	...
Lucile wt		59	1 1/4	− 5/8
LukMed		80	2	−1/16
Lunnl		255	7/8	...
LuthMed		11	3 1/4	+ 1/8
M-SysFD		201	3 7/8	+ 1/8
MBF		527	2	+1/16
MPTV		1871	5/8	...
MacG Sp		20	11/16	+1/16
MacroCh		70	1 11/16	...
Madden		1646	4 1/2	− 3/8
Madn wtA		20	1 1/2	− 1/8
MadisnG		166	11/16	−1/64
MagelPt		323	29/32	+ 1/8
MagelRst		136	2 1/4	...
MagRst		642	5/8	+1/16
MagnaLb		30	3	− 1/8
MagnL un		10	3 1/8	...
MajRty		10	1 7/8	...
Malvy		580	9/32	...
MgdHlth		65	15/32	...
MgtTech		1980	5/16	−1/16
ManBagel		64	7	...
Margate	.06	143	2 3/8	−1/16
MarkSol		858	2 5/16	−1/16
Marqst		89	1/2	...
Mascott		4	1	...
MstGlaz		1175	3 3/8	+ 3/8
MstG wtA		2880	1 5/16	+3/16
MstG wtB		1710	1 1/32	+1/16
Matritch		266	2 3/16	...
Maxserv		1	3 7/8	...
Mecklmd		383	6	...
MedWst		31	3 1/8	+ 1/8
MdWst wt		8	9/32	−1/16
Medcross		252	2 1/8	− 1/8
Medgrp		200	3/32	...
MediMal		1243	2 7/16	+1/16
MedVat		111	3 1/16	...
MedDyn		189	1 1/16	−1/16
MedInn		583	1 5/8	+1/16
MedResc		33	3 1/4	...
MedisE		50	1 3/4	+ 1/8
Medlwre		20	1 1/2	+3/16
Mdmarco		80	3 1/8	+ 1/8
MedPlus		59	8	+ 1/8
MrdnN wt		100	7/16	−1/16
MerdnNt		507	2 1/2	+ 1/4
MesaLb		83	2 1/4	−3/16

Source: *The Wall Street Journal*, January 19, 1995. Reprinted by permission of *The Wall Street Journal*, ©1995 Dow Jones & Company, Inc. All rights reserved worldwide.

27¾	6⅞	Aphton	APHT	...	...	511	9½	8¾	8⅞	− ⅝			
18½	11½	ApogeeEnt	APOG	.32f	2.0	29	45	16¼	15¾	16¼	...		
n 19¾	12	Apogee	APGG	...	...	96	16¾	16¼	16⅜	+ ⅛			
n 19	11	♠ApolloGp A	APOL	...	...	392	19	18⅛	18⅝	− ⅜			
48¹/₁₆	24⅝	AppleCptr	AAPL	.48	1.1	18	11398	45⅝	44¾	45⅝	+ ⅝	◄────	Apple Computer
s 18¾	10¾	AppleSouth	APSO	.02	.1	30	2146	14½	13¾	14	...		
s 25¼	11	Applebee	APPB	.05e	.3	34	4678	19¼	18¼	19	+ ¾		
14¾	3½	ApplncRecyc	ARCI	...	dd	109	3¾	3½	3½	− ¼			

Source: *The Wall Street Journal*, January 19, 1995. Reprinted by permission of *The Wall Street Journal*, ©1995 Dow Jones & Company, Inc. All rights reserved worldwide.

MUTUAL FUNDS

At this point you may feel that the discussion has strayed from the goals established in Chapters 1 and 8. If you've decided to pick stocks instead of gold, can the wisdom of that decision be offset by the selection of the wrong stock? If so, is there a way to get into the stock market without purchasing a particular stock?

Yes, and yes. Mutual funds provide a way to invest in the stock market indirectly. Investment companies establish mutual funds to pool the resources of many investors and thus create a large, shared portfolio of investments. Individuals invest in mutual funds by purchasing shares in the fund from the investment company. These mutual funds are open-ended, which means the investment companies are always willing to sell more shares to the public and to redeem outstanding shares. Therefore, the pool of capital, the number of investors, and the number of shares outstanding can expand or contract.

The value of the fund's assets divided by the number of shares outstanding determines the value of each share. Any gain in the fund's portfolio is passed through to the individual investors. Purchases of additional shares by new investors do not reduce the value of existing shares, because the purchaser makes a cash contribution equal to the value of the share.

This raises an important point: Mutual fund shares are not traded on the open market. They are purchased from, and sold back to, the investment company.

Mutual funds are popular with individual investors because they permit diversification in a wide variety of securities with very small capital outlay. In addition, a mutual fund lets you take advantage of the professional management skills of the investment company.

When you purchase a mutual fund share, you own a fraction of the total assets in the portfolio. The price of that share is equal to its net asset value (net value of assets held by the fund divided by the number of mutual fund shares outstanding plus any sales commission.). As with any pooled investment in common stock, price appreciation and dividends earned will determine the gain in net asset value.

Mutual funds are classified according to whether or not they charge a sales commission called a load. Every day, **Mutual Fund Quotations** lists the major funds available to investors, and it can be found using the indexes on the front pages of the first (Al) and third (Cl) sections. Pages 181–183 provide excerpts from the Thursday, January 19, 1995 edition of the *Journal*.

No-Load (NL) Funds don't require a commission to purchase or sell the shares of the fund. There is, however, a "management fee" on these funds', and all other funds', assets that is generally less than 1 percent of the investment. Net asset values are calculated after management takes its fee.

You can tell if a fund has no load by the symbol *NL* under the offer price. Even if the fund's offer price is the same as its net asset value, absence of the "NL" symbol indicates a sales commission (load). This is explained below.

Front-End Loaded Funds charge a one-time admission or sales fee to purchasers of their shares, as well as the management fee levied by all funds. This "sales" or commission fee can be as high as 8 percent, which will effectively reduce your overall rate of return, depending on how long you hold the fund. A *p* after the fund's name indicates there is a distribution charge, or front-load, on the fund.

Back-End Loaded Funds levy a fee of up to 8 percent when the shares are sold back to the investment company. An *r* indicates this *redemption* charge. Some back-loaded funds vary their fees according to the length of time the shares are held. If you sell your shares after one year, the fee may be as high as 8 percent. But if you hold the shares for a long time (say, 30 years), no fee may be charged. (Remember that *all* funds have built-in management fees in addition to any loads.)

Therefore, the net asset value and offer price of a back-loaded fund may be identical, yet the fund may still charge you a sales commission when it redeems your shares.

When both redemption and distribution fees are charged, the fund is identified by a *t* after the fund's name.

MUTUAL FUND QUOTATIONS

What These Listings Provide...

		NASD DATA			LIPPER ANALYTICAL DATA		
Monday	Inv. Obj.	NAV	Offer Price	NAV Chg.	%Ret YTD	Max Initl Chrg.	Total Exp Ratio
Tuesday	Inv. Obj.	NAV	Offer Price	NAV Chg.	YTD	——Total Return—— 4 wk　1 yr	Rank
Wednesday	Inv. Obj.	NAV	Offer Price	NAV Chg.	YTD	—— Total Return—— 13 wk　3 yr*	Rank
THURSDAY	Inv. Obj.	NAV	Offer Price	NAV Chg.	YTD	——Total Return—— 26 wk　4 yr*	Rank
Friday	Inv. Obj.	NAV	Offer Price	NAV Chg.	YTD	——Total Return—— 39 wk　5 yr*	Rank

Annualized

	Inv. Obj.	NAV	Offer Price	NAV Chg.	– Total Return – YTD 26 wks 4 yrs R
BramwellGrGRO 10.61		NL	+0.03	+3.5	NS .. NS ..
Brinson Fnds:					
Global	S&B 10.41	NL	−0.01	+1.0	+0.6 NS ..
GlblBond	WBD 9.62	NL	−0.01	0.0	NS ..
NUSEqty	ITL NA	NA	NA	NA	NA NS ..
USBalncd	... 10.15	NL	−0.01	NA	NA NA ..
USEqty	G&I 9.92	NL	−0.02	+2.6	+1.7 NS ..
Brndyw	GRO 24.02	NL	−0.03	+2.2	+6.0 +20.4 A
BrndywBl	GRO 17.53	NL	−0.04	+2.8	+6.5 +19.0 A
Bruce	CAP 91.25	91.25	+0.35	+0.8	−1.0 +4.1 E
BrundgSl	9.96	9.96	−0.01	+0.7	+0.4 +6.4 D
BuffBal	S&B 9.74	NL	−0.01	+1.4	NS NS ..
Bull & Bear Gp:					
Gold p	SEC 13.25	13.25	+0.42	−8.6	−9.1 +6.1 E
Glblinc p	WBD 7.62	7.62	−0.01	−4.4	−5.8 +8.3 A
GovtSc p	MTG 14.33	14.33	...	+1.0k	−2.2k +6.4k C
Muniinc p	GLM 15.50	15.50	+0.02	+1.9k	−0.1k +4.9k E
QualGth p	G&I 13.71	13.71	−0.01	+2.9	+1.9 NS ..
SpEq p	CAP 19.78	19.78	−0.02	+3.5	+8.9 +16.5 B
USOvs p	WOR 6.97	6.97	...	−1.6	−5.9 +6.8 E
Burnhm p	G&I 19.44	20.04	...	+1.4	+3.3 +8.7 E
C&SRlty	SEC 32.00	32.00	−0.07	−2.7	−2.7 NS ..
CG Cap Mkt Fnds:					
EmgMkt	ITL 7.45	7.45	−0.05	−6.1	−9.0 NS ..
IntrFx	BIN 7.72	NL	...	+0.7	+0.7 NS ..
IntlEq	ITL 9.78	9.78	−0.01	−1.5	−5.2 NS ..
IntlFx	WBD 8.14	NL	...	+0.6	+0.7 NS ..
LgGrw	GRO 9.93	NL	...	+2.1	+6.0 NS ..
LgVal	G&I 8.73	NL	−0.02	+2.9	+0.8 NS ..
LTBnd	BND 7.70	NL	...	+0.9	+0.6 NS ..
MtgBkd	MTG 7.51	NL	...	+0.9	+1.2 NS ..
Muni	GLM 7.75	NL	−0.02	+2.6	−0.4 NS ..
SmGrw	SML 13.81	NL	−0.12	+0.4	+19.8 NS ..
SmVal	SML 8.39	NL	−0.01	+1.1	−1.8 NS ..
CGM Funds:					
AmerTF	GLM 8.96	NL	...	+1.5	+0.5 NS ..
CapDv	GRO 21.59	NL	−0.08	+4.9	−11.4 +24.2 A
FxdInc	BND 9.79	NL	−0.03	+2.3	−2.8 NS ..
Mutl	S&B 25.33	NL	−0.01	+1.1	−3.8 +13.5 A
Realty	SEC 9.68	NL	...	−0.3	−0.1 NS ..
C&OAggG	SML 11.54	NL	+0.02	−1.5	−1.9 NS ..
CA TFin	ISM 9.86	9.86	+0.01	+1.1	−0.7 NS ..
California Trust:					
Callnc	MCA 11.51	NL	+0.02	+2.5	−0.1 +6.8 A
CalUS	MTG 9.95	NL	...	+1.1	+0.5 +8.3 A
S&P500	G&I 11.16	NL	...	+2.4	+5.1 NS ..
S&PMidCap	MID 11.37	NL	−0.02	+2.4	+2.7 NS ..
Calmos	S&B 12.04	12.61	−0.01	+1.9	+0.1 +13.0 A
Calvert Group:					
GlobEq	WOR 15.78	16.57	−0.03	−2.2	−7.5 NS ..
Inco	BND 15.63	16.24	...	+0.8	+0.6 +7.6 C
MuBdCAl	IDM 9.94	10.22	+0.02	+1.2	+0.3 NS ..
Munlnt	IDM 9.94	10.22	+0.02	+1.3	+1.2 NS ..
Social p	S&B 28.26	29.67	...	+1.4	+0.8 +6.7 E
SocBd	BND 15.32	15.92	...	+1.1	0.0 +7.1 D
SocEq	GRO 18.06	18.96	−0.08	−1.2	−5.8 −4.7 E
StrGwth	GRO 17.20	18.06	+0.01	−0.7	+17.6 NS ..
TxF Lt	STM 10.60	10.84	...	+0.3	+1.5 +4.5 E
TxF Ltc	STM 10.59	10.59	...	+0.3	NA NS ..
TxF Lg	GLM 16.06	16.69	+0.03	+1.5	+2.0 +6.8 B
TxF VT	SSM 15.55	16.16	+0.02	+1.4	+1.0 NS ..
US Gov	MTG 13.65	14.18	...	+0.9	+0.3 +5.3 E

	Inv. Obj.	NAV	Offer Price	NAV Chg.	– Total Return – YTD 26 wks 4 yrs R
Cambridge Fds:					
CapGrA	GRO 14.79	15.65	−0.01	+2.3	+3.3 NS ..
GvInA	MTG 12.49	13.11	−0.01	+0.8	+0.6 NS ..
GwthA	GRO 14.69	15.54	−0.02	+1.3	+1.5 NS ..
IncGrA	S&B 14.55	15.40	−0.02	+1.2	−1.5 NS ..
MuIncA	GLM 14.18	14.89	+0.02	+1.7	0.0 NS ..
CapGrB †	GRO 14.67	14.67	−0.01	+2.3	+2.9 NS ..
GlobB	WOR 13.65	13.65	...	−0.9	−4.0 NS ..
GvInB †	MTG 12.50	12.50	−0.01	+0.7	+0.3 NS ..
GwthB †	GRO 14.51	14.51	−0.01	+1.3	+1.1 NS ..
IncGrB †	S&B 14.56	14.56	−0.02	+1.2	−1.6 NS ..
MuIncB †	GLM 14.20	14.20	+0.02	+1.7	−0.3 NS ..
CapMkIdx	...11.22	11.22	−0.01	NA	NA NA ..
Cappiello-Rushmore:					
EmgGr	SML 12.14	12.14	+0.03	+4.2	+13.2 NS ..
Grwth	GRO 12.16	12.16	...	+1.3	+7.0 NS ..
Util	SEC 8.87	8.87	+0.01	+2.9	+5.5 NS ..
Capstone Group:					
Balanced	CAP 3.76	3.95	...	+2.5	−9.9 +6.6 E
GvtInc	BST 4.75	NL	...	−0.4	−1.4 +3.8 E
Grth	GRO 12.71	13.34	+0.01	+2.0	+1.7 +8.0 E
MedRs	SEC 17.23	18.09	+0.08	+2.0	+9.1 +15.2 B
NJapan	ITL 7.41	7.78	−0.03	−2.9	−13.8 +2.2 E
NZland	ITL 9.85	10.34	...	−0.5	−1.8 NS ..
Cardinal Family:					
Aggr Grth	CAP 10.26	10.86	−0.01	+2.6	+11.0 NS ..
Balanced	S&B 9.84	10.41	+0.01	+2.5	+2.5 NS ..
Fund	G&I 11.49	12.22	−0.03	+2.0	0.0 +10.8 D
Govt Oblg	MTG 7.86	8.22	−0.01	+0.9k	+1.4k +5.6k D
CariCa	S&B 11.76	12.38	−0.01	+0.4	+2.1 +12.0 B
CrnOHTE	MOH 9.26	9.70	+0.01	+1.1	+0.7 +6.5 E
Centura Funds:					
EqGrC	MID 9.97	10.44	+0.01	+5.1	+3.7 NS ..
FedSecC	BIN 9.74	10.02	−0.01	+0.6	+0.7 NS ..
NC TxFr	IDM 9.77	10.05	+0.02	+1.1	+0.9 NS ..
Cnt Shs	SEC 22.68	22.68	−0.11	+4.2	+4.7 +14.1 B
ChCapBC	GRO 12.34	NL	+0.01	+0.2	−4.2 +7.6 E
ChespkGr	GRO 14.49	14.93	+0.02	+2.3	−3.3 +13.8 NS ..
Chestnt	GRO 148.83	NL	+0.04	+3.0	+7.5 NA ..
ChicMilw	...141.44	NL	...	+2.7	+3.1 NS ..
ChubbGrIn	G&I 15.13	15.93	−0.04	+2.4	−0.5 +12.6 B
ChubbTR	S&B 13.49	14.20	−0.03	+2.0	−0.8 +11.3 B
Clipper	GRO 47.12	47.12	+0.01	+2.2	+3.3 +14.2 B
CloverCEq	GRO 13.20	NL	−0.05	+0.1	+0.3 NS ..
Colonial Funds:					
CalTE A	MCA 6.80	7.14	+0.01	+2.4k	−0.1k +5.7k E
ConTE A	SSM 7.02	7.37	+0.02	+2.3k	−0.2k NS ..
FedScA	MTG 9.93	10.43	−0.01	+1.1k	+0.7k +6.7k B
FL TE A	MFL 7.04	7.39	+0.01	+2.2k	+0.2k NS ..
FundA	G&I 7.46	7.92	...	+1.6	+1.2 +13.0 B
GIEqA	WOR 11.11	11.79	−0.03	−0.9	−0.8 NS ..
HiYldA	GRO 12.31	13.06	−0.01	+1.7	+0.4 +12.9 C
IncomeA p	BND 5.98	6.61	...	+0.5k	+0.9k +20.5k A
		6.28	...	+0.9k	+1.5k +8.8k B
IntGrA	ITL 9.38	9.95	...	−3.6	−8.5 NS ..
MATxA	DMA 7.31	7.67	+0.01	+2.3k	−0.1k +7.2k B
MI TE A	SSM 6.61	6.94	+0.02	+2.6k	+0.5k +6.5k C
MN TE A	SSM 6.79	7.13	+0.01	+2.1k	+0.5k +6.5k C
NatResA	SEC 11.83	12.55	+0.09	−0.8	−4.1 NS ..
NY TE A	DNY 6.59	6.92	...	+2.2k	−1.0k +6.4k D
OhTE A	MOH 6.88	7.22	+0.02	+2.2k	+0.0k +6.2k E
SmlStk	SML 18.71	19.85	−0.05	+1.8	+9.0 +16.5 D

(continued)

EXPLANATORY NOTES

Mutual fund data are supplied by two organizations. The daily Net Asset Value (NAV), Offer Price and Net Change calculations are supplied by the National Association of Securities Dealers (NASD) through Nasdaq, its automated quotation system. Performance and cost data are supplied by Lipper Analytical Services Inc.

Daily price data are entered into Nasdaq by the fund, its management company or agent. Performance and cost calculations are percentages provided by Lipper Analytical Services, based on prospectuses filed with the Securities and Exchange Commission, fund reports, financial reporting services and other sources believed to be authoritative, accurate and timely. Though verified, the data cannot be guaranteed by Lipper or its data sources and should be double-checked with the funds before making any investment decisions.

Performance calculations, as percentages, assuming reinvestment of all distributions, and after all asset based charges have been deducted. Asset based charges include advisory fees, other non-advisory fees and distribution expenses (12b-1). Figures are without regard to sales, deferred sales or redemption charges.

INVESTMENT OBJECTIVE (Inv. Obj.) – Based on stated investment goals outlined in the prospectus. The Journal assembled 27 groups based on classifications used by Lipper Analytical in the daily Mutual Fund Scorecard and other calculations. A detailed breakdown of classifications appears at the bottom of this page.

NET ASSET VALUE (NAV) – Per share value prepared by the fund, based on closing quotes unless noted, and supplied to the NASD by 5:30 p.m. Eastern time.

OFFER PRICE – Net asset value plus sales commission, if any.

NAV CHG. – Gain or loss, based on the previous NAV quotation.

TOTAL RETURN – Performance calculations, as percentages, assuming reinvestment of all distributions. Sales charges aren't reflected. Percentages are annualized for periods greater than one year. For funds declaring dividends daily, calculations are based on the most current data supplied by the fund within publication deadlines. A YEAR TO DATE (YTD) change is listed daily, with results ranging from 4 weeks to 5 years offered throughout the week. See chart on this page for specific schedule.

MAXIMUM INITIAL SALES COMMISSION (Max Init Chrg) – Based on prospectus; the sales charge may be modified or suspended temporarily by the fund, but any percentage change requires formal notification to the shareholders.

TOTAL EXPENSE RATIO (Total Exp Ratio) – Shown as a percentage and based on the fund's annual report, the ratio is total operating expenses for the fiscal year divided by the fund's average net assets. It includes all asset based charges such as advisory fees, other non-advisory fees and distribution expenses (12b-1).

RANKING (R) – Funds are grouped by investment objectives defined by The Wall Street Journal and ranked on longest time period listed each day. Performance measurement begins at either the closest Thursday or month-end for periods of more than one year. Gains of 100% or more are shown as a whole number, not carried out one decimal place. A=top 20%; B=next 20%; C=middle 20%; D=next 20%; E=bottom 20%.

QUOTATIONS FOOTNOTES

e-Ex-distribution. f-Previous day's quotation. s-Stock split or dividend. x-Ex–dividend.

p-Distribution costs apply, 12b-1 plan. r-Redemption charge may apply.

g-Footnotes x and s apply. i-Footnotes e and s apply. t-Footnotes p and r apply. v-Footnotes x and e apply. z-Footnotes x, e and s apply.

NA-Not available due to incomplete price, performance or cost data. NE-Deleted by Lipper editor; data in question. NL-No Load (sales commission). NN-Fund doesn't wish to be tracked. NS-Fund didn't exist at start of period.

k-Recalculated by Lipper, using updated data. I-No valid comparison with other funds because of expense structure.

Source: *The Wall Street Journal*, January 19, 1995. Reprinted by permission of *The Wall Street Journal*, ©1995 Dow Jones & Company, Inc. All rights reserved worldwide.

If there is no letter following the fund name and the offer price exceeds the net asset value, it is impossible to tell from the listing how the fund is loaded; the mutual fund company can provide that information.

Loaded funds are sold through brokers, which explains the commission fee. The investment company contracts with the broker to act as the fund's marketer.

Since no-load funds are directly marketed and have no outside sales force, there is no commission fee. In order to invest in a no-load fund, you must select the fund (e.g., in response to a newspaper ad or direct mail solicitation) and contact the investment company directly. A broker customarily will not act for you in the purchase of no-load funds, because he or she will not receive a commission fee of any kind.

The funds are grouped according to the investment company, and the individual funds listed also list the objective of each fund. The *Journal*

includes a table at the end of the Mutual Fund Quotations that lists the categories used to classify the objectives of mutual funds. See page 182. Some companies offer many funds, each with its own special objective. Take the *Calvert Group 's SocEq Fund* shown below, for example. In the first column, GRO indicates the fund's objective of growth. NAV, in the second column, stands for net asset value (per share). As you recall, this is calculated by totaling the market value of all securities owned by the fund, subtracting the liabilities (if any), and then dividing by the number of fund shares outstanding. In short, NAV equals the dollar value of the pool per mutual fund share. For instance, at the close of business on January 18, 1995, Calvert Group's Social Investment Equity Fund, which invests only in equity securities it considers to be socially responsible investments, had a net asset value of $18.06. The third column informs you that this was an 8 cent loss from the previous day.

Notice that the offer price of $18.96 is higher than the NAV, which indicates there is a load included. However, without a *t* or *p* after the fund's name, it is not clear how the load is determined. Also note that for $39.30 you could have bought a "share" in this fund, which includes hundreds of individual issues. Imagine the cost of buying a share in each of these companies.

Calvert Group:

GlobEq	WOR 15.78	16.57	−0.03	−2.2	−7.5	NS ..	
Inco	BND 15.63	16.24	...	+0.8	+0.6	+7.6 C	
MuBdCAl	IDM 9.94	10.22	+0.02	+1.2	+0.3	NS ..	
MunInt	IDM 9.94	10.22	+0.02	+1.3	+1.2	NS ..	
Social p	S&B 28.26	29.67	...	+1.4	+0.8	+6.7 E	
SocBd	BND 15.32	15.92	...	+1.1	0.0	+7.1 D	Calvert Social
SocEq	GRO 18.06	18.96	−0.08	+1.2	−5.8	+4.7 E	◀—— Investment Equity
StrGwth	GRO 17.20	18.06	+0.01	−0.7	+17.6	NS ..	Fund
TxF Lt	STM 10.62	10.84	...	+0.3	+1.5	+4.5 E	
TxF LtC	STM 10.59	10.59	...	+0.3	NA	NS ..	
TxF Lg	GLM 16.06	16.69	+0.03	+1.5	+2.0	+6.8 B	
TxF VT	SSM 15.55	16.16	+0.02	+1.4	+1.0	NS ..	
US Gov	MTG 13.65	14.18	...	+0.9	+0.3	+5.3 E	

The *Journal* publishes a report daily on the third-to-last page of the third (C) section called **Mutual Fund Scorecard**. (See the example from the Tuesday, February 21, 1995 *Wall Street Journal* on page 187). It lists the top and bottom performers of a wide variety of mutual funds. Here is a list of some of the different kinds of funds that are covered in the *Journal*'s **Mutual Fund Scorecard**:

A-Rated Bond	High Current Yield
Balanced	International
BBB-Rated Bond	Money Market
Capital Appreciation	Natural Resources and Gold
Closed End Bond	Short-Term Municipal Bond
Closed End Equity	Small Company Growth
Convertible Securities	Specialty and Miscellaneous
Equity Income	Tax-Exempt Money Funds
General Municipal Bond	U. S . Government Bond
Ginnie Mae	Variable Annuity Bond
Global	Variable Annuity Equity
Growth	World Income
Growth and Income	

At this point you may very well feel that the objective outlined in Chapters 1 and 8 has been lost. Mutual funds seem to have no advantage over individual stocks, because the choice among funds, even among different kinds of funds, has become tremendously difficult due to the proliferation of funds. What happened to gold vs. stocks?

Don't despair. You can still invest in the overall stock market by selecting an *index fund* that places your capital in one of the better known stock market barometers. For instance, Vanguard Group has an index fund, called Index 500, in which all of its resources are invested in the S & P 500. On Thursday, January 19, 1995, Vanguard's Index 500 had a net asset value of $43.99 (see page 186).

MUTUAL FUND OBJECTIVES

Categories used by The Wall Street Journal, based on classifications developed by Lipper Analytical Services Inc., and fund groups included in each:

STOCK FUNDS

Capital Appreciation (CAP): Capital Appreciation.
Growth & Income (G&I): Growth & Income, S&P 500 Index.
Growth (GRO): Growth.
Equity Income (EQI): Equity Income.
Small Company (SML): Small Company Growth
MidCap (MID): MidCap.
Sector (SEC): Health/Biotechnology; Natural Resources; Environmental; Science & Technology; Speciality & Miscellaneous; Utility; Financial Services; Real Estate; Gold Oriented.
Global (WOR): Global; Small Company Global.
International (non-U.S.) (ITL): International; European Region; Pacific Region; Japanese; Latin American; Canadian; Emerging Market; International Small Company.

TAXABLE BOND FUNDS

Short Term (BST): Adjustable Rate Mortgage; Ultrashort Obligation; Short U.S. Treasury; Short U.S. Government; Short Investment Grade.
Intermediate (BIN): U.S. Treasury; U.S. Government; Investment Grade Corporate.
General U.S. Taxable (BND): U.S. Treasury; General Bond; Target Maturity; Flexible Income; Corporate A-Rated; Corporate BBB-Rated.
High Yield Taxable (BHI): High Current Yield.
Mortgage (MTG): U.S. Government; GNMA; U.S. Mortgage.
World (WBD): Short World Multi-Market; Short World Single-Market; General World Income.

MUNICIPAL BOND FUNDS

Short Term (STM): Short Municipal Debt; Short term California.
Intermediate (IDM): Intermediate Municipal Debt; Intermediate California Muni Debt; Intermediate Florida Muni Debt; Intermediate Massachusetts Muni Debt; Intermediate Michigan Muni Debt; Intermediate New York Muni Debt; Intermediate Pennsylvania Muni Debt; Other States Intermediate Muni Debt.
General (GLM): General Municipal Debt.
California (MCA): California Municipal Debt.
Florida (MFL): Florida Municipal Debt.
Massachusetts (DMA): Mass. Municipal Debt.
New Jersey (MNJ): New Jersey Municipal Debt.
New York (DNY): New York Municipal Debt.
Ohio (MOH): Ohio Municipal Debt.
Pennsylvania (MPA): Pennsylvania Municipal Debt.
Single-State Municipal (SSM): All single-state municipal debt, except California, Florida, Massachusetts, New Jersey, New York, Ohio and Pennsylvania.
High Yield Municipal (HYM): High Yield Municipal Debt.
Insured, All Maturities, All Issuers (ISM): Insured Municipal Debt; California Insured Debt; New York Insured Debt.

STOCK & BOND FUNDS

Blended Funds (S&B): Flexible Portfolio; Global Flexible Portfolio; Balanced; Balanced Target Maturity; Convertible Securities; Income.

Source: *The Wall Street Journal*, January 19, 1995. Reprinted by permission of *The Wall Street Journal*, ©1995 Dow Jones & Company, Inc. All rights reserved worldwide.

Vanguard Group:

Fund	Type	NAV	Offer	Chg				Rank
AdmIT	BIN	9.51	NL	...	+1.0	+0.6	NS	..
AdmLT	BND	9.31	NL	...	+1.3	+1.4	NS	..
AdmST	BST	9.72	NL	...	+0.8	+1.1	NS	..
AssetA	S&B	13.78	NL	...	+1.8	+3.4	+11.1	C
Convrt	S&B	10.69	NL	+0.03	+1.3	+1.4	+14.6	A
EqInc	EQI	13.06	NL	+0.02	+2.3	+4.1	+12.3	C
Explr	SML	43.33	NL	−0.02	+1.1	+7.2	+20.7	B
LIFECon	S&B	10.01	NL	−0.01	+1.2	NS	NS	..
LIFEMod	S&B	9.99	NL	−0.01	+1.3	NS	NS	..
LIFEGro	S&B	10.07	NL	−0.01	+1.4	NS	NS	..
Morg	GRO	11.59	NL	−0.01	+2.0	+4.6	+11.2	D
Prmcp	GRO	20.58	NL	+0.05	+3.0	+9.1	+17.9	A
Quant	G&I	15.92	NL	−0.01	+2.3	+4.6	+12.9	B
STAR	S&B	12.84	NL	...	+1.8	+2.2	+11.5	B
TxMCap	GRO	10.19	NL	...	+2.4	NS	NS	..
TxMGI	G&I	10.00	NL	−0.01	+2.4	NS	NS	..
Trintl	ITL	30.74	NL	−0.02	−2.4	−6.1	+8.1	C
TrUS	G&I	29.99	NL	−0.02	+3.1	+1.7	+11.8	C
STTsry	BST	9.83	NL	−0.01	+0.7	+1.0	NS	..
STFed	BST	9.73	NL	−0.01	+0.7	+0.7	+6.1	B
STCorp	BST	10.35	NL	...	+0.8	+1.2	+6.8	A
ITTsry	BIN	9.69	NL	...	+0.9	+0.5	NS	..
GNMA	MTG	9.63	NL	−0.02	+0.9	+2.0	+7.0	A
ITCorp	BIN	9.01	NL	...	+1.0	+0.7	NS	..
LTTsry	BND	9.14	NL	...	+1.3	+1.3	+9.8	A
LTCorp	BND	8.11	NL	...	+1.1	+1.2	+9.5	A
HYCorp	BHI	7.21	NL	...	+0.6	+3.3	+14.7	D
Prefd	BND	8.39	NL	+0.01	+2.9	+0.2	+8.7	B
IdxTotB	BIN	9.22	NL	−0.01	+0.9	+1.2	+7.2	B
IdxSTB	BST	9.55	NL	...	+0.8	+1.0	NS	..
IdxITB	BIN	9.23	NL	−0.01	+0.9	+0.6	NS	..
Idx Bal	S&B	10.53	NL	...	+1.8	+3.2	NS	..
Idx 500	G&I	43.99	NL	−0.02	+2.4	+5.1	+12.5	C
IdxExt	MID	18.94	NL	−0.03	+2.3	+3.9	+16.7	C
IdxTot	GRO	11.65	NL	−0.01	+2.5	+4.8	NS	..
IdxGro	GRO	10.47	NL	...	+1.8	+7.7	NS	..
IdxVal	G&I	11.45	NL	−0.01	+3.0	+2.4	NS	..
IdxSmC	SML	15.12	NL	−0.03	+0.9	+3.7	+20.0	C
IdxEMkt	ITL	10.21	NL	−0.03	−6.1	−5.5	NS	..
IdxEur	ITL	11.83	NL	+0.04	+0.6	+0.5	+9.6	B
IdxPac	ITL	10.84	NL	−0.10	−4.2	−9.3	+6.9	D
IdxInst	G&I	44.24	NL	−0.02	+2.4	+5.1	+12.6	B
MuHY	HYM	9.82	NL	+0.02	+2.0	0.0	+7.9	A
MuInt	IDM	12.55	NL	+0.02	+1.6	+1.0	+7.5	A

Vanguard Index 500: Net Asset Value $43.99 →

Source: *The Wall Street Journal*, January 19, 1995. Reprinted by permission of *The Wall Street Journal*, ©1995 Dow Jones & Company, Inc. All rights reserved worldwide.

Finally, notice that the last four columns provide a summary of each fund's total return for the year to date (YTD), as well as for the previous 26 weeks and four years. The explanatory table and notes at the top of the first page of listings (see pages 181 and 182) shows that each day's listing provides a different length of time for the total return calculation. The last column ranks the funds (A = top 20%, B = next 20%, C = middle 20%, D = next 20%, and E = bottom 20%) for the longest time period listed in comparison with all other funds *with a similar investment objective*. Note the classification of investment objectives that regularly appears at the bottom of the last column on the first page of the mutual fund listings (see page 185).

You can see from the example on page 183 that Calvert Group's Social Investment Equity Fund's total return of 4.7% annually over the past four years placed its performance in the bottom fifth of all common-stock mutual funds that had growth as their objective. But keep in mind that you can not compare this fund's ranking with that of Vanguard's Index 500 which had a growth and income objective.

Mutual Fund Scorecard/Equity Income

INVESTMENT OBJECTIVE: Dividend income from a portfolio principally made up of equities; may hold some bonds. Bull/Bear ratings are figured over the latest two rising and two falling market cycles.

ASSETS SEPT. 30 (in millions)	BULL MKTS	BEAR MKTS	FUND NAME	4 WEEKS	52 WEEKS	5 YEARS*
TOP 15 PERFORMERS						
183.7	Med	Low	Fidelity Adv Inst Eq Inc [2,5]	2.74%	7.21%	10.18%
135.3	**	**	Fidelity Adv Eq Inc;A [4]	2.69	6.24	**
7.0	**	**	Delaware Div Growth;A [4]	4.71	5.31	**
3128.6	**	Med	T Rowe Price Eq Income [2]	2.90	4.69	9.73
10.5	**	**	Nicholas Equity Income [2]	2.85	4.35	**
762.7	**	**	STI Classic:Val Inc;Tr [2,4,5]	3.86	3.68	**
34.4	**	**	Riverfront:Income Equity [3]	3.70	3.10	**
7474.1	**	**	Fidelity Equity-Inc II [2]	3.13	2.46	**
62.0	Med	High	Analytic Optioned Eq [2]	2.52	2.34	5.85
44.6	**	**	Managers:Income Equity [2,5]	2.71	1.95	N.A.
195.7	**	Med	One Gp:Inco Eq;Fid [2,4,5]	2.62	1.74	7.60
50.2	**	**	Gabelli Eq:Eq Income [3]	2.89	1.47	**
318.6	Med	Low	Putnam Equity Income;A [4]	3.11	1.40	7.30
140.5	**	**	Galaxy:Equity Income;Rtl [2,4]	2.32	1.24	**
11376.5	Med	Med	Fidelity Puritan [2]	1.28	0.57	10.60
AVG. FOR CATEGORY				2.60%	−2.12%	7.23%
NUMBER OF FUNDS				116	98	52
BOTTOM 10 PERFORMERS						
6.3	Med	Low	Steadman Associated Fd [2]	−1.52%	−22.62%	−3.82%
69.2	**	**	Nich-App:Inc & Gr;B [2,4]	1.48	−8.94	**
359.2	**	**	Parkstone:Hi Inc;Instl [2,4]	3.36	−8.79	6.80
43.0	**	**	Westcore:Eq Income;Instl [2,4]	1.81	−8.38	6.20
17.8	**	**	Nich-App:Inc & Gr Instl [2]	1.59	−7.80	**
10.4	**	Med	Amana:Income Fund [2]	1.67	−5.70	4.86
30.2	**	**	Eaton Vance Equity-Inc [2]	0.29	−5.58	1.63
469.0	High	High	Flag Inv Tphn Inc;A [3,4]	2.23	−5.58	7.53
2.7	**	**	MIM Mutual:AFA Eq Inc [2]	2.82	−5.55	**
179.0	**	**	Pimco Adv:Eq Inc;C [2,4]	1.93	−5.34	6.51

TOTAL RETURN[1] IN PERIOD ENDING JAN. 5

[1] Change in net asset value with reinvested dividends and capital gains
[2] No initial load
[3] Low initial load of 4.5% or less
[4] Fund has other share classes
[5] Fund may not be open to all investors
** Fund track record is too short

Hi = Top third
Med = Middle third
Low = Bottom third
* Annualized

Source: *Lipper Analytical Services Inc.*

CLOSED-END FUNDS

The mutual funds described above are open-ended because they continually issue new shares in order to expand their pool of capital. They sell their shares to investors and buy them back. But after their initial offering, *closed-end funds* do not issue additional shares and do not buy them back. The shares of the closed-end fund trade on an organized exchange or over-the-counter and appreciate or depreciate with investor demand like any other share of stock. Meanwhile, the investment company has its initial (fixed) pool of capital with which to make investments.

The success of the fund's investments determines the net asset value of the fund's shares (a fluctuating numerator to be divided by a fixed denominator), which can differ from their market value (stock price) as determined by supply and demand. The stock price may be above net asset value, trading at a premium, or below, trading at a discount. Either way, the fund's management takes its fee for administering the fund.

Why would fund managers choose to be confined by a closed-end fund rather than grow with a conventional open-end mutual fund? Because their pool of capital is not subject to the volatile swings generated by purchases and redemptions. Why would investors buy this kind of fund? Because they can purchase a closed-end fund at a discount, at less than net asset value, and enjoy a substantial potential gain if the stock price climbs back up to net asset value.

The Wall Street Journal publishes a report on closed-end funds each Monday under the heading **Closed End Funds**. You can find it in the index on page C1. Page 189 has an example from the February 21, 1995 issue. Notice the broad array of investments and investment objectives. Notice also that you may be able to purchase shares in a fund at a substantial discount from its net asset value. This may signal an unusual and temporary investment opportunity.

CLOSED END FUNDS

Friday, February 17, 1995

Closed-end funds sell a limited number of shares and invest the proceeds in securities. Unlike open-end funds, closed-ends generally do not buy their shares back from investors who wish to cash in their holdings. Instead, fund shares trade on a stock exchange. The following list, provided by Lipper Analytical Services, shows the exchange where each fund trades (A: American; C: Chicago; N: NYSE; O: Nasdaq; T: Toronto; z: does not trade on an exchange). The data also include the fund's most recent net asset value, its closing share price on the day NAV was calculated, and the percentage difference between the market price and the NAV (often called the premium or discount). For equity funds, the final column provides 52-week returns based on market prices plus dividends. For bond funds, the final column shows the past 12 months' income distributions as a percentage of the current market price. Footnotes appear after a fund's name. a: the NAV and market price are ex dividend. b: the NAV is fully diluted. c: NAV, market price and premium or discount are as of Thursday's close. d: NAV, market price and premium or discount are as of Wednesday's close. e: NAV assumes rights offering is fully subscribed. v: NAV is converted at the commercial Rand rate. y: NAV and market price are in Canadian dollars. All other footnotes refer to unusual circumstances; explanations for those that appear can be found at the bottom of this list. N/A signifies that the information is not available or not applicable.

Fund Name	Stock Exch	NAV	Market Price	Prem /Disc	52 week Market Return
General Equity Funds					
Adams Express -a	N	18.58	16 1/4	−12.5	−0.1
Alliance All-Mkt	N	20.03	17 3/8	−13.3	N/A
Baker Fentress	N	18.05	15	−16.9	−2.6
Bergstrom Cap	A	100.58	91	− 9.5	6.4
Blue Chip Value	N	7.30	6 3/8	−12.7	−9.5
Central Secs	A	17.37	16 1/4	− 6.4	5.8
Specialized Equity Funds					
Alliance Gl Env	N	11.10	8 7/8	−20.0	−13.4
C&S Realty	A	8.27	8 3/4	+ 5.8	−0.1
C&S Total Rtn	N	12.60	12 7/8	+ 2.2	−6.2
Centrl Fd Canada -c	A	4.63	4 3/8	− 5.5	−22.0
Counsellors Tand	N	15.50	13 7/8	−10.5	−2.6
Delaware Gr Div	N	12.87	12 5/8	− 1.9	−5.3
Delaware Grp Gl	N	13.04	12 3/8	− 5.1	N/A
Convertible Sec's. Funds					
Amer Cap Conv	N	22.32	20 1/4	− 9.3	−3.2
Bancroft Conv	A	22.57	20 1/4	−10.3	−0.6
Castle Conv	A	25.26	24 3/8	− 3.5	8.2
Ellsworth Conv	A	9.47	8 3/8	−11.6	−0.1
Lincoln Conv -c	N	17.39	16 1/4	− 6.6	−13.0
Putnam Hi Inc Cv -a	N	8.82	9 3/8	+ 6.3	4.9
TCW Conv Secs	N	7.55	8 3/8	+10.9	−4.3
Dual-Purpose Funds					
Conv Hold Cap	N	11.65	9 7/8	−15.2	−5.9
Conv Hold Inc	N	9.45	10 1/8	+ 7.1	1.7
Gemini II Cap	N	21.01	18 7/8	−10.2	−0.7
Gemini II Inc	N	9.20	10 3/4	+16.8	7.1
Quest Value Cap	N	28.24	25	−11.5	7.9
Quest Value Inc	N	11.59	12 1/8	+ 4.6	4.5
World Equity Funds					
ASA Limited -acv	N	42.74	43 1/2	+ 1.8	−2.7
Americas All Sea	O	4.76	3 7/16	−27.8	−17.0
Anchor Gold&Curr	C	5.18	5 1/8	− 1.1	−25.5
Argentina	N	9.60	10 3/8	+ 8.1	−39.4
Asia Pacific	N	N/A	13 7/8	N/A	−23.2
Asia Tigers	N	N/A	10	N/A	−28.4
Austria	N	9.05	7 3/4	−14.4	−26.7
Royce Micro-Cap	O	7.71	6 3/4	−12.5	−10.8
SthEastrn Thrift	O	21.52	20 1/8	− 6.5	12.1
Templtn Gl Util	A	12.70	12	− 5.5	−18.4
U.S. Gov't. Bond Funds					
ACM Govt Inc	N	8.10	9 1/2	+17.3	11.7
ACM Govt Oppty	N	7.40	7 1/8	− 3.7	11.0
ACM Govt Secs	N	7.74	8 3/8	+ 8.2	13.1
ACM Govt Spec	N	6.56	7 1/8	+ 8.6	13.2
Amer Govt Income -c	N	5.42	6	+10.7	13.4
Amer Govt Port -c	N	6.55	7 1/8	+ 8.8	14.4
Dean Witter Govt	N	8.74	7 15/16	− 9.2	7.9
Excelsior Income -c	N	17.45	15	−14.0	8.1
Kemper Int Govt	N	7.84	7 5/16	− 6.7	9.2
MFS Govt Mkts	N	6.99	6 1/4	−10.6	6.3
Putnam Int Govt -a	N	8.13	7 3/8	− 9.3	8.3
RCM Strat Glbl	N	10.86	9 5/8	−11.4	N/A
U.S. Mortgage Bond Funds					
2002 Target Term -ac	N	13.04	11 1/4	−13.7	7.7
Amer Adj Rate 95 -c	N	9.72	9 1/2	− 2.3	3.2
Amer Adj Rate 96 -c	N	8.97	8 1/2	− 5.2	4.9
Amer Adj Rate 97 -c	N	8.76	8 1/8	− 7.2	6.1
Amer Adj Rate 98 -c	N	8.62	8 1/8	− 5.7	6.7
Amer Adj Rate 99 -c	N	8.43	7 7/8	− 6.6	7.1
Amer Govt Term -c	N	8.03	7 1/2	− 6.6	9.8
Amer Oppty Inc -c	N	6.23	7 3/8	+18.4	14.0
Amer Sel Port -c	N	11.64	11	− 5.5	10.2
Amer Str Inc II -c	N	12.33	12 1/8	− 1.7	11.5
Amer Str Inc III -c	N	11.94	11 7/8	− 0.5	11.3
Amer Str Income -c	N	12.62	13 1/8	+ 4.0	10.9
BlckRk 1998 Term -c	N	9.22	8 5/8	− 6.5	7.3

Fund Name	Stock Exch	NAV	Market Price	Prem /Disc	12 Mo Yield 1/31/95
Investment Grade Bond Funds					
1838 Bd-Deb	N	20.23	20 3/8	+ 0.7	8.6
All-American Tm -ac	N	13.52	12 3/8	− 8.5	10.1
Amer Cap Bond	N	19.22	17 7/8	− 7.0	8.7
CNA Income -c	N	9.26	10	+ 8.0	11.8
Circle Income -ac	O	11.20	9 7/8	−11.8	9.2
Current Inc Shs	N	12.81	11 1/4	−12.2	8.5
Fortis Secs -a	N	8.97	9	+ 0.3	9.9
Ft Dearborn Inc	N	15.40	14	− 9.1	8.1
Hatteras Income -a	N	15.48	15 1/2	+ 0.1	9.1
INA Investments	N	18.07	16	−11.5	8.7
Independence Sq	O	17.09	15 1/2	− 9.3	8.2
InterCap Income	N	16.98	16 7/8	− 0.6	9.0
Loan Participation Funds					
Eaton Vance Pr	z	10.04	N/A	N/A	N/A
Merrill Sen Fl	z	10.01	N/A	N/A	N/A
Pilgrim Pr Rate	N	9.63	8 3/4	− 9.1	8.5
Prime Income	z	9.98	N/A	N/A	N/A
VanKamp Prime	z	N/A	N/A	N/A	N/A
High Yield Bond Funds					
CIGNA High Inc	N	6.81	6 3/4	− 0.9	13.2
CIM High Yld	N	7.28	7 5/8	+ 4.7	11.5
Colonial Intmdt	N	6.31	6 1/4	− 1.0	10.9
Corp Hi Yld -a	N	12.37	12 3/4	+ 3.1	13.0
Corp Hi Yld II -a	N	11.57	12	+ 3.7	13.0
Franklin Univ -c	N	8.74	8 1/8	− 7.0	10.1
High Inc Adv	N	5.15	5 3/8	+ 4.4	11.7
High Inc Adv II	N	5.81	5 7/8	+ 1.1	10.5
High Inc Adv III	N	6.21	6 1/2	+ 4.7	11.1
High Yld Income	N	6.83	7 1/2	+ 9.8	12.3
Other Domestic Taxable Bond Funds					
ACM Mgd $	N	8.85	9 3/4	+10.2	15.0
ACM Mgd Income	N	7.46	7 5/8	+ 2.2	14.2
AIM Strategic	A	9.17	8	−12.8	5.8
Alliance Wld $	N	9.53	11 1/8	+16.7	15.5
Alliance Wld $ 2	N	10.21	10 3/8	+ 1.6	11.8
Allmerica Secs	N	10.89	10	− 8.2	8.7
Amer Cap Inc	N	7.42	7	− 5.7	9.5
Colonial Intrmkt	N	10.46	10 1/2	+ 0.4	9.8
Duff&Ph Util Cor	N	12.68	12 3/8	− 2.4	8.8
First Boston Inc	N	8.16	7 1/2	− 8.1	9.9
First Boston Str	N	9.40	8 5/8	− 8.2	9.7
Franklin Mul-Inc -c	N	9.56	8 3/4	− 8.5	9.1
Franklin Pr Mat -c	N	7.78	6 7/8	−11.6	8.7
Global Partners	N	10.08	10 1/4	+ 1.7	14.1
Highlander Inc -c	A	13.01	12 1/4	− 5.8	N/A
J Han Income	N	15.60	15 1/8	− 3.0	8.5
J Han Investors	N	20.44	19 1/2	− 4.6	8.6
Kemper Multi Mkt	N	10.15	9 1/2	− 6.4	10.2
Kemper Strat Inc	N	11.55	12 1/8	+ 5.0	N/A
World Income Funds					
ACM Mgd MultiMkt	N	7.76	7 3/8	− 5.0	9.8
Americas Inc Tr -c	N	7.65	6 7/8	−10.1	15.8
BlckRk North Am -c	N	9.75	9 1/8	− 6.4	11.7
Dreyfus Str Govt	N	9.91	9 1/4	− 6.7	9.6
Emer Mkts Float	N	11.99	11 7/8	− 1.0	N/A
Emer Mkts Inc	N	11.74	12 3/8	+ 5.4	9.8
Emer Mkts Inc II	N	9.34	10 3/8	+11.1	15.7
First Aust Prime	A	8.80	8 13/16	+ 0.1	11.3
First Commonwlth	N	11.87	10 3/8	−12.6	10.2
Global Govt	N	6.95	5 3/4	−17.3	7.9
Global Hi Inc $ -a	N	11.71	10 7/8	− 7.1	13.0
Global Income Pl	N	8.71	8 1/8	− 6.7	8.2
Global Total Ret	N	7.72	6 1/8	−20.7	7.7
National Muni Bond Funds					
ACM Muni Secs	N	11.74	11 1/8	− 5.2	8.1
Amer Muni Income -c	N	12.55	12 1/8	− 3.4	7.5
Amer Muni Tm II -c	N	10.78	10	− 7.2	6.4
Amer Muni Tm III -c	N	10.02	9 5/8	− 3.9	6.4
Amer Muni Tm Tr -c	N	10.99	10 1/4	− 6.7	6.5
Apex Muni -a	N	9.95	9 1/4	− 7.0	8.1
BlckRk Ins 2008	N	14.87	13 5/8	− 8.4	6.6
BlckRk Ins Muni	N	10.26	9 5/8	− 6.2	6.7
BlckRk Inv Q Mun	N	13.03	12 1/8	− 6.9	7.8
BlckRk Muni Tgt	N	10.46	9 5/8	− 8.0	6.5
Colonial Hi Inc	N	8.24	7 7/8	− 4.4	8.0
Colonial Inv Gr	N	10.34	9 7/8	− 4.5	6.7
Colonial Mu Inc	N	7.34	7 3/8	+ 0.5	8.5
Dreyfus Income	A	9.40	9 1/4	− 1.6	7.5
Dreyfus St Munis	N	9.73	10	+ 2.8	7.4
Dreyfus Str Muni	N	9.12	9 1/4	+ 1.4	7.4
Duff&Ph Util TF	N	15.06	14 1/4	− 5.4	7.1
Single State Muni Bond					
BlckRk CA Ins 08	N	14.64	13 5/8	− 6.9	6.1
BlckRk CA Inv	A	12.68	12	− 5.4	6.9
BlckRk FL Ins 08	N	14.91	13 7/8	− 6.9	6.1
BlckRk FL Inv	A	12.97	12	− 7.5	7.1
BlckRk NJ Inv	A	12.43	11 7/8	− 4.5	6.8
BlckRk NY Ins 08	N	14.76	13 3/4	− 6.8	6.3
BlckRk NY Inv	A	12.51	11 1/4	−10.1	7.0
Dreyfus CA Inc	A	8.81	8 3/8	− 4.9	6.9
Dreyfus NY Inc	A	9.87	9 1/4	− 6.3	6.2
Greenwich St CA	A	12.43	11 5/8	− 6.5	N/A
InterCap CA Ins	N	12.38	11 3/8	− 8.1	7.9
InterCap CA Qual	N	11.54	10 3/8	−10.1	8.2
InterCap Ins CA	N	14.06	12 3/8	−12.0	N/A

Source: *The Wall Street Journal*, February 21, 1995. Reprinted by permission of *The Wall Street Journal*,

RISKY BUSINESS

Margin and Option Trading

If you are confident a stock will rise, you may purchase it and realize your gain if your prediction proves true. But there are a number of ways you can *leverage* your purchase in order to increase your gain (i.e., you can capture the increase on a larger number of shares of stock than you can currently afford to purchase). Your *leverage* is the ratio between the value of the shares you control (and from which you will reap a profit) and the amount of capital (money) you have invested. The smaller your investment and the larger the value of the shares you control, the greater your leverage.

For instance, under current regulations set by the Fed, you may borrow from your broker up to half the initial value of the shares of stock you purchase, which provides leverage of two to one. It's called *buying on margin*. If you buy $200 worth of stock from your broker, with a margin (your capital) of $100 (50 percent margin) and a $100 loan from the broker, and the stock doubles in value (from $200 to $400), you have made $200 on a $100 investment (less interest and brokerage costs) instead of $100 on a $100 investment that was not margined. That's leverage.

Options provide another opportunity to leverage your investment. They give you the right (option) to buy or sell stock at a stated price for future delivery at a premium (cost to buy the option). People do this for the same reason they buy or sell any stock: They think it's going up or down in value. Only in this case, they believe the market price of the stock will be higher or lower than the price at which they agreed to buy or sell it. Investors stand to gain if they can buy a stock below its market price (and can then sell it at the market price), or can sell it above market price (after having purchased it below market price).

For instance, suppose you had the option to buy a share of stock for $25 in a few months' time that currently trades at 23½, and you were convinced the stock would be trading at 28 by then. Wouldn't you pay a premium for the right to buy a $28 stock for $25? That's a good deal, as long as the premium is smaller than the spread between $25 and the $28 price at which you think the stock will trade. Conversely, if you were convinced that a stock, currently trading at 23½, would fall to 18, wouldn't you pay a fee (premium) for the right to sell it at $20, knowing you could obtain it at $18?

LISTED OPTIONS QUOTATIONS

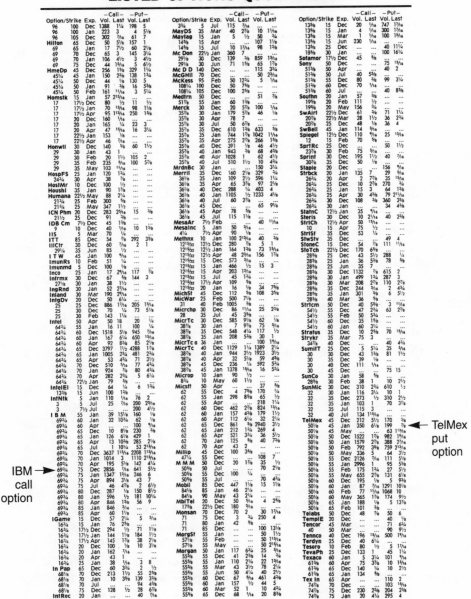

IBM → call option

TelMex → put option

IBM	55	Jan	39	$15\frac{1}{8}$	160	$\frac{1}{8}$
$69\frac{3}{4}$	60	Jan	32	$10\frac{3}{4}$	62	$\frac{1}{8}$
$69\frac{3}{4}$	60	Apr	...	...	100	$\frac{9}{16}$
$69\frac{3}{4}$	65	Dec	10	$8\frac{1}{8}$	230	$\frac{3}{8}$
$69\frac{3}{4}$	65	Jan	126	$6\frac{1}{8}$	429	1
$69\frac{3}{4}$	65	Apr	13	$10\frac{3}{8}$	285	$2\frac{1}{8}$
$69\frac{3}{4}$	65	Jul	1	$10\frac{1}{4}$	53	$2\frac{13}{16}$
$69\frac{3}{4}$	70	Dec	3637	$1\frac{13}{16}$	2208	$1\frac{15}{16}$
$69\frac{3}{4}$	70	Jan	1014	3	1110	$2\frac{13}{16}$
$69\frac{3}{4}$	70	Apr	195	$5\frac{1}{8}$	142	$4\frac{1}{4}$
$69\frac{3}{4}$	75	Dec	2856	$\frac{7}{16}$	641	$5\frac{1}{2}$
$69\frac{3}{4}$	75	Jan	1347	$1\frac{3}{16}$	246	6
$69\frac{3}{4}$	75	Apr	894	$3\frac{1}{8}$	43	7
$69\frac{3}{4}$	75	Jul	46	$4\frac{7}{8}$	2	$6\frac{1}{2}$
$69\frac{3}{4}$	80	Dec	287	$\frac{1}{8}$	150	$8\frac{1}{2}$
$69\frac{3}{4}$	80	Jan	596	$\frac{1}{2}$	181	$10\frac{1}{4}$
$69\frac{3}{4}$	80	Apr	846	$1\frac{5}{8}$	56	9
$69\frac{3}{4}$	85	Jan	846	$\frac{3}{16}$	...	...
$69\frac{3}{4}$	85	Apr	60	$1\frac{1}{8}$	...	...

← IBM call option at $1\frac{3}{16}$ on November 22, 1994

Source: *The Wall Street Journal*, November 23, 1994. Reprinted by permission of *The Wall Street Journal*,

The excerpt from the Wednesday, November 23, 1994 *Journal* shown above presents a summary of options trading on Tuesday, November 22, 1994. This report, called **Listed Options Quotations**, appears daily, and you can find it listed in the front-page indexes of the first (Al) and last (Cl) sections. This excerpt takes IBM as an example (first column).

The first column informs you that IBM closed at $69\frac{3}{4}$ on Tuesday, November 22, 1994.

The second column lists the *strike prices*—in five dollar increments from 55 to 85—at which you have the option of buying or selling the stock in the future. Note that some prices are higher and some are lower than the current price ($69\frac{3}{4}$). Think of the strike price as the price at which you strike a deal. The third column lists the month in the future—on the third Friday—that your option expires.

The last four columns list the volume of options traded and the premium you must pay per share to purchase the option to buy (*call*) or sell (*put*) IBM stock at the applicable strike price of the months listed. Take January as an example. You could purchase an option at a strike price of 75. On November 22, 1994, you had to pay a premium of \$1.1875 ($1\frac{3}{16}$) for the right (option) to buy a share of IBM stock at \$75.00 (75) by the close of trading on January 21, 1995 (third Friday of January). Once the deal was struck, the seller (writer) of the option would be bound to deliver the stock to you at that price at any time before the close of business on January 21, 1995, *at your option*. That is, the decision to purchase is up to you. You can take it or leave it once you have paid the premium.

Why would you buy such a contract? Because you were convinced that IBM would trade at more than $76.1875 (strike price of $75.00 plus premium of $1.1875) at any time before the third Friday in January. Then you would have the option to buy it at $75.00 (the strike price) from the option writer and sell it at the higher market price. When the call price rises above the strike price, an option is said to be *in the money*.

Trading is done in round lots of 100 shares. Thus, on November 22, 1994, when IBM was $69.75, you could have purchased an option for $118.75 (100 × $1.1875) to buy 100 shares at $75.00 by January 21, 1995. How would you have done?

Not bad. As you can see on page 194 in the excerpt from the Wednesday, January 18, 1995 *Journal*, IBM traded at $77.50 on January 17, 1995, a few days before the option expired. Back in November you paid a $118.75 premium (100 × $1.1875) for the option to call 100 shares at $75.00, and now exercise your option for $7,500 (100 × $75.00). Those shares are worth $7,750 (100 × $77.50) on the market. Thus you have obtained $7,750 of securities for $7,500, less your premium of $118.75, for a gain of $131.25 ($7,750 – $7,500 – $118.75 = $131.25) on your $118.75 investment. That's leverage.

Notice that purchasing the option provided you a much higher return than buying IBM stock at $69.75 on November 22, 1994. By January 17, that investment had appreciated by 11% ($77.50 – $69.75 return on $69.75 investment), considerably less than the 110.5% ($131.25 return on $118.75 investment) gain on the option. But notice that the option carried considerably greater risk. When a stock does not appreciate, you at least preserve your capital (you still have the stock). When an option expires, your money's gone (you have nothing).

You should know, however, that you need not purchase the stock underlying an option in order to realize your gain. You can sell the option instead. For instance, using the IBM example in the previous paragraphs, you will notice that the option was in the money a few days before its expiration and traded at $2.625 (2⅝), a little more than the difference ($2.50) between the strike price ($77.50) and the call price ($75.00). In other words, you could have sold the option for $2.625 on January 17, 1995 to another investor *and reaped your gain of $143.75 ($2.625 × 100 less the initial investment of $118.75) for a return of 121.1% ($143.25 ÷ $118.75) without purchasing the underlying stock*. As a matter of fact, most investors never intend to buy the underlying stock. Instead, they hope to sell their option at a profit.

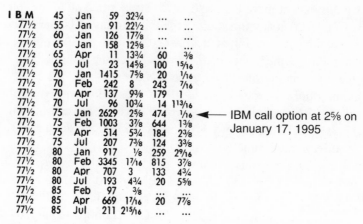

IBM	45	Jan	59	32¾	...	...
77½	55	Jan	91	22½	...	...
77½	60	Jan	126	17⅞	...	...
77½	65	Jan	158	12⅝	...	...
77½	65	Apr	11	13¾	60	⅜
77½	65	Jul	23	14⅝	100	15/16
77½	70	Jan	1415	7⅝	20	1/16
77½	70	Feb	242	8	243	7/16
77½	70	Apr	137	9⅜	179	1
77½	70	Jul	96	10¾	14	1 13/16
77½	75	Jan	2629	2⅝	474	1/16
77½	75	Feb	1003	3⅞	644	1⅜
77½	75	Apr	514	5¾	184	2⅜
77½	75	Jul	207	7⅜	124	3⅜
77½	80	Jan	917	⅛	259	2 9/16
77½	80	Feb	3345	1 7/16	815	3⅞
77½	80	Apr	707	3	133	4¾
77½	80	Jul	193	4¾	20	5⅝
77½	85	Feb	97	⅜	...	...
77½	85	Apr	669	1 7/16	20	7⅞
77½	85	Jul	211	2 15/16	...	...

IBM call option at 2⅝ on January 17, 1995

Thus, if you buy a call, you're speculating that the stock's price will rise sufficiently to earn you a return (spread) over and above the premium you must pay to buy the option. But suppose it doesn't? Suppose the stock rises only a little, or even falls in value, so that you have the option to buy a stock at a price greater than market value? What then? Would you have to buy the stock from the option writer at the strike price? No, because you have only purchased an option to buy. There's no requirement to do so. You can let the option expire without exercising it, and you have only lost your premium.

A rising market motivates investors to buy calls. They hope the price of their stock will shoot up and they will be able to exercise their option and recover their premium, and then some. This does not necessarily mean that option writers (people who sell the option) are counting on the market to stay flat or even fall. The call writer may have decided to sell a stock if it reaches a certain target level (i.e., take his or her gain after the stock rises a certain number of points). If it does rise, the call writer will receive the increment and the premium; even if it doesn't, he or she will still receive the premium. Thus, income is the primary motive for writing the option. Instead of waiting for the stock to move up to the target level, the seller writes a call. If it doesn't move up to that price, he or she will still have earned the premium. If it does, he or she will get premium plus capital gain.

TelMex	45	Dec	212	5½	170	⅜
50⅛	45	Jan	350	6⅛	199	⅞
50⅛	45	May	...	...	63	1¹³/₁₆
50⅛	50	Dec	1522	1⅞	982	1⁹/₁₆
50⅛	50	Jan	1579	2⅞	388	2⁷/₁₆
50⅛	50	Feb	792	3⅝	759	2¹³/₁₆
50⅛	50	May	336	5	64	3½
50⅛	55	Dec	2126	⁷/₁₆	111	5⅛
50⅛	55	Jan	2996	1	95	5⅜
50⅛	55	Feb	175	1¾	27	5½
50⅛	55	May	655	2⅞	131	6⅛
50⅛	60	Dec	195	⅛	5	9⅜
50⅛	60	Jan	87	⁷/₁₆	1291	10⅛
50⅛	60	Feb	77	¹¹/₁₆	1068	10
50⅛	60	May	365	1⅞	174	9½
50⅛	65	Jan	188	⅛	5	13⅞
50⅛	65	Feb	101	⅜	...	...

◄—— TelMex put option at ⅞ on November 22, 1994

Now let's consider the other kind of option and return to the November 23, 1994 issue of the *Journal* on page 196, using TelMex as our example. If you had believed on November 22, 1994 that TelMex stock would fall substantially below its current market value of $50.125 (50⅛), you could have purchased a put contract, and the option writer would have been obliged to buy TelMex from you at the strike price, regardless of current market value. Your option to sell at the strike price would give you an opportunity to buy at the lower market value (assuming your forecast was correct) and sell at the strike price to profit on the difference.

The last column in the example on page 196 provides the put contract premiums. Investors traded TelMex options for strike prices ranging from 45 to 65 for the months of December, January, February, and May. Suppose you were predicting a drop in TelMex's stock price in the next two months. Notice the $0.875 (⅞) premium for the January contract at a strike price of 45. If TelMex fell below $44.125 (Strike price less premium or $45 − $0.875) before the January 21 expiration date, you could buy TelMex at the (lower) market price and sell (put) it to the option writer at the (higher) contract price of 45. The difference, less the premium and any brokerage fees, would be your profit.

Let's see what happened. TelMex had fallen to $36.50 (36½) on January 17, 1995, and your put was *definitely* in the money. You could have purchased TelMex at the market price of $36.50 and sold it to the option writer for $45.00, for a gain of $8.50 per share less the $0.875 premium and any brokerage fees.

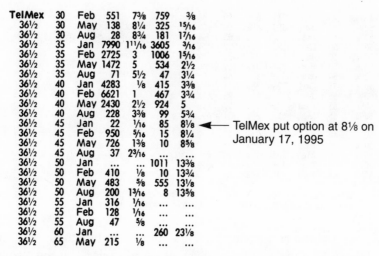

TelMex	30	Feb	551	7 3/8	759	3/8	
36 1/2	30	May	138	8 1/4	325	15/16	
36 1/2	30	Aug	28	8 3/4	181	1 7/16	
36 1/2	35	Jan	7990	1 11/16	3605	3/16	
36 1/2	35	Feb	2725	3	1006	1 5/16	
36 1/2	35	May	1472	5	534	2 1/2	
36 1/2	35	Aug	71	5 1/2	47	3 1/4	
36 1/2	40	Jan	4283	1/8	415	3 3/8	
36 1/2	40	Feb	6621	1	467	3 3/4	
36 1/2	40	May	2430	2 1/2	924	5	
36 1/2	40	Aug	228	3 3/8	99	5 3/4	
36 1/2	45	Jan	22	1/16	85	8 1/8	← TelMex put option at 8⅛ on January 17, 1995
36 1/2	45	Feb	950	5/16	15	8 1/4	
36 1/2	45	May	726	1 3/8	10	8 5/8	
36 1/2	45	Aug	37	2 3/16	...	...	
36 1/2	50	Jan	...	...	1011	13 3/8	
36 1/2	50	Feb	410	1/8	10	13 3/4	
36 1/2	50	May	483	5/8	555	13 1/8	
36 1/2	50	Aug	200	1 3/16	8	13 5/8	
36 1/2	55	Jan	316	1/16	...	...	
36 1/2	55	Feb	128	1/16	...	...	
36 1/2	55	Aug	47	5/8	...	...	
36 1/2	60	Jan	...	...	260	23 1/8	
36 1/2	65	May	215	1/8	...	...	

Source: *The Wall Street Journal*, January 18, 1995. Reprinted by permission of *The Wall Street Journal*,

To be precise, your premium would have been \$87.50 (100 × \$0.875). When TelMex fell to \$36.50 you could have purchased 100 shares at \$3,650 (100 × \$36.50) in the market and exercised your option to sell for \$4,500 (100 × \$45.00), for a gain of \$762.50 (\$850 of stock market appreciation less \$87.50 of premium). (Again, you have to subtract the broker's fee from your profit.)

Once again, you should be aware that most options buyers do not exercise their options. They sell them if they show a profit or let them expire if they do not. In this case, the premium had risen to 8⅛ for a net gain of 7¼ (8⅛ less ⅞) per share. For 100 shares, that works out to \$725. What a bonanza on an \$87.50 investment!

If you guessed wrong and TelMex rose, so that the market price exceeded the strike price, you wouldn't want to exercise your option to sell at a price below market. Instead, you would permit your option to expire without exercising it. Your loss would be only the premium you paid.

Why would someone write a put? Because he or she is prepared to buy a stock if it should drop to a particular price. The writer earns the premium whether or not the option is exercised. If he or she believes the stock will rise in price, then the writer has little concern that an option holder will put it to him or her at less than the market price. And the writer has

collected the premium. But if the market does fall, and falls sufficiently that the contract comes in the money, the writer will have to buy the stock at the contract price, which will be above market. That's not necessarily bad, since the writer had already planned to buy the stock if it fell to the strike price, and he or she has collected a premium, too.

In addition to simply playing the options market for profit, an investor can use options to hedge against price fluctuations of his or her investment in the underlying security. For instance, you can write (sell) call options against a stock you own. If the stock falls in value, you at least get to keep the premium. If it rises above the strike price, you keep the premium and realize a gain on the stock.

On the other hand, if you like a stock but think it will fall in value, write (sell) a put instead of buying the stock. If it doesn't fall, you collect the premium anyway. If it does fall, you still collect the premium and purchase the stock at a lower price.

These strategies involve *covered* options, i.e. stock you own or intend to buy. You can write *naked* options on stock you don't own and do not intend to buy. It seems like an easy way to collect a premium. But suppose you've written a call option thinking the stock couldn't possibly rise that far, and it does. You'll have to buy that stock at the market price if the option is exercised and then sell it at the lower strike price. That could hurt.

Conversely, you can write naked put options and collect your premium if you believe a stock could never fall *that* far. But if there's another crash like the one in 1987 and the market collapses, you may find yourself in the embarrassing position of having to buy stock at prices substantially above market. Where are you going to get the money?

That's one of the reasons options are risky business.

One more comment about leverage. You can minimize risk if you buy options whose strike price is close to the market price, but you also reduce your relative gain. Leverage increases as the strike price increasingly deviates from the market price. That is, not surprisingly, risk and reward move together.

You can spread the risk of options investing by purchasing *index options* (see page 198) in the entire market rather than an option on an individual stock. Instead of buying all the stocks in one of the stock market averages (or buying an index mutual fund), you can buy a put or call on an index option (such as the S & P 100), just as you can invest in options on individual stocks.

INDEX OPTIONS TRADING

Wednesday, January 18, 1995

Volume, last, net change and open interest for all contracts. Volume figures are unofficial. Open interest reflects previous trading day. p-Put c–Call

CHICAGO

S & P 100 index options →

S & P 100 INDEX(OEX)

Strike		Vol.	Last	Net Chg.	Open Int.
Feb	380p	296	3/16	...	11,335
Mar	380p	2,057	9/16	...	12,234
Apr	380p	39	1⅛	...	936
Feb	385p	930	¼	...	4,552
Mar	385p	100	11/16	...	5,138
Feb	390p	521	5/16	...	8,517
Mar	390p	2,536	13/16	– 1/16	3,282
Apr	390p	500	1 9/16	– 1/16	4,420
Feb	395p	367	⅜	...	12,650
Mar	395p	90	1	– 1/16	2,269
Jan	400p	3	1/16	...	25,430
Feb	400p	1,588	½	+ 1/16	13,215
Mar	400p	324	1 3/16	+ 1/16	3,941
Apr	400p	111	2 1/16	+ 1/16	1,411
Jan	405p	10	1/16	...	19,041
Feb	405p	1,723	9/16	+ 1/16	15,671
Mar	405p	115	1½	+ 1/16	3,061
Jan	410c	198	26⅜	– ¾	1,777
Jan	410p	353	1/16	...	30,117
Feb	410p	1,379	11/16	...	11,274
Mar	410c	5	30	+ 1¼	36
Mar	410p	2,606	1¾	– 1/16	9,175
Apr	410p	277	3	...	3,090
Jan	415c	501	21½	– ½	3,910
Jan	415p	1,858	1/16	...	27,945
Feb	415c	40	22	– ½	932
Feb	415p	5,799	⅞	...	14,207
Mar	415p	3,402	2 3/16	+ 1/16	2,152
Jan	420c	2,364	16⅜	– ⅝	12,497
Jan	420p	2,457	⅛	...	38,424
Feb	420c	263	17½	– ⅞	3,618
Feb	420p	4,057	1¼	...	20,712
Mar	420c	100	20	– ¾	3,756
Mar	420p	342	2⅞	+ ⅛	10,037
Apr	420c	2	23	+ ⅜	151
Apr	420p	1	4½	+ ¼	5,415
Jan	425c	3,587	11⅝	– ½	20,679
Jan	425p	10,660	3/16	...	44,064
Feb	425c	381	13¼	– ¼	16,849
Feb	425p	7,871	1⅞	...	27,039
Mar	425c	452	16	– ½	4,432
Mar	425p	924	3½	– ⅛	7,938
Jan	430c	19,992	6½	– ⅝	32,096
Jan	430p	23,179	5/16	...	55,937
Feb	430c	7,645	9¼	– ⅝	20,863
Feb	430p	12,426	2⅞	+ ⅛	28,406
Mar	430c	472	12¼	– ½	6,117
Mar	430p	1,286	4¾	+ ⅛	8,918
Apr	430c	36	14⅞	– ⅝	4,990
Apr	430p	113	6½	+ ¼	4,945
Jan	435c	49,239	2 5/16	– ⅝	37,210
Jan	435p	37,841	1 3/16	...	26,804
Feb	435c	6,908	5⅝	– ⅜	16,866
Feb	435p	12,905	4⅜	+ ⅛	12,506
Mar	435c	2,139	8¾	– ⅛	2,205
Mar	435p	2,535	6¼	...	2,218
Jan	440c	31,376	5/16	– ¼	44,238
Jan	440p	10,041	4¼	+ ½	6,378
Feb	440c	12,047	3	– ¼	31,176
Feb	440p	2,555	6¾	+ ¼	2,928
Mar	440c	1,405	5⅝	– ¼	9,107
Mar	440p	294	8⅜	+ ⅛	1,605
Apr	440c	62	8½	– ⅜	11,750
Apr	440p	183	10¼	+ ¼	1,169
Jan	445c	14,880	1/16	– 1/16	30,320
Feb	445c	8,486	1⅜	– ⅛	37,656
Feb	445p	40	10¾	+ ¾	234
Mar	445c	1,140	3½	– ⅛	6,649
Mar	445p	7	11¾	– ¼	78
Jan	450c	220	1/16	...	27,956
Feb	450c	2,949	⅝	– 1/16	39,000
Mar	450c	3,172	1⅞	– 1/16	14,098
Mar	450p	7	15¼	– ⅜	381
Apr	450c	24	3⅞	– ⅛	3,274
Apr	450p	3	16¼	+ ⅝	127
Feb	455c	1,182	¼	– 1/16	13,127
Feb	455p	3	19	+ ¼	3
Mar	455c	3,170	15/16	...	10,490
Jan	460c	1,110	1/16	...	18,983
Jan	460p	1	25	– 5¼	5
Feb	460c	365	⅛	...	7,626
Mar	460c	55	7/16	– 1/16	5,573
Apr	460c	190	1⅜	...	2,914
Feb	465c	200	⅛	...	1,058
Feb	470c	560	1/16	...	4,957

Call vol.....176,917 Open Int.......547,993
Put vol......156,715 Open Int.......610,835

S & P 500 index options →

S & P 500 INDEX-AM(SPX)

Strike		Vol.	Last	Net Chg.	Open Int.
Feb	350p	51	1/16	...	1,267
Mar	350p	42	⅛	...	3,864
Feb	400c	50	69½	+ 5⅝	240
Mar	400p	250	⅜	– 5/16	20,385
Mar	410p	150	11/16	...	4,061
Feb	420p	75	¼	...	11,480
Mar	425p	520	1⅛	+ ⅛	14,374
Feb	430p	35	⅜	...	22,980
Mar	430p	470	1¼	+ ⅛	9,209
Feb	435p	58	7/16	– ⅛	2,726
Jan	440p	1	1/16	– 1/16	29,931
Feb	440p	63	¾	+ ⅛	10,030
Mar	440p	1,886	1¾	+ ⅛	17,236
Jan	445c	304	25¾	+ 1	11,111
Jan	445p	294	1/16	...	29,389
Feb	445c	304	25½	– ¾	4,018
Feb	445p	6,277	13/16	– 1/16	13,927
Mar	445p	744	2¼	+ 1/16	16,200
Jan	450c	121	20	+ ½	10,723
Jan	450p	121	1/16	...	25,365
Feb	450c	120	21¾	+ ⅞	6,254
Feb	450p	4,230	1 1/16	...	18,738
Mar	450c	250	24	...	26,817
Mar	450p	2,059	2⅝	– 1/16	45,879
Jan	455c	1,419	14⅞	– ¼	12,232
Jan	455p	1,908	1/16	...	25,601
Feb	455c	180	16½	+ 1	8,039
Feb	455p	6,829	1¾	+ ¼	14,755
Mar	455c	20	19⅝	– ⅛	2,243
Mar	455p	56	3½	+ ⅛	4,939
Jan	460c	6,439	9⅝	– ⅝	19,545
Jan	460p	5,298	1/16	– 1/16	22,353
Feb	460c	5,937	12¼	...	17,212
Feb	460p	4,547	2¼	+ ⅛	17,387
Mar	460c	50	15	– ½	8,130
Mar	460p	579	4⅛	+ ⅛	12,335
Jan	465c	7,459	4¾	– ½	22,345
Jan	465p	11,830	¼	...	23,271
Feb	465c	4,946	8½	– ⅜	15,163
Feb	465p	6,364	3⅛	+ ⅛	8,878
Mar	465c	3,960	11⅝	– ¼	10,598
Mar	465p	3,697	5¾	+ ⅝	15,254
Jan	470c	14,597	1¼	– ⅜	30,684
Jan	470p	3,807	1¾	+ 3/16	15,497
Feb	470c	1,651	5¼	– ½	16,299
Feb	470p	556	5	+ ⅛	11,195
Mar	470c	3,164	8⅝	– ⅛	11,840
Mar	470p	2,790	7	– ¼	7,141
Jan	475c	13,977	⅛	– ⅛	26,399
Jan	475p	1,611	5¾	– ⅛	6,198
Feb	475c	1,455	2⅝	– ½	20,001
Feb	475p	288	7½	+ ½	1,970
Mar	475c	536	5½	– ⅛	27,645
Mar	475p	53	9⅝	– ¼	21,191
Jan	480c	1,561	1/16	– 1/16	15,045
Jan	480p	24	10¾	+ ¾	2,559
Feb	480c	719	1 5/16	– 1/16	21,652
Feb	480p	272	11	...	563
Mar	480c	30	3¼	– ¼	11,769
Mar	480p	27	11⅞	...	882
Jan	485p	100	16⅛	– ⅞	186
Feb	485c	173	7/16	– 3/16	35,657
Feb	485p	200	15⅝	...	...
Mar	485c	12,278	1 15/16	– 1/16	23,475
Mar	485p	7	15⅞	+ ⅞	1,293
Jan	490c	1,000	1/16	...	10,623
Feb	490c	20	¼	– 1/16	16,520
Mar	490c	10,712	15/16	– 1/16	24,817
Feb	495c	30	⅛	...	1,156
Mar	495c	100	½	...	4,953
Mar	520c	10	⅛	+ 1/16	7,025
Jan	525p	10	55½	– 5¾	53
Feb	525p	30	54	– 20⅝	61

Call vol.....106,360 Open Int.......726,394
Put vol.......75,650 Open Int.......856,967

S&P BANK INDEX(BIX)

Strike		Vol.	Last	Net Chg.	Open Int.
Feb	220c	50	7¼	– 2½	50
Mar	220p	1	3¾	– 2⅜	24
Jan	225c	25	⅜	– 1 11/16	160
Jan	225p	100	1 7/16	+ ¾	165
Feb	225p	5	4⅜	+ 1⅜	357
Jan	230p	30	6	+ 1¾	255

Call vol.............75 Open Int.............966
Put vol...........136 Open Int..........2,005

AMERICAN

AM MEXICO INDEX(MXY)

Strike		Vol.	Last	Net Chg.	Open Int.
Feb	90c	10	16¼	– 1⅝	20
Jan	100c	5	3/16	– ⅝	81
Jan	100p	10	6⅞	+ 1	55
Feb	100c	38	8⅛	– 1⅜	62
Jan	105c	25	11/16	– 1 5/16	40
Jan	105p	10	2	+ ⅞	107
Feb	105c	12	6⅛	– 2⅛	34
Jan	115p	10	11¾	+ 3⅛	22
Feb	115c	25	2	– 1⅝	135
Mar	115c	25	3½	– 2¾	75
Feb	120c	10	1	– ⅞	138
Mar	120c	25	2⅜	– 2⅝	42
Jan	125c	10	1/16	– 5/16	88
Mar	125c	65	1½	– 1⅝	114
Mar	140c	5	9/16	– ½	15

Call vol...........326 Open Int.........10,447
Put vol...........119 Open Int..........5,937

PHILADELPHIA

BIG CAP INDEX(MKT)

Strike		Vol.	Last	Net Chg.	Open Int.
Jan	210p	10	3⅝	– ½	102

Call vol.............0 Open Int.............234
Put vol.............10 Open Int.............535

GOLD/SILVER(XAU)

Strike		Vol.	Last	Net Chg.	Open Int.
Feb	95p	2	½	– 3/16	261
Jan	100c	52	7⅞	+ 1½	573
Jan	100p	64	1/16	...	1,917
Feb	100c	126	9¾	+ 2	429
Feb	100p	29	1¼	– ¼	200
Mar	100c	13	11	+ 1½	200
Jan	105c	156	3	+ 1¼	1,459
Jan	105p	89	¼	– 9/16	1,907
Feb	105c	93	5½	+ ⅜	1,690
Feb	105p	44	2¾	– ½	224
Mar	105c	27	7½	+ 1¼	566
Jan	110c	262	7/16	+ ⅛	2,100
Jan	110p	48	2½	– 1⅜	1,391
Feb	110c	90	3⅝	+ ½	789
Feb	110p	18	5⅛	– ⅞	234
Mar	110c	39	5	+ ⅞	2,426
Jan	115c	5	⅛	+ 1/16	1,043
Jan	115p	11	7½	– 2½	438
Feb	115c	130	1⅝	+ 1/16	1,383
Feb	115p	10	8¼	– 1⅝	46
Mar	115c	82	3¼	+ ½	1,010
Feb	120c	4	1	+ ⅜	188
Mar	125c	5	1	– ¼	145
Mar	130c	10	13/16	+ 1/16	206
Mar	135c	23	⅜	+ 1/16	58
Mar	140c	20	¼	...	68

Call vol........6,794 Open Int.........19,020
Put vol...........320 Open Int..........8,978

OTC INDEX(XOC)

Strike		Vol.	Last	Net Chg.	Open Int.
Mar	530p	2	1	+ 1/16	7
Jan	575p	60	1/16	– ⅛	300
Feb	575p	26	2	– 3⅛	25
Jan	580c	3	24	+ 4	25
Feb	580p	3	3¼	– ⅛	54
Mar	580p	4	5¾	– 1⅛	...
Feb	585p	35	3½	...	...
Feb	590p	31	5⅛	– ⅜	21
Jan	595c	51	6⅞	– ⅜	102
Jan	595p	10	¼	– 3/16	50
Jan	600c	79	5¼	+ ⅛	517
Jan	600p	123	⅞	– 1 7/16	82
Feb	600c	2	11⅜	– ⅞	79
Feb	600p	20	7¾	– ½	10
Jan	605c	171	2½	+ ⅜	94
Jan	605p	102	2⅜	– 2	27
Feb	605c	1	11	+ 2⅞	38

NEW YORK

NYSE INDEX new(NYA)

Strike		Vol.	Last	Net Chg.	Open Int.
Mar	250p	21	2 5/16	+ 3/16	36
Feb	260c	25	1 1/16	– ⅛	15
Jan	265p	5	9⅛	– 13¼	5
Jan	270p	3	14⅛	– 13⅛	3

Call vol.............25 Open Int..........3,085
Put vol.............32 Open Int.............526

LEAPS-LONG TERM

HONG KONG INDEX – AM

Strike		Vol.	Last	Net Chg.	Open Int.
Jan 96	20c	22	1⅛	+ 1/16	1275

Call vol.............22 Open Int..........1,727
Put vol...............0 Open Int..........1,525

MAJOR MARKET – AM

Strike		Vol.	Last	Net Chg.	Open Int.
Dec 95	40p	50	1 9/16	+ 1/16	2333
Dec 96	40p	1010	1⅞	...	5245

Call vol...............0 Open Int.............891
Put vol.........1,060 Open Int.........32,576

S & P 100 INDEX – CB

Strike		Vol.	Last	Net Chg.	Open Int.
Dec 95	35p	70	5/16	...	4727
Dec 95	40p	224	⅞	...	30585
Dec 95	42½c	4	3⅜	...	9420
Dec 95	42½p	177	1 9/16	...	24341
Dec 95	45p	139	2½	...	15351

Call vol...............4 Open Int.........37,229
Put vol.........1,657 Open Int.......124,775

S & P 500 INDEX – CB

Strike		Vol.	Last	Net Chg.	Open Int.
Dec 95	40p	20	½	...	5028
Dec 95	45p	262	1 5/16	...	20010
Dec 95	47½c	20	2¾	...	187
Dec 95	47½p	32	2	+ 1/16	6366
Dec 95	50p	25	3	...	5788

Call vol.............20 Open Int..........8,242
Put vol...........379 Open Int.......103,413

Source: *The Wall Street Journal*, January 19, 1995. Reprinted by permission of *The Wall Street Journal*,

S & P 100 INDEX(OEX)

Feb	380 p	296	3/16			5
Mar	390					7,626
			1/8	...		
	..UU c	55	7/16	−	1/16	5,573
Apr	460 c	190	1¾		...	2,914
Feb	465 c	200	1/8		...	1,058
Feb	470 c	560	1/16		...	4,957

Call vol. .... 176,917 Open Int 547,993
Put vol. ...... 156,715 Open Int 610,835

Source: *The Wall Street Journal*, January 19, 1995. Reprinted by permission of *The Wall Street Journal*, ©1995 Dow Jones & Company, Inc. All rights reserved worldwide.

Take a look at the Thursday January 19, 1995 excerpt from **Index Options Trading** above. You can see that options on both the S&P 100 and 500 permit you to speculate on changes in the broad market without purchasing a large number of stocks.

These index options are more widely traded than options on individual securities. Notice the trading volume for S&P 100 index call and put options of 333,632 (176,917 plus 156,715); it is considerably higher than any other option, index, or individual security. The S&P 100 was created to represent 100 companies among the S&P 500 stocks for which options are actively traded. This provides the investor with the opportunity to spread the risk over 100 options rather than exposing himself or herself to the risks inherent in a single option.

Finally, the investor can purchase longer-term options on some stocks. *The Journal* publishes a daily listing of **Leaps—Long Term Options**, as the example on page 201 illustrates. On Thursday, January 19, 1995, for instance, TelMex traded at $34.50, but you can see that investors willing to gamble on a doubling in TelMex's price by January 1997 could have purchased a call for $1.19 to buy TelMex at 70 anytime before the third Friday in January of 1997. That seems like a leap of faith, yet a 100 share contract would have been no more than $118.75. And if TelMex did surge and the premium doubled to $2.50, the investor could have doubled his or her money even if TelMex did not double in value. Remember, most options are traded without being exercised (the purchase of the underlying shares).

Many of these possibilities sound intriguing, easy, and potentially profitable. Keep in mind, however, that there are substantial commission costs. Furthermore, as in any leveraged situation, the potential for considerable loss exists. Options are not for novices, and even buying on margin exposes you to up to twice the risk of simply buying a stock with your own money. With leverage you can move a big rock with a small stick—

but the stick can also break off in your hands, and the rock can roll back over your feet.

In fact, the whole options game is tricky and multi-faceted. Consequently, before you can invest in options, your broker will evaluate your past investment experience and your current financial position. It will not be easy to qualify.

Short Interest

Instead of speculating on a price increase, some investors borrow stock from their broker in the hope of a price *decrease*. They sell the stock and leave the proceeds of the sale with their broker. If the stock falls, the borrower buys it back at the lower price and returns it to the broker, at which time the broker returns the funds from the original sale to the borrower. The advantage to the borrower is obvious: He or she pockets the difference between the high price when he or she borrowed and sold the stock and the low price when he or she bought and returned the stock.

For example, if you borrow a $2 stock from your broker and sell it, you have $2. If it falls to $1, you can buy it on the market and return the stock to the broker and you keep the other dollar. This is called *selling short*. But what advantage does the broker gain? Brokers lend stocks because you have to leave the cash from your sale of the stock with them as collateral for the borrowed stock, and they can then lend (or invest) the cash at interest.

If you borrow a $2 stock from your broker in the hope that it falls to $1, you can easily return the stock to your broker if the market heads south. But what happens if you guess wrong and the stock rises to $3? You have only $2 and, therefore, cannot repurchase the stock for $3 in order to return it to your broker. How can the broker protect him or herself?

Your broker will insist that you maintain a substantial deposit (margin) at the brokerage firm in order to cover that risk, and, if the stock does appreciate, you will be required to deposit additional margin. This risk can be substantially reduced if you have a buy-stop order with your broker that instructs the broker to repurchase the stock for your account as soon as it rises to a level slightly higher than the price at which you borrowed it. Your loss will be held to a minimum.

Around the twentieth of each month *The Wall Street Journal* reports **Short Interest Highlights** (check the front-page index of the first section). The Friday, January 20, 1995 *Journal* excerpt (see page 202) serves as an example.

LEAPS — LONG TERM OPTIONS

Option/Strike		Exp.	Call Vol.	Call Last	Put Vol.	Put Last
AMD	20	Jan 97	150	15 3/8	...	...
32	40	Jan 96	174	2 1/4	10	9 1/8
AT&T	50	Jan 97	27	7 1/8	72	4 1/8
48 7/8	55	Jan 96	47	2 1/4	205	6 1/2
48 7/8	60	Jan 96	121	1 1/16	20	11
48 7/8	70	Jan 96	125	1/4	...	...
Amoco	65	Jan 96	50	2 3/8	9	6 3/4
59	65	Jan 97	50	5 1/8	...	...
AppleC	50	Jan 96	121	5 3/8	2	7 1/4
AvonPd	60	Jan 96	465	3	465	5 1/2
Boeing	40	Jan 96	385	10 3/8	1	5/8
48 1/4	45	Jan 96	68	6 7/8	...	...
48 1/4	50	Jan 96	47	3 3/8	...	...
48 1/4	55	Jan 96	72	1 13/16	...	...
BrMySq	50	Jan 96	50	10 1/2	...	...
59 1/8	60	Jan 96	74	3 7/8	7	3 1/4
Caterp	50	Jan 96	83	10	70	2 3/4
Centocr	20	Jan 96	60	2 1/8	...	...
Chase	30	Jan 96	...	...	124	1 1/2
33 3/8	35	Jan 96	196	2 3/4	...	...
Chevrn	50	Jan 96	40	1 1/2	...	...
ChmBnk	30	Jan 96	47	8 3/8	30	3/4
37 1/4	40	Jan 97	45	4 1/4	...	...
Chrysl	50	Jan 96	79	6	12	5 1/4
49 1/8	50	Jan 97	35	9 1/4	...	...
49 1/8	60	Jan 96	60	2 5/8	...	...
Cisco	15	Jan 97	80	23 3/4	...	...
35 3/4	40	Jan 96	35	5 1/8	...	...
Citicp	35	Jan 96	46	6 3/4	17	1 1/2
39 3/8	40	Jan 96	72	4 1/8	20	3
39 3/8	45	Jan 96	50	2 1/2	5	6 1/2
39 3/8	50	Jan 96	25	1 1/8	34	9 7/8
CocaCl	50	Jan 96	31	5 1/8	...	...
50 7/8	55	Jan 96	169	2 7/8	...	...
Compaq	40	Jan 96	2	10 1/8	400	4 1/4
DellCptr	35	Jan 96	34	15 1/4	...	...
47 1/8	45	Jan 96	135	9 3/8	...	...
47 1/8	50	Jan 96	40	7	...	...
Digital	30	Jan 96	95	10 1/4	25	2
36 5/8	40	Jan 96	364	5 1/4	114	6 1/4
36 5/8	50	Jan 96	85	2 1/4	...	...
Disney	30	Jan 96	42	18	...	...
46 5/8	50	Jan 96	96	3 1/2	...	...
DuPont	60	Jan 96	99	4	6	4 7/8
57 1/2	70	Jan 96	52	1 5/16	...	...
EKodak	35	Jan 96	40	14 1/4	...	...
48	55	Jan 96	38	2	...	...
Exxon	70	Jan 96	25	1 1/4	50	8 5/8
FedNM	70	Jan 96	34	7	2	4 3/4
FedNMt	80	Jan 97	...	...	165	12 3/8
Ford	25	Jan 97	38	6 1/8	3	2 1/4
GTE	35	Jan 96	33	11/16	10	4 1/2
GaPac	55	Jan 96	33	26	...	...
GenEl	40	Jan 96	500	13 1/8	99	1/2
51	45	Jan 96	2	8 7/8	112	1 1/4
GnMill	40	Jan 96	50	20	...	...
GnMotr	40	Jan 96	108	5 3/4	34	3 5/8
40 1/4	50	Jan 96	60	2 1/8	...	...
HewlPk	120	Jan 96	43	7 1/4	...	...
HmeDep	55	Jan 96	217	2 1/4	...	...
Hmstke	15	Jan 97	50	5 5/8	...	...
IBM	50	Jan 96	39	28 3/4	18	3/8
76 1/2	60	Jan 96	32	19 3/4	...	...
76 1/2	70	Jan 96	76	12 1/2	6	3
76 1/2	80	Jan 96	169	7 1/8	5	6 7/8
76 1/2	80	Jan 97	101	11 1/4	20	8 3/8
76 1/2	90	Jan 96	184	3 5/8	10	13 1/2
76 1/2	90	Jan 97	372	7 7/8	...	...
IGame	15	Jan 96	37	2	...	...
13 1/4	20	Jan 96	36	1	...	...
IntGame	12 1/2	Jan 97	102	4 5/8	5	2
13 1/4	15	Jan 97	44	3 1/4	5	3 1/4
13 1/4	17 1/2	Jan 97	63	2 3/4	...	...
Intel	50	Jan 96	222	24 3/8	45	13/16
70 11/16	65	Jan 96	244	12 7/8	360	3 3/8
70 11/16	80	Jan 96	530	5	...	...
70 11/16	80	Jan 97	875	10 5/8	10	12 3/8
JohnJn	40	Jan 96	32	16 1/8	...	...
54 1/2	55	Jan 96	152	4 5/8	...	...
K mart	12 1/2	Jan 96	35	2 1/2	...	...
13 3/4	15	Jan 96	1113	1 1/4	...	...
13 3/4	15	Jan 97	53	2 5/8	...	...
LizClab	20	Jan 96	50	1 3/8	...	...
MCI	20	Jan 96	30	2 1/2	...	...
McDnld	25	Jan 97	...	...	40	1
MerLyn	50	Jan 97	34	3 1/8	...	...
Merck	30	Jan 96	22	9 3/8	30	1/2
38 1/8	40	Jan 96	44	2 15/16	...	...
38 1/8	45	Jan 96	248	1 5/16	...	...
38 1/8	45	Jan 97	8	3 1/4	80	7 3/8
MicrTc	45	Jan 96	125	10 3/8	364	6 1/4
MicrTc o	36	Jan 96	50	16 3/8	...	...
Micsft	60	Jan 96	127	11	28	3 3/8
97 3/4	60	Jan 97	60	16 1/2	10	5 3/8
63 1/2	65	Jan 96	38	8 3/8	13	6
97 3/4	65	Jan 97	63	13	1	7 5/8
63 1/2	75	Jan 96	31	4 3/8	11	12 3/8
Morgan	50	Jan 96	...	...	60	1 1/4
Motorla	70	Jan 96	144	4 5/8	7	9 1/4
OcciPt	20	Jan 97	53	2 3/4	...	...
Oracle	45	Jan 96	46	8 1/4	...	...
Pfizer	60	Jan 96	169	22 1/4	10	1/2
79 1/8	90	Jan 96	125	3	...	...
PhilMr	45	Jan 96	2	13	535	1 1/8
56 1/2	50	Jan 96	44	9 1/8	49	2 1/2
56 1/2	70	Jan 96	42	1 3/8	10	13 3/4
PlacrD	17 1/2	Jan 96	...	...	50	1
20 7/8	20	Jan 96	45	4	...	...
RJR Nb	5	Jan 96	50	1 3/8	40	3/8
5 5/8	5	Jan 97	...	...	100	9/16
Salomn	40	Jan 96	40	4	...	...
SchrPl	85	Jan 96	43	2 3/8	...	...
Sears	55	Jan 96	49	1 7/8	...	...
StorTch	40	Jan 96	125	3 7/8	17	9 1/2
SunMic	25	Jan 96	20	11 1/2	215	1 1/16
SwstA	25	Jan 96	...	...	39	5 3/4
TelMex	30	Jan 96	97	8 1/4	15	2 3/8
34 1/2	35	Jan 96	220	5 1/2	446	4 1/2
34 1/2	35	Jan 97	49	7 7/8	254	5 5/8
34 1/2	40	Jan 96	164	3 5/8	20	7 5/8
34 1/2	40	Jan 97	11	6	32	8 1/4
34 1/2	45	Jan 96	269	2 7/16	10	11
34 1/2	45	Jan 97	305	4 5/8	2	11 3/8
34 1/2	50	Jan 96	56	1 9/16	10	15 1/8
34 1/2	55	Jan 96	30	1 1/16	...	...
34 1/2	55	Jan 96	244	1 1/16	...	...
34 1/2	55	Jan 97	60	2 7/8	...	...
34 1/2	65	Jan 96	30	3/8	...	...
34 1/2	65	Jan 96	101	1/2	1400	30 1/4
34 1/2	70	Jan 97	501	1 3/16	...	... ← TelMex
34 1/2	75	Jan 96	51	1/4	...	...
34 1/2	85	Jan 96	138	1/8	...	...
34 1/2	85	Jan 96	115	1/8	...	1/4
Texaco	65	Jan 96	...	...	118	5 5/8
TmeWar	30	Jan 97	400	10 1/2	...	...
UAL	130	Jan 96	65	3 1/4	...	...
US Surg	20	Jan 96	314	6	80	2 5/16
22 3/8	40	Jan 96	40	7/8	...	...
USXMar	17 1/2	Jan 97	13	2 1/2	57	2 5/8
UnCarb	20	Jan 96	100	9 3/4	...	...
Upjohn	30	Jan 96	25	4 1/4	65	2 3/4
31 1/8	30	Jan 97	...	...	121	3 1/2
ViacmB	30	Jan 96	...	...	915	11/16
WMX Tc	35	Jan 97	302	2 1/16	...	...
WalMrt	25	Jan 96	43	1 7/16	...	...
Wolwth	25	Jan 96	100	5/16	...	...
WstgEl	10	Jan 96	79	4 3/4	...	...
14	12 1/2	Jan 97	205	4 1/4	20	1 3/8
14	15	Jan 96	129	1 5/8	...	...
14	20	Jan 96	56	7/16	...	...

VOLUME & OPEN INTEREST SUMMARIES

CHICAGO BOARD			
Call Vol:	11,007	Open Int:	764,152
Put Vol:	6,554	Open Int:	582,130
AMERICAN			
Call Vol:	6,502	Open Int:	459,695
Put Vol:	2,325	Open Int:	306,367
PHILADELPHIA			
Call Vol:	1,907	Open Int:	210,669
Put Vol:	473	Open Int:	102,573
PACIFIC			
Call Vol:	1,434	Open Int:	79,860
Put Vol:	1,215	Open Int:	42,866
NEW YORK			
Call Vol:	31	Open Int:	92,179
Put Vol:		Open Int:	51,191
TOTAL			
Call Vol:	20,881	Open Int:	1,606,555
Put Vol:	- 10,567	Open Int:	1,085,127

Source: *The Wall Street Journal*, January 20, 1995. Reprinted by permission of *The Wall Street Journal*, ©1995 Dow Jones & Company, Inc. All rights reserved worldwide.

	TelMex	30	Jan 96	97	8 1/4	15	2 3/8
	34 1/2	35	Jan 96	220	5 1/2	446	4 1/2
	34 1/2	35	Jan 97	49	7 7/8	254	5 5/8
	34 1/2	40	Jan 96	164	3 5/8	20	7 5/8
	34 1/2	40	Jan 97	11	6	32	8 1/4
	34 1/2	45	Jan 96	269	2 7/16	10	11
	34 1/2	45	Jan 97	305	4 5/8	2	11 3/8
	34 1/2	50	Jan 96	56	1 9/16	10	15 1/8
	34 1/2	55	Jan 96	30	1 1/16	...	...
	34 1/2	55	Jan 96	244	1 1/16	...	...
	34 1/2	55	Jan 97	60	2 7/8	...	...
	34 1/2	65	Jan 96	30	3/8	...	...
	34 1/2	65	Jan 96	101	1/2	1400	30 1/4
TelMex Leaps Option →	34 1/2	70	Jan 97	501	1 3/16	...	...
	34 1/2	75	Jan 96	51	1/4	...	...
	34 1/2	85	Jan 96	138	1/8	...	...
	34 1/2	85	Jan 96	115	1/8	...	...

Source: *The Wall Street Journal*, January 20, 1995. Reprinted by permission of *The Wall Street Journal*, ©1995 Dow Jones & Company, Inc. All rights reserved worldwide.

SHORT INTEREST HIGHLIGHTS

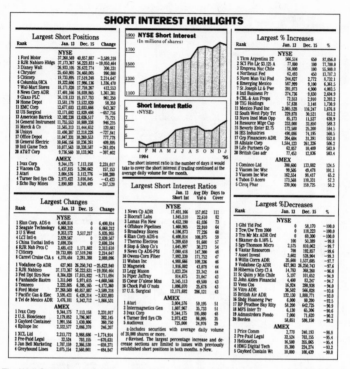

Source: *The Wall Street Journal*, January 20, 1995. Reprinted by permission of *The Wall Street Journal*, ©1995 Dow Jones & Company, Inc. All rights reserved worldwide.

Short interest is the number of borrowed shares that have not been returned to the lender. A great deal of short interest in a stock indicates widespread speculation that a stock will fall. Remember, however, that these shares must be repaid, and that those who owe stock must buy it in order to repay it. Their stock purchases could bid the stock up.

This ambivalence illustrates the difficulty in using short-interest data as an analytical tool. For instance, the charts under **Short Interest Highlights** indicate more than 1,700 million shares had not yet been returned to brokers (NYSE Short Interest) and that this was nearly seven times recent trading volume (Short Interest Ratio). Despite the fact that this indicates considerable sentiment that stocks will fall, a short-interest ratio of over two has been a rule of thumb that stocks will rise, because these borrowed stocks must be repurchased to be repaid. Now you can see why it is difficult to find meaning in the ratio.

Nonetheless, this does not mean that you should remain unconcerned if there is a substantial short interest increase in an individual stock in your portfolio. The forces that move the entire market may not be the same as those that move an individual stock. What does the smart money know about your stock that you don't? It's an important question, and one that you should ask. So follow this report each month in the *Journal*.

Foreign Markets

Finally, you can buy shares of stock on **Canadian Markets** and on **Foreign Markets**. *The Journal* provides daily listings, and you can find them in the front page indexes of the first and last sections. Representative samples are included on pages 209 and 210 from the Friday, February 10, 1995 edition. Remember, when you invest in foreign markets you must be concerned with the fluctuation of foreign currency values as well as the value of the shares you purchase. A rise in the dollar's value against the currency in which your shares are denominated can wipe out your gain, while a fall in the dollar's value could accentuate that gain. In addition, information on foreign stocks is often not as complete and accurate as on U.S. stocks. Let the buyer beware.

In any event, the disparities among the performances of the overseas markets have been huge. Each day the *Journal*'s **World Markets** feature (see the front page indexes) carries a report on foreign stock markets that provides detail on recent developments as well as historical trends. (See pages 204–206.) You will also notice a daily table under the World Markets feature called **Dow Jones World Stock Index**. See the example on page 207.

You should notice two things from the example on page 207. First, U.S. indexes and World indexes have different bases, making comparisons difficult. Second, the Mexican stock market fell over 60% when denominated in dollars in the twelve months preceding February 9, 1995.

If these disparities alarm you, there is a way you can invest in foreign firms while keeping your money in dollars and in the U.S. American Depository Receipts (ADRs) are negotiable instruments representing foreign securities that trade like stocks in the U.S. They are listed each day in the *Journal* at the end of the **NASDAQ Bid and Asked Quotations**. For instance, see the page 208 listing under **ADRS** from the February 17, 1995 edition.

WORLD MARKETS

Stocks Fall in Tokyo but Rebound in Hong Kong, While Many European Bourses Rack Up Gains

A WALL STREET JOURNAL *News Roundup*

Tokyo stocks dropped 1% Thursday, weighed down by selling in the construction sector and among blue chips, while the Hong Kong bourse rebounded.

London's benchmark index touched a new intraday high for this year and the market logged solid gains, buttressed by strong futures and bond markets. The Frankfurt bourse surged 1.2% on buying by foreign investors and Paris equities resumed their rally.

World-wide, stock prices fell in dollar terms. The Dow Jones World Stock Index was at 112.67, down 0.05, reflecting lower Asia/Pacific and American markets, and

DOW JONES WORLD STOCK INDEX

Thursday, February 9, 1995

REGION/ COUNTRY	DJ EQUITY MARKET INDEX, LOCAL CURRENCY	PCT. CHG.	CLOSING INDEX	CHG.	PCT. CHG.	12-MO HIGH	12-MO LOW	12-MO CHG.	PCT. CHG.	FROM 12/31	PCT. CHG.
Americas			112.77	− 0.25	− 0.22	113.88	105.21	− 1.04	− 0.91	+ 4.25	+ 3.91
Canada	113.01 + 0.30		93.42	+ 0.17	+ 0.18	104.16	88.37	− 8.55	− 8.38	− 1.81	− 1.90
Mexico	140.68 − 1.33		78.03	− 3.11	− 3.83	202.11	67.57	−124.08	− 61.39	− 29.02	− 27.11
U.S.	453.54 − 0.19		453.54	− 0.88	− 0.19	454.48	416.31	+ 6.03	+ 1.35	+ 20.47	+ 4.73
Europe			117.24	+ 1.17	+ 1.01	121.15	110.89	− 0.63	− 0.53	+ 1.54	+ 1.33
Austria	97.49 + 0.83		96.83	+ 0.92	+ 0.96	113.96	95.91	− 10.30	− 9.61	− 7.53	− 7.22
Belgium	115.00 + 0.09		114.83	+ 0.45	+ 0.39	123.30	111.37	− 1.04	− 0.89	− 0.92	− 0.79
Denmark	101.25 + 0.21		99.55	+ 0.26	+ 0.26	107.35	92.02	− 2.80	− 2.73	+ 1.39	+ 1.42
Finland	235.75 + 0.35		207.17	+ 0.92	+ 0.45	222.84	151.23	+ 36.36	+ 21.28	+ 1.26	+ 0.61
France	111.75 + 1.21		109.53	+ 1.45	+ 1.34	120.91	104.68	− 10.42	− 8.69	+ 0.36	+ 0.33
Germany	124.85 + 1.23		123.71	+ 1.72	+ 1.41	128.64	109.84	+ 13.70	+ 12.45	+ 1.14	+ 0.93
Ireland	151.38 + 0.56		126.16	+ 1.04	+ 0.83	128.67	106.32	+ 9.50	+ 8.15	+ 3.57	+ 2.91
Italy	156.81 + 0.07		120.03	+ 0.08	+ 0.07	143.55	98.43	+ 8.49	+ 7.61	+ 10.49	+ 9.58
Netherlands	138.59 + 0.24		136.17	+ 0.49	+ 0.36	139.37	121.03	+ 7.68	+ 5.97	+ 2.30	+ 1.72
Norway	136.96 + 0.39		122.44	+ 0.63	+ 0.52	123.93	101.45	+ 8.21	+ 7.19	− 0.16	− 0.13
Spain	123.73 + 0.57		91.32	+ 0.70	+ 0.77	103.47	84.89	− 12.09	− 11.69	+ 1.99	+ 2.23
Sweden	168.98 + 1.47		125.84	+ 1.85	+ 1.49	126.44	103.22	+ 8.15	+ 6.93	+ 6.42	+ 5.38
Switzerland	157.14 + 0.62		164.73	+ 1.39	+ 0.85	166.86	149.77	+ 1.30	+ 0.80	+ 1.74	+ 1.07
United Kingdom	129.41 + 0.84		107.86	+ 1.21	+ 1.14	113.87	100.94	− 4.85	− 4.30	+ 0.52	+ 0.49
Asia/Pacific			109.82	− 0.66	− 0.60	128.85	106.40	− 7.87	− 6.69	− 9.67	− 8.09
Australia	108.63 + 0.64		106.03	+ 0.19	+ 0.18	124.92	105.84	− 18.89	− 15.12	− 8.86	− 7.71
Hong Kong	181.69 + 1.43		182.62	+ 2.56	+ 1.42	260.42	158.20	− 77.77	− 29.87	− 1.32	− 0.72
Indonesia	187.45 − 0.16		168.03	− 0.28	− 0.17	242.05	156.97	− 68.12	− 28.85	− 7.68	− 4.37
Japan	83.67 − 0.91		105.60	− 0.93	− 0.87	125.50	103.50	− 4.11	− 3.74	− 10.61	− 9.13
Malaysia	203.59 + 0.85		217.47	+ 2.05	+ 0.95	268.37	182.57	− 14.28	− 6.16	+ 0.77	+ 0.36
New Zealand	136.62 − 0.21		159.66	− 0.46	− 0.29	169.86	141.27	− 7.77	− 4.64	+ 3.80	+ 2.44
Singapore	148.91 − 0.48		166.02	− 0.59	− 0.35	191.35	139.96	− 2.83	− 1.68	− 12.04	− 6.76
Thailand	209.24 − 0.14		196.92	− 0.17	− 0.09	237.09	176.16	− 10.33	− 4.98	− 10.74	− 5.17
Asia/Pacific (ex. Japan)			152.53	+ 0.97	+ 0.64	186.04	140.27	− 33.51	− 18.01	− 5.03	− 3.19
World (ex. U.S.)			111.34	+ 0.05	+ 0.05	124.28	108.30	− 6.29	− 5.35	− 5.24	− 4.49
DJ WORLD STOCK INDEX			112.67	− 0.05	− 0.04	119.86	109.40	− 3.32	− 2.86	− 1.27	− 1.12

Indexes based on 6/30/82=100 for U.S., 12/31/91=100 for World.   ©1995 Dow Jones & Co. Inc., All Rights Reserved

◄— 61% plunge in Mexican stocks

higher European markets.

Plantations stocks were the top gainers in the Dow Jones World Industry Groups, closing at 228.66, up 6.96, or 3.1%, with **High & Low** of Malaysia rising 5.4% in local currency. Biotechnology stocks trailed at 90.35, down 3.25, or 3.5%, with **Amgen** of the U.S. sliding 5.7%.

In Tokyo, the Nikkei 225-stock index, which lost 210.30 points Wednesday, retreated 190.70 to 18099.55. In trading Friday, the Nikkei rose 72.94 points to close the morning session at 18172.49. Thursday's first-section volume was estimated at 340 million shares, up from 327.4 million shares a day earlier. Losers outnumbered gainers, 588-376. The Tokyo Stock Price Index, or Topix, of all first-section issues, which fell 21.60 points Wednesday, dropped 11.04 to 1423.75.

The construction sector, which propelled rallies immediately after the Jan. 17 earthquake in Japan, was hit again by profit-taking, deepening its losses and pressuring the broader market. And blue-chip electronics issues, a sector that is pivotal to any market upturn, remained weak as the U.S. dollar slumped against the yen. Foreign investors continued to sell high-technology issues, which they viewed for now as having limited potential for gains, but· rather than bowing out, they shifted to pharmaceutical, food and other domestically oriented sectors. Only a few overseas mutual funds sold Japanese equities aggressively because of redemptions.

In London, the Financial Times-Stock Exchange 100-share index climbed 26.5 points to 3099.0, after scoring a session peak of 3102.7, which marked a 1994 high. The FT 30-stock index advanced 20.5 points to 2358.2. Volume was 682.6 million shares, compared with 528.7 million shares a day earlier.

The market slipped into the red briefly after the opening, then built steadily on gains for the rest of the day. Investors increasingly believed British lending rates are near their peaks in the battle against inflation. This sentiment, combined with strength in futures, British government bonds and other European bourses, enlivened London stocks after a restrained performance earlier this week. The market was cheered by data that showed Britain's trade deficit in November was narrower than expected.

In **Frankfurt,** the DAX 30-stock index gained 25.07 points to 2112.69, fractionally off the intraday high and far above the day's low of 2086.11. The sharp rise ended a two-day consolidation and pushed the DAX above a perceived barrier. Among institutional moves, insurers, which typically

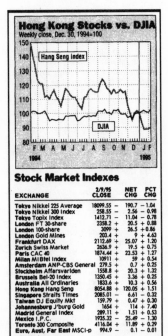

Stock Market Indexes

EXCHANGE	2/9/95 CLOSE		NET CHG		PCT CHG
Tokyo Nikkei 225 Average	18099.55	−	190.7	−	1.04
Tokyo Nikkei 300 Index	258.55	−	2.56	−	0.98
Tokyo Topix Index	1412.71	−	11.04	−	0.78
London FT 30-share	2358.2	+	20.5	+	0.88
London 100-share	3099	+	26.5	+	0.86
London Gold Mines	203.4	+	9	+	4.63
Frankfurt DAX	2112.69	+	25.07	+	1.20
Zurich Swiss Market	2636.9	+	19.5	+	0.75
Paris CAC 40	1874.44	+	23.53	+	1.27
Milan MIBtel Index	10911	+	59	+	0.54
Amsterdam ANP-CBS General	279.5	+	0.7	+	0.25
Stockholm Affarsvarlden	1558.8	+	20.3	+	1.32
Brussels Bel-20 Index	1350.45	+	3.36	+	0.25
Australia All Ordinaries	1833.6	+	10.3	+	0.56
Hong Kong Hang Seng	8054.88	+	120.06	+	1.51
Singapore Straits Times	2085.01	−	6.61	−	0.32
Taiwan DJ Equity Mkt	159.79	+	0.47	+	0.30
Johannesburg J'burg Gold	1654	+	114	+	7.40
Madrid General Index	289.11	+	1.51	+	0.53
Mexico I.P.C.	1935.32	−	25.49	−	1.30
Toronto 300 Composite	4116.04	+	11.89	+	0.29
Euro, Aust, Far East MSCI-p	994.9	−	0.1	−	0.01

p-Preliminary
na-Not available

await signs of corporate earnings improvements before buying, picked up positions.

In Paris, the market ratcheted up 1.3%, with gains accelerating on buying to cover short, or oversold, positions in robust volume; investors also were encouraged by the bullish performances in London and Frankfurt. **In Amsterdam,** prices finished mixed to higher in an erratic session, first boosted by gains for London stocks and German government bond futures, then pushed down by a listless dollar and early weakness on Wall Street, and finally lifted by some foreign buying.

In Milan, stocks rose in technical dealings, mainly affected by option prices ahead of their Friday expiration for the February account. **In Madrid,** the bourse rose, buoyed by bargain-hunting and purchases of baskets of issues linked to futures. **In Stockholm,** equities advanced sharply, propelled by strong interest in some blue chips, falling bond yields and climbing European bourses; turnover jumped. **In Zurich,** prices rose in quiet activity that focused on a few blue chips.

(continued)

In **Mexico City**, stocks tumbled 1.3% in light activity, as investors continued to wait for developments in the Mexican economic crisis; the market also was anxious prior to Sunday's gubernatorial elections in Jalisco state, where public-opinion polls indicate the governing Institutional Revolutionary Party could be defeated by the conservative National Action Party.

In **Sydney**, the main index rose in volatile trading, after falling at the opening because of sharp drops in metals prices and then rebounding because of bargain-hunting by institutional investors; in the overall market, though, declining issues slightly outnumbered rising issues.

In **Hong Kong**, stocks rallied 1.5% on volume that swelled with foreign orders, after an early decline was reversed when investors put aside their concerns about share-purchase warrant issues and a Sino-U.S. trade dispute. The recovery overcame the previous session's consolidation stemming partly from rumors, later confirmed, that securities firms were offering covered warrants on shares of two blue chips, a move usually considered to be a signal for a market decline. Financial stocks gained 1.8%, and the property and the commercial and industrial sectors each climbed 1.7%.

In **Singapore**, the market slipped as profit-taking continued and buying switched almost entirely to Malaysian shares traded over the counter; the property sector benefited from encouraging results from sales at the first major condominium opening since property shares collapsed in mid-January. In **Kuala Lum**-pur, equities rose, as profit-taking among blue chips was balanced by heavy buying of speculative issues.

In **Seoul**, prices ended higher, after sentiment improved when the benchmark index climbed through a perceived resistance level, signs of eased liquidity emerged, and investors concentrated on companies that expect good earnings. In **Taipei**, stocks edged up, despite some profit-taking that pushed turnover up, but momentum slowed when the main index neared a resistance mark. In **Manila**, the bourse advanced after Philippine investors followed suit when foreign funds bought positions, though activity was listless. In **Bangkok**, shares fell in dealings that were subdued as many investors awaited more U.S. economic data.

Among corporate developments, in Stockholm, **Ericsson** soared 15.5 kronor, or 3.8%, to 427.5 kronor ($57.29). The telecommunications company posted preliminary results for 1994, showing pretax profit jumped 81% to 5.61 billion kronor ($751.7 million) from a year earlier, slightly exceeding expectations. Ericsson said it would propose a 4-for-1 stock split.

Here are price trends on the world's major stock markets, as calculated by Morgan Stanley Capital International Perspective, Geneva. To make them directly comparable, each index, calculated in local currencies, is based on the close of 1969 equaling 100. The percentage change is since year-end.

	Feb. 8	Feb. 7	% This Year
U.S.	452.9	452.7	+ 5.0
Britain	932.5	932.3	− 0.5
Canada	442.6	442.1	− 1.9
Japan	841.4	854.8	− 9.2
France	570.5	575.7	− 1.1
Germany	298.6	299.4	− 1.1
Hong Kong	5421.1	5462.8	− 4.5
Switzerland	334.7	335.9	− 0.3
Australia	388.1	392.9	− 4.3
World Index	613.7	615.9	− 0.8

DOW JONES WORLD STOCK INDEX

Thursday, February 9, 1995

REGION/ COUNTRY	DJ EQUITY MARKET INDEX, LOCAL CURRENCY	PCT. CHG.	IN U.S. DOLLARS								
			CLOSING INDEX	CHG.	PCT. CHG.	12-MO HIGH	12-MO LOW	12-MO CHG.	PCT. CHG.	FROM 12/31	PCT. CHG.
Americas			112.77	− 0.25	− 0.22	113.88	105.21	− 1.04	− 0.91	+ 4.25	+ 3.91
Canada	113.01 + 0.30		93.42	+ 0.17	+ 0.18	104.16	88.37	− 8.55	− 8.38	− 1.81	− 1.90
Mexico	140.68 − 1.33		78.03	− 3.11	− 3.83	202.11	67.57	−124.08	− 61.39	−29.02	−27.11
U.S.	453.54 − 0.19		453.54	− 0.88	− 0.19	454.48	416.31	+ 6.03	+ 1.35	+20.47	+ 4.73
Europe			117.24	+ 1.17	+ 1.01	121.15	110.89	− 0.63	− 0.53	+ 1.54	+ 1.33
Austria	97.49 + 0.83		96.83	+ 0.92	+ 0.96	113.96	95.91	− 10.30	− 9.61	− 7.53	− 7.22
Belgium	115.00 + 0.09		114.83	+ 0.45	+ 0.39	123.30	111.37	− 1.04	− 0.89	− 0.92	− 0.79
Denmark	101.25 + 0.21		99.55	+ 0.26	+ 0.26	107.35	92.02	− 2.80	− 2.73	+ 1.39	+ 1.42
Finland	235.75 + 0.35		207.17	+ 0.92	+ 0.45	222.84	151.23	+ 36.36	+ 21.28	+ 1.26	+ 0.61
France	111.75 + 1.21		109.53	+ 1.45	+ 1.34	120.91	104.68	− 10.42	− 8.69	+ 0.36	+ 0.33
Germany	124.85 + 1.23		123.71	+ 1.72	+ 1.41	128.64	109.84	+ 13.70	+ 12.45	+ 1.14	+ 0.93
Ireland	151.38 + 0.56		126.16	+ 1.04	+ 0.83	128.67	106.32	+ 9.50	+ 8.15	+ 3.57	+ 2.91
Italy	156.81 + 0.07		120.03	+ 0.08	+ 0.07	143.55	98.43	+ 8.49	+ 7.61	+10.49	+ 9.58
Netherlands	138.59 + 0.24		136.17	+ 0.49	+ 0.36	139.37	121.03	+ 7.68	+ 5.97	+ 2.30	+ 1.72
Norway	136.96 + 0.39		122.44	+ 0.63	+ 0.52	123.93	101.45	+ 8.21	+ 7.19	− 0.16	− 0.13
Spain	123.73 + 0.57		91.32	+ 0.70	+ 0.77	103.47	84.89	− 12.09	− 11.69	+ 1.99	+ 2.23
Sweden	168.98 + 1.47		125.84	+ 1.85	+ 1.49	126.44	103.22	+ 8.15	+ 6.93	+ 6.42	+ 5.38
Switzerland	157.14 + 0.62		164.73	+ 1.39	+ 0.85	166.86	149.77	+ 1.30	+ 0.80	+ 1.74	+ 1.07
United Kingdom	129.41 + 0.84		107.86	+ 1.21	+ 1.14	113.87	100.94	− 4.85	− 4.30	+ 0.52	+ 0.49
Asia/Pacific			109.82	− 0.66	− 0.60	128.85	106.40	− 7.87	− 6.69	− 9.67	− 8.09
Australia	108.63 + 0.64		106.03	+ 0.19	+ 0.18	124.92	105.84	− 18.89	− 15.12	− 8.86	− 7.71
Hong Kong	181.69 + 1.43		182.62	+ 2.56	+ 1.42	260.42	158.20	− 77.77	− 29.87	− 1.32	− 0.72
Indonesia	187.45 − 0.16		168.03	− 0.28	− 0.17	242.06	156.97	− 68.12	− 28.85	− 7.68	− 4.37
Japan	83.67 − 0.91		105.60	− 0.93	− 0.87	125.50	103.50	− 4.11	− 3.74	−10.61	− 9.13
Malaysia	203.59 + 0.85		217.47	+ 2.05	+ 0.95	268.37	182.57	− 14.28	− 6.16	+ 0.77	+ 0.36
New Zealand	136.62 − 0.21		159.66	− 0.46	− 0.29	169.86	141.27	− 7.77	− 4.64	+ 3.80	+ 2.44
Singapore	148.91 − 0.48		166.02	− 0.59	− 0.35	191.35	139.96	− 2.83	− 1.68	−12.04	− 6.76
Thailand	209.24 − 0.14		196.92	− 0.17	− 0.09	237.09	176.16	− 10.33	− 4.98	−10.74	− 5.17
Asia/Pacific (ex. Japan)			152.53	+ 0.97	+ 0.64	186.04	140.27	− 33.51	− 18.01	− 5.03	− 3.19
World (ex. U.S.)			111.34	+ 0.05	+ 0.05	124.28	108.30	− 6.29	− 5.35	− 5.24	− 4.49
DJ WORLD STOCK INDEX			112.67	− 0.05	− 0.04	119.86	109.40	− 3.32	− 2.86	− 1.27	− 1.12

Indexes based on 6/30/82=100 for U.S., 12/31/91=100 for World.   ©1995 Dow Jones & Co. Inc., All Rights Reserved

◄── 61% plunge in Mexican stocks

Source: *The Wall Street Journal*, February 10, 1995. Reprinted by permission of *The Wall Street Journal*, ©1995 Dow Jones & Company, Inc. All rights reserved worldwide.

ADRS

Thursday, Feb. 16, 1995

AngSA 1.13e	255	47³/₈	−	⁷/₈
AngAG .42e	78	8⁵/₁₆	−	³/₁₆
ASEA 1.28e	21	73⅛		...
Blyvoor	207	1⁷/₁₆	−	¹/₁₆
Bowater .25e	32	6³/₈	+	³/₈
Buffels .87e	190	7³/₈		...
CPcMn	770	1¾	+	¼
Cortecs	50	1³/₈	−	¼
DBeer .85e	1777	21⁹/₆₄	−	¹⁵/₆₄
DriefC .28e	1417	13³/₁₆	−	¹⁹/₆₄
Fisons .21e	334	7½	+	³/₈
FreSCn .90e	1016	12	−	½
FujiPh .38e	39	43¾	−	1⅛
GoldFd .22e	3	23¼	−	⁶¹/₆₄
GrtCtrl	78	5³/₁₆	+	¹/₁₆
Highvld .14e	15	9¼		...
InstCp s .32e	24	9¾	−	⁵/₈
KirinBr 1.00e	15	109½	+	1½
KloofG .24e	223	11⁵/₈		...
Lydnbg .36e	30	17¼		...
Minorc .57e	277	21¹³/₁₆	−	⁷/₁₆
Nissan .14e	315	14³/₈	−	¼
PhrmPat	519	1³/₈		...
RankO s .50e	18	12	−	⅛
StHIGd .97e	4	8⅛	−	⅛
Santos .79e	12	10⅛	−	³/₈
Sasol .25e	1	7⁵/₈		...
Senetek	801	2¹/₃₂		...
SoPcPt	202	¹¹/₁₆	+	¹/₃₂
TelefMex .07e	14264	1¹⁷/₃₂	+	¹/₃₂
Toyota .56e	35	36¾	−	¼
TrnBio	439	1½	+	⅛
TrnBi wtB	10	⁵/₁₆		...
VaalRf .35e	641	7¹⁵/₆₄	−	¹/₆₄
Wacoal	4	52¾	−	1¾
WDeep 1.41e	121	32⁷/₈	−	¾

FOREIGN MARKETS

Thursday, February 9, 1995

TOKYO
(in yen)

	Close	Prev. Close
ANA	1020	1020
Aiwa	1950	2000
Ajinomoto	1170	1180
Alps Elec	1160	1150
Amada Co	980	993
Ando Elec	1190	1180
Anritsu	1110	1120
Asahi Chem	684	680
Asahi Glass	1130	1140
AT&T Global	1000	1010
Bank of Tokyo	1420	1450
Bk of Yokohama	790	790
Banyu Pharm	992	1000
Bridgestone	1370	1370
Brother Ind	558	560
CSK	2970	3000
Canon Inc	1470	1450
Canon Sales	2350	2430
Casio Computer	1070	1080
Chichibu Cement	583	592
Chubu Pwr	2310	2260
Chugai Pharm	999	1000
Citizen Watch	678	673
Dai Nippon Print	1540	1560
Dai-ichi Kangyo	1650	1670
Daiei	1010	1060
Daiichi Seiyaku	1500	1540
Dainippon Ink	436	442
Dainippon Pharm	1050	1060
Daiwa House	1470	1480
Daiwa Securities	1120	1160
Eisai	1520	1550
Ezaki Glico	951	949
Fanuc	4040	4080
Fuji Bank	2040	2080
Fuji Hi	388	393
Fuji Photo Film	2220	2220
Fujisawa Pharm	1110	1080
Fujitsu	895	913
Furukawa Elec	586	583
Green Cross	855	857
Haseko	591	581
Hirose Elec	5280	5180
Hitachi Cable	750	755
Hitachi Credit	1620	1630
Hitachi Ltd	850	856
Hitachi Maxell	1610	1560
Hitachi Metals	1040	1040
Hitachi Sales	593	579
Honda Motor	1500	1560
Hoya	2260	2260
IHI	401	409
Ind Bank Japan	2520	2450
Intec	1270	1290
Isetan	1420	1400
Isuzu	446	451
Ito-yokado	4620	4740
Itochu Corp	607	623
Iwatsu Elec	490	486
JAL	626	632
JEOL	667	670
JUSCO	1720	1750
Japan Aviat El	675	665
Japan Energy	362	367
Japan Radio	1410	1420
KDD	8920	8880
Kajima	873	897
Kandenko	1650	1630
Kansai Elec	2200	2200
Kao Corp	1050	1080
Kawasaki Hi	399	406
Kawasaki Steel	374	377
Kinden	1900	1920
Kirin	1040	1050
Kobe Steel	269	283
Kokusai Elec	1680	1710
Kokuyo	2380	2310
Komatsu Ltd	811	823
Konica	708	720
Kubota	648	662
Kumagai Gumi	510	500
Kuraray	1030	1060
Kureha Chem	456	455
Kyocera	6300	6430
Kyowa Hakko	946	955
Kyushu Matsushit	2060	2150
Lion	591	591
Makino Milling	781	785
Makita Elec	1650	1620
Marudai Food	720	725
Marui	1440	1490
Matsushita Com	2100	2160
Mats' Elec Ind	1390	1420
Mats' Elec Wrks	1060	1070
Mazda	505	506
Meiji Seika	583	588
Minolta	454	454
Misawa Homes	1090	1120
Mitsubishi Bank	2270	2290
Mitsubishi Chem	477	478
Mitsubishi Corp	1090	1140
Mitsubishi Elec	616	628
Mitsubishi Real	1010	1040
Mitsubishi Hi	640	644
Mitsubishi Matl	455	458
Mitsubishi Trust	1330	1340
Mitsubishi Whse	1570	1590
Mitsui Fudosan	1050	1080
Mitsui Mar&Fire	673	668
Mitsui Trust	931	938
Mitsui & Co	737	753
Mitsukoshi	930	939
Mochida Pharm	1830	1850
NEC	916	940
NGK Spark	1130	1120
NIFCO	1370	1370
NKK	264	267
NSK	632	646
NTN	592	590
NTT	745000	764000
New Oji Paper	935	938
Nihon Unisys Ltd	1220	1220
Nikko Securities	990	1000
Nikon Corp	815	805
Nintendo	5130	5100
Nippon Chemi-con	561	552
Nippon Columbia	603	598
Nippon El Glass	1700	1740
Nippon Express	892	901
Nippon Hodo	1730	1740
Nippon Meat	1270	1270
Nippon Oil	633	637
Nippon Paper	638	644
Nippon Sanso	491	487
Nippon Shinpan	770	774
Nippon Steel	346	349
Nissan Motor	733	735
Nissin Food	2220	2190
Nitsuko	1140	1190
Nomura Securities	1760	1810
OKK	370	365
Obayashi Corp	740	755
Odakyu Railway	715	716
Oki Elec Ind	596	605
Okuma Corp	860	870
Olympus Optical	955	961
Omron	1740	1740
Ono Pharm	4750	4860
Onward	1230	1240
Orient Corp	570	534
Pioneer Electron	2120	2130
Renown	405	400
Ricoh Co	831	836
Royal Co	1350	1360
Ryobi	520	520
SMK	612	612
Sakura Bank	1190	1200
Sankyo Co	2400	2410
Sanrio	1280	1280
Sanwa Bank	1900	1930
Sanyo Elec	509	504
Sapporo Brewery	900	902
Secom	5360	5410
Sekisui House	1180	1190
Seven-eleven	7140	7110
Sharp	1470	1500
Shimizu Corp	972	980
Shin-etsu Chem	1730	1750
Shionogi	864	871
Shiseido	1090	1090
Showa Denko	314	326
Skylark	1550	1550
Sony	4720	4720
Sumitomo Bank	1790	1820
Sumitomo Chem	463	470
Sumitomo Corp	897	931
Sumitomo Elec	1240	1270
Sumitomo Marine	793	762
Sumitomo Metal	292	298
Sumitomo Realty	581	585
Sumitomo Trust	1170	1200
Suzuki Motor	932	921
TDK	4220	4290
Taisei Corp	641	651
Taisho Pharm	1780	1780
Taiyo Yuden	961	978
Takeda Chem	1190	1170
Tanabe Seiyaku	760	753
Teijin	475	490
Toho Co	16000	16100
Tokio Mar&Fire	1050	1050
Tokyo Denki Kom	1150	1150
Tokyo Elec Power	2590	2600
Tokyo Electron	2630	2680
Tokyo Gas	397	400
Tokyo Style	1430	1460
Tokyu Corp	628	636
Tonen Corp	1520	1520
Toppan Print	1300	1300
Toray	616	625
Toshiba	625	633
Toto	1600	1630
Toyo Seikan	3020	3090
Toyobo	384	375
Toyoda Mach	740	740
Toyota Motor	1840	1870
Tsugami	469	470
Uny	1490	1520
Ushio	949	934
Wacoal	1040	1060
Yamaha	1160	1180
Yamaichi Sec	679	680
Yamanouchi Phm	1970	1990
Yamatake-Hnywl	1430	1420
Yamato Transport	1020	1020
Yamazaki Baking	1760	1760
Yasuda Fire	651	637
Yokogawa Elec	914	925

LONDON
(in pence)

	Close	Prev. Close
Abbey National	437	432
Albert Fisher	44	44
Allied-Domecq	518	513
Argyll Group	268	277.5
Arjo Wiggins	234	229.5
Assoc Brit Fds	604.5	602
BAA PLC	463	452
Barclays	601.5	599.5
Bass	518	516
BAT Indus	460	455.5
Blue Circle	283.5	281
BOC Group	722	715.5
Body Shop	168.25	168
Boots	484	477
Borland	563	563
Bowater Indus	396	387
BPB Indus	321	318
British Aero	473	475
British Airwys	384.5	384
British Gas	310	310
British Pete	423	419
British Steel	153	151
British Telcom	397.5	394.5
BTR	321.5	313
Burmah Castrol	853	837
Cable&Wireless	401	392
Cadbury Schwp	412	411
Caradon	251	245
Charter Cons	763	767
Coats Viyella	182	183
Commercial Un	517	497.5
Courtaulds	430	423
Dixons	213.5	215
Eng Ch Clay	372	363
Euro Tunnel	303	306
Fisons	111.5	108
Forte	244	243
GEC	295	293
Genrl Accidnt	538	527
GKN	587	582
Glaxo Hldgs	657	654
Granada	519.5	506
Grand Metrop	380	375
Gt Universal St	538	528
Guardian Royal	180.5	176
Guinness	433	426
Hanson PLC	244	237
Hillsdown	174	175
Imp Chem Ind	754	746
Inchcape PLC	307	308
Jefferson Smurf	404.5	397
Johnson Mathy	525	523
Kingfisher	431	432
Ladbroke Grp	175	174
Land Securs	584	576
LASMO	156	157
Legal & Genl	453	446
Lloyds Bank	550	549
Lonrho	152.5	151
Lucas	190	188
Marks&Spencer	400	394
MEPC	388	382
Nat Power PLC	479	474
Nat Wstmn Bk	490	485
NFC	171	165
P & O	595	581
Pearson	591	582
Pilkgtn Bros	156	149
PowerGen PLC	509	505
Prudential	303	304.5
Racal Elect	225	221
Rank Org	392	386
Reckit&Colman	646	637
Redland	446	439
Reed Intl	760	747
Reuters	455	454
RMC	941	935
Rolls Royce	164.5	160
Royal Insur	285	276
RTZ Corp	760	752
Stchi&Stchi	109	109
J Sainsbury	420	426
Sears	104	102
Sedgwick Grp	154	150
Severn Trent	512	496
Shell Trnspt	727	720
Siebe PLC	539	528
Smithkln Bchm	495	489
Smith&Nephew	167.5	165
Std Chartrd	268	264
Storehouse	231.5	229
Sun Alliance	316	300
TI Group	346	339
Tarmac	114	114.5
Tate & Lyle	428	427
Tesco	242.5	249
Thorn EMI	1040	1035
Tomkins	233	236
Trafalgar Hse	66	66.5
TSB Group	249	250
Utd Biscuits	340	338
Unilever	1177	1166
Vodafone	191	193
Warburg	747	733
Wellcome	1020	1022
Williams Hldgs	338	340.5
WPP Group	112.5	114
South African Mines (in U.S. dollars)		
Bracken	0.23	0.23
Deelkraal	1.08	1.18
Doornfontein	0.81	0.81
Durban Deep	9.50	9.75
E. Rand Gold	2.03	2.16
E. Rand Prop	1.06	1.06
Elandsrand	5.00	5.00
Grootvlei	2.03	2.13
Harmony	8.18	8.68
Hartebstfftn	3.82	3.88
Impala Pltm	20.13	20.31
Kinross	12.31	12.50
Leslie	1.50	1.55
Loraine	3.80	3.80
Randfontein	7.13	7.18
Rustenburg	22.31	22.31
Southvaal	24.88	24.88
Stilfontein	1.70	1.70
Unisel	2.10	2.21
West Areas	13.25	13.25
Winkelhaak	10.06	10.25

STOCKHOLM
(in krona)

	Close	Prev. Close
AGA	75.5	75.5
Asea	555	550
Astra	198	196.5
Atlas Copco	101.5	99
Electrolux	377.5	376.5
Ericsson	427.5	412
SE Bank	44	43.5
Skanska	168	167
SKF	135.5	134
Volvo	146.5	142.5

SWITZERLAND
(in Swiss francs)

	Close	Prev. Close
Alusuisse	643	643
Brown Boveri	1113	1108
Brown Bov reg	218	218
Ciba-Geigy br	808	805
Ciba-Geigy reg	808	805
CS Holding	546	544
Hof LaRoch br	11675	11650
Roche div rt	6740	6690
Nestle reg	1220	1209
Sandoz br	696	685
Sandoz reg	686	673
Sulzer	750	753
Swiss Bnk Cp	384	379
Swiss Reins br	752	748
Swiss Reins reg	755	752
Swissair	770	760
UBS	1037	1037
Winterthur br	660	655
Winterthur reg	632	626
Zurich Ins	1213	1210

BRUSSELS
(in Belgian francs)

	Close	Prev. Close
Arbed	4860	4790
BBL	4450	4450
Bekaert	20925	20900
CBR	11800	11800
Delhaize	1180	1184
Electrabel	5790	5720
GIB	1240	1236
Gevaert	1496	1490
Gen de Bnque	8220	8110
Petrofina	9330	9330
Soc Gen Belg	2060	2080
Solvay	15500	15525

PARIS
(in French francs)

	Close	Prev. Close
Accor	587	589
Air Liquide	751	740
Alcatel Alstm	457	460.6
AXA Group	236.9	237.2
BNP	249	240.6
Carnaud Metal	185.9	179.9
Carrefour	2199	2140
Club Med	426	428
Danone	773	760
Dassault Avitn	437	434
Elf Aquitaine	386.5	383.3
Euro Disneyld	11.55	11
Generale Eaux	486	477.1
Havas	381.4	365.5
Imetal	508	516
Lafarge Coppe	359.5	357.5
Lagardere Grp	125.9	122.3
LVMH	848	837
Michelin	210.5	210
L'Oreal	1187	1167
Paribas	337.4	334.2
Pernod Ricard	328.2	318.9
Peugeot	744	731
Renault	182.3	183
Saint Gobain	639	626
Sanofi	273	271
Schneider	371	365
Soc Generale	542	538
Suez	231.7	229.4
Thomson CSF	145	145
Total Francais	296	287.7

AMSTERDAM
(in guilders)

	Close	Prev. Close
ABN Amro	60.10	59.90
Aegon	111.9	112.1
Ahold	54.20	54
Akzo Nobel	195.4	195.2
AMEV	73.60	72.90
Bols Wessanen	33.60	33.90
DSM	136.8	135.6
Elsevier	16.90	16.60
Fokker	12.70	12.80
Gist-Brocades	45.40	45.30
Heineken	256.5	255.4
Hoogovens	75.30	74.60
Hunter Douglas	78.50	76.20
Intl Ndrlndn Gr	81.60	81.50
KLM	46.90	46.50
KNP BT	51.60	51.90
Nedlloyd	53.50	53.70
Oce-van Grntn	84.50	85.30
Pakhoed Hldg	49.30	49.70
Philips	54.50	54.60
Robeco	106.4	106.5
Rodamco	48.10	48.50
Rolinco	107.9	106.5
Rorento	83.50	83.30
Royal Dutch	193.1	192.1
Unilever	200.1	199.5
VOC	47.80	47.80
VNU	176	173.9
Wolters Kluwer	125.7	126.8

HONG KONG
(in Hong Kong dollars)

	Close	Prev. Close
Bank E Asia	25.50	24.60
Cathay Pacific	11.70	11.35
Cheung Kong	31.10	30.50
China L & P	37	36.40
Dairy Farm	8.95	9
Hang Seng Bk	46.50	45.70
HK Electric	23	22.85
HK Land	14.95	14.85
HK Telecom	14.25	14.20
HSBC Hldgs	80.25	79
Hutchsn Whmp	30.50	30.10
Hysan Develop	15.15	15.10
Sun Hung Kai	48.30	47.90
Swire Pacific	47.60	47.20
Tsingtao Brew	4.225	4
Wharf Holdings	25.85	25.35

MEXICO
(in pesos)

	Close	Prev. Close
Alfa A	52	52.90
Apasco A	20.50	20.50
Bimbo A	24.50	24.30
Banacci C	11.10	11
Cemex B	20.15	20.50
Cifra B	6.90	7.10
Cifra C	6.64	6.76
Femsa B	11	11.56
Gcarso A1	34.25	35.10
Kimber A	53.40	54.50
Maseca B	5.10	5.12
Tamsa	16.70	17
Televisa	57.20	59
Tolmex B2	21.70	21.25
Vitro	20.30	20

FRANKFURT
(in Marks)

	Close	Prev. Close
AEG	142.6	142
Allianz	2479	2428
Asko	668	670
BASF	332.2	328
Bayer	364.8	360.8
Byr Vereinsbk	442	436.5
BMW	772	748.5
Commerzbank	336.5	330.8
Continental	233	230
Daimler Benz	723.5	718.5
Degussa	467.5	461
Deutsche Bank	721.5	715.2
Dresdner Bank	402	399
Heidlbg Zemnt	1160	1130
Henkel	556	553
Hochtief	823	820
Hoechst	336	330
Karstadt	568	567
Kaufhof	473	472
Linde	938	930
Lufthansa	198	196.5
Mannesmann	428.5	426.3
MAN	420	417.5
Metallges	132.8	134.2
Munchen Ruck	2380	2400
Porsche	647	650
RWE	442	437
Schering	1130	1120
Siemens	677.5	673
Thyssen	305	297.7
Veba	533.5	530
VEW	425	423.5
Volkswagen	413	405.3

SYDNEY
(in Australian dollars)

	Close	Prev. Close
Amcor	9.05	9
ANZ Group	4.54	4.56
Ashton	2.05	2.10
Boral	3.56	3.50
Bougainville	0.60	0.58
Brambles Inds	11.76	11.80
Brokn Hill Prp	17.96	17.84
Burns Philp	3.37	3.35
Coles Myer	4.13	4.16
Comalco	4.34	4.30
Centrl Norsemn	0.82	0.83
CRA	16.32	16.40
CSR	4.55	4.46
Fletcher Chl-a	3.87	3.86
Foster's	1.13	1.12
Gld Mns Kalgo	0.86	0.81
Goodman	1.28	1.27
Leighton	1.80	1.75
Mayne Nickless	6.29	6.30
MIM Holdings	1.82	1.86
Nat Aust Bnk	10.42	10.34
News Corp	5.54	5.36
Normdy Poseidn	1.57	1.65
North Ltd	2.77	2.83
Orbital Engine	1.35	1.39
Pacific Dunlop	3.01	3.01
Pancontinental	1.41	1.40
Renison Gldflds	4.25	4.45
Santos	3.50	3.5
S Pac Pete	0.42	0.42
TNT Ltd	1.75	1.74
Western Mining	6.59	6.41
Westpac	4.62	4.71
Woodside	4.83	4.73

a-New Zealand quote; in New Zealand dollars.

MILAN
(in lire)

	Close	Prev. Close
Banca Com	4085	4050
Benetton	17500	17580
CIGA	926	923
CIR	1819	1805
FIAT Com	6625	6525
FIAT Pref	4355	4270
Generali	39950	39900
Mediobanca	14500	14320
Montedison	1305	1293
Olivetti Com	2020	2000
Olivetti NC	1400	1390
Pirelli Co	4230	4195
Pirelli SpA	2435	2410
Rinascente	9150	9160
RAS	18225	18140
Saipem	3215	3150
Snia	2060	2050
Stet	5160	5090
Telecom Ital	4545	4540

Source: *The Wall Street Journal*, February 10, 1995. Reprinted by permission of *The Wall Street Journal*,

CANADIAN MARKETS

Quotations in Canadian Funds
Quotations in cents unless marked $
Thursday, February 9, 1995

TORONTO

Sales	Stock	High	Low	Close	Chg.
99722	Abti Prce	$18½	18½	18½	
14225	Agnico E	$13½	13¼	13½	+ ¼
13018	Air Canada	$8	7⅞	7⅞	− ⅛
76496	Alt Energy	$18¼	18	18¼	+ ¼
17488	Alta Nat	$15⅝	15½	15⅝	+ ⅛
161800	Anderson	$12	11¾	12	+ ⅛
814541	Barick gld	$29⅝	29¼	29⅝	+ ¾
11600	Atco I f	$14⅝	14⅝	14⅝	+ ⅛
33698	Aur Res o	450	415	450	+30
43277	Avenor	$27⅜	27⅛	27¼	
189071	BCE Inc	$44⅛	43⅞	44	
32082	BC Gas	$13⅞	13⅝	13⅞	
6135	BGR A	$12⅞	12¾	12¾	− ¼
1131030	Bank Mtl	$27⅛	26½	26⅞	+ ⅛
871063	Bank N S	$27⅛	26⅝	27	+ ⅛
10050	BCE Mobl	$45⅞	45¾	45¾	
1058478	Bramalea	113	102	103	−12
19302	BC Telcom	$24⅝	24¼	24⅝	+ ¼
80650	CAE	$7¼	7	7⅛	
200000	CCL A	$11¼	11¼	11¼	+ ⅜
2806440	CCL B f	$11⅝	11¼	11⅜	+ ⅜
1023	Cabre	$12½	12⅜	12⅜	
4000	Cambridg	$12¼	12⅛	12⅛	
80038	Cameco	$31⅛	30¾	30¾	− ⅜
1276102	Ci Bk Com	$34⅛	33½	34	+ ⅜
223350	Cdn Nat Res	$12½	12¼	12½	
316857	CP Ltd	$20	19⅝	19⅞	
266444	CTire A f	$13⅝	13⅜	13½	
1500	C Util B	$23⅛	23	23	− ⅛
58656	Canfor	$17¾	17½	17¾	+ ¼
1050700	Cara	320	300	310	+10
175200	Celanese	$26⅛	26	26	− ⅛
14400	Cineplex	390	375	390	+20
41	Camdev	390	390	390	−30
255145	Co Steel	$25½	25	25⅛	− ⅛
95550	CocaCBev	$5⅝	5½	5½	
28050	Conwest	$21¼	20½	20½	− ¾
503249	Corel o	$17⅝	16⅞	17	− ⅝
11500	DY 4 syst	$11⅝	11½	11½	
249296	Delrina C o	$21¼	20½	21	+ ⅝
717900	Derlan	290	281	290	+ 4
195842	Dofasco	$18¼	18	18	− ¼
4557	Dundee A f	$9	8⅞	8⅞	
4550	Dupont A	$19	18¾	18¾	
92100	Dylex A f	20	18	18	−1½
3200	ELAN Eng	$7⅞	7⅞	7⅞	
41780	Euro Nev	$26⅞	26	26¼	− ⅝
5400	FCA Intl	325	325	325	− 5
7971	FPI Ltd	$7	6⅞	7	
1800	Fahnstk A f	$9⅜	9⅛	9⅛	
2600	Fairfax f	$68	68	68	
83200	Fed Ind A	$6	5⅞	6	
26190	Finning L	$18½	18⅛	18⅛	− ⅜
19959	Flet CCan A	$17⅞	17⅝	17⅝	− ⅛
237246	FSesn HI f	$16¼	16	16¼	+ ½
32210	Franco	$63	62¼	62⅝	
120515	Geac Comp	$17⅜	17	17⅜	+ ½
6732	Gendis A	$15⅞	15¾	15¾	
36073	Gentra Inc	59	57	57	
7800	Goldcorp A f	$7½	7¼	7¼	+ ⅛
1800	Hayes D	$12	11⅞	11⅞	− ⅜
67062	Hees Intl	$11⅞	11½	11⅞	+ ⅜
67581	Hemlo Gld	$12¼	11⅞	11⅞	
7600	Hollingr I	$11⅞	11¾	11⅞	− ⅛
1000	Horsham f	$17¼	17¼	17¼	+ ⅛
536183	H Bay Co	$27	26⅜	26⅞	+ ⅜
69267	Imasco L	$41⅜	41⅛	41⅜	
19900	IForest A f	$11⅝	11½	11½	− ⅛
77675	IPL eng	$28	27⅞	28	
3547	Inv Grp	$16	15⅞	15⅞	− ⅛
74300	Ipsco	$22¼	22	22⅛	− ¼
625	ISG Tech	$8⅞	8¾	8⅞	+ ⅛
232592	Ivaco A f	480	470	470	−10
6537	Jannock	$15	14¾	14⅞	− ¼
532989	Labatt	$20⅛	19¾	20⅛	+ ⅛
4900	Loblaw Co	$24⅜	24⅜	24⅜	− ⅛
21786	Mackenzie	$8⅝	8¼	8½	
59021	Magna A f	$51⅝	51¼	51⅝	+ ⅜
22800	M L Foods	$12	11⅞	11⅞	
6500	MDS H A	$13½	13½	13½	− ⅛
4601	Maritime f	$21½	21¼	21⅜	+ ⅛
2400	Mark Res	$6⅞	6⅞	6⅞	+ ⅛
28470	Molson A f	$19	18¾	19	− ⅛
200	Molson B	$19¼	19¼	19¼	− ½
159425	Morisn P	$7	6⅞	7	
117000	Mind Wlyn	$7½	7¼	7⅜	
1331800	Noma A f	490	480	480	
147966	Noranda F	$10⅝	10½	10⅝	+ ⅛
167358	Noranda I	$23⅝	23¼	23¼	− ⅜
26430	Norcen	$15⅞	15¾	15⅞	+ ⅛
947395	Nova Corp	$11⅞	11¾	11¾	− ⅛
23100	NS Power	$11½	11⅜	11⅜	
18288	Nowsco W	$13¼	13	13¼	+ ⅛
392900	Onex C f	$12¼	12⅛	12¼	+ ⅛
40270	Oshawa A f	$18¾	18½	18⅝	+ ⅛
414332	PWA Corp	39½	38½	39½	+ 1
16700	Pgurin A f	465	460	465	+ 5
2127	PanCan P	$38⅝	38⅝	38⅝	
29037	Petro Cdn	$11⅝	11½	11⅝	
673723	Placer Dm	$28	27½	28	+ ½
9613	Poco Pete	$7⅞	7¾	7¾	− ⅛
75088	Ptash Cor	$51¼	49¾	50¼	+ ½
1100	Rayrock f	$13	12½	13	− ¾
130930	Renisanc	$27	26¾	26⅞	− ⅛
300	Rogrs Cn bf	$37½	37½	37½	− ½
1848	Rogers A	$18½	18½	18½	− ¼
71161	Rogers B f	$17½	17¼	17½	+ ¼
1206940	Royal Bnk	$28⅜	27⅞	28	+ ⅛
23400	SemiT Af	$10¼	10	10¼	+ ⅛
2700	SemiT B	$10⅛	10	10⅛	+ ⅛
5777	Sceptre R	$9⅜	9⅛	9⅛	− ⅛
500	Scotts f	$7¼	7¼	7¼	− ¼
806	Sears Can	$7¾	7¾	7¾	+ ⅛
124763	SHL Systm	$8	7⅞	8	
40855	Shell Can	$40½	39⅝	40	− ½
1293387	Sherritt	$13⅞	13½	13¾	+ ⅝
41100	Southam	$13½	13¼	13⅜	+ ⅛
6900	Spar Aero	$10¼	10	10⅛	− ⅛
551060	Stelco A	$7⅝	7½	7⅝	
5000	Stone con d	$127	127	127	
96351	Talisman	$24½	23¾	24⅜	+ ⅜
135200	Teck Cor A	$22½	22½	22½	+ ¾
419514	Teck B f	$22¾	22¼	22½	+ ⅛
168726	Telus Cor	$16½	16⅛	16⅛	− ¼
97582	ThomCor	$17⅜	17	17⅜	+ ⅛
1248126	Tor Dm Bk	$22⅛	21⅝	21¾	
60349	TIPS	2205	2195	2205	+15
11650	Torstar B f	$20	19½	20	+ ⅝
34752	TrAlt corp	$14	13⅞	14	+ ⅛
144748	TrCan PL	$17⅞	17¾	17⅞	
13050	Trilon A	375	365	370	− 5
11250	Trimac	$10¼	10⅛	10¼	
146685	Wascana	$10¼	10	10⅛	− ⅛
2560	Westmin	$5½	5½	5½	− ⅛
3200	Weston	$40¼	40	40	− ¾

Total sales 65,737,603 shares

MONTREAL

Sales	Stock	High	Low	Close	Chg.
208765	Bio Pha	$20½	19⅞	20¼	+ ¼
7250	BombrdrA	$25⅝	25⅜	25⅜	+ ⅛
164593	BombrdrB	$25⅝	25⅜	25½	+ ⅛
18800	Cambior	$13½	13⅜	13½	+ ⅜
13300	Cascades	$ 7¾	7⅝	7⅝	
7511	DomTxtA	$ 8	8	8	
77200	Donohue A	$15⅞	15⅞	15⅞	− ⅛
939480	NatBk Cda	$ 9¾	9¼	9⅝	+ ⅜
1081800	Power Crp	$18¼	18	18	− ⅛
9200	Provigo	5¾	5½	5⅝	+ ⅛
81940	Quebecr B	$18½	18	18⅛	
6800	Teleglobe	$20¼	19⅞	20	− ¼
2762	Videotron	$12⅝	12½	12½	

Total Sales 11,434,850 shares; as of 4:00 pm.

F-No voting rights or restricted voting rights.

Source: *The Wall Street Journal*, February 10, 1995. Reprinted by permission of *The Wall Street Journal*, ©1995 Dow Jones & Company, Inc. All rights reserved worldwide.

EARNINGS AND DIVIDENDS

Many investors focus so heavily upon the potential capital gain (increase in price) of their stock that they ignore the dividends it pays. These dividends can be an important part of a stock's total return, so take a moment to consider corporate earnings and dividends.

Corporations issue stock to raise capital; investors buy shares of it to participate in the growth of the business, to earn dividends, and to enjoy possible capital gains. The ability of a corporation to pay dividends and the potential for increase in the value of a share of stock depend directly on the profits earned by the corporation: The greater the flow of profit (and anticipated profit), the higher the price investors will pay for that share of stock.

The ownership value of assets depends on the income they generate, just as the value of farmland reflects profits that can be reaped by raising crops on it and the value of an apartment building reflects rent that can be collected. Similarly, the value of a share in the ownership of a corporation ultimately depends on the ability of that corporation to create profits. Note that the value of an asset depends not only on the income it currently earns, but also on its potential for greater earnings and on investors' willingness to pay for these actual and potential earnings.

A corporation's profit is one of the most important measures of its success. Profit indicates the effectiveness and efficiency with which its assets

are managed and employed. Profits calibrate the ability of a firm to make and sell its product or service for more than the cost of production. Profit means that the firm has efficiently combined the labor, material, and capital necessary to produce and market its product at a price that people will pay and that will provide the owners with the financial incentive to expand the operation. When costs exceed revenues and the firm takes a loss, the amount that the public is willing to pay for the firm's product no longer justifies the cost of producing it.

If you are a stock owner, then, in addition to following the market indexes, you will need to monitor the earnings of particular stocks. You can do so by using *The Wall Street Journal*'s **Digest of Earnings Report**, listed as **Earnings Digest** in the front-page index of the first and last sections. The **Digest of Earnings Report** occasionally appears in the second section of the *Journal*.

Find Eli Lilly & Co in the February 15, 1995 reprint on pages 212 and 213. The statement reports earnings for the quarter ending December 31, 1994 and compares them with figures for the same period one year earlier. Look for revenues, net income, and net income per share (i.e., total earnings divided by total shares of stock outstanding). As you can see, Lilly sales revenue improved, and net income and net earnings per share reversed year earlier losses.

Improved earnings are important, because (among other things) they permit corporations to pay dividends, an important source of income for many stockholders. The stock pages list current annual dividends, and you can also use the *Journal*'s daily **Corporate Dividend News** (see the Wednesday, February 15, 1995 excerpt on page 214), listed in the front-page indexes of the first and last sections, to be informed of future dividend payments.

DIGEST OF EARNINGS REPORTS

EASTCO INDUST SAFETY (Nq)

Quar Dec 31:	1994	1993
Sales..............	$5,567,000	$4,918,000
Net income.....	35,000	(524,000)
Shr earns:		
Net income ..	.01	(.65)
6 months:		
Sales..............	11,396,000	10,000,000
Net income.....	(77,000)	(1,099,000)
Avg shares	3,477,383	800,143
Shr earns:		
Net income ..	(.02)	(1.37)

EASTERN ENVIRON SVCS (Nq)

Quar Dec 31:	1994	1993
Revenues	$2,046,955	$2,031,892
Inco cnt op....	(200,342)	(169,630)
Inco dis op....	....	a189,000
Net income.....	(200,342)	19,370
Avg shares	4,390,205	4,509,425
Shr earns:		
Inco cnt op ...	(.05)	(.04)
Net income ..	(.05)	....
6 months:		
Revenues	4,517,790	4,512,153
Inco cnt op ...	(393,223)	(134,170)
Inco dis op ...	....	a225,000
Net income.....	(393,223)	90,830
Avg shares	4,390,205	4,527,802
Shr earns:		
Inco cnt op ...	(.09)	(.03)
Net income ..	(.09)	.02

a-From disposal of discontinued operations.

EDUCATION ALTERNATIVES (Nq)

Quar Dec 31:	1994	1993
Revenues	$65,029,000	$8,756,000
Net income.....	201,000	549,000
Avg shares	7,573,947	8,077,184
Shr earns:		
Net income ..	.03	.07
6 months:		
Revenues	71,191,000	14,137,000
Net income.....	(35,000)	879,000
Avg shares	7,539,910	8,033,593
Shr earns:		
Net income ..	....	.11

→ Eli Lilly & Co.

ELI LILLY & CO. (N)

Quar Dec 31:	c1994	a1993
Sales..............	$1,548,400,000	$1,457,100,000
Inc ct op....	269,600,000	d(463,000,000)
Inco dis op ...	20,500,000	60,600,000
Net income .	290,100,000	(523,600,000)
Shr earns:		
Inc ct op........	.93	(1.57)
Net income ...	1.00	(1.77)
Year:		
Sales.........5,711,600,000		5,198,500,000
dInc ct op 1,185,100,000		464,800,000
Inco dis op....	101,000,000	26,300,000
Income 1,286,100,000		491,100,000
Acctg adj	....	b(10,900,000)
Net income .1,286,100,000		480,200,000
Shr earns:		
Inc ct op........	4.10	1.58
Income	4.45	1.67
Net income ..	4.45	1.63

a-Restated to reflect discontinued operations. b-Cumulative effect of an accounting change. c-Includes the results of Sphinx Pharmaceuticals Corp., acquired on September 9, 1994. d-Includes pre-tax non-recurring charges of $66,000,000 in the 1994 year, compared with $1,032,600,000 in the 1993 quarter and year.

EMONS TRANSPORTATION (Nq)

Quar Dec 31:	1994	a1993
Revenues	$3,775,011	$2,847,135
Net income.....	278,697	(338,587)
Avg shares	5,825,299	5,653,389
Shr earns (com & com equiv):		
Net income ..	.04	(.07)
6 months:		
Revenues	6,926,479	5,816,476
Income........	400,582	(169,408)
Acctg adj	....	b(750,000)
Net income.....	400,582	(919,408)
Avg shares	5,804,118	5,636,291
Shr earns (com & com equiv):		
Income	.05	(.05)
Net income ..	.05	(.18)

a-Restated. b-Cumulative effect of an accounting change.

EARNINGS SURPRISES

Companies listed below reported quarterly profit substantially different from the average of analysts' estimates. The companies are followed by at least three analysts. Results in parentheses are losses.

The percent difference compares actual profit on continuing operations, when applicable, with the 30-day estimate where at least three analysts have issued forecasts in the past 30 days. Otherwise, actual profit on continuing operations is compared with the 120-day estimate.

COMPANY NAME	ACTUAL EPS	ESTIMATE [≠ of analysts] 30-DAY	ESTIMATE [≠ of analysts] 120-DAY	% DIFF.
Positive				
Wolohan Lumber	$.38	....	8.18 [3]	111.11
Lubrizol	.54	....	.47 [11]	14.89
Landstar System	.57	....	.50 [4]	14.00
Sun Healthcare	.37	....	.33 [8]	12.12
National Gypsum	1.22	....	1.10 [4]	10.91
Outback Steakhouse	.25	....	.23 [10]	8.70
Performnce Food	.16	....	.15 [4]	6.67
Negative				
LCI International	($.75)	....	$.28 [5]	
Western Gas Resources	.01	....	.24 [9]	95.83
Barrett Resources	.02	....	.07 [6]	71.43
MedImmune	(.41)	....	(.33) [7]	24.24
20th Century Industries	(.95)	....	(.79) [7]	20.25
Liposome	(.47)	....	(.42) [3]	11.90

Source: Zacks Investment Research

FIRST PACIFIC NETWORKS (Nq)

Quar Dec 31:	1994	1993
Revenues	$573,000	$430,000
Net income.....	(7,172,000)	(6,493,000)
Avg shares	21,090,000	19,685,000
Shr earns:		
Net income ..	(.34)	(.33)
9 months:		
Revenues	1,843,000	1,049,000
Net income.....	(20,518,000)	(19,002,000)
Avg shares	20,298,000	18,794,000
Shr earns:		
Net income ..	(1.01)	(1.01)

FIRST PATRIOT BANKSHRS (Nq)

Quar Dec 31:	1994	1993
Net income.....	$341,000	$274,000
Avg shares	2,054,191	1,959,936
Shr earns (com & com equiv):		
Net income ..	.17	.14
Year:		
Net income.....	1,096,000	806,000
Avg shares	2,046,960	1,580,113
Shr earns (com & com equiv):		
Net income ..	.54	.51

FORUM GROUP INC. (Nq)

Quar Dec 31:	1994	1993
Revenues	$41,901,000	$28,307,000
Income..........	a3,087,000	b1,632,000
cExtrd chg	(262,000)	(1,360,000)
Net income.....	2,825,000	272,000
Avg shares	23,164,000	20,823,000
Shr earns & com equiv):		
Income	.13	.08
Net income ..	.12	.01
9 months:		
Revenues	107,504,000	80,636,000
Income..........	a11,168,000	b1,289,000
cExtrd chg	(262,000)	(1,772,000)
Net income.....	10,906,000	(483,000)
Avg shares	22,944,000	15,858,000
Shr earns (com & com equiv):		
Income	.49	.08
Net income ..	.48	(.03)

a-Includes non-recurring pre-tax

HANCOCK FABRICS INC. (N)

13 wk Jan 29:	1995	1994
Sales	$95,664,000	$92,316,000
Net income.....	4,334,000	1,234,000
Avg shares	21,061,000	21,126,000
Shr earns:		
Net income ..	.21	.06
Year:		
Sales	366,816,000	367,745,000
Net income.....	10,139,000	5,438,000
Avg shares	21,118,000	21,161,000
Shr earns:		
Net income ..	.48	.26

HANSON PLC (N)

Quar Dec 31:	1994	1993
Sales $5,022,000,000		$4,567,000,000
Net income.	330,000,000	199,000,000
ADR earns (primary):		
Net income ..	.32	.20
ADR earns (fully diluted):		
Net income ..	.31	.20

Converted by company using the December 31, 1994 exchange rate for the British pound.

HARMONY HOLDINGS INC. (Nq)

Quar Dec 31:	1994	1993
Revenues	$16,328,516	$9,530,845
Net income.....	402,216	(1,185,154)
Avg shares	5,451,878	5,396,780
Shr earns:		
Net income ..	.07	(.22)
6 months:		
Revenues	28,388,170	19,686,082
Net income.....	706,847	(1,987,217)
Avg shares	5,451,878	5,243,643
Shr earns:		
Net income ..	.13	(.38)

HIGHWOODS PROPERTIES (N)

Quar Dec 31:	1994	1993
Net income.....	$3,141,000	....
Shr earns:		
Net income ..	.35	....
a29 weeks:		

Eli Lilly ➤
& Co.

ELI LILLY & CO. (N)

Quar Dec 31:	c1994	a1993
Sales	$1,548,400,000	$1,457,100,000
Inc ct op......	269,600,000	d(463,000,000)
Inco dis op...	20,500,000	60,600,000
Net income .	290,100,000	(523,600,000)
Shr earns:		
Inc ct op........	.93	(1.57)
Net income ...	1.00	(1.77)
Year:		
Sales...........	5,711,600,000	5,198,500,000
dInc ct op....	1,185,100,000	464,800,000
Inco dis op...	101,000,000	26,300,000
Income	1,286,100,000	491,100,000
Acctg adj	....	b(10,900,000)
Net income .	1,286,100,000	480,200,000
Shr earns:		
Inc ct op........	4.10	1.58
Income	4.45	1.67
Net income ...	4.45	1.63

a-Restated to reflect discontinued operations. b-Cumulative effect of an accounting change. c-Includes the results of Sphinx Pharmaceuticals Corp., acquired on September 9, 1994. d-Includes pre-tax non-recurring charges of $66,000,000 in the 1994 year, compared with $1,032,600,000 in the 1993 quarter and year.

The February 15, 1995 report provides dividend news for February 14. The companies listed under the heading **Regular** will pay regular cash dividends on the payable date to all those who were stockholders on the record date.

For instance, the February 15 excerpt on page 215 reports that Navistar International announced a quarterly dividend of $1.50 per share payable on April 15, 1995 to all stockholders of record on April 5, 1995.

Some companies prefer to pay dividends in extra stock rather than cash. Returning to the report, you can see that Columbus Energy announced a ten percent stock dividend effective March 10, 1995 for all holders of record on February 24, 1995. That is, each stockholder received an additional amount of stock equal to ten percent of his or her holdings.

CORPORATE DIVIDEND NEWS

Dividends Reported February 14

Company	Period	Amt.	Payable date	Record date
REGULAR				
Albany Intl clA	Q	.08¾	4- 3-95	3-20
Amtech Corp	Q	.02	3-28-95	3-7
Aviall Inc	Q	.01	3-31-95	3-17
Baxter Intl	Q	.26¼	4- 3-95	3-15
Bridgford Foods	Q	.05	4- 4-95	3-7
Central VA Bnkshs	Q	.15	3-15-95	2-24
Chesapeake Corp	Q	.18	5-15-95	4-17
Colonial Gas	Q	.31½	3-15-95	3-1
Col/HCA Hlthcare	Q	.03	6- 1-95	5-1
Conagra Inc pfE	Q	.421⅛	4- 1-95	3-17
Cooper Industries	Q	.33	4- 3-95	3-1
CooperTire&Rubber	Q	.06	3-31-95	3-6
Cummins Engine	Q	.25	3-15-95	3-1
Enron Corp	Q	.20	3-20-95	3-6
Enron 10.50% pf2	Q	2.7304	4- 3-95	3-10
Enron Oil & Gas	Q	.03	4-28-95	4-13
Enserch Corp	Q	.05	3- 6-95	2-24
FHP Intl Corp pfA	Q	.31¼	3-15-95	2-28
FldcrestCannon pfA	Q	.75	3- 1-95	2-17
GP Finl Corp	Q	.20	3- 8-95	2-24
GeorgiaP $1.925pf	Q	.48⅛	4- 1-95	3-15
GeorgiaP $1.9375pf	Q	.4844	4- 1-95	3-15
GeorgiaP $2.125pf	Q	.53⅛	4- 1-95	3-15
GeorgiaP $7.72pf	Q	1.93	4- 1-95	3-15
GeorgiaP $7.80pf	Q	1.95	4- 1-95	3-15
GeorgiaP $1.90pf	Q	.47½	4- 1-95	3-15
GeoPwr $1.9875 pfA	Q	.4969	4- 1-95	3-15
GeorglaP adlpfA'93	Q	.42⅞	4- 1-95	3-15
GeorgP adlpfA2'93	Q	.39⅜	4- 1-95	3-15
Hecla Mining pfB	Q	.87½	4- 1-95	3-13
Intl Aluminum Corp	Q	.25	4-10-95	3-20
IntFlavs&Frags	Q	.31	4-11-95	3-27
Intl Paper Co	Q	.42	3-15-95	2-24
Investors Title	Q	.02	3-15-95	3-1
Kaman Corp clA	Q	.11	4-17-95	4-3
Kimball Intl clB	Q	.21	4-15-95	3-24
Lawson Products	Q	.12	4-19-95	4-5
MonarchMachineTool	Q	.05	3- 8-95	2-27
Nash Finch Co	Q	.18	3-10-95	2-24
Navistar Intl pfG ← Navistar	Q	1.50	4-15-95	4-5
North Amer Mtg Co	Q	.06	3- 8-95	2-24
Phillips Van Heusen	Q	.03¾	3-16-95	3-10
Portsmth BkShrs	Q	.12	3-15-95	3-1
Questar Corp	Q	.28½	3-13-95	2-24
Raven Industries	Q	.10½	4-14-95	3-24
SeaCont $1.4625pf	Q	.365⅜	3-15-95	3-1
SthCarolinaE&G5%pf	Q	.62½	4- 1-95	3-10
Trident NGL Hldg	Q	.01¼	3-21-95	3-7
VF Corp	Q	.34	3-20-95	3-10
Windmere Corp	Q	.05	3-15-95	3-1

Company		Amt.	Payable date	Record date
IRREGULAR				
Pitts & W Va RR		.13	3-31-95	3-13
FUNDS - REITS - INVESTMENT COS - LPS				
Allmerica Secs	Q	.21	3-31-95	2-28
Amer1st Tax Ex Mtg	M	.04½	3-27-95	2-28
Amer1st TaxEx Mtg2	M	.06¼	3-27-95	2-28
Am1st Partpfd Eqty	M	.0883	3-31-95	2-28
Bedford Prop Inv	Q	.09½	4-28-95	4-14
CIM Hi Yld Secs	M	.06½	3- 7-95	2-27
Glbl Hilnco Dollar	M	h.11½	2-28-95	2-24
Mid-Atlantic Rlty	Q	.22	3-15-95	2-28
Northeast Invst Tr	Q	h.24	2-16-95	2-15
Western Invest RE	Q	.28	3-15-95	2-24

STOCK				
Columbus Energy ← Columbus Energy		10%	3-10-95	2-24
Dalg Corp		nn	3- 8-95	2-24
nn-Two-for-one stock split.				
Portsmth BkShrs		2%	3-15-95	3-1

INCREASED		--Amounts--			
		New	Old		
Calif Bancshares	Q	.18	.14	4- 4-95	3-10
Hon Industries	Q	.12	.11	3- 1-95	2-23
Scana Corp	Q	.72	.70½	4- 1-95	3-10

FOREIGN				
British Petrol ADR		t.598	5- 9-95	3-9

RESUMED				
Trion Inc		.02	4- 3-95	3-1

OMITTED

IVF America pfd

A-Annual; b-Payable in Canadian funds; h-From income;
k-From capital gains; M-Monthly; Q-Quarterly; S-Semi-
annual; t-Approximate U.S. dollar amount per American
Depositary Receipt/Share.

REGULAR

Albany Intl clA	Q	.08¾	4 – 3 – 95	3 – 20
Amtech Corp	Q	.02	3 – 28 – 95	3 – 7
Aviall Inc	Q	.01	3 – 31 – 95	3 – 17
Baxter Intl	Q	.26¼	4 – 3 – 95	3 – 15
Bridgford Foods	Q	.05	4 – 4 – 95	3 – 7
Central VA Bnkshs	Q	.15	3 – 15 – 95	2 – 24
Chesapeake Corp	Q	.18	5 – 15 – 95	4 – 17
Colonial Gas	Q	.31½	3 – 15 – 95	3 – 1
Col/HCA Hlthcare	Q	.03	6 – 1 – 95	5 – 1
Conagra Inc pfE	Q	.42⅞	4 – 1 – 95	3 – 17
Cooper Industries	Q	.33	4 – 3 – 95	3 – 1
CooperTire&Rubber	Q	.06	3 – 31 – 95	3 – 6
Cummins Engine	Q	.25	3 – 15 – 95	3 – 1
Enron Corp	Q	.20	3 – 20 – 95	3 – 6
Enron 10.50% pf2	Q	2.7304	4 – 3 – 95	3 – 10
Enron Oil & Gas	Q	.03	4 – 28 – 95	4 – 13
Enserch Corp	Q	.05	3 – 6 – 95	2 – 24
FHP Intl Corp pfA	Q	.31¼	3 – 15 – 95	2 – 28
FldcrestCannon pfA	Q	.75	3 – 1 – 95	2 – 17
GP Finl Corp	Q	.20	3 – 8 – 95	2 – 24
GeorgiaP $1.925pf	Q	.48⅛	4 – 1 – 95	3 – 15
GeorgiaP $1.9375pf	Q	.4844	4 – 1 – 95	3 – 15
GeorgiaP $2.125pf	Q	.53⅛	4 – 1 – 95	3 – 15
GeorgiaP $7.72pf	Q	1.93	4 – 1 – 95	3 – 15
GeorgiaP $7.80pf	Q	1.95	4 – 1 – 95	3 – 15
GeorgiaP $1.90pf	Q	.47½	4 – 1 – 95	3 – 15
GeoPwr $1.9875 pfA	Q	.4969	4 – 1 – 95	3 – 15
GeorgiaP adipfA'93	Q	.42⅞	4 – 1 – 95	3 – 15
GeorgP adipfA2'93	Q	.39⅜	4 – 1 – 95	3 – 15
Hecla Mining pfB	Q	.87½	4 – 1 – 95	3 – 13
Intl Aluminum Corp	Q	.25	4 – 10 – 95	3 – 20
IntlFlavs&Frags	Q	.31	4 – 11 – 95	3 – 27
Intl Paper Co	Q	.42	3 – 15 – 95	2 – 24
Investors Title	Q	.02	3 – 15 – 95	3 – 1
Kaman Corp clA	Q	.11	4 – 17 – 95	4 – 3
Kimball Intl clB	Q	.21	4 – 15 – 95	3 – 24
Lawson Products	Q	.12	4 – 19 – 95	4 – 5
MonarchMachineTool	Q	.05	3 – 8 – 95	2 – 27
Nash Finch Co	Q	.18	3 – 10 – 95	2 – 24
Navistar Intl pfG	Q	1.50	4 – 15 – 95	4 – 5
North Amer Mtg Co	Q	.06	3 – 8 – 95	2 – 24
Phlips Van Heusen	Q	.03¾	3 – 16 – 95	3 – 10
Portsmth BkShrs	Q	.12	3 – 15 – 95	3 – 1
Questar Corp	Q	.28½	3 – 13 – 95	2 – 24
Raven Industries	Q	.10½	4 – 14 – 95	3 – 24
SeaCont $1.4625pf	Q	.365⅝	3 – 15 – 95	3 – 1
SthCarolinaE&G5%pf	Q	.62½	4 – 1 – 95	3 – 10
Trident NGL Hldg	Q	.01¼	3 – 21 – 95	3 – 7
VF Corp	Q	.34	3 – 20 – 95	3 – 10
Windmere Corp	Q	.05	3 – 15 – 95	3 – 1

Navistar
$1.50 quarterly
dividend → Navistar Intl pfG

Source: *The Wall Street Journal*, February 15, 1995. Reprinted by permission of *The Wall Street Journal*, ©1995 Dow Jones & Company, Inc. All rights reserved worldwide.

STOCK

Columbus Energy	10%	3 – 10 – 95	2 – 24
Daig Corp	nn	3 – 8 – 95	2 – 24
nn-Two-for-one stock split.			
Portsmth BkShrs	2%	3 – 15 – 95	3 – 1

Columbus Energy
10% stock dividend → Columbus Energy

Source: *The Wall Street Journal*, February 15, 1995. Reprinted by permission of *The Wall Street Journal*, ©1995 Dow Jones & Company, Inc. All rights reserved worldwide.

INDUSTRY GROUPS

This chapter began with a look at the **Markets Diary**, which appears on the first page (C1) of the Journal's third section (see page 156). That discussion mentioned the Dow Jones Equity Index (June 30, 1982 = 100) and the 700-odd companies that the index comprises.

Each day the *Journal* breaks out the performance of these stocks in the **Dow Jones Industry Groups** (you can find the index on pages A1 or C1). In addition, the five industries that enjoyed the greatest relative gain in value the previous trading day and the five that suffered the biggest loss are presented at the top of the report together with the three most important contributing firms in each case. You can use this information to compare the performance of your stock with the average for the entire industry or to compare the performance of a variety of industries.

For instance, under **Technology** in the Wednesday, February 15, 1995 report, note that Software had increased almost 40-fold since June 30, 1982, while under **Energy**, oil-drilling had fallen. That is, the index for software had risen to 3919.71 from a base of 100.0 in 1982, while oil drilling had fallen to 82.10 (see pages 218–219).

Test yourself, but be honest. Do you think you could have forecast these industry performances back in 1982?

INSIDER TRADING

Finally, if you want to see what the officers and directors of the company in which you own stock are doing, you can follow the **Insider Trading Spotlight** in Wednesday's *Wall Street Journal*. An example from the February 8, 1995 issue is provided on page 220.

If you have an interest in a particular company, it may be worth your while to know whether its key executives and members of its board of directors have purchased its stock recently. Sales are not as important, because they can occur for a variety of reasons. Sellers may wish to diversify their portfolios or need cash. Yet you should be alert for massive sell-offs by a number of insiders.

Insider purchases of a company's stock are a better indicator of long-term company prospects (why else buy the stock?) because insiders must keep their purchases for six months. The law forbids insiders from selling stock they have purchased until half a year has elapsed from the time of purchase. Nor may insiders sell stock short. This protects the public from insiders profiting from their knowledge at the public's expense.

DOW JONES WORLD INDUSTRY GROUPS

Tuesday, February 14, 1995

Groups Leading

GROUP Strongest Stocks	CLOSE		CHG.		PCT. CHG.
Water Utils	107.33	+	1.84	+	1.74
YkshirWat (UK)	5.26	+	0.22	+	4.37
AngiWtr (UK)	4.98	+	0.20	+	4.18
SevernTrent (UK)	5.27	+	0.21	+	4.15
Apparel Rtlrs	75.92	+	1.17	+	1.57
ChrmingShps (US)	6.38	+	0.38	+	6.25
Limited Inc (US)	18.25	+	1.00	+	5.80
ChowSang (HK)	2.80	+	0.10	+	3.70
Ins-Full Line	118.62	+	1.17	+	1.00
Cigna Corp (US)	74.38	+	3.13	+	4.39
Unitrin (US)	48.00	+	1.38	+	2.95
CrpMapfre (SP)	5380.00	+	110.00	+	2.09
Aluminum	122.24	+	1.15	+	0.95
Maxxam (US)	30.50	+	1.00	+	3.39
Alumax (US)	27.75	+	0.75	+	2.78
Reynolds Mtls (US)	51.88	+	1.13	+	2.22
Semiconductr	229.50	+	1.89	+	0.83
Micron Tech (US)	55.13	+	2.25	+	4.26
Intel Corp (US)	78.50	+	1.38	+	1.78
Analog Dev (US)	23.00	+	0.38	+	1.66
Oil Drilling	93.20	+	0.76	+	0.82
Global Marine (US)	3.75	+	0.13	+	3.45
Rowan Cos (US)	5.75	+	0.13	+	2.22
NaborsInd (US)	6.25	+	0.13	+	2.04

Groups Lagging

GROUP Weakest Stocks	CLOSE		CHG.		PCT. CHG.
Plantations	226.19	−	5.91	−	2.55
Asiatic (MA)	2.87	−	0.13	−	4.33
High&Low (MA)	4.52	−	0.16	−	3.42
UnitedPlant (MA)	5.75	−	0.20	−	3.36
Toys	77.36	−	1.45	−	1.84
SegaEntpr (JP)	4640.00	−	200.00	−	4.13
Mattel Inc (US)	22.75	−	0.63	−	2.67
Nintendo (JP)	5070.00	−	110.00	−	2.12
Overseas Trad	103.45	−	1.74	−	1.65
NichimenCp (JP)	410.00	−	18.00	−	4.21
ToyotaTsusho (JP)	607.00	−	20.00	−	3.19
MitsuiCo (JP)	712.00	−	22.00	−	3.00
Advertising	139.45	−	2.28	−	1.61
Intrpblc Grp (US)	33.38	−	1.25	−	3.61
TrueNoComm (US)	38.63	−	0.63	−	1.59
Omnicom Grp (US)	53.50	−	0.25	−	0.47
Hm Construct	121.24	−	1.73	−	1.41
Pelangi (MA)	3.06	−	0.14	−	4.38
HasekoCp (JP)	592.00	−	27.00	−	4.36
MisawaHomes (JP)	1100.00	−	40.00	−	3.51
Air Freight	134.76	−	1.89	−	1.38
Air Exprs Intl (US)	18.75	−	0.75	−	3.85
Fed Express (US)	62.75	−	1.63	−	2.52
Harper Group (US)	16.38	−	0.25	−	1.50

AU - Australia	FI - Finland	IR - Ireland	NV - Netherlands	SW - Sweden
AS - Austria	FR - France	IT - Italy	NZ - New Zealand	SZ - Switzerland
BE - Belgium	GR - Germany	JP - Japan	NW - Norway	TH - Thailand
CA - Canada	HK - Hong Kong	MA - Malaysia	SI - Singapore	UK - United Kingdom
DK - Denmark	IN - Indonesia	MX - Mexico	SP - Spain	US - United States

NOTE: Stock prices are in local currencies.   ©1995 Dow Jones & Co. Inc., All Rights Reserved

Industry Group Performance

WORLD			U.S.		AMERICAS		EUROPE		ASIA/PACIFIC	
CLOSE 02/14/95	% CHG. YTD		CLOSE 02/14/95	% CHG. YTD	CLOSE 02/14/95	% CHG. YTD	CLOSE 02/14/95	% CHG. YTD	CLOSE 02/14/95	% CHG. YTD
120.30 − 3.29		**Basic Materials**	463.53 + 1.53		121.80 − 0.46		133.43 + 2.04		111.45 − 9.78	
122.24 − 1.08		**Aluminum**	346.67 − 2.97		121.82 − 2.14		151.60 + 6.81		97.96 − 9.00	
108.55 − 8.32		**Other non-ferrous**	319.38 − 5.56		121.23 − 5.64		94.90 − 2.86		106.07 − 13.17	
122.21 − 1.62		**Chemicals**	552.47 + 2.07		122.50 + 1.58		130.04 + 2.81		114.89 − 11.12	
129.29 − 2.26		**Chem-commodity**	554.28 + 0.24		128.51 − 0.15		139.40 + 3.48		119.92 − 12.28	
108.21 − 0.16		**Chem-specialty**	566.60 + 6.15		110.52 + 5.63		108.49 + 1.14		105.72 − 8.78	
146.17 + 3.03		**Forest products**	398.78 + 7.38		139.07 + 5.49		0.00 0.00		418.27 − 1.31	
113.33 − 11.20		**Mining, diversified**	293.54 − 0.03		93.12 − 10.75		126.28 − 9.06		123.74 − 13.30	
114.68 − 0.21		**Paper products**	539.19 + 5.82		111.77 + 4.27		124.82 + 3.23		103.21 − 10.60	
122.90 − 10.01		**Precious metals**	236.68 − 9.35		127.48 − 9.26		158.31 + 1.71		104.88 − 15.81	
118.29 − 5.98		**Steel**	192.95 − 5.47		139.86 − 6.00		164.52 + 3.05		109.38 − 7.71	
123.25 − 3.41		**Independent**	663.31 + 3.96		129.18 + 1.40		109.69 + 2.26		124.38 − 9.40	
129.21 + 0.12		**Conglomerates**	663.31 + 3.96		129.18 + 1.40		111.94 + 3.70		150.75 − 6.08	
103.45 − 13.62		**Overseas Trading**	0.00 0.00		0.00 0.00		63.35 − 31.48		105.43 − 12.95	
226.19 − 2.09		**Plantations**	0.00 0.00		0.00 0.00		0.00 0.00		226.19 − 2.09	
120.24 − 3.28		**Consumer, Cyclical**	557.49 + 4.68		121.12 + 3.53		127.08 + 0.08		117.59 − 10.09	
139.45 + 1.39		**Advertising**	765.88 + 2.39		134.14 + 2.39		148.77 − 2.10		0.00 0.00	
101.74 − 0.85		**Airlines**	312.96 + 11.17		90.41 + 10.19		137.74 + 7.95		97.23 − 4.65	
95.27 − 6.13		**Apparel**	746.74 − 2.42		88.57 − 2.37		106.08 + 0.18		96.49 − 8.99	
95.22 − 6.17		**Clothing/Fabrics**	574.45 + 0.99		83.08 + 1.06		106.46 − 0.15		96.93 − 8.92	
93.30 − 5.94		**Footwear**	1000.73 − 5.71		95.99 − 5.71		104.50 + 3.53		93.47 − 10.00	
146.92 − 6.73		**Auto manufacturers**	382.73 − 5.80		180.47 − 5.80		127.38 + 3.62		146.23 − 12.06	
134.80 − 5.12		**Auto parts & equip**	388.52 + 5.78		138.93 + 5.26		160.93 + 2.72		128.34 − 11.05	

(continued)

Oil drilling ➤ (row: Oil drilling)

Software ➤ (row: Software)

		Name								
112.51	+ 2.06	Energy	294.79	+ 2.82	110.05	+ 2.68	119.52	+ 3.09	99.89	− 5.09
102.61	− 2.59	Coal	300.83	+ 4.11	127.48	+ 4.11	0.00	0.00	90.68	− 10.06
93.20	− 2.69	Oil drilling	82.10	− 2.69	122.82	− 2.69	0.00	0.00	0.00	0.00
115.87	+ 2.65	Oil cos, major	373.18	+ 2.51	111.35	+ 2.51	121.39	+ 2.82	0.00	0.00
102.17	− 0.90	Oil cos, secondary	185.51	+ 1.07	100.68	+ 0.75	105.39	+ 4.81	100.94	− 4.82
97.42	+ 5.99	Oilfield equip/svcs	135.53	+ 6.07	96.79	+ 5.91	111.98	+ 7.73	0.00	0.00
132.73	+ 4.74	Pipelines	265.69	+ 5.79	132.73	+ 4.74	0.00	0.00	0.00	0.00
111.76	− 0.91	Financial	449.21	+ 10.03	125.89	+ 9.11	114.72	+ 1.13	104.51	− 7.00
110.09	− 1.33	Banks, all	408.17	+ 10.83	132.03	+ 9.81	118.89	+ 1.77	102.59	− 6.19
108.31	− 3.48	Major int'l	302.52	+ 10.06	126.83	+ 7.64	120.42	+ 1.44	103.95	− 7.15
112.83	+ 2.05	Regional banks	485.86	+ 11.16	135.25	+ 11.09	116.43	+ 2.39	100.07	− 4.15
0.00	0.00	U.S. east	411.03	+ 13.55	0.00	0.00	0.00	0.00	0.00	0.00
0.00	0.00	U.S. central	681.10	+ 10.39	0.00	0.00	0.00	0.00	0.00	0.00
0.00	0.00	U.S. south	411.61	+ 9.84	0.00	0.00	0.00	0.00	0.00	0.00
0.00	0.00	U.S. west	601.01	+ 10.96	0.00	0.00	0.00	0.00	0.00	0.00
118.26	+ 3.24	Diversified financial	481.16	+ 11.25	121.40	+ 8.91	109.70	− 0.17	112.95	− 4.62
115.47	+ 2.38	Insurance, all	484.94	+ 7.95	127.43	+ 7.93	115.15	+ 1.47	86.95	− 10.15
118.62	+ 3.38	Full line	283.20	+ 11.44	127.17	+ 11.38	115.95	+ 2.05	117.51	− 8.62
113.99	+ 6.71	Life	667.39	+ 10.76	119.02	+ 10.76	104.22	+ 2.76	344.66	− 1.53
111.54	− 0.38	Property/Casualty	641.78	+ 5.87	130.53	+ 5.87	114.41	− 3.32	82.84	− 10.57
103.72	− 4.52	Real estate	351.79	+ 3.56	52.51	+ 0.36	88.52	− 3.89	116.26	− 5.18
95.80	+ 11.04	Savings & loan	425.80	+ 11.04	95.80	+ 11.04	0.00	0.00	0.00	0.00
127.89	− 8.51	Securities brokers	591.44	+ 11.03	122.84	+ 10.72	142.50	+ 2.39	130.53	− 14.29
110.13	− 1.90	Industrial	420.73	+ 5.24	111.30	+ 3.44	119.11	+ 0.70	106.24	− 5.71
134.76	− 1.47	Air freight	286.75	+ 3.24	146.64	+ 3.24	80.97	− 13.60	142.54	− 23.40
111.82	− 2.19	Building materials	505.39	+ 7.53	88.80	− 9.85	115.79	− 0.47	118.63	− 1.33
104.39	+ 1.02	Containers & pkging	786.81	+ 10.70	113.58	+ 10.70	91.92	− 2.59	107.24	− 5.70
119.35	− 4.17	Elec comps & equip	406.52	+ 7.23	112.63	+ 7.23	178.77	+ 1.36	115.38	− 9.54
98.02	− 10.67	Factory equipment	328.29	+ 1.07	104.25	+ 1.07	105.56	− 1.53	97.99	− 12.54
92.13	+ 5.53	Heavy construction	297.44	+ 8.05	100.97	+ 8.05	97.91	− 3.29	90.99	+ 7.95
130.63	− 5.02	Heavy machinery	281.32	+ 2.64	193.87	+ 2.64	82.02	− 10.61	110.86	− 9.15
123.65	− 1.43	Industrial, diversified	404.65	+ 5.54	124.36	+ 4.67	141.78	+ 3.18	103.91	− 15.02
104.13	− 5.02	Marine transport	436.72	− 3.75	91.90	− 3.75	109.36	+ 1.63	98.70	− 10.13
77.28	+ 0.99	Pollution control	641.38	+ 4.04	73.18	+ 3.97	60.16	+ 0.33	118.29	− 11.36
113.60	− 2.56	Other industrial svcs	389.35	+ 1.97	109.64	+ 0.26	120.52	+ 1.72	114.34	− 8.26
109.30	+ 1.82	Railroads	575.85	+ 9.02	121.70	+ 9.02	67.71	+ 3.96	105.75	− 1.88
116.61	− 4.77	Transportation equip	307.04	− 1.98	127.64	− 1.98	157.80	+ 6.13	103.09	− 8.57
107.50	− 7.97	Trucking	255.44	− 3.66	90.91	− 4.73	73.81	− 2.64	117.25	− 9.78
132.13	− 2.08	Technology	426.40	+ 4.90	138.90	+ 4.84	126.44	+ 5.09	120.83	− 15.56
138.07	+ 2.18	Aerospace/Defense	588.65	+ 4.04	144.64	+ 3.66	128.58	− 2.05	89.78	− 8.98
134.39	− 6.29	Commu-w/AT&T	623.68	+ 3.08	154.31	+ 3.06	100.83	+ 4.25	123.31	− 17.22
0.00	0.00	Commu-wo/AT&T	808.91	+ 3.31	0.00	0.00	0.00	0.00	0.00	0.00
110.18	− 1.70	Computers w/IBM	193.63	+ 2.72	109.19	+ 2.65	83.44	− 5.17	107.72	− 14.07
0.00	0.00	Computers wo/IBM	339.17	+ 2.70	0.00	0.00	0.00	0.00	0.00	0.00
131.47	− 1.79	Diversified technology	359.96	+ 3.53	127.08	+ 3.53	149.96	+ 6.83	122.04	− 13.70
110.30	− 8.57	Industrial technology	338.63	+ 10.50	110.35	+ 10.50	201.24	+ 4.52	106.33	− 17.16
90.29	+ 5.14	Medical/Bio tech	896.76	+ 5.89	88.77	+ 6.18	139.16	+ 1.14	96.66	− 13.36
91.82	+ 6.78	Advcd Med Devices	848.12	+ 6.78	91.03	+ 6.78	0.00	0.00	0.00	0.00
89.85	+ 4.47	Biotechnology	953.86	+ 5.74	88.31	+ 6.39	134.25	+ 1.14	96.66	− 13.36
130.85	− 4.51	Office equipment	392.07	+ 8.96	135.91	+ 8.96	131.86	+ 7.80	127.44	− 13.36
229.50	+ 5.14	Semiconductors	897.27	+ 18.74	303.06	+ 18.74	168.86	+ 4.26	154.47	− 16.12
153.51	+ 3.19	Software	3919.71	+ 3.97	163.95	+ 4.02	76.21	+ 5.99	86.03	− 12.25
103.23	+ 2.00	Utilities	289.70	+ 6.19	99.83	+ 4.62	126.19	+ 1.04	101.26	− 3.15
100.48	+ 1.78	Electric	222.67	+ 5.92	91.84	+ 5.79	152.25	+ 0.43	101.25	− 3.12
84.56	− 2.28	Gas	143.20	+ 4.15	89.40	+ 3.97	104.86	− 0.72	83.18	− 6.75
118.00	+ 3.35	Telephone	412.95	+ 6.54	107.69	+ 3.79	131.18	+ 3.97	178.27	− 0.92
107.33	− 3.34	Water	474.94	+ 4.44	102.19	+ 4.44	107.56	− 3.81	0.00	0.00
113.00	− 0.83	DJ Equity Market	455.71	+ 5.23	113.19	+ 4.30	117.96	+ 1.96	109.76	− 8.14

Indexes based on 6/30/82=100 for U.S., 12/31/91=100 for World

Oil drilling →

Software →

112.51 + 2.06 **Energy**	294.79 + 2.82	110.05 + 2.68	119.52 + 3.09	99.89 − 5.09	
102.61 − 2.59 **Coal**	300.83 + 4.11	127.48 + 4.11	0.00 0.00	90.68 − 10.06	
93.20 − 2.69 **Oil drilling**	82.10 − 2.69	122.82 − 2.69	0.00 0.00	0.00 0.00	
115.87 + 2.65 **Oil cos, major**	373.18 + 2.51	111.35 + 2.51	121.39 + 2.82	0.00 0.00	
102.17 − 0.90 **Oil cos, secondary**	185.51 + 1.07	100.68 + 0.75	105.39 + 4.81	100.94 − 4.82	
97.42 + 5.99 **Oilfield equip/svcs**	135.53 + 6.07	96.79 + 5.91	111.98 + 7.73	0.00 0.00	
132.73 + 4.74 **Pipelines**	265.69 + 5.79	132.73 + 4.74	0.00 0.00	0.00 0.00	
132.13 − 2.08 **Technology**	426.40 + 4.90	138.90 + 4.84	126.44 + 5.09	120.83 − 15.56	
138.07 + 2.18 **Aerospace/Defense**	588.65 + 4.04	144.64 + 3.66	128.58 − 2.05	89.78 − 8.98	
134.39 − 6.29 **Commu-w/AT&T**	623.68 + 3.08	154.31 + 3.06	100.83 + 4.25	123.31 − 17.22	
0.00 0.00 Commu-wo/AT&T	808.91 + 3.31	0.00 0.00	0.00 0.00	0.00 0.00	
110.18 − 1.70 **Computers w/IBM**	193.63 + 2.72	109.19 + 2.65	83.44 − 5.17	107.72 − 14.07	
0.00 0.00 Computers wo/IBM	339.17 + 2.70	0.00 0.00	0.00 0.00	0.00 0.00	
131.47 − 1.79 **Diversified technology**	359.96 + 3.53	127.08 + 3.53	149.96 + 6.83	122.04 − 13.70	
110.30 − 8.57 **Industrial technology**	338.63 + 10.50	110.35 + 10.50	201.24 + 4.52	106.33 − 17.16	
90.29 + 5.14 **Medical/Bio tech**	896.76 + 5.89	88.77 + 6.18	139.16 + 1.14	96.66 − 13.36	
91.82 + 6.78 **Advcd Med Devices**	848.12 + 6.78	91.03 + 6.78	0.00 0.00	0.00 0.00	
89.85 + 4.47 **Biotechnology**	953.86 + 5.74	88.31 + 6.39	134.25 + 1.14	96.66 − 13.36	
130.85 − 4.51 **Office equipment**	392.07 + 8.96	135.91 + 8.96	131.86 + 7.80	127.44 − 13.36	
229.50 + 5.14 **Semiconductors**	897.27 + 18.74	303.06 + 18.74	168.86 + 4.26	154.47 − 16.12	
153.51 + 3.19 **Software**	3919.71 + 3.97	163.95 + 4.02	76.21 + 5.99	86.03 − 12.25	

Source: *The Wall Street Journal*, February 15, 1995. Reprinted by permission of *The Wall Street Journal*, ©1995 Dow Jones & Company, Inc. All rights reserved worldwide.

Whereas insider trading may be a good clue to the fortunes of a particular company, that does not mean that insider trading can be used to successfully forecast stock market trends and turning points. They may know more than you do about their company, but that doesn't necessarily mean they know more than you do about the entire market. You're better off using the guidelines in this book.

GREED VERSUS FEAR

Perhaps this chapter has made clear to you how complex the stock market can be, and how many ways there are to invest in stocks. No wonder that even major investors feel they need an expert's advice before they venture their capital.

There is a saying, "Greed and fear drive the stock market." For example, greedy investors fueled the blaze of speculative gains before the crash of 1987, while fear held the market back after the crash.

So far, there has been no discussion of investors' psychological dynamics, the herd instinct created by greed and fear. Instead, these chapters treated the fundamentals of investing in terms of the analysis of the outlook for stocks vs. gold and then applied that analysis to a variety of stock market indicators. Here is a brief summary of these approaches.

INSIDER TRADING SPOTLIGHT

Biggest Individual Trades

(Based on reports filed with regulators last week)

COMPANY NAME	EXCH.	INSIDER'S NAME	TITLE	$ VALUE (000)	NO. OF SHRS. IN TRANS. (000)	% OF HLDNG. EXCLD. OPTNS.	TRANSACTION DATES
BUYERS							
Amer Wht Cross	O	R. M. Rodnick x	D	818	275.0	367.00	11/15-12/30/94†
Shelby Williams Inds I	N	M. Steinfeld	CB	800	100.0	4.00	1/4/95
Adams Express	N	A. R. Marusi x	D	789	50.5	467.00	12/30-30/94 †
Smithfield Foods	O	W. H. Murphy x	D	689	24.5	5.00	11/17-18/94 †
Shelby Williams Inds I	N	P. N. Steinfeld	O	394	50.0	7.00	1/18/95
Hutchinson Technology	O	H. C. Ervin Jr x	D	249	10.0	133.00	1/30/95
Mead Corp The	N	P. F. Miller Jr	D	184	4.0	39.00	12/6/94 †
Megatest	O	W. H. Chen	D	144	20.0	200.00	1/13/95
Doskocil Cos	O	R. R. Devening s	CB	102	12.0	n	1/18-24/95
Zenith Natl Insur	N	H. L. Silbert x	D	98	4.5	0.400	1/9-18/95
SELLERS							
Coleman Inc	N	L. M. Jones	D	3,359	100.7	66.00	1/3-11/95
Standex Intl	N	T. L. King	CB	2,603	83.6	32.00	1/17-30/95 r
Celadon Group	O	L. R. Bennett	P	2,501	164.0	15.00	1/24/95
Morton Intl	N	K. D. Holmgren x	O	1,197	40.0	51.00	1/23-26/95 r
Bristol-Myers Squibb	N	R. L. Davis	O	1,173	20.1	49.00	1/23/95
First Empire State	A	J. G. Pereira x	O	1,152	8.0	2.00	1/19-21/95
Bristol-Myers Squibb	N	K. E. Weg	O	993	17.0	28.00	1/23/95
UnitedVideoSatl COM A	O	R. L. Bliss	P	964	41.4	8.00	1/10-13/95
Bristol-Myers Squibb	N	J. Vonroy	O	887	15.0	54.00	1/25/95
Boca Research	O	T. Farris	O	735	80.0	2.00	1/11/95

Companies With Biggest Net Changes

(Based on actual transaction dates in reports received through Friday)

COMPANY NAME	EXCH./SYMBOL	NET % CHG. IN HOLDINGS OF ACTIVE INSIDERS¹		LATEST 12 WKS.		LATEST 24 WKS	
		LATEST 12 WEEKS	LATEST 24 WEEKS	NO. OF BUYERS-SELLERS	MULTIPLE OF HIST. NORM²	NO. OF BUYERS-SELLERS	MULTIPLE OF HIST. NORM²
BUYING							
Enron Glbl Pwr & Ppln	N/EPP	6508	6508	8-0	1.0	8-0	1.0
Megatest	O/MEGT	158	62	4-0	1.0	4-1	1.0
Allmerica Prop & Cas	N/APY	107	164	4-0	2.0*	4-0	1.0
Prins Recycling	O/PRNS	43	43	7-0	12.8*	7-0	6.4
Farr Co	O/FARC	36	101	3-0	7.2	3-0	3.6
GMIS Inc	O/GMIS	19	2001	7-0	32.7*	9-0	21.0
HamburgrHmltaRstrnt	O/HAMB	12	13	3-0	6.0	4-0	4.0
Piedmont Bankgroup	O/PBGI	11	14	4-0	3.2	7-1	2.8
Continental Can	N/CAN	7	10	5-1	5.5	5-1	2.7
SELLING							
Northeast Utilities	N/NU	− 45	− 26	0-3	1.3	0-5	1.1
Russ Berrie & Co	N/RUS	− 43	− 43	0-3	4.0	0-3	2.0
Digi Intl	O/DGII	− 17	− 17	0-3	1.5	0-3	0.8
UnitedVideoSatl COM A	O/UVSGA	− 14	− 16	0-5	1.0*	0-5	1.0
Manville	N/MVL	− 5	− 5	0-3	3.6	0-3	1.8
Integral Systems	O/ISYS	− 5	− 11	0-5	15.0	0-5	7.5

NOTE: Shows purchases and sales by most officers and directors, which must be reported to the SEC and other regulators by the 10th of the month following the month of the trade. Includes both open-market and private transactions involving direct and indirect holdings. Excludes stocks valued at less than $2 a share, acquisitions through options and companies being acquired.
n-No prior holdings. r-sale within two weeks of option exercise equal to 90% or more of shares sold. s-Holds other class of stock. x-Reflects shares held indirectly. †-Late filing. *-Base period is less than 3 years.
CB-chairman. P-president. D-director. VP-vice president. O-officer. Z-other.
¹Ranked by the change in shares held by those insiders who bought or sold during the last 12 weeks, expressed as a percentage change of only their holdings at the start of the period. Reflects companies for which filings made last week showed some insider activity during the latest 12 weeks. Excluded: companies with total trades valued under $75,000; option-related sales, unexercised options, companies with fewer than three buyers or sellers, or fewer buyers or sellers than the historical average for the period.
²Based on the previous three years.

Source: CDA/Investnet, Fort Lauderdale, Fla.

Source: *The Wall Street Journal*, February 8, 1995. Reprinted by permission of *The Wall Street Journal*, ©1995 Dow Jones & Company, Inc. All rights reserved worldwide.

Fundamental analysis tries to determine the intrinsic value of stocks by discovering their future earnings potential within the context of the business environment, and then concludes whether or not their present market value accurately reflects that intrinsic value.

This book's version of fundamental analysis began with a review of business cycle conditions and inflation's outlook and the impact of monetary and fiscal policy on them. From there, the analysis proceeded to a discussion of profits under a variety of cyclical and inflationary settings, and delved into the importance of these settings for stocks and gold. At the same time, it dealt with the importance of the price-earnings ratio and

the importance of current stock market valuation as a determinant of potential appreciation.

This chapter provided some additional assistance in the fundamental analysis of a particular stock. You learned how to compare that stock's performance to its industry's performance and then compare the industry to the overall market. A company's earnings and its price-earnings ratio are also ingredients in fundamental analysis. Final steps include an appraisal of a company's management and a forecast of future prospects founded upon its marketing and technological outlook and the ability to control costs.

If that makes sense, you must nonetheless keep in mind that *technical analysis*, a school with a number of passionate advocates, takes a different approach. It studies the historical price trend of the stock market, a group of stocks, or a single stock to forecast future trends. Technical analysis makes extensive use of charts to comprehend historical developments and thereby predict price movements. This reduces an understanding of the psychology of the market and the forces of greed and fear to an analysis of charts of past price movements. For instance, if stock prices (or the price of a stock) rise and then fall back, only to rise again above the previous high, one school of technical analysis views this as a sign of market strength. On the other hand, failure of the stock to surpass its earlier peak is viewed as a sign of weakness.

Investor's Tip

- To avoid greed and fear, take the long-run view developed in these chapters.

CONCLUSION

You can make money in the stock market if you have the time and expertise required to study it closely. But as you know from Chapters 1 and 8, timing is crucial. You have to know when to get in and when to get out, because it's very difficult to find a stock that will buck the market's trend for long. Just remember that, by investing in an index fund, you can invest in that trend without investing in an individual stock.

CHAPTER 10

COMMODITIES
AND PRECIOUS METALS

INTRODUCTION

Chapters 1 and 8 observed that stocks and gold move in opposite directions, each reacting differently to the rate of inflation. Chapter 9 reviewed investment opportunities in the stock market. It's now time to turn to gold as an investment opportunity. But before you do, let's take a historical step backward to gain a little perspective on commodity and commodity futures markets, where gold (among other things) is traded for delivery and payment at a later date.

Drastic price fluctuations plagued the farmers and producers of commodities throughout our nineteenth-century westward expansion. After a period of rapid western settlement, new farms and ranches flooded the market with their output. Prices plummeted, devastating farmers and ranchers who had hoped for higher prices to cover their debts. Only after the market absorbed the excess capacity did prices firm and rise again, instigating a new round of price increases and cyclical expansion.

Wildly fluctuating prices for cotton, grain, and meat hurt the farmer and rancher as well as the textile manufacturer, flour miller, and meat packer. In order to protect themselves from unpredictable swings in market prices, these "producers" and "consumers" began contracting to buy and sell output (*commodities*) at predetermined prices for future delivery (*forward contracts*). That way both parties could more accurately forecast revenues and costs and remove some of the uncertainty and risk from their operations.

The contracting parties custom tailored the quantity, quality, delivery date, and other conditions of the forward contracts. Soon, buyers and sellers felt the need for greater flexibility. Suppose either party wanted to get

out of the deal, for whatever reason. Who would take the cotton, hogs, or cattle? As a result, commodity producers and users established exchanges to trade these commodities, just as stock exchanges had been established to trade ownership in corporations. And just as a share of stock became a standardized unit of corporate ownership to be exchanged on the open market, commodity contracts were standardized with respect to quantity, quality (grade), delivery date, and price so that they could be traded, too. That established the modern *futures* contract, which can be bought and sold anonymously without any special reference to initial producer or ultimate user.

The futures contract is settled at the price initially agreed to when the contract is entered into, regardless of the commodity's market price (cash or spot price) at the time of future delivery and payment, and regardless of any subsequent change in the value of the contract due to changes in the market price. In this way, producers, such as farmers and ranchers, who contract to sell their output for future delivery, protect themselves from potentially lower spot (cash) prices, while foregoing the possibility that the actual cash prices might be higher at the time of delivery. Conversely, manufacturers, millers, meat packers, and other commodity processors who contract to buy goods for future delivery forego potentially low spot prices at time of delivery to avoid the possible risk of higher prices later. Futures contracts limit both the potential risk and the potential reward of the cash market for producers and consumers; the price risk is hedged.

For instance, if you are a wheat farmer and wheat's spot and future price is $4 a bushel, you can contract to sell it for the $4 futures price. If the spot price falls to $3, you have protected yourself by hedging (hemming in) your risk. You will have sold your wheat for $1 more than the spot price. Should the price rise to $5, you will not be able to take advantage of that opportunity, although you will have protected yourself (hedged) against the downside risk. In other words, hedging permits you to guarantee a good price while foregoing the risk and reward of extreme prices.

The miller may have the same motivation to lock in $4 with a futures contract and forego either high or low prices.

The futures market protects buyers and sellers of commodities, but it also provides a market for speculative trading. Speculators do not produce or consume the commodities they trade; they hope to profit from fluctuations in commodity prices. The possibility for speculative profits arises as futures prices fluctuate with spot prices.

If wheat sells for $4 a bushel in spot and futures markets, farmers and millers will contract for future delivery of the crop at that price. But if you are smart enough to correctly forecast that wheat will rise to $6 a bushel by the time of future delivery, you may wish to also contract to buy wheat for future delivery at $4 a bushel. Why? Because if you are right, the wheat you bought for delivery at $4 can be resold for $6 on the spot market at a gain of $2 when the day of future delivery arrives.

Moreover, you won't have to take delivery of the wheat, because as the spot price starts to rise, the price of futures contracts will also rise. After all, other speculators will begin to buy futures contracts when they see the spot price rise, bidding its price up. Therefore, when the price of the futures contract for which you paid $4 reaches $5, you can offset it by contracting for a futures sale at $5. You earn $1 by selling a bushel of wheat for $5 for which you paid only $4.

Conversely, if wheat is $6 a bushel and you correctly forecast that it will fall to $4, you can enter into a contract to sell wheat for future delivery at $6 and then fulfill your obligation on that date by purchasing wheat in the spot market for $4 and reselling it for $6 at a gain of $2. As the futures price falls to $5 with the spot price, you can make $1 with a $5 purchase of a contract for future delivery by using it to discharge your obligation to sell a contract for $6.

Speculation is important to the futures market because it provides liquidity by increasing sales and purchases of futures contracts. Speculative buying and selling broadens and deepens the market for producers and processors. As a result, fewer than 5 percent of futures contracts are held for actual delivery. The business of the exchange is conducted by traders who make a market for others and buy and sell on their own account.

LONG POSITION

Miller and manufacturer enter into futures contracts to buy commodities for future delivery at a set price. This is called a *long* position.

Investors also take long positions (i.e., purchase futures contracts that enable them to buy commodities at a stipulated price for future delivery) when they expect market prices at the time of delivery to be higher than the present futures price. If the investors' forecast of future cash prices is accurate, they will profit by selling at a high spot price the commodity they purchased for a low futures price. For instance, if you expect gold prices to be higher in October than the current October gold futures con-

tract, you will buy that contract. If you are correct, and in October the spot prices *are* higher than the October futures contract price, your gain will be the difference between the low futures price at which you purchased the gold and the high spot price at which you sell it.

In practice, however, fewer than 5 percent of all futures contracts are actually held to delivery; investors rarely trade the actual commodity. An investor who has taken a long position (i.e., bought a contract for future delivery) can sell the contract before the delivery date. Again, as above, if you are correct, and gold prices are rising, the October contract will have risen as well, because market forces push future prices toward spot prices as the date of delivery approaches. You will be able to sell your contract to buy gold to someone else at a higher price than you paid for it.

SHORT POSITION

Farmers, ranchers, and miners enter into futures contracts to sell commodities for future delivery at an agreed upon price. This is known as a *short* position.

Investors take short positions when they anticipate that spot prices will be lower than present futures prices. If, for example, you anticipate falling gold prices and feel that spot prices will be lower than present futures contract prices, you can take a short position in gold and thereby contract to sell gold at favorable futures prices. If you wait until the time of delivery, you can buy gold in the cash market at the low spot price and then complete or perform the contract to sell the gold at the higher contracted futures price.

But as you learned earlier, futures contracts are rarely performed; they are generally offset with an opposing trade. As gold prices fall, and therefore futures prices with them, you can buy a contract at the new low price and discharge your obligation to sell a contract at the old high price. Your gain is the difference between the two prices.

MARGIN

Finally, be aware that whether you buy (long position) or sell (short position) a futures contract, your broker will ask you for only a small portion (say, 10 percent) of the contract's value. This margin deposit will protect the broker in the event that prices fall, should you have gone long, or rise,

if you have sold short. The broker can liquidate your position quickly, as soon as prices move the wrong way, and cover the loss from your deposit. Obviously, your margin can disappear in a hurry.

If wheat's spot price is $4, and you go long because you think it will go to $6, but it falls to $3, will you be able to buy it at $3 in order to sell it at $4? That's why your broker will demand more margin.

But if wheat prices move the right way, your potential profits will accrue to your account.

INVESTING SHORT

The Wall Street Journal reports commodity prices on a daily basis (see the first or last section's index). **Futures Prices** provides quotes for future delivery of specified amounts of each commodity (see pages 228–230 for excerpts from the Wednesday, September 28, 1994 *Wall Street Journal*). The line in boldface across the top tells you the name of the commodity, the exchange where it is traded, the size of a contract, and the unit in which the price is quoted. Take **Gold** as an example. This commodity trades on the Commodity Exchange in New York City (CMX) in contracts of 100 troy ounces at prices quoted in dollars per troy ounce. The quotations are for delivery in October and December of 1994 and February, April, June and subsequent months of 1995, continuing through July of 1999.

Using February 1995 for an example from the top excerpt on page 230, note how the following information is provided by column:

Open—opening price: $401.80 for February 1995 delivery.

High—highest price for trading day: $404.80.

Low—lowest price for trading day: $404.40.

Settle—settlement price or closing price for the trading day: $404.70.

Change—difference between the latest settlement price and that of previous trading day: increase of $3.50 (+3.50) for February 1995 delivery.

FUTURES PRICES

Tuesday, September 27, 1994

Open Interest Reflects Previous Trading Day

GRAINS AND OILSEEDS

CORN (CBT) 5,000 bu.; cents per bu.

	Open	High	Low	Settle	Change	Lifetime High	Lifetime Low	Open Interest
Dec	216¼	216½	215½	215¾	− 1	277	215½	135,126
Mr95	226¼	226½	225¼	225¾	− 1	282½	225½	42,081
May	233¾	234	232¾	233	− 1	285	232½	16,975
July	238¼	238½	237¼	237¾	− ¾	285½	236½	17,443
Sept	242	242	241¼	241¼	− 1	270½	239	1,198
Dec	245¾	246	244¾	245¼	− ¾	263	235½	6,786
Dc96	....	....	....	243	....	257	239	133

Est vol 22,000; vol Mon 19,750; open int 219,838, +1,923.

OATS (CBT) 5,000 bu.; cents per bu.

	Open	High	Low	Settle	Change	Lifetime High	Lifetime Low	Open Interest
Dec	125½	126½	125¼	125¾	....	157¼	116	11,293
Mr95	130¾	131¼	130¾	131	....	152¾	121½	1,950
May	134	134	134	134	....	151	125	1,106
July	136	136	136	136	....	137¾	132	1,015

Est vol 750; vol Mon 446; open int 15,468, −33.

SOYBEANS (CBT) 5,000 bu.; cents per bu.

	Open	High	Low	Settle	Change	Lifetime High	Lifetime Low	Open Interest
Nov	553½	556½	552¾	554½	....	699	549½	78,272
Ja95	564	566½	563½	564¾	+ 1½	704	559	19,708
Mar	573¾	576¼	573	574¼	....	705	569	11,781
May	580½	582½	580	581	− ¼	705½	575½	5,926
July	587	589	585	586¾	....	706½	578½	11,695
Aug	....	....	....	587¾	....	608	579	269
Sept	....	....	....	588½	....	606	577	82
Nov	596½	598	594½	596	− ½	645	578½	4,274

Est vol 21,000; vol Mon 14,614; open int 132,040, +222.

SOYBEAN MEAL (CBT) 100 tons; $ per ton.

	Open	High	Low	Settle	Change	Lifetime High	Lifetime Low	Open Interest
Oct	164.50	165.60	164.30	165.40	+ .80	207.50	164.30	11,944
Dec	165.00	165.90	164.90	165.50	+ .40	209.00	164.90	44,087
Ja95	167.20	167.70	167.00	167.40	+ .40	207.50	166.90	10,622
Mar	170.80	171.40	170.50	171.00	+ .20	207.50	170.00	11,071
May	173.10	173.80	173.10	173.70	+ .50	207.00	172.00	5,896
July	176.00	176.90	176.00	176.60	+ .40	206.00	174.30	3,871
Aug	177.00	177.20	176.70	177.00	+ .40	182.60	175.20	611
Sept	177.00	178.00	177.00	178.00	+ 1.30	182.70	175.00	506
Dec	181.50	182.00	181.00	181.00	+ .80	182.00	176.50	179

Est vol 14,500; vol Mon 12,045; open int 88,791, −639.

SOYBEAN OIL (CBT) 60,000 lbs.; cents per lb.

	Open	High	Low	Settle	Change	Lifetime High	Lifetime Low	Open Interest
Oct	25.85	26.02	25.63	25.77	− .07	29.54	22.10	16,063
Dec	25.04	25.13	24.84	24.93	− .14	28.87	22.00	38,257
Ja95	24.75	24.80	24.55	24.64	− .11	28.55	22.65	8,535
Mar	24.42	24.43	24.25	24.30	− .14	28.30	22.95	8,584
May	24.05	24.15	24.00	24.01	− .12	28.05	22.93	5,679
July	23.90	23.90	23.90	23.80	− .08	27.85	23.00	3,911
Aug	23.85	23.85	23.75	23.75	− .10	27.20	22.95	569
Sept	23.70	23.75	23.65	23.65	− .08	24.75	22.95	201
Oct		....	....	23.50	− .13	23.80	23.10	124
Dec	23.60	23.65	23.50	23.50	− .20	23.75	22.80	432

Est vol 15,000; vol Mon 14,483; open int 82,418, +1,351.

WHEAT (CBT) 5,000 bu.; cents per bu.

	Open	High	Low	Settle	Change	Lifetime High	Lifetime Low	Open Interest
Dec	396¼	396¼	390¼	391¼	− 5½	399½	309	47,933
Mr95	402½	402¾	398	399	− 4¾	406½	327	19,305
May	389	389	384	386	− 3¼	393	325	2,611
July	359½	359¾	354	356½	− 3½	363¾	311½	4,619
Dec	370	370	370	367½	− 4½	375	331	81

Est vol 15,000; vol Mon 14,670; open int 74,648, −434.

LIVESTOCK AND MEAT

CATTLE–FEEDER (CME) 50,000 lbs.; cents per lb.

	Open	High	Low	Settle	Change	Lifetime High	Lifetime Low	Open Interest
Sept	73.25	73.25	72.85	72.85	− .45	81.70	71.00	1,148
Oct	73.55	73.55	73.00	73.15	− .40	82.35	70.95	2,950
Nov	74.17	74.17	73.57	73.65	− .55	81.85	72.40	3,766
Ja95	73.85	73.85	73.27	73.35	− .55	80.95	72.75	943
Mar	72.75	72.80	72.25	72.40	− .25	80.25	71.90	332
Apr	72.10	72.30	71.97	72.00	− .15	76.90	71.50	296
May	71.95	72.00	71.50	71.50	− .35	76.45	71.30	208

Est vol 1,070; vol Mon 1,578; open int 9,6617, +106.

CATTLE–LIVE (CME) 40,000 lbs.; cents per lb.

	Open	High	Low	Settle	Change	Lifetime High	Lifetime Low	Open Interest
Oct	69.90	69.90	69.07	69.15	− .85	74.10	65.70	24,455
Dec	69.00	69.12	68.60	68.70	− .42	74.30	67.20	21,021
Fb95	67.87	67.92	67.60	67.65	− .22	75.25	67.25	14,078
Apr	69.35	69.40	69.05	69.10	− .27	75.10	68.50	9,446
June	66.20	66.25	66.00	66.00	− .25	72.50	65.80	2,058
Aug	65.85	65.85	65.55	65.67	− .27	68.10	65.40	1,069
Oct	66.40	66.40	65.95	66.00	− .20	67.55	65.95	129

Est vol 11,852; vol Mon 11,541; open int 72,256, −826.

HOGS (CME) 40,000 lbs.; cents per lb.

	Open	High	Low	Settle	Change	Lifetime High	Lifetime Low	Open Interest
Oct	37.60	37.80	37.20	37.27	− .37	49.75	36.75	7,994
Dec	38.30	38.30	37.72	37.85	− .45	50.50	37.60	12,752
Fb95	39.15	39.17	38.55	38.62	− .57	50.80	38.55	4,401
Apr	39.20	39.25	38.72	38.75	− .45	48.80	38.72	2,640
June	44.30	44.30	43.90	44.02	− .37	51.55	43.75	875
July	44.32	44.32	43.80	43.90	− .45	49.00	43.72	243
Aug	43.05	43.05	42.82	42.82	− .25	47.00	41.65	118

Est vol 5,542; vol Mon 4,493; open int 29,119, −584.

PORK BELLIES (CME) 40,000 lbs.; cents per lb.

	Open	High	Low	Settle	Change	Lifetime High	Lifetime Low	Open Interest
Feb	39.07	39.60	38.90	39.10	− .15	60.05	38.45	7,772
Mar	39.10	39.55	38.97	39.20	− .07	60.20	38.50	679
May	40.25	40.45	40.10	40.10	− .20	61.15	39.65	159
July	41.30	41.40	40.85	40.90	− .20	54.00	40.60	205

Est vol 1,458; vol Mon 1,109; open int 8,860, −88.

FOOD AND FIBER

COCOA (CSCE) – 10 metric tons; $ per ton.

	Open	High	Low	Settle	Change	Lifetime High	Lifetime Low	Open Interest
Dec	1,352	1,361	1,347	1,350	+ 1	1,580	1,045	41,730
Mr95	1,401	1,411	1,398	1,400	− 1	1,605	1,077	15,731
May	1,428	1,440	1,428	1,430	....	1,612	1,111	5,164
July	1,450	1,462	1,460	1,458	− 5	1,600	1,225	2,639
Sept		....	....	1,485	− 5	1,611	1,265	1,304
Dec		....	....	1,511	− 5	1,633	1,290	4,920
Mr96		....	....	1,540	− 5	1,676	1,350	3,394
May		....	....	1,573	− 5	1,642	1,574	312

Est vol 5,198; vol Mon 47,157; open int 75,205, −423.

COFFEE (CSCE) – 37,500 lbs.; cents per lb.

	Open	High	Low	Settle	Change	Lifetime High	Lifetime Low	Open Interest
Dec	222.25	224.00	219.25	219.95	− 6.65	244.25	77.10	22,497
Mr95	225.50	226.50	223.00	223.50	− 6.45	244.00	78.90	8,962
May	226.75	227.50	224.85	225.00	− 5.85	244.40	82.50	3,498
July	227.75	228.00	226.00	225.25	− 6.00	245.10	85.00	1,117
Sept	228.50	228.50	226.00	225.75	− 6.00	238.00	89.00	450
Dec	229.00	229.00	227.00	226.25	− 6.00	242.00	188.00	627

Est vol 10,022; vol Mon 6,683; open int 37,151, −212.

SUGAR – WORLD (CSCE) – 112,000 lbs.; cents per lb. ← Sugar

	Open	High	Low	Settle	Change	Lifetime High	Lifetime Low	Open Interest
Oct	12.68	12.70	12.43	12.54	− .14	12.85	9.42	15,723
Mr95	12.58	12.60	12.35	12.45	− .15	12.70	10.56	102,539
May	12.57	12.58	12.34	12.46	− .14	12.65	10.57	16,443
July	12.45	12.46	12.23	12.35	− .14	12.52	10.57	10,457
Oct	12.24	12.24	12.05	12.12	− .11	12.29	10.57	6,873
Mr96	11.82	11.80	11.65	11.67	− .13	11.83	10.88	1,042

Est vol 25,577; vol Mon 24,292; open int 153,087, +433.

SUGAR – DOMESTIC (CSCE) – 112,000 lbs.; cents per lb.

	Open	High	Low	Settle	Change	Lifetime High	Lifetime Low	Open Interest
Nov	21.74	21.75	21.69	21.70	− .07	22.51	21.50	1,693
Ja95	21.92	21.92	21.87	21.88	− .04	22.28	21.65	2,720
Mar	22.00	22.01	21.99	21.99	− .01	22.18	21.70	2,867
May	22.20	22.22	22.20	22.22	....	22.23	21.87	1,442
July	22.30	22.31	22.30	22.32	+ .02	22.31	22.00	1,608
Sept	22.25	22.30	22.29	22.31	+ .02	22.30	22.00	1,197
Nov		....	....	22.15	+ .02	22.15	22.80	209

Est vol 956; vol Mon 350; open int 11,736, +110.

COTTON (CTN) – 50,000 lbs.; cents per lb.

	Open	High	Low	Settle	Change	Lifetime High	Lifetime Low	Open Interest
Oct	68.40	68.40	67.50	67.70	− .56	78.60	59.51	501
Dec	67.50	67.70	66.80	67.20	− .37	77.25	59.48	27,788
Mr95	69.35	69.40	68.65	68.95	− .42	78.15	64.00	10,443
May	70.77	70.77	70.00	70.20	− .57	78.55	64.00	5,689
July	71.85	71.85	70.91	71.25	− .60	78.75	69.30	3,961
Oct	68.90	68.90	68.80	68.80	− .20	74.70	66.80	468
Dec	68.10	86.25	67.75	67.90	− .30	72.80	66.25	1,735

Est vol 10,000; vol Mon 8,029; open int 50,585, −272.

ORANGE JUICE (CTN) – 15,000 lbs.; cents per lb.

	Open	High	Low	Settle	Change	Lifetime High	Lifetime Low	Open Interest
Nov	99.35	99.40	96.60	97.85	− 1.50	134.00	85.00	9,797
Ja85	101.50	103.00	100.25	101.10	− 1.65	132.00	89.00	6,677
Mar	105.70	105.70	103.70	104.35	− 1.60	124.25	93.00	4,466
May	109.20	109.20	107.00	107.70	− 1.75	114.25	97.50	1,039
Jly		....	....	110.75	− 1.20	119.00	100.50	609
Nov		....	....	115.75	− 1.20	112.60	110.45	431

Est vol 2,500; vol Mon 5,768; open int 23,095, −1,037.

METALS AND PETROLEUM

COPPER-HIGH (CMX) – 25,000 lbs.; cents per lb.

	Open	High	Low	Settle	Change	Lifetime High	Lifetime Low	Open Interest
Sept	127.80	128.00	123.00	124.30	− 3.50	128.90	74.90	1,725
Oct	121.00	121.00	120.20	120.25	− 1.00	122.10	75.20	2,351
Nov	118.40	118.40	118.40	118.80	− .20	118.80	77.75	711
Dec	118.00	118.40	117.60	118.35	+ .35	119.60	75.75	43,170
Ja95		....	....	117.80	+ .45	118.90	76.90	573
Feb		....	....	117.80	+ .45	117.60	87.85	439
Mar	116.20	116.65	116.00	117.20	+ .50	117.60	76.30	5,326
Apr		....	....	116.65	+ .55	116.50	90.10	583
May	115.20	115.20	114.80	116.10	+ .60	115.80	76.85	1,385
June	115.20	115.20	115.20	115.55	+ .60	115.20	106.30	287
July	114.00	114.10	113.90	115.00	+ .65	114.70	78.00	1,099
Sept	112.90	112.90	112.80	114.45	+ .65	113.30	79.10	776
Dec	111.30	111.60	111.30	113.15	+ .65	112.20	88.00	975
Mr96	109.80	109.80	109.80	111.65	+ .65	110.30	99.20	188

Est vol 8,000; vol Mon 7,059; open int 59,754, −1,378.

GOLD (CMX) – 100 troy oz.; $ per troy oz. ← Gold

	Open	High	Low	Settle	Change	Lifetime High	Lifetime Low	Open Interest
Sept		....	....	398.00	+ 3.70	395.00	377.10	30
Oct	395.10	398.50	395.00	398.10	+ 3.60	417.00	344.00	4,805
Dec	398.30	401.80	397.90	401.40	+ 3.60	426.50	343.00	107,255
Fb95	401.80	404.80	401.40	404.70	+ 3.50	411.00	363.50	16,079
Apr	406.10	408.30	405.50	408.20	+ 3.50	425.00	385.50	7,137
June	410.00	410.50	409.00	411.70	+ 3.50	430.00	351.00	10,388
Aug	414.50	414.50	412.30	415.30	+ 3.50	414.50	380.50	5,887
Oct		....	....	419.20	+ 3.50	413.30	401.00	1,282
Dec	420.90	421.60	420.90	423.10	+ 3.50	439.50	358.00	5,712
Fb96		....	....	427.10	+ 3.50	424.50	412.50	1,812
Apr		....	....	431.10	+ 3.50	430.20	418.30	1,398
June		....	....	435.40	+ 3.50	447.00	370.90	4,370
Dec		....	....	448.50	+ 3.50	447.50	379.60	2,980
Ju97		....	....	462.20	+ 3.50	456.00	436.00	1,255
Dec		....	....	476.20	+ 3.40	477.00	402.00	1,556
Ju98		....	....	490.70	+ 3.40	489.50	481.70	1,590
Dec	505.00	505.00	505.00	505.60	+ 3.40	505.00	468.00	1,964
Ju99		....	....	521.00	+ 3.40	520.00	511.00	661

Est vol 60,000; vol Mon 27,083; open int 176,161, −2,134.

PLATINUM (NYM) – 50 troy oz.; $ per troy oz.

	Open	High	Low	Settle	Change	Lifetime High	Lifetime Low	Open Interest
Oct	na	419.80	417.00	419.40	+ 1.10	435.40	368.00	7,156
Ja95	na	424.50	422.00	424.30	+ 1.10	435.50	374.80	13,218
Apr	na	427.00	426.50	427.50	+ 1.10	439.00	390.00	2,497

INTEREST RATE

TREASURY BONDS (CBT)–$100,000; pts. 32nds of 100%

	Open	High	Low	Settle	Change	Lifetime High	Lifetime Low	Open Interest
Dec	99-08	99-09	98-20	98-23	– 18	118-08	91-19	386,515
Mr95	98-18	98-19	97-31	98-01	– 18	116-20	97-31	22,041
June	97-27	97-27	97-10	97-11	– 18	113-15	97-10	10,609
Sept	....	....	....	96-23	– 18	112-15	97-09	237
Dec	96-20	96-20	96-04	96-04	– 18	111-23	96-04	126

Est vol 320,000; vol Mon 200,115; op int 454,481, +9,400.

TREASURY BONDS (MCE)–$50,000; pts. 32nds of 100%

	Open	High	Low	Settle	Change	Lifetime High	Lifetime Low	Open Interest
Dec	99-07	99-10	98-19	98-24	– 17	114-00	98-19	11,191

Est vol 3,000; vol Mon 1,774; open int 11,739, –38.

TREASURY NOTES (CBT)–$100,000; pts. 32nds of 100%

	Open	High	Low	Settle	Change	Lifetime High	Lifetime Low	Open Interest
Dec	101-23	101-26	101-12	101-15	– 8	114-21	100-25	256,544
Mr95	100-28	100-30	100-20	100-20	– 8	111-07	100-05	4,182
June	100-03	100-03	99-27	99-27	– 8	105-22	99-20	106

Est vol 87,000; vol Mon 35,661; open int 287,126, –1,628.

5 YR TREAS NOTES (CBT)–$100,000; pts. 32nds of 100%

	Open	High	Low	Settle	Change	Lifetime High	Lifetime Low	Open Interest
Dec	102-16	102-18	02-105	102-12	– 3.5	104-20	101-26	182,785
Mr95	101-28	101-28	101-23	101-23	– 3.5	103-09	101-23	198

Est vol 40,000; vol Mon 17,307; open int 186,980, –3,951.

2 YR TREAS NOTES (CBT)–$200,000, pts. 32nds of 100%

	Open	High	Low	Settle	Change	Lifetime High	Lifetime Low	Open Interest
Sept	02-202	102-21	02-202	102-21	....	104-31	102-04	890
Dec	01-317	02-015	101-31	01-312	....	102-25	101-30	31,839

Est vol 3,000; vol Mon 2,731; open int 32,729, +389.

30-DAY FEDERAL FUNDS (CBT)-$5 million; pts. of 100%

	Open	High	Low	Settle	Change	Lifetime High	Lifetime Low	Open Interest
Sept	95.23	95.25	95.23	95.25	+ .02	96.44	94.81	1,769
Oct	95.00	95.08	94.97	95.07	+ .08	95.63	94.63	3,597
Nov	94.83	94.87	94.81	94.86	+ .04	95.52	94.50	3,287
Dec	94.56	94.60	94.54	94.57	+ .02	96.00	94.46	1,060
Ja95	....	....	....	94.41	+ .01	94.66	94.24	119

Est vol 4,000; vol Mon 1,988; open int 9,840, +304.

TREASURY BILLS (CME)–$1 mil.; pts. of 100%

	Open	High	Low	Settle	Chg	Discount Settle	Discount Chg	Open Interest
Dec	94.64	94.69	94.62	94.66	+ .02	5.34	– .02	17,365
Mr95	94.25	94.28	94.25	94.25	....	5.75	....	8,863
June	93.93	93.93	93.92	93.93	+ .01	6.07	– .01	2,330

Est vol 2,131; vol Mon 3,155; open int 28,558, +1,299.

LIBOR-1 MO. (CME)–$3,000,000; points of 100%

	Open	High	Low	Settle	Chg	Discount Settle	Discount Chg	Open Interest
Oct	94.82	94.90	94.79	94.88	+ .07	5.12	– .07	24,451
Nov	94.65	94.69	94.61	94.65	+ .02	5.35	– .02	17,298
Dec	93.98	94.03	93.97	94.00	+ .03	6.00	– .03	7,486
Ja95	94.26	94.30	94.26	94.32	+ .06	6.68	– .06	1,781
Feb	....	....	....	94.16	+ .03	6.84	– .03	356
Mar	....	....	....	93.96	+ .01	6.04	– .01	161
Apr	....	....	....	93.79	+ .01	6.21	– .01	136
May	....	....	....	93.68	+ .01	6.32	– .01	250

Est vol 14,220; vol Mon 8,287; open int 51,929, +2,323.

MUNI BOND INDEX (CBT)-$1,000; times Bond Buyer MBI

	Open	High	Low	Settle	Chg	High	Low	Open Interest
Dec	87-17	87-21	87-00	87-07	– 13	91-17	87-00	18,588
Mr95	....	....	....	86-06	– 13	88-09	86-06	128

Est vol 4,000; vol Mon 1,739; open int 18,716, +36.
The index: Close 89-12; Yield 6.89.

EURODOLLAR (CME)–$1 million; pts of 100%

	Open	High	Low	Settle	Chg	Yield Settle	Yield Chg	Open Interest
Dec	94.09	94.15	94.08	94.12	+ .03	5.88	– .03	522,795
Mr95	93.74	93.79	93.71	93.75	+ .02	6.25	– .02	401,539
June	93.39	93.43	93.35	93.38	+ .01	6.62	– .01	282,804
Sept	93.09	93.14	93.07	93.09	....	6.91	....	228,210
Dec	92.79	92.82	92.76	92.78	– .01	7.22	+ .01	167,453
Mr96	92.73	92.77	92.70	92.72	– .01	7.28	+ .01	147,941
June	92.61	92.63	92.57	92.59	– .02	7.41	+ .02	117,244
Sept	92.51	92.52	92.46	92.49	– .02	7.51	+ .02	107,070
Dec	92.36	92.36	92.32	92.33	– .03	7.67	+ .03	86,217
Mr97	92.35	92.35	92.31	92.32	– .03	7.68	+ .03	75,786
June	92.26	92.27	92.23	92.24	– .03	7.76	+ .03	64,910
Sept	92.19	92.20	92.16	92.16	– .03	7.84	+ .03	53,404
Dec	92.05	92.05	92.01	92.02	– .03	7.98	+ .03	50,739
Mr98	92.04	92.05	92.01	92.02	– .03	7.98	+ .03	41,046
June	91.97	91.98	91.94	91.95	– .03	8.05	+ .03	34,717
Sept	91.91	91.91	91.88	91.89	– .03	8.11	+ .03	25,440
Dec	91.79	91.79	91.74	91.76	– .03	8.24	+ .03	23,057
Mr99	91.81	91.81	91.76	91.77	– .04	8.23	+ .04	19,796
June	91.75	91.75	91.71	91.71	– .04	8.29	+ .04	12,934
Sept	91.69	91.69	91.65	91.65	– .04	8.35	+ .04	8,946
Dec	91.56	91.56	91.51	91.52	– .04	8.48	+ .04	6,974
Mr00	91.57	91.57	91.53	91.54	– .04	8.46	+ .04	7,075
June	91.53	91.53	91.48	91.49	– .04	8.51	+ .04	5,479
Sept	91.49	91.49	91.44	91.44	– .05	8.56	+ .05	8,007

EXCHANGE ABBREVIATIONS
(for commodity futures and futures options)

CBT-Chicago Board of Trade; CME-Chicago Mercantile Exchange; CSCE-Coffee, Sugar & Cocoa Exchange, New York; CMX-Commodity Exchange, New York; IPE-International Petroleum Exchange; KC-Kansas City Board of Trade; LIFFE-London International Financial Futures Exchange; MATIF-Marche A Terme International De France; ME-Montreal Exchange; MCE-MidAmerica Commodity Exchange; MPLS-Minneapolis Grain Exchange; CTN-New York Cotton Exchange; NYM-New York Mercantile Exchange; SFE-Sydney Futures Exchange; TFE-Toronto Futures Exchange; WPG-Winnipeg Commodity Exchange.

CURRENCY

JAPAN YEN (CME)–12.5 million yen; $ per yen (.00)

	Open	High	Low	Settle	Change	Lifetime High	Lifetime Low	Open Interest
Dec	1.0186	1.0280	1.0180	1.0252	+ .0064	1.0490	.9525	44,990
Mr95	1.0320	1.0355	1.0315	1.0334	+ .0065	1.0560	.9680	2,580
June	....	....	....	1.0433	+ .0066	1.0670	.9915	452

Est vol 17,289; vol Mon 23,426; open int 48,112, –1,629.

DEUTSCHEMARK (CME)–125,000 marks; $ per mark

	Open	High	Low	Settle	Change	Lifetime High	Lifetime Low	Open Interest
Dec	.6439	.6509	.6438	.6484	+ .0045	.6606	.5351	71,350
Mr95	.6462	.6505	.6462	.6493	+ .0045	.6595	.5798	4,087
June	....	....	....	.6503	+ .0046	.6595	.5980	476

Est vol 26,359; vol Mon 28,035; open int 75,924, –1,228.

INDEX

S&P 500 INDEX (CME) $500 times index

	Open	High	Low	Settle	Chg	High	Low	Open Interest
Dec	463.05	465.15	461.20	463.95	+ .80	487.10	438.85	203,042
Mr95	466.25	468.25	464.80	467.25	+ .80	484.00	441.45	6,854
June		....	....	470.75	+ .75	487.40	449.50	2,049
Sept		....	....	475.00	+ .60	486.00	470.90	116

Est vol 71,591; vol Mon 51,103; open int 212,061, +237.
Indx prelim High 462.75; Low 459.83; Close 462.05 +1.23

S&P MIDCAP 400 (CME) $500 times index

	Open	High	Low	Settle	Chg	High	Low	Open Interest
Dec	174.10	174.80	173.40	174.25	– .35	187.05	163.50	13,326

Est vol 525; vol Mon 747; open int 13,338, +331.
The index: High 173.25; Low 172.42; Close 172.81 –.11

NIKKEI 225 STOCK AVERAGE (CME)–$5 times index

	Open	High	Low	Settle	Chg	High	Low	Open Interest
Dec	19580.	19625.	19570.	19585.	– 0315.	21800.	17030.	25,826

Est vol 1,832; vol Mon 850; open int 25,828, +136.
The index: High 19822.16; Low 19414.08; Close 1968.89 –345.47

GSCI (CME)–$250 times nearby index

	Open	High	Low	Settle	Chg	High	Low	Open Interest
Oct	169.70	170.20	168.90	169.00	– 1.10	184.40	168.90	4,703
Dec	179.30	179.30	178.20	178.20	– 1.00	187.20	176.20	718

Est vol 1,103; vol Mon 805; open int 5,441, +49.
The index: High 170.20; Low 168.81; Close 169.04 –1.12

MAJOR MARKET INDEX (CME)–$500 times index

	Open	High	Low	Settle	Chg	High	Low	Open Interest
Oct	400.50	402.60	400.00	402.20	+ 1.50	409.30	378.45	2,292
Dec		....	....	402.70	+ 1.50	408.20	361.75	193

Est vol 152; vol Mon 130; open int 2,514, –22.
The index: High 401.78; Low 399.13; Close 401.73 +2.31

NYSE COMPOSITE INDEX (NYFE)–500 times index

	Open	High	Low	Settle	Chg	High	Low	Open Interest
Dec	255.80	256.75	254.40	256.15	+ .40	264.50	244.15	3,673
Mr95	257.20	258.00	257.05	257.55	+ .40	264.60	248.50	195

Est vol 3,088; vol Mon 1,496; open int 3,932, +18.
The index: High 255.30; Low 253.92; Close 254.87 +.48

KR-CRB INDEX (NYFE)–500 times index

	Open	High	Low	Settle	Chg	High	Low	Open Interest
Dec	234.50	234.50	233.85	234.45	– .05	241.00	225.00	2,147
Mr95	235.80	235.80	235.40	235.95	+ .05	242.75	228.70	1,691
May	237.30	237.30	237.30	237.35	+ .05	240.75	234.00	757
July	238.20	238.30	238.20	238.65	– .05	240.10	238.20	125

Est vol 143; vol Mon 117; open int 4,720, –39.
The index: High 232.35; Low 231.34; Close 231.65 –.59

CAC-40 STOCK INDEX (MATIF)–FFr 200 per index pt.

	Open	High	Low	Settle	Chg	High	Low	Open Interest
Sept	1897.	1914.	1896.	1896.	....	2127.	1863.5	22,467
Oct	1902.	1921.	1902.	1904.5	– 0.5	2058.	1902.	15,285
Nov	1928.5	1928.5	1928.5	1913.5	....	1928.5	1928.5	100
Dec	1920.5	1938.	1920.5	1923.	– 0.5	2195.	1920.5	20,811
Mr95	1962.	1962.	1962.	1949.5	– 0.5	2044.5	1950.	4,826
June	1955.5	1956.5	1952.5	1940.	– 2.5	2042.	1952.5	250

Est vol 35,230; vol Mon 37,506; open int 63,739, +19.

FT–SE 100 INDEX (LIFFE)–£25 per index point

	Open	High	Low	Settle	Chg	High	Low	Open Interest
Dec	3014.	3030.	3000.	3018.	+ 9.0	3292.	2965.	51,158
Mr95	3038.5	3038.5	3038.5	3041.5	+ 8.0	3131.	3038.5	2,105

Est vol 10,424; vol Mon 17,425; open int 53,263, –245.

ALL ORDINARIES SHARE PRICE INDEX (SFE)
A$25 times index

	Open	High	Low	Settle	Chg	High	Low	Open Interest
Sept	2023.	2024.	1995.	1997.	– 22.0	2330.	1704.	43,453
Dec	2023.	2023.	1986.	1989.	– 30.0	2300.	1940.	33,961
Mr95	2030.	2030.	2030.	2015.	– 30.0	2242.	1974.	3,304
June	2050.	2050.	2050.	2037.	– 30.0	2175.	1990.	3,691

Est vol 12,315; vol Mon 9,171; open int 84,409, –8,938.
The index: High 2031.20; Low 2013.70; Close 2013.80 –16.20

OTHER FUTURES

Settlement prices of selected contracts. Actual volume (from previous session) and open interest of all contract months.

BARLEY (WPG) 20 metric tons; Can. $ per ton

	Vol.	High	Low	Close	Net Change	Lifetime High	Lifetime Low	Open Interest
Nov	787	111.80	111.00	111.60	+ 1.50	111.80	88.50	10,172

BRITISH POUND (MCE) 12,500 pounds; $ per pound

	Vol.	High	Low	Close	Net Change	Lifetime High	Lifetime Low	Open Interest
Dec	42	1.5826	1.5710	1.5784	+ .0094	1.5850	1.4646	442

CANADIAN GOVT. BONDS (CBT) C$100,000; $ per C$

	Vol.	High	Low	Close	Net Change	Lifetime High	Lifetime Low	Open Interest
Dec	1	98.86	98.85	98.86	– .20	101.25	98.40	785

CATTLE-LIVE (MCE) 20,000 lb.; ¢ per lb.

	Vol.	High	Low	Close	Net Change	Lifetime High	Lifetime Low	Open Interest
Oct	52	69.05	68.65	68.70	– .42	74.25	65.75	247

CORN (MCE) 1,000 bu.; cents per bu.

	Vol.	High	Low	Close	Net Change	Lifetime High	Lifetime Low	Open Interest
Dec	561	216½	215½	215¾	– 1	277	215½	4,800

DEUTSCHEMARK (MCE) 62,500 marks; $ per mark

	Vol.	High	Low	Close	Net Change	Lifetime High	Lifetime Low	Open Interest
Dec	174	.6504	.6447	.6486	+ .0009	.6590	.5045	608

DEUTSCHEMARK–FR. FRANC CROSSRATE (FINEX)
500,000 Dmarks; FFr per DM

	Vol.	High	Low	Close	Net Change	Lifetime High	Lifetime Low	Open Interest
Dec	4	3.4207	3.4200	3.4175	– .0025	3.4511	3.4200	597

DEUTSCHEMARK–JAP. YEN CROSSRATE (FINEX)
125,000 marks; yen per mark

	Vol.	High	Low	Close	Net Change	Lifetime High	Lifetime Low	Open Interest
Dec	45	63.09	62.90	63.25	+ .05	63.90	62.66	626

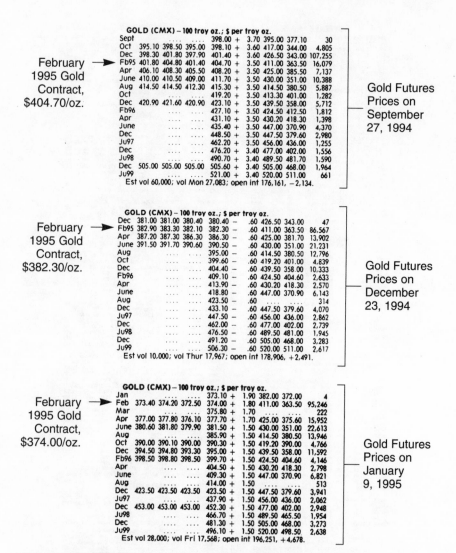

February 1995 Gold Contract, $404.70/oz.

February 1995 Gold Contract, $382.30/oz.

February 1995 Gold Contract, $374.00/oz.

Gold Futures Prices on September 27, 1994

Gold Futures Prices on December 23, 1994

Gold Futures Prices on January 9, 1995

GOLD (CMX) – 100 troy oz.; $ per troy oz.

	Open	High	Low	Settle	Change	Lifetime High	Lifetime Low	Open Int
Sept				398.00	+ 3.70	395.00	377.10	30
Oct	395.10	398.50	395.00	398.10	+ 3.60	417.00	344.00	4,805
Dec	398.30	401.80	397.90	401.40	+ 3.60	426.50	343.00	107,255
Fb95	401.80	404.80	401.40	404.70	+ 3.50	411.00	363.50	16,079
Apr	406.10	408.30	405.50	408.20	+ 3.50	425.00	385.50	7,137
June	410.00	410.50	409.00	411.70	+ 3.50	430.00	351.00	10,388
Aug	414.50	414.50	412.30	415.30	+ 3.50	414.50	380.50	5,887
Oct				419.20	+ 3.50	413.30	401.00	1,282
Dec	420.90	421.60	420.90	423.10	+ 3.50	439.50	358.00	5,712
Fb96				427.10	+ 3.50	424.50	412.50	1,812
Apr				431.10	+ 3.50	430.20	418.30	1,398
June				435.40	+ 3.50	447.00	370.90	4,370
Dec				448.50	+ 3.50	447.50	379.60	2,980
Ju97				462.20	+ 3.50	456.00	436.00	1,255
Dec				476.20	+ 3.40	477.00	402.00	1,556
Ju98				490.70	+ 3.40	489.50	481.70	1,590
Dec	505.00	505.00	505.00	505.60	+ 3.40	505.00	468.00	1,964
Ju99				521.00	+ 3.40	520.00	511.00	661

Est vol 60,000; vol Mon 27,083; open int 176,161, −2,134.

GOLD (CMX) – 100 troy oz.; $ per troy oz.

	Open	High	Low	Settle	Change	Lifetime High	Lifetime Low	Open Int
Dec	381.00	381.00	380.40	380.40	− .60	426.50	343.00	47
Fb95	382.90	383.30	382.10	382.30	− .60	411.00	363.50	86,567
Apr	387.20	387.30	386.30	386.30	− .60	425.00	381.70	13,902
June	391.50	391.70	390.60	390.50	− .60	430.00	351.00	21,231
Aug				395.00	− .60	414.50	380.50	12,796
Oct				399.60	− .60	419.20	401.00	4,839
Dec				404.40	− .60	439.50	358.00	10,333
Fb96				409.10	− .60	424.50	404.60	2,633
Apr				413.90	− .60	430.20	418.30	2,570
June				418.80	− .60	447.00	370.90	6,143
Aug				423.50	− .60			314
Dec				433.10	− .60	447.50	379.60	4,070
Ju97				447.50	− .60	456.00	436.00	2,862
Dec				462.00	− .60	477.00	402.00	2,739
Ju98				476.50	− .60	489.50	481.00	1,945
Dec				491.20	− .60	505.00	468.00	3,283
Ju99				506.30	− .60	520.00	511.00	2,617

Est vol 10,000; vol Thur 17,967; open int 178,906, +2,491.

GOLD (CMX) – 100 troy oz.; $ per troy oz.

	Open	High	Low	Settle	Change	Lifetime High	Lifetime Low	Open Int
Jan				373.10	+ 1.90	382.00	372.00	4
Feb	373.40	374.20	372.50	374.00	+ 1.80	411.00	363.50	95,246
Mar				375.80	+ 1.70			222
Apr	377.00	377.80	376.10	377.70	+ 1.70	425.00	375.60	15,952
June	380.60	381.80	379.90	381.50	+ 1.50	430.00	351.00	22,613
Aug				385.90	+ 1.50	414.50	380.50	13,946
Oct	390.00	390.10	390.00	390.30	+ 1.50	419.20	390.00	4,766
Dec	394.50	394.80	393.30	395.00	+ 1.50	439.50	358.00	11,592
Fb96	398.50	398.80	398.50	399.70	+ 1.50	424.50	404.60	4,146
Apr				404.50	+ 1.50	430.20	418.30	2,798
June				409.30	+ 1.50	447.00	370.90	6,821
Aug				414.00	+ 1.50			513
Dec	423.50	423.50	423.50	423.50	+ 1.50	447.50	379.60	3,941
Ju97				437.90	+ 1.50	456.00	436.00	2,062
Dec	453.00	453.00	453.00	452.30	+ 1.50	477.00	402.00	2,948
Ju98				466.70	+ 1.50	489.50	465.50	1,954
Dec				481.30	+ 1.50	505.00	468.00	3,273
Ju99				496.10	+ 1.50	520.00	498.50	2,638

Est vol 28,000; vol Fri 17,568; open int 196,251, +4,678.

Source: *The Wall Street Journal*, September 28, 1994, December 27, 1994, and January 10, 1995. Reprinted by permission of *The Wall Street Journal*, ©1994–1995 Dow Jones & Company, Inc. All rights reserved worldwide.

Lifetime High—highest price ever for the February 1995 contract: $411.00.

Lifetime Low—lowest price ever for the February 1995 contract: $363.50.

Open Interest—number of contracts outstanding for February delivery (for the previous trading day): 16,079 contracts have not been offset by an opposing trade or fulfilled by delivery.

The bottom line provides the estimated volume (number of contracts) for the day (60,000) as well as the actual volume for the previous trading day (27,083). Finally, the total open interest is given for all gold contracts (176,161), along with the change in the open interest from the previous trading day (–2,134).

Recall that you sell (short) futures contracts when you expect commodity prices to fall, because you anticipate a lower spot price than the futures contract price for which you are obligated. If you held the contract to maturity, you could buy at the (lower) spot price and sell at the (higher) contract price. But you also recall that contracts are usually not held to maturity. If your forecast of falling prices proves accurate, you can offset your short position to sell (*at the contract price that has remained unchanged*) with an offsetting purchase of a lower-priced long position. The price difference is your profit per ounce. Follow the step-by-step example below in order to sharpen your understanding.

1.   Turn to page 230 (top excerpt), and note from the excerpt of the Wednesday, September 28, 1994 *Wall Street Journal* the $404.70 price on Tuesday, September 27, 1994 of the February 1995 gold contract. Suppose at that time you sold short a February 1995 gold futures contract because you believed gold prices would fall. Your broker would adjust your account by $40,470 ($404.70 × 100 troy ounces) to reflect the sale and ask for a good faith deposit (margin) of, say, 10 percent ($4,047) in the event prices rose.

2.   By Friday, December 23, 1994 (see the Tuesday, December 27, 1994 *Journal* excerpt on page 230), your forecast proved accurate, as the February 1995 gold contract price dropped to $382.30 per ounce.

3.   On Monday, January 9, 1995 (see the Tuesday, January 10, 1995 excerpt on page 230), the February 1995 gold contract traded for $374.00. You then instructed your broker to purchase a long position to buy gold for February 1995 delivery at that price in order to offset your obligation

to sell at $404.70. In other words, you bought a contract in order to meet your need to sell a contract.

4.   In that way, you realized the difference ($30.70) between the original high futures price at which you sold ($404.70) and the present low price ($374.00) at which you bought. Your net gain on January 9, 1995, after about five months, is $3,070 ($30.70 per ounce × 100 ounces), reflecting the difference between the contract's original value of $40,470 (see #1 above) and its current value of $37,400 ($374.00 per ounce × 100 ounces).

Keep in mind that you need never take possession of the commodity or actually buy or sell it. Your broker handles all transactions and maintains a running record of your gain or loss.

Return for a moment to your margin deposit of $4,047. This is a performance bond or good faith money, not a down payment. It says you are prepared to meet your contractual obligation to sell gold at the contract price. But remember that you must first buy gold in order to sell it. Since you agreed to deliver gold at $404.70 an ounce, a higher spot price would have placed you in the embarrassing position of buying high in order to sell low. Had gold increased rather than fallen in value, your broker would have asked you to deposit additional margin to cover the difference in price.

For instance, if the spot and futures price rises to $424.70, how does your broker know that you will be able to meet the $2,000 difference ($20 per ounce × 100 ounces) between the $424.70 price you will pay for gold and the $404.70 price at which you must deliver it? Your broker will demand a bigger margin as the price of gold increases.

Should the price surge suddenly and unexpectedly before you can respond to your broker's call for more margin, your broker will liquidate your position to cover the difference and protect his or her own position. After all, your broker is liable for the orders he or she exercises on your behalf. You will lose your margin before your broker takes a loss on your behalf.

Commodities trading is risky.

On the other hand, as noted above, your broker will add your potential profits to your margin account if gold prices fall.

Finally, note the higher contract prices in the examples above as settlement dates extend further into the future. Does that mean that traders always anticipated a price increase despite continuously falling prices? No. The increases reflect the time value of money. A dollar tomorrow

is worth less than a dollar today at any positive rate of interest. There-fore, the price of an ounce of gold for delivery a year from now must be greater than the price of an ounce of gold today in order to compensate the owner for the interest foregone by holding gold instead of an interest earning asset.

INVESTING LONG

Commodities prices do not always march in lock step. Sugar prices rose at the same time that gold prices fell in the examples above. Use the excerpts below from the *Journal* to track sugar futures on the same dates.

Test your understanding of these concepts by asking yourself (and answering) these questions:

1.   What were the prices for the March 1995 (September 28 and December 27, 1994 and January 10, 1995 excerpts) contracts on page 234, and by how much did they change?
2.   How could an investor have profited from these price movements by purchasing long contracts? By how much would the investor have prof-ited in each case? Note that prices are quoted in dollars per pounds and that a contract is 112,000 pounds.

OTHER FUTURES AND OPTIONS
ON FUTURES CONTRACTS

Turn once again to the excerpt from the Wednesday, September 28, 1994 *Journal* on page 229 and notice that you can purchase futures contracts on investments other than commodities. For instance, futures contracts are available on Treasury bonds, Eurodollars, the S&P 500, the NYSE com-posite index, and the Major Market Index (which closely tracks the Dow). Whereas futures began with commodities like wheat, trading activity is now far heavier for instruments like Treasury bonds. *Futures options* let you buy options on futures contracts.

Examine the excerpts from the September 28, 1994 *Journal* that portray trading on Tuesday, September 27, 1994 for Futures and Futures Options on the S&P 500 Index, which closed at 462.05 that day (see pages 235–237).

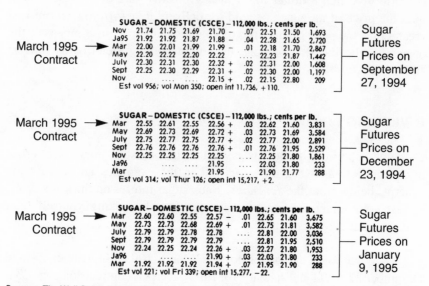

1.   You could have purchased a *long* contract on S&P 500 futures if you had forecast sharply rising stock prices, or a *short* contract if you had anticipated the index's decline. The same principles apply as discussed above in the sections on commodity trading. (See page 237.)

2.   As an alternative, you could have purchased either call or put options on the S&P 500 futures index; calls to take advantage of rising prices and puts to take advantage of falling prices. (See page 236.)

INDEX

S&P 500 INDEX (CME) $500 times index

	Open	High	Low	Settle	Chg	High	Low	Open Interest
Dec	463.05	465.15	461.20	463.95	+ .80	487.10	438.85	203,042
Mr95	466.25	468.25	464.80	467.25	+ .80	484.00	441.45	6,854
June	....	....		470.75	+ .75	487.40	449.50	2,049
Sept	....	....		475.00	+ .60	486.00	470.90	116

Est vol 71,591; vol Mon 51,103; open int 212,061, +237.
Indx prelim High 462.75; Low 459.83; Close 462.05 +1.23

S&P MIDCAP 400 (CME) $500 times index

Dec	174.10	174.80	173.40	174.25	− .35	187.05	163.50	13,326

Est vol 525; vol Mon 747; open int 13,338, +331.
The index: High 173.25; Low 172.42; Close 172.81 −.11

NIKKEI 225 STOCK AVERAGE (CME) −$5 times index

Dec	19580.	19625.	19570.	19585.	− 0315.	21800.	17030.	25,826

Est vol 1,832; vol Mon 850; open int 25,828, +136.
The index: High 19822.16; Low 19414.08; Close 1968.89 − 345.47

GSCI (CME) −$250 times nearby index

Oct	169.70	170.20	168.90	169.00	− 1.10	184.40	168.90	4,703
Dec	179.30	179.30	178.20	178.20	− 1.00	187.20	176.20	718

Est vol 1,103; vol Mon 805; open int 5,441, +49.
The index: High 170.20; Low 168.81; Close 169.04 −1.12

MAJOR MARKET INDEX (CME) −$500 times index

Oct	400.50	402.60	400.00	402.20	+ 1.50	409.30	378.45	2,292
Dec	....	....		402.70	+ 1.50	408.20	361.75	193

Est vol 152; vol Mon 130; open int 2,514, −22.
The index: High 401.78; Low 399.13; Close 401.73 +2.31

NYSE COMPOSITE INDEX (NYFE) −500 times index

Dec	255.80	256.75	254.40	256.15	+ .40	264.50	244.15	3,673
Mr95	257.20	258.00	257.05	257.55	+ .40	264.60	248.50	195

Est vol 3,088; vol Mon 1,496; open int 3,932, +18.
The index: High 255.30; Low 253.92; Close 254.87 +.48

KR-CRB INDEX (NYFE) −500 times index

Dec	234.50	234.50	233.85	234.45	− .05	241.00	225.00	2,147
Mr95	235.80	235.80	235.40	235.95	+ .05	242.75	228.70	1,691
May	237.30	237.30	237.30	237.35	+ .05	240.75	234.00	757
July	238.20	238.30	238.20	238.65	− .05	240.10	238.20	125

Est vol 143; vol Mon 117; open int 4,720, −39.
The index: High 232.35; Low 231.34; Close 231.65 −.59

CAC-40 STOCK INDEX (MATIF) − FFr 200 per index pt.

Sept	1897.	1914.	1896.	1896.	....	2127.	1863.5	22,467
Oct	1902.	1921.	1902.	1904.5	− 0.5	2058.	1902.	15,285
Nov	1928.5	1928.5	1928.5	1913.5	....	1928.5	1928.5	100
Dec	1920.5	1938.	1920.5	1923.	− 0.5	2195.	1920.5	20,811
Mr95	1962.	1962.	1962.	1949.5	− 0.5	2044.5	1950.	4,826
June	1955.5	1956.5	1952.5	1940.	− 2.5	2042.	1952.5	250

Est vol 35,230; vol Mon 37,506; open int 63,739, +19.

FT−SE 100 INDEX (LIFFE) −£25 per index point

Dec	3014.	3030.	3000.	3018.	+ 9.0	3292.	2965.	51,158
Mr95	3038.5	3038.5	3038.5	3041.5	+ 8.0	3131.	3038.5	2,105

Est vol 10,424; vol Mon 17,425; open int 53,263, −245.

ALL ORDINARIES SHARE PRICE INDEX (SFE)
A$25 times index

Sept	2023.	2024.	1995.	1997.	− 22.0	2330.	1704.	43,453
Dec	2023.	2023.	1986.	1989.	− 30.0	2300.	1940.	33,961
Mr95	2030.	2030.	2030.	2015.	− 30.0	2242.	1974.	3,304
June	2050.	2050.	2050.	2037.	− 30.0	2175.	1990.	3,691

Est vol 12,315; vol Mon 9,171; open int 84,409, −8,938.
The index: High 2031.20; Low 2013.70; Close 2013.80 −16.20

FUTURES OPTIONS PRICES

AGRICULTURAL

CORN (CBT)
5,000 bu.; cents per bu.

Strike	Calls–Settle			Puts–Settle		
Price	Dec	Mar	May	Dec	Mar	May
200	16	25¾	33	⅝	1	....
210	8⅛	17½	....	2½	2	1½
220	3⅛	10⅝	16½	7¼	5	3½
230	1	6	11	15½	10¼	8
240	½	3⅛	7	24¼	17¼	14
250	¼	1⅞	4½	34¼	26	20

Est vol 3,500 Mon 2,932 calls 719 puts
Op int Mon 147,451 calls 60,252 puts

SOYBEANS (CBT)
5,000 bu.; cents per bu.

Strike	Calls–Settle			Puts–Settle		
Price	Nov	Jan	Mar	Nov	Jan	Mar
500	54½	65½	....	⅜	1⅛	....
525	31	43	53	1¾	3½	4¼
550	11¾	23	34	7½	8¾	10¼
575	2⅝	10½	19	23½	20½	19
600	½	4¾	10½	46¼	39	35¾
625	¼	2	6	70¾	61½	56

Est vol 5,750 Mon 4,058 calls 2,230 puts
Op int Mon 155,354 calls 51,605 puts

SOYBEAN MEAL (CBT)
100 tons; $ per ton

Strike	Calls–Settle			Puts–Settle		
Price	Dec	Jan	Mar	Dec	Jan	Mar
155	11.00	12.90	....	....	....	....
160	6.75	....	....	1.20	....	....
165	3.20	5.25	8.50	2.60	2.70	2.25
170	1.50	3.00	5.25	6.00	5.30	4.25
175	.80	1.75	3.50	10.10	9.00	7.50
180	.35	1.05	2.30	14.75	13.40	11.10

Est vol 400 Mon 406 calls 276 puts
Op int Mon 10,903 calls 7,069 puts

SOYBEAN OIL (CBT)
60,000 lbs.; cents per lb.

Strike	Calls–Settle			Puts–Settle		
Price	Dec	Jan	Mar	Dec	Jan	Mar
2450	.940	.900	.880	.520	....	....
2500	.680	.690	.750	.760	1.050	1.430
2600	.350	.440	.500	1.450	1.750	....
2700	.220	....	.350	2.290	....	....
2800	.140	.180	....	3.200	....	....
2900	.100	....	....	....	....	....

Est vol 500 Mon 245 calls 290 puts
Op int Mon 10,491 calls 9,255 puts

OIL

CRUDE OIL (NYM)
1,000 bbls.; $ per bbl.

Strike	Calls–Settle			Puts–Settle		
Price	Nov	Dec	Jan	Nov	Dec	Jan
1650	1.13	1.39	....	.08	.23	.37
1700	.73	1.05	1.29	.18	.38	.53
1750	.42	.77	1.02	.37	.60	.75
1800	.24	.55	.82	.69	.88	1.05
1850	.12	.40	.63	1.07	1.23	1.36
1900	.07	.28	.49	1.52	1.60	1.71

Est vol 12,688 Mon 9,771 calls 11,
138 puts
Op int Mon 190,011 calls 125,854 puts

HEATING OIL No.2 (NYM)
42,000 gal.; $ per gal.

Strike	Calls–Settle			Puts–Settle		
Price	Nov	Dec	Jan	Nov	Dec	Jan
47	....	....	....	.0080	.0110	....
48	.0169	.0315	....	.0125	.0145	.0160
49	.0120	.0261	....	.0176	.0190	....
50	.0085	.0216	.0316	.0241	.0245	.0250
51	.0055	....	....	....	....	....
52	.0040	.0150	.0240	.0395	.0378	.0373

Est vol 3,013 Mon 1,765 calls 1,197 puts
Op int Mon 46,713 calls 14,947 puts

GASOLINE – Unlead (NYM)
42,000 gal.; $ per gal.

Strike	Calls–Settle			Puts–Settle		
Price	Nov	Dec	Jan	Nov	Dec	Jan
42	....	....	....	.0105	....	....
43	....	....	....	.0140	....	....
44	.0170	....	....	.0182	....	....
45	.0130	....	....	.0242	....	....
46	.0100	....	....	.0311	.0040	.0060
47	.0070	....	....	.0381	....	....

Est vol 889 Mon 670 calls 169 puts
Op int Mon 14,188 calls 9,672 puts

NATURAL GAS (NYM)
10,000 MMBtu.; $ per MMBtu.

Strike	Calls–Settle			Puts–Settle		
Price	Nov	Dec	Jan	Nov	Dec	Jan
160	....	....	....	.041	....	....
165	....	....	....	.058	....	....
170	.094	....	....	.079	....	....
175	.073	....	....	.108	....	....
180	.053	....	....	.138	.041	....

LIVESTOCK

CATTLE-FEEDER (CME)
50,000 lbs.; cents per lb.

Strike	Calls–Settle			Puts–Settle		
Price	Sep	Oct	Nov	Sep	Oct	Nov
71	....	....	....	....	....	....
72	0.85	1.80	2.40	0.00	0.65	0.75
73	0.05	....	....	0.20	....	....
74	0.00	0.70	1.25	1.15	1.55	1.60
75	0.00	....	....	2.15	....	....
76	0.00	0.17	0.50	3.15	3.05	2.85

Est vol 419 Mon 104 calls 40 puts
Op int Mon 3,328 calls 4,197 puts

CATTLE-LIVE (CME)
40,000 lbs.; cents per lb.

Strike	Calls–Settle			Puts–Settle		
Price	Oct	Dec	Feb	Oct	Dec	Feb
67	2.22	....	....	0.07	0.92	....
68	1.35	2.00	2.12	0.20	1.30	2.47
69	0.67	1.47	....	0.52	1.77	....
70	0.25	1.02	1.30	1.10	2.32	3.60
71	0.10	0.70	....	1.95	2.97	....
72	0.05	0.47	0.72	2.90	3.75	5.00

Est vol 1,999 Mon 510 calls 748 puts
Op int Mon 17,827 calls 23,564 puts

HOGS – LIVE (CME)
40,000 lbs.; cents per lb.

Strike	Calls–Settle			Puts–Settle		
Price	Oct	Dec	Feb	Oct	Dec	Feb
35	....	....	....	0.15	0.45	....
36	....	....	....	0.35	0.75	0.97
37	0.97	....	....	0.70	1.10	....
38	0.50	1.40	2.35	1.22	1.55	1.75
39	0.25	1.00	....	1.97	2.15	....
40	0.12	0.70	1.50	2.85	2.82	2.85

Est vol 518 Mon 265 calls 202 puts
Op int Mon 8,070 calls 3,511 puts

METALS

COPPER (CMX)
25,000 lbs.; cents per lb.

Strike	Calls–Settle			Puts–Settle		
Price	Nov	Dec	Mar	Nov	Dec	Mar
114	5.70	6.60	7.30	1.30	2.25	4.65
116	4.25	5.35	6.25	1.90	3.00	5.60
118	3.15	4.15	5.30	2.80	3.80	6.65
120	2.25	3.25	4.45	3.90	4.90	7.80
125	0.90	1.55	3.00	7.55	8.20	11.35
130	0.25	0.75	1.95	11.90	12.40	15.30

Est vol 375 Mon 195 calls 172 puts
Op int Mon 5,177 calls 4,473 puts

GOLD (CMX)
100 troy ounces; $ per troy ounce

Strike	Calls–Settle			Puts–Settle		
Price	Nov	Dec	Feb	Nov	Dec	Feb
380	21.50	21.80	26.00	0.10	0.70	1.80
390	12.50	13.50	17.60	0.90	2.40	3.80
400	5.50	7.60	12.40	4.10	6.20	7.70
410	2.00	4.30	7.80	10.60	12.80	13.10
420	0.70	2.30	5.00	19.30	20.70	20.00
430	0.30	1.10	3.30	28.90	29.60	28.10

Est vol 6,500 Fri 1,962 calls 1,413 puts
Op int Fri 101,717 calls 39,108 puts

SILVER (CMX)
5,000 troy ounces; cts per troy ounce

Strike	Calls–Settle			Puts–Settle		
Price	Nov	Dec	Mar	Nov	Dec	Mar
525	51.5	53.1	68.3	0.5	2.5	9.7
550	28.9	34.3	51.5	2.9	8.3	17.5
575	12.5	20.5	37.5	11.5	19.5	28.2
600	5.0	12.0	28.0	29.0	36.0	43.3
625	2.0	7.4	21.1	51.1	56.2	60.2
650	1.0	4.8	15.9	74.6	78.5	79.4

Est vol 5,600 Fri 2,594 calls 1,613 puts
Op int Fri 72,677 calls 24,927 puts

INDEX

S&P 500 STOCK INDEX (CME)
$500 times premium

Strike	Calls–Settle			Puts–Settle		
Price	Oct	Nov	Dec	Oct	Nov	Dec
455	11.75	....	16.95	2.85	5.85	8.10
460	8.10	11.20	13.65	4.15	7.30	9.75
465	5.00	8.15	10.65	6.05	9.20	11.70
470	2.55	5.50	7.95	8.60	11.50	13.95
475	1.15	3.40	5.70	12.15	14.35	16.65
480	0.40	1.90	3.80	16.40	17.85	19.70

Est vol 6,055 3,125 calls 4,964 puts
Op int Mon 59,604 calls 121,958 puts

GSCI (CME)
$250 times Prem.

Strike	Calls–Settle			Puts–Settle		
Price	Oct	Nov	Dec	Oct	Nov	Dec
167	2.80	....	....	0.80	....	....
168	....	....	....	1.10	....	....
169	....	....	....	....	....	....

CURRENCY

JAPANESE YEN (CME)
12,500,000 yen; cents per 100 yen

Strike	Calls–Settle			Puts–Settle		
Price	Oct	Nov	Dec	Oct	Nov	Dec
10150	1.54	2.11	2.65	0.52	1.10	....
10200	1.23	1.83	2.38	0.71	1.31	1.87
10250	0.96	1.57	2.14	0.94	1.55	2.12
10300	0.73	1.35	1.92	1.21	1.83	2.39
10350	0.55	1.15	1.71	1.53	....	....
10400	0.42	0.98	1.52	1.90	2.45	2.98

Est vol 9,845 Mon 4,343 calls 3,737 puts
Op int Mon 44,206 calls 59,376 puts

DEUTSCHEMARK (CME)
125,000 marks; cents per mark

Strike	Calls–Settle			Puts–Settle		
Price	Oct	Nov	Dec	Oct	Nov	Dec
6400	1.05	1.46	1.76	0.21	0.62	0.94
6450	0.71	1.16	1.50	0.37	0.82	1.16
6500	0.45	0.90	1.25	0.61	1.06	1.41
6550	0.27	0.69	1.05	0.93	1.35	....
6600	0.16	0.52	0.87	1.32	1.67	2.02
6650	0.09	0.38	0.71	1.75	2.03	2.35

Est vol 5,083 Mon 5,149 calls 4,087 puts
Op int Mon 79,040 calls 79,644 puts

CANADIAN DOLLAR (CME)
100,000 Can.$, cents per Can.$

Strike	Calls–Settle			Puts–Settle		
Price	Oct	Nov	Dec	Oct	Nov	Dec
7350	0.79	1.01	1.18	0.04	0.26	0.44
7400	0.40	0.69	0.88	0.15	0.44	0.63
7450	0.15	0.44	0.64	0.40	0.69	0.89
7500	0.04	0.27	0.47	....	....	1.21
7550	0.01	0.15	0.31	....	....	1.55
7600	0.00	....	0.21	....	....	....

Est vol 645 Mon 378 calls 340 puts
Op int Mon 9,316 calls 5,985 puts

INTEREST RATE

T-BONDS (CBT)
$100,000; points and 64ths of 100%

Strike	Calls–Settle			Puts–Settle		
Price	Nov	Dec	Mar	Nov	Dec	Mar
97	2-14	....	....	0-32	....	....
98	1-34	1-63	....	0-52	1-18	2-35
99	0-63	....	....	1-17	....	....
100	0-38	1-02	....	1-56	2-19	3-40
101	0-19	....	....	2-37	....	....
102	0-09	0-28	....	3-27	3-44	4-61

Est. vol. 70,000;
Mon vol. 18,661 calls; 19,619 puts
Op. int. 267, 165 calls; 264,233 puts

T-NOTES (CBT)
$100,000; points and 64ths of 100%

Strike	Calls–Settle			Puts–Settle		
Price	Nov	Dec	Mar	Nov	Dec	Mar
99	....	....	....	0-10	0-25	1-15
100	....	2-06	....	0-20	0-40	1-39
101	1-06	1-28	1-46	0-39	0-62	2-04
102	0-36	0-59	1-17	1-06	1-28	2-37
103	0-16	0-34	0-58	1-50	2-03	....
104	0-06	0-18	0-40	....	2-51	....

Est vol 25,000 Mon 2,767 calls 2,994 puts
Op int Mon 67,757 calls 92,326 puts

MUNICIPAL BOND INDEX (CBT)
$100,000; pts. & 64ths of 100%

Strike	Calls–Settle			Puts–Settle		
Price	Oct	Nov	Dec	Oct	Nov	Dec
85	....	....	....	....	....	....
86	....	....	....	0-25	....	....
87	....	....	....	0-46	....	1-39
88	....	....	....	....	....	....
89	....	....	....	....	....	2- 48
90	....	....	....	....	....	....

Est vol 0 Mon 0 calls 0 puts
Op int Mon 115 calls 87 puts

OTHER OPTIONS

Final or settlement prices of selected contracts. Volume and open interest are totals in all contract months.

CORN (MCE)
1,000 bu.; cents per bu.

Strike	Calls–Settle			Puts–Settle		
Price	Dec	Mar	May	Dec	Mar	May
220	3⅛	10⅝	....	7¼	5	....

Est vol 5 Mon 23 calls 0 puts
Op int Mon 540 calls 121 puts

EASTERN CATASTROPHE INS. (CBT)
$25,000 times ratio of losses/prem.

Strike	Calls–Settle			Puts–Settle		
Price	Mar	Jun	Sep	Mar	Jun	Sep
60.0	.1	.1	2.3	....	....	....

Est vol 0 Mon 80 calls 0 puts
Op int Mon 3,987 calls 0 puts

Source: *The Wall Street Journal*, September 28, 1994. Reprinted by permission of *The Wall Street Journal*,

INDEX

S&P 500 INDEX (CME) $500 times index

	Open	High	Low	Settle	Chg	High	Low	Open Interest
Dec	463.05	465.15	461.20	463.95 +	.80	487.10	438.85	203,042
Mr95	466.25	468.25	464.80	467.25 +	.80	484.00	441.45	6,854
June	....	....		470.75 +	.75	487.40	449.50	2,049
Sept	....	....		475.00 +	.60	486.00	470.90	116

Est vol 71,591; vol Mon 51,103; open int 212,061, +237.
Indx prelim High 462.75; Low 459.83; Close 462.05 +1.23

TRACKING COMMODITIES

Every day, on the first page (Cl) of the third section, *The Wall Street Journal* summarizes recent **Commodities** activity under the **Markets Diary** heading. A sample from the Monday, September 26, 1994 edition appears on page 238. The chart presents the Knight Ridder-Commodities Research Bureau's (KR-CRB) Futures Index, and spot prices for gold, oil, wheat, and steers are also given.

The Wall Street Journal carries a commodities article daily in the third section; on Mondays it includes the Dow Jones Commodity Indexes. See the example from the Monday, September 26, 1994 issue on pages 239 and 240.

You can use the daily or weekly indexes to follow commodity price movements. These indexes will be your most sensitive barometers of inflation.

The Wall Street Journal reports Cash Prices for immediate delivery on a wide variety of commodities on a daily basis. On Tuesday, January 24, 1995, the *Journal* published cash prices for Monday, January 23, 1995 (see page 241).

All of these series can be located using the indexes on the front pages of the first and last sections.

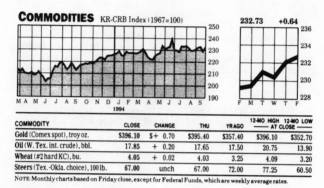

COMMODITIES KR-CRB Index (1967=100)

232.73   +0.64

COMMODITY	CLOSE	CHANGE	THU	YR AGO	12-MO HIGH AT CLOSE	12-MO LOW
Gold (Comex spot), troy oz.	$396.10	$+ 0.70	$395.40	$357.40	$396.10	$352.70
Oil (W. Tex. int. crude), bbl.	17.85	+ 0.20	17.65	17.50	20.75	13.90
Wheat (#2 hard KC), bu.	4.05	+ 0.02	4.03	3.25	4.09	3.20
Steers (Tex.-Okla. choice), 100 lb.	67.00	unch	67.00	72.00	77.25	60.50

NOTE: Monthly charts based on Friday close, except for Federal Funds, which are weekly average rates.

Source: *The Wall Street Journal*, September 26, 1994. Reprinted by permission of *The Wall Street Journal*, ©1994 Dow Jones & Company, Inc. All rights reserved worldwide.

CONCLUSION

Commodities investing is far riskier than stock market investing, because positions are highly leveraged. You can lose your entire investment if prices move the wrong way. Moreover, individual commodities can be drastically affected by random events—droughts, floods, wars, political upheavals. Yet these markets also present tremendous opportunities for those who can accurately forecast inflation's trend.

Rift Grows Between Factions at CBOT

By STEVEN E. LEVINGSTON
Staff Reporter of THE WALL STREET JOURNAL

CHICAGO – As the boom in financial futures squeezes old-guard commodity traders, tensions are building over how the exchanges should adapt.

The latest clash came last week when the membership of the **Chicago Board of Trade** voted down a proposal to reorganize the exchange into a for-profit corporation that would pay dividends to members. The proposal, initiated by former CBOT Chairman Leslie R. Rosenthal, would largely have favored traders of soybeans, wheat and other commodity futures, whose fortunes haven't kept pace with their colleagues in the financial futures pits.

"It's a tug of war," said Hans Stoll, professor of finance and director of the Financial Markets Research Center at the Owen School of Management of Vanderbilt University. "The old-line members would like to have some of the gains from the new business."

However, the fact that the reorganization was rejected out of hand tells a lot about who has the most clout in the futures markets today. John Damgard, president of the Futures Industry Association, sees the conflict as a Darwinian struggle between the industry's past and its future.

"The old guard wants to turn back the clock and trade futures in the old ways – they want to do business the way it was done around World War II," he says. "These kinds of transitions are painful in every kind of business."

In the past 10 years, interest-rate, stock-index and currency futures have grown at such a break-neck rate that they now dwarf the commodity pits. At the CBOT, the world's largest futures market, financial futures now account for 83% of the exchange's trading volume – about double their 1983 market share. The numbers are even more staggering at the **Chicago Mercantile Exchange**, where financial futures account for nearly 97% of trading.

Making the CBOT a for-profit reorganization would have tended to enrich agricultural traders by redistributing the exchange's wealth through dividend payments. In lobbying for the change, traditionalists had contended that the exchange's mushrooming size required the exchange's board to be more accountable to its old-line membership.

"We're saying . . . we're going to make you accountable," Mr. Rosenthal said. "Let's run our exchange like a business."

Exchange officials lobbied heavily against the measure, arguing the plan would siphon off money for development and hinder the exchange's competitiveness both at home and overseas. That struck a chord with financial futures traders – including powerful commercial banks, Wall Street firms and other big institutions, which rely on those contracts as a cheap, efficient way to manage their risks.

"There are those – and I count myself among them – who want to reinvest in our

Changing of the Guard

How total trading volume on U.S. futures exchanges divides up between financial contracts and traditional commodity contracts. *

■ *Financials*
▩ *Commodities*

Financials include interest-rate, currency and stock-index products; commodities include grains, oils, energy, metals, food, fiber and livestock.

Source: Chicago Board of Trade

(continued)

future like a growth company," said CBOT Chairman Patrick H. Arbor. "But there are others who want to suck out of the exchange temporary dividends."

The CBOT's board and many of its members also feared that a for-profit conversion would endanger their plans to build a new, state-of-the-art trading floor. That project, estimated at $171 million, is seen as crucial to the exchange's continued growth and competitiveness – particularly against fast expanding foreign rivals.

"We're trading some of the world's largest futures contracts on the world's oldest and smallest futures floor," Mr. Arbor complained. "We are choking our growth by not addressing these floor needs."

Trading volume at the **London International Financial Futures and Options Exchange,** or Liffe, and the **Marche a Terme International de France,** or MATIF, is surging as those exchanges take steps to attract business. In the for-profit battle, the CBOT emphasized that transaction fees would rise under the reorganization, possibly scaring away the big financial dealers who account for the lion's share of the exchange's business.

"There are many markets trading many of the same products that are ready and willing to take away the Chicago markets' share," said the Futures Industry Association's Mr. Damgard. "Brokers and dealers can take their business over-the-counter or offshore — wherever it's most efficiently done."

The CBOT debate isn't the only example of the internal strains created by the boom in financial futures. Pressure to address the new realities cuts across the industry. This month, for instance, the Chicago Merc's board approved a plan aimed at leveling the playing field between the old guard and the new by granting them equal voting rights. The exchange's members still have to approve the plan.

While financial futures are driving the Merc's growth, agricultural traders are concentrated in the exchange's full-membership seats, which have three times the voting power of the "International Monetary Market" seats that are mostly held by financial traders. To compensate the full members, the exchange will make one-time payments of between $60,000 and $70,000, roughly the difference between the current cost of a full seat and an IMM seat.

The restructuring recognizes the growing clout of the banks, brokers and other dealers that trade financial contracts. But it also aims at reinvigorating the agricultural pits. Along with their enhanced votes,

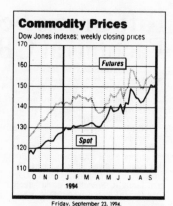

Commodity Prices

Dow Jones indexes: weekly closing prices

Friday, September 23, 1994.

	Close	Net Chg.	Yr. Ago
Dow Jones Futures	156.14	– 0.32	127.95
Dow Jones Spot	151.73	+ 1.28	120.61
Reuter United Kingdom	2126.2	+ 0.3	1604.5
K R-C R B Futures	232.73	+ 0.64	217.42
*Division of Knight-Ridder.			

IMM members gain equal access to trade agricultural products.

Indeed, big gains in commodity prices this year — a time when stock and bond prices have been swooning – are attracting more Wall Street players to the metal, energy and agricultural pits. Several big Wall Street dealers have launched commodity indexes recently to measure returns from these markets, and to lure traditional stock and bond clients into commodity investing.

The Merc's chairman, Jack F. Sandner, said the new voting parity paves the way for the exchange to study other critical issues, including a for-profit plan and a pension program for members. "We have to change as the market changes," Mr. Sandner said. "First, the real priority is to harmonize the institution. Then when we look at issues down the road, we look through the same eyeglasses."

So far, the only exchange that seems to favor the for-profit route is the **New York Mercantile Exchange.** Swelling profits from trading in energy futures, rather than financial products, prompted the board of directors to agree to put the issue to a ballot. But voting has been postponed indefinitely, as the exchange deals with the more immediate challenge of executing its merger with New York's **Commodity Exchange.**

Even despite the defeat of the for-profit measure at the CBOT, the struggle to control the exchange's fate isn't over. Says Mr. Rosenthal, the former chairman, "Everybody is examining these issues."

CASH PRICES

Monday, January 23, 1995

(Closing Market Quotations)

	Mon	Fri	Yr.Ago
GRAINS AND FEEDS			
Barley, top-quality Mpls., bu	2.75-.85	2.85	2.55
Bran, wheat middlings, KC ton	50.-53.0	52.-55.0	98.00
Corn, No. 2 yel. Cent. Ill. bu	bp2.22	2.22½	2.88
Corn Gluten Feed, Midwest, ton	76.-85.0	76.00	86.00
Cottonseed Meal, Clksdle, Miss. ton	95.-100.	100.00	170.25
Hominy Feed, Cent. Ill. ton	70.00	70.00	90.00
Meat-Bonemeal, 50% pro. Ill. ton.	na	190.-195.	220.00
Oats, No. 2 milling, Mpls., bu	147¾-58¾	148¼-59¼	z
Sorghum, (Milo) No. 2 Gulf cwt	4.63	4.63-.65	5.54
Soybean Meal, Cent. Ill., 44% protein-ton	144-149	145.-153.	182.50
Soybean Meal, Cent. Ill., 48% protein-ton	156-159	157.-161.	196.00
Soybeans, No. 1 yel Cent.-Ill. bu	bp5.43½	5.41½	6.85
Wheat, Spring 14%-pro Mpls. bu	4.20½-30½	4.24½-29½	5.35½
Wheat, No. 2 sft red, St.Lou. bu	bp3.71½	3.68½	3.76½
Wheat, hard KC, bu	na	3.98¼	3.79½
Wheat, No. 1 sft wht, del Port Ore	4.26	4.20	3.69
FOODS			
Beef, Carcass, Equiv. Index Value, choice 1-3,550-700lbs.	107.15	106.31	108.10
Beef, Carcass, Equiv. Index Value, select 1-3,550-700lbs.	103.80	103.00	105.20
Broilers, Dressed "A" NY lb	x.4883	.4830	.5470
Broilers, 12-Cty Comp Wtd Av	.5122	.5120	.5310
Butter, AA, Chgo., lb.	.65	.65	.65
Cocoa, Ivory Coast, $metric ton	g1,661	1,686	1,471
Coffee, Brazilian, NY lb.	n1.61½	1.61½	.64½
Coffee, Colombian, NY lb.	n1.80	1.80	.81½
Eggs, Lge white, Chgo doz.	.57-.62	.57-.62	.59½
Flour, hard winter KC cwt	10.70	10.60	na
Hams, 17-20 lbs, Mid-US lb fob	.53	.53	.60
Hogs, Iowa-S.Minn. avg. cwt	40.50	39.50	.45¼
Hogs, Omaha avg cwt	40.50	39.00	.45
Pork Bellies, 12-14 lbs Mid-US lb	.40	.39	.50
Pork Loins, 14-18 lbs. Mid-US lb	.95-1.02	1.02	1.13½
Steers, Tex.-Okla. ch avg cwt	74.00	74.00	73.00
Steers, Feeder, Okl Cty, av cwt	81.25	82.75	89.25
Sugar, cane, raw, world, lb. fob	.1489	.1519	.1016
FATS AND OILS			
Coconut Oil, crd, N. Orleans lb.	xxn.29½	.30	.28
Corn Oil, crd wet/dry mill, Chgo.	.28-.28½	.28-.28¼	.28¼
Grease, choice white, Chgo lb.	.18	.18	.13¾
Lard, Chgo lb.	n.21¼	.21¼	.14½
Palm Oil, ref. bl. deod. N.Orl. lb.	n.33½	.33½	.22
Soybean Oil, crd, Central Ill. lb.	.27⅝-.28⅛	.27⅝-.28¾	.3016
Tallow, bleachable, Chgo lb.	.21	.21	.15¼
Tallow, edible, Chgo lb.	n.26½	.26½	.16¾
FIBERS AND TEXTILES			
Burlap, 10 oz 40-in NY yd	n.2920	.2920	.2725
Cotton 1 1/16 str lw-md Mphs lb	.8653	.8733	.6906
Wool, 64s, Staple, Terr. del. lb.	2.37½	2.37½	1.32½
METALS			
Aluminum ingot lb. del. Midwest	q99½-101½	97½-98½	.58
Copper cathodes lb.	p1.47	1.48	.89
Copper Scrap, No 2 wire NY lb	h1.06	1.06	.71
Lead, lb.	q.42920	.42910	.34½
Mercury 76 lb. flask NY	q240.00	240.00	175.00
Steel Scrap 1 hvy mlt Chgo ton	145.-149.	145.-149.	139.50
Tin composite lb.	q4.3198	4.3046	3.3550
Zinc Special High grade lb	p.63750	.63750	.48275
MISCELLANEOUS			
Rubber, smoked sheets, NY lb.	n.89½	.88	.44¾
Hides, hvy native steers lb., fob	.88¼-.91	.88¼-.91	.72
PRECIOUS METALS			
Gold, troy oz			
Engelhard indust bullion	383.65	385.15	380.90
Engelhard fabric prods	402.83	404.41	399.09
Handy & Harman base price	382.35	383.85	378.80
Handy & Harman fabric price	383.85	385.35	z
London fixing AM 385.10 PM	382.35	383.85	378.80
Krugerrand, whol	a385.00	388.00	384.00
Maple Leaf, troy oz.	a394.00	398.00	394.00
American Eagle, troy oz.	a394.00	398.00	394.00
Platinum, (Free Mkt.)	415.50	420.50	381.00
Platinum, indust (Engelhard)	417.00	419.00	380.00
Platinum, fabric prd (Engelhard)	517.00	519.00	480.00
Palladium, indust (Engelhard)	159.00	157.00	124.00
Palladium, fabrc prd (Englhard)	174.00	172.00	139.00
Silver, troy ounce			
Engelhard indust bullion	4.840	4.880	5.080
Engelhard fabric prods	5.227	5.270	5.486
Handy & Harman base price	4.815	4.865	5.070
Handy & Harman fabric price	4.839	4.889	z
London Fixing (in pounds)			
Spot (U.S. equiv. $4.9150)	3.0965	3.0560	3.3760
3 months	3.1420	3.1010	3.4195
6 months	3.1965	3.1540	3.4615
1 year	3.3240	3.2845	3.5455
Coins, whol $1,000 face val	a3,427	3,485	3,744

a-Asked. b-Bid. bp-Country elevator bids to producers. c-Corrected. d-Dealer market. e-Estimated. f-Dow Jones International Petroleum Report. g-Main crop, ex-dock, warehouses, Eastern Seaboard, north of Hatteras. h.-Reuters. i.-f.o.b. warehouse. k-Dealer selling prices in lots of 40,000 pounds or more, f.o.b. buyer's works. n-Nominal. p-Producer price. q-Metals Week. r-Rail bids. s-Thread count 78x54. x-Less than truckloads. z-Not quoted. xx-f.o.b. tankcars.

Source: *The Wall Street Journal*, January 24, 1995. Reprinted by permission of *The Wall Street Journal*,

CHAPTER 11

LONG-TERM INTEREST RATES

INTRODUCTION

"Gold versus stocks" is shorthand for the concept that paper assets do well in times of low inflation while tangible assets do not, and vice versa.

Chapter 9 investigated the stock market; this chapter will examine long-term debt instruments. You will discover why they, like stocks, appreciate when prices are stable, but become poor investments when inflation turns severe. Begin your investigation with a general discussion of the origin of these investments.

Governments and businesses turn to the credit markets and issue long-term debt instruments to raise large sums whenever their internally generated funds, such as tax revenues or profits, fall short of their current or capital expenditures. The federal government, for instance, began the 1990s by annually borrowing hundreds of billions of dollars in the capital markets, because recession suppressed revenue growth while expenditures continued to climb.

Corporations, on the other hand, issue debt (i.e., sell bonds that are redeemed after a long period throughout which they pay interest) in order to finance the purchase of new plant and equipment. Take public utilities for example. Profits cannot cover the cost of new generating and switching stations, satellites, and transmission lines, so the difference has to be made up by borrowing. Since the projects of public utility companies are long-term and generate income for these companies over several decades of useful life, it's appropriate that the financing be long-term too. The stretch-out in earnings on these assets will provide for the regular payment of interest and principal.

You already know that corporations can raise funds by selling shares via the stock market (see Chapter 9). In that process, the ownership of a corporation is subdivided by the issue of new stock. The situation is very

different when corporations borrow funds in the credit markets. Ownership does not change hands, although, of course, the debt burden is increased.

New credit market debt, whether sold by government or business, is subdivided into discrete units called notes or bonds and is issued for a specified length of time. At the conclusion of that period, the issuer redeems the note or bond and repays the initial purchase price. Notes are medium-term debt instruments that are redeemed in one to ten years, whereas bonds are issued with maturities of more than ten years. (Chapter 12 discusses debt instruments with maturities of less than a year.)

Notes and bonds are sold or auctioned in the *primary* (initial issue) market and then traded on the *secondary* market until they mature (redeemed by the issuer). They have a specific face or *par value* (such as $1,000) and pay a specified annual, semiannual, or quarterly amount, known as *coupon interest.* When you purchase a bond, expect to receive an interest return (called the *current* or *true* yield) determined by the relationship between the fluctuating market price of the bond (more, less, or equal to its fixed $1,000 par value) and the fixed periodic payment of coupon interest. If you hold the bond to maturity (i.e., until it is redeemed by the issuer), you will also receive back its par value.

But you need not hold the note or bond to maturity, because there is a secondary market for notes and bonds that is separate from the initial-issue market. The existence of this secondary or resale market makes it much easier for government and business to sell bonds in the initial primary market. If note and bond buyers could not sell and resell these instruments over and over again, it would be very difficult for government and business to issue them in the first place. Now you know why these instruments are issued in discrete units (such as $1,000) for convenient trading.

Trading on the secondary market determines all notes' and bonds' market prices and thereby determines their current yields. The secondary market dog wags the primary market tail. Not only are primary market auction or issue prices determined by secondary market trading, but primary market coupon rates will quickly reflect true yields established in the secondary market.

There are three principal issuers of bonds: the United States government and its agencies; corporations; and state and local governments. Examine each of their issues in turn.

TREASURY AND AGENCY ISSUES

Both the U.S. Treasury and a variety of federal agencies issue long-term debt instruments. Treasury debt is classified as bonds, notes, and bills. The Treasury bill will be discussed in Chapter 12. Treasury notes (maturities of 1 to 10 years) and bonds (over 10 years) are issued in $1,000 denominations and pay a stated coupon interest payment semiannually.

Treasury bills, bonds, and notes are referred to collectively as Treasury Securities. These securities are the safest of all debt instruments, because they are backed by the full taxing power of the U.S. Government.

The government sells Treasury securities when it needs funds. These primary market sales are made at auction to securities dealers. Dealers then resell them on the secondary market to investors, where they are traded freely until maturity. By the early 1990s, the secondary market, an over-the-counter market in New York, traded $150 billion of Treasury securities daily, about 15 times daily New York Stock Exchange volume. *The Wall Street Journal* reports activity in the primary and secondary markets for long-term Treasury securities in its daily **Credit Markets** article in the third (C) section (see front page index).

The Treasury announces its auction of 2-year notes once a month. The auction takes place during the last full week of the month, and the notes are issued on the last day. Five-year, two-month (62 month) notes are auctioned and issued with the two-year notes.

The Treasury generally auctions 3-year notes and 10-year notes quarterly, during the first week of February, May, August, and November and issues them shortly afterward, on the 15th of the same month. 30-year bonds are issued twice a year in February and August.

Bonds and notes are almost always issued in denominations of $1,000, which is referred to as the par value of the bond. Each bond has a coupon rate indicating the dollar amount the security will pay annually until maturity. Interestingly, bonds are seldom auctioned at precisely their par value ,because market conditions will influence buyers' bids at the auction.

The Treasury entertains bids at the primary auction and arrays them from highest to lowest. The Treasury accepts bids starting at the highest price and works down until it has accepted a sufficient number of bids to realize its target funding. The par value and coupon interest rate are established before the auction begins, but the true yield is determined by the price established at the auction. It can be higher or lower than the $1,000 par value. If higher, the true yield will be less than the coupon rate. If lower, the true yield will be more than the coupon rate.

The Treasury awarded the $11 billion of five-year notes at a yield of 6.994%, compared with 7.125% at the previous five-year note auction Feb. 23. The bid-to-cover ratio, a measure of demand comparing total bids to those accepted, was just 2.17-to-1, compared with a ratio of 2.47-to-1 at last month's sale. Noncompetitive bids, which reflect interest from outside the Wall Street community, totaled $649 million, down from $952 million last month.

Here are results from the Treasury auction:

All bids are awarded at a single price at the market-clearing yield. Rates are determined by the difference between that price and the face value.

On March 29, 1995, the 7-year note auctioned by the Treasury in the primary market yielded 6.994%.

Applications	$23,876,606,000
Accepted bids	$11,002,166,000
Tenders submitted at market-clearing yld	37%
Accepted noncompetitively	649,000,000
Auction price (rate)	99.505 (6.994%)
Interest rate	6⅞%
CUSIP number	912827T44

The notes are dated March 31, and mature March 31, 2000.

Source: *The Wall Street Journal*, March 30, 1995. Reprinted by permission of *The Wall Street Journal*, ©1995 Dow Jones & Company, Inc. All rights reserved worldwide.

Look at the Thursday, March 30, 1995 *Journal* excerpt above from the **Credit Markets** article (see front page index) that reports on the previous Wednesday's 6.994 percent five-year note issue. Noncompetitive bids totalled $649 million. These small bidders took the market (average) price established at the auction. Notice that on the average successful bidders paid 99.505 percent of par, so that a $1,000 one year note cost $995.05 (on the average), which is $4.95 less than par. The coupon rate was 6.875 percent or $68.75 annually per $1,000 note, but since successful bidders paid only $995.05 on the average, the true yield was a higher 6.994 percent. Therefore, the 6.994% yield on these five-year notes was slightly higher than the coupon rate of 6.875%.

Major financial institutions, not individuals, bid in the primary market for Treasury securities, but your bank or broker can act as your agent if you wish to purchase a Treasury note or bond in the secondary (resale)

market. This market is very liquid, which means that you should have no trouble buying or selling securities on any business day. The third section of *The Wall Street Journal* reports trading on the secondary market for Treasury notes and bonds on a daily basis under **Treasury Bonds, Notes & Bills**. (See the report on page 248 for Monday, January 30, 1995 in the Tuesday, January 31, 1995 *Wall Street Journal*. You can locate it using the front-page index of the first or last section.)

In the first section, labeled **Govt. Bonds & Notes**, turn to the *bellwether* (named after the lead sheep in the flock that wears a bell) 30-year Treasury bond in the bottom blowup on page 249. It is listed last because it has the most recent date of issue and, therefore, has the longest span of time until maturity. The first two columns describe the bond or note in question. Begin with the coupon rate in column one (*Rate*). Since it is 7½, a $1,000 note or bond will pay $75 annually (7.5% of $1,000). The second column, titled *Maturity-Mo/Yr* (maturation date), provides the year and month of maturity: November 2024. If the security has two maturity dates, such as 05–10, the bond matures in 2010 but can be called (redeemed) by the Treasury as early as 2005. Thus, if market interest rates drop below the 2005–10 bond's rate, the Treasury may redeem the security in 2005 and reissue the debt at the lower interest rate. For instance, the 13⅞ May 2006–11 pays $138.75 per $1,000 bond. If in 2006 the current interest rate is less than 13 percent, the Treasury can redeem the 13⅞ 2006–11 bonds and reissue new securities with lower coupon payments, thus reducing the Treasury's annual coupon obligation.

The letter *n* following the date indicates that the security is a note. All other issues are bonds. You will notice in the example on page 248 that there are no *n*'s after November 2004, because there are no notes with maturities greater than 10 years. The bond issues that mature in less than 10 years (those with no letter following the month) are seasoned issues, sold sometime in the past.

The third (*Bid*) and fourth (*Asked*) columns represent the prices buyers bid or offered and sellers asked. The price quoted is a percentage of par ($1,000) value, with the number after the colon representing 32nds. Thus, a price of 96:31 for the November 2024 (bellwether) bond means that on January 30, 1995 buyers were willing to pay 96³¹⁄₃₂ percent of the par value, or $969.69 (96 + 0.96875 percent of par, or $1,000 × 0.9696875). Whenever the price exceeds par value, the security trades at a *premium*; securities priced below par trade at a *discount*. Thus, the bellwether bond on page 249 traded at a discount on January 30, 1995.

TREASURY BONDS, NOTES & BILLS

Monday, January 30, 1995

Representative Over-the-Counter quotations based on transactions of $1 million or more.

Treasury bond, note and bill quotes are as of mid-afternoon. Colons in bid-and-asked quotes represent 32nds; 101:01 means 101 1/32. Net changes in 32nds. n-Treasury note. Treasury bill quotes in hundredths, quoted on terms of a rate of discount. Days to maturity calculated from settlement date. All yields are to maturity and based on the asked quote. Latest 13-week and 26-week bills are boldfaced. For bonds callable prior to maturity, yields are computed to the earliest call date for issues quoted above par and to the maturity date for issues below par. *-When issued.

Source: Federal Reserve Bank of New York.

U.S. Treasury strips as of 3 p.m. Eastern time, also based on transactions of $1 million or more. Colons in bid-and-asked quotes represent 32nds; 101:01 means 101 1/32. Net changes in 32nds. Yields calculated on the asked quotation. ci-stripped coupon interest. bp-Treasury bond, stripped principal. np-Treasury note, stripped principal. For bonds callable prior to maturity, yields are computed to the earliest call date for issues quoted above par and to the maturity date for issues below par.

Source: Bear, Stearns & Co. via Street Software Technology Inc.

GOVT. BONDS & NOTES

Rate	Mo/Yr	Bid	Asked	Chg.	Ask Yld.
3	Feb 95	99:24	100:24	....	0.00
5½	Feb 95n	99:31	100:01	- 1	4.56
7¼	Feb 95n	100:02	100:04	- 1	4.30
7⅞	Feb 95-00	100:05	100:09	....	0.46
10½	Feb 95	100:05	100:07	- 2	4.52
11¼	Feb 95n	100:07	100:09	- 1	3.66
3⅞	Feb 95n	99:27	99:29	....	5.05
3⅞	Mar 95n	99:22	99:24	....	5.39
8½	Apr 95n	100:14	100:16	- 1	5.71
3⅞	Apr 95n	99:14	99:16	....	5.90
5⅞	May 95n	99:29	99:31	....	5.91
8½	May 95n	100:20	100:22	- 1	5.93
10¾	May 95	101:05	101:07	- 1	5.89
11¼	May 95n	101:14	101:16	- 1	5.75
12⅝	May 95	101:28	102:00	- 1	5.34
4⅛	May 95n	99:10	99:12	+ 1	6.13
4⅛	Jun 95n	99:04	99:06	....	6.13
8⅞	Jul 95n	101:02	101:04	- 1	6.29
4¼	Jul 95n	98:30	99:00	....	6.32
4⅝	Aug 95n	99:01	99:03	+ 1	6.36
8½	Aug 95n	101:01	101:03	....	6.40
10½	Aug 95n	102:04	102:06	....	6.31
3⅞	Aug 95n	98:17	98:19	+ 2	6.40
3⅞	Sep 95n	98:07	98:09	....	6.57
8⅝	Oct 95n	101:10	101:12	+ 1	6.59
3⅞	Oct 95n	97:31	98:01	+ 1	6.63
5⅛	Nov 95n	98:25	98:27	....	6.66
8½	Nov 95n	101:10	101:12	....	6.68
9½	Nov 95n	102:02	102:05	....	6.64
11½	Nov 95	103:20	103:24	....	6.53
4¼	Nov 95n	97:31	98:01	....	6.73
4¼	Dec 95n	97:23	97:25	+ 1	6.80
9¼	Jan 96n	102:05	102:07	+ 2	6.81
4	Jan 96n	97:08	97:10	+ 1	6.83
7½	Jan 96n	100:21	100:23	+ 2	6.74
4⅝	Feb 96n	97:23	97:25	+ 1	6.87
7⅞	Feb 96n	100:29	100:31	+ 1	6.89
8⅞	Feb 96n	101:30	102:00	+ 2	6.85
4⅝	Feb 96n	97:21	97:23	+ 2	6.86
7½	Feb 96n	100:19	100:21	+ 2	6.86
5⅛	Mar 96n	97:30	98:00	+ 2	6.95
7¾	Mar 96n	100:27	100:29	+ 3	6.92
9⅜	Apr 96n	102:21	102:23	+ 1	6.98
5⅜	Apr 96n	98:06	98:08	+ 2	6.99
8⅞	Apr 96n	100:23	100:25	+ 4	6.96
4¼	May 96n	96:19	96:21	+ 3	7.01
7⅞	May 96n	100:12	100:14	+ 2	7.01
5⅞	May 96n	98:16	98:18	+ 2	7.03
7⅞	May 96n	100:30	100:31	+ 4	7.04
6	Jun 96n	98:18	98:20	+ 4	7.04
7⅞	Jun 96n	101:03	101:05	+ 4	7.00
7⅞	Jul 96n	101:03	101:05	+ 3	7.02
6⅛	Jul 96n	98:20	98:22	+ 3	7.06
7⅞	Jul 96n	101:03	101:05	+ 3	7.05
4⅜	Aug 96n	96:01	96:03	+ 3	7.10
6¼	Aug 96n	98:21	98:23	+ 3	7.12
7¼	Aug 96n	100:04	100:06	+ 2	7.12
6½	Sep 96n	98:30	99:00	+ 2	7.15
7	Sep 96n	99:24	99:26	+ 2	7.12
8	Oct 96n	101:08	101:10	+ 2	7.17
6⅛	Oct 96n	99:15	99:17	+ 3	7.17
4⅜	Nov 96n	95:10	95:12	+ 4	7.18
7¼	Nov 96n	100:01	100:03	+ 2	7.19
6½	Nov 96n	98:26	98:28	+ 3	7.17
7¼	Nov 96n	100:02	100:04	+ 3	7.18
6½	Dec 96n	98:05	98:07	+ 3	7.14
7½	Dec 96n	100:16	100:18	+ 3	7.18
8	Jan 97n	101:12	101:14	+ 3	7.20
6¼	Jan 97n	98:06	98:08	+ 3	7.21
7½	Jan 97n*	100:16	100:18	+ 4	7.19
4¾	Feb 97n	95:08	95:10	+ 4	7.27

Rate	Mo/Yr	Bid	Asked	Chg.	Ask Yld.
8⅞	May 00n	105:22	105:24	+ 6	7.54
8⅜	Aug 95-00	100:17	100:21	+ 7	7.11
7¼	Aug 04n	97:07	97:09	....	7.66
13¾	Aug 04	140:11	140:15	- 1	7.69
7⅞	Nov 04n	101:18	101:20	+ 2	7.64
11⅝	Nov 04	126:17	126:21	+ 1	7.70
8⅛	May 00-05	101:30	102:02	....	7.77
12	May 05	129:31	130:03	- 5	7.71
10¾	Aug 05	121:16	121:20	- 5	7.71
9⅜	Feb 06	112:09	112:13	- 5	7.69
7⅝	Feb 02-07	98:13	98:17	- 5	7.82
7⅞	Nov 02-07	100:20	100:24	- 3	7.74
8⅜	Aug 03-08	103:06	103:10	- 4	7.84
8¾	Mar 03-08	105:19	105:23	- 4	7.84
9⅛	May 04-09	108:12	108:16	- 5	7.82
10⅜	Nov 04-09	117:09	117:13	- 5	7.80
11¾	Feb 05-10	127:08	127:12	- 7	7.77
10	May 05-10	115:06	115:10	- 4	7.81
12¾	Nov 05-10	135:20	135:24	- 6	7.79
13⅞	May 06-11	145:00	145:04	- 7	7.79
14	Nov 06-11	147:04	147:08	- 8	7.80
10¾	Nov 07-12	120:04	120:08	- 11	7.84
12	Aug 08-13	134:08	134:12	- 11	7.84
13¼	May 09-14	146:00	146:04	- 17	7.83
12½	Aug 09-14	140:04	140:08	- 10	7.82
11¾	Nov 09-14	134:01	134:05	- 8	7.81
11¼	Feb 15	133:31	134:01	- 10	7.85
10⅝	Aug 15	127:31	128:01	- 7	7.85
9⅞	Nov 15	120:16	120:18	- 5	7.85
9¼	Feb 16	114:05	114:07	- 5	7.86
7¼	May 16	93:27	93:29	- 6	7.84
7½	Nov 16	96:11	96:13	- 7	7.85
8¾	May 17	109:07	109:09	- 6	7.86
8⅞	Aug 17	110:17	110:19	- 6	7.86
9⅛	May 18	113:09	113:11	- 7	7.87
9	Nov 18	112:01	112:03	- 8	7.87
8⅞	Feb 19	110:26	110:28	- 7	7.86
8⅛	Aug 19	102:26	102:28	- 7	7.86
8½	Feb 20	106:30	107:00	- 7	7.86
8¾	May 20	109:23	109:25	- 7	7.85
8¾	Aug 20	109:24	109:26	- 8	7.85
7⅞	Feb 21	100:08	100:10	- 7	7.85
8⅛	May 21	103:03	103:05	- 10	7.84
8⅛	Aug 21	103:06	103:08	- 7	7.84
8	Nov 21	101:29	101:31	- 7	7.82
7¼	Aug 22	93:23	93:25	- 7	7.80
7⅝	Nov 22	97:31	98:01	- 8	7.80
7⅛	Feb 23	92:14	92:16	- 6	7.79
6¼	Aug 23	82:18	82:20	- 5	7.77
7½	Nov 24	96:31	97:01	- 6	7.76

U.S. TREASURY STRIPS

Mat.	Type	Bid	Asked	Chg.	Ask Yld.
Feb 95	ci	99:26	99:26	....	5.18
Feb 95	np	99:26	99:26	....	5.18
May 95	ci	98:13	98:13	- 4	5.70
May 95	np	98:12	98:12	+ 1	5.82
Aug 95	ci	96:24	96:24	+ 1	6.21
Aug 95	np	96:21	96:21	....	6.39
Nov 95	ci	95:02	95:02	+ 1	6.55
Nov 95	np	94:31	94:31	+ 1	6.67
Nov 95	ci	93:08	93:09	+ 1	6.80
Feb 96	ci	93:05	93:06	+ 1	6.91
Feb 96	np	91:17	91:18	+ 3	6.99
May 96	ci	91:15	91:17	+ 2	7.02
May 96	np	90:00	90:01	+ 2	7.09
Nov 96	np	88:04	88:05	+ 2	7.09
Nov 96	ci	88:08	88:10	+ 2	7.09
Feb 97	ci	86:18	86:19	+ 2	7.29
May 97	np	84:27	84:29	+ 2	7.33
May 97	np	84:25	84:27	+ 2	7.33

Maturity Rate Mo/Yr		Bid	Asked	Chg.	Ask Yld.
Nov 02	ci	55:15	55:19	- 2	7.69
Feb 03	ci	54:10	54:14	- 2	7.71
Feb 03	np	54:15	54:19	- 2	7.67
May 03	ci	53:09	53:13	- 2	7.72
Aug 03	ci	52:07	52:12	- 3	7.72
Aug 03	np	52:15	52:19	- 3	7.67
Nov 03	ci	51:09	51:13	- 3	7.72
Feb 04	ci	50:07	50:11	- 3	7.74
Feb 04	np	50:16	50:20	- 3	7.67
May 04	ci	49:08	49:13	- 3	7.74
Aug 04	ci	49:18	49:22	- 3	7.68
Aug 04	ci	48:10	48:14	- 3	7.75
Aug 04	np	48:20	48:24	- 3	7.67
Nov 04	ci	47:13	47:17	- 3	7.75
Nov 04	bp	47:10	47:14	- 4	7.77
Nov 04	np	47:29	48:02	- 3	7.63
Feb 05	ci	46:12	46:16	- 3	7.77
May 05	ci	45:16	45:20	- 3	7.78
May 05	bp	45:16	45:20	- 3	7.78
Aug 05	ci	44:20	44:24	- 3	7.78
Nov 05	bp	44:20	44:24	- 3	7.78
Nov 05	ci	43:24	43:29	- 3	7.78
Feb 06	ci	42:26	42:31	- 4	7.80
Feb 06	bp	43:05	43:10	- 4	7.73
May 06	ci	42:00	42:04	- 4	7.81
Aug 06	ci	41:05	41:10	- 4	7.81
May 06	ci	40:11	40:15	- 4	7.82
Feb 07	ci	39:16	39:20	- 4	7.84
May 07	ci	38:23	38:28	- 4	7.84
Aug 07	ci	37:31	38:03	- 4	7.85
Nov 07	ci	37:07	37:11	- 4	7.85
May 08	ci	36:14	36:19	- 4	7.86
May 08	ci	35:24	35:28	- 4	7.87
Aug 08	ci	35:01	35:05	- 4	7.87
Nov 08	ci	34:11	34:15	- 4	7.88
Feb 09	ci	33:21	33:25	- 4	7.88
May 09	ci	32:31	33:04	- 4	7.89
Aug 09	ci	32:11	32:15	- 4	7.89
Nov 09	ci	31:22	31:27	- 4	7.89
Nov 09	bp	31:10	31:15	- 3	7.98
Nov 09	ci	31:02	31:07	- 3	7.91
Nov 20	ci	13:12	13:16	- 3	7.91
Feb 21	bp	13:11	13:14	- 3	7.86
May 21	ci	13:01	13:04	- 3	7.88
May 21	bp	13:05	13:08	- 3	7.84
Aug 21	ci	12:27	12:30	- 3	7.86
Aug 21	bp	12:31	13:02	- 3	7.82
Nov 21	ci	12:23	12:26	- 3	7.82
Feb 21	bp	12:27	12:30	- 3	7.78
Feb 22	ci	12:16	12:19	- 3	7.82
Feb 22	ci	12:11	12:14	- 3	7.79
Aug 22	ci	12:10	12:13	- 2	7.72
Nov 22	ci	12:13	12:17	- 2	7.69
Nov 22	ci	12:04	12:07	- 2	7.71
Nov 22	bp	12:05	12:08	- 2	7.70
Feb 23	ci	11:30	12:01	- 2	7.70
Feb 23	ci	12:01	12:04	- 2	7.67
Aug 23	ci	11:24	11:27	- 2	7.68
Aug 23	ci	11:19	11:23	- 2	7.66
Nov 23	ci	11:22	11:25	- 2	7.64
Nov 23	ci	11:16	11:19	- 2	7.63
May 24	ci	11:14	11:17	- 2	7.51
Nov 24	ci	10:25	10:28	- 3	7.52
Nov 24	bp	10:28	10:31	- 3	7.56

(Right-margin annotations with arrows: "August 2004 T-Bond", "November 2004 T-Bond", "May 2016 T-Bond", "Bellwether Strip", "Bellwether T-Bond")

TREASURY BILLS

Maturity	Days to Mat.	Bid	Asked	Chg.	Ask Yld.
Feb 02 '95	1	4.86	4.76	- 0.24	4.83
Feb 09 '95	8	5.33	5.23	+ 0.10	5.31
Feb 16 '95	15	5.37	5.27	+ 0.09	5.35
Feb 23 '95	22	5.01	4.91	- 0.04	4.99
Mar 02 '95	29	5.02	4.98	- 0.20	5.07
Mar 09 '95	36	5.39	5.35	- 0.02	5.45
Mar 16 '95	43	5.39	5.35	....	5.46
Mar 23 '95	50	5.36	5.32	- 0.02	5.43
Mar 30 '95	57	5.31	5.27	+ 0.03	5.39
Apr 06 '95	64	5.61	5.59	....	5.72
Apr 13 '95	71	5.67	5.65	....	5.79
Apr 20 '95	78	5.68	5.66	- 0.03	5.81
Apr 27 '95	85	5.73	5.71	- 0.03	5.87
May 04 '95	92	5.78	5.76	- 0.05	5.93
May 11 '95	99	5.80	5.78	- 0.07	5.95
May 18 '95	106	5.83	5.81	- 0.05	5.99
May 25 '95	113	5.88	5.86	- 0.02	6.05
Jun 01 '95	120	5.90	5.88	- 0.02	6.08
Jun 08 '95	127	5.94	5.92	- 0.05	6.13
Jun 15 '95	134	5.97	5.95	- 0.02	6.17
Jun 22 '95	141	5.99	5.97	....	6.20
Jun 29 '95	148	5.97	5.95	- 0.03	6.18
Jul 06 '95	155	5.96	6.04	- 0.02	6.29
Jul 13 '95	162	6.07	6.05	- 0.03	6.31
Jul 20 '95	169	6.07	6.05	- 0.03	6.31

8⁷/₈	May 00n	105:22	105:24	+	6	7.54
8³/₈	Aug 95-00	100:17	100:21	+	7	7.11
7¹/₄	Aug 04n	97:07	97:09	....		7.66
13³/₄	Aug 04	140:11	140:15	−	1	7.69
7⁷/₈	Nov 04n	101:18	101:20	+	2	7.64
11⁵/₈	Nov 04	126:17	126:21	+	1	7.70
8¹/₄	May 00-05	101:30	102:02	....		7.77
12	May 05	129:31	130:03	−	5	7.71
10³/₄	Aug 05	121:16	121:20	−	5	7.71
9³/₈	Feb 06	112:09	112:13	−	5	7.69
7⁵/₈	Feb 02-07	98:13	98:17	−	5	7.82
7⁷/₈	Nov 02-07	100:20	100:24	−	3	7.74

August 2004 T-Bond
$137.50 annual coupon payment,
◀—— $1,403.44 price, 7.69 yield

November 2004 T-Bond
$116.53 annual coupon payment,
$1,261.70 price, 7.70% yield

Source: *The Wall Street Journal*, January 30, 1995. Reprinted by permission of *The Wall Street Journal*, ©1995 Dow Jones & Company, Inc. All rights reserved worldwide.

8³/₈	Aug 95-00	100:17	100:21	+	7	7.11
7¹/₄	Aug 04n	97:07	97:09	....		7.66
13³/₄	Aug 04	140:11	140:15	−	1	7.69
7⁷/₈	Nov 04n	101:18	101:20	+	2	7.64
11⁵/₈	Nov 04	126:17	126:21	+	1	7.70

August 2004 T-Bond
◀—— $1,403.44 price

9⁷/₈	Nov 15	120:16	120:18	−	5	7.85
9¹/₄	Feb 16	114:05	114:07	−	5	7.86
7¹/₄	May 16	93:27	93:29	−	6	7.84
7¹/₂	Nov 16	96:11	96:13	−	7	7.85
8³/₄	May 17	109:07	109:09	−	6	7.86

◀—— May 2016 T-Bond
$938.44 price

Source: *The Wall Street Journal*, January 30, 1995. Reprinted by permission of *The Wall Street Journal*, ©1995 Dow Jones & Company, Inc. All rights reserved worldwide.

7¹/₄	Aug 22	93:23	93:25	−	7	7.80
7⁵/₈	Nov 22	97:31	98:01	−	8	7.80
7¹/₈	Feb 23	92:14	92:16	−	6	7.79
6¹/₄	Aug 23	82:18	82:20	−	5	7.77
7¹/₂	Nov 24	96:31	97:01	−	6	7.76

Bellwether 30 year T-Bond
◀—— Nov 2024, 7.76% yield

Aug 23	bp	11:22	11:25	−	2	7.64
Nov 23	ci	11:16	11:19	−	2	7.63
May 24	ci	11:14	11:17	−	2	7.51
Nov 24	ci	10:25	10:28	−	3	7.59
Nov 24	bp	10:28	10:31	−	3	7.56

Bellwether Strip
◀—— $1087.50 price

Source: *The Wall Street Journal*, January 30, 1995. Reprinted by permission of *The Wall Street Journal*, ©1995 Dow Jones & Company, Inc. All rights reserved worldwide.

The second to last column is the change in bid price, expressed in 32nds, from the previous trading day. The bellwether bond on page 249 fell $1.88 on January 30 ($\%_{32}$ of 1% of $1,000 = $1.875).

The last column is the yield to maturity of 7.76%, which is slightly more than the coupon rate of 7.5% because the bond trades at $969.69, somewhat below its $1,000 par.

Here's a rough and ready way to approximate the yield:

$$\text{Approximate yield } = \frac{\text{Coupon rate}}{\text{Market price}}$$

$$= \frac{\$75}{\$969.69}$$

$$= 7.734\%$$

In this particular example, the approximate yield to maturity does not equal the actual yield to maturity, but it nonetheless offers a good approximation.

Why do securities sell at premiums (prices above the $1,000 par value) and discounts (prices below par)? Once again, market forces provide the answer. If the economy is awash in cash and, therefore, demand for Treasury securities (the next best thing to cash) is strong on the part of those who desire an interest return, securities buyers will bid their price up. Since the coupon rate is fixed, a higher market price will reduce the yield (see the approximate yield example above). Conversely, a cash shortage will prompt sales of securities on the part of those who need cash, reducing their price and increasing yields.

To illustrate this, note on page 249, that two Treasury bonds with similar maturities can have markedly different coupon rates, although they have similar yields. For example, the 13¾ August 2004 bond yields 7.69 percent, whereas the 11⅝ November 2004 bond yields 7.70 percent. Why is there so little difference in the yields when there is a large ($137.50 − $116.25 = $21.25) difference in the coupon payments? Because these securities have different prices. The August bond's bid price is 140¹¹⁄₃₂, or $1,403.44, while the November bond's price is 126¹⁷⁄₃₂, or $1,265.31. In other words, the $21.25 coupon difference is offset by a $138.13 difference in market price. Thus, differing prices will ensure that Treasury bonds and notes with similar maturity dates and features will have similar yields, whether the coupon is markedly different or not.

Treasury bonds are almost risk-free when held to maturity, yet their value will fall when interest rates rise, and you will suffer a loss if you must sell your bonds before they mature. For instance, the 7¼ May 2016 bond traded at $938.44 on January 30, 1995 (see page 249), or $61.56 below par, because interest rates had increased somewhat since its issue in 1986. If you had purchased it then, and had been obliged to sell it six years later, you would have suffered a loss.

On the other hand, returning to the 13¾ August 2004 bond, its price had risen to $1,403.44, a handsome gain since its 1984 issue at high interest rates. Substantial capital gains can be earned in low-risk Treasuries, while enjoying a comfortable yield (13¾ percent at issue or $137.50 annually in this case).

Bond prices converge on par and fluctuate very little as the maturity date approaches. Thus, bonds with the longest time to maturity offer the greatest opportunities for speculation, the greatest risk of loss, and (usually) the highest yields.

Finally, examine the data on page 248 under **U.S. Treasury Strips**. You can purchase Treasuries in the secondary market that pay no annual interest but are offered at a deep discount so that you receive the equivalent of interest as the price appreciates. For instance, turning to the January 31, 1995 data for January 30, you can see that the most recently issued (bellwether) bond traded at $108.75 ($10^{28}/_{32}$). If you had purchased it that day, you could count on it appreciating about ten-fold by maturity. Many investors purchase these securities in order to accumulate a nest egg for a special purpose, such as a child's college education.

Investor's Tip

- Bonds are a good investment in low inflation times, because falling interest rates send bond prices upward.
- Unload your bonds when inflation threatens, because rising interest rates will depress bond prices.

Since fluctuations in market interest rates are crucial in determining the value of your investment, make a habit of tracking **Key Interest Rates** in Tuesday's *Wall Street Journal* (check the last section's index). See Tuesday, January 10, 1995's report on page 252 for the week ending Friday, January 4, 1995.

Key Interest Rates

Annualized interest rates on certain investments as reported by the Federal Reserve Board on a weekly-average basis:

	Week Ended:	
	Jan. 6, 1995	Dec. 30, 1994
Treasury bills (90 day)-a	5.67	5.52
Commrcl paper (Dealer, 90 day)-a	6.29	6.29
Certfs of Deposit (Resale, 3 month)	6.36	6.36
Certfs of Deposit (Resale, 6 month)	6.87	6.88
Federal funds (Overnight)-b	5.40	5.45
Eurodollars (90 day)-b	6.34	6.34
Treasury bills (one year)-c	7.24	7.21
Treasury notes (two year)-c	7.66	7.69
Treasury notes (three year)-c	7.81	7.79
Treasury notes (five year)-c	7.86	7.81
Treasury notes (ten year)-c	7.86	7.81
Treasury bonds (30 year)-c	7.89	7.83

a-Discounted rates. b-Week ended Wednesday, January 4, 1995 and Wednesday December 28, 1994. c-Yields, adjusted for constant maturity.

Source: *The Wall Street Journal*, January 10, 1995. Reprinted by permission of *The Wall Street Journal*, ©1995 Dow Jones & Company, Inc. All rights reserved worldwide.

The Treasury is not the only government agency that issues long-term debt. The *Journal* publishes a **Government Agency & Similar Issues** report daily, which you can find using the front-page index of the first or last sections (under Treasury/Agency Issues). The Monday, January 30, 1995 edition (see page 254) covered Friday, January 27, 1995 trading activity for these agencies: FNMA, Federal Home Loan Bank, World Bank Bonds, Financing Corporation, InterAmerican Development Bank, GNMA Mortgage Issues, Tennessee Valley Authority, Farm Credit Financial Assistance Corporation, Resolution Funding Corporation, Federal Land Bank, Federal Farm Credit Bank, and Student Loan Marketing. The columns read **Rate**, **Mat.**, **Bid**, **Asked**, and **Yld**, and provide the same information as Treasury securities. The discussion below deals with some of these issues.

FNMA (called "Fannie Mae") stands for the Federal National Mortgage Association, a publicly owned corporation sponsored by the federal government and established to provide a liquid market for mortgage investors. Fannie Mae buys mortgages from mortgage bankers and other mortgage writers, earns the interest payments made by homeowners, and pays for these mortgages with the sale of bonds (debentures) to investors in $10,000 and $5,000 denominations. Pension funds, insurance

companies, mutual funds, and other large institutional investors are the principal purchasers of these bonds, which are called Fannie Maes.

The **Federal Home Loan Bank** (FHLB) is a federally chartered, privately owned company charged with regulating the S&L industry. The FHLB borrows by issuing bonds in $10,000 denominations to provide funds to weaker S&Ls with temporary liquidity problems.

The **Federal Farm Credit Bank** assists farmers by helping financial institutions, such as small commercial banks and savings and loan associations (S&Ls), provide credit to farmers for the purchase and sale of commodities and the financing of buildings and new equipment. It is an independent agency of the U.S. Government primarily funded by short-term debt, although it also issues longer-term notes that trade in the secondary market and are listed in the report.

Student Loan Marketing ("Sallie Mae") is a privately owned, government-sponsored corporation that provides a secondary market for government-guaranteed student loans. Sallie Mae sells bonds to investors to raise funds for the purchase of these student loans from financial institutions. The yields on these issues tend to be higher than other government agency issues because of the higher risk of default on student loans.

World Bank Bonds are debt instruments issued by the International Bank for Reconstruction and Development (World Bank) to finance its lending activities to less-developed countries.

GNMA ("Ginnie Mae"), the Government National Mortgage Association, is a government-owned corporation that purchases, packages, and resells mortgages and mortgage purchase commitments in the form of mortgage-backed securities called Ginnie Maes. Each Ginnie Mae bond is backed by a package of residential mortgages, and the holder of a GNMA bond thereby owns a portion of these underlying mortgages. New GNMA bonds cost $25,000, but older, partially repaid GNMAs can cost as little as $5,000.

Mortgage payments of interest and principal are "passed through" to the Ginnie Mae holders. Thus, unlike holders of Treasuries, who receive their principal at maturity, investors in Ginnie Maes are paid interest and principal each month.

GOVERNMENT AGENCY & SIMILAR ISSUES

Friday, January 27, 1995

Over-the-Counter mid-afternoon quotations based on large transactions, usually $1 million or more. Colons in bid-and-asked quotes represent 32nds; 101:01 means 101 1/32.

All yields are calculated to maturity, and based on the asked quote. * -- Callable issue, maturity date shown. For issues callable prior to maturity, yields are computed to the earliest call date for issues quoted above par, or 100, and to the maturity date for issues below par.

Source: Bear, Stearns & Co. via Street Software Technology Inc.

FNMA Issues

Rate	Mat.	Bid	Asked	Yld.
11.50	2-95	100:04	100:06	4.50
8.85	3-95	100:09	100:11	5.55
11.70	5-95	101:09	101:11	6.60
11.15	6-95	101:15	101:17	6.77
4.75	8-95	98:23	98:25	7.03
10.50	9-95	101:29	102:01	7.01
8.80	11-95	101:11	101:15	6.79
10.60	11-95	102:24	102:28	6.69
9.20	1-96	102:01	102:05	6.79
7.00	2-96	99:30	100:02	6.93
9.35	2-96	102:03	102:07	7.07
8.50	6-96	102:00	102:04	6.82
8.75	6-96	102:10	102:14	6.83
8.00	7-96	100:25	100:29	7.32
7.90	8-96	100:17	100:21	7.44
8.15	8-96	100:28	101:00	7.44
7.70	9-96	100:08	100:12	7.44
8.63	9-96	101:20	101:24	7.44
7.05	10-96	99:10	99:14	7.40
8.45	10-96	101:17	101:21	7.40
6.90	11-96*	98:28	99:00	7.50
7.70	12-96	100:03	100:07	7.56
8.20	12-96	101:11	101:15	7.35
6.20	1-97*	97:15	97:21	7.52
7.60	1-97	100:07	100:13	7.37
7.05	3-97*	98:26	99:00	7.57
7.00	4-97*	98:18	98:24	7.62
6.75	4-97	98:09	98:15	7.50
9.20	6-97	103:21	103:27	7.39
8.95	7-97	102:29	103:03	7.53
8.80	7-97	102:23	102:29	7.49
9.55	9-97	104:15	104:21	7.54
5.70	9-97*	95:06	95:12	7.68
5.35	10-97*	94:09	94:15	7.66
6.05	10-97*	95:24	95:30	7.72
6.05	11-97	95:31	96:05	7.61
9.55	11-97	104:21	104:27	7.57
7.10	12-97*	98:20	98:26	7.57
9.55	12-97	104:26	105:00	7.57
6.30	12-97*	96:11	96:17	7.67
6.05	1-98	95:27	96:01	7.58
8.65	2-98	102:22	102:28	7.57
8.20	3-98	101:12	101:18	7.62
5.30	3-98*	93:03	93:09	7.77
5.25	3-98	93:04	93:10	7.68
9.15	4-98	103:18	103:24	7.79
8.38	4-98*	100:25	100:31	4.09
8.15	5-98	101:00	101:06	7.73
5.25	5-98*	92:20	92:26	7.77
5.40	5-98*	92:31	93:05	7.77
5.38	6-98	92:26	93:00	7.78
5.10	7-98*	92:00	92:06	7.70
8.20	8-98*	100:10	100:16	7.20
5.35	8-98*	92:21	92:27	7.70
4.70	9-98*	90:11	90:17	7.76
7.85	9-98	100:08	100:14	7.70
4.95	9-98*	90:30	91:04	7.78
4.88	10-98*	90:19	90:25	7.78
5.05	11-98	91:11	91:17	7.67
5.30	12-98*	91:21	91:27	7.78
7.05	12-98*	97:10	97:16	7.81
7.05	12-98*	96:13	96:19	8.09
5.55	2-99*	91:29	92:03	7.88
7.50	3-99*	98:18	98:24	7.86
9.55	3-99	105:28	106:02	7.79
8.70	6-99	103:13	103:19	7.71
8.45	7-99	102:16	102:22	7.72
6.35	8-99	94:16	94:22	7.76
7.00	8-99*	96:13	96:19	7.91
8.55	8-99	103:00	103:06	7.71
8.35	11-99	102:08	102:14	7.72
6.10	2-00	92:31	93:07	7.76
9.30	2-00*	100:00	100:08	9.24
9.05	4-00	105:08	105:16	7.74
9.80	5-00*	102:00	102:08	1.63
8.90	6-00	104:15	104:23	7.80
9.20	9-00	106:08	106:16	7.75
8.25	12-00	101:25	102:01	7.81
8.63	4-01*	101:04	101:12	7.38
8.70	6-01*	100:22	100:30	7.95
8.88	7-01*	101:10	101:18	7.70
7.80	12-01*	96:25	97:01	8.38
7.20	1-02*	93:26	94:02	8.34
7.50	2-02	97:00	97:08	8.02
7.90	4-02*	96:25	97:01	8.46
7.55	4-02	96:23	96:31	8.11
7.80	6-02*	95:31	96:07	8.50
7.30	7-02*	94:00	94:08	8.35
7.00	8-02*	92:24	93:00	8.27
6.93	8-02*	92:10	92:18	8.27
6.95	9-02*	93:10	93:18	8.10
7.30	10-02*	93:31	94:07	8.32
6.80	10-02*	92:12	92:20	8.10
7.05	11-02	93:13	93:21	8.16
6.80	1-03	91:26	92:02	8.18
6.40	3-03*	88:19	88:27	8.31
6.63	4-03*	89:28	90:04	8.31
6.45	6-03*	90:06	90:14	8.04
6.20	7-03*	88:21	88:29	8.03
6.25	8-03*	88:29	89:05	8.03
5.45	10-03	84:24	85:00	7.86
6.20	11-03*	88:10	88:18	8.04
5.80	12-03	86:20	86:28	7.89
6.40	1-04*	89:05	89:13	8.09
6.90	3-04*	91:24	92:00	8.16
6.85	4-04	93:07	93:15	7.86
7.60	4-04*	95:07	95:15	8.31
7.65	4-04*	95:17	95:25	8.31
7.55	6-04*	95:13	95:21	8.22
7.40	7-04	96:25	97:01	7.85
8.05	7-04*	97:23	97:31	8.36
7.70	8-04*	96:11	96:19	8.22
7.85	9-04*	97:05	97:13	8.24
8.25	10-04*	99:12	99:20	8.30
8.40	10-04*	100:05	100:13	8.29
8.63	11-04*	101:06	101:14	8.25
8.55	12-04*	100:08	100:16	8.34
8.50	2-05*	100:25	101:01	8.2[illegible]
0.00	7-14	19:15	19:23	8.53
10.35	12-15	123:01	123:09	8.03
8.20	3-16	100:03	100:11	8.16
8.95	2-18	109:01	109:09	8.06
8.10	8-19	100:00	100:08	8.08
0.00	10-19	13:01	13:09	8.35
9.65	8-20*	106:19	106:27	8.96
9.50	11-20*	105:03	105:11	8.96

Federal Home Loan Bank

Rate	Mat.	Bid	Asked	Yld.
5.94	2-95	99:31	100:01	5.39
8.60	2-95	100:05	100:07	5.47
6.45	3-95	100:01	100:03	5.73
7.88	3-95	100:04	100:06	6.50
9.00	3-95	100:13	100:15	5.83
6.04	4-95	99:26	99:28	6.47
8.88	6-95	100:25	100:27	6.68
10.00	6-95	101:06	101:08	6.77
10.30	7-95	101:17	101:19	6.90
4.60	8-95	98:20	98:22	7.00
4.50	9-95	98:09	98:13	7.05
5.00	10-95	98:18	98:22	6.86
5.38	11-95	98:25	98:29	6.75
9.50	12-95	102:07	102:11	6.76
4.89	3-96	97:24	97:28	6.91
8.10	3-96	100:28	101:00	7.16
9.80	3-96	102:22	102:26	7.19
6.68	4-96	99:03	99:07	7.35
4.36	4-96*	96:09	96:13	7.46
7.75	4-96	100:17	100:21	7.17
8.25	5-96	100:31	101:03	7.35
8.25	6-96	101:00	101:04	7.38
6.13	7-96	98:09	98:13	7.32
4.41	7-96*	96:00	96:04	7.30
8.00	7-96	100:21	100:25	7.43
6.40	8-96*	98:14	98:18	7.43
6.13	8-96	98:01	98:05	7.44
7.70	8-96	100:08	100:12	7.44
6.36	9-96	98:07	98:11	7.45
8.25	9-96	101:06	101:10	7.38
7.10	10-96	99:12	99:16	7.40
8.25	11-96	101:08	101:12	7.42
6.85	2-97	98:23	98:29	7.43
7.65	3-97	100:02	100:08	7.51
9.15	3-97	103:05	103:11	7.43
6.99	4-97	98:29	99:03	7.43
6.34	6-97	97:06	97:12	7.59
9.20	8-97	103:19	103:25	7.55
6.86	10-97	98:05	98:11	7.55
7.25	10-97*	98:30	99:04	7.60
5.26	4-98*	92:23	92:29	7.78
9.25	11-98	104:19	104:25	7.77
9.30	1-99	104:29	105:03	7.79
5.43	2-99	91:27	92:01	7.75
8.60	6-99	103:02	103:08	7.71
7.05	7-99*	96:24	96:30	7.89
8.45	7-99	102:16	102:22	7.73
7.35	8-99*	97:23	97:29	7.91
8.60	8-99	103:05	103:11	7.72
7.12	9-99*	97:01	97:07	7.85
8.38	10-99	102:08	102:14	7.74
8.60	1-00	103:06	103:14	7.76
9.50	2-04	109:16	109:24	7.97

World Bank Bonds

Rate	Mat.	Bid	Asked	Yld.
8.63	10-95	100:26	100:30	7.13
7.25	10-96	99:21	99:25	7.38
8.75	3-97	102:08	102:14	7.46
5.88	7-97	96:02	96:08	7.57
9.88	10-97	105:09	105:15	7.56
8.38	10-99	102:13	102:19	7.70
8.13	3-01	100:23	100:31	7.92
6.75	1-02	95:16	95:24	7.55
12.38	10-02	124:19	124:27	7.99
8.25	9-16	100:25	101:01	8.15
8.63	10-16	104:14	104:22	8.16
9.25	7-17	110:25	111:01	8.17
7.63	1-23	94:31	95:07	8.06
8.88	3-26	107:05	107:13	8.21

Financing Corporation

Rate	Mat.	Bid	Asked	Yld.
10.70	10-17	126:08	126:16	8.12
9.80	11-17	117:02	117:10	8.12
9.40	2-18	113:00	113:08	8.12
9.80	4-18	117:05	117:13	8.12
10.00	5-18	119:08	119:16	8.12
10.35	8-18	123:00	123:08	8.12
9.65	11-18	115:23	115:31	8.12
9.90	12-18	118:12	118:20	8.12
9.60	12-18	115:08	115:16	8.12
9.65	3-19	115:26	116:02	8.12
9.70	4-19	116:11	116:19	8.12
9.00	6-19	109:01	109:09	8.12
8.60	9-19	104:27	105:03	8.12

Inter-Amer. Devel. Bank

Rate	Mat.	Bid	Asked	Yld.
11.38	5-95	101:03	101:05	6.54
7.50	12-96	100:07	100:11	7.29
9.50	10-97	104:14	104:20	7.57
8.50	5-01	102:11	102:19	7.96
12.25	12-08	133:16	133:24	8.14
8.88	6-09	109:01	109:09	7.79
8.50	3-11	103:00	103:08	8.13

GNMA Mtge. Issues a-Bond

Rate	Mat.	Bid	Asked	Yld.
6.00	30Yr	84:22	84:30	8.16
6.50	30Yr	88:00	88:08	8.30
7.00	30Yr	91:07	91:15	8.37
7.50	30Yr	94:08	94:16	8.46
8.00	30Yr	97:03	97:11	8.54
8.50	30Yr	99:21	99:29	8.66
9.00	30Yr	101:30	102:06	8.77
9.50	30Yr	104:07	104:15	8.79
10.00	30Yr	106:06	106:14	8.84
10.50	30Yr	107:21	107:29	8.61
11.00	30Yr	109:02	109:10	8.69
11.50	30Yr	110:01	110:09	8.88
12.00	30Yr	111:03	111:11	9.16

Tennessee Valley Authority

Rate	Mat.	Bid	Asked	Yld.
4.38	3-96*	96:30	97:02	7.22
8.25	11-96	101:01	101:05	7.54
4.60	12-96*	94:25	94:29	7.57
6.00	1-97*	97:09	97:15	7.41
6.25	8-99*	93:25	93:31	7.87
7.63	9-99*	98:18	98:24	7.95
8.38	10-99	102:12	102:18	7.71
7.88	9-01*	99:00	99:08	8.02
7.45	10-01*	97:08	97:16	7.93
6.88	1-02*	94:08	94:16	7.92
6.88	8-02*	93:29	94:05	7.92
7.63	9-22*	92:08	92:16	8.32
7.75	12-22*	93:19	93:27	8.32
8.05	7-24*	97:00	97:08	8.30
8.63	11-29*	99:21	99:29	8.63
8.25	9-34*	95:25	96:01	8.60
8.25	4-42*	97:12	97:20	8.45
7.25	7-43	85:28	86:04	8.44
6.88	12-43*	81:20	81:28	8.43

Farm Credit Fin. Asst. Corp.

Rate	Mat.	Bid	Asked	Yld.
9.38	7-03	108:27	109:03	7.88
9.45	11-03*	104:27	105:03	7.87
8.80	6-05	105:25	106:01	7.93
9.20	9-05	103:00	103:08	8.72

Resolution Funding Corp.

Rate	Mat.	Bid	Asked	Yld.
8.13	10-19	99:26	100:02	8.12
8.88	7-20	109:11	109:19	7.99
9.38	10-20	113:29	114:05	8.06
8.63	1-21	105:28	106:04	8.06
8.63	1-30	107:22	107:30	7.95
8.88	4-30	110:19	110:27	7.95

Federal Land Bank

Rate	Mat.	Bid	Asked	Yld.
6.00	7-96	98:03	98:07	7.34
7.95	10-96	100:24	100:28	7.39
7.35	1-97	99:22	99:28	7.42

Federal Farm Credit Bank

Rate	Mat.	Bid	Asked	Yld.
3.53	2-95	100:00	100:02	0.00
5.17	2-95	100:00	100:02	0.00
5.38	2-95	100:00	100:02	0.00
5.60	2-95	100:00	100:02	3.89
5.19	3-95	99:29	99:31	5.44
5.66	3-95	100:00	100:02	4.89
6.05	4-95	99:30	100:00	6.02
6.38	4-95	99:30	100:00	6.25
4.43	4-95	99:20	99:22	6.15
5.49	4-95	99:26	99:28	6.10
5.16	5-95	99:18	99:20	6.58
5.85	5-95	99:23	99:25	6.63
6.20	5-95	100:00	100:02	5.95
5.47	6-95	99:14	99:16	6.93
6.15	6-95	99:25	99:27	6.56
6.67	7-95	100:02	100:04	6.34
5.38	8-95	99:08	99:10	6.80
6.65	8-95	100:01	100:03	6.46
5.70	9-95	99:05	99:07	7.08
5.79	10-95	99:02	99:06	7.04
6.33	11-95	99:19	99:23	6.70
6.70	12-95	99:26	99:30	6.76
5.50	12-95	98:23	98:27	6.91
7.21	1-96	100:07	100:11	6.81
5.08	1-96	98:10	98:14	6.80
7.11	2-96	100:04	100:08	6.85
6.65	5-96	98:30	99:02	7.44
4.55	2-97*	94:12	94:18	7.52
5.12	3-97*	95:08	95:14	7.52
11.90	10-97	110:13	110:19	7.51
5.27	2-99*	90:28	91:02	7.92
5.79	3-99*	92:28	93:02	7.80
8.65	10-99	103:06	103:12	7.77
7.95	4-02*	97:02	97:10	8.45

Student Loan Marketing

Rate	Mat.	Bid	Asked	Yld.
8.55	2-95	100:00	100:02	0.00
5.28	2-95	100:00	100:02	0.00
7.63	3-95	100:05	100:07	5.62
9.80	9-00*	101:25	102:01	6.45
7.00	12-02	92:30	93:06	8.19
0.00	5-14	17:07	17:15	9.25
0.00	10-22	10:01	10:09	8.39

Source: *The Wall Street Journal*, January 30, 1995. Reprinted by permission of *The Wall Street Journal*,

Ginnie Maes don't have stated maturity dates, because the bond's flow of income depends on the repayment of the underlying mortgages. If all homeowners pay their mortgages regularly for the mortgage's life, with no prepayments, the Ginnie Mae holder receives regular monthly checks for 30 years. However, a homeowner may choose to pay off his or her mortgage prior to maturity, or may pay additional principal in some months. The prepayment or excess principal payments are passed through to the Ginnie Mae holder, who receives a larger monthly check. This prepayment reduces the subsequent monthly payments and the Ginnie Mae's par value.

Ginnie Maes offer higher rates than Treasury bonds because of the unpredictable nature of interest and principal payments. The U.S. Treasury backs these government bonds to remove the risk of homeowner default.

Finally, you can see the mortgage interest rates associated with the various Ginnie Mae pools, as well as the range of prices that determine these bonds' yields.

Federal Land Banks are privately owned organizations, backed by the federal government, that are organized to finance agricultural activities. They primarily provide first mortgage loans on farm properties with original maturities of around 20 years and fund these mortgages by issuing Consolidated Federal Farm Loan Bonds. The Federal Farm Credit Agency examines the activities of the Federal Land Bank.

CORPORATE BONDS

Corporations are the second principal issuer of long-term debt, and they, like the government and government agencies, issue credit instruments in order to finance long-term needs.

Most bonds are exchanged over-the-counter, like Treasury securities, by large investment banking firms on behalf of institutional investors. A limited amount of small-lot trading is conducted on the New York Stock Exchange by brokerage firms for individual investors. If you wish to track a corporate bond that is listed on the New York Stock Exchange, you will find it in *The Wall Street Journal* under **New York Exchange Bonds**. Consult the front page of the first or last section for the daily listing. An example from the Thursday, February 2, 1995 issue appears on pages 256–258. (American Stock Exchange Bonds appear under **Amex Bonds** on page 259.)

NEW YORK EXCHANGE BONDS

Quotations as of 4 p.m. Eastern Time
Wednesday, February 1, 1995

Volume $31,385,000

	Domestic Wed.	Domestic Tue.	All Issues Wed.	All Issues Tue.
Issues traded	391	345	399	354
Advances	185	195	187	202
Declines	123	77	127	77
Unchanged	83	73	85	75
New highs	8	7	8	7
New lows	7	4	7	4

SALES SINCE JANUARY 1
(000 omitted)

1995	1994	1993
$612,599	$759,335	$1,024,444

Dow Jones Bond Averages

−1994− High	−1994− Low	−1995− High	−1995− Low		−−−1995−−− Close	−−−1995−−− Chg.	−−−1995−−− %Yld	−−1994−− Close	−−1994−− Chg.
105.61	93.56	95.06	93.63	20 Bonds	95.06	+0.39	8.02	105.32	−0.06
103.43	88.99	90.23	89.08	10 Utilities	90.23	+0.52	8.50	103.30	−0.03
107.93	97.93	99.96	98.08	10 Industrials	99.89	+0.26	7.55	107.34	−0.10

CORPORATION BONDS
Volume, $30,844,000

AT&T ➔

Bonds	Cur Yld	Vol	Close	Net Chg.
AMR 9s16	9.4	41	95¼	...
AMR 6⅛24	cv	16	86	− ½
ATT 7½06	7.8	75	95⅞	...
ATT 8.35s25	8.5	63	98½	− ⅜
ATT 4⅜96	4.6	50	95⅝	+ ½
ATT 4⅜99	5.0	8	88¼	+ ¼
ATT 6s00	6.5	204	91⅝	...
ATT 5⅛01	5.9	39	86¼	+ ⅜
ATT 8⅝31	8.6	50	100	− ¼
ATT 7⅛02	7.5	339	95½	− ⅛
ATT 8⅛22	8.4	143	97¼	+ ⅜
ATT 8⅛24	8.4	31	97⅛	+ ⅛
ATT 4½96	4.6	20	97½	− ⅛
ATT 6¾04	7.3	118	91⅞	− ¼
Actava 9½98	10.3	27	91⅞	− ⅛
Actava 10s99	10.7	1	93½	− 2½
Advst 9s08	cv	30	89¼	...
AirbF 6¾01	cv	21	94½	...
AlskAr zr06	...	51	43½	+ ½
AlbnyInt 5s02	cv	18	86¼	− ¼
AlldC zr2000	...	123	64½	+ 1⅛
AlldC zr97	...	35	82	...
AlldC zr09	...	15	30¾	− ⅜
AlegCp 6½14	cv	10	93	+ 1
Allwst 7¼14	cv	26	85½	+ 1
AForP 5s30	9.2	1	54⅝	+ ⅜
AmBrnd 9⅛16	8.9	10	103	− ½
AmBrnd 8½03	8.3	5	103	+ 2¼
AmBrnd 8⅝21	8.7	36	99⅜	+ ¼
AmHme 6⅞97	7.0	12	98⅛	+ ⅛
AMedia 11⅝04	11.2	100	103½	+ ¼
Amoco 8⅝16	8.3	10	103⅝	+ ½
Amsco 2002	cv	25	83¼	+ ¾
Ancp 13⅞02f	cv	7	100	...
Arml 11⅜99	11.3	10	100¾	− ¼
Arrow 5¾02	cv	55	118	+ 2
Arvin 7½14	cv	25	99¼	− ¼
Ashlnd 6¾14	cv	21	91	+ ½
ARich 5⅝97	5.9	5	95	− 1⅝
AutDt zr12	...	1	42	− ½
Avnet 6s12	cv	10	101½	...
BPAmer 7⅞02	7.9	15	99⅜	+ ⅜
BkrHgh zr03	...	1	54	...
BkNY 7½01	cv	21	154	− ½
Barnet 8½07	8.5	30	100½	+ ½
BellPa 7⅛12	8.1	10	88½	+ ¼
BellsoT 8¼32	8.5	107	97	+ ½
BellsoT 7⅞32	8.5	95	92⅝	...
BellsoT 6½00	6.8	30	95	+ ⅝
BellsoT 6¼03	7.0	84	89⅞	+ ½
BellsoT 6¾33	8.3	10	81⅜	+ ⅝
BstBuy 8⅝00	9.4	280	92⅛	− ½
BethSt 9s00	9.0	18	100¼	...
BethSt 8.45s05	9.2	10	91⅝	− ⅛
BethSt 8⅜01	8.9	2	94	+ ½
Bevrly 7⅝03	cv	36	97	...
BoisC 7s16	cv	20	89½	...
Bordn 8⅜16	9.7	60	86	+ ¾
BorgWS 9⅛03	11.4	12	79⅞	+ ¼
BwnFer 6¼12	cv	197	96½	...
BurN 8.15s20P	8.9	3	92	...
BurNo 3.20s45	8.1	35	39½	+ 1
CIGNA 8.2s10	cv	46	105	...
CarnCp 4½97	cv	7	125⅛	...
CaroFrt 6¼11	cv	10	67¼	+ ¼
Caterplnc 6s07	7.3	5	82	+ 1⅞
Caterplnc 9¾19	9.3	32	105⅛	− 1⅞
Caterplnc 9⅛96	8.8	40	103½	+ 1½
Champ 6½11	cv	15	114¾	+ 2¾
ChsCp 8s99	8.0	126	99⅝	...
ChsCp 8s04	8.3	25	96⅜	− ⅝
ChsCp 7⅞04	8.3	40	94½	...
CPoV 7¼12	8.3	5	87¾	− 1¾
CPoWas 7¾	8.5	35	91½	+ ¾
Chvrn 9⅜16	8.9	14	105⅛	...
Chiquta 10½04	10.4	109	100⅞	− ⅛
ChckFul 7s12	cv	4	80½	...
ChryF 13¼99	10.9	3	121¼	...
ChryF 12¾99	10.8	10	117⅝	+ ¾
ChryF 6⅝00	7.1	3	94	+ 1¼
Chryslr 13cld	...	50	100 9/32	...
Chryslr 10.95s17	10.0	8	109	− ½
Chryslr 10.4s99	9.8	8	105¾	+ ⅛
Clardge 11¾02	17.4	60	67½	...
ClrkOil 9½04	9.8	25	96¾	...
ClevEl 8¾05	9.6	47	91½	− ⅜
ClevEl 8⅜11	9.9	9	84⅞	+ ⅝
ClevEl 8⅜12	10.0	64	84	+ ¼
Coeur 7s02	cv	36	110	+ 3½
Coeur 6⅜04	...	12	80¼	+ 1¼
ColeWld zr13	...	71	26½	− ½
vjColuG 9s94f	...	7	121	+ ¼
vjColuG 8¾s95f	...	24	120¼	− ½
vjColuG 8⅜s96f	...	3	119⅛	+ ⅛
vjColuG 7½97M f	...	15	116	+ 1
vjColuG 7½97O f	...	28	115	+ 1⅛
vjColuG 9⅞99f	...	14	124	+ 3¼
vjColuG 9⅛96f	...	20	121	+ 3
vjColuG 9s93f	...	43	123	+ 4⅛
vjColuG 10¼11f	...	9	130	+ 1
vjColuG 10½12f	...	10	128⅛	+ ½
CmwE 8s03	8.2	11	97	+ ¼
CmwE 8⅛07J	8.7	41	93⅞	+ ½
CmwE 8⅛07D	8.6	78	94⅛	+ ⅝
CmwE 8¼07	8.7	15	94⅞	+ ⅜
CompUSA 9½00	10.8	1188	87¾	+ ¾
ConrPer 6¾01	cv	13	74¼	+ ½
ConrPer 6½02	cv	40	73½	...
Consec 8⅛03	9.0	10	90	+ 1
ConNG 7¼15	cv	61	97¾	+ ½
CnPw 5⅞96	6.0	5	97⅞	+ 1½
CnPw 6⅞98	7.2	10	95⅛	− ½
Cooptn 7.05s15	cv	60	99½	+ ½
DataGn 01	cv	6	83	− 1
Datpnt 8⅞06	cv	11	27¾	+ ½
Dole 6¾00	7.3	15	92	+ ⅞
Dow 6.85s13	8.3	17	83	...
duPnt dc6s01	6.7	109	89¾	− ⅛
EMC 4¼01	cv	18	103	− 6
Eckerd 9¼04	9.5	121	97⅞	...
ElanInt zr12	...	21	41	+ 1¼
Enron 10¾98	10.4	20	102⅞	− ⅛
viF&M 11½03f	...	221	15½	+ ⅛
FairCp 13⅛06	16.0	1	82¼	+ ¼
FedDS 10s01	9.9	36	101¼	...
FidNtl 09	...	20	34¼	+ ⅛
Fldcst 6s12	cv	68	73½	− 1½
FFnMgt 5s99	cv	35	106½	+ ½
FstRep 7¼02	cv	25	91	− 1
Florsh 12¾02	14.5	31	88	− 1
Frpt dc6.55s01	cv	2	90¼	...
FreptM zr06	...	51	36⅛	+ ⅜
FremntGn zr13	...	71	32¾	− ¼
GMA dc6s11	7.9	40	76¼	+ 1¼
GMA zr12	...	47	226¾	− ¼
GMA zr15	...	68	185	− ½
GMA 8¼16	8.8	211	94⅛	− ¼
GMA 8⅜97	8.3	80	101	...
GPA Del 8¾98	11.8	330	74	− 1
Ganett 5¼98	5.7	15	92⅝	...
GElCap 7⅞06	8.0	35	98¾	− ½
GHost 11½02	12.6	139	91½	− 2
GHost 8s02	cv	250	81½	...
GnInst 5s00	cv	25	125½	− 1½
Gene 10⅜03	13.9	55	74¾	− ⅝
Genrad 7¼11	cv	26	68	+ ¾
GaGlf 15s00	14.8	86	101⅝	...
GaPw 6⅞02	7.3	10	94	+ 1¼
GaPw 6⅛99	6.6	5	92¼	+ 1
Grancre 6½03	7.9	27	82½	+ ½
Hallb zr06	...	1	50½	+ ¼
Hallwd na13½09	...	25	37¾	− ¼
Hallwd 7s00	10.0	21	69⅞	− ⅝
Hawn 7⅝02	8.1	20	94⅝	− 1⅞
Hlthso 9½01	9.7	55	98	− ¼
Hilhvn 7¾02	4.8	15	160½	+ 1½
HomeDp 4½97	cv	28	122¼	+ ¼
HorMan 6½99	cv	5	93¼	...
HostM 10⅝00	10.6	216	100¼	− ½
HostM 9⅛00	9.4	22	97½	− ⅛
HostM 9⅞01	9.8	10	100¾	...
HostM 10⅞01	10.9	28	100¼	+ ¼
HostM 11¼05	11.2	36	100½	...
HostM 11s07	11.0	101	100	− ⅜
ICN Ph 8½99	cv	322	101	+ 2
ICN 12⅞98	12.5	282	102¾	+ ⅝
IMC Glb 6¼01	cv	39	92½	...
IllBel 7⅝06	7.9	11	96⅞	+ 1⅜
IntgHlt 6s03	cv	10	122	− 2
IBM 9s98	9.0	121	100½	...
IBM 8⅜19	8.5	292	98⅜	− ⅛
IBM 6⅜97	6.6	148	96⅝	− ¼
IBM 7¼02	7.6	82	95	+ ¼
IBM 6⅜00	6.9	162	92¾	− ¼
IBM 7½13	8.2	75	91¼	+ ¾
IntShip 9s03	9.8	65	92¼	− ¼
IntTch 9⅜96	9.7	10	97⅛	− ¼
Interpool 5¼18	...	3	75	...
JCP 6¾25	8.6	5	78¼	...
KaufB 9⅜03	10.6	310	88¾	+ ⅜
Kroger 9s99	9.0	74	100⅜	...
LehmnBr 8¾02	8.8	5	99⅜	+ ⅛
LehmnBr 10¾96	10.4	2	103¼	+ ⅜
Leucadia 10⅜02	9.9	15	105	+ ⅞
Leucadia 5¼03	...	1	96½	+ 1½
LibPrp 8s01	cv	93	100	+ ⅛
Lilly 8⅛01	8.0	10	101½	− ⅛
Litton 12⅝cld	...	23	105 9/32	− 3/32
LomasFn 9s03	cv	3	66	− 1
LglsLt 9⅝24	10.3	10	93¼	+ ¾
LglsLt 9¾21	10.4	10	94	− ¼
LglsLt 7.3s99	7.9	23	92¼	+ ⅜
LglsLt 8.9s19	10.7	26	83⅜	...
LslsLt 9s22	10.8	214	83½	...
LglsLt 7½07	9.4	30	80⅛	+ ⅝
LglsLt 7.05s03	8.5	9	82½	+ ¼
LglsLt 8.2s23	10.5	67	77¾	...
MACOM 9¼06	cv	5	93	− ¾
MGM Grd 11¾99	11.1	500	105⅞	...
MGM Grd 12s02	11.0	44	109	...
Magntx 8s01	cv	5	98	...
MarO 8½00	8.5	15	100	...
MarO 8.5s06	8.9	25	96	− ½
MarO 9¾99	9.5	67	102⅜	+ ¾
MarO 7s02	7.7	25	90½	+ ½
Masco 5¼12	cv	12	79¼	+ ¼
Mascotch 03	cv	138	68½	...
vjMcCro 7¾95f	...	13	7	+ 1

NASDAQ

Convertible Debentures

Wednesday, February 1, 1995

Issue	Vol.	Close	Net Chg.
Argosy 12s01	20	95	+ ½
BFrkRet cv03	22	81	+ 2½
Bindly 6½10	5	95½	− ½
BoxEngy 8¼02	22	99	+ 4¾
BuildT 8s05	5	87½	...
BuildT 6½11	10	72½	− 2½
Commnet 6¾09	85	100	+ 4
DrgEmp 7¾14	48	70	...
EagleH cv01	25	66½	...
Hechng 5½12	5	61	...
Intfce 8s13	10	100	+ 5½
Jacobsn 6¾11	22	71	− 1
MidlBk 8¼10	20	94¼	+ ¾
PrceCo 6¾01	23	92½	+ ½
RPM zr12	100	38¾	− ⅛
SCI Sy 5⅝12	10	98½	+ 2
Sanifil 7½06	28	101½	...
Synetic 7s01	100	108	+ ½
Trenwck 99	30	100⅛	+ 1⅛
VLSI 7s12	15	88	− 1½
WstwdOne 6¾11	10	66½	...

Bonds	Cur Yld	Vol	Close	Net Chg.
McDnl 9¾99	9.5	60	102⅞	– ⅛
McDnl 9⅜97	9.3	23	101¼	...
McDnl 7⅜02	7.6	22	97	+ ⅜
McDnlDg 8⅝97	8.5	20	101¼	– ⅜
McDnlDg 9¼02	9.0	70	103¼	– ¾
MichB 7¾11	8.2	4	95	– ¼
MichB 7s12	8.1	3	86¼	+ ¼
MPac 4¼05	5.8	12	73½	+ 3½
MPac 4¼05r	5.8	10	73½	+ 1
MPac 4¾20f	...	8	60	+ 1¼
MPac 4¾30f	...	19	56	– 2
MPac 5s45f	...	20	57	+ 1
Mobil 8s32	8.3	24	96	+ 2
Motrla zr09	...	8	108	– 3
Motrla zr13	...	46	73	+ 1
NJBTl 7¼11	8.1	5	89⅛	– ⅞
NRUt 9s16	9.1	25	99	...
Nabis 7¾s01	7.9	7	98	– ½
NtEdu 6½11	cv	25	54	+ 1
NETelTel 4⅝05	6.2	35	75	+ 1
NETelTel 8⅝01	8.3	20	103⅞	+ 1⅞
NYTel 4⅝02	5.7	4	80¾	+ 1½
NYTel 4⅝04	6.1	20	75⅝	...
NYTel 4⅞06	6.6	10	74¼	+ ⅛
NYTel 7½09	8.3	5	90¾	+ ⅛
NYTel 7⅜11	8.2	6	90	+ 1⅞
NYTel 7⅞17	8.5	8	92⅞	+ ⅝
NYTel 6½00	7.6	10	86	– 2¾
NYTel 5¼98	5.7	25	91⅝	+ ¼
NYTel 7¼24	8.4	15	85⅞	...
NYTel 6¼04	7.1	25	87½	+ ½
NoPac 3s47	4.6	24	65	– 12⅛
Novacr 5½2000	cv	129	80	+ ½
OcciP 10¾98	10.6	50	101	– ¾
OcciP 11⅛19	10.1	5	110	+ ⅛
OcciP 9⅝99	9.4	15	102¼	– ¼
OcciP 10⅛09	9.3	83	108¾	+ ⅜
OcciP 10⅛01	9.3	4	108⅝	+ ⅝
OffDep zr08	...	24	57	+ 1
OldRep 5¾02	cv	4	100	+ ½
Olsten 4⅞03	4.6	1	106½	– 2
Oryx 9¾98	9.8	4	99	...
Oryx 10⅜18	11.1	35	93⅝	– ⅜
OwnIll 10¼99	10.3	120	99⅝	+ ½
OwIll 11s03	10.5	15	104⅝	– ⅛
OwnIll 10s02	10.3	108	97¼	+ ⅛
OwnIll 9¾04	10.3	11	95	+ ¼
PhilEl 6⅛97	6.5	5	94¾	– ½
PhilEl 7¾23	8.7	5	88¾	– ¼
PacTT 7.8s07	8.1	50	95⅞	– ⅛
PacBell 7¼02	7.6	10	96	– ⅛
PacBell 7½33	8.5	15	88	+ ¾
PacBell 7⅛26	8.3	100	86¼	+ ⅛
PacBell 6⅝34	8.3	80	79⅞	– ⅛
PacSci 7¾03	cv	30	109	+ 6½
ParCm 7s03A	8.3	48	84⅛	– ⅜
ParCm 7s03B	8.3	22	84⅜	+ ¼
Pathmk zr03	...	133	51⅛	+ ⅛
Paten 8¼12	cv	5	76½	+ ¼
PaylCsh 9⅛03	10.1	15	90⅝	...
PennTr 9⅝05	10.8	70	89½	– ¼
Pennzl 6½03	5.8	30	112½	– 1½
PepBoys 4s99	cv	8	97	+ ½
Pepsic 7⅝98	7.7	65	99	– 1¼
PeryDr 8½cld	cv	85	100⅝	+ ⅜
Pier1 6⅞02	cv	13	98	+ 1¼
PionFn 8s00	cv	25	95½	...
PogoP 8s05	cv	48	98	...
PotEl 7s18	cv	13	88	+ 1

EXPLANATORY NOTES
(For New York and American Bonds)

Yield is Current yield.

cv-Convertible bond. cf-Certificates. cld-Called. dc-Deep discount. ec-European currency units. f-Dealt in flat. il-Italian lire. kd-Danish kroner. m-Matured bonds, negotiability impaired by maturity. na-No accrual. r-Registered. rp-Reduced principal. st, sd-Stamped. t-Floating rate. wd-When distributed. ww-With warrants. x-Ex interest. xw-Without warrants. zr-Zero coupon.

vi-In bankruptcy or receivership or being reorganized under the Bankruptcy Act, or securities assumed by such companies.

USAir

Bonds	Cur Yld	Vol	Close	Net Chg.
Primark 8¾00	9.3	90	94	+ ⅜
PSEG 8¾21	8.8	10	98⅞	...
PSEG 8¾22	8.8	10	99¾	+ ⅜
PSEG 8½22	8.7	3	98	+ 2½
PSEG 7½23	8.6	25	87¼	– ¾
PSEG 6s00	6.6	80	90¾	+ 1⅜
RJR Nb 8.3s99	8.4	170	98½	– ½
RJR Nb 8¾04	9.2	167	95¼	+ ½
RJR Nb 8⅝02	9.1	90	95⅛	– ⅜
RJR Nb 7⅝03	8.7	305	87⅝	– 1¼
RJR Nb 8s00	8.4	280	95¼	– ⅞
RJR Nb 8¾05	9.3	261	94	– ¼
RJR Nb 9¼13	10.0	1778	92¾	– ⅞
Rallys 9⅞00	20.3	138	48¾	+ 1⅛
RalsP 9s96	8.7	10	103	+ 1
RltyInco 01t	...	76	84⅛	+ 1⅛
RegHS 6½03	cv	125	116	+ 10
RelGrp 9s00	9.7	199	92⅜	...
RelGrp 9¾03	10.9	122	89¼	+ ¼
Revl 10⅞10	11.6	70	93⅞	+ 1¼
Revl 9½99	10.2	115	92¾	+ ⅛
Rexene 11¾04	11.4	22	102⅞	+ ½
RiteA zr06	cv	5	46¼	...
Rivrwdlnt 11¼02	10.9	25	103½	+ ½
Roadmst 8s03	cv	86	101	– 1½
RocInt 8⅞99	8.6	5	103⅝	+ 1⅛
Rohr 7s12	cv	8	72	...
Rowan 11⅞01	11.5	10	103¼	+ ⅝
Royce 5¾04	cv	31	93¾	...
Safwy 10s01	9.6	80	104⅛	– ½
Safwy 9.65s04	9.3	20	103¼	– ¼
Safwy 9.35s99	9.2	181	101½	– 1½
Safwy 9⅞07	9.6	15	102¾	– ¼
SallM zr14	...	90	18⅜	+ 1/16
Seagte 6¾12	cv	49	88	+ 2⅛
Sears 9½99	9.0	94	105⅛	...
Sequa 9⅝99	10.1	50	95	...
Sequa 9⅜03	10.8	20	87	...
SvcMer 9s04	11.2	1157	80⅜	+ ½
ShellO 7¼02	7.6	13	94⅞	– 2⅞
Showboat 9¼08	10.8	220	85¾	+ ⅛
Snyder 7s01	cv	28	88	...
SoCnBel 7⅜12	8.1	5	91¼	+ 1¼
SoCnBel 8½29	8.7	46	97¼	– ¾
SouBell 6s04	6.9	10	87	+ 1¼
SouBell 7⅝13	8.4	24	91	– ½
SouBell 8⅛17	8.4	105	96½	+ ½
SouBell 8⅝26	8.8	121	98½	– ½
SouBell 8¾24	8.7	30	100¼	+ 1¼
SouBell 8½29	8.7	35	97¾	+ ⅛
SoCG 6⅞02	7.5	25	92¼	+ ¼
StdCmcl 07	cv	1	69¼	...
StdPac 10½00	10.6	59	99⅛	+ ⅝
StoneC 11½99	11.4	124	100¾	– ¼
StoneCn 11⅞98	11.4	130	104	...
StoneCn 6¾07	cv	50	80	+ ½
StoneC 10¾02A	11.2	282	96⅛	+ ⅛
StoneC 10¾97	10.6	48	101¾	+ ⅜
StoneCn 11s99	11.2	116	98½	...
StoneC 9⅞01	10.5	84	94	...
StoneC 10¾02O	10.8	55	99½	– ⅛
StrTch 8s15	cv	160	88¾	+ ¼
SunCo 7.95s01	8.1	10	98½	+ 1
SwBell 6⅛00	6.7	25	92	– ⅛
Teledy 10s04A	10.1	53	98¾	– ¼
Teledy 10s04C	10.1	302	98¾	...
Tesor dc12¾01	12.7	35	100⅛	– ⅛
TexEst 10⅛11	10.1	30	100	– 2½
Texfi 8¾99	12.0	5	73	– 3
TmeWar 8¾17	10.0	175	87¾	– ¾
TmeWar zr02	...	807	95¼	...
TmeWar 7.45s98	7.7	267	96¾	– ⅛
TmeWar 9⅛13	10.1	283	90⅝	– ¼
TmeWar 7.95s00	8.4	168	95	– ¼
TmeWar 9.15s23	10.3	172	89¼	...
TmeWar 8¾15	cv	882	96⅜	– ⅛
TmeWar zr13	...	295	36⅝	...
TitanWh 4¾01	cv	11	105	...
TolEd 7½02	8.9	10	84¼	+ 1
TolEd 8s03	9.2	31	87⅛	+ ¾
Toll 9½03	10.5	119	90⅝	+ 1
TollCp 4¾04	cv	2	71¼	+ ¼
Trvlr 7⅝97	7.6	5	100¼	+ 1⅛
TucEP 8⅛01	8.7	10	92⅞	+ 2⅞
TucEP 7.55s02	8.5	10	89	+ 1
TucEP 7.65s03	8.6	6	88⅞	+ 1⅜
Tyco 10⅛02	13.5	1541	75¼	...
US West zr11	...	1	31	...
USAir 12⅞00	13.7	247	94	+ ⅛
USLICO 8s11	cv	10	99½	+ ½

Bonds	Cur Yld	Vol	Close	Net Chg.
USX 4⅝96	4.8	7	97 1/16	+ 1/16
USX 5¾01	cv	91	82	+ ½
USX 7s17	cv	26	81¾	...
USX zr05	cv	1	44½	...
Unisys 8¼00	cv	101	103¾	+ ¼
UtdAir 10.67s04	10.2	20	104⅜	+ ¾
Valhi zr07	...	90	31⅝	– ⅜
Vencor 6s02	cv	1	118	– 1½
WhlPit 9⅜03	10.7	1020	88	– ½
WMS 5¾02	cv	74	85½	...
WMX dc2s05	cv	478	81¼	– ½
WasteM zr12	...	29	35½	...
Waban 6½02	cv	10	92	+ 1
Watrhse 6s03	cv	13	73	+ ½
Webb 10⅞00	11.0	134	98¾	+ ¼
Webb 9¾03	11.3	147	86½	– ½
Webb 9s06	11.5	30	78½	– ¾
Wendys 7s06	cv	24	137	– ½
WstCNA 7¼15	cv	10	104½	+ ¼
WstDig 9s14	cv	51	114½	+ 2
WisBl 7¼07	7.8	11	92⅜	– 1⅛
Zapt 10⅞01f	...	4	95⅛	– 1⅝
Zapt 10¼97f	...	4	100	...
Zenith 6¼11	cv	68	66½	+ ⅝

FOREIGN BONDS
Volume, $541,000

Bonds	Cur Yld	Vol	Close	Net Chg.
AmocoCda 7⅜13	6.6	190	112¼	– 1¾
CdnPc4s perp	8.5	1	47⅛	...
Inco 7¾16	7.9	10	97½	– 1½
SeaCnt 12½04A	11.9	15	105	...
SeaCnt 9½03	10.4	30	91½	– ½
EmplCA 5s04	...	84	45½	– ½
CGDina 8s04	18.4	65	43½	+ 1½
TelArg 11⅞04	13.2	125	89¾	+ ¼

AMEX BONDS

Volume $2,762,000

SALES SINCE JANUARY 1

1995	1994	1993
$69,191,000	$75,143,000	$75,760,000

	Wed.	Tue.	Mon.	Fri.
Issues traded	30	34	31	34
Advances	10	13	7	22
Declines	11	13	15	6
Unchanged	9	8	9	6
New highs	1	0	1	1
New lows	0	2	3	0

Bonds	Cur Yld	Vol	Close	Net Chg
AirExp 6s03	cv	30	99½	+ ½
AHaagn 7½01	8.5	5	88¾	...
AFtMtg 10½02	15.4	27	68	+ 8
Atari 5¼02	cv	100	50¾	...
CII Fn 7½01	cv	76	68	– 1
CVD Fn 9¼08t	19.7	90	47	– 3
ChckFul 8s06	cv	16	89	+ 1
DrPep11½02f	...	385	83	...
FruitL 7s11	8.5	10	82	...
Greyhnd 10s01f	...	95	66	– 1
Greyhnd 8½07f	cv	3	55	+ 2½
KelleyOG 8½00	cv	33	81½	+ 2
MacNS 7⅞04	cv	18	89	...
Maxam 12½99	11.9	6	101⅝	– ⅜
PlainRs 12s99	12.2	35	98	...
RstIntl 11s03	14.5	41	76	...
RstIntl 11⅜04	16.8	7	67¾	– 1¼
Sage 8½05	cv	10	78½	– 1½
SwBell 6⅞11	8.0	38	86¼	+ ⅜
SwBell 7¾09	8.2	45	94	+ ½
SwBell 8¼14	8.5	65	97	...
SwBell 8¼17	8.5	20	97¼	+ ¾
TmeWar 12	...	12	31	– ¼
TWA 10s98f	...	165	62½	...
TWA 8s00f	...	496	21½	+ ½
TTai un 11.35s99f	...	72	69½	+ ⅛
Trump 11¾03	19.4	288	60½	– 1⅛
Viacom 10¼01	9.9	107	104	– ¼
Viacm 9⅛99	9.1	205	100	– 1
Viacom 8s06	9.2	243	86¾	– ½

Source: *The Wall Street Journal*, February 2, 1995. Reprinted by permission of *The Wall Street Journal*, ©1995 Dow Jones & Company, Inc. All rights reserved worldwide.

ATT 8⅛22	8.4	143	97¼	+	⅜
ATT 8⅛24	8.4	31	97⅛	+	⅛
ATT 4½96	4.6	20	97½	–	⅛
ATT 6¾04	7.3	118	91⅞	–	¼
Actava 9½98	10.3	27	91⅞	–	⅛
Actava 10s99	10.7	1	93½	–	2½
Advst 9s08	cv	30	89¼		...
AirbF 6¾01	cv	21	94½		...

On 2/1/95 the AT&T Bond that will mature in 2004 was worth $918.75 and paid a $67.50 annual coupon interest rate for a yield of 7.3%

TucEP 8⅛01	8.7	10	92⅞	+	2⅞
TucEP 7.55s02	8.5	10	89	+	1
TucEP 7.65s03	8.6	6	88⅞	+	1⅜
Tyco 10⅛02	13.5	1541	75¼		...
US West zr11	...	1	31		...
USAir 12⅞00	13.7	247	94	+	⅛
USLICO 8s11	cv	10	99½	+	½

On 2/1/95 the USAir Bond that will mature in 2000 was worth $940.00 and paid a $128.75 annual coupon interest rate for a yield of 13.7%

Source: *The Wall Street Journal*, February 2, 1995. Reprinted by permission of *The Wall Street Journal*, ©1995 Dow Jones & Company, Inc. All rights reserved worldwide.

The top portion of the New York Exchange Bonds quotations provides important information about the previous trading day. **Volume** is the par value of bonds traded on Wednesday, February 1, 1995: $31,385,000. **Issues traded** lists the number of different bonds sold on that day. **Advances** is the number of bonds that traded at a price higher than the previous day; **Declines** is the number that traded at a price below the previous trading day's, and **Unchanged** is the number of bonds whose price did not change. **New highs** lists the number trading at all-time highs. **Dow Jones Bond Averages** is a straight arithmetic summary and average of 20 selected utility and industrial bonds.

If you wish to follow the performance of a particular bond, consider the following illustration from the Thursday, February 2, 1995 edition.

Bonds	*Cur. Yld.-*	*Vol.*	*Close*	*Net Chg.*
AT&T 6¾ 04	7.3	118	91⅞	–¼
USAir 12⅞ 00	13.7	247	94	+⅛

You will find a key to all footnotes under **Explanatory Notes** at the bottom of the listing.

In the case of the AT&T bond shown above, the coupon rate at issue per $1,000 bond (6¾ or 6.75 percent) and the year of maturity (2004, the year the bond is due for redemption) follows the company's name. (You'll find an "s" after the interest rate when a fraction is absent.)

AMEX BONDS

Volume $2,762,000

SALES SINCE JANUARY 1		
1995	1994	1993
$69,191,000	$75,143,000	$75,760,000

	Wed.	Tue.	Mon.	Fri.
Issues traded	30	34	31	34
Advances	10	13	7	22
Declines	11	13	15	6
Unchanged	9	8	9	6
New highs	1	0	1	1
New lows	0	2	3	0

Bonds	Cur Yld	Vol	Close	Net Chg.
AirExp 6s03	cv	30	99½	+ ½
AHaagn 7½01	8.5	5	88¾	...
AFtMtg 10½02	15.4	27	68	+ 8
Atari 5¼02	cv	100	50¾	...
CII Fn 7½01	cv	76	68	− 1
CVD Fn 9¼08t	19.7	90	47	− 3
ChckFul 8s06	cv	16	89	+ 1
DrPep11½02f	...	385	83	...
FruitL 7s11	8.5	10	82	...
Greyhnd 10s01f	...	95	66	− 1
Greyhnd 8½07f	cv	3	55	+ 2½
KelleyOG 8½00	cv	33	81½	+ 2
MacNS 7⅞04	cv	18	89	...
Maxam 12½99	11.9	6	101⅝	− ⅜
PlainRs 12s99	12.2	35	98	...
RstIntl 11s03	14.5	41	76	...
RstIntl 11⅜04	16.8	7	67¾	− 1¼
Sage 8½05	cv	10	78½	− 1½
SwBell 6⅞11	8.0	38	86¼	+ ⅜
SwBell 7¾09	8.2	45	94	+ ½
SwBell 8¼14	8.5	65	97	...
SwBell 8¼17	8.5	20	97¼	+ ¾
TmeWar 12	...	12	31	− ¼
TWA 10s98f	...	165	62½	...
TWA 8s00f	...	496	21½	+ ½
TTai un 11.35s99f	...	72	69½	+ ⅛
Trump 11¾03	19.4	288	60½	− 1⅛
Viacom 10¼01	9.9	107	104	− ¼
Viacm 9⅛99	9.1	205	100	− 1
Viacom 8s06	9.2	243	86¾	− ½

Source: *The Wall Street Journal*, February 2, 1995. Reprinted by permission of *The Wall Street Journal*, ©1995 Dow Jones & Company, Inc. All rights reserved worldwide.

Corporate bonds are issued in denominations of $1,000, and this particular AT&T bond originally paid an annual fixed-dollar interest return of $67.50 (6.75 percent of $1,000 = $67.50). Thus, AT&T promised to pay the bearer $67.50 a year until it redeemed the bond at maturity.

You can see from the next column that the current yield is 7.3 percent. Volume is reported in thousands of dollars: 118 bonds with a face value of $1,000 were traded on February 1, 1995. The closing price for the day follows. Since bonds are issued in denominations of $1,000, the reported prices are a percentage of the face value of $1,000. Thus, 91⅞ means this bond traded at a price of $918.75 (91.875 percent of $1,000 = $918.75) at the day's close. The last column informs you that the February 1 closing price was ¼ ($2.50 = ¼% of $1,000) lower than the previous close.

Now, if you bought this bond on February 1, 1995, your yield would be 7.3 percent, slightly *more* than the coupon rate of 6¾ (6.75) percent, because on February 1 the bond had a value of $918.75, *less* than its par value of $1,000. An annual payment of $67.50 on an investment of $918.75 provides a higher yield than a payment of $67.50 on an investment of $1,000.

If the current yield on securities of similar risk and maturity as the AT&T bond rises above the coupon rate of 6¾ percent (as they have here), an investor will pay less than the par value for the bond. When commentators speak of the bond market rising and falling, they mean the *price* of the bond, not the *interest rate*. Bondholders want interest rates to fall so that the value of their bonds will rise. You can see that the AT&T bond went from $1,000 to $918.75 as its yield rose from 6¾ percent to 7.3 percent.

Investor's Tip

- Rising inflation, or fear of inflation, which drives interest rates up, hurts corporate bonds as well as Treasuries. Bond prices fall as interest rates rise.

You may have noticed that some of these bonds carry a "cv" notation in the *current yield* column. These bonds can be converted to a designated amount of common stock at the discretion of the bond holder, who will ordinarily make the conversion when the stock rises above a certain level. Because of this added feature, convertible bonds trade at a higher price and lower yield than bonds of comparable maturity and credit-worthiness. They are attractive to investors who are drawn to a company's stock but wish to earn interest while waiting to see whether the stock will appreciate.

Not only interest rates, but also the relative strength of the issuing company will affect the price of its bonds. AT&T is an investment of high quality because of its healthy financial condition and secure earnings potential. On the other hand, the USAir 12⅞ 00 bond (pages 257–258) carries a higher coupon payment *and* yield than AT&T, because USAir, a much weaker company in severe financial difficulty, had to pay a higher yield to attract investors' funds.

"Junk" bonds (like USAir) offer higher rates of interest because of their inherently risky nature. They are issued by companies that have high debt-to-equity ratios and high debt-to-cash flow ratios and must therefore pay high interest rates to attract investors' money. Any fluctuation in the business of the issuing corporation could affect the timely payment of interest and the repayment of principal on the bonds.

Junk, or high-yield bonds, have been around for a long time and should be distinguished from their well-heeled cousins, the investment-grade bonds issued by financially secure corporations. Interest in junk bonds, especially on the part of institutions such as insurance companies and savings and loan companies, grew in the early 1980s, when falling interest rates boosted the prices of all bonds. Investors used the proceeds from the sale of junk bonds to purchase the stock of corporations, particularly conglomerates, that had fallen on hard times. These new owners often hoped to service their junk-bond debt by selling off divisions of the company they had purchased. Sometimes the company was worth more dead than alive and was dismembered. Sometimes top management bought a company from stockholders (called "going private") and then shrank it down to a profitable base. Often, however, the highly-leveraged surviving company was burdened with a huge, high-yield debt. Many companies failed and defaulted on their bonds, so that by the end of the 1980s, and especially during the 1990–91 recession, junk bonds fell out of favor and their prices sank and their yields soared. But the 1992 recovery and falling interest rates resuscitated many of these bonds, so that some investors realized strong capital gains as their prices soared. The example on page 262 serves as a case in point.

Junk bonds can bring substantial speculative rewards if a troubled company works its way out of difficulty and survives. Compare the USAir bond listing in the October 11, 1994 *Journal* (see the excerpt on page 262) with the February 2, 1995 listing on page 258. On October 10, 1994, the USAir 12⅞ 00 traded at $782.25 (78¼). By February 1, 1995, less than four months later, its value had increased by twenty percent to $940.

Every day the *Journal* publishes **High Yield Bonds** (see the January 27, 1995 example from the January 30, 1995 *Journal* on page 263) that summarizes activity in key junk bonds. You should note from the index values that in early 1995, all junk bonds had appreciated over the past four and a half years to 165.70 (July 1, 1990 = 100).

```
TmeWar zr13      ...  101  36    +  ¼
TolEd 8s03       9.4   12  85    − 1¾
Toll 9½03       10.6  117  89⅝      ...
TollCp 4¾04       cv    5  75    −  ¾
Trnstex 10½00   10.6   35  98⅞   +  ⅜
TucEP 8⅛01       8.7   10  93    +  1
USAir 12⅞00     16.5  190  78¼   + 1⅛
USX 5¾01          cv  101  84    −  ¼
USX zr05          cv    6  43⅞      ...
Unisys 8¼00       cv    1  120   +  1
UtdAir 10.67s04 10.5   20  101⅞     ...
```

◄— On October 10, 1994, USAir 12⅞ 00 bond traded at $782.25 for a yield of 16.5%

Source: *The Wall Street Journal*, October 11, 1994. Reprinted by permission of *The Wall Street Journal*, ©1994 Dow Jones & Company, Inc. All rights reserved worldwide.

The *Journal* can help you sort bonds according to credit-worthiness. Each day it publishes **Credit Ratings** (check the last section's index), summarizing the actions of Standard & Poor's and Moody's, the nation's major bond-rating services. (See the example from the January 30, 1995 *Journal* on page 264.) These services rate bonds according to the likelihood of payment of principal and interest. The rating services arrive at their decision by investigating the profitability and strength of the companies issuing the bonds. You will notice that different companies pay varying rates of interest on their debt according to the ratings they have received.

The table below summarizes the format used by the two major-rating services.

Bond Ratings

Moody's	Standard & Poor's	Rating
Aaa	AAA	
Aa	AA	Investment Grade
A	A	
Baa	BBB	
Ba	BB	
B	B	
Caa	CCC	Junk
Ca	CC	
C	C	

Junk bond index up 65.7% since July 1, 1990 ➤

HIGH-YIELD BONDS

Friday January 27, 1995

	Total Daily Return	Index Value	Average Price Change	Vol.
Flash Index	+ 0.07%	165.70	+ 0.04	M
Cash Pay	+ 0.06	167.32	+ 0.03	M
Deferred Int	− 0.08	157.19	− 0.05	M
Distressed	+ 0.40	117.96	+ 0.22	M
Bankrupt	+ 0.05	144.00	unch	M

Volume Key: H = Heavy, M = Moderate, L = Light
The Flash Index comprises more than 650 issues.
July 1, 1990 = 100

Key Gainers

	Type/Coup.	Mat.	3:00P.M. Bid Price	Price Change	Principal Return	Yld.-y
Nextel	g/ 0.000	8/04	34 1/2	+ 3/4	+ 2.22	18.53
SvcMerch	c/ 9.000	12/04	78	+ 1 1/2	+ 1.93	13.02
NL Ind	g/ 0.000	10/05	62	+ 1/2	+ 0.81	13.15
OwensIll	b/11.000	12/03	104 1/2	+ 3/4	+ 0.71	10.07
Hollywood	d/14.000	4/98	101	+ 1/2	+ 0.49	13.60

Key Losers

Grand Union	c/12.250	7/02	34	− 1/2	− 1.43	z
Ralphs	c/ 9.000	4/03	95 1/4	− 3/4	− 0.76	9.86

Name	Type/Rating	Coup.	Mat.	3 PM Bid	Net Chg.	Yld.-y
Aramark	a /BB+	8.500	6/03	91 1/2	unch	10.03
AdelphComm	b /B	11.875	9/04	88	unch	14.19
Amer Stand	c /B	9.875	6/01	97 3/4	unch	10.36
BethSteel	b /B+	10.375	9/03	98 3/4	unch	10.60
Comcast	c /B+	10.625	7/12	97 3/4	unch	10.91
ContCablevsn	b /BB	9.500	8/13	91	unch	10.62
ContainerCrp	b /B+	9.750	4/03	95	unch	10.68
Flagstar	b /B	10.750	9/01	92	unch	12.56
Grand Union	b /D	11.250	7/00	98 1/2	+ 1/2	z
Healthtrust	a /B	8.750	3/05	97	unch	9.21
InlandSteel	b /B+	12.750	12/02	107 1/4	unch	10.79
Kaiser Alum	b /B+	9.875	2/02	93 1/2	unch	11.23
KaufmanBrd	c /BB-	9.375	5/03	87	unch	11.88
Kroger	d /BB	8.500	6/03	95 1/2	unch	9.28
MFS Comm	e /B	0.000	1/04	61 3/8	unch	11.03
MGM Grand	d /BB-	11.750	5/99	105 3/4	unch	9.63
Maxus Energy	b /BB-	9.375	11/03	86 1/2	− 1/2	11.89
Nextel Comm	e /CCC·	0.000	9/03	37	+ 1/2	20.14
OrNda	c /B-	12.250	5/02	106 1/2	unch	10.60
OwensIll	b /B-	11.000	12/03	104 1/2	+ 3/4	10.07
Revlon	c /B-	10.500	2/03	88 1/2	unch	12.83
Safeway	d /BB-	9.650	1/04	101 1/2	unch	9.40
SouthPacRail	b /BB-	9.375	8/05	96	unch	10.00
StoneCont	c /B-	10.750	4/02	95 1/4	unch	11.74
TreasureIsl	d /BBB	9.875	10/00	104 1/2	unch	8.56
UnirovalChem	f /B+	9.000	9/00	93 1/2	unch	10.57
Unisys	b /BB-	10.625	10/99	100 3/4	unch	10.36
WeirtonStl	b /B	11.500	3/98	100 1/4	unch	11.39

Volume indicators are based solely on the traders' subjective judgment given the relative level of inquiry and trading activity on any given day.

Bid Prices are indicative only and may not represent actual bids by a dealer.

Price quotes follow accrued interest conventions.

a–Subordinated. b-Senior. c-Senior Sub. d-Secured. e-Senior, Zero To Full. f-Senior, Var Rt. g-Secured, Zero To Full. y-yield is the lower of yield to maturity and yield to call. z-omitted for reset or bankrupt bonds, negative yields, or yields above 35%.

Source: Salomon Brothers

Source: *The Wall Street Journal*, January 30, 1995. Reprinted by permission of *The Wall Street Journal*, ©1995 Dow Jones & Company, Inc. All rights reserved worldwide.

CREDIT RATINGS

CONTINENTAL AIRLINES (Houston) — Standard & Poor's Ratings Group said it placed its single-B-minus preliminary senior debt rating of Continental Airlines' $1 billion Rule 415 shelf registration, filed June 4, on CreditWatch with negative implications. The ratings agency said the move is based on serious operational and financial problems the airline has experienced in implementing its "Lite" service, leading to about a $400 million fourth-quarter charge, and its suspension of some rentals pending negotiations to revise those aircraft leases. Continental declined to comment.

*   *   *

NUI Corp. (Bedminster, N.J.) — Moody's Investors Service Inc. said it lowered its ratings of the company's industrial revenue bonds to Baa-2 from Baa-1, and lowered the rating on its shelf registration for unsecured debt to (P)-Baa-2 from (P)-Baa-1. About $160 million of debt is affected. The rating service said the downgrade and outlook reflect the gas-distribution company's poor returns, and the expectation of little or no near-term improvement. The ratings also reflect NUI's high debt load and limited flexibility in reducing that debt. David Vincent, chief financial officer at NUI, said the previous ratings carried a negative outlook, which has now stabilized. "I'm pleased that Moody's has noted the company is not increasing its debt load, as we have cut the dividend and are reducing expenses," he said.

*   *   *

UPJOHN Co. (Kalamazoo, Mich.) — Moody's Investors Service Inc. said it is reviewing Upjohn's long-term debt rating. The review, which may include a downgrade, affects $650 million of industrial revenue bonds, medium-term notes and guaranteed amortizing notes. Moody's said Upjohn's Prime 1 rating for commercial paper isn't being reviewed. Moody's said the loss of market exclusivity for several top-selling pharmaceutical products has damaged the drug maker's financial performance. What's more, Moody's said it believes that "weak sales of pharmaceuticals may continue in view of Upjohn's mature product line and the fact that there appear to be no new compounds of significance that will be marketed in the intermediate term to take up the slack." Upjohn officials weren't available to comment.

*   *   *

HECHINGER Co. (Landover, Md.) — Moody's Investors Service Inc. confirmed its long-term ratings of this home-improvement store chain, saying it expects the home-center chain operator to show stronger earnings and cash flow over the next several years. Moody's earlier this month said it was considering a possible ratings downgrade following Hechinger's announcement of planned store closings and layoffs. At the time, Moody's said its review was prompted by "continuing competitive challenges" in the home-center industry. Moody's rates about $325 million of long-term debt, including the Baa3-rated senior debt of Hechinger.

Source: *The Wall Street Journal*, January 30, 1995. Reprinted by permission of *The Wall Street Journal*, ©1995 Dow Jones & Company, Inc. All rights reserved worldwide.

You can also follow **New Securities Issues** daily in the *Journal* (check the index in the first or last section). It lists all new corporate, municipal, government agency, and foreign bonds issued on the previous day and provides pertinent information regarding these securities, including their ratings. (See the excerpt from the January 31, 1995 *Journal* on page 265.)

Finally, Monday's **Securities Offering Calendar** (see the excerpt from the February 13, 1995 edition on page 266) provides information on the week's new issues (check the third section's index under New Offerings).

MUNICIPAL BONDS

You may wish to purchase municipal (state and local government) or tax-exempt bonds, as they are sometimes called, because earnings from these bonds are not subject to federal income tax and may not be subject to income tax in your state. These bonds were granted tax exemption in order to reduce the borrowing cost of the states, cities, and local districts that issue them. Investors purchase them knowing their return is not taxable, and they will therefore be satisfied with a yield below that of comparable federal or corporate bonds. State and local governments save billions in interest costs as a result of this indirect subsidy.

NEW SECURITIES ISSUES

The following were among yesterday's offerings and pric-
ings in U.S. and non-U.S. capital markets, with terms and
syndicate manager, as compiled by Dow Jones Capital Markets Report:

CORPORATE

Federal National Mortgage Association – $125 million of
medium-term notes due Feb. 6, 1997, priced at par to yield
7.37%, according to MCM CorporateWatch. The noncallable
issue was priced at a spread of 14 basis points above Treasurys
and will be sold through underwriters led by Morgan Stanley &
Co.

Merrill Lynch & Co. -- $150 million of notes due Feb. 9, 2000,
priced at par to yield 8.375%, according to MCM CorporateWatch. The noncallable issue was priced at a spread of 82
basis points above Treasurys. Rated single-A-1 by Moody's
Investors Service Inc. and single-A-plus by Standard & Poor's
Ratings Group, the issue will be sold through underwriters led
by Merrill Lynch & Co.

EUROBOND

General Electric Capital Corp. (U.S. parent) – £100 million
of 9% Eurobonds due Feb. 14, 2000, at issue price 101.795 via
Goldman Sachs International. Reoffered at 100.17 to yield
8.96%, a margin of 20 basis points above the comparable U.K.
gilt. The borrower's outstanding senior debt is rated triple-A
by Moody's and S&P. General Electric Capital Corp. is the
financing arm of **General Electric** Co. Fees 1.875.

Colonial Finance Ltd. (Australian parent) – $150 million of
step-up floating-rate Euronotes due February 2005 at issue and
fixed reoffer price par via Goldman Sachs International.
Bonds pay interest semiannually at the six-month London
Interbank Offered Rate plus 0.75 point for the first five years,
stepping up to Libor plus 1.75. Callable after three years at par
if financed out of the proceeds of an issue of capital securities.
Guarantor the Australian mutual-fund manager **Colonial Mutual Life Assurance Society** Ltd. Fees undisclosed.

Source: *The Wall Street Journal*, January 31, 1995. Reprinted by permission of *The Wall Street
Journal*, ©1995 Dow Jones & Company, Inc. All rights reserved worldwide.

Each Friday, the *Journal* publishes a **Municipal Bond Index** prepared
by Merrill Lynch (see the last section's index). The excerpt from the
January 27, 1995 *Journal* on page 267 serves as an example. In addition
to an overall index, this report presents the latest yield on a variety of
municipal bond categories.

Also, the *Journal* publishes a weekly listing of actively traded municipal bonds on Tuesday, under the heading **Weekly Tax-Exempts**. (See the
excerpt from the February 21, 1995 *Journal* on page 268.)

Before deciding on the purchase of a tax-exempt municipal bond, an
investor must weigh four considerations: the yield available on the municipal bond, the yield on a taxable bond with the same maturity, the
investor's tax bracket, and whether the bond is callable.

If, for example, you are in a 28 percent tax bracket, use the "equivalent
tax-exempt yield formula" to calculate your after-tax yield on a security
whose income is taxable. This will be the minimum yield a municipal
bond must pay you to be of equivalent value to the taxable bond.

SECURITIES OFFERING CALENDAR

The following U.S. Treasury, corporate and municipal offerings are tentatively scheduled for sale this week, according to Dow Jones Capital Markets Report and Dow Jones News Service:

TREASURY
Today
$27.6 billion of three- and six-month bills.
CORPORATE
One Day in the Week
Adco Technologies Inc. – initial 2 million shares, via Kemper Securities Inc.
American Home Products Corp. – $500 million each of five-year and 10-year debt, via Goldman Sachs & Co.
Aspen Technology Inc. – 1.075 million shares, via Montgomery Securities.
Asyst Technology Inc. – 1 million shares, via Needham & Co.
California Energy Co. – 16.67 million shares, via Alex. Brown & Sons Inc.
City of Barcelona – $200 million of 10-year debt, via Morgan Stanley.
Federal National Mortgage Association – $500 million of a 10-year global bond, via J.P. Morgan Securities & Morgan Stanley & Co.
Globalstar Telecommunications Ltd. – initial 10 million shares, via Lehman Brothers.
HCIA Inc. – initial 1.75 million shares , via Alex. Brown & Sons Inc.
Highwoods Properties Inc. – 4 million shares, via Merrill Lynch & Co.
Medisense Inc. – 5.32 million shares, via Smith Barney Inc.
National Medical Enterprises Inc. – $300 million of seven-year senior notes and $700 million of 10-year senior notes via Donaldson Lufkin & Jenrette.
Northwest Natural Gas Co. – 1 million shares, via Merrill Lynch & Co.
Oak Technology Inc. – initial 4.75 million million shares, via Hambrecht & Quist Inc.
Rockwell International Corp. – $300 million of three-year debt and $200 million of five-year debt, via Morgan Stanley & Co.
STB Systems Inc. – initial 1.75 million shares, via Rauscher Pierce Refsnes Inc.

Sunglass Hut International Inc. – 1.985 million shares, via Montgomery Securities.
U.S. Office Products Co. – initial 3.25 million shares, via Mabon Securities Corp.
Westbridge Capital Corp. – 2.5 million shares, via Chicago Corp.

MUNICIPAL
Today
Cedar Springs, Mich., School District – $27.5 million of improvement bonds, via competitive bid.
Tomorrow
Milwaukee – $92.3 million securities, via competitive bid.
Los Angeles Municipal Improvement Corp. – $31.5 million of sanitation equipment charge revenue bonds, via competitive bid.
Tualatin Hills, Ore., Park and Recreation District – $25.9 million of general obligation bonds, via competitive bid.
Wednesday
Rankin County, Miss., School – $34 million of general obligation bonds, via competitive bid.
Thursday
Louisiana – $200 million of general obligation bonds, via competitive bid.
Fresno, Calif. – $36.1 million of water system revenue bonds, via competitive bid.
One Day in the Week
New York State Thruway Authority – $335 million of revenue bonds, via a PaineWebber Inc. group.
Texas Public Finance Authority – $300 million refunding bonds, via a Grigsby Brandford & Co. group.
Westchester County, N.Y. – $75 million of tax anticipation notes, via a Chemical Securities Inc. group.
Ohio Housing Finance Agency – $70 million of housing bonds, via a Lehman Brothers group.
Ashland, Ky. – $55 million of revenue bonds, via a Goldman, Sachs & Co. group.
Massachusetts Health and Education Facilities Authority – $31.1 million series A bonds, via Goldman. Sachs & Co.
Idaho Housing Agency – $30 million of mortgage bonds, via a Goldman Sachs & Co. group.
Illinois Development Finance Authority – $27.9 million of revenue bonds, via an A.G Edwards & Sons Inc. group.
Brevard County, Fla., Housing Finance Agency – $27 million housing revenue bonds, via a William R Hough & Co. group.

Source: *The Wall Street Journal*, February 13, 1995. Reprinted by permission of *The Wall Street Journal*, ©1995 Dow Jones & Company, Inc. All rights reserved worldwide.

Here's an example using a 10 percent yield on the security whose interest is taxable.

$$
\begin{aligned}
\text{Equivalent tax-exempt yield} &= (1 - \text{Tax bracket}) \times \text{Taxable yield} \\
&= (1 - .28) \times .10 \\
&= .072 \\
&= 7.2 \text{ percent}
\end{aligned}
$$

Thus, in your 28 percent tax bracket, a 7.2 percent tax-exempt yield is the equivalent of a 10 percent taxable yield.

Therefore, if you had the opportunity, you would purchase an 8 percent tax-exempt bond rather than a 10 percent taxable bond with similar maturity and credit-worthiness.

Municipal Bond Index

Merrill Lynch 500

Week ended January 24, 1995

The following index is based on yields that about 500 major issuers, mainly of investment grade, would pay on new long-term tax-exempt securities. The securities are presumed to be issued at par; general obligation bonds have a 20-year maturity and revenue bonds a 30-year maturity. The index, prepared by Merrill Lynch, Pierce, Fenner & Smith Inc., is calculated using yields on major outstanding bonds in the market. Yields are obtained from an internal source.

—500 MUNICIPAL BOND INDEX—
6.56   0.02

— REVENUE BONDS—
Sub-Index   6.60   0.02

	1-24	Change In Week
—25-YEAR REVENUE BONDS—		
AAA-Guaranteed ...	6.44	0.02
Airport	7.00	0.02
Power	6.38	0.02
Hospital	6.47	0.02
Housing-		
Single Family	6.88	0.02
Housing-		
Multi Family	6.97	0.01
Miscellaneous	N/A	....
Pollution Control/		
Ind. Dev.	6.75	0.03
Transportation	6.59	0.02
Water	6.38	0.02
Advance Refunded .	5.93	0.03
—20-YEAR GENERAL OBLIGATIONS—		
Sub-Index 6.37 0.04		
Cities	6.60	0.02
Counties	6.45	0.04
States	6.10	0.04
Other Districts	N/A	....

The transportation category excludes airports; other districts include school and special districts.

WEEKLY TAX-EXEMPTS

Market quotations for some actively traded municipal issues. Yield is to maturity.

Issue	Coupon	Mat.	Bid	Ask	Yld.
Calif Rev Antcptn Wrnts C4	5.75	4/25/96	100¾	LOCK	4.97

Source: J.J. Kenny Drake Inc./McGraw-Hill Municipal Screen Service

Municipal bond buyers should always determine if the issuing agency can call (redeem) the bond before maturity. It may wish to do so when interest rates are low in order to issue new debt at lower rates. Meanwhile, the purchaser is forced to find another investment at a disadvantageous time. Therefore, an investor that plans to hold a bond until maturity should not purchase a bond that is callable before that date.

TRACKING THE BOND MARKET

It's now time to wrap up this discussion by detailing how you can use the *Journal* every day to follow the bond market. You should begin your daily analysis of bond market activity with a glance at the **Bonds** reports on the first page of the third section under **Markets Diary** (see the excerpt from the Monday, January 30, 1995 edition on page 269), which lists five important indexes that track bond market performance and provide current yields. The graph portrays the Lehman Brothers T-Bond Index, a composite index of Treasury securities' yield and price performance. The DJ 20 Bond Index provides the average price and yield of 10 public utility bonds and 10 industrial bonds. You became acquainted with it in the discussion of NYSE bonds. The Salomon mortgage-backed index covers mortgage-backed securities such as Ginnie Maes, Fannie Maes, and Freddie Macs. The Bond Buyer municipal index is compiled by *The Bond Buyer*, a publication that specializes in fixed-income securities, and covers AA-rated and A-rated municipal bonds. The Merrill Lynch corporate bond index, like the Dow index, is a corporate bond composite.

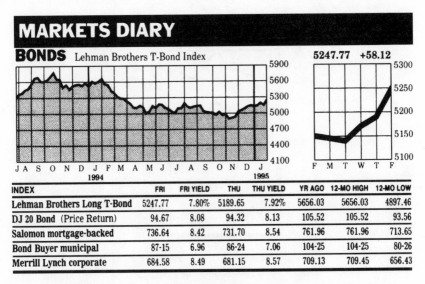

MARKETS DIARY

BONDS Lehman Brothers T-Bond Index

5247.77 +58.12

INDEX	FRI	FRI YIELD	THU	THU YIELD	YR AGO	12-MO HIGH	12-MO LOW
Lehman Brothers Long T-Bond	5247.77	7.80%	5189.65	7.92%	5656.03	5656.03	4897.46
DJ 20 Bond (Price Return)	94.67	8.08	94.32	8.13	105.52	105.52	93.56
Salomon mortgage-backed	736.64	8.42	731.70	8.54	761.96	761.96	713.65
Bond Buyer municipal	87-15	6.96	86-24	7.06	104-25	104-25	80-26
Merrill Lynch corporate	684.58	8.49	681.15	8.57	709.13	709.45	656.43

The **Bond Yields** chart appears in Monday's *Wall Street Journal* with the Credit Markets article, as shown in the sample on page 270 from the January 30, 1995 issue. It depicts three series: the top line portrays the yield paid by financially healthy public utilities on debt instruments maturing in 10 years or more, the second series depicts the yield on 15-year and longer Treasury bonds, and the bottom line shows municipal bond yields.

The *Journal* publishes its **Bond Market Data Bank** (find it in the front page index of the first and last sections) daily toward the center of Section C, as in the example from the Monday, January 30, 1995 issue on pages 271 and 272. The Data Bank thoroughly covers the bond market for the preceding trading day and contains more information than you may ever want to know.

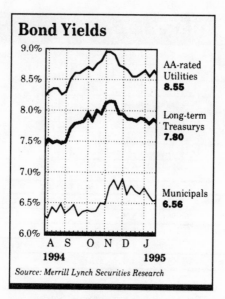

Bond Yields

Source: Merrill Lynch Securities Research

Finally, you can compare the yield on a variety of long-term instruments by using the **Yield Comparisons** table that appears daily with the **Credit Markets** article; also check the yield on the entire range of Treasury securities in the **Treasury Yield Curve** (see the excerpts from the January 30, 1995 issue on page 273). Notice the normal shape of the yield curve: Yields increase with length of maturity.

BOND MARKET DATA BANK 1/27/95

MAJOR INDEXES

HIGH	LOW (12 MOS)		CLOSE	NET CHG	% CHG	12-MO CHG	% CHG	FROM 12/31	% CHG
U.S. TREASURY SECURITIES (Lehman Brothers indexes)									
4158.35	3966.84	Intermediate	4093.64	+ 17.53	+ 0.43	− 64.71	− 1.56	+ 61.21	+ 1.52
5656.03	4897.46	Long-term	5247.77	+ 58.12	+ 1.12	− 408.26	− 7.22	+ 117.75	+ 2.30
1602.67	1307.21	Long-term(price)	1373.28	+ 14.94	+ 1.10	− 229.39	− 14.31	+ 22.47	+ 1.66
4500.55	4199.01	Composite	4358.62	+ 26.00	+ 0.60	− 141.93	− 3.15	+ 73.22	+ 1.71
U.S. CORPORATE DEBT ISSUES (Merrill Lynch)									
709.45	656.43	Corporate Master	684.58	+ 3.43	+ 0.50	− 24.55	− 3.46	+ 10.32	+ 1.53
518.52	487.79	1-10 Yr Maturities	508.36	+ 1.97	+ 0.39	− 10.03	− 1.93	+ 7.41	+ 1.48
544.83	490.84	10+ Yr Maturities	516.43	+ 3.51	+ 0.68	− 27.79	− 5.11	+ 8.74	+ 1.72
332.37	317.57	High Yield	324.96	+ 0.68	+ 0.21	− 5.79	− 1.75	+ 3.90	+ 1.21
520.54	477.83	Yankee Bonds	496.63	+ 2.51	+ 0.51	− 23.91	− 4.59	+ 6.63	+ 1.35
TAX-EXEMPT SECURITIES (Bond Buyer; Merrill Lynch: Dec. 31, 1986 = 100)									
104-25	80-26	Bond Buyer Municipal	87-15	+ ·23	+ 0.83	− 17-10	− 16.52	+ 2-6	+ 2.57
108.32	100.33	7-12 yr G.O.	104.58	+ 0.62	+ 0.60	− 3.50	− 3.24	+ 1.37	+ 1.33
109.89	97.44	12-22 yr G.O.	103.93	+ 0.77	+ 0.75	− 5.96	− 5.42	+ 2.65	+ 2.62
108.16	95.67	22+ yr Revenue	102.15	+ 0.90	+ 0.89	− 6.01	− 5.56	+ 3.41	+ 3.45
MORTGAGE-BACKED SECURITIES (current coupon; Merrill Lynch: Dec. 31, 1986 = 100)									
216.20	197.64	Ginnie Mae(GNMA)	208.00	+ 1.35	+ 0.65	− 8.20	− 3.79	+ 4.11	+ 2.02
214.73	197.82	Fannie Mae(FNMA)	207.71	+ 1.22	+ 0.59	− 7.02	− 3.27	+ 3.92	+ 1.92
130.84	120.58	Freddie Mac(FHLMC)	126.64	+ 0.74	+ 0.59	− 4.20	− 3.21	+ 2.31	+ 1.86
CONVERTIBLE BONDS (Merrill Lynch: Dec. 31, 1986 = 100)									
189.40	177.60	Investment Grade	188.76	+ 0.07	+ 0.04	+ 0.85	+ 0.45	+ 4.67	+ 2.54
210.43	188.27	High Yield	194.44	+ 0.01	+ 0.01	− 13.52	− 6.50	+ 3.90	+ 2.05

CORPORATE BONDS

Quotes of representative taxable issues at mid-afternoon New York time, provided by CS First Boston

ISSUE (RATING: MOODY'S/S&P)	COUPON	MATURITY	PRICE	CHANGE	YIELD	CHANGE
FINANCIAL						
Citicorp (A3/A−)	7.125	03/15/04	90.842	0.354	8.590	− 0.060
Chase Manhattan (Baa1/A−)	7.500	02/01/03	93.778	0.330	8.590	− 0.060
Ford Credit Co (A2/A)	6.250	02/26/98	95.270	0.316	8.010	− 0.120
GMAC (Baa1/BBB+)	7.000	03/01/00	94.282	0.239	8.400	− 0.060
UTILITY						
BellSouth Telecomm (Aaa/AAA)	6.500	02/01/00	94.179	0.434	7.930	− 0.110
Pacific G&E (A1/A)	7.250	03/01/26	84.963	1.017	8.650	− 0.110
So Calif Gas (A2/A+)	6.500	12/15/97	96.515	0.325	7.870	− 0.130
Phila Electric (Baa1/BBB+)	7.125	09/01/02	93.572	0.850	8.280	− 0.160
Pacific Bell (Aa3/AA−)	7.125	03/15/26	86.075	1.150	8.390	− 0.120
INDUSTRIAL						
Lockheed (Baa1/A−)	6.750	03/15/03	91.005	0.332	8.290	− 0.060
Amer Home Pdts (A2/A−)	7.250	03/01/23	87.176	1.049	8.450	− 0.111
USX (Baa3/BB+)	9.125	01/15/13	97.452	1.144	9.420	− 0.137
DuPont (Aa2/AA)	7.950	01/15/23	94.561	1.018	8.460	− 0.101
Philip Morris (A2/A)	7.125	12/01/99	95.032	0.229	8.390	− 0.060
FOREIGN						
Hanson Overseas (A1/A+)	7.375	01/15/03	94.570	0.333	8.320	− 0.060
Int Bk Recon Dev (Aaa/AAA)	7.625	01/19/23	94.453	0.728	8.130	− 0.070
Hydro-Quebec (A1/A+)	8.400	01/15/22	94.429	0.767	8.950	− 0.080
Ex-Im Bank of Korea (A1/A+)	6.500	05/15/00	91.710	0.282	8.470	− 0.070
KFW Intl Fin (Aaa/AAA)	7.000	03/01/13	87.838	0.589	8.310	− 0.070

TAX-EXEMPT BONDS

Representative prices for several active tax-exempt revenue and refunding bonds, based on institutional trades. Changes rounded to the nearest one-eighth. Yield is to maturity. n-New. Source: The Bond Buyer.

ISSUE	COUPON	MAT	PRICE	CHG	BID YLD	ISSUE	COUPON	MAT	PRICE	CHG	BID YLD
Anne Arundel Md Ser94	6.000	04-01-24	92⅝	+ 1⅛	6.56	NYC Indus Dev Agcy	6.000	01-01-15	88⅝	+ ¾	7.06
CA Pub Wrks Bd rev ser	7.000	03-01-19	100⅝	+ ⅝	6.95	NYC Indus Dev Agcy	6.125	01-01-24	87½	+ 1	7.14
Calif Health Fac	5.550	08-15-25	82½	+ ¾	6.93	NYC Lcl Govt Asst Cp	5.500	04-01-18	85¾	+ ⅞	6.71
Calif Pub Wrks 94a	7.000	11-01-19	100⅝	+ ½	6.95	Nys Energy Ser 94A	7.125	12-01-29	99¾	+ ¾	7.14
Chgo Ill Gen Arpt	6.375	01-01-15	98⅛	+ 1	6.54	NYS Envr Facs 94D	6.900	11-15-15	103½	+ ½	6.59
Clv Ohio pub pwr mtg	7.000	11-15-24	104	+ ¾	6.69	NYS Med Cr mtg 94 Se	6.800	08-15-24	101⅛	+ ½	6.71
Douglas Co SD RE-1	6.500	12-15-16	100¼	+ ¾	6.48	NYS Med Cr mtg 94 Se	6.900	08-15-34	101⅛	+ ½	6.82
Florida St Bd Ed	5.800	06-01-24	91⅛	+ ½	6.48	NYS Thruway Auth	6.000	04-01-14	92⅞	+ ¾	6.66
Florida St Bd Ed Ser9	6.100	06-01-24	96⅛	+ ⅞	6.39	Orange Co Fla	6.000	10-01-24	94½	+ ⅞	6.41
Ga Muni Elec Auth	6.500	01-01-26	99	+ 1	6.57	Penn Intergovt Auth	6.750	06-15-21	100¾	+ ¾	6.68
Harris Co Hlth Fac	6.375	10-01-24	96¼	+ ¾	6.66	Portland Ore 94 Ser A	6.250	06-01-15	97¾	+ ⅞	6.45
Hawaii Hsng Fin & Dev	6.000	07-01-26	86⅞	+ ⅜	7.08	PuertoRico pub im go 94	6.500	07-01-23	98¼	+ ¾	6.64
Ill Fin Auth Ser 94d	6.750	03-01-15	101	+ ½	6.66	S.F. Cal. Sewr Ref Rev	5.375	10-01-22	83¾	+ ¾	6.66
Ill Regional TA	6.250	06-01-24	94⅝	+ ⅞	6.66	Salam Co Poll Ctrl	6.250	06-01-31	94⅞	+ 1	6.62
Kansas City Util Sys	6.375	09-01-23	98⅝	+ ⅞	6.48	Salem Co Poll Ctrl	6.550	10-01-29	98⅞	+ ⅞	6.63
Lehigh Ind Dev Auth Pa	6.400	09-01-29	97¾	+ 1⅛	6.56	Santa Clara CA Fin	6.750	11-15-20	101¼	+ ¾	6.65
MTA NY Series O	6.375	07-01-20	98⅛	+ 1	6.53	Santa Clara Wtr Calif	6.000	02-01-24	92½	+ ⅞	6.58
N.J. Econ Dev Auth PCR	6.400	05-01-32	95⅛	+ 1	6.76	TBTA NY	5.000	01-01-24	78⅛	+ ⅝	6.71
NJ Econ Dv wtr facil	6.875	11-01-34	100⅛	+ 1	6.87	Texas GOs Ser 94A	7.000	12-01-25	99	+ ½	7.08
NYC G.O. 95 Series B	7.250	08-15-19	99¾	+ ½	7.28	Valdez Al Marine Term	5.650	12-01-28	83¼	+ 1⅛	6.94

(continued)

MORTGAGE-BACKED SECURITIES

Representative issues, quoted by Salomon Brothers Inc.

	REMAINING TERM (Years)	WTD-AVG LIFE (Years)	PRICE (FEB) (Pts.-32ds)	PRICE CHANGE (32ds)	CASH FLOW YIELD*	YIELD CHANGE (Basis pts.)
30-YEAR						
GNMA 6.0%	28.7	13.0	84-24	+ 36	8.21%	− 18
FHLMC Gold 6.0%	28.6	10.4	86-11	+ 28	8.32	− 16
FNMA 6.0%	28.0	10.3	86-07	+ 28	8.33	− 16
GNMA 7.0%	28.3	11.8	91-07	+ 28	8.41	− 15
FHLMC Gold 7.0%	28.3	9.9	92-09	+ 24	8.40	− 14
FNMA 7.0%	27.9	9.8	92-03	+ 24	8.41	− 14
GNMA 8.0%	27.9	10.5	97-02	+ 24	8.58	− 13
FHLMC Gold 8.0%	27.8	9.1	97-08	+ 20	8.58	− 12
FNMA 8.0%	27.8	9.1	97-04	+ 20	8.57	− 12
15-YEAR						
GNMA 6.0%	13.9	6.1	90-06	+ 16	8.29%	− 12
FHLMC Gold 6.0%	13.6	6.1	90-24	+ 16	8.13	− 12
FNMA 6.0%	13.7	6.2	90-16	+ 16	8.15	− 12

*Based on projections from Salomon's prepayment model, assuming interest rates remain unchanged from current levels

COLLATERALIZED MORTGAGE OBLIGATIONS

Spread of CMO yields above U.S. Treasury securities of comparable maturity, in basis points (100 basis points = 1 percentage point of interest)

MAT	SPREAD	CHG FROM PREV DAY
SEQUENTIALS		
2-year	95	unch
5-year	100	unch
10-year	105	unch
20-year	100	unch
PACS		
2-year	64	unch
5-year	61	unch
10-year	70	unch
20-year	80	unch

INTERNATIONAL GOVERNMENT BONDS

Prices in local currencies, provided by Salomon Brothers Inc.

COUPON	MATURITY (Mo./yr.)	PRICE	CHANGE	YIELD*	COUPON	MATURITY (Mo./yr.)	PRICE	CHANGE	YIELD*
JAPAN (3 p.m. Tokyo)					**GERMANY** (5 p.m. London)				
#119 4.80%	6/99	103.914	+ 0.070	3.82%	7.25%	10/97	101.353	+ 0.109	6.56%
#145 5.50	3/02	105.810	+ 0.022	4.54	8.25	9/01	104.400	+ 0.169	7.24
#164 4.10	12/03	96.396	+ 0.063	4.60	7.00	10/99	100.157	+ 0.126	6.83
#89 5.10	6/96	103.349	+ 0.001	2.63	6.25	1/24	82.280	+ 0.294	7.66
#105 5.00	12/97	104.570	+ 0.039	3.33	7.50	11/04	100.480	+ 0.282	7.29
UNITED KINGDOM (5 p.m. London)					**CANADA** (3 p.m. EDT)				
10.00%	11/96	103.406	+ 0.031	7.91%	8.00%	6/23	87.150	+ 0.900	9.29%
8.75	8/17	102.938	+ 0.594	8.46	7.75	9/96	98.780	+ 0.330	8.56
6.75	11/04	87.844	+ 0.312	8.60	9.00	12/04	98.420	+ 0.790	9.24
7.25	3/98	96.656	+ 0.094	8.47	8.50	3/00	97.850	+ 0.750	9.03
8.00	12/00	97.406	+ 0.219	8.55	9.00	6/25	97.100	+ 1.050	9.29

*Equivalent to semi-annual compounded yields to maturity

GUARANTEED INVESTMENT CONTRACTS

Source: T. Rowe Price GIC Index

	1 YEAR RATE CHG	2 YEARS RATE CHG	3 YEARS RATE CHG	4 YEARS RATE CHG	5 YEARS RATE CHG
High	7.17% −0.06	7.87% unch	8.05% −0.08	8.15% −0.13	8.25% −0.11
Low	6.26 unch	6.96 −0.12	7.34 −0.14	7.61 −0.06	7.86 unch
INDEX	6.86 −0.08	7.52 −0.09	7.80 −0.08	7.97 −0.07	8.08 −0.06
TOP QUARTILE RANGE	7.17% - 7.17%	7.87% - 7.68%	8.05% - 7.98%	8.15% - 8.10%	8.25% - 8.18%
SPREAD vs. TREASURYS	+0.04	+0.21	+0.34	+0.38	+0.45

GIC rates quoted prior to 10:30 am (Eastern) net of all expenses, no broker commissions. Rates represent best quote for a $2-$5 million immediate lump sum deposit with annual interest payments. Yield spreads based on U.S. Treasury yields, as of 10:30 am (Eastern), versus the index rate unadjusted for semi vs. annual interest payments. CHG reflects change in rate from previous day. INDEX is average of all rates quoted. Universe is investment grade.

Total Rates of Return on International Bonds

In percent, based on Salomon Brothers' World Government Bond Index

	— LOCAL CURRENCY TERMS —				— U.S. DOLLAR TERMS —			
	INDEX VALUE-a	1 DAY	1 MO	3 MOS	SINCE 12/31	INDEX VALUE-a	1 DAY	1 MO	3 MOS	SINCE 12/31
Japan	189.11	+ 0.05	+ 0.32	+ 2.15	+ 0.30	480.31	+ 0.33	+ 1.66	− 0.12	+ 0.98
Britain	289.09	+ 0.31	+ 0.08	+ 2.90	+ 1.10	397.37	+ 0.33	+ 3.04	+ 0.03	+ 2.87
Germany	198.63	+ 0.17	+ 1.12	+ 2.42	+ 1.50	414.23	+ 0.35	+ 5.46	+ 1.42	+ 4.06
France	272.15	+ 0.06	+ 0.85	+ 3.17	+ 1.54	500.63	− 0.10	+ 4.63	+ 0.73	+ 3.25
Canada	284.63	+ 0.59	+ 0.15	+ 0.99	+ 0.12	265.02	+ 0.41	− 0.89	− 3.73	− 0.74
Netherlands	203.04	+ 0.20	+ 1.08	+ 2.17	+ 1.80	426.55	+ 0.34	+ 5.25	+ 1.18	+ 4.24
Non-U.S.	226.03	+ 0.15	+ 0.61	+ 2.34	+ 0.93	414.91	+ 0.25	+ 3.11	− 0.13	+ 2.21
World*	242.65	+ 0.28	+ 0.87	+ 2.40	+ 1.18	326.75	+ 0.35	+ 2.46	+ 0.81	+ 2.02

*Includes 14 international government bond markets   NA=Not Applicable   a-Dec. 31, 1984=100

EURODOLLAR BONDS

Provided by CS First Boston

ISSUE (RATING: MOODY'S/S&P)	COUPON	MATURITY	PRICE	CHANGE	YIELD	CHANGE
Quebec (A1/A+)	9.125	08/22/01	103.094	0.725	8.301	− 0.140
Belgium (Aa1/NR)	9.625	07/10/98	105.148	0.379	7.687	− 0.121
IntBkReconDev (Aaa/AAA)	9.000	08/12/97	103.031	0.283	7.468	− 0.120
UnitedKingdom (Aaa/AAA)	7.250	12/09/02	96.907	0.687	7.639	− 0.118
IBMJapan (A3/A)	6.500	12/03/97	96.348	0.306	7.817	− 0.121
Sweden (Aa2/AA+)	5.500	12/01/95	98.361	0.162	7.364	− 0.193

YIELD COMPARISONS

Based on Merrill Lynch Bond Indexes, priced as of midafternoon Eastern time.

	1/27	1/26	52 Week High	52 Week Low
Corp.-Govt. Master	7.78%	7.89%	8.09%	5.46%
Treasury 1-10yr	7.39	7.51	7.79	4.55
10+ yr	7.93	8.03	8.36	6.36
Agencies 1-10yr	7.91	8.03	8.17	5.14
10+ yr	8.16	8.25	8.51	6.73
Corporate				
1-10 yr High Qlty	8.05	8.14	8.34	5.67
Med Qlty	8.37	8.46	8.65	6.00
10+yr High Qlty	8.49	8.56	8.84	7.08
Med Qlty	8.91	8.98	9.24	7.42
Yankee bonds(1)	8.44	8.52	8.65	6.62
Current-coupon mortgages (2)				
GNMA 8.50%	8.67	8.79	9.13	6.39
FNMA 8.50%	8.66	8.77	9.04	6.40
FHLMC8.50%	8.67	8.79	9.05	6.40
High-yield corporates	11.24	11.26	11.37	8.87
New tax-exempts				
7-12-yr G.O. (AA)	6.12	6.21	6.45	4.65
12-22-yr G.O. (AA)	6.27	6.36	6.69	4.96
22+yr revenue (A)	6.41	6.50	6.89	5.31

Note: High quality rated AAA-AA; medium quality A-BBB/Baa; high yield, BB/Ba-C.
(1) Dollar-denominated, SEC-registered bonds of foreign issuers sold in the U.S. (2) Reflects the 52-week high and low of mortgage-backed securities indexes rather than the individual securities shown.

Source: *The Wall Street Journal*, January 30, 1995. Reprinted by permission of *The Wall Street Journal*, ©1995 Dow Jones & Company, Inc. All rights reserved worldwide.

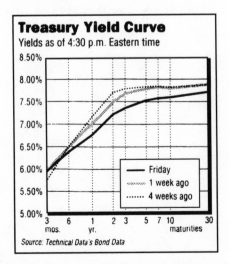

Source: *The Wall Street Journal*, January 30, 1995. Reprinted by permission of *The Wall Street Journal*, ©1995 Dow Jones & Company, Inc. All rights reserved worldwide.

MUTUAL FUNDS

If you recall the discussion of mutual funds in Chapter 9, you will remember that mutual funds often specialize in particular types of investments. Bond funds are mutual funds that invest primarily in debt instruments, permitting you to diversify your bond investments without venturing a large sum of capital. For example, new Ginnie Mae issues require a $25,000 minimum investment, which would be out of the reach of the small investor. Mutual funds pool large sums of money in order to invest in instruments like Ginnie Maes, from which small individual investors can then benefit.

Recall as well Chapter 9's description of two types of mutual funds. Open-end funds issue shares as needed, while closed-end fund's shares are limited and fixed. Once all the shares are sold, no more shares will be issued. On Mondays, the *Journal* reports on Closed-End Bonds (find them in the last section's index), as in the example from the February 13, 1995 edition (page 275).

CONCLUSION

If all this detail has set your head swimming, regain your perspective by recalling that stocks' and bonds' values should move together in the long haul and that both are paper investments that thrive in low inflation.

CLOSED END FUNDS

Friday, February 10, 1995

Closed-end funds sell a limited number of shares and invest the proceeds in securities. Unlike open-end funds, closed-ends generally do not buy their shares back from investors who wish to cash in their holdings. Instead, fund shares trade on a stock exchange. The following list, provided by Lipper Analytical Services, shows the exchange where each fund trades (A: American; C: Chicago; N: NYSE; O: Nasdaq; T: Toronto; z: does not trade on an exchange). The data also include the fund's most recent net asset value, its closing share price on the day NAV was calculated, and the percentage difference between the market price and the NAV (often called the premium or discount). For equity funds, the final column provides 52-week returns based on market prices plus dividends. For bond funds, the final column shows the past 12 months' income distributions as a percentage of the current market price. Footnotes appear after a fund's name. a: the NAV and market price are ex dividend. b: the NAV is fully diluted. c: NAV, market price and premium or discount are as of Thursday's close. d: NAV, market price and premium or discount are as of Wednesday's close. e: NAV assumes rights offering is fully subscribed. v: NAV is converted at the commercial Rand rate. y: NAV and market price are in Canadian dollars. All other footnotes refer to unusual circumstances; explanations for those that appear can be found at the bottom of this list. N/A signifies that the information is not available or not applicable.

Fund Name	Stock Exch	NAV	Market Price	Prem /Disc	52 week Market Return
Friday, February 10, 1995					
General Equity Funds					
Adams Express	N	18.75	16 1/2	− 12.0	−0.1
Alliance All-Mkt	N	20.16	17 1/2	− 13.2	N/A
Baker Fentress	N	18.49	14 7/8	− 19.6	−2.6
Bergstrom Cap	A	101.09	90	− 11.0	3.6
Blue Chip Value	N	7.28	6 1/4	− 14.1	−11.1
Central Secs	A	17.33	16 1/8	− 7.0	8.3
Charles Allmon	N	10.11	8 5/8	− 14.7	−8.0
Engex	A	10.10	N/A	N/A	N/A
Equus II	A	19.91	12 5/8	− 36.6	−25.9
Gabelli Equity	N	9.79	10 1/8	+ 3.4	4.9
General American	N	22.91	20	− 12.7	1.9
Inefficient Mkt	A	12.16	9 1/2	− 21.9	−10.4
Jundt Growth	N	15.47	14 3/8	− 7.1	6.8
Liberty All-Star	N	9.69	9 1/8	− 5.8	−6.5
Specialized Equity Funds					
Alliance Gl Env	N	11.07	8 7/8	− 19.8	−11.3
C&S Realty	A	8.24	8 3/4	+ 6.2	−0.1
C&S Total Rtn -a	N	12.58	13 1/8	+ 4.3	−1.2
Centrl Fd Canada -c	A	4.62	4 1/2	− 2.6	−16.1
Counsellors Tand	N	15.51	13 3/4	− 11.3	−1.8
Delaware Gr Div -a	N	12.81	12 1/2	− 2.4	−6.1
Delaware Grp Gl -a	N	13.00	12 3/8	− 4.8	N/A
Preferred Inc Op	N	10.84	10 1/2	− 3.1	−0.6
Preferred IncMgt	N	12.56	12 1/8	− 3.5	0.1
Preferred Income	N	14.03	13 5/8	− 2.9	−3.0
Putnam Divd Inc	N	10.26	9 1/4	− 9.8	1.3
Royce Micro-Cap	O	7.72	6 3/4	− 12.6	−8.6
SthEastrn Thrift	O	21.49	19 3/4	− 8.1	10.1
Templtn Gl Util -a	A	12.74	11 7/8	− 6.8	−21.4
Convertible Sec's. Funds					
Amer Cap Conv	N	22.28	20 1/8	− 9.7	−5.4
Bancroft Conv	A	22.50	20 1/4	− 10.0	−2.8
Castle Conv	A	25.12	24 1/4	− 3.5	6.1
Ellsworth Conv -a	A	9.44	8 3/8	− 11.3	−0.1
Lincoln Conv -c	N	17.35	16 3/4	− 3.5	−8.8
Putnam Hi Inc Cv	N	8.82	9 1/4	+ 4.9	2.3
TCW Conv Secs	N	7.56	8 1/8	+ 7.5	−5.6
Dual-Purpose Funds					
Conv Hold Cap	N	11.58	9 7/8	− 14.7	−4.7
Conv Hold Inc	N	9.42	10 1/8	+ 7.5	4.1
Gemini II Cap	N	20.96	18 3/8	− 12.3	−3.3
Gemini II Inc	N	9.16	10 5/8	+ 16.0	7.1
Quest Value Cap -a	N	28.08	24 7/8	− 11.4	8.5
Quest Value Inc -a	N	11.58	12 1/8	+ 4.7	4.5
World Equity Funds					
ASA Limited -cv	N	44.47	44 1/2	+ 0.1	−4.4
Americas All Sea	O	4.75	3 5/16	− 30.3	−25.5
Anchor Gold&Curr	C	5.17	5 1/8	− 0.9	−25.5
Argentina	N	10.54	11 1/4	+ 6.7	−34.2
Asia Pacific	N	13.18	13 7/8	+ 5.3	−25.3
Asia Tigers	N	11.20	10	− 10.7	−31.4
Austria	N	8.84	7 3/8	− 16.6	−27.9
BGR Prec Metals -cy	T	16.02	12 3/4	− 20.4	−15.0
U.S. Gov't. Bond Funds					
ACM Govt Inc	N	8.08	9 1/2	+ 17.6	11.7
ACM Govt Oppty	N	7.36	7 1/4	− 1.5	11.0
ACM Govt Secs	N	7.73	8 1/2	+ 10.0	13.1
ACM Govt Spec	N	6.54	7 3/8	+ 12.8	13.2
Amer Govt Income -c	N	5.34	6 1/4	+ 17.0	13.4
Amer Govt Port -c	N	6.50	7 1/4	+ 11.5	14.4
Dean Witter Govt -a	N	8.64	7 7/8	− 8.9	7.9
Excelsior Income -c	N	17.28	15 1/4	− 11.7	8.1
Kemper Int Govt -a	N	7.76	7 1/4	− 6.6	9.2
MFS Govt Mkts -a	N	6.93	6 1/4	− 9.8	6.3
Putnam Int Govt	N	8.10	7 1/2	− 7.4	8.3
RCM Strat Glbl -a	N	10.79	9 15/16	− 7.9	N/A
U.S. Mortgage Bond Funds					
2002 Target Term -c	N	12.99	11	− 15.3	7.7
Amer Adj Rate 95 -c	N	9.70	9 1/2	− 2.1	3.2
Amer Adj Rate 96 -c	N	8.95	8 1/4	− 7.8	4.9
Amer Adj Rate 97 -c	N	8.70	7 7/8	− 9.5	6.1
Amer Adj Rate 98 -c	N	8.58	7 3/4	− 9.7	6.7
Amer Adj Rate 99 -c	N	8.41	7 5/8	− 9.3	7.1
Amer Govt Term -c	N	7.95	7 3/8	− 7.2	9.8
Amer Oppty Inc -c	N	6.16	7 1/2	+ 21.8	14.0
Amer Sel Port -c	N	11.60	11 1/8	− 4.1	10.2
Amer Str Inc II -c	N	12.26	11 7/8	− 3.1	11.5
Amer Str Inc III -c	N	11.88	11 1/2	− 3.2	11.3
Amer Str Income -c	N	12.55	12 7/8	+ 2.6	10.9
Investment Grade Bond Funds					
1838 Bd-Deb	N	20.04	20 1/8	+ 0.4	8.6
All-American Tm -c	N	13.46	12 1/4	− 9.0	10.1
Amer Cap Bond	N	19.04	17 7/8	− 6.1	8.7
CNA Income -c	N	9.22	9 7/8	+ 7.1	11.8
Circle Income -c	O	11.16	10 1/8	− 9.3	9.2
Current Inc Shs	N	12.70	11 1/2	− 9.4	8.5
Fortis Secs	N	8.88	9 1/8	+ 2.8	9.9
Ft Dearborn Inc	N	15.24	14 1/8	− 7.3	8.1
Hatteras Income	N	15.44	16	+ 3.6	9.1
INA Investments	N	17.89	16	− 10.6	8.7
Independence Sq	O	17.05	15 1/2	− 9.1	8.2
InterCap Income -a	N	16.64	17 3/8	+ 3.2	9.0
Montgomery St	N	18.06	17 5/8	− 2.4	8.2
Op Fd Multi-Gov	N	7.56	7	− 7.4	9.1
Pac Amer Income -c	N	N/A	14 5/8	N/A	8.5
Pioneer Int Shs	N	12.88	13 1/4	+ 2.9	8.8
Transam Income	N	22.87	22 3/8	− 2.2	9.0
Vestaur Secs -c	N	13.81	12 3/4	− 7.7	8.7
Loan Participation Funds					
Eaton Vance Pr	z	10.04	N/A	N/A	N/A
Merrill Sen Fl	z	10.01	N/A	N/A	N/A
Pilgrim Pr Rate -a	N	9.61	8 3/4	− 8.9	8.5
Prime Income	z	9.99	N/A	N/A	N/A
VanKamp Prime	z	10.04	N/A	N/A	N/A
High Yield Bond Funds					
CIGNA High Inc	N	6.72	6 3/4	+ 0.4	13.2
CIM High Yld	N	7.22	7 1/4	+ 0.4	11.5
Colonial Intmdt	N	6.25	6 1/4	+ 0.0	10.9
Corp Hi Yld	N	12.31	13	+ 5.6	13.0
Corp Hi Yld II	N	11.52	12 1/8	+ 5.3	13.0
Franklin Univ -ac	N	8.64	8 1/8	− 6.0	10.1
High Inc Adv -a	N	5.09	5 3/8	+ 5.6	11.7
High Inc Adv II -a	N	5.75	5 7/8	+ 2.2	10.5
High Inc Adv III -a	N	6.14	6 1/2	+ 5.9	11.1
High Yld Income -a	N	6.74	7 1/8	+ 5.7	12.3
High Yld Plus	N	7.78	7 7/8	+ 1.2	11.3
Kemper High Inc -a	N	8.39	8 3/4	+ 4.3	10.9
Managed High Inc	N	10.72	10 1/2	− 2.1	11.3
Morgan St Hi Yld	N	12.23	12 1/2	+ 2.2	11.9
New Amer Hi Inc -a	N	4.20	4 1/4	+ 1.2	13.0
PaineWbr Pr High -a	N	12.62	12 1/4	− 2.9	11.0
Prospect St High	N	3.60	3 5/8	+ 0.7	12.3
Putnam Mgd HiYld	N	12.47	12 3/8	− 0.8	10.8
SB High Inc Opp	N	10.83	10 3/4	− 0.7	11.0
Salomon HIF -a	N	N/A	13 1/4	N/A	10.6
Senior Strat Inc	N	9.21	8 7/8	− 3.6	N/A
USF&G Pacholder -ch	A	17.13	16	− 6.6	12.4
VanKamp Int Hi -a	N	5.67	5 7/8	+ 3.6	16.2
VanKamp Ltd Hi -a	N	7.42	7 5/8	+ 2.8	15.2
Zenix Income	N	5.73	6 3/8	+ 11.3	13.8
Other Domestic Taxable Bond Funds					
ACM Mgd $	N	8.92	10	+ 12.1	15.0
ACM Mgd Income	N	7.35	7 7/8	+ 7.1	14.2
AIM Strategic -a	A	9.18	8 1/8	− 11.5	5.8
Alliance Wld $	N	9.54	11	+ 15.3	15.5
Alliance Wld $ 2	N	10.22	11 1/8	+ 8.9	11.8
Allmerica Secs	N	N/A	10	N/A	8.7
Amer Cap Inc -a	N	7.34	7 1/8	− 2.9	9.5
Colonial Intrmkt -a	N	10.38	10 1/4	− 1.3	9.8
Duff&Ph Util Cor -a	N	12.49	12 1/2	+ 0.1	8.8
First Boston Inc	N	8.06	7 1/2	− 6.9	9.9
First Boston Str	N	9.30	8 5/8	− 7.3	9.7
Franklin Mul-Inc -c	N	9.47	8 5/8	− 8.9	9.1
Franklin Pr Mat -c	N	7.75	6 3/4	− 12.9	8.7
Global Partners -a	N	N/A	10 5/8	N/A	14.1
Highlander Inc -c	A	12.85	11 7/8	− 7.6	N/A
J Hancock Income	N	N/A	15 5/8	N/A	8.5
J Hancock Invest	N	N/A	19 5/8	N/A	8.6
Kemper Multi Mkt -a	N	10.07	9 5/8	− 4.4	10.2
Kemper Strat Inc -a	N	11.46	12 1/4	+ 6.9	N/A
Lincoln Income -c	N	12.67	12	− 5.3	10.6
MFS Charter -a	N	9.68	8 7/8	− 8.3	6.8
MFS Intmdt -a	N	7.24	6 5/8	− 8.5	7.6
MFS Multimkt -a	N	6.95	6 1/4	− 10.1	8.0
MFS Special Val -a	N	12.32	14 1/4	+ 15.7	0.6
MassMutual Part	N	N/A	7 1/4	N/A	8.8
Op Fd Multi-Sec -a	N	9.64	9 5/8	− 0.2	10.1
Putnam Mas Inc	N	8.44	7 7/8	− 6.7	9.6
Putnam Mas Int	N	7.90	7 1/8	− 9.8	9.6
Putnam Prem Inc	N	7.96	7 3/8	− 7.3	9.9
Senior Hi Inc	N	8.91	8 1/2	− 4.6	8.9
Senior Hi Inc II	N	9.15	8 5/8	− 5.7	9.9

Source: *The Wall Street Journal*, February 13, 1995. Reprinted by permission of *The Wall Street Journal*,

CHAPTER 12

MONEY MARKET
INVESTMENTS

INTRODUCTION

Maybe the risk and bother of investing in stocks, bonds, and commodities inhibit you. If that's so, you may be satisfied with an investment whose yield just covers the rate of inflation, provided that you can readily convert it to cash. In other words, you want your money's purchasing power to be unchanged a year or two from now, and you want the assurance that you can get your hands on your money at will.

Many circumstances might justify this point of view. Everyone's future involves some degree of uncertainty. If you are retired, your nest egg may have to meet unexpected medical bills. You don't want to be penalized for cashing out in a hurry. And investors of every age may wish to park their money for brief periods in anticipation of other planned uses of their funds. Whatever the situation, you might have a number of good reasons not to tie up your funds in riskier investments, even if they offer higher returns.

If you wish to make a short-term investment that is relatively risk-free and can be quickly converted to cash, the money market offers a variety of selections that range from one day to one year and may be obtained for large or small amounts. Most of these are probably familiar to you: bank savings accounts, interest-bearing checking accounts (money market checking accounts), certificates of deposit, money market mutual funds, and Treasury bills (T-bills). Market forces determine their yields, and the markets for all are interrelated.

As a general rule, the greater the liquidity (ease with which it is converted into cash) and safety of an investment, the lower the yield. A

smaller investment commitment and a shorter maturity also reduce the yield.

This chapter describes the money market investments available to individual investors and shows you how to track those investments in *The Wall Street Journal*.

CONSUMER SAVINGS AND INTEREST-EARNING CHECKING ACCOUNTS

Your interest-earning checking account or savings account at the bank or savings and loan company (S&L) is a short-term liquid investment, because you can withdraw your funds quickly and easily with relatively few restrictions. Moreover, these accounts are insured up to $100,000 by the Federal Deposit Insurance Corporation (FDIC). In the hierarchy of short-term interest rate yields, consumer checking and savings rates tend to be on the bottom because of their liquidity and safety and because of the inertia that prevents many savers from shopping for the higher yields available on alternative investments.

BANK MONEY MARKET ACCOUNTS

You can open a money market account with a minimum daily balance ranging from $500 to $5,000, depending on the bank. This is a highly liquid investment, because you can withdraw from the account at any time simply by writing a check, although most banks have restrictions regarding the number and frequency of checks written. These accounts offer relatively low yields because of their check-writing privileges, although the yields do tend to be a little higher than on savings accounts due to higher required minimum balances. They are also insured up to $100,000 by the FDIC.

Every Thursday *The Wall Street Journal* publishes **Consumer Savings Rates** (check the third section's index), a listing prepared by the *Bank Rate Monitor* that reports on the average rate paid by 100 banks on the previous day for a variety of money market and certificate of deposit (CD) accounts. See the page 279 excerpt from the February 2, 1995 *Journal*. According to this report, money market deposits paid 2.78 percent on February 1, 1995, Interest Checking paid less, and a variety of certificates of deposit, as well as U.S. Savings Bonds, earned more.

Consumer Savings Rates	
Money Market Deposits-a	2.78%
Interest Checking-a	1.49%
Six-month Certificates-a	4.72%
One-year Certificates-a	5.65%
Thirty-month Certificates-a	6.21%
Five-Year Certificates-a	6.63%
U.S. Savings Bonds-b	5.92%

a-Average rate paid yesterday by 100 large banks and thrifts in the 10 largest metropolitan areas as compiled by Bank Rate Monitor.
b-First of 10 or more rates to be averaged if held five years or longer. Guaranty is 4% if held less than five years.

Source: *The Wall Street Journal*, February 2, 1995. Reprinted by permission of *The Wall Street Journal*, ©1995 Dow Jones & Company, Inc. All rights reserved worldwide.

On Wednesday of each week, on the next to the last page of the last section, the *Journal* publishes **Banxquote Money Markets** together with **High Yield Savings** and **High Yield Jumbos** (see the excerpt from the February 15, 1995 *Journal* on page 280). The Banxquote Money Market report lets you compare your yield on a variety of money market accounts and certificate of deposit accounts at different maturities with the average earned nationally (Bank Average) and in six key states: New York, California, Pennsylvania, Illinois, Texas, and Florida. You can also find the weekly change in the national average. In the week ended February 14, 1995, for instance, the average short-term three-month account earned 4.28 percent and had risen 0.02 percent over the previous week. The **High Yield Savings** figures represent the rates available at individual institutions for accounts requiring a small minimum balance (some as low as $500), and the **High Yield Jumbos** are rates offered with minimum balances of $95,000 to $100,000.

Banks and S&Ls created the money market accounts to stem withdrawals of funds lost to competing money market mutual funds offering higher rates than savings accounts. Although interest paid by the money market accounts fluctuates with short-term market rates, these accounts do not enjoy yields as high as those paid by money market mutual funds. Your account will, however, be insured by the FDIC, which is not the case with money market mutual funds. Remember: The smaller the risk, the smaller the reward.

The average short-term account earned 4.28% in the week ending February 14, 1995 →

Broker Average → 5.86%

Southern Pac → T&L 6.18%

BANXQUOTE® MONEY MARKETS

Survey ended Tuesday, February 14, 1995

AVERAGE YIELDS OF MAJOR BANKS

	MMI*	One Month	Two Months	Three Months	Six Months	One Year	Two Years	Five Years
NEW YORK								
Savings	3.49%	z	z	4.51%	5.39%	6.00%	6.61%	7.01%
Jumbos	5.23%	5.23%	5.32%	5.10%	5.55%	6.11%	6.69%	6.95%
CALIFORNIA								
Savings	2.44%	z	z	3.71%	4.35%	5.81%	6.01%	6.28%
Jumbos	2.79%	3.11%	3.30%	4.06%	4.70%	5.99%	6.97%	7.25%
PENNSYLVANIA								
Savings	3.36%	z	z	3.69%	4.93%	5.63%	6.28%	6.83%
Jumbos	4.46%	5.35%	5.34%	5.45%	5.85%	6.29%	6.50%	z
ILLINOIS								
Savings	4.15%	z	z	5.18%	5.51%	6.13%	6.47%	7.05%
Jumbos	4.70%	5.44%	5.49%	5.94%	6.25%	6.81%	7.24%	7.52%
TEXAS								
Savings	4.14%	z	z	4.15%	4.73%	5.53%	6.55%	7.01%
Jumbos	4.33%	4.27%	4.31%	4.60%	4.83%	5.65%	6.55%	7.05%
FLORIDA								
Savings	2.98%	z	z	4.45%	5.18%	5.90%	6.32%	6.70%
Jumbos	3.35%	4.60%	4.67%	5.20%	5.82%	6.30%	6.55%	6.95%
BANK AVERAGE								
Savings	3.43%	z	z	4.28%	5.02%	5.83%	6.36%	6.81%
Jumbos	4.14%	4.58%	4.65%	5.06%	5.50%	6.19%	6.77%	7.14%

WEEKLY CHANGE (in percentage point)

Savings	+0.01	z	z	+0.02	+0.02	−0.01	−0.03	−0.12
Jumbos	+0.02	+0.03	+0.05	+0.10	+0.08	+0.05	+0.01	−0.02

SAVINGS CD YIELDS OFFERED THROUGH LEADING BROKERS

	Three Months	Six Months	One Year	Two Years	Five Years
BROKER AVERAGE	5.86%	6.09%	6.52%	6.98%	7.22%
WEEKLY CHANGE	−0.01	−0.03	+0.05	+0.10	+0.15

*Money Market Investments include MMDA, NOW, savings deposits, passbook and other liquid accounts.
Each depositor is insured by the Federal Deposit Insurance Corp. (FDIC) up to $100,000 per issuing institution.
COMPOUND METHODS: c-Continuously. d-Daily. w-Wkly. m-Mthly. q-Qrtly. s-Semi-annually. a-Annually.
SIMPLE INTEREST: sl-Paid Monthly. e-Paid Semi-annually. y-Paid at Maturity.
OTHER SYMBOLS: APY-Annual percentage yield. F-Floating rate P-Prime CD. T-T-Bill CD. BD-Broker-

Dealer. pp-Priced below par.
YIELD BASIS: A-365/365. B-360/360. C-365/360.
The information included in this table has been obtained directly from broker-dealers, banks and savings institutions, but the accuracy and validity cannot be guaranteed. Rates are subject to change. Yields, terms and capital adequacy should be verified before investing. Only well capitalized or adequately capitalized depository institutions are quoted.
z-Unavailable.

HIGH YIELD SAVINGS

Small minimum balance/opening deposit, generally $500 to $25,000

Money Market Investments*	Rate		APY	Six Months CDs	Rate		APY
Eastern American, Herndon Va	5.87%	mA	6.03%	Heritage Bank, Willmar Mn	6.40%	yA	6.50%
Harris Bank, Chicago Il	5.83%	mA	5.99%	Beal Bank, Dallas Tx	6.36%	slA	6.46%
Lincoln National, Chicago Il	5.82%	mA	5.98%	South Pac T&L, Los Angeles Ca	6.25%	dA	6.45%
Citicorp Invest, Sioux Falls Sd	5.73%	dC	5.98%	Calif Thrift, Santa Barbara Ca	6.23%	dA	6.43%
MBNA America, Newark De	5.62%	dA	5.78%	First Commnwlth, Alexandria Va	6.15%	qA	6.29%

One Month CDs	Rate		APY	One Year CDs	Rate		APY
South Pac T&L, Los Angeles Ca	5.25%	dA	6.05%	Washington Savings, Waldorf Md	7.10%	qA	7.29%
Firstrust Bank, Philadelphia Pa	5.22%	slA	5.35%	Northern Trust, Chicago Il	6.97%	dA	7.22%
New South FSB, Birmingham Al	5.00%	slA	5.12%	New York Federal, New York NY	7.00%	slC	7.10%
Republic Bank, New York NY	4.75%	dA	4.86%	South Pac T&L, Los Angeles Ca	6.85%	dA	7.09%
Northern Trust, Chicago Il	4.75%	dA	4.86%	Calif Thrift, Santa Barbara Ca	6.81%	dA	7.05%

Two Months CDs	Rate		APY	Two Years CDs	Rate		APY
South Pac T&L, Los Angeles Ca	5.50%	dA	5.65%	Washington Savings, Waldorf Md	7.30%	dA	7.57%
New South FSB, Birmingham Al	5.00%	slA	5.11%	East New York, New York NY	7.23%	dA	7.50%
Standard Pac, Newport Beach Ca	4.79%	dA	4.91%	Washington Savings, Waldorf Md	7.30%	qA	7.50%
Northern Trust, Chicago Il	4.75%	dA	4.86%	South Pac T&L, Los Angeles Ca	7.20%	dA	7.46%
Safra National, New York NY	4.55%	dA	4.65%	Calif Thrift, Santa Barbara Ca	7.17%	dA	7.43%

Three Months CDs	Rate		APY	Five Years CDs	Rate		APY
South Pac T&L, Los Angeles Ca	6.00%	dA	6.18%	Washington Savings, Waldorf Md	7.90%	dA	8.14%
Smith Barney (BD), New York NY	5.75%	yA	5.88%	Northern Trust, Chicago Il	7.72%	dA	8.02%
Paine Webber (BD), New York NY	5.75%	yA	5.88%	Eastern Savings, Baltimore Md	7.53%	mA	7.80%
Merrill Lynch (BD), New York NY	5.75%	yA	5.88%	Broadway National, New York NY	7.50%	dA	7.79%
Fidelity Invsmt (BD), Boston Ma	5.70%	yA	5.82%	Key Bank USA, Albany NY	7.50%	mA	7.76%

HIGH YIELD JUMBOS

Large minimum balance/opening deposit, generally $95,000 to $100,000

Money Market Investments*	Rate		APY	Six Months Jumbo CDs	Rate		APY
Mbna America, Newark PR	5.87%	dA	6.03%	Firstbank, Santurce PR	6.85%	slA	6.97%
Eastern American, Herndon Va	5.87%	mA	6.03%	Provident Savings, Riverside Ca	6.75%	slA	6.86%
Stearns County NB, Albany Mn	5.84%	mA	6.00%	Providian National, Concord NH	6.63%	dA	6.85%
Harris Bank, Chicago Il	5.83%	mA	5.99%	Hurley State Bank, Sioux Falls SD	6.65%	slA	6.76%
Lincoln National, Chicago Il	5.82%	mA	5.98%	Turnberry Sav, N Miami Beach Fl	6.60%	slA	6.71%

One Month Jumbo CDs	Rate		APY	One Year Jumbo CDs	Rate		APY
Plaza Home, Santa Ana Ca	6.65%	slC	6.95%	First USA, Wilmington De	7.25%	slC	7.35%
Hurley State Bank, Sioux Falls SD	6.10%	slA	6.27%	Providian National, Concord NH	7.09%	dA	7.35%
Resource Bank, Virginia Beach Va	6.00%	slA	6.17%	Firstbank, Santurce PR	7.25%	slA	7.25%
First Commnwlth, Alexandria Va	6.00%	slA	6.17%	First Deposit, Tilton NH	7.00%	dA	7.25%
Greenwood Trust, Wilmington De	5.90%	yA	6.06%	Calif Thrift, Santa Barbara Ca	6.99%	dA	7.24%

Two Months Jumbo CDs	Rate		APY	Two Years Jumbo CDs	Rate		APY
Plaza Home, Santa Ana Ca	6.65%	slC	6.93%	Calif Thrift, Santa Barbara Ca	7.34%	dA	7.62%
Hurley State Bank, Sioux Falls SD	6.20%	slA	6.36%	Key Bank USA, Albany NY	7.35%	mA	7.60%
First Commnwlth, Alexandria Va	6.10%	slA	6.26%	Northern Trust, Chicago Il	7.30%	mA	7.55%
Equitable Federal, Wheaton Md	6.05%	slA	6.20%	Providian National, Concord NH	7.23%	dA	7.50%
Colonial National, Wilmington De	6.00%	slA	6.15%	Standard Pac, Newport Beach Ca	7.23%	dA	7.50%

Three Months Jumbo CDs	Rate		APY	Five Years Jumbo CDs	Rate		APY
Hurley State Bank, Sioux Falls Sd	6.30%	slA	6.45%	Northern Trust, Chicago Il	7.72%	mA	8.00%
Firstbank, Santurce PR	6.25%	slA	6.40%	Key Bank USA, Albany NY	7.70%	mA	7.98%
Provident Savings, Riverside Ca	6.25%	slA	6.40%	Eastern Savings, Baltimore Md	7.58%	mA	7.85%
Providian National, Concord NH	6.11%	dA	6.30%	MBNA America, Newark De	7.55%	dA	7.84%
First Federal, Detroit Mi	6.15%	yA	6.29%	Heritage Bank, Willmar Mn	7.80%	aA	7.80%

For more information call MASTERFUND at (800) 666-2000. MASTERFUND is registered with the FDIC as a deposit broker.
For BanxQuote® Institutional Jumbo CDs see Dow Jones Telerate pages 22300-99.

Source: BANXQUOTE, Millburn N.J.
BANXQUOTE is a registered trademark and service mark of MASTERFUND INC.

MONEY MARKET MUTUAL FUNDS

Investment companies establish mutual funds to pool the capital of many investors and thus create a large shared portfolio of investments. (Recall the earlier discussions of mutual funds in Chapter 9.) Individuals invest in mutual funds by purchasing shares in the fund, and the return on the portfolio is passed through to the investor according to the number of shares held. An enormous variety of mutual funds is available, designed for different types of investors and bearing a wide variety of yields.

Money market mutual funds invest principally in short-term investment instruments such as Treasury bills, commercial paper, bank certificates of deposit, bankers acceptances, and other liquid assets denominated in large amounts and therefore unavailable to the small investor. A money market mutual fund permits you to participate in the return on a variety of short-term investments and enjoy the benefits of diversification without employing large sums of your own capital. You also take advantage of the professional management skills of the investment company.

Most money market mutual funds are *no-load funds*. They do not charge a sales commission fee, because they are directly marketed by the investment company. However, "management" fees are subtracted from the yield you receive. Money market mutual funds are issued and trade at a par value of one dollar. The dividends you receive are expressed as percentage yield.

Although money market funds sell their shares for a dollar each, most have minimum investment requirements ranging from $1,000 to $25,000. As an incentive, many money market funds also have check-writing privileges. Although these funds are not insured by the federal government, they are safe and liquid investments whose yields tend to be higher than the yields on bank money market accounts.

In the early 1980s, when the Federal Reserve applied a chokehold on the economy and interest rates climbed to the sky, money market mutual funds became popular among investors and savers. Since banks and S&Ls were, at the time, prohibited from offering above-passbook rates to small depositors, huge sums poured into the money market funds as their yields climbed above the legal passbook minimums. When the interest rate ceilings were removed from small denomination accounts at banks and S&Ls, and these accounts began to offer rates that moved with market conditions (and thus competed with the money market mutual funds), some investors deserted the money market funds. Once again, however, money market fund (not insured) rates generally outdo those at the banks (insured) and consequently remain very popular.

Assets of Money Funds Slipped in Latest Week

WASHINGTON — Money-market mutual fund assets fell $4.21 billion to $641.27 billion from a revised $645.48 billion for the week ended Wednesday, the Investment Company Institute said.

Money-Market Funds
Assets, in billions of dollars

Source: Investment Company Institute

Assets of 679 retail money market mutual funds dipped by $1.87 billion to $454.93 billion, the trade group said.

Among retail funds, the assets of 417 taxable money-market funds fell by $1.07 billion to $359.74 billion while assets of 262 retail tax-exempt funds slid by $796.6 million to $95.19 billion.

Assets of 296 institutional money market funds decreased $2.34 billion to $186.34 billion. Among institutional funds, the assets of 232 taxable money-market fund assets fell by $1.89 billion to $162.95 billion while assets of 64 tax-exempt funds dropped by $446.9 million to $23.39 billion.

Source: *The Wall Street Journal*, February 17, 1995. Reprinted by permission of *The Wall Street Journal*, ©1995 Dow Jones & Company, Inc. All rights reserved worldwide.

Money-Market Funds

The report from the February 17, 1995 *Journal* informs you that money fund assets fell in the latest week, although the accompanying charts show their rise with interest rates in late 1994. You can use a variety of reports in *The Wall Street Journal* to compare the performance of your money fund with others.

Every Thursday the *Journal* publishes a report and a chart called **Yields for Consumers** that compares money market fund yields with yields on bank certificates of deposit and money market accounts and provides a report on the size of money market funds' assets. As you can see from the February 9, 1995 excerpt on page 283, yields rose substantially and assets fell in the latest week. Notice that the average maturity of the investments in these funds (T-bills, CDs, commercial paper, etc.) "lengthened by three days to 38 days." If they think interest rates will fall many fund managers lock in longer yields on longer maturities in order to enjoy those higher yields for as long as possible; they choose shorter maturities when they believe rates will rise. Since the length of maturity changed significantly, the author of the article felt that money fund managers did not expect the Fed "to raise interest rates again any time soon."

Taxable Money Funds Report Big Increase In Yields for Week

By a WALL STREET JOURNAL Staff Reporter

NEW YORK — Yields on taxable money funds rose substantially in the week ended Tuesday, in the wake of last week's interest-rate increase by the Federal Reserve.

Taxable Yield

IBC/Donoghue's average seven-day compound yield on taxable money funds jumped to 5.52% from 5.37%, according to Money Fund Report, an Ashland, Mass., newsletter. Compound yields assume reinvestment of dividends.

Yields for Consumers

Average compounded yields in percent; money market funds' yield is 7-day average; CD yields are for deposits of $50,000 or less at major banks

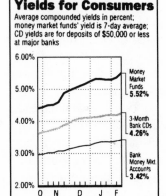

Sources: Banxquote Money Markets; Money Fund Report

Taxable Yield

The seven-day simple yield on taxable funds leaped to 5.37% from 5.23%. The 30-day simple yield rose to 5.23% from 5.19%, while the 30-day compound yield increased to 5.37% from 5.32%.

Total assets of the 706 taxable funds (one more than the previous week) reporting to Money Fund Report, decreased by $372.8 million to $528.48 billion, according to the newsletter. Institutional investors took out $1.96 billion, while individual investors actually put in $1.58 billion.

Average Maturity

The average maturity of the taxable funds' investments, which include commercial paper, or short-term corporate IOUs, and Treasury bills, lengthened by three days to 38 days.

This would indicate that portfolio managers don't expect the Federal Reserve to raise interest rates again anytime soon, nor do they expect yields to go up much higher than they are now, said Walter Frank, chief economist for Money Fund Report. Lengthening the portfolio maturity allows fund managers to lock in current yields for a longer period of time, he noted.

Tax-Exempt Yield

The average seven-day compound yield on tax-exempt money funds crept up to 3.21% from 3.19% in the latest week, according to Money Fund Report. The latest tax-free yield is equivalent to a taxable 5.02% for someone paying 36% in taxes and to 5.31% for those who pay 39.6%.

Total assets of the 378 tax-exempt funds (one more than the previous week) reporting to Money Fund Report increased by $1.11 billion to $117.47 billion, the newsletter said.

Money Fund Report is published by IBC/Donoghue Inc., a subsidiary of **IBC USA (Publications)** Inc.

Average Maturity—Fifth Paragraph

The average maturity of the taxable funds' investments, which include commercial paper, or short-term corporate IOUs, and Treasury bills, lengthened by three days to 38 days.

Yield–Sixth Paragraph

The average seven-day compound yield on tax-exempt money funds crept up to 3.21% from 3.19% in the latest week, according to Money Fund Report. The latest tax-free yield is equivalent to a taxable 5.02% for someone paying 36% in taxes and to 5.31% for those who pay 39.6%.

Money Market Mutual Funds, published every Thursday in the *Journal*, lists the most popular money market mutual funds (see the index on page C1). Several statistics are given for each: the average maturity (in days) of the investments in the fund, the 7-day yield for the week (average yield), and the total assets in millions of dollars as of the previous day. (See the examples from the February 9, 1995 *Journal* on pages 285–286.)

You can track the performance of your money market mutual fund and most others with this report. For instance, Merrill Lynch's Cash Management fund had an average maturity of 59 days, yields of 5.34 percent, and assets of $28.61 billion. Finally, note that tax-exempt funds are listed separately and have lower yields.

CERTIFICATES OF DEPOSIT

Certificates of deposit (CDs) are like savings accounts for which you receive a "certificate of deposit" from the bank or savings and loan company. Banks and S&Ls issue certificates of deposit to compete with Treasury bills and commercial paper for the investor's dollar. CDs that have maturities of one year or less are part of the money market.

MONEY MARKET MUTUAL FUNDS

The following quotations, collected by the National Association of Securities Dealers Inc., represent the average of annualized yields and dollar-weighted portfolio maturities ending Wednesday, February 8, 1995. Yields don't include capital gains or losses.

Fund	Avg. Mat.	7Day Yld.	Assets
Money Market:			
AALMny	24	4.69	68
AARP HQ	30	5.28	382
AFD ExRsv A	25	4.84	39
AFD ExResB	25	4.34	94
AIM MM C	25	5.20	274
AIM MMA	25	5.22	129
AVESTA Tr	41	5.32	51
AccUSGov	78	5.24	12
ActAsGv	42	5.26	541
ActAsMny	63	5.67	5106
AetnaAdvs	31	5.86	63
Aetna Sel	31	5.86	173
AlexBwn	47	5.52	1413
AlxBTr	48	5.12	535
BiltPrCshlst	28	5.86	826
BILTmm	36	5.68	141
BiltTrInst	30	5.62	121
BiltTrInv	30	5.32	67
BiltMMIv	36	5.38	92
BishopStA	54	5.63	259
WmBlrRdy	51	5.54	547
BlnchGv	73	4.51	177
BradGovObl	21	4.94	40
Bradfd	38	5.31	747
BrentonUS	38	5.07	25
BullBDlr	87	4.67	69
CRTGovt	20	5.05	980
CRTMMkt	29	5.23	266
CalvSoc	42	5.20	142
CapCash	26	5.40	2
CapPre II	1	5.17	261
CapPrsv	46	5.20	2850
CapitolTreas	24	5.70	24
CapitolMM	46	5.88	152
CardGvt	12	4.88	396
Carnegie	19	4.79	14
CshActMM	18	4.99	384
CshAcctGv	12	5.01	123
CashEqv	23	5.18	3502
CshEqGv	12	5.23	1602
CashMgt	22	5.44	2816
CshTrGv	36	4.98	413
CshTrPr	35	5.17	979
CshTrTreas	34	4.90	404
CshTrII	34	5.04	203
CentnGv	21	5.20	721
Centen	34	5.49	3469
ChchCsh	28	5.45	197
ColonlMMB	42	4.14	45
ColonlMM A	42	5.83	68
DryGvt	35	5.02	466
DryInG	24	5.22	232
DryInst	43	5.54	273
DryfLA	66	5.36	475
DryWld	58	5.41	2244
DryInstGv1	32	5.65	446
DryInstPrm1	23	5.71	781
DryInstUST1	45	5.55	646
DryPrimeR	12	5.32	313
DryUSTOnl2	57	5.34	24
DryUSTR	25	4.73	296
EatVCsh	31	5.30	116
ElfunMM	53	5.84	107
EnterMM	36	4.98	35
EvgrnM	47	5.36	248
ExcelsrMM	75	5.83	327
ExcelsrTM	53	5.12	162
FBL	32	4.50	19
FFB Csh	41	5.41	637
FFB US Gvt	31	5.44	225
FFB US Tr	38	5.26	717
FFBLexicn	19	5.39	111
FGICTreas	11	5.43	152
FidUSTI	52	5.54	1179
FMBCons	15	5.20	9
FMBInst	15	5.20	108
FdShtUS	35	5.59	977
FedMstr	36	5.70	810
FidInDom	17	5.82	1012
FidInGov	41	5.82	3337
FidInMM	24	5.87	5334
FidInTr	33	5.78	1212
FidInTrII	29	5.76	4717
FidCRMM	33	5.07	769
FidCRGv	34	4.90	198
FidCsRes	29	5.55	15891
FidDMM	25	5.29	1937
FidDUS	31	5.34	1972
FidDom	21	5.64	289
Fid FDIT	32	5.52	2197
FidGvRes	40	5.57	1142
FidGvPr	36	5.57	203
FidUS Tr	36	5.52	154
FidRetGov	37	5.55	1993
FidRetMM	32	5.64	3777
FidSpGov	38	5.54	738
FidSpMM	33	5.61	7595
FidSpUSTr	54	5.30	1687
HTInsgtCs	21	5.46	633
HTInsgtGv	63	5.52	232
HanvCsh	39	5.34	1031
HanvGov	12	5.46	1305
HanvUSTr	13	5.02	1363
HanvTreas	26	4.79	893
Harbor	65	5.61	72
HrtgCsh	24	5.20	1075
HiMrkUSFid	39	5.04	180
HiMrkTrsFid	41	4.77	230
HiMrkDvFid	37	5.19	346
HilrdGovt	49	5.27	241
HmestdDly	41	5.35	41
HorznPr	22	5.92	2559
HorznTr	29	5.65	1896
Liq Ins Gv	26	5.56	54
LiqInt	10	5.53	183
LiqInstSec	13	5.64	28
LiqCapital	35	5.10	273
LiqCshTr f	3	5.82	315
LordAbbCR	28	5.32	151
LuthrnBr	33	4.93	290
MASCashRes	19	5.57	31
MFSGovMonA	22	4.89	38
MFSMonMkA	22	5.32	429
MIMLIC a	28	5.03	29
MainStay A	44	5.50	15
MainStay B	44	5.50	225
MngdCsh	26	5.51	390
MngdGv	34	5.40	66
Map Gvt	33	5.26	84
MarinCsh	53	5.30	217
MarineGv	25	5.14	130
MarinerUS	38	5.01	120
MrkTwGovtT	24	5.15	184
MarquisTrI	10	5.40	426
MarquisTrR	10	5.20	167
Marshall A	30	5.74	1112
MedalistMM	41	5.34	120
MedalistTr	42	5.20	428
ML CBAMon	56	5.14	1419
ML CMAGv	56	5.18	3165
ML CMAMn	59	5.34	28611
MerLyGv	44	5.62	1483
MerLITr	44	5.33	389
MerLyIn	58	5.69	4950
MerLyRdy	55	5.23	6482
MerLyRet	59	5.34	7453
ML CMATr	54	5.06	1434
MerLyUSA	45	4.85	522
ML US Tr	39	4.72	64
NatnsPrInvB	54	5.58	132
NatnsTrInvA	28	5.16	106
NatnsPrInvA	54	5.39	668
NatnsGvMMTrA	34	5.55	452
NatnsTreTrA	28	5.53	3087
NatwMM	35	5.46	529
NeubCsh	48	5.36	309
NeubGvt	50	5.00	254
NewEngCMTUSG	37	5.04	63
NewEngCMT	46	5.26	663
Newpoint Gv	52	4.99	55
Nicholas	23	5.60	109
Northern	28	5.59	908
NorthernGvSl	42	5.78	53
NorthernMun	34	3.35	949
NorthernUSGv	37	5.59	247
NorwestCash	44	5.68	1456
NorwestMunII	26	3.53	274
NorwestRdy	37	5.36	211
NorwestRdyI	37	5.70	383
NorwestTr	41	5.09	706
NorwestUS	28	5.41	1036
OLDE MM	38	4.89	221
OLDE PrPl	41	6.05	638
OLDE Prem	36	5.31	101
OneGrGovt	24	5.61	696
OneGrPr A	47	5.48	122
OneGrPr	47	5.72	1931
OneGrUST A	39	5.11	67
OneGrUSTSc	39	5.36	1117
OneGrTresOn	53	5.44	246
OppMoney	32	5.53	874
Oppenh Csh	21	5.00	93
OvldExTrs	39	4.90	201
OvldExMM	37	5.64	350
PIMCO AdvI	20	5.49	9
PIMCO Adv	18	5.45	77
PNCGovtS	21	5.36	553
PNC GvI	21	5.66	65
PNCMoneyS	29	5.48	623
PNCMoneyI	29	5.78	706
PcfCptlCshAs	29	5.34	514
PcfCptlUSTrs	41	5.08	67
PcHrzGvHor	26	5.93	891
PacAmerMM	66	5.64	511
PacAmerUST	36	5.45	904
PcHrzGvPH	26	5.61	891
PcHrzPr	22	5.60	2559
QualivestA	35	5.42	173
QualivestGvA	44	4.70	62
QualivestY	35	5.82	69
QltyCsh	47	5.17	101
QuestCshGov	32	5.02	104
QuestCshPr	42	5.22	1504
RNC Liq	42	4.99	36
RegisDSI	15	5.20	106
RemTaxTr	29	5.51	468
RemTreasTr	25	5.06	114
RemGovtTr	29	5.47	168
RenaisGvt	24	5.17	47
RenaisMM	21	5.15	338
ResrveFd Gvt	11	4.92	734
ReserveFd	27	5.08	1424
RimcoTrs	48	4.89	109
RIMCOPrm	57	5.39	316
RiverUSGv	43	5.47	151
RiversdeCap	48	4.91	173
RdSqMM	29	5.55	687
RdSqUS	19	5.42	384
RshFGI	53	5.15	502
StarbGovT	38	5.24	158
StarbMMT	35	5.48	152
SteinroeCRs	49	5.38	527
SteinroeGvt	45	5.11	104
StepstnInst	20	5.36	522
StepstnInv	20	5.16	112
StepstnTrInst	22	5.32	129
StepstnTrInv	22	5.07	145
Strong	49	6.24	937
StrongUST	48	4.70	53
SumtCsh	53	5.02	95
SunAmMMA	34	5.03	271
TCW MM	31	5.62	118
TRowPRF	34	5.38	3898
TRowUST	39	5.01	705
TempltnM	26	5.07	235
ThmNtl	21	5.38	793
TowerUSTreas	28	5.26	77
TowerCsh	26	5.18	205
TrstShtGv	36	5.54	1030
TCU MMP	3	5.73	227
TrGvCsh	34	5.47	1110
TrstUSTrOb	32	5.45	3413
TSR FD DP	17	5.34	132
TSR FD UST	33	5.31	99
TwCntPrCapR	31	5.51	76
TwCntCs	31	5.31	1350
231 Prime	26	5.90	1426
231 Trsy	27	5.47	107
UMB Fed	35	5.49	197
UMB Prim	36	5.51	188
USGvtSec	33	5.67	571
US TreSec	6	4.66	208
US Tr Am	36	4.81	201
US Treasry	35	4.91	43
USAA Mutl	39	5.86	1345
VistaGovPS	22	5.46	605
VistaGov VS	22	5.21	337
VistaGovtInt	22	5.74	609
VistaPrInst	12	5.83	167
VistaPrimeP	12	5.66	81
VistaTrInst	15	5.52	22
WPG GovMM	34	5.14	187
WarburgPCR	46	5.58	426
WestcrCs	13	5.37	304
WestcrGv	17	5.18	60
WestcrPr	16	5.70	301
WestcrTr	31	5.59	482
WoodTreas	18	5.32	813
WoodGv	29	5.33	365
WoodMM	40	5.39	1334
WorkAsets	18	4.87	107
ZweigGvt	32	5.11	68
Tax Exempt:			
AARPHTe	37	2.80	128
AIMTx	32	3.03	31
ATOhioMuni	47	3.22	371
ActAsCal	42	2.92	297
ActAstTx	33	3.09	1544
ALMuni	49	3.49	139
AlxB TF	45	3.11	407
AllMuNJ	48	2.88	66
AllMunCal	38	2.68	227
AllMuCT	46	2.65	65
AllianMuVA	18	3.21	58
AllMuNY	36	2.64	184
AlliaMun	27	2.70	1192
AmAAdMuni	16	3.46	6
AmSouth TxEx	52	3.23	63
AmbTxFrF	43	3.13	33
AmbTxFrI	43	2.98	204
AmbTxFrA	43	2.88	4
ArchFd	22	2.78	6
ARKTaxFr A	49	3.60	63
AtlasCA	48	3.25	43
BT InvNY	44	2.86	82
BT InvTxFr	57	3.10	122
BdfdTxFr	29	2.81	202
BedfordNY	25	2.82	47
BenCAMu	30	3.24	207
BenCaTF	26	3.11	366
BenNaTF	30	3.01	103
Benchmrk TE	24	3.38	647
BenhFlorida	47	3.80	31
FidCapRsMu	32	2.95	114
FidInTxEx	37	3.57	2074
FidCA	24	3.13	689
FidCT	46	2.99	313
FidDlyTE	39	3.20	447
FidMA	28	2.88	729
FidMI	28	3.12	221
FidNJ	54	3.11	428
FidNY	41	3.14	741
FidOH	54	3.28	303
FidSpCA	24	3.49	1177
FidSpCT	48	3.11	155
FidSpNJ	53	3.44	452
FidSpNY	40	3.25	567
FidSpPA	36	3.32	234
FidTxEx	37	3.28	3644
FidSpFL	30	3.34	418
FidSpMA	29	3.05	412
FidSpMu	35	3.50	2196
FtInvTax	52	3.04	26
FtPraMu	45	3.18	193
FLMuniCash	35	3.45	135
MarinTx	48	2.95	21
MDMuniCsh	41	3.12	58
MedalistTxF	58	3.41	27
ML CMAMI	24	2.86	233
ML CMAOH	31	3.11	223
MLCMA Cal	39	2.95	1127
MLCMA CT	32	2.80	274
ML CMA MA	27	2.74	154
ML CMA NC	22	2.97	317
ML CMA NJ	26	2.84	522
MLCMA NY	23	2.98	935
ML CMA PA	22	2.95	370
MLCMA TE	40	3.10	7630
ML Inst TE	28	3.36	306
MichDly	31	2.99	57
MdwCATF	63	3.09	19
MdwRoyPFL	73	3.28	28
MdwstGrp	58	3.17	28
MdwOHTF	68	3.20	222
MnyMgt	9	3.28	68
MonitorOhM	52	3.45	40
MonitOhInv	52	3.34	38
MontCalMon	50	3.40	49
MS Muni	30	3.17	384
ML CMA AZ	24	3.20	101
NCMuniCsh	38	3.27	98
NCC TER	26	3.12	54
NCC TEI	26	3.22	192
NCarol Dly	50	2.98	144
NYMuniCshII	36	3.16	163
NYDlyTF	45	2.99	232
NatnsTEInvA	37	3.08	179
NatnsTETrA	37	3.35	908
NeubBMu	44	3.15	156
NewEngTxETr	58	3.33	74
NJDlyMun	56	2.92	106
PW KP CalT	33	2.94	147
PW KP NJ	22	2.61	36
PW KP NY	16	2.58	58
PW KP TxE	37	2.91	488
PWRMA NY	43	3.02	195
PW RM Tx	43	3.23	1584
ParkTFInvA	39	2.95	43
ParkTxFInst	39	3.05	93
PierpontTE	52	3.27	1116
PillarTE A	40	3.16	42
PilotSTTxDP	32	3.51	408
PilotSTTEP	37	3.20	233
PiperTF	47	2.90	195
PorticoTE	42	3.21	72
PrincrTE	36	3.05	101
PIFMnNY	42	3.46	214
PIFMuni	46	3.50	780
PIFMCs	42	3.68	300
PruCA	38	2.97	209
PruCdTx	56	3.25	952
PruNJ	62	3.14	170
PruNY	44	3.03	300
PruTax	57	3.16	528
PruMuniCT	60	3.09	58
PruMuniMA	61	3.08	39
PutCA	31	2.68	53
PutNY	37	3.23	43
PutTE	44	3.26	85
QualivestTFA	64	2.94	38
QuestCAMu	38	2.85	64
QuestGenMu	34	2.90	125
QuestNYMu	43	3.04	53
RemTx-ExTr	43	3.47	172
RepubNY TF	34	3.25	59
RsrvConn	49	2.57	33
ResrvInt	58	2.92	338
ResrvNY	50	2.63	153
RshFTx	54	2.66	24
SEIBainbrge	53	3.56	187
SEI CalifC	42	2.74	315
SEI InTF	60	3.58	842
SEI TECA	43	3.23	28
SEITxFr t	44	3.29	340
STITxExptIv	32	3.04	66
STITxExptTr	32	3.18	256
SAFC TF	60	3.35	85
Salomon NY	36	3.35	274
ShwbTE	40	3.03	3105

Source: *The Wall Street Journal*, February 9, 1995. Reprinted by permission of *The Wall Street Journal*, ©1995 Dow Jones & Company, Inc. All rights reserved worldwide.

MarquisTrR	10	5.20	167
Marshall A	30	5.74	1112
MedalistMM	41	5.34	120
MedalistTr	42	5.20	428
ML CBAMon	56	5.14	1419
ML CMAGv	56	5.18	3165
ML CMAMn	59	5.34	28611	◄─── Merrill Lynch's Cash Management Account
MerLyGv	44	5.62	1483
MerLlTr	44	5.33	389
MerLyln	58	5.69	4950
MerLyRdy	55	5.23	6482
MerLyRef	59	5.34	7453

Source: *The Wall Street Journal*, February 9, 1995. Reprinted by permission of *The Wall Street Journal*, ©1995 Dow Jones & Company, Inc. All rights reserved worldwide.

CDs offer higher rates than bank money market accounts, but you pay a price in penalties for early withdrawal of funds. Jumbo ($90,000–$100,000) certificates purchased through a broker are the only exception, and then only if the broker can sell the CD to another investor. When you tie up your funds until maturity, the CD becomes a non-liquid asset. This disadvantage is offset to some extent by FDIC deposit insurance.

You can often get a higher CD rate from your broker than your local bank or S&L, because your broker can shop nationally for the highest CD rate. You won't pay a fee for this service, because the bank pays the broker.

Every Wednesday *The Wall Street Journal* publishes an article on current certificates of deposit yields which accompanies the Banxquote Money Markets Table. Page 287 provides an example from the February 15, 1995 issue.

On the same day, the *Journal* publishes the more comprehensive **Banxquote Money Markets**, **High Yield Savings**, and **High Yield Jumbos** discussed earlier. Return to the February 15, 1995 example on page 280 (and blown up on page 287). It reports CD interest rates by locale, maturity, and size. Note that CDs are quoted by rate and yield in the "high yield" portions of the table. The more frequently interest is compounded, the higher the yield for each rate.

It pays to shop, too. You can see on page 280 that, while the average 3-month CD paid 4.28 percent, the broker average was 5.86 percent, and Southern Pac T&L's yield was 6.18 percent.

Yields on CDs Mixed
During Latest Week

By a WALL STREET JOURNAL *Staff Reporter*
NEW YORK — Yields on certificates of
deposit at major banks and brokerage
firms were mixed in the week ended
yesterday.

The average yield on six-month small-
denomination "savings" CDs crept up to
5.02% from 5%, according to a survey by
BanxQuote Money Markets. The average
yield on five-year savings CDs declined
to 6.81% from 6.93%, the Millburn, N.J.,
information service said.

The average yield on six-month broker-
sold CDs edged down to 6.09% from 6.12%,
while yields on five-year CDs rose to 7.22%
from 7.07%, BanxQuote said.

On large-denomination, "jumbo" CDs,
which typically require deposits of $95,000
or more, the average yield on six-month
certificates rose to 5.50% from 5.42%. On
five-year jumbos, the average slipped to
7.14% from 7.16%, according to Banx-
Quote.

HIGH YIELD SAVINGS
Small minimum balance/opening deposit, generally $500 to $25,000

Money Market Investments*	Rate		APY	Six Months CDs	Rate		APY
Eastern American, Herndon Va	5.87%	mA	6.03%	Heritage Bank, Willimar Mn	6.40%	yA	6.50%
Harris Bank, Chicago Il	5.83%	mA	5.99%	Beal Bank, Dallas Tx	6.36%	siA	6.46%
Lincoln National, Chicago Il	5.82%	mA	5.98%	Southn Pac T&L, Los Angeles Ca	6.25%	dA	6.45%
Citicorp Invest, Sioux Falls Sd	5.73%	dC	5.98%	Calif Thrift, Santa Barbara Ca	6.23%	dA	6.43%
MBNA America, Newark De	5.62%	dA	5.78%	First Commnwlth, Alexandria Va	6.15%	qA	6.29%

One Month CDs	Rate		APY	One Year CDs	Rate		APY
Southn Pac T&L, Los Angeles Ca	5.25%	dA	5.39%	Washington Savings, Waldorf Md	7.10%	qA	7.29%
Firstrust Bank, Philadelphia Pa	5.22%	siA	5.35%	Northern Trust, Chicago Il	6.97%	dA	7.22%
New South FSB, Birmingham Al	5.00%	siA	5.12%	New York Federal, New York NY	7.00%	siC	7.10%
Republic Banks, New York NY	4.75%	dA	4.86%	Southn Pac T&L, Los Angeles Ca	6.85%	dA	7.09%
Northern Trust, Chicago Il	4.75%	dA	4.86%	Calif Thrift, Santa Barbara Ca	6.81%	dA	7.05%

Two Months CDs	Rate		APY	Two Years CDs	Rate		APY
Southn Pac T&L, Los Angeles Ca	5.50%	dA	5.65%	Northern Trust, Chicago Il	7.30%	dA	7.57%
New South FSB, Birmingham Al	5.00%	siA	5.11%	East New York, New York NY	7.23%	dA	7.50%
Standard Pac, Newport Beach Ca	4.79%	dA	4.91%	Washington Savings, Waldorf Md	7.30%	qA	7.50%
Northern Trust, Chicago Il	4.75%	dA	4.86%	Southn Pac T&L, Los Angeles Ca	7.20%	dA	7.46%
Safra National, New York NY	4.55%	dA	4.65%	Calif Thrift, Santa Barbara Ca	7.17%	dA	7.43%

Three Months CDs	Rate		APY	Five Years CDs	Rate		APY
Southn Pac T&L, Los Angeles Ca	6.00%	dA	6.18%	Washington Savings, Waldorf Md	7.90%	qA	8.14%
Smith Barney (BD), New York NY	5.75%	yA	5.88%	Northern Trust, Chicago Il	7.72%	dA	8.02%
Paine Webber (BD), New York NY	5.75%	yA	5.88%	Eastern Savings, Baltimore Md	7.53%	mA	7.80%
Merrill Lynch (BD), New York NY	5.75%	yA	5.88%	Broadway National, New York NY	7.50%	dA	7.79%
Fidelity Invsmt (BD), Boston Ma	5.70%	yA	5.82%	Key Bank USA, Albany NY	7.50%	mA	7.76%

TREASURY BILLS

Our national debt made the news when it passed $4 trillion, and it continues to grow. Treasury bills (T-bills) constitute about a quarter of the total national debt, and this huge dollar volume makes Treasury bills one of the most important short-term investment instruments.

The U.S. Treasury borrows by selling bills at auction (primary market) every Monday in New York, and in the following day's *Journal* you will find a summary at the end of the **Credit Markets** article of the U.S. Treasury's Monday auction of 13- and 26-week bills (see the indexes at the front of the first and last sections). An example drawn from the Wednesday, January 18, 1995 edition of the *Journal* appears on page 289.

Treasury bills are sold on a discount basis. Buyers pay less than the $10,000 face value (par value), the amount they will receive when the bill matures and is redeemed by the U.S. Treasury. If bidding is strong and the price is high, the effective rate of interest will be low, and vice versa.

To understand how this works, place yourself in the role of a buyer. If you pay $9,750 for a bill maturing in 91 days (about a quarter of a year), your effective annual yield is approximately 10 percent. Remember, $250 in a quarter-year is the equivalent of $1,000 in a year, or 10 percent of a $10,000 base. (Use $10,000 as the base for calculating the discount rate, rather than $9,750, because Treasury bills' yields are usually quoted on a discount basis; that is, the discount—$250—is measured against face value—$10,000.) If strong bidding drives the price to $9,875, your yield falls to 5 percent. If weak bidding or selling pressure permits the price to fall to $9,500, the effective yield rises to 20 percent. The more you pay for the Treasury bill, the lower your yield, and vice versa. These examples are summarized here. You can easily approximate the following discount rates using this simple table.

Face (redemption) Value	$10,000	$10,000	$10,000
Selling Price	$9,875	$9,750	$9,500
(note: prices falling)			
Discount (difference)	$125	$250	$500
Approximate Yield (Discount Rate)	5%	10%	20%
(note: yield rising)			

CREDIT MARKETS

Meanwhile, the Treasury sold 13-week and 26-week bills. Here are the results:

Rates are determined by the difference between the purchase price and face value. Thus, higher bidding narrows the investor's return while lower bidding widens it. The percentage rates are calculated on a 360-day year, while the coupon-equivalent yield is based on a 365-day year.

	13-Week	26-Week
Applications	$70,942,884,000	$47,321,886,000
Accepted bids	$13,452,915,000	$13,498,766,000
Accepted at low price	6%	36%
Accepted noncompet'ly	$1,549,285,000	$1,692,420,000
Average price (Rate)	98.541 (5.77%)	96.871 (6.19%)
High price (Rate)	98.541 (5.77%)	96.876 (6.18%)
Low price (Rate)	98.539 (5.78%)	96.871 (6.19%)
Coupon equivalent	5.94%	6.48%
CUSIP number	912794R63	912794U28

Both issues are dated Jan. 19. The 13-week bills mature April 20, 1995, and the 26-week bills mature July 20, 1995.

YIELD COMPARISONS

Based on Merrill Lynch Bond Indexes, priced as of midafternoon Eastern time.

	1/17	1/16	–52 Week– High	Low
Corp.-Govt. Master	7.90%	7.86%	8.09%	5.46%
Treasury 1-10yr	7.55	7.49	7.79	4.55
10+ yr	7.98	7.99	8.36	6.36
Agencies 1-10yr	8.03	7.96	8.17	5.14
10+ yr	8.20	8.20	8.51	6.73
Corporate				
1-10 yr High Qlty	8.15	8.12	8.34	5.67
Med Qlty	8.47	8.44	8.65	6.00
10+yr High Qlty	8.52	8.51	8.84	7.08
Med Qlty	8.95	8.94	9.24	7.42
Yankee bonds(1)	8.48	8.46	8.65	6.62
Current-coupon mortgages (2)				
GNMA 8.50%	8.75	8.75	9.13	6.39
FNMA 8.50%	8.75	8.74	9.04	6.40
FHLMC8.50%	8.76	8.75	9.05	6.40
High-yield corporates	11.22	11.22	11.37	8.88
New tax-exempts				
7-12-yr G.O. (AA)	6.16	6.09	6.45	4.65
12-22-yr G.O. (AA)	6.34	6.33	6.69	4.91
22+yr revenue (A)	6.50	6.48	6.89	5.31

Note: High quality rated AAA-AA; medium quality A-BBB/Baa; high yield, BB/Ba-C.
(1) Dollar-denominated, SEC-registered bonds of foreign issuers sold in the U.S. (2) Reflects the 52-week high and low of mortgage-backed securities indexes rather than the individual securities shown.

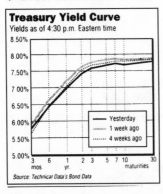

Treasury Yield Curve

Yields as of 4:30 p.m. Eastern time

Yesterday
1 week ago
4 weeks ago

Source: Technical Data's Bond Data

On Monday, January 17, 1995, the U.S. Treasury auctioned 13-week bills in the primary market at an average price of $9,854.10 and a discount of $145.90, for a discount rate of 5.77% and a coupon equivalent of 6.19%. ➤

Meanwhile, the Treasury sold 13-week and 26-week bills. Here are the results:

Rates are determined by the difference between the purchase price and face value. Thus, higher bidding narrows the investor's return while lower bidding widens it. The percentage rates are calculated on a 360-day year, while the coupon-equivalent yield is based on a 365-day year.

	13-Week	26-Week
Applications	$70,942,884,000	$47,321,886,000
Accepted bids	$13,452,915,000	$13,498,766,000
Accepted at low price	6%	36%
Accepted noncompet'ly	$1,549,285,000	$1,692,420,000
Average price (Rate)	98.541 (5.77%)	96.871 (6.19%)
High price (Rate)	98.541 (5.77%)	96.876 (6.18%)
Low price (Rate)	98.539 (5.78%)	96.871 (6.19%)
Coupon equivalent	5.94%	6.48%
CUSIP number	912794R63	912794U28

Both issues are dated Jan. 19. The 13-week bills mature April 20, 1995, and the 26-week bills mature July 20, 1995.

Take a moment to review the method used to compute the discount rate in the bottom row of the table on page 288. The following calculations show how the 10 percent rate was obtained. Discount rate (Yield) = Discount expressed as a percentage of par (yield) × Time factor multiplier (which is needed to generate the annual rate).

$$
\begin{array}{l}
\text{Approximate} \\
\text{discount rate} \\
\text{(yield)}
\end{array}
= \frac{\text{Discount}}{\text{Face or par value}} \times 4
\quad
\begin{array}{l}
\text{(Because 91 days} \\
\text{are about a quarter} \\
\text{of a 365-day year)}
\end{array}
$$

$$
= \frac{\$250}{\$10,000} \times 4
$$

$$
= 2.5\% \times 4
$$

$$
= 10\%
$$

The true discount-rate formula is very close to this approximation. The "time factor multiplier" is somewhat different, because the "year" is 360 days. Returning to the example, the discount rate would be calculated as follows:

$$
\text{Discount rate} = \frac{\text{Discount}}{\text{Par value}} \times \text{Time multiplier}
$$

$$
= \frac{\$250}{\$10,000} \times \frac{360}{91}
$$

$$
= 0.0989
$$

$$
= 9.89\%
$$

You can see that the true discount rate of 9.89 is less than the 10 percent approximation calculated above, because the time multiplier ($360/91$) is less than 4.

The discount rate is only an approximation of the true yield to maturity or coupon equivalent. In the first place, the purchase price of the T-bill was $9,750, not $10,000. In the fraction below, $9,750 replaces $10,000. And secondly, a year is 365 days, not 360. Thus, the correct time multiplier is $365/91$.

Now calculate the actual yield, called the investment yield to maturity, for the same example.

$$\text{Yield to maturity} = \frac{\text{Discount}}{\text{Purchase price}} \times \text{Time factor}$$

$$= \frac{\$250}{\$9,750} \times \frac{365}{91}$$

$$= 0.1029$$

$$= 10.29\%$$

You can see that the discount rate of 9.89% is less than the true yield of 10.29 percent, because the discount is expressed as a percentage of the purchase price rather than par, and the year is calculated at 365 rather than 360 days.

Why are T-bills quoted on a discount rather than true-yield basis? Because the arithmetic is much easier to deal with, and that was important years ago before the advent of data processing equipment.

Now that you understand the relationship between the discount rate and the yield to maturity (coupon equivalent), look at the illustration on page 289 from the Wednesday, January 18, 1995 *Journal*. Potential buyers submitted $70,942,884,000 in bids, of which the Treasury accepted $13,452,915,000. The Treasury took the highest bid of $9,854.10 (98.541 percent of par) and then accepted progressively lower bids until it generated the required funds, stopping at the low bid of $9,853.90 (98.539 percent of $10,000). On the average, the U.S. Treasury received $9,854.10 (98.541 percent of face value) for each $10,000 bill auctioned (same as the high price) on Monday, January 16, 1995, for a discount rate of 5.77 percent and a coupon equivalent yield of 5.94 percent. Note that in over $13 billion of successful bids, only 20 cents separated the high and low bids. It's a tough business.

Here is how you calculate the discount rate using the Treasury auction figures on page 289.

$$\text{Discount rate} = \frac{\text{Discount}}{\text{Par value}} \times \text{Time multiplier}$$

$$= \frac{\$145.90 \text{ (i.e., } \$10,000 - \$9,854.10)}{\$10,000} \times \frac{360}{91}$$

$$= 0.00577$$

$$= 5.77\%$$

You can also compute the true (coupon equivalent) yield as follows.

$$\text{Yield to maturity} = \frac{\text{Discount}}{\text{Purchase price}} \times \text{Time factor}$$

$$= \frac{\$145.90}{\$9,854.10} \times \frac{365}{91}$$

$$= 0.0593867$$

$$= 5.94\%$$

Your motivation for buying Treasury bills is probably quite simple: You have idle cash on which you wish to earn an interest return. If you and all other bidders for Treasury bills have ample funds and are eager to buy, you will drive the price close to $10,000 and earn a low rate of return. If you and all other bidders do not have ample funds, you can be enticed only by a very low price for the right to receive $10,000 in 91 days, and you will earn a high rate of return.

Now, this discussion has been presented as if you could participate in the bidding for Treasury bills. Well, you can't. The auction is conducted in New York by the Fed, acting as the Treasury's agent, and bidding is conducted by large firms that deal in, and make a market for, Treasury bills. They bid for the bills at the weekly Monday auction (primary market), so they can resell them at a markup on any business day (secondary market).

You *can* go to your local regional Federal Reserve Bank and buy Treasury bills, but you'll have to do so noncompetitively at the average rate (discount) established at the New York auction. (For instance, the 5.77 percent discount rate and 5.94 percent yield in the example on page 289.) Note that the Treasury accepted $1,549,285,000 of bids noncompetitively on January 16, 1995. These were bids made directly to the Fed by individuals and small institutions who could not participate in the auction.

There are two ways to buy T-bills from the Fed: immediately or by opening an account that permits purchases at a later date.

If you want to purchase Treasuries right away, obtain what is called a "Tender" form from the Fed or your bank, fill out the "Direct Deposit" section, and include a money order or certified check for $10,000. The IFed will mail you your change (the discount) and return the $10,000 at maturity (91 days).

If you wish to open an account to purchase Treasuries in the near future, complete and return the "New Account Application." Once the application

is received and you are given an account number, you can then contact the Fed by phone and purchase Treasuries with a tender offer and certified check for the exact amount.

If you purchase a Treasury bill from the Fed, you must hold it to maturity, which is not the case if you have purchased it from your bank or broker in the secondary market. Your bank or broker can sell it on the open or secondary market for you at any time, but be prepared to pay a flat fee of $25 to $50 per transaction. In order to gain clients with large assets, however, some brokerage houses do not charge a fee if an investor purchases more than $100,000 of Treasury bills.

The Wall Street Journal reports on activity in the secondary market each day, under the heading **Treasury Bonds, Notes & Bills**. Find this table by using the index on the front page or the index on the first page of Section C.

Look at the excerpts from the Friday February 3, 1995 *Journal* on pages 294 and 295. The data represent quotations for Thursday, February 2, 1995. Keep in mind that these bills are auctioned on Mondays, issued on Thursdays, and mature 13 weeks later (also on a Thursday). Thus, using the February 2, 1995 report, you know that the latest 91-day bill included in the report was auctioned on Monday, January 30, 1995, and issued on Thursday, February 2, 1995. It will mature 13 weeks later, on Thursday, May 4, 1995. (Note the boldface type for the 13- and 26-week maturity dates.)

On February 2, that bill carried a discount rate (bid) of 5.85 percent. This figure is located in the row opposite the date under the column headed "Bid." Buyers (bidders) paid a price (less than $10,000) that would yield 5.85 percent if the Treasury bill were held to maturity and cashed in for $10,000. Sellers on February 2 were asking a higher price (lower interest rate), equivalent to 5.83 percent. The last column gives the true yield of 6.0 percent. (The other maturity dates are for older bills and for bills with maturities of more than 91 days.)

It is now time to complete this discussion of short-term interest rates with a description of how you can track the yield on your own interest-earning investments and compare them with market rates.

TREASURY BONDS, NOTES & BILLS

Thursday, February 2, 1995

Representative Over-the-Counter quotations based on transactions of $1 million or more.

Treasury bond, note and bill quotes are as of mid-afternoon. Colons in bid-and-asked quotes represent 32nds; 101:01 means 101 1/32. Net changes in 32nds. n-Treasury note. Treasury bill quotes in hundredths, quoted on terms of a rate of discount. Days to maturity calculated from settlement date. All yields are to maturity and based on the asked quote. Latest 13-week and 26-week bills are boldfaced. For bonds callable prior to maturity, yields are computed to the earliest call date for issues quoted above par and to the maturity date for issues below par. *-When issued.

Source: Federal Reserve Bank of New York.

U.S. Treasury strips as of 3 p.m. Eastern time, also based on transactions of $1 million or more. Colons in bid-and-asked quotes represent 32nds; 101:01 means 101 1/32. Net changes in 32nds. Yields calculated on the asked quotation. ci-stripped coupon interest. bp-Treasury bond, stripped principal. np-Treasury note, stripped principal. For bonds callable prior to maturity, yields are computed to the earliest call date for issues quoted above par and to the maturity date for issues below par.

Source: Bear, Stearns & Co. via Street Software Technology Inc.

GOVT. BONDS & NOTES

Rate	Maturity Mo/Yr	Bid	Asked	Chg.	Ask Yld.
3	Feb 95	99:29	100:29	....	0.00
$5\frac{1}{2}$	Feb 95n	99:31	100:01	....	4.11
$7\frac{3}{4}$	Feb 95n	100:01	100:03	....	3.77
$7\frac{7}{8}$	Feb 95-00	100:03	100:07	− 2	0.00
$10\frac{1}{2}$	Feb 95	100:04	100:06	....	2.69
$11\frac{1}{4}$	Feb 95n	100:05	100:07	− 1	2.18
$3\frac{7}{8}$	Feb 95n	99:28	99:30	+ 1	4.82
$3\frac{7}{8}$	Mar 95n	99:22	99:24	....	5.53
$8\frac{3}{8}$	Apr 95n	100:12	100:14	....	5.85
$3\frac{7}{8}$	Apr 95n	99:14	99:16	....	6.02
$6\frac{7}{8}$	Apr 97n	98:27	98:29	− 3	7.42
$6\frac{1}{2}$	May 97n	98:00	98:02	− 3	7.44
$8\frac{1}{2}$	May 97n	102:04	102:06	− 6	7.44
$6\frac{3}{4}$	May 97n	98:15	98:17	− 4	7.45
$6\frac{3}{8}$	Jun 97n	97:20	97:22	− 4	7.45
$8\frac{1}{2}$	Jul 97n	102:07	102:09	− 4	7.46
$5\frac{1}{2}$	Jul 97n	95:18	95:20	− 4	7.46
$6\frac{1}{2}$	Aug 97n	97:24	97:26	− 3	7.47
$8\frac{5}{8}$	Aug 97n	102:19	102:21	− 4	7.45
$5\frac{5}{8}$	Aug 97n	95:22	95:24	− 4	7.48
$5\frac{1}{2}$	Sep 97n	95:07	95:09	− 5	7.50
$8\frac{3}{4}$	Oct 97n	102:30	103:00	− 4	7.50
$5\frac{3}{4}$	Oct 97n	95:22	95:24	− 6	7.50
$7\frac{3}{8}$	Nov 97n	99:21	99:23	− 7	7.49
$8\frac{7}{8}$	Nov 97n	103:09	103:11	− 5	7.52
6	Nov 97n	96:04	96:06	− 5	7.53
6	Dec 97n	96:02	96:04	− 5	7.51
$7\frac{7}{8}$	Jan 98n	100:27	100:29	− 7	7.53
$5\frac{5}{8}$	Jan 98n	94:28	94:30	− 4	7.55
$8\frac{1}{8}$	Feb 98n	101:15	101:17	− 6	7.55
$5\frac{1}{8}$	Feb 98n	93:12	93:14	− 8	7.57
$5\frac{1}{8}$	Mar 98n	93:07	93:09	− 8	7.56
$7\frac{7}{8}$	Apr 98n	100:26	100:28	− 9	7.56
$5\frac{1}{8}$	Apr 98n	92:31	93:01	− 5	7.60
9	May 98n	104:01	104:03	− 5	7.56
$5\frac{3}{8}$	May 98n	93:17	93:19	− 7	7.60
$5\frac{1}{8}$	Jun 98n	92:21	92:23	− 5	7.60
$8\frac{1}{4}$	Jul 98n	101:29	101:31	− 6	7.59
$5\frac{1}{4}$	Jul 98n	92:27	92:29	− 5	7.61
$9\frac{1}{4}$	Aug 98n	105:01	105:03	− 7	7.58
$4\frac{3}{4}$	Aug 98n	91:05	91:07	− 5	7.61
$4\frac{3}{4}$	Sep 98n	91:00	91:02	− 8	7.60
$7\frac{1}{8}$	Oct 98n	98:23	98:25	− 5	7.51
$4\frac{3}{4}$	Oct 98n	90:24	90:26	− 7	7.63
$3\frac{1}{2}$	Nov 98	88:25	89:25	− 2	6.60
$8\frac{7}{8}$	Nov 98n	104:02	104:04	− 8	7.60
$5\frac{1}{8}$	Nov 98n	91:28	91:30	− 7	7.60
$5\frac{1}{8}$	Dec 98n	91:23	91:25	− 4	7.60
$6\frac{3}{8}$	Jan 99n	95:26	95:28	− 5	7.61
5	Jan 99n	91:03	91:05	− 9	7.62
$8\frac{7}{8}$	Feb 99n	104:09	104:11	− 8	7.60
$5\frac{1}{2}$	Feb 99n	92:24	92:26	− 6	7.59
$5\frac{7}{8}$	Mar 99n	93:27	93:29	− 6	7.62
7	Apr 99n	97:26	97:28	− 6	7.60
$6\frac{1}{2}$	Apr 99n	95:31	96:01	− 6	7.61
$9\frac{1}{8}$	May 99n	105:11	105:13	− 7	7.62
$6\frac{3}{4}$	May 99n	96:24	96:26	− 8	7.63
$6\frac{3}{4}$	Jun 99n	96:23	96:25	− 8	7.62
$6\frac{3}{8}$	Jul 99n	95:09	95:11	− 8	7.63
$6\frac{7}{8}$	Jul 99n	97:04	97:06	− 7	7.63
8	Aug 99n	101:13	101:15	− 5	7.61
$6\frac{7}{8}$	Aug 99n	97:03	97:05	− 8	7.62
$7\frac{1}{8}$	Sep 99n	97:31	98:01	− 7	7.64
6	Oct 99n	93:19	93:21	− 10	7.63
$7\frac{1}{2}$	Oct 99n	99:13	99:15	− 6	7.64
$7\frac{7}{8}$	Nov 99n	100:29	100:31	− 8	7.63
$7\frac{3}{4}$	Nov 99n	100:12	100:14	− 7	7.64
$7\frac{3}{4}$	Dec 99n	100:13	100:15	− 8	7.63
$6\frac{3}{8}$	Jan 00n	94:27	94:29	− 5	7.63
$7\frac{3}{4}$	Jan 00n	100:16	100:18	− 9	7.61
$8\frac{1}{2}$	Feb 00n	103:17	103:19	− 1	7.63
$5\frac{1}{2}$	Apr 00n	91:00	91:02	− 1	7.62
$8\frac{7}{8}$	May 00n	105:11	105:13	− 3	7.61
$8\frac{3}{8}$	Aug 95-00	100:14	100:18	− 1	7.26
$8\frac{3}{4}$	Aug 00n	104:29	104:31	− 3	7.63
$8\frac{1}{2}$	Nov 00n	103:29	103:31	− 3	7.64
$7\frac{3}{4}$	Feb 01n	100:14	100:16	− 3	7.64
$11\frac{3}{4}$	Feb 01	119:15	119:19	− 4	7.63
8	May 01n	101:22	101:24	− 7	7.64
$13\frac{1}{8}$	May 01	126:28	127:00	− 4	7.63
$7\frac{7}{8}$	Aug 01n	101:03	101:05	− 5	7.65
8	Aug 96-01	100:10	100:14	− 15	7.69

U.S. TREASURY STRIPS

Mat.	Type	Bid	Asked	Chg.	Ask Yld.
Feb 95	ci	99:28	99:28	+ 1	5.66
Feb 95	np	99:27	99:27	+ 2	5.76
May 95	ci	98:13	98:13	+ 1	5.93
May 95	np	98:12	98:12	+ 1	6.08
Aug 95	ci	96:25	96:25	+ 1	6.34
Aug 95	np	96:22	96:22	+ 2	6.52
Nov 95	ci	95:01	95:02	+ 1	6.70
Nov 95	np	95:00	95:00	+ 1	6.75
Feb 96	ci	93:07	93:08	+ 1	6.95
Feb 96	np	93:06	93:07	+ 1	6.99
May 96	ci	91:14	91:15	− 1	7.15
May 96	np	91:13	91:14	....	7.17
Aug 96	ci	89:29	89:31	....	7.06
Nov 96	ci	88:04	88:05	− 1	7.24
Nov 96	np	87:30	87:31	− 2	7.37
Feb 97	ci	86:13	86:14	− 1	7.33
May 97	ci	84:21	84:23	− 1	7.44
May 97	np	84:20	84:22	− 2	7.46
Aug 97	ci	83:02	83:04	− 2	7.46
Aug 97	np	82:31	83:01	− 2	7.51
Nov 97	ci	81:15	81:17	− 3	7.50
Nov 97	np	81:13	81:15	− 2	7.54
Feb 98	ci	79:28	79:30	− 2	7.54
Feb 98	np	79:25	79:27	− 3	7.58
May 98	ci	78:12	78:14	− 3	7.56
May 98	np	78:10	78:12	− 3	7.59
Aug 98	ci	76:27	76:30	− 2	7.58
Aug 98	np	76:24	76:27	− 2	7.62
Nov 98	ci	75:14	75:17	− 2	7.58
Nov 98	np	75:11	75:14	....	7.62
Feb 99	ci	73:31	74:02	− 3	7.61
Feb 99	np	73:29	74:00	− 3	7.63
May 99	ci	72:18	72:21	− 3	7.62
May 99	np	72:16	72:19	− 3	7.64
Aug 99	ci	71:12	71:15	− 4	7.56
Aug 99	np	71:06	71:09	− 3	7.62
Nov 99	ci	70:01	70:04	− 4	7.58
Nov 99	np	69:28	69:31	− 4	7.63
Feb 00	ci	68:23	68:26	− 4	7.58
Feb 00	np	68:16	68:19	− 4	7.65
May 00	ci	67:17	67:20	− 4	7.56
May 00	np	67:10	67:13	− 4	7.63
Aug 00	ci	66:04	66:08	− 4	7.60
Aug 00	np	65:30	66:02	− 4	7.65
Nov 00	ci	64:30	65:01	− 4	7.60
Nov 00	np	64:23	64:27	− 4	7.65
Feb 01	ci	63:21	63:25	− 3	7.61
Feb 01	np	63:15	63:19	− 3	7.66
May 01	ci	62:16	62:20	− 3	7.61
May 01	np	62:08	62:12	− 3	7.67
Aug 01	ci	61:10	61:14	− 3	7.61
Aug 01	np	61:04	61:07	− 3	7.66
Nov 01	ci	60:07	60:11	− 3	7.60
Nov 01	np	60:00	60:03	− 3	7.66
Feb 02	ci	58:26	58:30	− 4	7.67
May 02	ci	58:00	58:04	− 3	7.60
May 02	np	57:24	57:28	− 3	7.67
Aug 02	ci	56:18	56:22	− 3	7.69
Aug 02	np	56:17	56:21	− 3	7.70
Nov 02	ci	55:15	55:19	− 3	7.70
Feb 03	ci	54:09	54:13	− 3	7.73
Feb 03	np	54:14	54:18	− 3	7.70
May 03	ci	53:08	53:12	− 3	7.74
Aug 03	ci	52:07	52:11	− 3	7.74
Aug 03	np	52:13	52:18	− 3	7.69
Nov 03	ci	51:08	51:12	− 3	7.74
Feb 04	ci	50:05	50:10	− 3	7.76
Feb 04	np	50:14	50:19	− 3	7.70
May 04	ci	49:07	49:11	− 4	7.77
May 04	np	49:16	49:20	− 4	7.70
Aug 04	ci	48:08	48:12	− 4	7.77
Aug 04	np	48:18	48:23	− 4	7.70
Nov 04	ci	47:11	47:15	− 4	7.77
Nov 04	bp	47:08	47:12	− 4	7.79
Nov 04	np	47:27	48:00	− 4	7.66
Feb 05	ci	46:09	46:14	− 4	7.80
May 05	ci	45:14	45:18	− 3	7.80
May 05	bp	45:12	45:17	− 4	7.81
Aug 05	ci	44:18	44:22	− 2	7.80
Aug 05	bp	44:16	44:21	− 4	7.81
Nov 05	ci	43:21	43:26	− 3	7.81
Feb 06	ci	42:25	42:29	− 3	7.82
Feb 06	bp	43:05	43:09	− 3	7.74
May 06	ci	41:31	42:03	− 3	7.83
Aug 06	ci	41:05	41:09	− 3	7.83
Nov 06	ci	40:10	40:15	− 3	7.84
Feb 07	ci	39:16	39:20	− 2	7.85
May 07	ci	38:23	38:28	− 2	7.85
Aug 07	ci	37:30	38:03	− 2	7.86
Nov 07	ci	37:07	37:11	− 2	7.86
Feb 08	ci	36:14	36:19	− 2	7.87
May 08	ci	35:23	35:28	− 2	7.88
Aug 20	bp	13:28	14:00	....	7.86
Nov 20	ci	13:16	13:19	....	7.89
Feb 21	ci	13:10	13:14	....	7.87
Feb 21	bp	13:15	13:18	....	7.83
May 21	ci	13:04	13:08	....	7.85
May 21	bp	13:09	13:12	....	7.81
Aug 21	ci	12:30	13:02	....	7.83
Aug 21	bp	13:03	13:06	....	7.79
Nov 21	ci	12:26	12:29	....	7.79
Nov 21	bp	12:31	13:02	....	7.75
Feb 22	ci	12:20	12:24	+ 2	7.77
May 22	ci	12:15	12:18	+ 1	7.75
Aug 22	ci	12:14	12:17	+ 2	7.69
Aug 22	bp	12:17	12:21	+ 2	7.66
Nov 22	ci	12:08	12:12	+ 1	7.67
Nov 22	bp	12:12	12:15	+ 3	7.64
Feb 23	ci	12:04	12:07	+ 3	7.65
Feb 23	bp	12:06	12:09	+ 2	7.63
May 23	ci	11:27	11:30	+ 1	7.66
Aug 23	ci	11:22	11:25	....	7.64
Aug 23	bp	11:25	11:28	+ 1	7.61
Nov 23	ci	11:19	11:22	+ 1	7.60
May 24	ci	11:17	11:20	+ 1	7.49
Nov 24	ci	10:29	11:00	+ 1	7.56
Nov 24	bp	10:31	11:02	+ 1	7.53

TREASURY BILLS

← Treasury Bills

Maturity	Days to Mat.	Bid	Asked	Chg.	Ask Yld.
Feb 09 '95	3	5.27	5.17	−0.09	5.24
Feb 16 '95	10	5.32	5.22	−0.12	5.30
Feb 23 '95	17	5.14	5.04	−0.05	5.12
Mar 02 '95	24	5.22	5.12	−0.07	5.21
Mar 09 '95	31	5.46	5.42	−0.11	5.52
Mar 16 '95	38	5.47	5.43	−0.11	5.54
Mar 23 '95	45	5.48	5.44	−0.12	5.55
Mar 30 '95	52	5.46	5.42	−0.06	5.54
Apr 06 '95	59	5.61	5.59	−0.17	5.72
Apr 13 '95	66	5.67	5.65	−0.15	5.79
Apr 20 '95	73	5.78	5.76	−0.09	5.91
Apr 27 '95	80	5.79	5.77	−0.07	5.93
May 04 '95	**87**	**5.85**	**5.83**	**−0.05**	**6.00**
May 11 '95	94	5.87	5.85	−0.04	6.02
May 18 '95	101	5.90	5.88	−0.04	6.06
May 25 '95	108	5.91	5.89	−0.03	6.08
Jun 01 '95	115	5.93	5.91	−0.04	6.11
Jun 08 '95	122	5.98	5.96	−0.05	6.17
Jun 15 '95	129	6.00	5.98	−0.05	6.20
Jun 22 '95	136	6.01	5.99	−0.05	6.21
Jun 29 '95	143	6.01	5.99	−0.04	6.22
Jul 06 '95	150	6.07	6.05	−0.06	6.29
Jul 13 '95	157	6.13	6.11	−0.02	6.36
Jul 20 '95	164	6.16	6.14	−0.01	6.40
Jul 27 '95	171	6.17	6.15	−0.01	6.42
Aug 03 '95	**178**	**6.19**	**6.17**	**−0.02**	**6.45**
Aug 24 '95	199	6.24	6.22	....	6.51
Sep 21 '95	227	6.27	6.25	....	6.55
Oct 19 '95	255	6.37	6.35	−0.06	6.68
Nov 16 '95	283	6.41	6.39	−0.04	6.74
Dec 14 '95	311	6.42	6.40	....	6.77
Jan 11 '96	339	6.51	6.49	−0.01	6.90

← 91-day T-Bill (May 04 '95)

Source: *The Wall Street Journal*, February 3, 1995. Reprinted by permission of *The Wall Street Journal*, ©1995 Dow Jones & Company, Inc. All rights reserved worldwide.

TREASURY BILLS				
Maturity	Days to Mat.	Bid	Asked	Chg.	Ask Yld.

Maturity	Days to Mat.	Bid	Asked	Chg.	Ask Yld.
Feb 09 '95	3	5.27	5.17	−0.09	5.24
Feb 16 '95	10	5.32	5.22	−0.12	5.30
Feb 23 '95	17	5.14	5.04	−0.05	5.12
Mar 02 '95	24	5.22	5.12	−0.07	5.21
Mar 09 '95	31	5.46	5.42	−0.11	5.52
Mar 16 '95	38	5.47	5.43	−0.11	5.54
Mar 23 '95	45	5.48	5.44	−0.12	5.55
Mar 30 '95	52	5.46	5.42	−0.06	5.54
Apr 06 '95	59	5.61	5.59	−0.17	5.72
Apr 13 '95	66	5.67	5.65	−0.15	5.79
Apr 20 '95	73	5.78	5.76	−0.09	5.91
Apr 27 '95	80	5.79	5.77	−0.07	5.93
May 04 '95	**87**	**5.85**	**5.83**	**−0.05**	**6.00**
May 11 '95	94	5.87	5.85	−0.04	6.02
May 18 '95	101	5.90	5.88	−0.04	6.06
May 25 '95	108	5.91	5.89	−0.03	6.08
Jun 01 '95	115	5.93	5.91	−0.04	6.11
Jun 08 '95	122	5.98	5.96	−0.05	6.17
Jun 15 '95	129	6.00	5.98	−0.05	6.20
Jun 22 '95	136	6.01	5.99	−0.05	6.21
Jun 29 '95	143	6.01	5.99	−0.04	6.22
Jul 06 '95	150	6.07	6.05	−0.06	6.29
Jul 13 '95	157	6.13	6.11	−0.02	6.36
Jul 20 '95	164	6.16	6.14	−0.01	6.40
Jul 27 '95	171	6.17	6.15	−0.01	6.42
Aug 03 '95	**178**	**6.19**	**6.17**	**−0.02**	**6.45**
Aug 24 '95	199	6.24	6.22	....	6.51
Sep 21 '95	227	6.27	6.25	....	6.55
Oct 19 '95	255	6.37	6.35	−0.06	6.68
Nov 16 '95	283	6.41	6.39	−0.04	6.74
Dec 14 '95	311	6.42	6.40	....	6.77
Jan 11 '96	339	6.51	6.49	−0.01	6.90

On Thursday, February 2, 1995, the 91-day T-bill rate on the open (secondary) market was 5.85% for bills auctioned on Monday, January 30, issued on Thursday, February 2, and maturing 13 weeks later on Thursday, May 4.

TRACKING SHORT-TERM INTEREST RATES

Every day you can use the **Markets Diary** report on the left side of the first page (Cl) of the *Journal*'s last section to follow some of the most important short-term interest rates. Consult the excerpt from the Friday, February 3, 1995 edition on page 296, starting with the chart labeled **Interest**, which displays the *federal funds* rate for the preceding 18 months. This is the rate banks charge one another for overnight loans of reserves in amounts of $1 million or more. The federal funds rate was 5.97 percent on February 2, 1995. Four more interest rates follow. Except for Treasury bills, which were discussed above, these quotes are for instruments purchased by financial institutions in very large amounts. Nonetheless, they provide a good daily snapshot of current short-term rates. Note that the yields increase with increased risk and reduced liquidity. The February 2, 1995 rates were 3-month T-bills, 5.85 percent (as noted above); new 3-month certificates of deposit, 5.54 percent; 90-day *commercial paper* (short-term corporate debt), 6.24 percent; and 3-month *Eurodollar deposits* ("dollar" denominated deposits held at European banks), 6.31 percent.

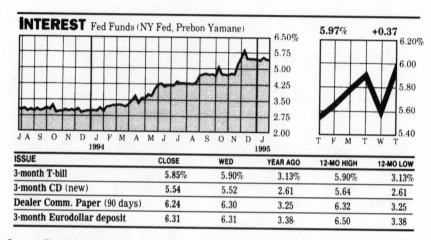

ISSUE	CLOSE	WED	YEAR AGO	12-MO HIGH	12-MO LOW
3-month T-bill	5.85%	5.90%	3.13%	5.90%	3.13%
3-month CD (new)	5.54	5.52	2.61	5.64	2.61
Dealer Comm. Paper (90 days)	6.24	6.30	3.25	6.32	3.25
3-month Eurodollar deposit	6.31	6.31	3.38	6.50	3.38

Source: *The Wall Street Journal*, February 3, 1995. Reprinted by permission of *The Wall Street Journal*, ©1995 Dow Jones & Company, Inc. All rights reserved worldwide.

You can follow an even larger array of interest rates each day in **Money Rates**, a report that lists the current yields on most of the major money market interest-rate instruments. Look for it in the front-page index of the first and last sections. The example from the Thursday, January 26, 1995 *Journal* on page 297 reports the rates for Wednesday, January 25, 1995. **Money Rates** tracks the following domestic rates: *Prime Rate* (rate banks charge their corporate customers), *Federal Funds* (defined above), *Discount Rate* (rate the Federal Reserve charges its member banks), *Call Money* (rate banks charge brokers), *Commercial Paper, Certificates of Deposit* (defined above), *Bankers Acceptances* (rates on corporate or business credit used in international trade, backed by a bank), *Treasury Bills* (defined above), *Federal Home Loan Mortgage Corp.* (rates on a variety of mortgages), *Federal National Mortgage Association* (also rates on a variety of mortgages), and *Merrill Lynch Ready Assets Trust* (a money market mutual fund). **Money Rates** also tracks foreign money market rates, including: *London Late Eurodollars* (defined above), *London Interbank Offered Rates* (similar to federal funds), and *Foreign Prime Rates* (defined above) of different countries. These interest rates are discussed more thoroughly below.

MONEY RATES

Wedesday, January 25, 1995

The key U.S. and foreign annual interest rates below are a guide to general levels but don't always represent actual transactions.

PRIME RATE: 8½%. The base rate on corporate loans posted by at least 75% of the nation's 30 largest banks.

FEDERAL FUNDS: 5 9/16% high, 5 7/16% low, 5 7/16% near closing bid, 5½% offered. Reserves traded among commercial banks for overnight use in amounts of $1 million or more. Source: Prebon Yamane (U.S.A.) Inc.

DISCOUNT RATE: 4¾%. The charge on loans to depository institutions by the Federal Reserve Banks.

CALL MONEY: 7¼%. The charge on loans to brokers on stock exchange collateral. Source: Dow Jones Telerate Inc.

COMMERCIAL PAPER placed directly by General Electric Capital Corp.: 5.85% 30 to 59 days; 6% 60 to 89 days; 6.17% 90 to 119 days; 6.25% 120 to 149 days; 6.41% 150 to 179 days; 6.48% 180 to 259 days; 6.72% 260 to 270 days.

COMMERCIAL PAPER: High-grade unsecured notes sold through dealers by major corporations: 5.96% 30 days; 6.13% 60 days; 6.26% 90 days.

CERTIFICATES OF DEPOSIT: 5.26% one month; 5.43% two months; 5.57% three months; 6.03% six months; 6.61% one year. Average of top rates paid by major New York banks on primary new issues of negotiable C.D.s, usually on amounts of $1 million and more. The minimum unit is $100,000. Typical rates in the secondary market: 5.95% one month; 6.30% three months; 6.75% six months.

BANKERS ACCEPTANCES: 5.91% 30 days; 5.98% 60 days; 6.07% 90 days; 6.16% 120 days; 6.29% 150 days; 6.37% 180 days. Offered rates of negotiable, bank-backed business credit instruments typically financing an import order.

LONDON LATE EURODOLLARS: 6 1/16% - 5 15/16% one month; 6 3/16% - 6 1/16% two months; 6⅜% - 6¼% three months; 6½% - 6⅜% four months; 6 11/16% - 6 9/16% five months; 6 13/16% - 6 11/16% six months.

LONDON INTERBANK OFFERED RATES (LIBOR): 6 1/16% one month; 6⅜% three months; 6 13/16% six months; 7½% one year. The average of interbank offered rates for dollar deposits in the London market based on quotations at five major banks. Effective rate for contracts entered into two days from date appearing at top of this column.

FOREIGN PRIME RATES: Canada 9.25%; Germany 5.10%; Japan 3%; Switzerland 5.62%; Britain 6.25%. These rate indications aren't directly comparable; lending practices vary widely by location.

TREASURY BILLS: Results of the Monday, January 23, 1995, auction of short-term U.S. government bills, sold at a discount from face value in units of $10,000 to $1 million: 5.80%, 13 weeks; 6.24%, 26 weeks.

FEDERAL HOME LOAN MORTGAGE CORP. (Freddie Mac): Posted yields on 30-year mortgage commitments. Delivery within 30 days 9.24%, 60 days 9.30%, standard conventional fixed-rate mortgages; 6.375%, 2% rate capped one-year adjustable rate mortgages. Source: Dow Jones Telerate - Inc.

FEDERAL NATIONAL MORTGAGE ASSOCIATION (Fannie Mae): Posted yields on 30 year mortgage commitments (priced at par) for delivery within 30 days 9.20%, 60 days 9.28%, standard conventional fixed rate-mortgages; 8.15%, 6/2 rate capped one-year adjustable rate mortgages. Source: Dow Jones Telerate Inc.

MERRILL LYNCH READY ASSETS TRUST: 5.13%. Annualized average rate of return after expenses for the past 30 days; not a forecast of future returns.

Federal Funds Rate

Banks lend reserves to one another overnight at the federal funds rate. This practice is profitable for lender banks, because they earn interest on funds ($1 million or more) that would otherwise be idle, and it is profitable for the borrower banks, because they acquire reserves that enable them to make additional loans and still meet their reserve requirement.

Notice that under *Federal Funds* in the *Money Rates* column on page 297, four different percentages are listed: 5⁹⁄₁₆ percent high, 5⁷⁄₁₆ percent low, 5⁷⁄₁₆ percent near closing bid, and 5½ percent offered. These numbers show that during trading on Wednesday, January 25, 1995, 5⁹⁄₁₆ percent was the highest interest rate proposed by a potential lender bank, and 5⁷⁄₁₆ percent was the lowest interest rate proposed by a prospective borrower. The last two percentages describe the state of trading near the end of the day: Lender banks were offering 5½ percent, and borrower banks were bidding 5⁷⁄₁₆ percent. Use the closing bid (5⁷⁄₁₆ percent) when following this interest rate.

This rate is closely watched as an indicator of Federal Reserve monetary policy. A rising federal funds rate is a sign that the Fed is draining reserves from the banks via its open market operations, forcing some banks to borrow excess reserves from other banks and thereby driving up the federal funds rate. A falling rate would indicate an easy money policy. But beware: Sharp fluctuations occur from day to day. This is such a short-term market that the rate changes on an "as needed" basis.

Investor's Tip

• Follow the federal funds chart under Interest in the Markets Diary on page C1, because it presents a weekly average that smoothes out sharp daily movements.

Commercial Paper

The excerpt on page 297 lists 6.26 percent as the going rate for 90-day commercial paper (second set of quotes) on January 25, 1995. Commercial paper is short-term, unsecured debt issued by the very largest

corporations. It is the equivalent of the Treasury bill, so in order to attract investors, its rate of interest has to be higher.

Corporations issue commercial paper to avoid the higher interest rate (prime rate) levied by banks on business borrowers, and it is issued for maturities up to 270 days. There are very large minimums set on commercial paper purchases (often in excess of $1 million), and this instrument is very popular with money market funds.

Prime Rate

This is the rate that large commercial banks charge their best corporate customers. Although it does not change as frequently as other market rates, it is an important indicator of supply and demand in the capital markets. Banks raise the prime rate whenever they have difficulty meeting the current demand for funds or when the Federal Reserve drains away their reserves through its open market operations.

Bankers Acceptances

Bankers Acceptances are used to finance international trade. Large institutions, investment companies, and money market mutual funds purchase bankers acceptances because they offer high yields for relatively short periods of time. Individual investors benefit from the higher yields when they invest in funds that include these instruments.

Call Rates

The call rate is the rate that banks charge brokers, who generally add 1 percent on loans to their clients.

Key Interest Rates

Annualized interest rates on certain investments as reported by the Federal Reserve Board on a weekly-average basis:

	Week Ended:	
	Feb. 10, 1995	Feb. 3, 1995
Treasury bills (90 day)-a	5.79	5.82
Commrcl paper (Dealer, 90 day)-a	6.14	6.23
Certfs of Deposit (Resale, 3 month)	6.16	6.22
Certfs of Deposit (Resale, 6 month)	6.46	6.58
Federal funds (Overnight)-b	5.95	5.63
Eurodollars (90 day)-b	6.13	6.21
Treasury bills (one year)-c	6.79	6.88
Treasury notes (two year)-c	7.22	7.27
Treasury notes (three year)-c	7.39	7.41
Treasury notes (five year)-c	7.47	7.54
Treasury notes (ten year)-c	7.56	7.62
Treasury bonds (30 year)-c	7.66	7.72

a-Discounted rates. b-Week ended Wednesday, February 8, 1995 and Wednesday February 1, 1995. c-Yields, adjusted for constant maturity.

Source: *The Wall Street Journal*, February 14, 1995. Reprinted by permission of *The Wall Street Journal*, ©1995 Dow Jones & Company, Inc. All rights reserved worldwide.

Key Interest Rates

Every Tuesday, under the heading **Key Interest Rates**, the *Journal* reports the weekly average of most important interest rates, including long-term rates. See the example above from the February 14, 1995 edition of the *Journal*. In the week ended February 10, Treasury bills averaged 5.79 percent; commercial paper, 6.14 percent; CDs, 6.16 percent; and federal funds, 5.95 percent. Once again, notice the interest rate hierarchy.

Short-Term Interest Rates Chart

The *Journal* provides a **Short-Term Interest Rates** chart each Thursday in the daily **Credit Markets** report (consult the front-page index of the first and last sections for location of the *Credit Markets* article), as in the example from the January 19, 1995 edition of the *Journal* on page 301. The **Short-Term Interest Rate** chart portrays Federal Funds, 3-Month Commercial Paper, and 3-Month T-Bill rates over the past six months.

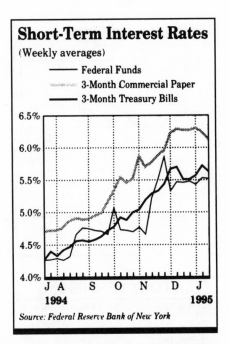

Short-Term Interest Rates
(Weekly averages)

—— Federal Funds
········ 3-Month Commercial Paper
—— 3-Month Treasury Bills

J A   S   O   N   D   J
1994   **1995**

Source: Federal Reserve Bank of New York

Source: *The Wall Street Journal*, January 19, 1995. Reprinted by permission of *The Wall Street Journal*, ©1995 Dow Jones & Company, Inc. All rights reserved worldwide.

Treasury Yield Curve

The yield curve charts the relationship between interest rates and length of maturity for all debt instruments at a particular time. A normal yield curve slopes upward, so that longer-term investments have higher yields. Thus, short-term Treasury bill rates are usually lower than long-term Treasury bond rates. Abnormal yield curves can be flat, inverted, or peaked in the middle (higher short-term rates than long-term rates).

The Wall Street Journal publishes a **Treasury Yield Curve** chart daily with the **Credit Markets** article. See the excerpt from the Wednesday, January 18, 1995 edition on page 302. You can see the normal pattern of rising rates associated with longer maturities.

A **Yield Comparisons** table accompanies the chart.

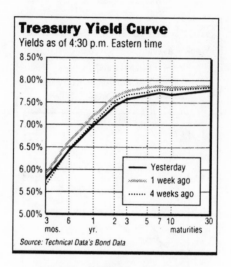

Treasury Yield Curve
Yields as of 4:30 p.m. Eastern time

Legend: Yesterday — 1 week ago — 4 weeks ago

Source: Technical Data's Bond Data

YIELD COMPARISONS

Based on Merrill Lynch Bond Indexes, priced as of midafternoon Eastern time.

	1/17	1/16	—52 Week— High	Low
Corp.-Govt. Master	7.90%	7.86%	8.09%	5.46%
Treasury 1-10yr	7.55	7.49	7.79	4.55
10+ yr	7.98	7.99	8.36	6.36
Agencies 1-10yr	8.03	7.96	8.17	5.14
10+ yr	8.20	8.20	8.51	6.73
Corporate				
1-10 yr High Qlty	8.15	8.12	8.34	5.67
Med Qlty	8.47	8.44	8.65	6.00
10+yr High Qlty	8.52	8.51	8.84	7.08
Med Qlty	8.95	8.94	9.24	7.42
Yankee bonds(1)	8.48	8.46	8.65	6.62
Current-coupon mortgages (2)				
GNMA 8.50%	8.75	8.75	9.13	6.39
FNMA 8.50%	8.75	8.74	9.04	6.40
FHLMC8.50%	8.76	8.75	9.05	6.40
High-yield corporates	11.22	11.22	11.37	8.88
New tax-exempts				
7-12-yr G.O. (AA)	6.16	6.09	6.45	4.65
12-22-yr G.O. (AA)	6.34	6.33	6.69	4.91
22+yr revenue (A)	6.50	6.48	6.89	5.31

Note: High quality rated AAA-AA; medium quality A-BBB/Baa; high yield, BB/Ba-C.

(1) Dollar-denominated, SEC-registered bonds of foreign issuers sold in the U.S. (2) Reflects the 52-week high and low of mortgage-backed securities indexes rather than the individual securities shown.

CONCLUSION

If the risk and bother of investing in stocks, bonds, and commodities seems excessive to you, a wide variety of relatively risk-free and highly liquid money market instruments is available to you. Use *The Wall Street Journal*'s data services to check the hierarchy of rates, and then choose the instrument that's right for you.

PART III

FINE TUNING: REFINING YOUR SENSE OF THE ECONOMY AND THE RIGHT INVESTMENT DECISION

CHAPTER 13

LEADING ECONOMIC
INDICATORS

Now that you have examined the business cycle in detail and learned to use *The Wall Street Journal*'s statistical series, you may be looking for a device to make analysis somewhat easier. Perhaps, while wading through the stream of data, you felt the need for a single indicator that could predict changes in the business cycle. You wanted something akin to the meteorologist's barometer, to inform you of rain or shine without a detailed examination of cloud formations.

Unfortunately, economists have never agreed on a single economic indicator to predict the future. Some indicators are better than others, but none is consistently accurate; all give a false signal on occasion. To deal with this, economists have devised a composite, or combination, of statistical series drawn from a broad spectrum of economic activity, each of which tends to move up or down ahead of the general trend of the business cycle. These series are referred to as leading indicators because of their predictive quality, and 11 have been combined into the *composite index of leading economic indicators*.

The components of the index are:

1. Average weekly hours of production or non-supervisory workers, manufacturing.
2. Average weekly initial claims for unemployment insurance.
3. Manufacturers' new orders in 1987 dollars, consumer goods and materials industries.
4. Vendor performance—slower deliveries diffusion index.
5. Contracts and orders for plant and equipment in 1987 dollars.
6. New private housing units authorized by local building permits.
7. Change in manufacturers' unfilled orders in 1987 dollars, durable goods industries.

8. Change in sensitive materials prices.
9. Stock prices, 500 common stocks.
10. Money supply—M2—in 1987 dollars.
11. Index of consumer expectations.

There are three general criteria for inclusion in the index. First, each series must accurately lead the business cycle. Second, the various series should provide comprehensive coverage of the economy by representing a wide and diverse range of economic activity. And, third, each series must be available monthly, with only a brief lag until publication, and must be free from large subsequent revisions.

The leading indicators meet these criteria, and weaving these series into a composite provides a statistic that is more reliable and less erratic than any individual component by itself.

Finally, some of the indicators measure activity in physical units, others in current dollars, still others in constant dollars, and some with an index form. This variety of measurements is reduced to an index with 1987 assigned a base value of 100. All other months and years are expressed as a percentage of the base year.

The July index, published in the Thursday, September 1, 1994 issue of *The Wall Street Journal*, is representative. The series usually appears around the first of the month. The chart accompanying the article and the second paragraph (see page 310) inform you that the index was unchanged (1987 = 100) in July.

Note that the chart accompanying the article correctly identifies 1987 as the base year, while the statistical summary at the end of the article (see page 310) incorrectly continues to report 1982 as the base year.

Chart 13–1 on page 311 complements the chart on page 310 that accompanied the article. Both show the 1990–91 recession's dip as well as the recovery's stall in late 1991.

You can see that the index did a good job of forecasting recession except in 1981–1982 and 1990–91. For all other instances, the index forecast the downturn by at least five months. In 1981–82, you should observe that the two-month lead is a difficult call, because the index double-clutched just prior to the recession's start. The first pump on the clutch is at least a half-year before the downturn begins. For 1990–91 there was no advance warning, although the index had been lethargic in the late 80s. This lends credence to the observation made earlier that there would have been no recession in 1990–91 had it not been for the Persian Gulf crisis.

Economy Loses Some Strength, New Data Show

Index of Leading Indicators Was Unchanged in July As Factory Orders Fell

---

By LUCINDA HARPER

Staff Reporter of THE WALL STREET JOURNAL

WASHINGTON—Evidence is mounting that the economy is cooling off.

Index of Leading Economic Indicators

The index of leading indicators, which is meant to gauge the future health of the economy, was unchanged in July, the Commerce Department said. The department also said factory orders, an indication of manufacturing plans, tumbled 2.3% in July, the biggest drop in nearly three years.

Taken together, analysts said, the reports suggest that the economy has lost

Leading Indicators

Index (1987 = 100)

some steam. "It doesn't signal an end to the expansion, but it does foreshadow a bit of a slowdown ahead," said Stuart Hoffman, chief economist of PNC Bank Corp. in Pittsburgh. Recent statistics have also shown weakness in consumer spending and home sales, and drops in consumer confidence.

The leading-indicator index for several months has shown only slight increases or no change at all. In July, only three of the 11 indicators that make up the index made

positive contributions. They were the change in prices of sensitive materials, building permits and average weekly claims for initial unemployment insurance. The index was hurt the most by a decline in factory orders for consumer goods and materials, suggesting factories are expecting consumer spending to remain on the weak side.

Orders for durable goods fell 4.3% and orders for nondurables fell a slight 0.1%, the department said. Although big, the drop in orders was expected since the department estimated last week that durable-goods orders were off substantially during the month.

What was new, and surprising to at least some economists, was that manufacturing inventories jumped 0.9% in July. In the second quarter, when stockpiles rose sharply, much of the buildup was in the wholesale and retail sectors. "This may suggest that an inventory problem has filtered down to the manufacturing sector," said Donald Maude, chief U.S. economist for ScotiaMcLeod in New York.

But the July buildup in stockpiles, while widespread, was pretty much in line with sales. The major exception was in the transportation sector. Model changeovers in the auto industry mean that car factories are buying supplies but not yet selling the finished product. "It's nothing to worry about," said Priscilla Luce Trumbull, head of industrial analysis at WEFA Group in suburban Philadelphia.

Unfilled orders also fell 0.2% in July, after three straight months of increases. This decline suggests that factories are more easily meeting demand and that the manufacturing sector may not have needed to add many new workers in August.

All figures have been adjusted for normal seasonal variations.

LEADING INDICATORS

Here are the net contributions of the components of the Commerce Department's index of leading indicators. After various adjustments, they produced no change in the index for July and a 0.2% increase in June.

Statistical Summary

	July 1994	June 1994
Workweek	−.04	−.04
Unemployment claims	.02	.11
Orders for consumer goods	−.12	−.03
Slower deliveries	−.07	−.03
Plant and equipment orders	−.04	.07
Building permits	.02	−.04
Durable order backlog	.00	.08
Materials prices	.27	.20
Stock prices	−.02	.02
Money supply	.00	−.06
Consumer expectations	−.08	−.03

The seasonally adjusted index numbers (1982=100) for July, and the change from June, are:

Index of leading indicators	101.5	0.0%
Index of coincident indicators	113.3	0.2%
Index of lagging indicators	97.3	−0.1%

The ratio of coincident to lagging indicators was 1.16, unchanged from 1.16 in June.

Index of Leading Indicators—Second Paragraph

The index of leading indicators, which is meant to gauge the future health of the economy, was unchanged in July, the Commerce Department said. The department also said factory orders, an indication of manufacturing plans, tumbled 2.3% in July, the biggest drop in nearly three years.

Statistical Summary—End of Article

LEADING INDICATORS

Here are the net contributions of the components of the Commerce Department's index of leading indicators. After various adjustments, they produced no change in the index for July and a 0.2% increase in June.

	July 1994	June 1994
Workweek	−.04	−.04
Unemployment claims	.02	.11
Orders for consumer goods	−.12	−.03
Slower deliveries	−.07	−.03
Plant and equipment orders	−.04	.07
Building permits	.02	−.04
Durable order backlog	.00	.08
Materials prices	.27	.20
Stock prices	−.02	.02
Money supply	.00	−.08
Consumer expectations	−.08	−.03

The seasonally adjusted index numbers (1982=100) for July, and the change from June, are:

Index of leading indicators	101.5	0.0%
Index of coincident indicators	113.3	0.2%
Index of lagging indicators	97.3	−0.1%

The ratio of coincident to lagging indicators was 1.16, unchanged from 1.16 in June.

CHART 13–1
Composite Index of 11 Leading Indicators

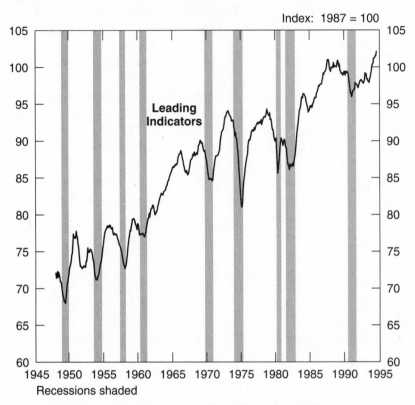

Index: 1987 = 100

Leading
Indicators

Recessions shaded

Source: U.S. Department of Commerce, *Business Cycle Indicators*, Series 910.

But you can also see the false alarms of 1962, 1966, 1984, and 1987. In each case the index fell for at least three consecutive months, although no recession followed. The 1962 decline followed on the heels of President Kennedy's forced rollback of Big Steel's price increase.

The stock market went into shock and business activity slowed, but you can see that the setback was brief. This decline was clearly a random event and of no cyclical significance.

The indicators' 1966 setback was more like developments in the 1980s. The Vietnam War had begun and inflation was climbing. The Fed tightened in response, in order to raise interest rates and curb consumer and business demand. Housing starts crashed, and it was "nip-and-tuck" for a while, but the Fed quickly eased when alarm spread so that recession never took hold.

The Fed faced similar conditions and tightened in 1984 as the cycle came roaring back from the 1981–1982 recession. The economy went into the doldrums temporarily, and the leading indicators fell, but once again the Fed eased as soon as inflation subsided and the economy emerged with only a scratch.

The October 1987 stock market crash was as severe as 1962's decline, but this time the market's own dynamic created the problem, rather than the actions of the president. Nonetheless, fears of recession swirled about for several months, and the composite index headed south. Soon, however, everyone realized the crash had nothing to do with the economy's fundamentals, and concern evaporated as the index snapped back.

Moreover, keep in mind that this statistic is not an analytical tool that permits you to probe beneath the cycle's surface in order to analyze its dynamic. The composite does not provide a step-by-step diagnosis that reveals the cycle's rhythm. It does not disclose the forces that lead from one set of conditions to another. It only averages a number of convenient series that are themselves leading indicators, but are otherwise unrelated.

This series is of interest solely because it provides an omen of future events. You need all the statistical reports appearing in the Journal in order to build an understanding of the timing, direction, and strength of the business cycle. After all, a meteorologist needs more than a barometer, and most Americans who make decisions in the business community, or wish to be fully informed of current economic events, need far more than a crude, general directional signal to guide their long-range planning.

Investor's Tip

- The composite index of leading economic indicators is not the square root of the universe. There is no single index or formula that provides all the answers to the problem of business forecasting.

CHAPTER 14

INVENTORIES

A DESTABILIZING FORCE

Inventories are stocks of goods on hand: raw materials, goods in process, or finished products. Individual businesses use them to bring stability to their operations, and yet you'll see that they actually have a destabilizing effect on the business cycle.

Businesses view inventories as a necessary evil. A manufacturer, wholesaler, or retailer can't live from hand to mouth, continually filling sales orders from current production. Stocks of goods "on the shelf" are a cushion against unexpected orders and slowdowns in production. On the other hand, inventories are an investment in working capital and incur an interest cost. If the firm borrows capital to maintain inventories, the direct interest cost is obvious. Even if the firm has not borrowed, however, working capital tied up in inventories represents an interest cost. Any funds invested in inventories could have earned the going interest rate in the money market, and this loss can substantially crimp profits.

Therefore, business attempts to keep inventories at an absolute minimum consistent with smooth operations. For a very large business, literally millions of dollars are at stake. This is why you see modern automated cash registers (i.e., the ones that automatically "read" the black and white bar code on packages) in large chain supermarkets and retail establishments. These cash registers came into use not chiefly because they record your purchases more quickly (which of course they do), but because they also tie into a computer network that keeps track of inventories of thousands of items on a daily basis.

But why do inventories, so necessary to the smooth functioning of an individual business, exacerbate the business cycle?

Consider the upswing of the cycle first. As demand increases rapidly, businesses must boost production to meet the growing volume of orders.

If they are not quick enough, and sales grow more rapidly than output, an unplanned drawdown of inventories will occur as orders are filled. This known as involuntary inventory depletion. If inventories are severely depleted, shortages can result and sales may be jeopardized. To protect itself against such developments once it is confident of the unfolding expansion, business will boost output and defensively accumulate inventories more rapidly than its sales are growing. Since all firms are stockpiling to prevent shortages, industrial production increases more vigorously than it otherwise would, accentuating the cylical expansion and the swift rise in capacity utilization. For the entire economy, production grows more rapidly than sales. This, of course, hastens the inevitable decrease in labor productivity and increase in unit labor costs associated with this phase of the cycle. Hence, inventory accumulation adds to inflationary pressures.

Now consider the downswing of the cycle. No firm willingly maintains production in a sales slump because unsold goods would pile up on the shelf. As sales weaken and fall, business curtails production in order to prevent involuntary inventory accumulation. Indeed, once business recognizes the severity of the slump, it will begin to liquidate the large volume of (now unnecessary) inventories built up during the previous expansion. These stockpiles of goods are no longer needed and can be disposed of. But as goods are sold from inventories, output and employment are reduced more than sales, since orders can be filled from inventories rather than from current production. This aggravates the cycle's downturn.

Thus, inventories play an important destabilizing role in the cycle through their influence on industrial production, boosting output during expansion and depressing it during slump. This destabilizing influence is compounded by inventory's impact on inflation. When rapid expansion is heightened by inventory accumulation, contributing to inflationary pressures, business firms increase their inventory buildup. They want to stockpile goods at current prices and sell them later at inflated prices. And when inventory liquidation in a recession contributes to deflationary pressures, falling prices can trigger a panic sell-off, which drives prices down even more steeply.

Here's how it works. Business stockpiles goods during the expansionary phase of the cycle to prevent involuntary inventory depletion and shortages, and prices start to rise. Firms quickly discover that goods held in inventory increase in value along with the general rise in prices. They have an incentive to buy now while prices are low, hold the goods in inventory, and sell them later at higher prices and profits. If prices are ris-

ing rapidly enough, widespread speculation can set in, which adds to the general increase in production and reinforces the inflation.

Recall, for example, the rapid increase in sugar prices in 1973–1974. Sugar manufacturers and industrial users of sugar (canners, soft drink bottlers, confectioners, and bakers) produced sugar and sweetened products and held them in inventory while their prices were low, hoping to make large profits from sales when their prices increased. This speculative stockpiling contributed to the price increase by bidding up production (and costs) out of proportion to sales.

Of course, when the inevitable contraction comes, liquidation of the inventory overhang helps halt the inflationary spiral. Businesses panic when faced with the prospect of selling at a price that will not recoup interest costs. If sufficiently severe, the sell-off can force prices down. More important, output plummets and layoffs mount as orders are filled from the shelf. Liquidation continues until inventories are in proper relation to sales.

Thus, speculative inventory accumulation and liquidation become a self-fulfilling prophecy. Firms pile up inventories in anticipation of a price increase, and the large volume of orders bids prices upward. When the recession begins, firms sell inventories in haste, afraid of a drop in prices, and the sell-off forces prices downward.

Now you understand why inventories and their relationship to sales are such important economic indicators. They not only confirm the stage of the cycle, they also provide advance warning of turning points and of the strength or severity of impending boom and bust.

And you also understand the irony that inventories exacerbate the business cycle, even though individual businesses use inventories to smooth operations. Production will rise more rapidly than sales during cyclical expansion, the difference accumulating as inventories, thereby forcing capacity utilization and costs up more rapidly, intensifying the expansion and hastening inflation and recession. After recession begins, firms will reduce output more rapidly than the drop in sales, drawing upon inventories to make up the difference. Therefore, the cycle's downswing will be more severe.

RECENT EXPERIENCE

Inventory accumulation and liquidation reinforce the business cycle. The consumer sets the cycle's pace; inventories exacerbate it. The cyclical

experience of the early 1970s will serve as an illustration, followed by an examination of more recent developments.

To begin with, *The Wall Street Journal* publishes the Commerce Department's inventory, sales, and inventory/sales ratio data around the middle of each month (see page 317).

In the excerpt on page 318 from the *Journal*'s Friday, September 16, 1994 edition, the statistical summary at the end of the article informs you that inventories were $891.50 billion, sales were $627.68 billion, and inventories were 1.42 times sales.

Inventories and sales are straightforward concepts. The inventory-sales ratio tells you how many months it would take to sell off inventories at the prevailing sales pace. You can calculate the ratio by dividing monthly inventory by monthly sales. Typically, inventories have been roughly 1.5 times sales over the cycle. A rise in the ratio indicates that inventories are growing out of proportion to sales and that inventory liquidation and recession are imminent. A fall in the ratio informs you that sales are out-pacing inventory growth and that economic expansion is under way. This is a key indicator; you should follow it closely.

Return to the *Journal* article after examining the inventory cycle of the early 1970s (see Chart 14–1 on page 319). This cycle concluded with a good example of inventory accumulation and speculation followed by inventory liquidation. To trace these events, follow the steep rise in inventories from 1972 through 1974 and the 1975 liquidation; note the decline in the inventory-sales ratio in 1971–72 and the increase in 1973 and 1974; and note that the inventory and sales curves are nearly congruent, with inventories lagging behind sales by a year or so.

You can observe the decline of the inventory-sales ratio as the business cycle moved from recovery to expansion in 1971–1972. Sales were expanding, but it was still too early for business to rebuild inventories.

As increasing demand boosted sales, 1973 displayed all the symptoms of the expansion-to-peak phase of the cycle: strong and rapidly growing sales, strained capacity utilization and slower deliveries, and a rising rate of inflation. Under these circumstances, business sought to defend itself against possible shortages by adding to inventories more rapidly than sales grew. The long decline in the inventory-sales ratio was reversed, and speculation began. Business boosted inventories in the expectation of rising prices, hoping to make a profit as goods increased in value. This intensified inflationary pressure (recall sugar), as a share of production went on the shelf instead of toward satisfying consumer demand. You can see that the inventory run-up dwarfed all other postwar increases up to that date.

Inventories Rose In July as Sales By Business Fell

Increase in Stockpiles Was The Fourth in a Row, Sign of Slower Growth

By CHRISTOPHER GEORGES
Staff Reporter of THE WALL STREET JOURNAL
WASHINGTON — Business inventories rose modestly in July, marking the fourth consecutive month in which stockpiles increased.

The 0.3% increase — to a seasonally adjusted $891.5 billion — is evidence, economists said, that while the economy is still expanding, the pace of growth appears to be slowing.

At the same time, the Commerce Department said, business sales decreased 0.8%, the largest drop since August 1992 and a turnaround from increases of 0.9% in June and 0.4% in May. Sales in July were a seasonally adjusted $627.68 billion.

The combination of the rise in inventories and decrease in sales caused the inventory-to-sales ratio — the number of months it would take to deplete inventories at the current sales pace — to rise to 1.42 from 1.40 in June.

Although business inventories have been expanding for most of the year, they are still at historically low levels, analysts said.

"Right now, the economy is well-balanced," said Joseph Liro, chief economist of S.G. Warburg & Co. "Three and a half years after the recession's trough, we are not seeing an excessive buildup in inventories."

Inventory buildup can be interpreted either as a sign that businesses are optimistically stockpiling in preparation for future sales, or as an early signal of slackening demand. But economists said the July rise wasn't large enough to warrant pessimism about demand.

"The level of inventories reflects confidence among business that the recovery will sustain itself," Mr. Liro said. "Businesses are comfortable about laying on more stock to meet demand."

While most sectors were increasing stockpiles or recording slight declines, auto dealers saw a 2% drop in inventories. Jose Rasco, an economist at Merrill Lynch & Co., said dealers may have been letting inventories decline in anticipation of the new model year.

Separately, a drop last week in initial unemployment claims continued the recent trend of improvement in the job market. First-time claims for unemployment benefits fell 3,000, to 327,000 from 330,000 the previous week, the Labor Department said. The four-week moving average increased slightly, to 328,250 from 327,750 the previous week.

Both reports are adjusted for normal seasonal variations.

Here is a summary of the Commerce Department's report on business inventories and sales in July. The figures are in billions of dollars, seasonally adjusted:

	July 1994	June 1994	July 1993
Total business inventories	891.50	889.10	857.69
Manufacturers	386.41	383.11	381.56
Retailers	280.21	282.90	263.03
Wholesalers	224.88	223.10	213.11
Total business sales	627.68	632.86	585.56
Inventory/sales ratio	1.42	1.40	1.46

Statistical Summary

As the cycle's peak approached, in 1974, sales stopped growing. Unplanned inventory accumulation became a problem; the inventory sales ratio rose even more rapidly; and business firms had to deal with ever-larger stockpiles of goods. Sensing that a sell-off was around the corner, they tried to bring inventories under control. Unfortunately, this was more easily said than done. Orders had to be canceled and production curtailed more than once because business underestimated the situation's severity.

Statistical Summary–End of Article

Here is a summary of the Commerce Department's report on business inventories and sales in July. The figures are in billions of dollars, seasonally adjusted:

	July 1994	June 1994	July 1993
	(billions of dollars)		
Total business inventories	891.50	889.10	857.69
Manufacturers	386.41	383.11	381.56
Retailers	280.21	282.90	263.03
Wholesalers	224.88	223.10	213.11
Total business sales	627.68	632.86	585.56
Inventory/sales ratio	1.42	1.40	1.46

But beginning in late 1974 and continuing into 1975, inventory liquidation finally began. Under panic conditions, business desperately dumped goods on the market. Despite the sell-off, you'll notice that the inventory-sales ratio remained high until early 1975. This is evidence of the collapse in sales and the recession's severity—the reason business went to such lengths to unload its stocks of goods. Other postwar recessions had been mild by comparison. Industrial production plunged, as business firms cut output sharply and filled the meager volume of orders from overstocked inventories. Two million workers were laid off between the fall of 1974 and the spring of 1975, and the unemployment rate brushed 10 percent. There is no doubt that inventory accumulation and liquidation played a key role in the recession's harshness.

Unlike the cycle of the early 70s, the 1981–82 recession can't be used as a typical example of inventory accumulation and liquidation because of the Fed's role in aborting the 1981 recovery. Sales were doing well and the inventory-sales ratio was low when the Fed's tight money policy clamped a vise on the economy in 1981. Sales shrank and involuntary inventory accumulation drove up both inventories and the inventory-sales ratio. As soon as possible, business began a massive inventory liquidation program that continued through early 1983. As you can tell from Chart 14–1 on page 319, a desperate bout of inventory liquidation accompanied the worst recession since World War II.

CHART 14–1
Manufacturing and Trade Inventory/Sales Ratio (constant dollars),
and Change in Book Value of Manufacturing and Trade Inventories
(current dollars)

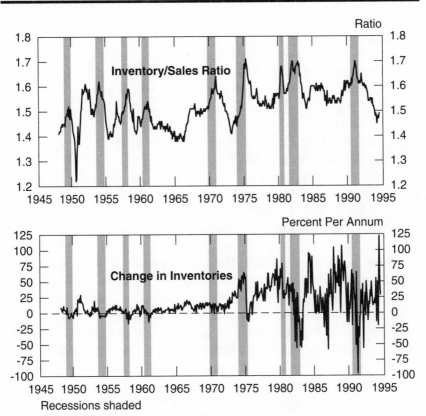

Recessions shaded

Source: U.S. Department of Commerce, *Business Cycle Indicators*, Series 31, 77.

Recovery began as soon as the Fed provided easier credit conditions. And you can see that business did not wait long before it began restocking its depleted inventories. By early 1984, inventory accumulation set a new record. Massive inventory accumulation contributed impressively to the economy's explosive growth immediately after the 1981–82 recession, yet sales were so strong that the inventory-sales ratio declined throughout 1983 and remained low in 1984. There was no indication that inventory growth had outstripped sales or that the economy was near a cyclical peak.

Nevertheless, the Fed became concerned that the recovery and expansion were proceeding too rapidly. It fine-tuned the slowdown of mid-84,

and inventory accumulation began to subside. By 1985 and early 1986, economic conditions were slack and inventory accumulation had fallen to a moderate level.

To a large extent, the inventory run-up of 1984 and the subsequent drop to a moderate pace in 1985–86 were a one-time reaction to the extreme inventory depletion during the 1981–82 recession. These developments were not part of the ordinary cyclical scene; they were a reaction to the credit conditions imposed on the economy by the Fed. In a way, the decks were cleared for a resumption of normal cyclical patterns by the second half of the 80s.

As the economy's pace improved in the late 80s, inventory accumulation picked up once again. Although inflation, and perhaps speculation, was minimal, inventory accumulation turned robust by 1988 and then declined as the Fed tightened up once again. By the end of the decade, circumstances were similar to 1985–86: A jump in interest rates had led to slack conditions and the absence of inventory build-up.

Then Iraq invaded Kuwait, and the economy plunged into recession. Businesses were caught by surprise, and the inventory-sales ratio climbed as unsold goods piled up on shelves. But businesses brought the unintended inventory accumulation under control by sharply reducing inventories in 1991. By early 1992, the inventory-sale ratio was back to normal levels and inventories had begun to expand once again.

Another glance at Chart 14–1 on page 319 will demonstrate the 1990–91 recession's peculiar nature. No signs of serious speculation, such as a rising inventory-sales ratio, can be seen before the recession's start. Even after the slump begins, and despite massive inventory liquidation, the inventory-sales ratio's rise is moderate by the standard of previous recessions. Many observers ventured that the ratio's relatively smooth sailing provided evidence of business's better inventory-control methods and that relatively low inventory levels coming out of recession meant a snappy recovery and expansion.

They were wrong. Recovery was sluggish and expansion late.

THE OUTLOOK

By the mid-1990s, the inventory-sales ratio had fallen to an unusually low level, as sales gains continued to outstrip inventory growth.

Return to the September 16, 1994 *Journal* article on pages 317 and 318. It informs you of a 1.42 inventory-sales ratio, and Chart 14–1 on page 319

confirms that this was fairly low figure. This is partly a consequence of the improved technology that enables business to keep a closer watch over its inventories. But it's also a sign of a lean economy.

How long will the inventory-sales ratio remain low, and how long will it be before inventory accumulation exacerbates the expansion and contributes to the next recession? That depends on the strength of the expansion as determined by the growth in consumer demand. If demand grows too quickly and inflation speeds up, business will begin stockpiling for self-protection and speculation, and the inventory-sales ratio will start to climb. This will be a dead giveaway that inventory accumulation is contributing to boom conditions and that the peak of the cycle cannot be far off. On the other hand, if the expansion is restrained, the inventory-sales ratio should remain flat for a long time. In that case, inventory accumulation will not aggravate the expansion and the business cycle will not be brought to a peak prematurely.

Investor's Tip

- Watch these figures carefully. If boom conditions drive
  inventories out of moderate proportion to sales and the
  inventory-sales ratio rises rapidly and exceeds 1.6, you know
  recession can't be far behind.

CHAPTER 15

BUSINESS CAPITAL EXPENDITURES

WHY BUSINESS INVESTS

John Maynard Keynes could not have known America's modern consumer economy when he wrote his General Theory in 1936 (see Chapters 3 and 5). Keynes assumed the absence of any dynamic in British consumer expenditures and believed consumption behaved passively, expanding and contracting with consumer income. As far as Keynes was concerned, business investment determined the cycle's dynamic. So Keynes built his theory of aggregate economic activity around the forces that determine business investment in plant and equipment.

But business's expenditures on factories, warehouses, offices, machinery, and equipment, like its accumulation of inventories, reinforce the business cycle; they do not lead it. Business waits for its signal from the economy before committing its capital. Similarly, only after the expansion is over does business begin to cut back on capital expenditures in anticipation of reduced sales.

There are six principal factors influencing business decisions to spend on new plant and equipment.

First, old facilities may wear out and need to be replaced.

Second, the rate of capacity utilization may be high. Putting it simply, if sales are strong, business will invest in new machinery and equipment in order to have the capacity necessary to fill the orders. During a recession, however, the rate of capacity utilization is low and business has more than enough plant and equipment on hand to satisfy the low volume of orders. Why add to plant and equipment when the existing level is already more than adequate?

Third, old facilities, whether fully utilized or not, will be scrapped and replaced by new facilities if operating costs can be sufficiently reduced

through innovation in the process of production. Competition leaves business no choice: If equipment is no longer cost-effective, it must be replaced, even though it could still be used.

Fourth, new plant and equipment may be required to produce a new or redesigned product, even if existing facilities are operating at full capacity and have a continued useful life. Model and style changes have forced the automobile industry to spend billions replacing still-functional equipment, for instance.

Fifth, spending on plant and equipment is sensitive to current and anticipated profits. Business will invest in additional facilities if it expects long-range profit growth beyond any short-run cyclical fluctuation. In addition, profits plowed back into the business provide the cash flow necessary to finance capital expenditures. A recession will limit business's ability to finance capital expenditures; an expansion will generate the necessary cash flow.

The final factor is interest rates. Business must borrow to finance plant and equipment expenditures if internally generated funds are not adequate. When interest rates are very high, the cost of borrowing may be prohibitive, and so business firms postpone or cancel their capital expenditure plans. Or they may feel that, for the time being, they can get a better return by investing their own funds at high rates of interest than by making expenditures on new productive facilities.

Keep these factors in mind when evaluating business's capital expansion plans and their role in the current cycle. You can keep abreast of capital expenditures by following a series published monthly in *The Wall Street Journal*: the Commerce Department report on new orders for nondefense capital goods.

NONDEFENSE CAPITAL GOODS

The Wall Street Journal publishes preliminary data for nondefense capital goods on the Thursday or Friday of the next-to-the-last week of the month, such as the Thursday, September 29, 1994 release (see page 325), and then publishes the final report about a week later. You will have to keep your eyes open for the preliminary figures, because they are part of an overall report on durable goods. The revised data, appearing a week later, is included with a general release on factory orders. The October 6, 1994 article on page 328–329, covering the previous month, is a good example.

Durable-Goods Orders in August Increased 6%

But Analysts Link Much Of Jump to 19.1% Rise In Transportation Sector

By CHRISTOPHER GEORGES
Staff Reporter of THE WALL STREET JOURNAL
WASHINGTON — Evidence that the economy is still expanding briskly continues to mount, with a new report that orders for big-ticket factory items surged in August.

The 6% increase in orders for durable goods, reported by the Commerce Department yesterday, was the largest since December 1992 and the 11th rise in the past 13 months.

Some economists cautioned that, combined with July's 4% decline, the August orders increase paints a more tempered picture of economic growth. In addition, analysts note, the August rise was just 2.3% excluding a sharp 19.1% increase in orders in automotive and aircraft equipment. Orders for transportation equipment are normally highly volatile and thus not as reliable an indicator of overall economic activity as other sectors are.

"Without transportation, it's a mixed bag," said Stephen S. Roach, co-director of economic analysis at Morgan Stanley & Co. "There's momentum, but no dramatic sea change."

Non-defense Capital Goods —
For example, the rise in orders for nondefense capital goods, excluding aircraft, was just 1.5%, following a 3% drop in July.

While yesterday's report helped fuel speculation of an increase in inflation— and with it a greater likelihood that the Federal Reserve would move to raise interest rates — economists said they expected no immediate action.

"Does it call for an immediate tightening? Probably not," said Joseph R. Liro of S.G. Warburg & Co. "But it does add to the evidence that the Fed will move to raise rates in a month or two."

The Fed's Open Market Committee, which met Tuesday, decided then not to raise rates for the time being. But the Fed chairman, by custom, has the authority to move rates by at least one quarter percentage point between meetings without a formal committee vote. The next scheduled meeting is Nov. 15.

According to the August durable-goods report, widespread gains in orders were reported in primary metals, up 4.8%; electrical machinery, up 1.2%; and nonelectrical machinery, up 4%. Orders in both primary metals and nonelectrical machinery had declined in July, while electrical machinery had remained unchanged.

Unfilled orders, an indication of how well manufacturers are keeping up with demand, fell 0.3% in August, matching the percentage they fell in July.

All figures have been adjusted for seasonal variations.

Here are the Commerce Department's latest figures on new orders for durable goods (seasonally adjusted, in billions):

	Aug.	July	% Chg.	
Total	$154.00	$145.23	+ 6.0%	Statistical
Primary Metals	$13.62	$13.00	+ 4.8%	Summary
Nonelect. machinery	$29.62	$28.50	+ 4.0%	
Electrical machinery	$22.46	$22.18	+ 1.2%	
Transportation equip.	$38.47	$32.30	+19.1%	
Capital goods	$43.41	$41.86	+ 3.7%	
Nondefense	$37.43	$36.32	+ 3.0%	
Defense	$5.98	$5.54	+ 7.9%	

Durable Goods

In billions of dollars

NEW ORDERS received by manufacturers of durable goods rose in August to a seasonally adjusted $153.99 billion from a revised $145.23 billion a month earlier, the Commerce Department reports.

You will notice that the fifth paragraph (see page 326) of the September 29, 1994 durable goods article states that orders for nondefense capital goods rose 1.5 percent in August and that the statistical summary at the end of the article (page 326) reports a figure of $37.43 billion. The statistical summary at the end of the October 6, 1994 article on page 329 presents a slightly revised figure of $37.63 billion.

Nondefense Capital Goods—Fifth Paragraph

For example, the rise in orders for nondefense capital goods, excluding aircraft, was just 1.5%, following a 3% drop in July.

Statistical Summary—End of Article

Here are the Commerce Department's latest figures on new orders for durable goods (seasonally adjusted, in billions):

	Aug.	July	% Chg.
Total	$154.00	$145.23	+ 6.0%
Primary Metals	$13.62	$13.00	+ 4.8%
Nonelect. machinery	$29.62	$28.50	+ 4.0%
Electrical machinery	$22.46	$22.18	+ 1.2%
Transportation equip.	$38.47	$32.30	+19.1%
Capital goods	$43.41	$41.86	+ 3.7%
Nondefense	$37.43	$36.32	+ 3.0%
Defense	$5.98	$5.54	+ 7.9%

This series presents new orders received by manufacturers of durable goods other than military equipment. (Durable goods are defined as those having a useful life of more than three years.) Nondefense capital goods represent approximately one fifth to one third of all durable goods production. The series includes engines; construction, mining, and materials handling equipment; office and store machinery; electrical transmission and distribution equipment and other electrical machinery (excluding household appliances and electronic equipment); and railroad, ship and aircraft transportation equipment. Military equipment is excluded because new orders for such items do not respond directly to the business cycle.

CHART 15–1
Nondefense Orders for Capital Goods

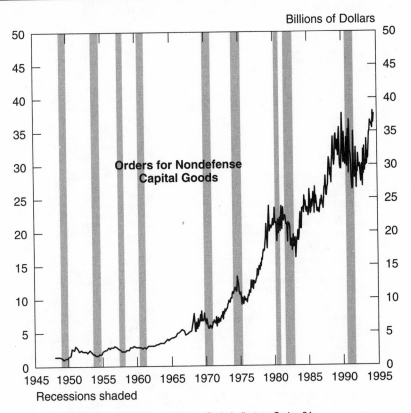

Billions of Dollars

Orders for Nondefense
Capital Goods

Recessions shaded

Source: U.S. Department of Commerce, *Business Cycle Indicators*, Series 24.

Chart 15–1 above provides a good illustration of the relationship between nondefense capital goods orders and the business cycle. We track orders rather than shipments in order to obtain maximum advance notice of business cycle developments and turning points.

By the late 80s, nondefense orders were hovering around $35 billion and had advanced rapidly over the past half-decade. Yet you should notice, in a development remarked upon earlier in the discussion on inventories, that the 1980s expansion stumbled in the middle and end of the decade. Then nondefense orders dropped into the $30 billion range with the 1990–91 recession.

August Factory Orders Surged 4.4%, Latest Sign of Strong Economic Growth

By CHRISTOPHER GEORGES
Staff Reporter of THE WALL STREET JOURNAL

WASHINGTON — The economy is expanding at a healthy clip — faster, in fact, than most economists had predicted just a few months ago.

Yesterday's report of a 4.4% surge in factory orders for August was just the latest in a series of upbeat reports about economic growth, most of which have led economists to forecast continued expansion into next year.

"The summer slowdown we saw was a blip," said Kurt Karl, an economist at the WEFA Group, a Bala Cynwyd, Pa., economic-consulting firm. "The latest information shows us back on track for 3% growth rate" in gross domestic product.

But the recent strong indicators—which include increases in areas as varied as manufacturing, personal income, durable-goods orders, vehicle sales and investments by businesses in machinery — haven't only sent encouraging signals to business but have also rekindled fears among some economists of an uptick in inflation. And with those fears come predictions of further interest-rate increases by the Federal Reserve.

As a result, stock and bond prices continued to tumble yesterday. The Dow Jones Industrial Average closed down 13.79, at 3787.34, while the 30-year Treasury bond fell ⅝ of a point (see article on page C1).

The August rise in new factory orders marked the largest gain in nearly two years, the Commerce Department reported. It was also the 11th increase in the past 13 months.

Though the increase was broad-based, economists said they were particularly surprised by the relatively large 2.5% jump in orders of nondurable goods. For example, nondurables were led by a 4.5% increase in paperboard containers and boxes, a 4.7% increase in rubber and plastic products, and a 3% increase in chemical products.

"Nondurable goods don't usually show these kinds of swings," said Peter E. Kretzmer, an economist with NationsBanc Capital Markets Inc. "It shows that manufacturers are expecting strong demand from consumers."

Yesterday's overall rise in new manufactured goods also reflected a 6.1% increase in durable goods, led primarily by large gains in autos and heavy machinery. While indicative of robust growth, those gains, especially in the volatile auto sector, were largely expected, analysts said.

With the spike in factory orders and the recent series of reports suggesting strong growth have come predictions from analysts of increasing inflationary pressures.

"As far as inflation goes, all indicators are pointing upward. The concern is how far upward," Mr Karl said.

Until now, inflation has stayed largely in check, thanks primarily to brisk competition, increases in interest rates by the Fed, and modest wage increases. But, some analysts, noting slight increases in unit labor costs in the second quarter, predict that may soon change.

In addition, while growth in some sectors of the U.S. economy, especially housing, may be slowing, some of the slack is being picked up by increased exports, economists said. That trend, they said, should continue as the economic recovery in Europe continues and as long as the dollar remains relatively weak.

The receptive market overseas has already helped boost sales for companies such as **Brown-Forman** Corp., a Louisville, Ky., marketer of alcoholic beverages. While domestic sales have slowed recently, according to a company spokesman, the company has recorded double-digit increases in overseas sales of such products as Jack Daniel's brand whiskey.

Yet another hint of future inflation, economists said, comes from increases in producer prices. "Those prices are heading up and that will eventually affect consumer prices," Mr. Karl said. "We expect producer prices to filter down to the consumer level over the next few months."

Administration officials, however, said yesterday that the recent economic reports didn't alter their overall predictions for future growth.

"Looking at all the numbers, there's more strength in some sectors but moderation elsewhere, such as in housing," said Laura D'Andrea Tyson, chairman of the Council of Economic Advisers. "We continue to see the economy on the same course we have been predicting."

Even so, the combination of strong economic reports and heightened concerns about inflation has fueled speculation among economists of an imminent interest-rate increase by the Fed.

"The Fed could easily make the case now that the economy is stronger than they thought it was at their last meeting and move rates sooner rather than later," said Mr. Kretzmer. "Growth at the level we're seeing now is what one might call . . . of concern to the Fed."

Some economists, however, remain more reserved about future economic growth. Shrugging off the recent numbers, David Levy, director of forecasting at the Jerome Levy Economics Institute in Mount Kisco, N.Y., noted that the recent slowdown in the housing sector, combined with a historically low savings rate among consumers, could check future growth.

In addition, he said, business investment in new equipment, which has helped fuel the recent expansion, should soon level off.

"There may not be a recession, but I do see a significant slowdown," Mr. Levy said."

New Factory Orders

In billions of dollars.

NEW ORDERS reported by manufacturers in August rose to a seasonally adjusted $286.46 billion from a revised $274.31 billion in July, the Commerce Department reports. The 12-month moving average rose to $271.26 billion in August from a revised $268.51 billion in July.

FACTORY ORDERS
Here are the Commerce Department's latest figures for manufacturers in billions of dollars, seasonally adjusted.

	August 1994	July 1994		%Chg.
All industries	286.46	274.31	+	4.4
Durable goods	154.18	145.25	+	6.1
Nondurable goods	132.28	129.05	+	2.5
Capital goods industries	43.60	41.86	+	4.2
Nondefense	37.63	36.31	+	3.6
Defense	5.97	5.55	+	7.7
Total shipments	287.86	275.49	+	4.5
Inventories	387.10	386.65	+	0.1
Backlog of orders	447.19	448.59	−	0.3

Statistical Summary

Statistical Summary—End of Article

FACTORY ORDERS
Here are the Commerce Department's latest figures for manufacturers in billions of dollars, seasonally adjusted.

	August 1994	July 1994		%Chg.
All industries	286.46	274.31	+	4.4
Durable goods	154.18	145.25	+	6.1
Nondurable goods	132.28	129.05	+	2.5
Capital goods industries	43.60	41.86	+	4.2
Nondefense	37.63	36.31	+	3.6
Defense	5.97	5.55	+	7.7
Total shipments	287.86	275.49	+	4.5
Inventories	387.10	386.65	+	0.1
Backlog of orders	447.19	448.59	−	0.3

SUMMARY

In conclusion, Chart 15–1 illustrates business cycle developments in the 1970s, when expenditures, like inventory accumulation, reinforced the cycle rather than initiated it. Business responded to consumer orders by adding plant and equipment. As the expansion developed into the peak of the cycle and productive capacity became strained, business added facilities and equipment. Their completion swelled the level of demand and contributed to generally inflationary conditions.

After recession begins, some of the investment projects are canceled, but most are completed, and these expenditures ease the downturn. Time elapses before a new cycle's expansionary phase encourages another round of capital expenditures. Until this occurs, the depressed level of plant and equipment expenditures holds demand down and prevents the economy from heating up too quickly. When capital expenditures do recover, the economy is once again approaching the cycle's peak.

Returning one last time to the articles and charts for an overview of the process, it's clear that the cycle developed differently in the 1980s than it had in the 1970s. The economy did not overheat in the 80s, because the Fed's fine-tuning cooled it at the middle and end of the decade. Unfortunately, conditions were still chilly when the Persian Gulf crisis began, and then quickly slipped into recession.

Investor's Tip

• Treat these statistics like inventory accumulation: Too much of a good thing is dangerous.

CHAPTER 16

U.S. INTERNATIONAL
TRANSACTIONS

POSTWAR PERSPECTIVE

The phrases of international commerce were continuously in the financial news in the early and mid 1990s. Foreign exchange rates, devaluation, IMF, NAFTA, balance of trade, balance of payments, and the other terms used to discuss America's international economic relations can certainly be defined and described in the context of current events. But to understand them thoroughly, you must think back to World War II. Most of our modern international economic institutions were formed at the end of the war and immediately afterward, when the American dollar assumed the central role in the world's economy that it still plays today. Take the time to review postwar international economic developments before plunging into the current data and terminology.

In the summer of 1944, in the resort town of Bretton Woods, New Hampshire, well before World War II came to a close, the United States hosted a conference to plan international monetary affairs for the postwar years, since the Allies were already certain of victory. The United States knew that the war was taking a drastic toll on the rest of the world's economies, while the U.S. economy was growing stronger. Both victor and vanquished would need food, fuel, raw materials, and equipment, but only the United States could furnish these requirements. How were other nations to pay for these imports? They had very little that Americans wanted. If they sold their money for dollars in order to buy goods from us, the strong selling pressure on their currencies and their strong demand for dollars would drive their currencies down in value and the dollar up. Soon the dollar would be so expensive, in terms of foreign currency, that

the rest of the world could not afford to buy the American goods necessary to rebuild.

It would have been very easy to say that this was everyone else's problem, not ours, but America's statesmen knew that it was our problem as well. This lesson had been learned the hard way during the aftermath of World War I. Following that war, the United States had washed its hands of international responsibilities; consequently, the world economy had suffered a severe dollar shortage. Many nations were forced to devalue their currencies. Other nations used gold in desperation to settle their accounts with the United States, so America ended up with most of the world's gold supply. Moreover, each nation sought shelter in shortsighted protectionist devices, shattering the world economy. Economic nationalism spilled into the diplomatic arena, where its malevolent force accelerated the world into the second global war.

Determined to avoid these mistakes the second time around, the United States convened the Bretton Woods Conference to anticipate such problems and establish institutions to handle them. The conference's principal task was to prevent runaway depreciation of other currencies after the war. It therefore created the International Monetary Fund (IMF), a pool of currencies to which all nations (but mostly the United States) contributed and from which any nation could borrow in order to shore up the value of its own currency. If a nation's currency was under selling pressure, and weak and falling in value compared to other currencies, buying pressure designed to drive its price upward could be implemented with strong currencies borrowed from the IMF. For instance, Britain could borrow dollars from the IMF to buy pounds, thus supporting the price of the pound.

The dollar was pegged to gold at $35 an ounce, and all other currencies were pegged to the dollar (e.g., a dollar was worth a fixed number of francs or pounds). At the time, the United States had most of the world's gold and other nations had hardly any, so the entire system was tied to gold through the U.S. dollar. This system of fixed exchange rates was constructed to provide stability in international economic relationships. Traders and investors knew exactly what a contract for future delivery of goods or future return on investment was worth in terms of the foreign exchange in which a contract was written. There was no incentive to speculate on shifting exchange rates, which could wipe out profit margins or generate large losses.

To draw an analogy, consider a shipment of oranges from California to New York and investments made by Californians on the New York Stock Exchange. Californians must be concerned about the price of oranges in

New York and the price of a share of stock on the exchange, but they need not be concerned about fluctuations in the value of New York currency versus California currency, since both states use dollars.

Now think how much more difficult selling and investing in New York would be for Californians if the exchange rate between their currencies fluctuated. The diplomats wished to avoid precisely that problem after World War II, and that's why the Bretton Woods Conference established the IMF and a system of fixed exchange rates.

Unfortunately, after the war, the U.S. balance-of-trade surplus (the amount by which the revenue of all exports exceeds the cost of all imports) created a greater dollar shortage than the conference had anticipated. Other nations were continually selling their currencies in order to buy American dollars with which to purchase American goods. Selling pressure forced down the price of other currencies despite the IMF, which was not large enough to bail them out, and many of these currencies faced runaway depreciation against the dollar.

The United States responded to this crisis with the Marshall Plan. George C. Marshall, a career soldier, had been chairman of the Joint Chiefs of Staff during the war. At the war's end, President Truman appointed him Secretary of State. Marshall understood that a shortage of essential items such as food, fuel, raw materials, and machinery and equipment hobbled Europe's recovery. Only the United States could supply Europe's needs in sufficient quantities. He further understood that the dollar shortage prevented Europe from importing what it needed from the United States.

He proposed, and President Truman and Congress approved, a plan whereby the European nations drew up a list of their needs and the United States gave (not loaned) them the dollars they required to satisfy those needs. This reduced the strain on Europe's balance of payments and freed their currencies from the pressure of devaluation. American exports, of course, benefited, as our dollars bounced right back to us for purchases of American goods.

By the time of the Korean War, everyone was talking about the "economic miracle of Europe." The Marshall Plan had been extended to victor and vanquished alike, probably history's greatest example of benevolence as enlightened self-interest. The United States had learned from its mistakes following World War I. Isolationism was myopic; the United States had to play an active role in world affairs. And our generosity would be repaid many times over, as foreign markets for our goods recovered rapidly.

The Marshall Plan became a cornerstone of American foreign policy. The United States provided the rest of the world with desperately needed dollars in this and also a number of other ways, not all of them purposeful. For example, the United States began to maintain a substantial military presence overseas, and our foreign bases salted their host countries with dollars when native civilians were employed at the bases and American personnel spent their paychecks. In addition, American business firms resumed overseas investing, especially in Europe, spending dollars to purchase subsidiaries and to build facilities. Finally, Americans started to travel abroad in great numbers, seeding Europe with funds. All of these activities meant that dollars were sold for foreign exchange (foreign currency), and so they helped offset the constant sale by other nations of their currency in order to buy American goods.

Furthermore, whenever foreign banks, businesses, or individuals received more dollars than were immediately required, they were delighted to deposit those dollars in either American or foreign banks in order to hold them for a rainy day. Since dollars were in vigorous demand because of the continuing need to buy American exports, those dollars could always be sold in the future, and, meanwhile, they were a handy private reserve.

To summarize, there were four principal outflows of dollars from the United States: foreign aid (such as the Marshall Plan), foreign investment, military presence overseas, and tourism. Two principal influxes of foreign exchange offset these outflows: foreign purchase of American exports, which greatly exceeded our purchases of imports, and foreigners' willingness to hold dollars as a liquid investment. The four outflows of dollars (roughly) equaled the two influxes of foreign exchange.

By the late 50s and early 60s, however, some foreign banks, businesses, and individuals found that they had more dollars than they could use. They did not wish to buy American goods, and they had found making other investments more attractive than holding dollars, so they decided to sell them.

The United States did not have to rely on the IMF to support the dollar and maintain a fixed exchange rate between the dollar and other currencies. Rather, the U.S. Treasury stood ready to redeem dollars with gold whenever selling pressure on the dollar became heavy: The United States propped up the price of the dollar relative to other currencies by buying the dollar for gold. Since a foreign holder of dollars could buy gold at $35 per ounce and sell that gold for foreign exchange anywhere in the world, there was no need to sell dollars below the fixed rate of exchange. When-

ever the dollar fell a little, foreigners would buy gold with their dollars and cash that gold in for other currencies at full value, which kept the dollar up. And the U.S. price of $35 per ounce of gold set the world price for gold, simply because the United States had most of the world's supply. As more and more dollars were redeemed for it, a stream of gold started to leave the United States. American holdings of gold were cut almost in half by the time increasing alarm was voiced in the early 60s.

An alternative solution had to be found, or else the U.S. supply of gold would disappear. The foreign central banks stepped in and agreed to support the price of the dollar as part of their obligation to maintain fixed exchange rates under the Bretton Woods agreement. They had potentially limitless supplies of their own currencies. If a bank, business, or individual in another nation wanted to sell dollars, and this selling pressure tended to force the price of the dollar down in terms of that nation's currency, the foreign central bank would buy the dollars for its currency and thus support the price of the dollar.

Neither the U.S. Treasury or the Federal Reserve System could support the dollar in this way, because neither had limitless supplies of foreign currency. As long as the foreign central banks were willing to buy and accumulate dollars, private citizens, banks, and businesses in other countries were satisfied. In this way, the system of fixed exchange rates survived.

However, by the late 60s and early 70s the situation had once again become ominous. The United States no longer had a favorable balance of trade. Other nations were selling more to, and buying less from, the United States. America's favorable balance of trade had been the single big plus in its balance of payments, offsetting the outflows of dollars mentioned earlier: foreign aid (the Marshall Plan), American tourism, foreign investment, and the American military presence overseas. Now the dollar holdings of foreign central banks began to swell ever more rapidly, as their citizens liquidated dollar holdings. These central banks realized that they were acquiring an asset that ultimately would be of little value to them. Having been put in a position of continually buying dollars they would never be able to sell, they insisted that the United States do something to remedy the situation.

The French suggested that the dollar be officially devalued as a first step, because it had had a very high value in terms of other currencies ever since World War II. They reasoned that if the dollar were worth less in terms of other currencies, American exports would be cheaper for the rest of the world, imports would be more expensive in the United States, and

thus the U.S. balance of trade would shift from negative to positive as the United States exported more and imported less. In addition, if foreign currencies were more expensive, Americans would be less likely to travel and invest overseas. This would partially stem the dollar hemorrhage. Others suggested that the foreign central banks stop supporting (buying) the dollar and that the dollar be allowed to float downward to a more reasonable level as foreigners sold off their holdings.

For many years, the United States resisted both devaluation and flotation, until, in a series of developments between 1971 and 1973, the U.S. ceased redeeming the dollar for gold and permitted it to float. It promptly fell, relative to other currencies, because foreign central banks no longer felt obliged to purchase it in order to support its price.

At the same time, the price of gold increased, because the United States would no longer redeem dollars with gold. The willingness of the United States to sell gold virtually without limit at $35 per ounce had kept its value from rising, but now the price of gold could increase according to the forces of private supply and demand. Consequently, it fluctuated with all other commodity prices, rising rapidly during the general inflation at the end of the 1970s and then falling with commodity prices after 1980.

The dollar fell until the summer of 1973, and then it fluctuated in value until the end of the 1970s. Although foreign central banks no longer felt an obligation to buy dollars, they occasionally did so to keep it from plummeting too far or too fast. They took this action in their own interest at the suggestion of exporters, who knew that a low value for the dollar and a high value for their own currencies made it difficult to export to the United States. Nevertheless, by the end of the 70s the dollar's value was at a postwar low.

The history of the dollar in the 1980s through the mid-1990s is a roller coaster ride. At first, the dollar's value headed steeply up and rose to a new postwar high by mid-decade. After that it fell once again, so that by the late 80s and early 90s it had retreated back down to its late 70s level. What caused these ups and downs, and what does the future hold? You can find an answer in *The Wall Street Journal*'s coverage of the balance of payments, the balance of trade, and foreign exchange rates.

These few statistical series portraying America's international transactions have generated more confusion in public perception than perhaps any others, but you will see that they are really not difficult to grasp and follow on a regular basis.

BALANCE OF PAYMENTS AND BALANCE OF TRADE

In order to comprehend the *balance-of-payments* accounts, think of yourself as representing the United States in all dealings with the rest of the world. If you wish to do business with the rest of the world, you must buy its currencies (called *foreign exchange*). Likewise, in order to do business in the United States, the rest of the world must buy dollars.

Now set up an accounting statement. The left side will include all the uses you had for all the foreign exchange you purchased. The right side of the account will include all the uses for the dollars that the rest of the world purchased. The two sides must balance: *For every dollar's worth of foreign exchange that you buy with a dollar, the rest of the world must use a dollar's worth of foreign exchange to buy that dollar*. There are no leaks. It is impossible for you to buy any amount of foreign currency without the seller of that currency buying an equivalent value of dollars. It doesn't matter what you do with the foreign exchange you bought, nor what they do with the dollars they bought (even if both of you do *nothing* with your newly purchased money). The balance of payments statement merely records what both parties do with their funds.

Congratulations. You have just constructed a balance-of-payments statement.

U.S. Balance of Payments

Money going out (–)	Money coming in (+)
Uses by United States for all foreign exchange purchased with U.S. dollars	Uses by rest of world for all U.S. dollars purchased with foreign exchange

Once the accounting statement has been set up, you may add other details. Each side of the statement will have a *current account* and a *capital account*. Subdivide the current account into merchandise trade, services, and foreign aid; subdivide the capital account into private investment and central bank transactions.

U.S. Balance of Payments

U.S. purchase of foreign money (debit) (–)	Foreign purchase of U.S. money (credit) (+)
Current account payments by United States to rest of world Goods and services imports by United States Merchandise trade imports Services for which United States pays rest of world Foreign aid payments by United States to rest of world Capital account outflows of funds from United States Private investment by United States in rest of world Central bank transactions such as Fed buys foreign currencies	Current account payments to United States by rest of world Goods and services exports by United States Merchandise trade exports Services United States sells rest of world Foreign aid payments by rest of world to United States Capital account inflows of funds to United States Private investment by rest of world in United States Central bank transactions such as foreign central banks buy dollars

To summarize: the left side of this account (*debit*) shows what you, representing the United States, are doing with the foreign exchange you purchased with American dollars. The right side of the account (*credit*) shows what the rest of the world is doing with the dollars it purchased with its money. Remember, *the two sides must be equal*; a transaction can take place only if things of equal worth are exchanged. Although the *total* for each side must be equal, however, the individual categories need not be. Thus, you can balance one category against another in order to arrive at a merchandise trade balance, goods and services balances, and so on. Each category in the balance of payments will be examined in turn.

The Current Accounts

Balance on Goods and Services

Merchandise Trade
You can use the foreign exchange you have purchased to buy foreign goods, and the rest of the world can use dollars to buy American goods.

Thus, if you import goods into the United States, you have incurred a debit (–), because you have sold dollars to buy foreign currency in order to make the transaction; in other words, money has left the United States. On the other hand, if the rest of the world buys American goods, you have earned a credit (+). It is customary to talk about the *balance on merchandise trade* by netting imports against exports to determine whether we have an export (+) surplus or an import (–) deficit.

Services

If you use your dollars to buy foreign currency in order to travel in a foreign country, or to use a foreign air carrier, or to pay interest on a foreign debt, all this would be classified as an outflow of funds, or a debit (–). On the other hand, if the rest of the world uses the dollars it buys to travel in the United States, or to fly with an American air carrier, or to pay interest on a debt to the United States, that flow of money into the United States would be a credit (+).

If the net credit (+) or debit (–) balance on this account is added to the credit (+) or debit (–) balance of the merchandise trade account, this subtotal is referred to as the *balance on goods and services*.

Foreign Aid

If you use the foreign money you have purchased to make a gift to the rest of the world, that's a debit (–); if the rest of the world uses the dollars it has purchased to make a gift to the United States, that's a credit (+). Until the Persian Gulf war, and our request to our allies that they compensate us for Operation Desert Storm, foreign aid had always been a debit (–) entry for the U.S. But in 1991 it temporarily switched to credit (+) and, as you will see, made a big difference in our balance of payments that year.

When the foreign aid transaction is combined with the balance on goods and services, it completes the *balance on current account*, which will be a debit (–) balance or a credit (+) balance, depending on whether more funds flowed out of or into the United States.

The Capital Accounts

Private Investments

As a private investor, you may wish to sell U.S. dollars and buy foreign exchange in order to make an investment somewhere else in the world.

This could be a direct investment in the form of plant and equipment expenditures or the purchase of a foreign company, or it could be a financial asset, either long-term or short-term. (Stocks and bonds, for instance, are long-term investments, while a foreign bank account or a holding in foreign currency is a short-term investment.)

Any of these transactions will be a debit (–) in the American account, because dollars have left the United States. Conversely, when a private investor in another country sells foreign exchange in order to have U.S. dollars to make a direct or financial investment in the United States, whether long-term or short-term, this is classified as a credit (+).

Central Bank Transactions

If, as a representative of the Federal Reserve System, you sell dollars in order to buy foreign currency, this too is a debit (–), and when foreign central banks buy dollars, it is a credit (+).

These central bank transactions conclude the discussion of balance-of-payments components.

A further point must be made before you plow into the data. References are constantly being made to deficits or surpluses in the balances on trade, goods and services, and current account. Now and then you may encounter a comment about a deficit or a surplus in the balance of payments, despite this chapter's assertion that it always balances. How can you explain this apparent paradox?

Trade, goods and services, and current account are easy. You already know that there can be a surplus (+) or a deficit (–) in these separate accounts. But how could anyone speak of a deficit in the total balance of payments when it *must always balance*? Because that is the shorthand way of saying that the nation's currency is under selling pressure and that the value of the currency will fall unless some remedial action is taken.

For instance, at the time the foreign central banks supported the value of the dollar, their purchases of dollars constituted a "plus" (+) in the American balance of payments, because they sopped up the excess dollars that their own economies didn't need. (Had they not done so, the dollar would have fallen in value.) Obviously, if you remove a plus from an accounting system that is in the balance, what remains has a negative bottom line. Since a remedial action made the account balance, and since without it the account would have been negative, reference was made to a deficit in the balance of payments.

When the United States still sold gold internationally in order to redeem the dollar, these sales were plus (+) entries in our balance of payments. If

you wonder why the loss of gold is a plus, remember that anything sold by the United States is a plus, because the rest of the world must pay us for it. When you remove gold sales from the balance of payments, the remaining items must net out to a negative balance. Therefore, people often referred to the size of the U.S. gold loss as the deficit in the U.S. balance of payments.

And now for one final tip before you look at the data: Keep your eyes on the money. That's the best way to determine whether something is a plus (+) or minus (–) in the balance of payments. If *we* pay for it, it's a minus, because money is going out. If *they* pay for it, it's a plus.

The Wall Street Journal regularly publishes two Commerce Department reports dealing with the balance of payments and the balance of trade that will be useful to you.

1. *Balance-of-payments* figures for the previous *quarter* appear in the third week of the last month of each quarter.
2. *Monthly balance-of-trade* figures for the previous month are also released in the third week of each month.

According to the September 14, 1994 *Balance on Current Account* article on page 342, the current account deficit was $36.97 billion in the second quarter of 1994.

Use Chart 16–1 (on page 343) to focus on recent balance of payments developments.

First, the merchandise trade balance dropped like a stone in the early 80s, dragging the current account deficit with it.

Second, the merchandise trade deficit stopped falling in the late 80s, halting the deterioration in the current account balance.

Third, the current account balance moved back above zero in 1991, although the merchandise trade balance lagged behind.

Service income, such as the net earnings that the United States receives from foreign investments, the sale of banking, transport, and insurance services, and foreign tourism in the United States, comprises most of the gap between the current account and merchandise trade balance. Notice that, until the late 70s and early 80s, U.S. service earnings grew so rapidly that the balance on current account remained positive (+) despite a negative (–) merchandise trade balance.

U.S. Trade Gap Widens Broadly For 2nd Period

Current Account Deficit Surges to $36.97 Billion; Short-Term Vigor Seen

By Bob Davis
Staff Reporter of The Wall Street Journal

WASHINGTON — The U.S. current account deficit — the broadest measure of a nation's trade position — widened to $36.97 billion in the second quarter, the biggest shortfall since 1987.

So is that good news or bad news? Oddly enough, in the short term, at least, it may be a sign of strength.

Current Account Deficit {
The current account gap reflects the relative vigor of the U.S. and foreign economies, economists said. With the U.S. economy perking along while Europe, Japan and some big developing countries are just beginning to recover, U.S. imports have been surging faster than exports. So the gap has been widening.

"We have that famous 'sucking sound,'" said Robert Dederick, chief economist at Northern Trust Co. in a reference to Ross Perot's assertion that freer trade with Mexico would "suck" jobs out of the U.S. "We have a high propensity to import," especially during an expansion.

The current account trade figure covers merchandise, services, investment income and government payments. Overall, the deficit widened by $4.65 billion in the second quarter compared with the first quarter. That tracks almost exactly with the $4.81 billion rise in the merchandise trade deficit during the same period. The numbers are adjusted for season variations.

Michael Aho, a senior economist at Prudential Securities Inc., predicted that the current account gap will narrow "appreciably" in the early part of 1995, as foreign economies pick up steam. Mr. Dederick said he expects the turnaround will begin later next year.

But both economists warned that the trade deficit, whether measured as current account or merchandise trade, can help undermine the value of the dollar. That's the bad news. A weaker dollar boosts the cost of foreign goods, potentially adding to inflation.

When the U.S. buys more goods from other countries than it sells, it blankets the world with dollars. "We're living beyond our means," Mr. Aho said. "We're buying more from the rest of the world, and we're borrowing the money from the rest of the world" to pay for the splurge.

But in some ways, a weak U.S. currency can be good news, too.

For instance, the current account numbers show a $2.13 billion increase in the services trade *surplus*. Two thirds of that increase is because of a strengthening of the tourist trade here. Foreign tourists are spending more money here, and U.S. tourists are spending less abroad — partly because of the falling value of dollar. Said Mr. Dederick, who returned recently from a vacation on Cape Cod, Mass.: "It's the first time that I saw a meaningful foreign presence there."

Current Account Deficit – First Paragraph

WASHINGTON — The U.S. current account deficit — the broadest measure of a nation's trade position — widened to $36.97 billion in the second quarter, the biggest shortfall since 1987.

CHART 16–1
Balance of Payments (quarterly data): Current Account Balance,
Goods and Services Balance, and Merchandise Trade Balance.

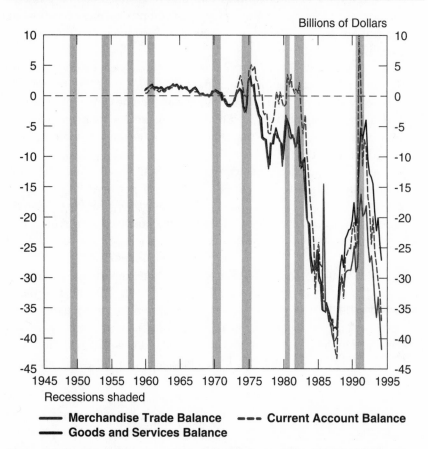

Billions of Dollars

Recessions shaded

—— **Merchandise Trade Balance**   ––– **Current Account Balance**
—— **Goods and Services Balance**

Source: U.S. Department of Commerce, *Business Cycle Indicators*, Series 622, 627; U.S. Department
of Commerce Business Statistics

Then the U.S. merchandise trade balance and the balance on current
account dropped off the end of the world, so that by the mid-80s
both numbers exceeded $150 billion at annual rates. (The numbers in
Chart 16–1 are quarterly.) The following circumstances can explain this
development.

1. The Fed's contractionary, anti-inflationary stand in the early 80s
drove U.S. interest rates above world market levels. Consequently,
Americans were reluctant to sell dollars, and the rest of the world was
eager to buy them. Strong demand for the dollar drove its price up, mak-

ing imports relatively attractive to Americans and our goods relatively less attractive in the rest of the world.

2. Even after U.S. interest rates fell, the dollar remained an attractive haven because of President Reagan's perceived pro-business position and the fear of left-wing governments elsewhere. A strong dollar hurt our balance on merchandise trade.

3. Recovery from the 1981–82 recession proceeded earlier and more swiftly in the U.S. than in the rest of the world. Therefore, our demand for imports grew more rapidly, because American incomes grew more rapidly.

4. As the U.S. led the world out of recession, our economy attracted foreign investment, further boosting the dollar and hurting our trade and current account balances.

At this point you should return to page 338 and review the balance of payments statement. If the current account is negative, as it was all through the 1980s, then the capital account must be positive. Otherwise, the balance of payments cannot balance. But a positive balance on capital account means that the rest of the world is acquiring American assets. In other words, if we buy Toyotas, they buy Rockefeller Center.

Put it in simple terms. If we export $2 and import $3, the rest of the world has at its disposal an additional dollar. Why? Because of the $3 it earned selling goods to us, it used only $2 to buy our goods. Keeping the extra dollar in its pocket constitutes a foreign investment by the rest of the world in the U.S. But of course, the rest of the world won't just keep the dollar in its pocket. Instead, it will purchase U.S. Treasury securities or a baseball team, or some other investment.

The U.S. ran a balance of trade and current account surplus for most years in the first three-quarters of the twentieth century and thereby became the world's greatest creditor nation. Reversing the example in the previous paragraph, we had extra money to invest in the rest of the world. But after 1980 we became the world's greatest debtor nation, as the flow of capital into the U.S. offset our deficit in the current account.

By the mid-1980s, President Reagan and his advisers viewed the situation with alarm. Free traders, they didn't want Congress imposing tariffs in order to reduce imports. So, we proposed that our major trading partners dump some of the dollars they had accumulated in the 1970s, thereby forcing down the dollar's value. As our export prices fell and import prices rose, the problem would take care of itself.

This agreement, negotiated at New York's Plaza Hotel in 1985, became known as the Plaza Accord and began to work in 1987. You can see

from Chart 16–1 on page 343 that our trade and current account balances began to improve in 1987 and that by the early 90s these deficits had shrunk considerably.

But they had help. Europe's economies began to break out of their malaise by the end of the 80s. As their incomes grew more rapidly, so did their imports of American goods. This helped stabilize our balance of trade.

In any event, you can see that even though the dollar had fallen all the way back down to its pre-1980 level, our balance of trade deficit persisted in the early 1990s and then escalated to record levels in the middle of the decade. The dollar's fall had not cured America's traded imbalance. Obviously, more was involved than the dollar's value and the relative health of the European economy.

But one last point remains regarding the current account before turning to the trade data in *The Wall Street Journal.* Our balance on current account popped back up above zero briefly in 1991 because of payments made to us by our Desert Storm allies. Those payments offset the continued trade deficit and momentarily pushed the current account into the black.

You can use the *Journal* to follow the Commerce Department's monthly merchandise trade report. The January 20, 1995 article provides data for November 1994. Focus your attention on imports, exports, and the balance between the two. (See pages 346–348).

According to the second and eighth paragraphs and the statistical summary at the end of the article, the United States ran a $10.53 billion trade deficit in November 1994 due to exports of $61.20 billion and imports of $71.70 billion.

Trade Deficit Widened Again In November

U.S. Gap for Year Heads For Record as Imports Stay in Strong Demand

ECONOMY

By CHRISTOPHER GEORGES

Staff Reporter of THE WALL STREET JOURNAL

WASHINGTON—The U.S. trade imbalance widened again in November, putting the nation on track for its worst annual deficit ever.

[Merchandise Trade Balance] The trade gap for both goods and services grew to $10.53 billion from a revised $10.10 billion in October, the Commerce Department reported. With just one month to go, America's trade deficit in goods only was running at an annual rate of $152.5 billion, which would top the old mark of $152.1 billion set in 1987.

"The only good news, if you want to call it good, is that the deficits with China and

Regional Trade Balances

U.S. merchandise trade balances by region: in billions of U.S. dollars, not seasonally adjusted

	NOV. 1994	OCT. 1994	NOV. 1993
Japan	−$6.19	−$6.66	−$5.71
China	− 2.89	− 3.48	− 2.12
Canada	− 2.02	− 1.69	− 1.06
Western Europe	− 1.96	− 1.50	− 0.76
Mexico	− 0.38	− 0.09	+ 0.18
NICs*	− 1.22	− 1.60	− 1.29

*Newly industrialized countries: Singapore, Hong Kong, Taiwan, South Korea

Source: Commerce Department

Japan were not enormous—just extremely high," said Lawrence Chimerine of the Economic Strategy Institute.

The widening gap, analysts said, stems from many of the same factors that have plagued the U.S. trade picture in recent months, such as economic growth in the U.S. combined with economic struggles abroad. Although several U.S. trading partners, such as Japan and European nations, have seen their economies pick up recently, the increased demand abroad is unlikely to trickle into the trade picture for several months, economists said.

Situation in Mexico

"We're upbeat for U.S. exports in 1995," said Brian Horrigan, a trade expert at Loomis Sayles & Co. in Boston. "We also expect that, as the economy here slows, U.S. demand for imports will slow."

Analysts, however, said that in coming months a worsening trade imbalance with Mexico will curb any improvement. Even if a $40 billion U.S. rescue package for Mexico succeeds in stabilizing the market turmoil, analysts said, the sharp fall in the value of the peso—making U.S. goods more expensive in Mexico and Mexican products cheaper in the U.S. — would likely widen the bilateral gap.

Even before the currency crisis, the U.S. trade performance with Mexico was deteriorating, yesterday's figures showed. The deficit with Mexico jumped to $378 million from $89 million in October.

In November, overall U.S. exports rose 2.2% to a record $61.20 billion, led by an

U.S. Trade Deficit

In billions of dollars

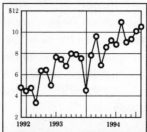

increase in big-ticket items, particularly commercial aircraft. But imports were up an even larger 2.5% to $71.70 billion, boosted in part by a jump in oil imports.

The U.S. deficit with Japan narrowed to $6.19 billion from $6.66 billion but remains the third-largest on record for any country. The second-biggest deficit in November—$2.89 billion — was with China, down from $3.48 billion in October.

Efforts to Open Markets

Over the past two years the Clinton administration has sought to force Japan and other Asian nations to open their markets further to American products.

[Merchandise Exports and Imports]

With Japan, however, the administration has achieved only partial success, especially in the auto sector, which accounts for two-thirds of the U.S. deficit with Japan.

That pattern continued in trade talks last week as the administration softened its recent rhetoric on forcing Japan to open its markets. President Clinton, in his meeting with Japanese Prime Minister Tomiichi Murayama, instead sought to emphasize agreements already reached.

"The administration's ideas are right, and its approach is right," Mr. Chimerine said. "They just haven't been tough enough in following through."

While damage to factories in Japan caused by Tuesday's earthquake may lead to a temporary decline in imports from Japan, the disaster may have less-direct but longer-term trade implications. "They may use this as an excuse to beg for more time" to complete trade agreements, Mr. Chimerine said.

In a separate report, the Labor Department said the number of Americans filing first-time claims for unemployment benefits dropped by 31,000 last week to 323,000, the lowest figure in three weeks. The four-week average for seasonally adjusted claims during the Jan. 14 week was 334,000, down from a revised 334,500 the previous week.

Here are the Commerce Department's monthly trade figures, in billions of dollars.

	November 1995	October 1995	
Total Exports	$61.16	$59.85	Statistical
Goods	44.54	43.38	Summary
Services	16.63	16.47	
Total Imports	71.69	69.94	
Goods	60.10	58.43	
Services	11.59	11.51	
Overall trade balance	– 10.53	– 10.10	
Goods	– 15.56	– 15.05	
Services	5.03	4.95	

Merchandise Trade Balance—Second Paragraph

The trade gap for both goods and services grew to $10.53 billion from a revised $10.10 billion in October, the Commerce Department reported. With just one month to go, America's trade deficit in goods only was running at an annual rate of $152.5 billion, which would top the old mark of $152.1 billion set in 1987.

Exports and Imports—Eighth Paragraph

In November, overall U.S. exports rose 2.2% to a record $61.20 billion, led by an increase in big-ticket items, particularly commercial aircraft. But imports were up an even larger 2.5% to $71.70 billion, boosted in part by a jump in oil imports.

Statistical Summary—End of Article

Here are the Commerce Department's monthly trade figures, in billions of dollars.

	November 1995	October 1995
Total Exports	$61.16	$59.85
Goods	44.54	43.38
Services	16.63	16.47
Total Imports	71.69	69.94
Goods	60.10	58.43
Services	11.59	11.51
Overall trade balance	− 10.53	− 10.10
Goods	− 15.56	− 15.05
Services	5.03	4.95

Source: *The Wall Street Journal*, January 20, 1995. Reprinted by permission of *The Wall Street Journal*, ©1995 Dow Jones & Company, Inc. All rights reserved worldwide.

Investor's Tip

- There is no long-run correlation between our balance of trade and the stock market's or gold's performance. If the trade figures improve, less and less attention will be paid to them. And when the balance of trade is no longer a headline-grabber, the stock and gold markets will pay less attention to it.

FOREIGN EXCHANGE RATES

Each day *The Wall Street Journal* publishes several reports on foreign exchange trading activity. Start with the report on the last section's first page, under the **Markets Diary** heading, labeled **U.S. Dollar**. The excerpt on page 349 from the Friday, February 10, 1995 issue is an example. The Chart provides a record of the dollar's value compared with a trade-weighted average of 15 currencies. Below that is a record of the dollar's value against five major currencies.

The *Journal* also publishes daily a table on **Currency Trading** (check the front-page index of the first and last sections under **Foreign Exchange**). The February 10, 1995 table appears on page 350. You can use it to keep abreast of the dollar's value against a wide range of curren-

cies. For instance, on Thursday, February 9, 1995, the British pound was worth approximately $1.55, the Canadian dollar about $0.72, the French franc approximately $0.19, the Japanese yen about $0.01, the Swiss franc approximately $0. 77, and the German mark approximately $0.65.

You can see that these quotations portray the value of a single unit of foreign exchange in terms of the American dollar. However, foreign currencies are usually quoted in units per American dollar. Thus, on February 9, 1995 the dollar was worth 98.90 Japanese yen and 1.528 German marks.

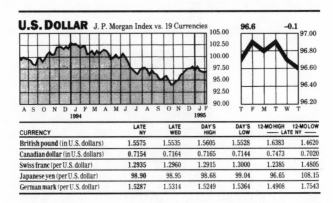

CURRENCY	LATE NY	LATE WED	DAY'S HIGH	DAY'S LOW	12-MO HIGH —— LATE NY ——	12-MO LOW
British pound (in U.S. dollars)	1.5575	1.5535	1.5605	1.5528	1.6383	1.4620
Canadian dollar (in U.S. dollars)	0.7154	0.7164	0.7165	0.7144	0.7473	0.7020
Swiss franc (per U.S. dollar)	1.2935	1.2960	1.2915	1.3000	1.2385	1.4805
Japanese yen (per U.S. dollar)	98.90	98.95	98.68	99.04	96.65	108.15
German mark (per U.S. dollar)	1.5287	1.5314	1.5249	1.5364	1.4908	1.7543

Source: *The Wall Street Journal*, February 10, 1995. Reprinted by permission of *The Wall Street Journal*, ©1995 Dow Jones & Company, Inc. All rights reserved worldwide.

Most foreign exchange trading is conducted by banks on behalf of their customers. Banks will also provide future delivery of foreign exchange for customers who want a guaranteed price in order to plan their operations and limit risk due to exchange rate fluctuation. The price for future delivery is known as the forward rate, and you can see forward quotes for the major currencies immediately beneath the current rate.

On Mondays, the *Journal* also provides exchange rates for major currencies in terms of each other's value and a weekly comparison of the dollar's value against almost every currency in the world. See **Key Currency Cross Rates** on page 351 and **World Value of the Dollar** from the February 10, 1995 issue on page 352.

Recall the brief outline of the dollar's postwar history presented earlier.

CURRENCY TRADING

EXCHANGE RATES

Thursday, February 9, 1995
The New York foreign exchange selling rates below apply to trading among banks in amounts of $1 million and more, as quoted at 3 p.m. Eastern time by Bankers Trust Co., Dow Jones Telerate Inc. and other sources. Retail transactions provide fewer units of foreign currency per dollar.

Country	U.S. $ equiv. Thur.	U.S. $ equiv. Wed.	Currency per U.S. $ Thur.	Currency per U.S. $ Wed.
Argentina (Peso)	1.00	1.00	1.00	1.00
Australia (Dollar)	.7416	.7444	1.3485	1.3435
Austria (Schilling)	.09297	.09273	10.76	10.78
Bahrain (Dinar)	2.6526	2.6525	.3770	.3770
Belgium (Franc)	.03180	.03176	31.45	31.49
Brazil (Real)	1.1997600	1.1976048	.83	.84
British Pound → Britain (Pound)	1.5577	1.5532	.6420	.6438
30-Day Forward	1.5570	1.5527	.6423	.6441
90-Day Forward	1.5558	1.5515	.6428	.6445
180-Day Forward	1.5440	1.5495	.6477	.6454
Canadian Dollar → Canada (Dollar)	.7152	.7166	1.3982	1.3956
30-Day Forward	.7142	.7156	1.4001	1.3974
90-Day Forward	.7122	.7138	1.4042	1.4011
180-Day Forward	.7095	.7113	1.4094	1.4060
Czech. Rep. (Koruna) Commercial rate	.0360984	.0360373	27.7021	27.7490
Chile (Peso)	.002436	.002443	410.45	409.30
China (Renminbi)	.118534	.118526	8.4364	8.4370
Colombia (Peso)	.001183	.001182	845.50	846.19
Denmark (Krone)	.1662	.1659	6.0180	6.0290
Ecuador (Sucre) Floating rate	.000423	.000422	2365.00	2372.00
Finland (Markka)	.21200	.21148	4.7170	4.7285
French Franc → France (Franc)	.18904	.18879	5.2900	5.2970
30-Day Forward	.18913	.18888	5.2875	5.2944
90-Day Forward	.18930	.18904	5.2828	5.2898
180-Day Forward	.18954	.18928	5.2758	5.2833
German Mark → Germany (Mark)	.6542	.6527	1.5287	1.5321
30-Day Forward	.6547	.6533	1.5274	1.5307
90-Day Forward	.6561	.6564	1.5241	1.5234
180-Day Forward	.6585	.6569	1.5187	1.5224
Japanese Yen → Japan (Yen)	.010111	.010109	98.90	98.93
30-Day Forward	.010141	.010139	98.61	98.63
90-Day Forward	.010211	.010207	97.93	97.97
180-Day Forward	.010326	.010321	96.85	96.89
Swiss Franc → Switzerland (Franc) ...	.7732	.7715	1.2933	1.2962
30-Day Forward	.7747	.7729	1.2909	1.2938
90-Day Forward	.7777	.7759	1.2858	1.2888
180-Day Forward	.7823	.7805	1.2782	1.2812
SDR	1.46625	1.46468	.68201	.68274
ECU	1.23470	1.23230	....	....

Special Drawing Rights (SDR) are based on exchange rates for the U.S., German, British, French and Japanese currencies. Source: International Monetary Fund.
European Currency Unit (ECU) is based on a basket of community currencies.

Chart 16–2 on page 353 provides graphic evidence that the value of foreign currencies in terms of dollars has risen dramatically (i.e., the dollar has fallen in value) since the mid-80s. The French franc has jumped from $0.10 to $0.19; the British pound from a little over $1.00 to $1.55; the Swiss franc from $0.35 to $0.77; the Japanese yen from $0.004 to $0.01; and the German mark from $0.30 to $0.65. The balance-of-payments discussion will aid your understanding of the dollar's decline.

Key Currency Cross Rates Late New York Trading Feb. 9, 1995

	Dollar	Pound	SFranc	Guilder	Peso	Yen	Lira	D-Mark	FFranc	CdnDlr
Canada	1.3978	2.1771	1.08063	.81576	.25300	.01413	.00087	.91437	.26443	....
France	5.2860	8.233	4.0866	3.0849	.95674	.05345	.00327	3.4578	....	3.7817
Germany	1.5287	2.3810	1.1818	.89215	.27669	.01546	.00095	....	.28920	1.0936
Italy	1614.8	2515.0	1248.36	942.37	292.26	16.327	....	1056.29	305.48	1155.2
Japan	98.90	154.04	76.459	57.718	17.900	....	.06125	64.695	18.710	70.75
Mexico	5.5250	8.6052	4.2714	3.2244	....	.05586	.00342	3.6142	1.0452	3.9526
Netherlands ..	1.7135	2.6688	1.3247	....	.31014	.01733	.00106	1.1209	.32416	1.2259
Switzerland ...	1.2935	2.0146	....	.75489	.23412	.01308	.00080	.84614	.24470	.9254
U.K.	.64205	....	.49637	.37470	.11621	.00649	.00040	.42000	.12146	.45933
U.S.	....	1.5575	.77310	.58360	.18100	.01011	.00062	.65415	.18918	.71541

Source: Dow Jones Telerate Inc.

The dollar fell to its post-World War II low against most currencies in the late 70s (see Chart 16–2) because of severe inflation here at home and its impact on our trade balance. (You can observe the increase in value of the key currencies in Chart 16–2.) The merchandise trade balance sank dramatically, as rising prices impeded our ability to sell and whetted our appetite for imports (Chart 16–1 on page 343). Since people in the rest of the world needed fewer dollars (because they weren't buying as many of our goods) and we needed more foreign exchange (because we were buying more of their goods), the dollar's value plunged. The dollar's rally in the early 80s was a two-phase process. The first phase in 1981–82 had two major causes.

First, high interest rates strengthened the dollar. When interest rates in the United States are higher than interest rates elsewhere, foreign exchange is sold for dollars, and the capital accounts will show a net flow of private investment into the United States. The Fed's tight money policy pushed interest rates in the United States higher than those in Europe and Japan, prompting heavy dollar purchases by foreign investors who wished to enjoy the high interest rates available here.

Second, the U.S. balance on current account improved dramatically until late 1982 because of rapidly growing service income and despite a sharply negative balance of trade. This positive element in the American balance of payments not only generated a flow of dollars into the United States, but also encouraged private businesses and individuals in the rest of the world to invest in dollars, because they believed that the dollar would remain strong in the future.

World Value of the Dollar

The table below, compiled by Bank of America, gives the rates of exchange for the U.S. dollar against various currencies as of Friday February 10, 1995. Unless otherwise noted, all rates listed are middle rates of interbank bid and asked quotes, and are expressed in foreign currency units per one U.S. dollar. The rates are indicative and aren't based on, nor intended to be used as a basis for, particular transactions.
BankAmerica International doesn't trade in all the listed foreign currencies.

Country (Currency)	Value 2/10	Value 2/3
Afghanistan (Afghani -c)	3463.03	3463.03
Albania (Lek)	100.49	100.49
Algeria (Dinar)	42.44	42.45
Andorra (Peseta)	131.70	132.17
Andorra (Franc)	5.289	5.2692
Angola (New Kwanza)	556973.00	551458.00
Antigua (E Caribbean $)	2.70	2.70
Argentina (Peso)	1.00	1.00
Aruba (Florin)	1.79	1.79
Australia (Australia Dollar)	1.3414	1.3262
Austria (Schilling)	10.752	10.69
Bahamas (Dollar)	1.00	1.00
Bahrain (Dinar)	0.377	0.377
Bangladesh (Taka)	40.3875	40.08
Barbados (Dollar)	2.0113	2.0113
Belgium (Franc)	31.44	31.77
Belize (Dollar)	2.00	2.00
Benin (C.F.A. Franc)	528.90	526.92
Bermuda (Dollar)	1.00	1.00
Bhutan (Ngultrum)	31.3725	31.81
Bolivia (Boliviano -f)	4.74	4.74
Bolivia (Boliviano -o)	4.75	4.75
Botswana (Pula)	2.71	2.7067
Bouvet Island (Norwegian Krone)	6.688	6.656
Brazil (Real)	0.834	0.84
Brunei (Dollar)	1.4525	1.4415
Bulgaria (Lev)	66.56	66.596
Burkina Faso (C.F.A. Franc)	528.90	526.92
Burma (Kyat)	5.8027	5.7939
Burundi (Franc)	244.3617	243.9923
Cambodia (Riel)	2608.00	2608.00
Cameroon (C.F.A. Franc)	528.90	526.92
Canada (Dollar)	1.4013	1.4056
Cape Verde Isl (Escudo)	82.97	82.97
Cayman Islands (Dollar)	0.8282	0.8282
Centrl African Rp (C.F.A. Franc)	528.90	526.92
Chad (C.F.A. Franc)	528.90	526.92
Chile (Peso -m5)	409.56	409.06
Chile (Peso -o5)	418.10	417.79
China (Renminbi Yuan)	8.436	8.4384
Colombia (Peso-o)	847.04	855.76
Commwlth Ind Sts (Rouble -m)	4191.00	4115.00
Comoros (Franc)	396.675	395.19
Congo, People Rp (C.F.A. Franc)	528.90	526.92
Costa Rica (Colon)	167.83	167.30
Croatia (Kuna)	5.5478	5.5099
Cuba (Peso)	1.00	1.00
Cyprus (Pound *)	2.1149	2.1269
Czech (Koruna)	27.67	27.56
Denmark (Danish Krone)	6.019	5.9955
Djibouti (Djibouti Franc)	177.72	177.72
Dominica (E Caribbean $)	2.70	2.70
Dominican Rep (Peso -d)	13.78	13.43
Ecuador (Sucre -o)	2346.50	2355.00
Ecuador (Sucre -d4)	2375.00	2370.00
Egypt (Pound)	3.3945	3.3935
El Salvador (Colon -d)	8.76	8.76
Equatorial Guinea (C.F.A. Franc)	528.90	526.92
Estonia (Kroon)	12.23	12.14
Ethiopia (Birr -o)	5.43	5.43
Faeroe Islands (Danish Krone)	6.019	5.9955
Falkland Islands (Pound *)	1.5564	1.5736
Fiji (Dollar)	1.4289	1.4172
Finland (Markka)	4.6953	4.7098
France (Franc)	5.289	5.2692
French Guiana (Franc)	5.289	5.2692
French Pacific Isl (C.F.P. Franc)	96.1635	95.8035
Gabon (C.F.A. Franc)	528.90	526.92
Gambia (Dalasi)	9.77	9.78
Germany (Mark)	1.528	1.5188
Ghana (Cedi)	1065.00	1065.00
Gibraltar (Pound *)	1.5564	1.5736
Greece (Drachma)	238.11	237.04
Greenland (Danish Krone)	6.019	5.9955
Grenada (E Caribbean $)	2.70	2.70
Guadeloupe (Franc)	5.289	5.2692
Guam (U.S. $)	1.00	1.00
Guatemala (Quetzal)	5.5492	5.707
Guinea Bissau (Peso)	13569.00	13569.00
Guinea Rep (Franc)	1014.54	1002.11
Guyana (Dollar)	143.76	142.00
Haiti (Gourde)	19.90	19.90
Honduras Rep (Lempira -d)	9.28	9.27
Hong Kong (Dollar)	7.7325	7.7325
Hungary (Forint -8)	111.74	111.22
Iceland (Krona)	67.22	67.20
India (Rupee)	31.3725	31.81
Indonesia (Rupiah)	2221.50	2219.75
Iran (Rial -o)	1749.00	1748.00
Iraq (Dinar)	0.60	0.60
Ireland (Punt *)	1.5521	1.5581
Israel (New Shekel)	3.0236	3.01
Italy (Lira)	1616.75	1607.50
Ivory Coast (C.F.A. Franc)	528.90	526.92
Jamaica (Dollar)	32.05	32.38
Japan (Yen)	98.94	99.57
Jordan (Dinar)	0.702	0.70
Kenya (Shilling)	44.5222	44.4167
Kiribati (Australia Dollar)	1.3414	1.3262
Korea, North (Won)	2.15	2.15
Korea, South (Won)	790.80	788.90
Kuwait (Dinar)	0.2999	0.2988
Laos, People DR (Kip)	724.00	724.00
Latvia (Lat)	0.55	0.54

Country (Currency)	Value 2/10	Value 2/3
Lebanon (Pound)	1641.50	1642.50
Lesotho (Maloti)	3.5492	3.5493
Liberia (Dollar)	1.00	1.00
Libya (Dinar -9)	0.3574	0.3574
Liechtenstein (Franc)	1.2925	1.2846
Lithuania (Litas)	4.00	4.00
Luxembourg (Lux.Franc)	31.44	31.77
Macao (Pataca)	7.9877	7.9877
Madagascar DR (Franc)	3760.00	3735.00
Malawi (Kwacha)	15.53	15.34
Malaysia (Ringgit)	2.5498	2.5605
Maldive (Rufiyaa)	11.77	11.77
Mali Rep (C.F.A. Franc)	528.90	526.92
Malta (Lira *)	2.7329	2.7507
Martinique (Franc)	5.289	5.2692
Mauritania (Ouguiya)	122.00	122.00
Mauritius (Rupee)	17.95	17.84
Mexico (New Peso -1)	5.63	5.45
Monaco (Franc)	5.289	5.2692
Mongolia (Tugrik -o)	411.96	411.96
Montserrat (E Caribbean $)	2.70	2.70
Morocco (Dirham)	8.875	8.8408
Mozambique (Meticai)	6906.67	6822.00
Namibia (Rand -c)	3.5492	3.5493
Nauru Islands (Australia Dollar)	1.3414	1.3262
Nepal (Rupee)	49.40	49.40
Netherlands (Guilder)	1.7129	1.7021
Netherlands Ant'les (Guilder)	1.79	1.79
New Zealand (N.Z.Dollar)	1.5778	1.5662
Nicaragua (Gold Cordoba)	7.1804	7.1804
Niger Rep (C.F.A. Franc)	528.90	526.92
Nigeria (Naira -o)	22.00	22.00
Norway (Norwegian Krone)	6.688	6.656
Oman, Sultanate of (Rial)	0.385	0.385
Pakistan (Rupee)	30.98	30.94
Panama (Balboa)	1.00	1.00
Papua N.G. (Kina -11)	1.1813	1.1696
Paraguay (Guarani -d)	1947.00	1930.00
Peru (New Sol -d)	2.225	2.185
Philippines (Peso)	24.775	24.655
Pitcairn Island (N.Z.Dollar)	1.5778	1.5662
Poland (Zloty -o4)	2.4634	2.4422
Portugal (Escudo)	157.58	156.98
Puerto Rico (U.S. $)	1.00	1.00
Qatar (Rival)	3.639	3.639
Republic of Yemen (Dinar)	0.461	0.461
Republic of Yemen (Rial)	12.00	12.00
Reunion, Ile de la (Franc)	5.289	5.2692
Romania (Leu)	1798.00	1788.00
Rwanda (Franc)	137.4517	137.4436
Saint Christopher (E Caribbean $)	2.70	2.70
Saint Helena (Pound Sterling *)	1.5564	1.5736
Saint Lucia (E Caribbean $)	2.70	2.70
Saint Pierre (Franc)	5.289	5.2692
Saint Vincent (E Caribbean $)	2.70	2.70
Samoa, American (U.S. $)	1.00	1.00
Samoa, Western (Tala)	2.4771	2.4771
San Marino (Lira)	1616.75	1607.50
Sao Tome & Principe (Dobra)	1610.05	1610.05
Saudi Arabia (Rival)	3.7503	3.7506
Senegal (C.F.A. Franc)	528.90	526.92
Seychelles (Rupee)	4.9338	4.9264
Sierra Leone (Leone)	622.50	622.50
Singapore (Dollar)	1.4525	1.4515
Slovak (Koruna)	30.97	30.79
Slovenia (Tolar)	121.93	121.93
Solomon Islands (Solomon Dollar)	3.3156	3.3156
Somali Rep (Shilling -o)	2620.00	2620.00
South Africa (Rand -f)	4.06	4.065
South Africa (Rand -c)	3.5492	3.5493
Spain (Peseta)	131.70	132.17
Sri Lanka (Rupee)	50.01	49.94
Sudan Rep (Dinar)	38.46	38.46
Sudan Rep (Pound -c 10)	384.62	384.62
Surinam (Guilder -3)	419.00	417.00
Swaziland (Lilangeni)	3.5492	3.5493
Sweden (Krona)	7.437	7.4575
Switzerland (Franc)	1.2925	1.2846
Syria (Pound)	42.00	42.00
Taiwan (Dollar -o)	26.31	26.25
Tanzania (Shilling)	518.99	545.00
Thailand (Baht)	25.06	25.055
Togo, Rep (C.F.A. Franc)	528.90	526.92
Tonga Islands (Pa'anga)	1.3414	1.3262
Trinidad & Tobago (Dollar)	5.685	5.675
Tunisia (Dinar)	0.9833	0.9815
Turkey (Lira)	41264.00	41008.00
Turks & Caicos (U.S. $)	1.00	1.00
Tuvalu (Australia Dollar)	1.3414	1.3262
Uganda (Shilling -i)	929.39	925.00
Ukraine (Karbovanet -7)	117100.00	117100.00
United Arab Emir (Dirham)	3.671	3.671
United Kingdom (Pound Sterling *)	1.5564	1.5736
Uruguay (Peso Uruguayo -n)	5.72	5.69
Vanuatu (Vatu)	111.75	111.75
Vatican City (Lira)	1616.75	1607.50
Venezuela (Bolivar -d 2)	170.00	170.00
Vietnam (Dong -o)	11142.00	11142.00
Virgin Is, Br (U.S. $)	1.00	1.00
Virgin Is, US (U.S. $)	1.00	1.00
Yugoslavia (New Dinar)	1.528	1.5188
Zaire Rep (New Zaire)	3221.70	3360.00
Zambia (Kwacha)	740.00	710.00
Zimbabwe (Dollar)	8.40	8.42

*U.S. dollars per National Currency unit. (a) Free market central bank rate. (b) Floating rate. (c) Commercial rate. (d) Free market rate. (e) Controlled. (f) Financial rate. (g) Preferential rate. (h) Nonessential imports. (i) Floating tourist rate. (j) Public transaction rate. (k) Agricultural products. (l) Priority rate. (m) Market rate. (n) Essential imports. (o) Official rate. (p) Exports. (n.a.) Not available.

(1) Mexico, 23 December 1994: Currency allowed to float. (2) Venezuela, 7 July 1994: New fixed single exchange rate introduced (3) Surinam, 9 October 1994: Foreign Currency rate freed. (4) Ecuador, 21 December 1994: Central Bank to implement a crawling peg technique. (5) Chile, 30 November 1994: Peso REVALUED by approx 3.5%. (6) Poland, 1 January 1995: Currency rebased. (7) Ukraine, 5 September 1994: Karbovanet devalued by approx 7.3%. (8) Hungary, 1 January 1995: Forint devalued by approx 1.4% (9) Libya, 7 November 1994: Dinar devalued by approx 18.56% (10) Sudan Rep, 29 June 1994: Pound revalued by approx 3.22% (11) Papua N.G., 10 October 1994: Kina allowed to float.

Further information available at BankAmerica International.

Source: Bank of America Global Trading, London

CHART 16–2
Foreign Exchange Rates

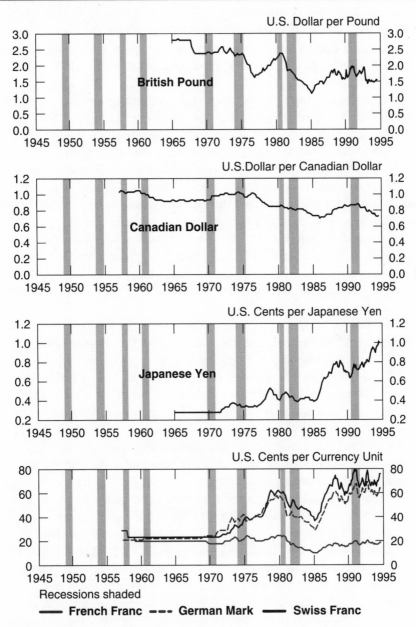

Recessions shaded

——— **French Franc** --- **German Mark** ——— **Swiss Franc**

Source: Standard & Poor's, *Statistical Service.*

The second phase in 1983–84 is somewhat more complex. The interest rate differential between the United States and the rest of the world had narrowed since mid-1982 (see the first cause listed on page 353), while the balance on current account deteriorated rapidly (see the second cause listed above) due to the plunge in our merchandise trade balance (see Chart 16–1 on page 343). Under these circumstances, the dollar's value should have fallen.

Nevertheless, it improved, because of the continuing flow of investment dollars into the United States and the continuing reduced flow of our investment dollars to the rest of the world. The rest of the world believed America to be the safest, most profitable home for its funds. To foreigners (indeed, to many Americans), President Reagan symbolized America's protection of, and concern for, business interests. Certainly, the United States was a secure haven: Investments would not be expropriated, nor would their return be subject to confiscatory taxation. And the return was good; even if the interest rate differential between here and abroad had narrowed, U.S. rates were still higher than those in most other countries. Moreover, profits had been strong, and the stock market reflected this. Foreign investors who had a stake in American business were rewarded handsomely.

Thus, the dollar remained strong because the huge net capital flow into the United States bid the dollar's price up and forced other currencies down. The rise in the dollar's value, together with the quicker economic expansion here than abroad, depressed our exports and stimulated our imports. Consequently, the deterioration in our merchandise trade balance in 1983 and 1984 was a result of the dollar's appreciation, not a cause of it.

But by 1985 the merchandise trade balance had deteriorated to such an extent, while American interest rates continued to slide, that the dollar began to weaken. Foreign demand for our currency was not strong enough to offset our demand for the rest of the world's currencies. In addition, we began to pressure our major trading partners, requesting their assistance in reducing our trade deficit by driving the dollar's value down. They (i.e., their central banks) complied by agreeing to the Plaza Accord and sold dollars, contributing to the dollar's slide. As a result, by the late 80s, the dollar had lost most of the increase of the early 80s.

The dollar stabilized at the end of the decade because our balance-of-trade deficit stopped growing due to rapid export growth. American interest rates rose, and foreign central banks actively supported the dollar once

again. These developments stimulated dollar purchase and helped halt the dollar's decline. The foreign central banks had begun to respond to their own industrial interests and were no longer willing to let the dollar fall in order to protect our markets.

The dollar remained low in the early 1990s, but resumed falling in mid-decade as America's balance of trade deteriorated further. By then the American economy operated at higher levels than our trading partners', drawing vast quantities of imports once again. Foreign exchange speculators responded by dumping dollars, thereby driving the dollar to new lows.

Investor's Tip

- This brief history should warn you how hard it is to predict the dollar's value and the course of international economic events. That's why foreign exchange speculation is not for amateurs. Even some pros go broke doing it.

CHAPTER 17

SUMMARY AND PROSPECT

So what will you have for the 1990s? Stocks and other paper securities, or gold and similar tangible assets? The best investment all depends on the course of inflation and the business cycle.

But, you may ask, didn't we tame both inflation and the business cycle in the 1980s? The decade came to an end after seven good years of steady expansion, with both low unemployment and low inflation. Wasn't this evidence that the Fed had done a great job?

Yes, the Fed did perform admirably and effectively in the 1980s, so that, by the end of the decade, escalating debt and inflation and the business cycle's roller coaster ride appeared to be mere relics of the past, confined to the years 1965 through 1980. Could it be that those years, with all their problems, were an exception, a kind of rough patch that is now behind us? Once again, we must turn to the historical record for some perspective.

The early 1960s followed the Eisenhower years, which President Kennedy and his advisers criticized severely for sluggish economic performance and too many recessions. They excoriated the fiscal policy of President Eisenhower's administration and the monetary policy of the Federal Reserve for excessive concern with inflation and complacency about slow economic growth and unemployment. These critics charged that, because of the attempt to restrain demand in order to combat "creeping inflation," the economy's growth rate had fallen and recovery from frequent recessions in the 1950s had been weak.

Yet the Eisenhower years had been the best of times for stock market investors. The Dow climbed from 200 in 1950 to almost 1,000 in 1965, a fivefold increase in 15 years. Some said that stocks had been a good hedge against the negligible inflation of those years. In truth, they had done well because of inflation's absence.

But as the middle 60s approached, the economy rapidly gained steam. The low level of inflation (inherited from the Eisenhower years) and the Fed's easy money policy (in response to Kennedy administration requests) were the most important ingredients in the rapid economic expansion that began in the 1960s.

Modest increases in the CPI permitted strong growth in real consumer income. As a result, consumer sentiment steadily improved. This, together with the ready availability of loans at low interest rates, prompted consumers to resort to record levels of mortgage borrowing and consumer credit. Home construction and automobile production set new highs. Business responded by investing heavily in new plant and equipment, so that general boom conditions prevailed by the middle of the decade.

The tax cut proposed by President Kennedy has received most of the credit for this prosperity. Inconveniently, however, it was not enacted until 1964, after his death, and it is difficult to understand how an expansion that began in 1962 can be attributed to a tax cut two years later.

The expansion's relaxed and easy progress was its most important early feature. There was no overheating. Housing starts, auto sales, consumer credit, and retail sales gradually broke through to new highs. By 1965, there had been three solid years of expansion, reflected in a strong improvement in labor productivity and a solid advance in real compensation.

The problems began in the late 60s, when the Fed did not exercise enough restraint on the boom. Its half-hearted measures were too little and too late. Most observers blamed the Vietnam War for the inflation, but the federal deficit never exceeded $15 billion in the late 60s. Meanwhile, private borrowing hit $100 billion annually, thereby dwarfing federal fiscal stimuli. Private borrowing and spending on residential construction, autos, and other consumer durables and business capital expenditures—not federal borrowing and spending on the Vietnam War—generated the inflation of the late 60s.

As the inflation progressed, it created a nightmare for stock and bond holders in the 1970s. During the entire decade, their investments did not gain in value; some even fell. Meanwhile, real estate boomed and gold and other precious metals went through the roof.

And as you know from the earlier discussion, the Fed's attempts to deal with inflation remained inadequate throughout the 70s, so that its stop-go policies only exacerbated inflation over the course of the cycle.

It was not until Paul Volcker persuaded the Fed to take a stand in the early 80s with a policy of continued restraint that inflation was brought

under control and stability ensured for the rest of the decade. By the end of the 80s, Americans enjoyed better economic conditions than at any time since the early 60s.

And, as had happened during the good old days of low inflation, paper assets such as stocks and bonds did well in the low inflation 80s, while gold and precious metals collapsed. Real estate appeared to be an anomaly. because it did well in key urban areas which enjoyed strong demographic and job growth. But that obscured real estate's weakness in most markets. Real estate was a bad investment all across rural America, in oil-producing regions, and in many metropolitan areas in the 1980s.

Will the 1990s be like the late 80s and the early 60s? Will the economy expand slowly and gradually, bringing prosperity without severe fluctuation and inflation? And will stocks and bonds do better than real estate and precious metals?

Yes. The rate of inflation remains low, with substantial slack in the economy. The Fed's change in direction in the early 1980s means that the years from 1965 to 1980 were an anomaly, a bad patch that is now behind us. Spiraling debt and inflation should be a thing of the past as we look forward to continued monetary restraint.

But that doesn't mean that the U.S. faces a rosy economic future. Long-run forces are at work that will weaken America's future growth unless they are dealt with soon. The U.S. economy can't compete the way it once did, and many Americans have noticed that their shares of the income pie are shrinking. That's a bad sign that became increasingly clear as we emerged from the 1990-91 recession. The old confidence was lacking.

The economy eventually recovered and expanded strongly in the mid 1990s. Once again, the Fed forced interest rates upward to prevent inflation's resurrection, and everyone hoped for a soft landing. But some of the old symptoms of robust conditions were absent. Although motor vehicle sales were strong, housing starts couldn't break through the 1.5 million range. Fewer people could aspire to the American dream.

Capitalism is a moving target, always changing and always evolving— constrained by indigenous institutions and shaped by contemporary events. The description of its dynamic, contained in these chapters, is appropriate for the present time and place. This dynamic would not have explained conditions 50 years earlier, nor will it describe them 50 years hence. The system will evolve in ways that no one can predict. Yet for the time being, the Fed has managed to wrestle the business cycle and inflation to the mat, so that they will be restrained, although not absent, in the 1990s.

APPENDIX A

MISCELLANEOUS
STATISTICAL INDICATORS

A number of statistical indicators have not yet been discussed although they appear regularly in *The Wall Street Journal*. These indicators are not directly applicable to the earlier chapters' analyses. They are important, however, and the following commentary should help you put them in perspective.

EMPLOYMENT DATA

The Wall Street Journal usually publishes the Labor Department's *monthly employment report* on Monday of the second week. August 1994 data appeared in the Tuesday, September 6, 1994 *Wall Street Journal* (see page 362). The third paragraph said, "the unemployment rate was unchanged at 6.1 percent of the workforce." The chart accompanying the article illustrates the drop in the unemployment rate since the end of the recession.

You should also track the *average workweek* and *factory overtime,* because they, too, portray the economy's strength and are important determinants of consumer sentiment. They appear in the statistical summary at the end of the article, as in the example drawn from the July story (see pages 362 and 363). Charts A–1 and A–2 on pages 364 and 365 clearly show that by the end of 1994 both the workweek and overtime were at record levels. You should also observe that these indicators generally improve during expansion, flatten with boom conditions, and plummet in recession. A strong economy provides big paychecks.

Wage Pressures And Inflation Stay in Check

August's 6.1% Jobless Rate Fails to Raise Specters Despite the Textbooks

By Lucinda Harper
Staff Reporter of The Wall Street Journal

WASHINGTON — For academic economists, two specters arise when unemployment falls to around 6%: wage increases and inflation that eventually could threaten business expansion.

But so far in this economic recovery, things haven't been so scary.

In August, the Labor Department said, the unemployment rate was unchanged at 6.1% of the work force, marking the fourth month in a row that joblessness has been at a level generally viewed as sparking wage increases and higher prices. But wage pressures are virtually absent from the picture; the latest unemployment rate shows that average hourly earnings in the nonfarm sector rose just 0.2% last month and were up only 2.5% from a year ago, a bit lower than the inflation rate. The number of jobs grew by 179,000 last month, with gains mostly in the service industries.

What gives?

Unemployment Rate

For one thing, economists say it's too soon for wages to start picking up. Despite isolated cases of wage increases, they say, wage pressures aren't likely to appear in a broad way until early next year. "There is usually a lag time between a low unemployment rate and inflation problems," says Paul Mastroddi, managing director of U.S. economic research for Morgan Guaranty Trust Co.

But analysts say that even given a lag time, wage pressures are still quite low. Unit labor costs, which take productivity into account, are usually rising at a 5.2% annual rate 13 quarters into a recovery. But at that stage in this recovery — this year's second quarter — they increased at only a 0.4% rate, says Stephen Roach, senior economist for Morgan Stanley & Co.

Many economists say international competition, low job security and weak union bargaining power have all helped to hold wage increases down. Mr. Roach notes that much of the job growth of recent months, strong as it has been, has been concentrated in temporary-help service firms, restaurants and retailers. "That's just not where wage pressures are going to start," he says. Wages usually go up first at manufacturing, transportation and finance companies, he says.

Labor Secretary Robert Reich says, "There is still some slack in the labor market. Eight million people are out of work, and several hundred thousand more are discouraged about finding jobs."

But these mitigating forces may not be at work for much longer, especially with strong increases in new jobs. "The bargaining balance is about to shift to labor, given the advanced stage of the cycle and the scarcity of skilled workers," says Gene Sherman, director of research for M.S. Schapiro & Co.

Indeed, problems are popping up in certain areas of the country. The Federal Reserve, small-business associations and employment agencies have noted labor shortages — particularly in the Midwest, which is about the strongest economic region of the country. Mr. Mastroddi notes that wages in the government's employment-cost index have risen in a range of 3%-3.5% in the Midwest. That compares with 2%-2.5% two years ago.

This rise in wages in the Midwest puts a hole in the argument that international competition will help keep labor costs low. The heart of U.S. manufacturing beats in the Midwest, with large companies such as Caterpillar Inc. and General Motors Corp. that do a large amount of exporting. "This is the place that should be affected most by

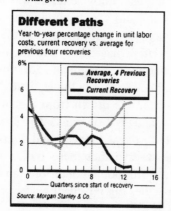

Different Paths

Year-to-year percentage change in unit labor costs, current recovery vs. average for previous four recoveries

- Average, 4 Previous Recoveries
- Current Recovery

Quarters since start of recovery

Source: Morgan Stanley & Co.

international competition," Mr. Mastroddi says. "And already, this is where we are seeing" wages accelerate. He says that although wages are still quite tame in the South, another strong spot, "This may be the next area to pick up."

Factories added 32,000 jobs in August after hardly adding any in July. With several indicators suggesting the manufacturing sector is slowing, many analysts expected factories to add far fewer workers. As usual, much of the employment growth last month was in the service sector, which added 123,000 jobs. Retailers added no jobs at all last month, after adding 100,000 in July. Construction employment dropped.

All figures have been adjusted for normal seasonal variations.

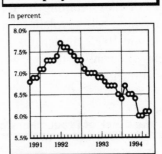

Unemployment Rate

In percent

UNEMPLOYMENT in August was unchanged at a seasonally adjusted 6.1% of the civilian labor force, the Labor Department reports.

Statistical Summary

Here are excerpts from the Labor Department's employment report. The figures are seasonally adjusted.

	August 1994	July 1994
	(millions of people)	
Civilian labor force	131.2	130.5
Civilian employment	123.2	122.5
Unemployment	8.0	8.0
Payroll employment	113.7	113.6
Unemployment:	(percent of labor force)	
All civilian workers	6.1	6.1
Adult men	5.4	5.6
Adult women	5.4	5.3
Teenagers	17.5	17.7
White	5.3	5.4
Black	11.5	11.2
Black teenagers	36.8	38.1
Hispanic	10.2	10.1
Average weekly hours:	(hours of work)	
Total private nonfarm	34.5	34.7
Manufacturing	42.0	41.9
Factory overtime	4.8	4.6

Employment Data—Statistical Summary

Here are excerpts from the Labor Department's employment report. The figures are seasonally adjusted.

	August 1994	July 1994
	(millions of people)	
Civilian labor force	131.2	130.5
Civilian employment	123.2	122.5
Unemployment	8.0	8.0
Payroll employment	113.7	113.6
Unemployment:	(percent of labor force)	
All civilian workers	6.1	6.1
Adult men	5.4	5.6
Adult women	5.4	5.3
Teenagers	17.5	17.7
White	5.3	5.4
Black	11.5	11.2
Black teenagers	36.8	38.1
Hispanic	10.2	10.1
Average weekly hours:	(hours of work)	
Total private nonfarm	34.5	34.7
Manufacturing	42.0	41.9
Factory overtime	4.8	4.6

True, manufacturing production workers typically do not control the length of their workweek or whether they will work overtime. Yet the extra income afforded by overtime is welcome and bolsters the consumer sentiment of those earning it. Together with the low rate of inflation, strong overtime helps explain robust consumer sentiment's strong recovery in the mid 1990s. In general, marginal employment adjustments are a reinforcing element of the business cycle through their impact on consumer sentiment.

CHART A–1
Average Workweek of Production Workers, Manufacturing

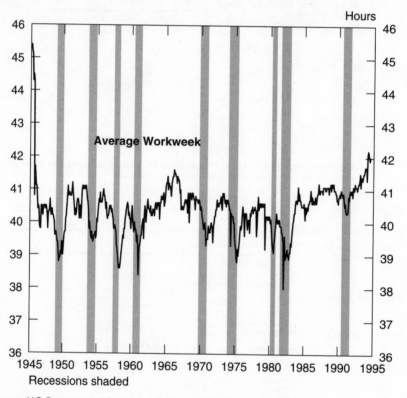

Source: U.S. Department of Commerce, *Business Cycle Indicators*, Series 1.

CHART A–2
Average Weekly Overtime of Production Workers, Manufacturing

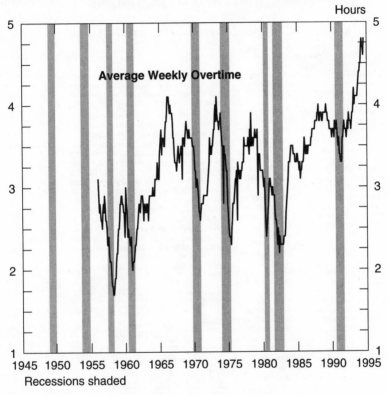

Recessions shaded

Source: U.S. Department of Commerce, *Business Cycle Indicators*, Series 21.

PERSONAL INCOME

The Commerce Department's monthly personal income report appears in *The Wall Street Journal* during the fourth week or the following week. The chart and statistical summary of the October 3, 1994 *Journal* article on page 366 informs you that personal income rose to a seasonally adjusted rate of $5.727 trillion. These are current, not constant dollars; there is no adjustment for inflation. The statistical summary at the end of the article also breaks out the major components of personal income and its disposition.

Consumer Spending, Income Increased In August, Signaling Economic Growth

By Christopher Georges
Staff Reporter of The Wall Street Journal

WASHINGTON — Americans earned more and spent more in August, indicating there still is considerable strength in the economy.

Disposable income rose 0.4% in the month, the seventh straight increase, while consumer spending jumped 0.9%, the largest gain since a 1.3% rise in February, the Commerce Department reported.

These figures, combined with last week's reported increases in durable-goods orders, new-home sales and revised Gross Domestic Product, all painted a picture of faster growth. But economists said they expect the pace of growth to slacken in coming months. Analysts concluded that inflationary pressure may continue to grow, but at a moderate rate.

"Yes, the economy is expanding, but as it does, we are bound to hit price pressure," said Charles Renfro of Alphametrics Corp., an economics consulting firm in Bala Cynwyd, Pa. "It's a given we will have some inflation, but the data do not suggest a dramatic increase in prices."

The Commerce Department's personal consumption expenditure report showed that spending on long-lasting items such as cars and appliances rose 4.2% in August, while spending on nondurable goods, such as food and fuel, rose 0.5%. Spending on services increased 0.4%.

The combination of rising incomes and spending meant that Americans' savings rate — savings as a percentage of disposable income — fell to 3.8% in August from 4.2% the previous month.

Wages and salaries, the most closely watched component of income, increased $7.9 billion in August after a $14.4 billion rise in July. Economists have kept an especially close eye on wages in recent months as a key indicator of potential inflation, but most agreed Friday that August's rise wasn't dramatic.

Analysts said that they didn't expect any immediate action by the Federal Reserve Board on interest rates in light of last week's economic data.

The Fed's Open Market Committee, which met Tuesday, decided not to raise rates for the time being. But the Fed chairman, by custom, has the authority to raise rates at least one-quarter percentage point between meetings without a formal committee vote. The next scheduled meeting is Nov. 15, and many analysts say they expect the Fed to boost rates for the sixth time this year at that time.

The central bank disclosed Friday that its most recent decision to increase rates by one-half percentage point, made at its Aug. 16 meeting, was unanimous.

According to a summary of the meeting released Friday, members of the Open Market Committee believed that "the rise in interest rates since the beginning of the year had had some restraining effects on interest-sensitive expenditures, notably housing and perhaps to a lesser extent some consumer durables, but to date these effects had not been large."

The report also noted that "despite some differing views, the members generally concluded that the economy was probably operating at a level that was close to, if not already at, its long-run potential."

PERSONAL INCOME

Here is the Commerce Department's latest report on personal income. The figures are at seasonally adjusted annual rates in trillions of dollars.

	Aug. 1994	July 1994
Personal income	5.727	5.703
Wages and salaries	3.290	3.282
Factory payrolls	.619	.616
Transfer payments	.969	.965
Disposable personal income	4.984	4.962
Personal outlays	4.796	4.755
Consumption expenditures	4.667	4.627
Other outlays	.129	.128
Personal saving	.188	.207

Statistical Summary

Personal Income

Annual rate, in trillions of dollars.

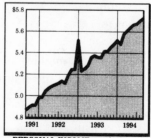

PERSONAL INCOME rose in August to a seasonally adjusted rate of $5.727 trillion from a revised $5.703 trillion a month earlier, the Commerce Department reports.

Personal Income—Statistical Summary

PERSONAL INCOME

Here is the Commerce Department's latest report on personal income. The figures are at seasonally adjusted annual rates in trillions of dollars.

	Aug. 1994	July 1994
Personal income	5.727	5.703
Wages and salaries	3.290	3.282
Factory payrolls	.619	.616
Transfer payments	.969	.965
Disposable personal income	4.984	4.962
Personal outlays	4.796	4.755
Consumption expenditures	4.667	4.627
Other outlays	.129	.128
Personal saving	.188	.207

Personal income is all the income we earn (wages, salaries, fringe benefits, profit, rent, interest, and so on) plus the transfer payments we receive (such as veterans' benefits, social security, unemployment compensation, and welfare), minus the social security taxes we pay to the government. Therefore, the federal government's ability to borrow from banks and use these borrowed funds to pay out to us in transfer payments more than it receives from us in taxes provides a cushion that keeps personal income growing even in recession, when earned income is down.

The huge federal deficits generated by the 1990–91 recession helped maintain personal income's growth trend (see chart accompanying article on page 366) despite rising unemployment in those years. This kept a floor under personal consumption expenditures.

For this reason, as you can see from the historical data (Chart A–3 on page 367), personal income has grown so steadily that it is difficult to use as a cyclical indicator, even after adjustments for inflation.

CHART A–3
Personal Income (constant dollars)

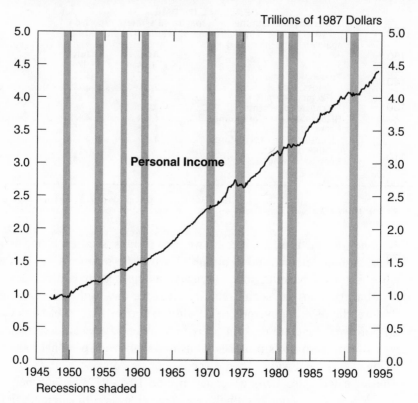

Trillions of 1987 Dollars

Personal Income

Recessions shaded

Source: U.S. Department of Commerce, *Business Cycle Indicators*, Series 52.

RETAIL SALES

The U.S. Department of Commerce's monthly release on *retail sales* appears in *The Wall Street Journal* around the second week of the month. Retail sales are reported in current dollars and include merchandise for personal or household consumption, but do not include services (such as haircuts, drycleaning, and restaurant meals). You can see from the chart accompanying the Thursday, September 15, 1994 article on page 370 that retail sales rose in August 1994.

Because retail sales has not been a volatile series (see Chart A–4 on page 369), even when measured in constant dollars, using retail sales to trace the course of the business cycle is not as easy or satisfactory as using auto sales, housing starts, or consumer credit.

CHART A–4
Retail Sales (constant dollars)

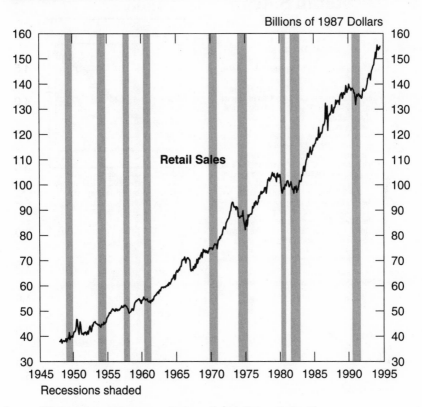

Billions of 1987 Dollars

Retail Sales

Recessions shaded

Source: U.S. Department of Commerce, *Business Cycle Indicators*, Series 59.

Retail Sales Are Brisk

By Lucinda Harper
And Josh Chetwynd
Staff Reporters of The Wall Street Journal

Meanwhile, in a sign that consumers are continuing to buy goods and services at a fairly brisk pace, the Commerce Department said retail sales rose 0.8% in August to $186.56 billion. Auto sales rose 1.2%, after falling 1.6% the month before. But there was considerable strength outside the auto sector as well. Sales of building materials surged 2.2%, and home-furnishing purchases were up 1.7%. Sales in the nondurable-good sector were up 0.4% in August, with apparel and accessory stores posting the strongest increases.

Sandra Shaber, retailing analyst for the WEFA Group in suburban Philadelphia, said new jobs are helping to combat the effect of higher interest rates on consumer spending. "If you give consumers jobs and paychecks, they are going to spend it," she said.

Retail Sales

In billions of dollars, seasonally adjusted.

RETAIL SALES rose in August to a seasonally adjusted $186.56 billion from a revised $185.14 billion in July, the Commerce Department reports.

Source: *The Wall Street Journal*, September 15, 1994. Reprinted by permission of *The Wall Street Journal*, ©1994 Dow Jones & Company, Inc. All rights reserved worldwide.

APPENDIX B

STATISTICAL SERIES PUBLISHED IN *THE WALL STREET JOURNAL* IN ALPHABETICAL ORDER

Chapter Introduced	Series Description	Publication Schedule
9	American Stock Exchange composite transactions	Daily
11	Amex bonds	Daily
16	Balance on current account	Quarterly
16	Balance of trade	Monthly
12	Banxquote money markets	Weekly
11	Bond market data bank	Daily
11	Bond yields (chart)	Weekly
9	Canadian markets (stocks)	Daily
7	Capacity utilization	Monthly
10	Cash prices (commodities)	Daily
11	Closed-end bond funds	Weekly
9	Closed-end funds (stocks & bonds)	Weekly
10	Commodities (article)	Daily
10	Commodity indexes	Daily
6	Consumer confidence	Monthly
6	Consumer credit	Monthly
12	Consumer savings rates	Weekly
6	Consumer price index	Monthly
9	Corporate dividend news	Daily
8	Corporate profits (Commerce Department)	Quarterly
8	Corporate profits (*The Wall Street Journal* survey)	Quarterly
11 and 12	Credit markets (article)	Daily
11	Credit ratings	Daily
16	Currency trading	Daily
9	Digest of earnings report	Daily
9	Dow Jones averages (six-month charts)	Daily

Chapter Introduced	Series Description	Publication Schedule
10	Dow Jones commodity indexes (chart)	Weekly
9	Dow Jones U.S. industry groups	Daily
9	Dow Jones world industry groups	Daily
15	Durable goods orders	Monthly
Appendix A	Employment	Monthly
15	Factory orders	Monthly
16	Foreign exchange (article)	Daily
9	Foreign markets (stocks)	Daily
10, 11, 12	Futures options prices	Daily
10, 11, 12	Futures prices	Daily
7	GDP	Quarterly
11	Government agency issues	Daily
11	High yield bonds	Daily
6	Housing starts	Monthly
9	Index options trading	Daily
7	Industrial production	Monthly
9	Insider trading spotlight	Weekly
14	Inventories	Monthly
16	Key currency cross rates	Daily
11 and 12	Key interest rates	Weekly
13	Leading indicators	Monthly
9	Leaps—long term options	Daily
9	Listed options trading	Daily
9 to 12	Markets diary	Daily
12	Money-fund yields	Weekly
12	Money market funds (chart)	Weekly
12	Money market mutual funds	Weekly
12	Money rates	Daily
11	Municipal bond index	Weekly
9	Mutual fund quotations	Daily
9	Mutual fund scorecard	Daily
9	NASDAQ national market issues	Daily
9	NASDAQ small cap issues	Daily
11	New securities issues	Daily
6	New-vehicle sales	Monthly
11	New York exchange bonds	Daily
9	NYSE composite transactions	Daily
9	NYSE highs/lows	Daily
9	Odd-lot trading	Daily
Appendix A	Personal income	Monthly
8	P/E Ratios	Weekly
7	Producer price index	Monthly
7	Productivity	Quarterly
Appendix A	Retail sales	Monthly
11	Securities offerings calendar	Weekly
9	Short interest (stocks)	Monthly
12	Short-term interest rates (chart)	Weekly

Chapter Introduced	Series Description	Publication Schedule
9	Stock market data bank	Daily
11 and 12	Treasury-bill auction	Weekly
11 and 12	Treasury bonds, notes, and bills	Daily
11 and 12	Treasury yield curve	Daily
11	Weekly tax-exempts (bonds)	Weekly
10	World markets (stocks article)	Daily
16	World value of the dollar	Daily
12	Yields on CDs	Weekly
11 and 12	Yield comparisons	Daily
12	Yields for consumers (chart)	Weekly

APPENDIX C

STATISTICAL SERIES PUBLISHED IN *THE WALL STREET JOURNAL* IN CHAPTER ORDER

Chapter Introduced	Series Description	Publication Schedule
6	Consumer confidence	Monthly
6	Consumer credit	Monthly
6	Consumer price index	Monthly
6	Housing starts	Monthly
6	New-vehicle sales	Monthly
7	Capacity utilization	Monthly
7	GDP	Quarterly
7	Industrial production	Monthly
7	Producer price index	Monthly
7	Productivity	Quarterly
8	Corporate profits (Commerce Department)	Quarterly
8	Corporate profits (*The Wall Street Journal* survey)	Quarterly
8	P/E Ratios	Weekly
9	American Stock Exchange composite transactions	Daily
9	Canadian markets (stocks)	Daily
9	Closed-end funds (stocks & bonds)	Weekly
9	Corporate dividend news	Daily
9	Digest of earnings report	Daily
9	Dow Jones averages (six-month charts)	Daily
9	Dow Jones U.S. industry groups	Daily
9	Dow Jones world industry groups	Daily
9	Foreign markets (stocks)	Daily
9	Index options trading	Daily
9	Insider trading spotlight	Weekly
9	Leaps—long term options	Daily
9	Listed options trading	Daily

Chapter Introduced	Series Description	Publication Schedule
9	Mutual fund quotations	Daily
9	Mutual fund scorecard	Daily
9	NASDAQ national market issues	Daily
9	NASDAQ small cap issues	Daily
9	NYSE composite transactions	Daily
9	NYSE highs/lows	Daily
9	Odd-lot trading	Daily
9	Short interest (stocks)	Monthly
9	Stock market data bank	Daily
9 to 12	Markets diary	Daily
10	Cash prices (commodities)	Daily
10	Commodities (article)	Daily
10	Commodity indexes	Daily
10	Dow Jones commodity indexes (chart)	Weekly
10, 11, 12	Futures options prices	Daily
10, 11, 12	Futures prices	Daily
10	World markets (stocks article)	Daily
11	Amex bonds	Daily
11	Bond market data bank	Daily
11	Bond yields (chart)	Weekly
11	Closed-end bond funds	Weekly
11 and 12	Credit markets (article)	Daily
11	Credit ratings	Daily
11	Government agency issues	Daily
11	High yield bonds	Daily
11 and 12	Key interest rates	Weekly
11	Municipal bond index	Weekly
11	New securities issues	Daily
11	New York exchange bonds	Daily
11	Securities offerings calendar	Weekly
11 and 12	Treasury-bill auction	Weekly
11 and 12	Treasury bonds, notes and bills	Daily
11 and 12	Treasury yield curve	Daily
11	Weekly tax-exempts (bonds)	Weekly
11 and 12	Yield comparisons	Daily
12	Banxquote money markets	Weekly
12	Consumer savings rates	Weekly
12	Money-fund yields	Weekly
12	Money market funds (chart)	Weekly
12	Money market mutual funds	Weekly
12	Money rates	Daily
12	Short-term interest rates (chart)	Weekly
12	Yields for consumers (chart)	Weekly
12	Yields on CDs	Weekly
13	Leading indicators	Monthly
14	Inventories	Monthly
15	Durable goods orders	Monthly

Chapter Introduced	Series Description	Publication Schedule
15	Factory orders	Monthly
16	Balance on current account	Quarterly
16	Balance of trade	Monthly
16	Currency trading	Daily
16	Foreign exchange (article)	Daily
16	Key currency cross rates	Daily
16	World value of the dollar	Daily
Appendix A	Employment	Monthly
Appendix A	Personal income	Monthly
Appendix A	Retail sales	Monthly

APPENDIX D

LISTING OF STATISTICAL SERIES ACCORDING TO *THE WALL STREET JOURNAL* PUBLICATION SCHEDULE

Day of Month Usually Published in The Wall Street Journal	Series Description	Chapter Introduced
	Quarterly	
Middle of last month of quarter	Balance on current account	16
25th	GDP	7
25th of last month of quarter	Corporate profits (Commerce Department)	8
A month after end of quarter	Productivity	7
Two months after close of quarter	Corporate profits (*The Wall Street Journal* survey)	8
	Monthly	
1st	Leading indicators	13
1st week	Consumer confidence	6
1st week	Factory orders	15
5th, 15th, 25th	New-vehicle sales	6
Monday of second week	Employment	Appendix A
2nd week	Consumer credit	6
Middle of 2nd week	Retail sales	Appendix A
Midmonth	Capacity utilization	7
Midmonth	Consumer price index	6
Midmonth	Industrial production	7
Midmonth	Inventories	14
Midmonth	Producer price index	7
3rd week	Balance of trade	16
17th to 20th	Housing starts	6

Day of Month Usually Published in The Wall Street Journal	Series Description	Chapter Introduced
	Monthly (concluded)	
20th	Short interest (stocks)	9
Thursday or Friday of next-to-last week	Durable goods orders	15
Last week	Personal income	Appendix A
	Weekly	
Monday	Bond yields (chart)	11
Monday	Closed-end bond funds	11
Monday	Closed-end funds (stocks & bonds)	9
Monday	Dow Jones commodity indexes (chart)	10
Monday	P/E Ratios	8
Monday	Securities offerings calendar	11
Tuesday	Key interest rates	11 and 12
Tuesday	Treasury-bill auction	11 and 12
Tuesday	Weekly tax-exempts (bonds)	11
Wednesday	Banxquote money markets	12
Wednesday	Insider trading spotlight	9
Wednesday	Yields on CDs	12
Thursday	Consumer savings rates	12
Thursday	Money-fund yields	12
Thursday	Money market funds (chart)	12
Thursday	Money market mutual funds	12
Thursday	Short-term interest rates (chart)	12
Thursday	Yields for consumers (chart)	12
Friday	Municipal bond index	11

Series Description—Daily	Chapter Introduced
American Stock Exchange composite transactions	9
Amex bonds	11
Bond market data bank	11
Canadian markets (stocks)	9
Cash prices (commodities)	10
Commodities (article)	10
Commodity indexes	10
Corporate dividend news	9
Credit markets (article)	11 and 12
Credit ratings	11
Currency trading	16

Series Description—Daily	Chapter Introduced
Digest of earnings report	9
Dow Jones averages (six-month charts)	9
Dow Jones U.S. industry groups	9
Dow Jones world industry groups	9
Foreign exchange (article)	16
Foreign markets (stocks)	9
Futures options prices	10,11,12
Futures prices	10,11,12
Government agency issues	11
High yield bonds	11
Index options trading	9
Key currency cross rates	16
Leaps—long term options	9
Listed options trading	9
Markets diary	9 to 12
Money rates	12
Mutual fund quotations	9
Mutual fund scorecard	9
NASDAQ national market issues	9
NASDAQ small cap issues	9
New securities issues	11
New York exchange bonds	11
NYSE composite transactions	9
NYSE highs/lows	9
Odd-lot trading	9
Stock market data bank	9
Treasury bonds, notes, and bills	11 and 12
Treasury yield curve	11 and 12
World markets (stocks article)	10
World value of the dollar	16
Yield comparisons	11 and 12

APPENDIX E

FURTHER REFERENCES*

These references were selected to assist you with further research into the many topics covered in this book. The listings include some of the best books and other resources on numerous investment topics. In certain cases, a title may be out-of-print, but copies will be available at most larger public and educational facility libraries.

All Irwin Professional Publishing titles are available in bookstores or directly from Irwin Professional Publishing, 1333 Burr Ridge Parkway, Burr Ridge, IL 60521. Customer Service can be reached at 1-800-634-3966.

BASICS

American Association of Individual Investors
625 North Michigan Avenue, Suite 1900
Chicago, IL 60611
(312) 280-0170

Member benefits include a subscription to the excellent monthly, *AAII Journal*. The Association also publishes home study courses and audio tapes and presents seminars. There is a local chapter network.

Taking Control of your Financial Future: Making Smart Investment Decisions with Stocks and Mutual Funds by Thomas E. O'Hara and Helen J. McLane. Burr Ridge, IL: Irwin Professional Publishing.

---

*The Author gratefully acknowledges the assistance of Bob Meier of DeKalb, Illinois, in compiling these references.

The New Century Family Money Book by Jonathan D. Pond. New York: Dell Publishing.

Asset Allocation: Balancing Financial Risk, 2nd Edition by Roger C. Gibson. Burr Ridge, IL: Irwin Professional Publishing.

Classics: An Investor's Anthology and *Classics II: Another Investors Anthology*, edited by Charles D. Ellis and James Vertin.

These two volumes are the most comprehensive, yet compact, source of Wall Street wisdom. They present the best practical ideas and commentaries of over 100 gifted economists and investment industry thinkers on financial analysis, investing, and economic history, from the past 200 years.

CHART SERVICES

Chartcraft, Inc.
Investors Intelligence
30 Church Street, Box 2046
New Rochell, NY 10802

Fifteen different chart service combinations, featuring the point and figure charting method.

Securities Research Company
208 Newbury Street
Boston, MA 02116

Monthly and quarterly chart services covering 1,000 stocks each, plus wall charts and books.

Standard & Poor's Corporation
25 Broadway
New York, NY 10004

Comprehensive subscriber package, including the Trendline Chart Service, tracking over 1,400 active stocks, and the Security Owner's Stock Guide, presenting statistics on over 5,300 stocks.

Futures Chart Service
Commodity Trend Service
P.O. Box 32309
Palm Beach Gardens, FL 33420

A weekly or bi-weekly service offering comprehensive daily, weekly, and monthly range charts for all commodities, important domestic and foreign stock indexes, bonds, money market instruments, energy markets, and precious and industrial metals. Subscription includes periodic monthly chart anthologies and numerous educational "how to" reports and videos.

STOCKS

Raging Bull: How to Invest in the Growth Stocks of the 90s by David Alger. Homewood, IL: Business One Irwin.

The Dow Jones Investor's Handbook 1995 edited by Phyllis Pierce. Burr Ridge, IL: Irwin Professional Publishing.

All About Stocks: From the Inside Out by Esme Faerber. Burr Ridge, IL: Irwin Professional Publishing.

Outsmarting Wall Street by Daniel Alan Seiver. Burr Ridge, IL: Irwin Professional Publishing.

Small Cap Stocks by Robert Klein and Jess Lederman. Burr Ridge, IL: Irwin Professional Publishing.

Stock Market Probability by Joseph E. Murphy, Jr. Burr Ridge, IL: Irwin Professional Publishing.

TECHNICAL ANALYSIS

Technical Analysis Explained by Martin J. Pring
Pring Market Review
P.O. Box 329
Washington, CT 06794

One of the most definitive and comprehensive references on technical analysis. The book, now in its third edition, features over 150 charts and illustrations. Danish, Italian, German, and Japanese editions are also available.

The Handbook of Technical Analysis by Darrell R. Jobman. Burr Ridge, IL: Irwin Professional Publishing.

Using Technical Analysis: A Step-by-Step Guide to Understanding and Applying Stock Market Charting Techniques, Rev. ed. by Clifford Pitolese. Burr Ridge, IL: Irwin Professional Publishing.

PRECIOUS METALS

Gold and Liberty by Richard Salsman. American Institute for Economic Research, Great Barrington, MA 01230.

A detailed, historical analysis of gold as an investment and monetary medium. Extensive charts and tables.

Gold Newsletter
Jefferson Financial
2400 Jefferson Highway, Suite 600
Jefferson, LA 70121

In publication for over 25 years, this monthly newsletter covers all aspects of the precious metals (gold, silver, platinum and palladium): fundamental and technical analysis, coins, bullion, and mining shares. Interviews with prominent analysts and precious metal industry figures are also presented.

Silver Bonanza: How to Profit From the Coming Bull Market In Silver by James U. Blanchard III. New York: Simon & Schuster.

CONSUMER PROTECTION

What Every Investor Should Know
Consumer Information Center K
P.O. Box 100
Pueblo, CO 81002

Basic information on choosing and safeguarding investments, trading securities, and protections guaranteed by law. Written by the Securities & Exchange Commission. When ordering, make checks payable to the "Superintendent of Documents" and include the publication number, #146V. (35 pages, $1.25)

INTERNATIONAL INVESTING AND FOREIGN CURRENCIES

FullerMoney
Chart Analysis Ltd.
7 Swallow Street
London W1R 7HD
United Kingdom

A monthly newsletter featuring long-term charts and commentary for 27 world stock and bond markets, all major currencies, and precious metals. This service is one of the best resources for the serious international investor.

The Handbook of Emerging Markets by Robert Lloyd George. Burr Ridge, IL: Irwin Professional Publishing.

Investor's World
Phillips Publishing, Inc.
7811 Montrose Road
Potomac, MD 20854

Practical, long-term recommendations for foreign stocks, bonds, mutual funds, currencies, precious metals, and special situations in emerging markets in every monthly issue.

The Investor's Guide to Emerging Markets by Mark Mobius. Burr Ridge, IL: Irwin Professional Publishing.

PSYCHOLOGY

Investment Psychology Consulting
337 Lochside Drive
Cary, NC 27511

Books and audio cassettes by Dr. Van K. Tharp to help investors and traders overcome the psychological barriers to objective interpretation of economic news and successful investment decisions. (Write for catalog.)

GENERAL REFERENCE

Investment Policy, 2nd Edition by Charles Ellis. Burr Ridge: Irwin Professional Publishing.

The Intelligent Investor by Benjamin Graham. New York: Harper & Row.

The Irwin Business and Investment Almanac by Sumner Levine. Burr Ridge, IL: Irwin Professional Publishing.

A Random Walk Down Wall Street, 4th Edition by Burton G. Malkiel. New York: W.W. Norton & Company.

FUTURES AND OPTIONS

Futures & Options Trading Kit
Fox Investments
Attn: Susan Rutsen, Consumer Affairs
Suite 1800A
141 West Jackson Blvd.
Chicago, IL 60604

Collection of basic "how to" brochures, article reprints, and other information on the potential risks and rewards of futures and options trading,

including managed accounts and funds. Indicate any special areas of interest.

All About Futures: From the Inside Out by Russell Wasendorf and Thomas McCafferty. Burr Ridge, IL: Irwin Professional Publishing.

LEAPS: What They Are and How to Use Them for Profit and Protection by Harrison Roth. Burr Ridge, IL: Irwin Professional Publishing.

Options: Essential Concepts and Trading Strategies, 2nd Edition by the Options Institute. Burr Ridge, IL: Irwin Professional Publishing.

The Senmontier Strategy
Marketing & Publishing Associates
23-00, Route 208
Fair Lawn, NJ 07410

Comprehensive monthly newsletter and hotline service featuring fixed-risk option and futures strategies for all agricultural and financial markets.

Technical Traders Guide to Computer Analysis of the Futures Market by Charles LeBeau and David Lucas. Burr Ridge, IL: Irwin Professional Publishing.

BONDS, LONG-TERM INTEREST RATES, AND MONEY MARKET INSTRUMENTS

The Bond Market: Trading and Risk Management by Christina Ray. Burr Ridge, IL: Irwin Professional Publishing.

Money Market Calculations: Yields, Break Evens and Arbitrage by Marcia Stigum with John Mann. Burr Ridge, IL: Irwin Professional Publishing.

Fixed Income Calculations, Volume One: Money Market Paper and Bonds by Marcia Stigum and Franklin Robinson. Burr Ridge, IL: Irwin Professional Publishing.

IBC's Investing for Income
P.O. Box 9104
Ashland, MA 01721

In-depth coverage of money market mutual funds, no-load municipal and taxable bond mutual funds, as well as Treasury markets. Other features include tax tips and economic trends.

IBC/Donoghue Money Fund Directory
P.O. Box 9104
Ashland, MA 01721

Complete details on more than 1,100 money market mutual funds. The exhaustive information on each fund includes investment minimums; privileges, like check writing and toll-free customer lines; and up to a 10-year performance record.

Fixed Income Masterpieces: Insights From America's Great Investors edited by Livingston G. Douglas. Burr Ridge, IL: Irwin Professional Publishing.

The Bond Book: Everything You Need to Know About Treasuries, Municipals, GNMAs, Corporates, Zeroes, Funds and More by Annette Thau. Burr Ridge, IL: Irwin Professional Publishing.

COMPUTERS & DATABASES

Technical Analysis of Stocks & Commodities
3517 SW Alaska Street
Seattle, WA 98126

This monthly magazine has articles and case studies on a wide range of computerized investing topics, plus reviews of the newest hardware, software and databases. Various special product and services directories are issued throughout the year.

The Global Directory of Financial Information Vendors by James Essinger and Joseph Rosen. Burr Ridge, IL: Irwin Professional Publishing.

Wall Street & Technology
600 Harrison Street
San Francisco, CA 94107

A monthly magazine with two bonus supplement issues, including an annual Buyer's Guide to financial planning and portfolio management software, trading systems, online quotes, and news services.

Fixed Income Masterpieces: Insights From America's Great Investors edited by Livingston G. Douglas. Burr Ridge, IL: Irwin Professional Publishing.

The Bond Book: Everything You Need To Know About Treasuries, Municipals, GNMAs, Corporates, Zeroes, Funds and More by Annette Thau. Burr Ridge, IL: Irwin Professional Publishing.

FINANCIAL PLANNING

Your Retirement Benefits by Peter Gaudio and Virginia Nicols. New York: John Wiley & Sons.

The Seven Secrets of Financial Success: Applying the Time-Tested Principles of Creating, Managing, and Building Personal Wealth by Jack Root and Douglas Mortensen. Burr Ridge, IL: Irwin Professional Publishing.

The Price Waterhouse Personal Financial Adviser by Price Waterhouse LLP. Burr Ridge, IL: Irwin Professional Publishing.

Secure Your Future: Your Personal Companion for Understanding Lifestyle and Financial Aspects of Retirement by Price Waterhouse LLP. Burr Ridge, IL: Irwin Professional Publishing.

Investing During Retirement: The Vanguard Guide to Managing Your Retirement Assets by The Vanguard Group of Investment Companies. Burr Ridge, IL: Irwin Professional Publishing.

The Vanguard Retirement Investing Guide by The Vanguard Group of Investment Companies. Burr Ridge, IL: Irwin Professional Publishing.

The ABC's of Managing Your Money by Jonathan D. Pond. Denver: The National Endowment for Financial Education. (Distributed by Irwin Professional Publishing.)

GENERAL REFERENCE

Business Cycle Indicators and Measures by George Hildebrand. Burr Ridge, IL: Irwin Professional Publishing.

Handbook of Key Economic Indicators by R. Mark Rogers. Burr Ridge, IL: Irwin Professional Publishing.

The Practical Forecasters' Almanac edited by Edward Renshaw. Burr Ridge, IL: Irwin Professional Publishing.

MUTUAL FUNDS

All About Mutual Funds: From the Inside Out by Bruce Jacobs. Burr Ridge, IL: Irwin Professional Publishing.

Morningstar Closed-End 250 (annual publication). Burr Ridge, IL: Irwin Professional Publishing.

Morningstar Mutual Fund 500 (annual publication). Burr Ridge, IL: Irwin Professional Publishing.

Sheldon Jacobs' Guide to Successful No-Load Funds Investing by Sheldon Jacobs. Burr Ridge, IL: Irwin Professional Publishing.

FINANCIAL AND ECONOMIC
ONLINE DATA RETRIEVAL

A number of computer information subscription services provide up-to-the-minute financial and economic information.

Dow Jones News Retrieval (DJN/R): 1-609-452-1511
Compuserve: 1-800-848-8990
GEnie: 1-800-638-9636
The Source: 1-800-336-3366

These services will give you access to many of the following:

- S & P Online
- Value Line Data Base
- Futures Focus
- Money Market Services
- OTC News
- Bond Prices and Volumes
- Stock Quotes
- Commodities Futures Prices
- Company Information
- and much more

INDEX